FROM TELECOMMUNICATIONS TO ELECTRONIC SERVICES:

A GLOBAL SPECTRUM OF DEFINITIONS, BOUNDARY LINES, AND STRUCTURES

FROM TELECOMMUNICATIONS TO ELECTRONIC SERVICES:

A GLOBAL SPECTRUM OF DEFINITIONS, BOUNDARY LINES, AND STRUCTURES

Robert R. Bruce
Jeffrey P. Cunard
Mark D. Director

Debevoise & Plimpton
Washington, D.C.

BUTTERWORTHS

The Butterworth Group of Companies

United States
Butterworth Legal Publishers, Austin
Butterworth Legal Publishers, Boston
Butterworth Legal Publishers, Seattle
Butterworth Legal Publishers, St. Paul
D&S Publishers, Clearwater

Canada
Butterworth & Co. (Canada) Ltd., Toronto and Vancouver

United Kingdom
Butterworth & Co. (Publishers) Ltd., London

Australia
Butterworth Pty. Ltd., Sydney

New Zealand
Butterworths of New Zealand Ltd., Wellington

South Africa
Butterowrth & Co. (South Africa) Pty. Ltd., Durban

Publisher's Note

This Butterworth edition is identical to the two-volume, spiral-bound version published by the International Institute of Communications (IIC) in October 1985. The IIC and the twelve sponsoring organizations have supported the publication of this hardcover version so that the important observations and conclusions it contains might be considered by a wide readership.

ISBN 0-88063-103-1

Printed in the United States of America

SPONSORS

AT&T COMMUNICATIONS (United States)

CABLE & WIRELESS plc (United Kingdom)

CITICORP (United States)

COMMISSION OF THE EUROPEAN COMMUNITIES

DEPARTMENT OF COMMUNICATIONS (Canada)

DIRECTION GÉNÉRALE DES TÉLÉCOMMUNICATIONS (France)

FEDERAL MINISTRY OF POSTS AND TELECOMMUNICATIONS (Federal Republic of Germany)

INIZIATIVA ME.T.A. - DIVISION OF GRUPPO MONTEDISON (Italy)

JAPAN INFORMATION PROCESSING DEVELOPMENT CENTRE (Japan)

MTV OY/TALOUDELLINEN TIEDOTUSTOIMISIO/NOKIA OY (Finland)

NIPPON TELEGRAPH AND TELEPHONE (Japan)

REUTERS (United Kingdom)

This report reflects the views of its authors and not necessarily those of the sponsors nor of the International Institute of Communications and its members.

TABLE OF CONTENTS

FOREWORD

Worldwide, telecommunications technologies and services are evolving rapidly. Distinctions between various forms of electronic communication—once discrete—have now become blurred as a result. Telephony has merged with computer communications creating new opportunities, not only for national administrations, but for competitive service providers and users. The convergence of technology and the blurring of distinctions between services have placed growing pressure on domestic and international telecommunications structures and policies. Governments and corporations are faced with a range of vexing issues when considering future policies.

The International Institute of Communications (IIC), by carrying out this major Study of Telecommunications Structures (STS), has identified complex domestic and international issues and has pointed towards a number of realistic policy options. As a worldwide members' organisation the Institute is a most suitable forum for this kind of research and policy analysis. Both the particular way in which the study has been conducted and this final report are proof.

The IIC appreciates the support and encouragement of the law firm Debevoise & Plimpton, and in particular its partner, Robert R. Bruce, who directed the study. He and his colleagues, Jeffrey P. Cunard and Mark D. Director, have shown great intellect and insight throughout the project. We are indebted to them for their important contribution to the work of the Institute.

As President of the IIC it has been my particular pleasure to have had a direct involvement with this study as Chairman of the Steering Committee which consisted of representatives of the twelve sponsors. Our meetings produced lively discussion which contributed to the quality of this report. I would like to express my gratitude for their substantive involvement during the course of this eighteen-month study.

Thomas P. Hardiman
President

PREFACE

This study could never have been undertaken—let alone completed—without the assistance and support of dozens, if not hundreds, of people. Listing them with any hope of comprehensiveness is an impossible task. So many contributed—and in so many different ways.

Everywhere in the IIC there were many people who were critical to bringing the project to fruition. Of these, foremost is Tom Hardiman, the President of the IIC, who unfailingly supported the idea from the start and who agreed to take an active role as the Chairman of the Steering Committee of the study sponsors.

Throughout, the staff of the IIC offered invaluable support, guidance, and assistance. It was Bill Sweeney, then the Executive Director of the IIC, who, in the very beginning, first seized on the idea of attempting this study. It was his unflagging trust in us and in the importance of this study, and his dedication to realizing the potential of the IIC, that has made this study a reality.

During the final preparations and throughout the research and writing, John Howkins, IIC Executive Director since 1984, made available his extraordinary range of contacts and supplied an immeasurably useful perspective on global developments in telecommunications. The Officers and Trustees of the Institute also supported the idea, and made many significant efforts to assure that the participants in the study represented a diverse and international group. Pierre Braillard, coordinator of the IIC Section Francaise, and Mikio Momiyama, NHK, coordinator of the IIC's Japanese members, deserve a special mention.

All these contributed to what is hoped will be a more lasting result of the study—the emergence of the IIC as a forum for discussion of the important telcommunications policy issues of the coming decade.

It is no overstatement to say that, without the extraordinary interest and administrative support offered by the sponsors, this study simply could not have been undertaken. It would be remiss not to mention the contributions of the sponsors and of their representatives.

Citicorp, at the outset, through Eduard Berlin, Citibank Vice President, early on expressed an interest in the study and worked closely with the IIC to bring it about. Derrick Nicholas, Citicorp Vice President in Brussels, offered useful advice and insightful commentary throughout the work. As well, Bill Halley in Citibank's New York office, Kathleen White, Deborah Tumey, Dan Sullivan, and others in Citibank offices worldwide offered time, effort, and expertise.

Similarly, Reuters, through the interest of its Managing Director, Glen Renfrew, took an early interest in and then supported the work in every practical way. In particular, a strong leadership role was taken by Peter Smith with the support of his colleagues Tony Cornish in London and Mike Salamon in Tokyo.

Cable & Wireless, likewise, contributed significantly, as a result of the initiative of Joe Crouch, its Director of Marketing. Incisive advice and counsel were supplied by David Wilkinson, Head of the Strategic Studies Group, along with significant contributions by his colleagues Peter Moulson and Paul Kirby.

In the United States, AT&T offered generous assistance and ongoing advice through its representatives, IIC member Marc Epstein and Paul Quinlan. In addition, Dwight Jasmann, Director, International Correspondent Relations, AT&T Communications, and Bobby Boone, Director, International Policy and Plans, AT&T Communications, made critical contributions during the effort.

The Canadian Department of Communications, of course, has been involved in many IIC activities of significance. Over the years, the DOC has contributed financial backing, key personnel, and the expertise of its extraordinary staff. Not surprisingly, then, the Canadian contribution is unique in scope. Bill Montgomery, Director, International Relations, made the original decision to participate. Vince Hill, Director General, Telecommunications Policy Branch, who has had the lead role in the Department's recent efforts to draft a comprehensive new telecommunications statute, offered invariably wise and insightful counsel on Canadian and international developments as the DOC's representative to the Steering Committee of sponsors. Leonard Bellam, Bob Tritt, and many others in the Department also made significant and noteworthy contributions.

Beyond all this, however, the DOC also took an active role in setting up meetings in Canada at the highest level. At the annual meeting of the Canadian chapter of the IIC, in June 1985, it organized a symposium, chaired by IIC Trustee David Golden, Chairman of the Board of Telesat Canada, to discuss the issues raised in the Canadian country report.

In Japan, Nippon Telegraph & Telephone and the Japan Information Processing Development Center (JIPDEC) were both active sponsors and worked in close conjunction with the Japanese chapter of the IIC to arrange meetings with the broadest spectrum of public and private sector decisionmakers in the telecommunications sector. Since June 1984, when the initial interviews were conducted in Japan, the extraordinary and rich participation of Japanese IIC members and other important figures in the field set the tone and standard for the meetings in other countries. Innumerable staff members at NTT made substantial contributions to the work; however, particular mention should be made of Nobuki Hori, Kiyotaka Matsubara, and Kageo Nakano. At JIPDEC, Toshihiko Nishiwaki, Executive Managing Director, offered sage insight into Japanese telecommunications policy and institutions; the active interest of Takao Nakayama, Managing Director, was greatly appreciated, as were the important contributions of many others affiliated with that organization.

In Finland there was broad-based participation by a consortium of sponsors, with the Finnish effort being coordinated by Seppo Sisatto, Vice President of Mainos TV and a long-time member of the IIC. The presence of

Finland in this study is ample testimony to its special and innovative place in global telecommunications and to the enthusiasm and vigor of the Finnish members of the IIC. Pentti Hanski, the now-retired President of MTV, spurred Finnish involvement. The Economic Information Bureau joined the work and was well-represented by Leif Fast, its Executive Director, and by Sakari Kumpulainen.

There was extremely active participation, as well, by Nokia Corporation, the largest industrial corporation in Finland. Throughout Nokia there was great interest and involvement in the study. Nevertheless, particular mention should be made of Harry Mildh, the Executive Vice President of Nokia Corporation, Kurt Wikstedt, the now-retired President of Nokia Electronics, and his successor Timo Koski; also key to the work in Finland were Nokia's Jorma Nieminen, President of Mobira, its rapidly expanding mobile communications subsidiary; Pentti Korkka, Vice President, Corporate Planning; Viljo Hentinen, Director, Research and Development; Juhani Vuori, Director, and Jan-Peter Paul, Manager, Corporate Planning and Business Development, who were all unstinting in making their time and good counsel freely available.

Worthy of special mention were the efforts of the Finnish chapter of the IIC in arranging an informal symposium on Finnish telecommunications issues in which industry leaders were brought together one summer afternoon in August 1984.

In Germany, the role of the Deutsche Bundespost as a sponsor was coordinated by Hartmut Nitsch and Dr. Karl-Heinz Neumann under the direction of Dr. Otto Kaiser, Ministerial Director, Deutsche Bundespost. The Bundespost freely made available many key members of its staff and facilitated meetings with industry leaders and policy advisers who had a wide range of views, some of which were, indeed, critical of the Bundespost itself. Of particular note was a May 1985 informal meeting of the German and Japanese sponsors that took place during a visit by a Bundespost delegation to Japan. Dr. Neumann, it should be stressed, is an extraordinarily prolific and incisive observer of developments in Germany and elsewhere; the study benefited greatly from his insights and perspective.

Of equal importance in assuring that a wide range of views was reflected in the work was the French Direction generale des telecommunications (D.G.T.); its Director General, Jacques Dondoux, has also taken an interest in other IIC activities in the past. The representative of the D.G.T. was Olivier Froissart, of the Direction des affaires industrielles et internationales, which is headed by Jean Grenier, one of today's keenest observers of the global telecommunications scene. Many in the top management of the D.G.T. were exceptionally generous in making time available for sharing their perspectives on developments in France and in other nations. Warranting special mention is Jean Voge, a long-time member and trustee of the IIC and counselor to the D.G.T. on strategic matters, whose insights and advice were especially appreciated.

Montedison, the Italian multinational enterprise, made an exceptionally important contribution by offering the perspective of a large European user of telecommunications services. Participating actively in the study was Iniziativa ME.T.A., a division of Montedison that integrates the company's information and service-related business activities. Montedison's involvement was led by Mathilde Bernabei, ME.T.A. Director of Strategies and Development, with the collaboration of Renato Mariano, and of Daniele Fano of F.O.R., Montedison's research and consulting arm. Dr. Fano's participation in the study and, in particular, his contribution to its analysis of European issues were especially noteworthy. Montedison also made two unique contributions by arranging, through F.O.R., a special seminar in Rome in February 1985 and, thereafter, a press briefing in Milan on the IIC and the study in April 1985.

Finally, but by no means last in importance, was the involvement of the Commission of the European Communities through its Task Group on Information and Telecommunications Technologies, which is headed by Michel Carpentier. Dr. Herbert Ungerer, the head of Strategy and Studies of the telecommunications directorate of the Task Group, was a forceful advocate for incorporating a European perspective on the issues raised by the study. Upon his suggestion, and with his encouragement, a number of additional interviews with policymakers in Belgium, Luxembourg, and the Netherlands were arranged to focus more clearly on the European dimension. In April 1985, a special seminar was arranged in Brussels to discuss the future development of European telecommunications.

When cumulated, this recitation of the sponsors' participation, incomplete as it necessarily must be, can only begin to convey their tremendous involvement in the study. At the same time, the sponsors recognized throughout the work that the perspectives and analysis of the study must remain independent.

From the outset it was understood that ultimate editorial responsibility would rest with the authors of the study and with the IIC. The sponsors were scrupulous in observing this understanding; thus, the project benefited from their enthusiastic and active role in setting up meetings and in reviewing plans, outlines, and drafts, while they respected its unique nature as a report of an independent, nonprofit, international institute. The final product, therefore, does not necessarily reflect the views of the sponsors, either individually or collectively, or, indeed, of the IIC.

The independence of perspective also results from the diversity of interests reflected in the group of sponsors: carriers, users, policymakers, and regulators from Europe, Japan, Canada, and the United States. Ultimately, the sponsors resolved that all points of view should be expressed, with the goal of assuring maximum objectivity. The expectation was that the final document would serve as a point of departure for additional discussion and future dialogue.

No review of the study would approach completeness if it failed to acknowledge the help of many others who were not sponsors but who provided documentation, offered insights, and gave so much of their time. Although not able to recognize everyone who contributed, a few individuals and groups might be mentioned and may suggest the scope and range of assistance received.

George McKendrick, Chairman of the International Telecommunications Users Group (INTUG), and Ernie Weiss, INTUG's President, offered advice and counsel and provided user group contacts. On several occasions, Henry Ergas and Ann Reid of the OECD shared perspectives on the issues addressed by the study and readily agreed to participate in the April 1985 Brussels seminar. Andrea Caruso, Secretary General of Eutelsat, and David Leive, General Counsel of Intelsat, offered useful perspectives on the future of regional and transoceanic satellite systems. Kent Combs, of IBM Europe, offered his insights and provided access to information and personnel in the IBM organization.

In the United Kingdom, Bill Wigglesworth, the Deputy Director of the Office of Telecommunications, along with Nick Hartley and his colleagues at OFTEL, and Jim Cowie, Director, Strategic Issues, of British Telecommunications, were especially generous with their time. In the Department of Trade and Industry, of special assistance were Ian Ellison, Assistant Secretary, Telecommunications Division, his successor, John Avery, and Greg Faulkner, Assistant Secretary, International Telecommunications.

In Japan, gracious with their time and energies were Yasuo Iwasaki, Chief Secretary to the Prime Minister, and Hirofumi Nakasone, both of the Office of Prime Minister Nakasone; Akira Konishi, Machinery and Information Industries Bureau, Ministry of International Trade and Industry; Kaoru Kanazawa, Director, Information and Industry Research Department, Ministry of Posts and Telecommunications; Seisuke Komatsuzaki, Managing Director, Research Institute of Telecommunications and Economics (RITE), and his colleagues Etsuzo Masuda and Hirofumi Takahashi. RITE is one of the most important research centers for telecommunications policy and the generous cooperation of that organization and its staff was particularly appreciated.

In Finland, the individual contributions were so numerous and significant that they virtually defy specific mention. Of very special note, however, were the time and perspectives of Christoffer Taxell, the Minister of Justice and the Chairman of the Cabinet Committee on Communications; Matti Luttinen, Minister of Communications; Dr. Pekka Tarjanne, the Director General of the Finnish PTT; Reijo Svensson and his former colleague (now with Nokia) Gunnulf Martenson, of The Association of Telephone Companies in Finland; Osmo Wiio, Professor, University of Helsinki; Ulla Sirkeinen, of the Confederation of Finnish Industries; Ilkka Pulkkinen, Managing Director, and Juhani Salonius, Director, of the Finnish Employers' Confederation; Veikko Loyttyniemi, Managing Director of The Finnish Newspaper Publishers Association; Jaakko Hannuksela, Vice President, Planning, Sanoma Corporation; Jukka Liedes, Special Adviser, Ministry of Education; Pekka Nurmi, Director of Legislation, Ministry of Justice; Jukka

Ojala, Matti Reunanen, and Sirkku Sivonen of the K.O.P. bank; Jaakko Iloniemi, of the Union Bank of Finland; Sakari Kiuri, Director General, Finnish Broadcasting Company; and Eero Pilkama, President of MTV, along with many of his top managers. The broad participation of Finnish leaders in industry and government is deserving of special note because it afforded the unique opportunity of providing access to almost all of the key decisionmakers in the telecommunications sector.

In the Federal Republic of Germany, the contributions of many individuals should be recognized. Special mention must be made of Dr. Jurgen Muller, Deutsches Institut fur Wirtschaftsforschung; Dr. Wolfgang Hoffmann-Reim, Professor, Public Law, Hamburg University; and Dr. Joachim Scherer of the Institute for Public Law, Johann Wolfgang Goethe University, all of whom gave freely of their time, insights, and documentation.

Finally, in France, a further note must be made of the role of Henri Pigeat, the President Director General, Agence France Presse, a long-time trustee of the IIC, and head of the IIC Section Francaise. With Henri Pigeat's encouragement and active support, Pierre Braillard played a special role in arranging meetings and offering an array of significant notes and observations on the French telecommunications scene as well as the broader issues addressed by the study. Pierre's incisive contributions are reflected throughout the French country report and the entire study.

Any mention of individuals who were important to the progress and completion of the study would be incomplete without highlighting the contributions of colleagues at Debevoise & Plimpton. Of special note are my partners, who tolerated my absences but approved the enormous investment of the firm's resources—including my time and that of my colleagues. They recognized the significance of the IIC, the importance of the issues addressed in the study, and the special opportunity of having an international law firm make a contribution to a dialogue on those issues.

Given this perspective, the firm made it possible for the project to work for six months with Philippe Peters, a young Belgian communications lawyer. Philippe gathered material on developments in the Benelux countries and was instrumental in setting up some important meetings in Brussels. The project benefited substantially from his perspective as a European lawyer and as a result of his assistance in reviewing background materials for the French and other country reports.

Functioning as a hub for the study in France and on the Continent, collecting documentation, and participating in many meetings, was the Debevoise & Plimpton European office. In particular, my partners in Paris, Jim Kiernan and Dominique Blanco, and their associate, Ann Baker, were of special assistance.

The study would never have seen the light of day if several members of the Debevoise & Plimpton staff had not worked literally night and day on at least two separate and extended occasions. Particular thanks for their special dedication and professional skills are owed to Donna Kinnaman, Elaine Foster, Jessica Herman, Helen Fiori, Mike Howell, and others who were called in when needed.

Finally, enough cannot be said about my co-authors and colleagues, Jeff Cunard and Mark Director, who each made immense contributions to this document. They drafted country reports, edited and honed the text, and collaborated in the analysis that set out the framework for the study. With the background of their work on this study and with their analytic and writing skills, both Jeff and Mark, though not yet in their thirties, must surely be among the most talented and promising young communications lawyers in this country.

R.R. Bruce
Washington, D.C.
August 1985

CHAPTER I
SUMMARY

I. OVERVIEW AND INTRODUCTION

Over the last few years, telecommunications and information policies have been reviewed in several major industrialized countries. Such policies are now seen as having great impact on productivity, economic growth, and on the economic, if not the political, relationships among the United States, Canada, Japan, and Europe. Policymakers perceive that technological and economic pressures are forcing change and that the status quo cannot be maintained.

Technological developments have created the potential for new services. Clusters of computers with incompatible standards can be linked together. New electronic markets for information, commodities, securities, and other services are competing with traditional markets—stock and commodities exchanges. Satellite networks for data and other services are leapfrogging national terrestrial networks and challenging past pricing policies.

Such new services cannot easily be fitted into old legal and regulatory schemes. Thus, the emergence of new services and service providers requires reviewing both industry and institutional structures, as well as the mechanisms for the oversight and control of the industrial sector.

So, too, economic pressures are forcing an end to historic subsidies and an upward realignment of prices affecting the general public. Policymakers are being confronted with the agonizing dilemma of weighing the short-term political costs of implementing new price structures against the long-term economic benefits likely to result therefrom.

It has, however, become increasingly clear that inaction and indecision are not viable policy responses to these pressures.

Similarly, in the international context, policymakers cannot choose inaction. The pace of change at the national level threatens to disrupt and destabilize traditional arrangements by which international telecommunications services have been provided. If anarchy and conflict are to be avoided, and stable relationships in international telecommunications assured, efforts to address an array of problems are needed on an urgent basis.

This study is an attempt to describe in a comprehensive way what is happening in eight major industrialized countries, what are the international consequences of those developments, and how international economic and technological pressures are requiring changes in national policy. The study is intended to assist government policymakers, users, and service providers in deciding how to respond in an era of unprecedented change.

II. GLOBAL CHANGE AND THE PROCESS OF REVIEW

Policies are being reviewed globally as a result of significant changes in telecommunications structures and policies in major industrialized countries.

In the U.S., AT&T has been restructured as a result of the settlement of the antitrust suit brought by the Department of Justice; the Modified Final Judgment ("MFJ") embodying the terms of that settlement has become a regulatory instrument rivaling the Communications Act of 1934 in establishing the industry structure and service arrangements. In the United Kingdom and Japan, new telecommunications laws were enacted in 1983 and 1984, respectively, and in both countries the previously dominant service providers, British Telecommunications ("BT") and Nippon Telegraph & Telephone ("NTT"), will face stiff challenges from new entrants providing both telecommunications facilities and services.

In Canada and Finland, telecommunications laws dating from 1906 and 1886, respectively, are under high-level review. Similarly, in the Federal Republic of Germany, a governmental commission is studying the future of the Deutsche Bundespost. In Italy and France, and the Benelux countries, the evolution of telecommunications policy is being monitored closely. And, as to Europe, the development of telecommunications and information services is one of the highest priorities of the Commission of the European Communities.

It is, moreover, becoming increasingly apparent that shifts in policy are emulative. Deregulation and divestiture in the U.S., along with privatization and liberalization in the U.K. and Japan, have effects on other nations. Thus, one country's policies and policy shifts are inextricably linked to the development of the industrial sectors and the formulation of policy elsewhere.

Beyond the emulative and inexorable nature of the changes that are taking place, several other forces are at work in pushing or reshaping traditional telecommunications policies. Some of these pressures are economic, some technological, others political or ideological.

The pricing of telecommunications services is undergoing significant review as a result of structural changes in the U.S., Japan, and Europe. The price of services is moving toward costs, thereby undermining historic pricing subsidies. Although these changes are occurring at the national level, they are exercising a gravitational pull on adjacent countries, with economic consequences rippling outward on a regional and international basis.

The consequences of these economic forces must be addressed in a complex web of institutional mechanisms that filter and focus the political and social pressures that are brought to bear on pricing decisions. Application of those pressures traditionally may have caused the pricing of some services—international and long distance, for example—above cost. Such policies have been intended to maintain low prices for local exchange services and to assure uniform national pricing. Consequently, any upward readjustment of prices to compensate for subsidies "lost" as a result of international competitive presssures inevitably will have an impact on the public at large.

The vexing dilemma confronting policymakers, therefore, is how to choose between short-term political pressure and cost-based pricing that may advance the long-term goal of stimulating economic efficiency and growth. Certain industrialized nations, Japan, for example, are beginning to make some hard choices by resolving to encourage economic development by significantly reducing the price of telecommunications services.

Technological changes are also having a pervasive impact on policymaking. It is conventional wisdom that the communications and computer sectors are becoming fused. Intertwined with communications and computer services, however, is an emerging array of transactional and financial services. The resultant blurring of sectoral distinctions is creating significant opportunities both for computer companies, which are entering the telecommunications field, and for communications providers, which are raising their profile in the related-services sector. As these differences, then, are becoming ever more difficult to discern, policymakers are confronted with the task of refereeing a game that has rules that are in constant flux.

The rapid emergence of satellite technology is, moreover, eroding national or geographic-based distinctions among services. Satellites are challenging the historic segmentation in national telecommunications industries between domestic and international services. Although the evolution of satellite services are creating market openings for both private and public entrepreneurs, they are also disrupting traditional pricing structures and are having a significant impact on the role of regional and international organizations such as Intelsat.

These numerous and conflicting national and regional forces have also created significant strain on the system by which international telecommunications services are provided. Over the years, the international environment has been relatively stable—a small number of providers offering telephone, telex, and telegram services within a structure of bilateral agreements. With the emergence of new providers, new services, and uncertainty in structural arrangements, the international regime is facing unpredictability, if not chaos.

As a result of this instability, there may be a shift toward a trade-oriented environment. Politics may come to characterize a regime of short-term agreements. Services may increasingly be provided on an end-to-end basis. Telecommunications policymakers will need to be more attentive to the trade-related aspects of their decisions and trade negotiators will have to become attuned to telecommunications and related-industry issues.

This study hopes to make a contribution to understanding and assessing some of the dynamics of the changes that are taking place. Nevertheless, the extraordinary rapidity of those changes ensures that even a study as comprehensive as this represents only a snapshot—a momentary portrait of an industry sector.

In the weeks and months immediately prior to this study becoming final, changes were occurring in and among many countries—the initiation of a *Computer III* proceeding in the U.S., the release of a new consultative document on value-added network services in the U.K., the authorization of private transoceanic satellite services and the crystallization of policy options by existing providers of satellite services, the implementation of a competitive structure in Japan, and extensive and ongoing reviews of telecommunications and information policies in Canada, the Federal Republic of Germany, Finland, Italy, the Netherlands, and at the Commission of the European Communities.

III. DEFINITIONAL ISSUES

Central to the review of the policies of the countries studied are the definitions of telecommunications and information services. Definitional issues are of critical importance because they determine who (and how many) can provide services—the public or private sectors, monopoly or competitive—and on what terms and conditions—regulated or not. It is no exaggeration to say, therefore, that service definitions have a profound influence on industry structure.

This study, therefore, has examined a number of critical definitional "boundary lines." Policymakers must, for example, distinguish between "basic" and "enhanced," or value-added, services. Other distinctions significant for the evolution of policy are between "telecommunications" and "information" services, between the provision of "facilities" and of "services," and between "telecommunications" and "cable television" services.

The development of definitions is, therefore, of considerable importance. At the same time, however, it is apparent that the convergence of communications and computer technologies is complicating the task of demarcating boundary lines. Further contributing to the difficulty facing policymakers is the emergence of communications and computer facilities as the infrastructure for financial and other market services. The prices, terms, and conditions of access to telecommunications services are fundamentally tied to the availability of such new services. Thus, as noted above, it is increasingly difficult to maintain divisions among several interrelated industry sectors—telecommunications, data processing, information, and other electronic services.

Throughout the course of this study, there has been an attempt to identify and compare the differing national approaches to definitional and structural issues in telecommunications policy. There has, of course, never been any presupposition that there is one "right" answer or that one nation's approach is preferable to that of any other. Rather, the assumption underlying the analysis is that national policies would, quite naturally, differ, given distinctive national values and priorities. The goal has been to shed some understanding on these differences, so as to facilitate the provision of international telecommunications, information, and related transactional services.

The study has focused on eight countries, the U.S., Canada, Japan, the U.K., Finland, France, the Federal Republic of Germany, and Italy. A series of country reports have been prepared; they are preceded herein by a synthetic section that attempts to focus on themes common to the experience of each country and on substantive and procedural issues raised by the provision of international telecommunications services. The guiding principle has been to focus on the differences and similarities in the national approaches while attempting to compare national policies. There are, in addition, a range of issues that are confronting policymakers around the world.

Some of the more important conclusions of the project are summarized in brief below.

A. "Basic" versus "Enhanced" or "Value-Added" Services

Many administrations have been wrestling with distinctions between "basic" and "enhanced" or "valued-added" services. The proliferation of computer devices operating with different standards has created both the need and the opportunity for protocol conversion or computer-controlled networks that are based on transmission capacity leased from an underlying carrier. Such services can be offered by entities unaffiliated with the transmission carrier; therefore, it is important to delineate what services can be provided outside the traditional monopoly of a service provider and what services must be offered by that carrier to new service providers.

Among the countries studied, there is a variety of approaches to establishing lines of demarcation between basic and enhanced services. Some of these boundary lines are based on technological distinctions; others are drawn on the basis of the market served by the new service provider, or its likely economic impact on the underlying carrier. All these efforts at drawing lines, however, ultimately have had to come to grips with unique and practical concerns facing each administration.

In the U.S., for example, the "basic" and "enhanced" distinction embedded in the *Computer II* decision of the Federal Communications Commission ("FCC") was influenced both by the terms of the then-effective 1956 Consent Decree, which set forth limits on AT&T's ability to offer services other than basic common carriage, and by the dominant market position of the pre-divestiture AT&T.

In the U.K., the concept of "value-added" services has evolved as a consequence of the government's rejection of the proposed BT-IBM venture to offer managed data network services. In Germany, the focus is on devising a definition of enhanced services that would minimize the possibility that new services, based on leased lines, might "cream skim" from the public network. The Japanese have established two categories of service providers—Type I offering facilities, Type II utilizing leased services—in an attempt to avoid the definitional dilemmas that have confronted regulators in the U.S., Canada, and elsewhere. These efforts at avoiding service-based distinctions have not succeeded in practice. The Japanese have found that it is necessary to identify Type II services that can be offered by Type I carriers through subsidiaries. In addition, distinctions among Type II services may have to be formulated to minimize the impact of resale by Type II entities on NTT's public switched services, and to provide for value-added services on an international basis.

Even as administrations elsewhere are struggling with the "basic"/ "enhanced" dichotomy, the FCC has just initiated its *Computer III* inquiry; the focus of the proceeding will not be on the failure of the *Computer II* distinction but on the continuing fairness and efficacy of applying the separate subsidiary requirements to AT&T. Thus, regulatory developments in the U.S. may, once again, unsettle and accelerate international consideration of the concept of "enhanced" services that, in large part, had been precipitated by the *Computer II* proceeding.

The diversity in approaches and ongoing regulatory ferment is creating an urgent need to catalogue and compare the various national definitions and concepts of valued-added or enhanced services. Simultaneously, there are efforts either to encourage a more uniform approach to defining enhanced services or to structure viable interconnection arrangements for international services. The first steps in addressing these issues will, necessarily, be taken among countries where new value-added services have evolved. The issues will be dealt with bilaterally—between the U.S. and Japan, or with the U.K.—but their resolution in a bilateral context will have implications for administrations worldwide, as well. The process of reaching an accommodation among varying national approaches ultimately will test the resilience and flexibility of traditional international mechanisms such as the CCITT.

B. Information and Hybrid Services: Definitional Issues

In the past, the regulatory focus of attention has been on the "basic"/"enhanced" dichotomy. Consequently, the impact of this distinction on the treatment accorded information or other hybrid or transaction-related services has been given very little attention by policymakers. This inattention has sometimes resulted in such hybrid information services—traditionally free from regulation and unrelated to pure communications services—becoming entangled in a scheme of regulation, albeit one that is "liberalized." This result may be entirely inappropriate for information vendors who, unlike many enhanced or value-added service suppliers, do not intend to compete with the providers of communications services; rather, they offer a distinct electronic service that may, incidentally, involve communications capabilities.

These services, based on the sale and dissemination of information to users, may permit them to execute transactions. The networks utilized in providing the services may resemble those used for basic transmission or protocol conversion networks.

Thus, although there may be some similarity between these offerings, information and transactional services have a distinctly different function—they market information or specific financial or brokerage services through electronic means. The offering of some communications capability to their customers is, then, quite incidental to their primary business purpose.

Increasingly, providers of these new business services are trying to avoid entanglement in policies and regulatory strictures intended to apply to communications-oriented enhanced services. Their concern is that they might be subject to carrier-like regulation as they add transactional (*i.e.*, customer-to-customer) capabilities to their information offerings. Thus, as administrations are beginning to focus on "value-added" services as a regulatory classification, information and transaction-based service providers hope that they will not inadvertently, or otherwise, be swept into a regulatory process of prior approval.

The concerns of these information vendors are not without foundation. Regulatory attention was drawn away from them with the shift from the "hybrid" category of *Computer I* to the dichotomy of *Computer II*. With respect to these offerors, the distinction between enhanced and information services was essentially unimportant as neither category was regulated. The MFJ, however, has imposed restrictions on the provision of information services by AT&T and its divested operating companies. Thus, the definitional bounds of such services are a focal point of concern for both suppliers and users.

Outside the U.S., it is more critical to establish regulatory distinctions between information and enhanced services. Enhanced services, even if less stringently regulated than transmission services, are still subject to a more structured scheme of regulation than has customarily been the case with information or transactional services. In the U.K., for example, suppliers of information-related services must determine whether they are subject to licensing either as a value-added service or, under the proposal of the government's consultative document, as a managed data network service. Similarly, in Japan, Type II approval of certain transactional services may be required.

In short, then, the spillover from liberalization may, ironically enough, be of some concern to information providers. One of the leitmotifs of the study, therefore, is an examination of the need for definitions for a spectrum of electronic and information services.

C. "Facilities" versus "Services": Industry Structure

Another key dichotomy that is evolving in many countries is the distinction between the provision of facilities and that of services. The study assesses a spectrum of approaches to industry structure.

At one end of the range is the U.S. model of open entry in both facilities and services and, at the other, is the traditional European preference for maintaining an integrated infrastructure. With respect to European administrations, more latitude is now being accorded users and others to provide service-based competition; however, it is unlikely that there soon will be competitive entry in basic network facilities. And, somewhere between the U.S. and traditional European approaches are numerous variations involving competition in either or both facilities and services.

From the European perspective, one of the most interesting case studies is that of Japan. NTT, the traditional provider of facilities and services on a monopoly basis, will be faced with competition in both the long-haul facilities and services markets. The Japanese objective, in starkest terms, is to drive down the cost of communications and to stimulate the development of new telecommunications and information services.

A similar transition is occurring in the U.K., but in a different industrial and institutional setting. The British government has opted for a policy of limited entry in the facilities market; it has authorized only Mercury to compete with BT, at least for the immediate future. To manage the transition, the British have created a new regulatory institution, OFTEL, while endeavoring to steer clear of the more formal procedures of the FCC and the U.S. experience. The Japanese have declined to move toward either the U.S. or British regulatory model, relying on the more traditional approach of consensus-building. Over the next few months and years, comparing the efficacy with which the British and the Japanese will manage their respective transitions to a competitive market structure will be instructive.

Both the British and Japanese approaches to regulation highlight one of the major observations of the study. That is, it is extremely difficult to revise historic policies toward competition and industry structure without commensurate changes in the arrangements for oversight or regulation. Often this nexus, between competition and regulatory policies, is not seen clearly by policymakers. The synthesis section of the study explores these relationships in detail.

Although much attention has been focused on recent initiatives in the U.K. and Japan, the Canadians for some time have regarded their market as liberalized. CNCP has long provided private line voice and data services. Now, with the CNCP application for the offering of public switched interexchange services, Canadian policymakers are wrestling with the issue of whether Telecom Canada and its members, the traditional providers of such services, should have a facilities-based competitor. Some of the impetus for movement toward a competitive environment has been from the U.S., from the economic consequences and gravitational pull of deregulation and from pricing changes. The complex jurisdictional questions raised by the federal-provincial relationship have made it difficult to achieve a consensus in Canada on such important issues as pricing and industry structure.

Diverse policy options are also undergoing examination elsewhere in the world. In Finland, there is, for example, a delicate balance between the

Finnish PTT, which is moving to modernize itself both institutionally and technologically, and the privately-owned telephone companies. Opportunities for enhanced competition between these two interests are increasing due to the emergence of satellite, fiber optic cable, and computer technologies. In particular, new models for offering data services are starting to develop in a market that many would have viewed as too small to support competition; however, it appears that a competitive environment is on the verge of successful evolution.

In Italy, too, the government is in the midst of reviewing a complex industry structure and is taking steps toward reorganization. At the same time, it is also assessing the potential of joint venture arrangements or of other innovative entrepreneurial steps to encourage the development of new services for business and other users.

In the Netherlands, a government commission is currently studying the experiences of other countries. It is considering whether enhanced services should be provided on a competitive basis. Movement in the Netherlands is, moreover, quite likely to stimulate examination and review in Belgium and elsewhere in Europe.

In the meantime, there is nothing stagnant about the traditional postal and telecommunications administrations of Germany and France. In Germany, there has been a series of studies and appraisals of the role of the Deutsche Bundespost and the viability of some limited service competition. The newly-established governmental commission is likely to focus on this issue. At the same time, the Bundespost has been modernizing its infrastructure by installing equipment that looks toward the implementation of an integrated services digital network environment ("ISDN").

In France, the Direction generale des telecommunications ("D.G.T.") has taken several steps to meet the competitive challenge it faces nationally and in Europe. Over the last few years, it has taken significant steps to upgrade its network infrastructure. By developing technical standards it has, moreover, encouraged the emergence of new software and information-based services. Concurrently, the D.G.T. has been pragmatic in assessing the economic consequences of deregulation internationally. It has restructured itself, creating subsidiaries to foster innovation and to respond to the competitive international challenges that are emerging. Furthermore, even as it faces the possibility of a shift in French industrial policy after the parliamentary elections of next year, it is continuing to seek autonomy to manage its telecommunications operations from an entrepreneurial perspective.

Although the national experiences in implementing more competitive industry structures or responding to international competitive pressures are diverse, many common issues are being faced. These issues are discussed in some detail in the country reports and in the synthesis. The study concludes that there is no global convergence toward a single industrial structure—no gravitation toward the U.S., British, Japanese, Canadian, German, or French model. The principal conclusion that can be stated is that the sector will continue to be marked by diverse approaches to structural issues and by substantial change in institutional and industry structure and in the mechanisms for regulatory control. This rapid change adds to the complexity of working out business arrangements and international agreements.

There is, therefore, a great need to make a comparative assessment of the directions of change. First, the experience of one country is often instructive to others. Moreover, it is difficult to agree on international services without a full exploration of developments at the national levels. Differences will not be resolved unless there is a complete understanding of the various institutional settings, the sources of the initiatives for any policy shifts, and the nature of any obstacles to change.

IV. SOME BROADER TRENDS: INTERNATIONAL POLICY ISSUES

The international telecommunications environ- ment is affected by a combination of centrifugal and centripetal forces that are at work concurrently.

Unsettling the status quo is a confluence of changes in national policies that are spilling over into the international arena. Such changes disrupt consensus, prevent the development of new rules, and create anarchy in the international telecommunications arena. Divergent national policies are forcing nations farther apart as they alter or deviate from traditional policies.

Simultaneously, however, there are forces that are drawing policymakers together to focus on a common agenda of issues. Even as economic pressures for cost-based pricing structures are intensifying competition among national administrations, they are creating incentives to address the common issue of how to remain competitive in a gradually liberalizing environment. Satellite technology is requiring administrations to join together to reevaluate strategies for pricing and marketing facilities and services.

A. International Impact of Pricing Pressures

The economic pressures resulting from deregulation, liberalization, and newly-emerging industry structures have an important effect on international telecommunications. In the U.S., for example, deregulation has moved prices closer to costs, but the impact of changes in U.S. pricing practices is international in scope. The emergence of new and vigorous competitors to AT&T in the international telephony market is driving down prices. Moreover, many Canadians regard their market as effectively deregulated because Canadian users have the option of bypassing Canadian facilities for trans-Canada communications by routing traffic via leased lines and switching facilities located in the U.S. More broadly, the lower cost and greater flexibility of the telecommunications facilities available in the U.S. are causing business users in other countries to seek similar advantages.

In Europe, liberalization in the U.K., with concomitant price reductions, is having a strong ripple effect on the Continent. Administrations are aware that multinational enterprises are looking to locate their network nodes to take advantage of the most flexible regulatory environments. Thus, the D.G.T. model—of creating subsidiaries—is intended, in part, both to permit greater flexibility in offering or tailoring services and to price services to meet international competition.

These economic pressures are international in scope and impact. It is, therefore, virtually impossible to insulate national pricing policies from them. In particular, when other administrations are determined to base pricing decisions on cost and efficiency, it can be difficult to pursue such important national political and social values as universal service or the redistribution of income between business and residential users.

In Germany, for example, some policymakers believe that movement toward a cost-based pricing system is important for maintaining international competitiveness, but that it is difficult to achieve given the subsidies built into the pricing structure and the fear of diverting services from the public network. In Canada, policymakers face a similar dilemma; they are being forced to choose between traditional pricing practices and subsidies, on the one hand, or the possibility of seeing traffic diverted over non-Canadian telecommunications facilities, or business opportunities lost by Canadian companies in global markets, on the other.

Cost-based pricing proposals, then, force difficult choices between reducing interexchange costs, for competitive reasons, and increasing local exchange costs to the general public. Thus, although political pressure might militate in favor of postponing adoption of proposals to restructure prices, the international forces at work are increasingly difficult to resist. A failure to bring prices and terms and conditions of national telecommunications services in line with levels and practices in the U.S., Japan, or other major industrialized countries may have severe economic consequences for all business and industrial sectors dependent on them.

National responses to pricing issues are of critical import to understanding the ebb and flow of policymaking at the transnational level. The steps taken by the U.S.—divestiture, access charges, unlimited resale—are dramatic and their consequences are spilling across borders. The Japanese see the thrust of their recent initiatives as a "supply side" measure intended to stimulate entrepreneurial activity by lowering the cost of telecommunications services. Pricing issues are caught up in intense debates in Canada and Germany; in both countries it is apparent that action is needed on an urgent basis, but that it is difficult to achieve a consensus. By contrast, the French and the British have been able to move ahead in restructuring their pricing without major political obstacles.

A study of this type may, then, be important because it focuses attention on these dilemmas. Knowing that other nations are grappling with pricing issues, and attempting to understand how they do so, may not make domestic policymaking any easier. Such an understanding may, however, lay the foundation for a consensus with respect to the importance of the pricing issues and the possible consequences of failing to address them head-on.

The movement toward cost-based pricing, particularly for national interexchange and international services, will have, as well, significant consequences for the providers of telecommunications services. It will create more pressure for efficiency, entrepreneurial independence, and institutional innovation by the PTTs. This process is underway in France, Finland, Japan, the U.K., now Germany, and elsewhere. Nevertheless, service providers will also be squeezed by the same dilemma that confronts policymakers—how to accommodate, on the one hand, pressures for a restructuring of prices that would diminish traditional subsidies and, on the other, the inevitable political resistance to upward adjustments in the pricing of local services.

B. Technological Pressures and Challenges

Further complicating the ability of service providers to respond to pricing pressures is the need to develop new technologies and services based on them. As administrations are struggling with pricing issues, industrial policymakers are urging investment in new infrastructure. Users are demanding new technology-based services. The ability of service providers to respond to pricing pressures can, therefore, be significantly limited by capital costs that are rapidly escalating as a result of investment in and development of fiber optic and satellite services.

These complicating cross-currents are particularly intense among European administrations. There is a proliferation of national satellite services; there are plans for major new broadband services at the European level. There is, however, no entirely adequate mechanism for coordination and planning of infrastructure development.

It remains to be seen whether a surplus of capacity will, in fact, evolve. Combined with pricing pressures, the costs and risks of investing in and developing new services will raise a formidable set of choices for decisionmakers and businesses. In light of growing uncertainties with respect to the use of new capacity, service providers may explore several options to minimize their risks; they could be inclined to shift such risks to public-private joint ventures or to the private sector entirely.

The response to technological and economic pressures may well be to spur innovation in developing and marketing new services. Relationships among service providers are likely to become more competitive at the international level. National administrations may come to woo multinational enterprises to base corporate networks in their countries or to develop new services themselves. Economic and technological factors may encourage service providers to become both more collaborative and more competitive. There may, for example, be movement toward using national satellite systems for transborder services in Europe and elsewhere.

Satellite technologies, in particular, are having a significant effect on the international environment. Inherently, satellite services challenge traditional pricing structures for services provided by conventional microwave or cable links. That is, the cost of such services, unlike that of terrestrial services, is no longer related to distance.

In Europe, the challenges may be especially difficult. Eutelsat, for example, currently provides the facilities infrastructure for satellite services but there is no single European mechanism for marketing or pricing those services. Arrangements must be made through the individual administrations and are, in large part, a result of the efforts of users, who seek both uniformity in marketing practices and more flexibility in conducting business on a transnational basis. Moreover, if Eutelsat does not move toward offering new services on a competitive basis, then Intelsat, itself faced with new competitive challenges, may step in to offer a set of options to users.

Satellite technology is also challenging such traditional institutional arrangements as Intelsat. National, regional, and, in the near future, private satellite systems can and will offer transoceanic services. The pressures actually to offer such international services may arise not only from the fact that they are now feasible or offer economic opportunities, but also because they may be necessary to sustaining the national systems. Many policymakers believe, for example, that Japanese satellite systems would not be viable without also being able to offer transoceanic services.

Beside the challenge of new satellite services, Intelsat must also confront the impact of transoceanic fiber optic cables. Fiber optic systems are being constructed by traditional service providers; soon, however, private fiber optic cables will offer competitive or new transoceanic services. Such cables pose a formidable economic challenge to Intelsat, which offers service to users on the basis of an integrated global pricing scheme. Fiber optic cable systems, by contrast, can set prices that reflect the economies of serving high-density routes.

The challenges posed by private, regional, and national satellites and by fiber optic cables will not abate. It will be critical for Intelsat, therefore, to rethink its role and to reassess its pricing practices. Although there is now increasing attention paid to the need for enhanced pricing flexibility, Intelsat must also plan for a shift in its institutional responsibilities. It must anticipate playing a larger role—that of coordinator, not just procurer, of satellite facilities. Intelsat may, as well, want to develop a broader role in the planning of international facilities.

C. Interlocking National Policies: The International Environment

The international environment, in short, is affected by economic and technological pressures that influence and often severely limit the options available to national policymakers. At the same time, national policy decisions spill over and fundamentally affect the international arena. Until recently, it was only deregulation in the U.S. that was the rock disturbing the still pond that once was the international telecommunications environment. Now, however, liberalization in the U.K. is having a similar impact on Europe. The international system will have to accommodate the new regulatory concepts embedded in the Japanese Telecommunications Business Law, such as that of a "Type II" provider. Plans for Japanese national satellites will surely have implications for the price and availability of facilities in the Pacific region. National policy shifts in France, Germany, and Canada are having similar international consequences.

The system or process by which international telecommunications are provided is extremely complex. It is comprised of an intermeshing of national systems, any one of which, by itself, is a web of economic and institutional relationships. National policy processes and economic pressures flow outward into the regional and international arena and are, in turn, influenced by international economic and technological pressures.

A keen assessment of these relationships is critical to developing a strategic perspective on the telecommunications and information industries. Domestic policymakers, however, understand little about the impact of their actions in the international arena. Conversely, it is not well understood how the international environment affects the course of national policy. Policymakers, providers, users, and businesses relying on telecommunications must come to understand the workings of the global political economy that is the international telecommunications market.

To establish policy or make business decisions without such a perspective is like setting sail without charts of the shoals and tides. Today, however, all these relationships are poorly understood. This study is only the first step toward such an understanding.

V. INTERNATIONAL INSTITUTIONAL IMPLICATIONS

The international environment is, quite clearly, no longer the static regime of the past in which long-term agreements were seldom renegotiated. There is now a pro- liferation of new players: new service providers, new policymakers, new regulators, and new services. Thus, as substantive policies have changed domestically so, too, is there a need to develop new institutional mechanisms to explore and address the impact of economic and technological changes at the international level.

Regulators and service providers in Europe, Japan, Canada, and the U.S. are focusing on the international telecommunications marketplace. Users, increasingly able to configure many of their own services, also want to be represented in discussions on international policy. Also having a stake in the international arena is a spectrum of data processing vendors and suppliers of information and transactional services.

As the flow of telecommunications and information-services across boundaries becomes more critical to national and international economies, traditional telecommunications regulators are joined by trade officials. Telecommunications and trade policymakers, however, come from different realms and often have difficulties in understanding each other. While those from the telecommunications sector perceive the complexity of economic and technological systems, trade officials see the urgency of making institutional adjustments. What is required, then, is a fusion of perspectives amongst policymakers at both the national and international levels.

For all such policymakers, there is a growing agenda of complex issues that must be addressed in a comprehensive, yet expeditious, fashion. The synthetic section of the study, which reviews overall trends, focuses on these issues. They include the need to restructure interconnection arrangements in light of the entry of multiple suppliers of interexchange public switched services and how to devise schemes for the interconnection of enhanced or value-added services.

Another major issue is Intelsat's future, which must be charted in an institutional framework broader than that of Intelsat itself. Policymakers must define and understand all the economic, technological, and political forces that are affecting the future of the organization. To address the role of Intelsat may require instituting new mechanisms to bring together telecommunications and political officials.

Further challenges are presented by the spread of transaction-oriented services heavily dependent on international telecommunications networks. Due to the absence of a flexible set of international tariff and regulatory principles applicable to such services, it may be difficult for them to evolve rapidly and in a unified way. Another possible pitfall is that telecommunications regulation—purportedly addressing technical standards and interconnection arrangements—can affect the structure and regulation of new electronic financial or brokerage services.

Mechanisms are needed to bring together telecommunications officals and those who have an interest in the regulation of the other aspects of newly-emerging electronic market services. The CCITT, which traditionally has dealt with the telecommunications sector, may not be best suited for accomplishing this important task. What institutional arrangements will be required or may ultimately develop is currently unclear, in large part because the scope of the problems and the issues is not yet completely delineated.

The difficulty and challenge for international institutions that deal with telecommunications is that the issues have become complex, interrelated, and involve the interests of many diverse parties. New fora for discussions are needed to prevent changes in the international environment from erupting into conflict and anarchy. Even for those administrations firmly committed to relying on the market and the forces of technology, there is nothing inconsistent in establishing better mechanisms for understanding and interpreting the direction of events. Collecting and analyzing information, and developing perspectives, are necessary to guide entrepreneurial initiative and for governmental decisionmaking, even where governments are committed to a minimally-regulated international system.

Users are not confident that government officials can or will create a framework for innovation. They believe that they must rely on their own resources for structuring new services and resolving regulatory obstacles. This task, however, could almost be insurmountable without a better and broader dialogue with and among international telecommunications officials.

There are, however, not many fora where users, along with service providers and policymakers, can gather to share views. Nor are there many satisfactory institutional frameworks in which Europeans, North Americans, and Japanese can be brought together. Representatives of a diverse set of interests must be given the opportunity to assess the future and discuss options, whatever might be the role of bilateral discussions, multilateral exchanges, trade talks, CCITT deliberations, or long-range OECD reviews. It may, therefore, ultimately be necessary to develop both formal mechanisms and informal processes to address the spectrum of issues in light of broader policy concerns, and not merely from technocratic or fragmented perspectives.

Of great importance, too, is that the gap in perceptions and experience between the OECD countries and other nations directly or indirectly affected by developments must be closed. If all elements of the global telecommunications puzzle are to be considered fully, and for there to be any hope of an integrated environment, it will be critical to consider the experiences and needs of nations that are in the process of developing their telecommunications and information infrastructures.

It is hoped that this study is a contribution toward launching the discussions on global telecommunications and information policies that are now so critical. The project was conceived as both an end in itself—an initial attempt at chronicling, examining, and appraising developments in eight countries and worldwide—and as a process of informal dialogue with representation from various elements of the telecommunications and information sectors. In this latter objective, it is hoped that the study is, at the end, only the beginning.

CHAPTER II
SYNTHESIS

TABLE OF CONTENTS

PART I

NATIONAL DEVELOPMENTS: SOME COMMON THEMES AND A COMPARATIVE ANALYSIS

CHAPTER II
SYNTHESIS

PART I

NATIONAL DEVELOPMENTS: SOME COMMON THEMES AND A COMPARATIVE ANALYSIS

I. A Comparative Assessment of Definitional and Boundary Line Issues

A. Introduction

The role of definitions—of boundary lines between services and regulatory classification—is increasingly important in telecommunications law and regulation around the world. Demarcating the border between "telecommunications" and "data processing" or "information services, between "basic" and "enhanced" services is critical because these definitions stake out who may provide a service, and under what terms and conditions. In some countries, the definitions both establish the limits of a state-controlled telecommunications monopoly and determine the role of the private sector in providing information or data processing services. Elsewhere, where some degree of competition or multiple entry may be authorized, definitions establish the texture of relationships between sectors subject to limited competitive entry and those without entry restrictions.

In the past, these definitional concepts were, it was assumed, to be of relative unimportance and of little controversy or consequence. In the 1934 Communications Act in the United States, for example, the definitions of such basic terms as "broadcasting" or "common carriage" were defined in either an unrevealing or wholly circular manner. Over the past twenty years, however, some of the most heated regulatory and judicial battles have been fought over just the meaning and scope of these seminal statutory and regulatory concepts.

The imprecision of statutory or regulatory definitions is not only a characteristic of older telecommunications statutes. For example, even the recently enacted telecommunications laws in the United Kingdom and Japan have, in some cases, not confronted basic definitional questions with complete clarity or precision. Consequently, there is some uncertainty in those countries as to what kind of value-added services can be provided, and on what basis.

B. Erosion of Boundary Lines Between Industry Sectors

The haziness of definitional boundary lines reflects, in some sense, the modern economic reality that it is becoming more difficult to draw—or perceive—traditional distinctions between industry sectors themselves. There is an increasing interdependence between the information or financial services sectors and the telecommunications and information processing industries, the facilities and services of which they rely. Financial institutions and providers of economic, marketplace, or other information have established networks of transmission lines and switching capacity to offer a wide-range of services to their customers on a national and global basis. Customers will also utilize these networks to interact with vendors of services. Almost inevitably, therefore, the business of communicating over such specialized networks is becoming closely intertwined with the businesses of financial services or the sale of information.

As the distinctions between and among businesses gradually erode, user pressures to make the most efficient use of the terminal—the customer's access to the services—escalate. Users may not want an office cluttered with an array of specialized terminals. Traditionally, of course, pressures for efficiency and "universality" in terminal devices have come from monopoly telecommunications service providers. Nevertheless, once the dominance of such suppliers over terminal supply has eroded, the pressures—to establish the measures of universal utility—remain. The dynamics of these pressures are not like those coming from a dominant entity; rather, the pressures are generated by competitive and private sector forces and industrial and technological developments.

The interdependence of communications, terminals, and services that is increasingly coming to characterize the offerings of financial and information services vendors is also characteristic of the remote access data processing services sector. Remote access data processing is, as well, often closely tied with banking, or the provision or marketing of information. Such companies market their services to a diverse set of customers who may have significantly disparate terminal devices or computer processing facilities on their own premises. As the robust and open terminal equipment and computer market has evolved, there is, concurrently, a variety of standards and protocols that influence the capability to communicate between these devices or with the central processing facilities of the data processing or information service vendors.

These service providers, therefore, typically will have established mechanisms by which different terminal devices can communicate. These vendors also intend that their customers have the ability to make the fullest use of informational or financial services offerings. Thus, they expect that users can negotiate and consummate transactions, with terminals executing orders or otherwise having access to business-related information. Communications services are often critical to the functioning of the core processing or information-services activity. In these cases, it may be appropriate to determine whether the services can be characterized in any way as "communications" or partake of another industry sector or business altogether.

The boundaries between communications and other businesses are imprecise, as well, in the case of service vendors who only intend to provide protocol or format conversion among diverse communities of users. Sometimes these services consist of storing or forwarding data. Utilizing similar configurations of leased lines as the financial, information, or data processing service providers, these services are, nevertheless, not necessarily part of any particular business activity. They might, however, be marketed to serve particular industry sectors. In general, these activities would be distinguished from the provision of pure transmission "pipe line" services that involve no change in the format, protocols, standards or content of the information conveyed.

A final critical distinction is not purely "service-based," but is between those who construct or operate facilities for the transmission of communications and those who merely lease that capacity from the owner and operator. Of special note is that the provider of the underlying transmission service can often be distinguished from the provider of the facilities for transmission. For example, the owner of communications satellite facilities is not necessarily the provider of satellite service.

A series of often subtle distinctions can, therefore, be drawn between 1) the owner of a facility, 2) the operator of that facility—who may or may not provide a communications service, and 3) other entities who act as retailers or marketers of communications services—often in a way that a retailer obtains goods from wholesalers and markets them more generally. Thus, distinctions between the provision of facilities and services may be of importance in determining what competitive relationships can be established between suppliers, marketing agents, and users.

C. *National Approaches to Drawing Lines*

The increasing availability of all these communications and interdependent business activities is a worldwide phenomenon. In each nation, of course, availability of the range of facilities, and communications, value-added, financial, or information services varies in accordance with particularized circumstances that may be political, economic, social, or technological in nature. Accordingly, each of the countries examined has taken a different approach to drawing the definitional lines of demarcation between and among these disparate—though intimately related—activities.

In comparing these various national approaches, it appears that the process of line-drawing is based on divergent criteria or rationales. At least two major approaches are evident. The first focuses on technological factors, the second on economic or marketplace criteria; both approaches are often tempered with an array of legal, pragmatic, and political considerations that vary by country.

1. Technological Approach. The first—technological—approach endeavors to distinguish among services on the basis of the functions carried out, or on a qualitative description of technological characteristics. This methodology depends on an examination of the formats, protocols, or content of information. The distinctions often grow out of sophisticated classifications based on functions described in such conceptual frameworks as the seven-layer Open Systems Interconnection ("OSI") model of the International Standards Organisation ("ISO").

2. Economic Approach. The second approach toward distinguishing between services is based on the economic relationship between a particular service and the existing offering of the monopoly provider. One method of defining "value-added services," for example, is to describe them in terms of activities in which the primary service supplier does not engage. This may have been the early approach in the U.K. toward "value-added network services" ("VANS"), which were defined to include electronic mailbox or information services that could be provided through the attachment—or addition—of computer processing capability to the underlying transmission offerings. Similarly, the French Law on Audiovisual Communication distinguishes between "public" services, on the one hand, and, on the other, message switching or other services that are incidental to information services and that do not rely on public transmission facilities.

The Deutsche Bundespost ("DBP"), however, has utilized some of the most sophisticated analyses of economic-based definitions for classifying new services. For example, DBP analysts point out that tariffs for public switched services are priced at a level above cost for several reasons—obligations to support postal activities, universal availability of service, and to increase payments to the general treasury accounts. Given that price/cost differential, the resale of leased line services—alone or in conjunction with information or data processing services—is seen as likely to encourage arbitrage or "cream skimming." In the DBP, it is argued that providers of service to third parties could have substantial economic incentives to induce users to abandon public network services.

Concomitantly, the DBP also recognizes that there may be significant differences between "simple" or "pure" resale of transmission capacity and the provision of new or value-added services that utilize such capacity. Such services are usually acknowledged as having some potential advantages for both users and the DBP. For example, permitting such services to evolve could facilitate the exploration of new markets without having the DBP bear any associated financial risks. The cost basis for tariffing leased line offerings may provide economic incentives that balance the risks involved in launching new services. Another possible benefit is that private entities, as they establish new networks, can begin to develop de facto technical standards or procedures that might be difficult to formulate in theory.

The adverse economic effects of revenue losses from resale of private lines are of critical importance for the DBP. Thus, the DBP is considering a strategy to reduce the economic incentives for "cream skimming" by defining the permissible limits of new services in conjunction with tariffing policies calling for the "harmonization" of leased line and public switched tariffs. The premise of the policy relies on the degree of substitution between the two—leased line and public switched—offerings. In principle, at least, a rational pricing strategy should attempt to establish tariff differentials between services that are based on possible substitution effects. Such distinctions are exceedingly difficult to draw in the abstract—almost as difficult as making technological distinctions among service categories.

It is important, nevertheless, to identify benchmarks or simplifying criteria that can be utilized to assess the likely impact of defining service classifications on a economic basis. In this regard, for example, in 1982, in the second phase of the Japanese liberalization process, small scale value-added networks ("VANs") limited to small- or medium-sized user groups were permitted. The VANs could not be used by companies over a particular size as the intent was to make available to smaller companies services that could be implemented by large integrated ventures. In addition, all VAN participants were to be affiliated companies. Thus, the ability of VAN providers to offer services to third parties—or extend the reach of their economic impact on third parties—was significantly circumscribed.

Some European Postal, Telegraph, and Telephone authorities ("PTTs") that have been studying issues relating to the economic impact of service classifications have considered, as one option, a parallel strategy of limiting services to related companies or industry clusters. This policy would allow service providers to serve particular sectors on a restricted basis. In some respects the rationale for such an approach follows one way in which the Federal Communications Commission ("FCC") in the U.S. distinguished unregulated "enhanced service" providers from "common carriers": the former provide services on an individualized basis and do not hold themselves out to serve the public at large.

In Finland, an early draft of new telecommunications legislation proposed to distinguish between "specialized networks" and "common networks," which served the public at large. Specialized networks were conceived as being usually available to participants in affiliated or like industries. There would be no obligations imposed on specialized network operators to deal with third parties. From the early drafts it was not entirely clear what services could be provided by specialized networks, *i.e.*, whether they would be restricted to "data," as opposed to "voice," services or whether there might be some additional criteria for measuring the extent to which the services were value-added.

The practical difficulty with such benchmark economic tests is that they may not, in fact, readily limit the economic impact of service classification of the established PTTs. An industry sector—such as banking—may be of considerable economic significance. Therefore, allowing multiple providers to serve that industry may have severe economic consequences for the existing provider.

The actual economic effects of such a policy may, as well, depend on the substitution effects between services. Consequently, an effort to distinguish between different categories of service—between those involving pure arbitrage or those offering new services—may be unavoidable.

3. Legal or Pragmatic Considerations. Boundaries may also be established on the basis of legal, institutional, or entirely pragmatic considerations. Distinctions grounded on such considerations may, of course, be disguised or justified with economic or technological rationales. For example, it is often emphasized that the distinction between "basic" and "enhanced" services had a technological underpinnning. Nevertheless, it is important that the unique legal factors militating toward that particular dichotomy not be ignored.

Before the *Computer II* decision of 1980, the scope of FCC's authority to refrain from regulating certain services was not at all clear. A recent appellate decision had left clouded the FCC's ability to "forbear" from regulating services that were defined under statute and case law as "common carrier" services. By contrast, it seemed more likely that the FCC could not regulate a service that was not a "common carrier" offering. The already complex legal situation faced by the FCC was made more so by the fact that the 1956 Consent Decree between the United States and AT&T expressly limited AT&T to providing only "common carrier communications services," defined in the Decree as communications services and facilities, "the charges for which are subject to public regulation under the Communications Act of 1934. . . . " The Consent Decree specifically did not limit AT&T to services regulated pursuant to Title II of the Communications Act (the provisions addressing common carrier services).

Thus, the legal and policy dilemma confronting the FCC was to define a service category that (1) was not a "common carrier" offering under Title II (which might have to be regulated); (2) yet was still a "common carrier communications service" within the meaning of the 1956 Consent Decree, *i.e.*, "the charges for which are subject to public regulation under the Communications Act of 1934"; (3) would be free from regulation (*i.e.*, consist essentially of unregulated data services; and (4) would not prevent AT&T from participating in an emerging market.

The problem was, in fact, to thread the very small eye of a legal/policy needle with a well-reasoned agency decision that could survive review by the appellate courts and the court with supervisory jurisdiction over the implementation of the 1956 Consent Decree. If such a decision could not be achieved, some at the FCC and in industry feared that Congress might intervene to enact legislation that would be less likely to take account of and balance evolving economic and competitive realities. A further possible consequence of such legislative intervention might have been to end the then-pending antitrust litigation brought by the Department of Justice against AT&T. The failure by the FCC to reach an administrative solution could have resulted in both legislative deadlock and intransigence on the part of the Department of Justice, which might not have wanted to concede any potential negotiating advantage, *i.e.*, the question of AT&T entry into unregulated markets, in the event of settlement discussions.

The FCC devised a solution that was tailored to these disparate legal and practical considerations. As the decision would have to pass judicial muster, it was buttressed with both economic and technological rationales. Nevertheless, the pragmatic or legal considerations, grounded in the complexity of the U.S. judicial and legislative environment, were crucial to the ultimate regulatory approach adopted.

This approach delineated a new category of services—"enhanced services"—which were not common carrier services under Title II but were "subject to public regulation," *i.e.*, FCC jurisdiction, under its "ancillary jurisdiction." Although asserting some jurisdiction was critical for purposes of satisfying the 1956 Consent Decree, under the "ancillary jurisdiction" doctrine the FCC is not bound to a rigid—Title II—regulatory formula. That is, it can regulate in any manner intended to preserve or promote objectives set forth in the Communications Act. The regulatory scheme must be justified, as serving statutory goals, both on the basis of a reasoned explanation and on the basis of a demonstrable record.

One of the difficulties of this approach was that it left unsettled whether the FCC could regulate various "enhanced services," non-essential elements of which were existing common carrier or regulated services. Concerns regarding this ambiguity were highlighted by representatives from the computer, data processing, and information service sectors. In its *Computer II* Reconsideration Order, therefore, the FCC emphasized that it was asserting jurisdiction over only those "enhanced services" that were offered by the regulated common carriers—AT&T and other telephone companies. Conversely, it stated, it was not deciding to what extent it possessed jurisdiction over "enhanced services" offered by entities that were not common carriers.

These legal and pragmatic considerations did define "enhanced services" as new combinations of transmission and computer services that were, in practice, difficult to separate. Beyond these pragmatic reasons, however, the FCC also sought, in some principled way, to distinguish "enhanced" from other services. It was thought that AT&T—then not a divested but an integrated company—might have an economic incentive to engage in certain kinds of anticompetitive pricing practices. Because a significant element of the FCC's approach was to devise effective restraints against such behavior, AT&T was required to establish a fully separated subsidiary to offer new, competitive services. Although the principal rationale for the subsidiary was largely a concern for possible anticompetitive practices, decisions regarding the inclusion or exclusion of particular services were based on an array of technological criteria.

The FCC's launching of the *Computer III* proceeding in July 1985 was also, in large part, an outgrowth of legal and structural factors that had emerged since the 1980 *Computer II* decision. As AT&T's dominance and the 1956 Consent Decree had been critical to the development of the 1980 policy, both increases in competition and the implementation of the antitrust settlement by the divestiture of AT&T, said the FCC in its *Computer III* Notice, have diminished the justification for adhering to a strict regime of structural separation for AT&T and its former operating subsidiaries. Moreover, pragmatic considerations—having to review repeated petitions seeking waivers of *Computer II* rules (with concomitant inefficiencies or delays in providing new services to the public)—have led the agency to question the special requirements governing AT&T and the operating companies.

Examples from the experience of other countries can usefully illustrate the legal and pragmatic elements of formulating classifications or definitions. Nevertheless, this rather extended discussion of the circumstances surrounding, and the rationale for, the U.S. approach to creating regulatory classifications is intended to highlight the degree to which legal, legislative, or institutional problems faced by decisionmakers can force often arbitrary service distinctions.

Despite the great differences in the institutional, legal, and economic settings of the U.S. and Canada, there are some parallels and sharp differences that might be illuminating in sketching out how pragmatic concerns can play a roll in developing a national approach to line-drawing. In Canada, in July 1984, the Canadian Radio-television and Telecommunications Commission ("CRTC") essentially adopted the FCC's definitional distinction between "basic" and "enhanced" services.

In Canada, there were a series of pragmatic pressures, as well, to establish a definitional line along the lines of the FCC's *Computer II* decision. First, although neither Bell Canada nor any other telephone company was as dominant as AT&T, it was deemed important that new companies would be able to enter and compete freely in the enhanced services market. Second, there was a clear desire to limit regulation of information service companies, particularly to ensure that comparable services would be available in both Canada and the U.S. Third, the problem faced by the CRTC was how existing telephone companies could provide new services, on the one hand, and, on the other, how to avoid subjecting the telephone companies—and the new services—to a strict regulatory regime.

By creating a category of "enhanced services," then, the CRTC solved its problem as did the U.S. In Canada, the CRTC may be free to forbear from regulating "enhanced" services not offered by common carriers because its jurisdiction is limited to "companies that operate a telephone or telegraph system." There are, however, complicated legal problems arising from the jurisdictional mandate of the CRTC. The obligation of the CRTC to regulate enhanced services provided by telephone companies is unsettled.

The CRTC also seized on the FCC's distinction in part to avoid forcing a discussion of repricing of long distance services, which would have strained yet further the federal-provincial relationship. Instead of focusing on the issue as one of "resale" per se, the CRTC wanted to couch the issues in the "basic"/"enhanced" dichotomy. To do otherwise, to distinguish between the provision of services and the "resale" of such services, would have opened up the much knottier question of resale. The CRTC hoped to sidestep the "resale" issue because the general authorization of resale could create opportunities for pure arbitrage of private line services, with resulting severe pressures on the existing public switched voice tariff.

Early implementation of resale might, in short, well have led to repricing of interexchange services, a subject certain to generate significant tension in the Canadian political structure. By creating an "enhanced" services category, the CRTC would not prejudice its ability to confront the resale and thorny repricing issues in separate regulatory proceedings. Again it was in light of this pragmatic consideration, *i.e.*, the desire to avoid opening up a sensitive economic and political issue, that the FCC's definitional category seemed attractive to the CRTC.

In the U.K., as well, legal or pragmatic forces have played a major role in defining "value-added network services." The approach has been guided by a number of constraints, including an intention not to allow "resale"—or at least simple resale—of services and the desire to encourage development of an open and competitive environment.

The proposed venture between British Telecommunications ("BT") and IBM forced a pragmatic expansion of the government's views on the scope of value-added services. The proposed BT-IBM network was based on using BT leased lines to link a web of IBM processors that would perform protocol conversion functions. Before the advent of the proposal, the restrictions on resale left it unclear whether leased lines would be available to establish such managed data communications networks. The Department of Trade and Industry ("DTI") had not previously confronted the issue of whether the use of lines for such purposes should be regarded as resale, or be viewed merely as part of a larger service, such as is used for remote access data processing networks.

The DTI declined to approve the venture in light of the anticompetitive issues it presented. Instead, it noted that both BT and IBM—as well as others—could provide the services independently. In so concluding, however, the DTI essentially determined that leased lines would be available for value-added services.

The DTI adopted the position that the service was similar to remote access data processing or other unregulated services that did not involve "simple" resale. This modification of its approach to resale had already been recognized as a result of its issuance in August 1984 of branch licenses for various corporate shared use networks. As it became more evident that BT had, over the years, tolerated a wide array of shared use practices, DTI had to couch its approval for these networks in a way that suggested it was not opposed to resale per se. Rather, it adopted a posture of gradually permitting various exceptions to its general policy against resale.

As in Canada, decisionmakers in the U.K. avoided a head-on confrontation with the issues raised by resale. The difficulty of allowing resale did not arise from the concern—as in Germany—that there would be significant economic consequences therefrom. Instead, the dilemma was political: in its policy pronouncements—particularly in connection with the privatization of BT—the government had stated that it would not permit resale until

1989. Thus, the U.K. policy toward "enhanced" service networks was formed by a series of policy and political constraints and marketplace realities that resulted in pragmatic decisionmaking.

In Finland, too, it appears that pressures created by the existing, antiquated legal framework will be key to drawing distinctions between services. That framework, which is based on an 1886 czarist decree and a 1919 telegraphy law, arguably establishes only a prior approval procedure for the establishment of a "telephone line." Neither statute seems to create a legal monopoly or approval procedure for data services, regardless of whether they utilize new or existing transmission facilities. In addition, historic industry practices, and the legal framework, create a sharp division between the private telephone companies and the PTT. Consequently, customers who need specialized, especially data, services are required to take independent steps to assure that they will be available. This burden may eventually cause users to take the initiative, to set up services to serve their particularized needs. Once again, the "definitions" of services will be a product of economic or user pressures channeled through the constraints imposed by the legal environment.

In Japan, there is an effort to root the new regulatory scheme on a clearly defined set of legal categories that are not based on technological or economic criteria that may shift over time. Consequently, the Telecommunications Business Law separates Type I carriers, who construct, own, and operate transmission facilities and lines, from Type II carriers, who use the transmission capacity of Type I entities to provide service. There was an effort to distinguish Nippon Telegraph & Telephone Co. ("NTT")—and any second "NTT" (*e.g.*, Daini Denden)—from other service providers. The Japanese viewed such an approach as being more progressive and clear cut than that of the U.S. regulatory distinction between "basic" and "enhanced" services.

The thrust toward simplification has foundered, principally due to institutional pressures to afford Type I carriers, such as NTT, the flexibility to compete with Type II carriers in emerging markets. Absent steps that would allow NTT to identify certain competitive services, and provide them apart from its Type I offerings, NTT would be required to adhere to a more stringent regime of prior tariff approval for those services. Its new competitors, by contrast, could change tariffs or pricing practices upon simple notification.

In Japan, for activities likely to be subject to particularly intense competitive pressures, *i.e.*, "computer services" and "data communications," proposed guidelines on cross-subsidization have been identified as separate accounting categories. Legal considerations have created the need for distinctions to differentiate services subject to competition and a less restrictive regulatory regime from those originally intended as central to a Type I provider. Thus, pressures to accommodate institutional pressures have delineated certain key boundaries in Japan.

D. Imprecision in the Line-Drawing Process

Having noted some of the general approaches toward line-drawing, it might also be pointed out that there is enormous imprecision in the process, and in the result. That is, the more closely observed are the boundaries—the more heightened the "resolution" of analysis—the fuzzier becomes their sharpness.

Although various administrations and regulators have struggled with a variety of different approaches, hoping to achieve rational, clear-cut distinctions, their quests are often elusive. Definitional precision—as it relates to particular services or activities—is usually unobtainable. Thus, the focus of regulators and suppliers must be on a far-reaching conceptual commitment to creating service distinctions.

Of substantial importance is the recognition that an administration—or some decisionmaking body—will ultimately have to make decisions in setting boundaries. As regulatory authorities propose distinctions, it may be as important to focus on what are the dividing lines as on the process by which those boundaries are established. These perceptions have given rise to what one high-level British telecommunications policymaker has described as the "Red Queen" principle. He referred, of course, to the Red Queen in *Alice in Wonderland,* whose own definitional approach to decisionmaking was arbitrary but decisive.

A key telecommunications analyst at the Organization for Economic Cooperation and Development stresses that there must be "transparency" in establishing regulations or boundary lines. By "transparency," he means that the basis for deriving and setting distinctions—and, consequently, differing operational practices—must be articulated by an administration and accessible to users. Being able to understand a definition, its origin and its intent, is critical for those who wish to use and plan for services. "Transparency" also implies that users have some access and influence with respect to the institutional process of setting boundaries. One critical implication of "transparency," therefore, would be a willingness by administrations to strive for adopting guidelines or configuring restrictions in light of the needs or circumstances of users. Whether the "Red Queen" or "transparency" principles apply to the process of line-drawing over the last two decades is, in part, the focus of the following discussion.

II. Critical Definitional Issues: Where Are the Boundaries Drawn?

Given that there are differing general approaches and principles that are relied on by different administrations, it is now appropriate to examine more closely some of the actual definitional distinctions that have been or are being established in the countries studied. This analysis will, of necessity, distill some of the issues addressed in the country reports. Importantly, however, it is also intended to set each national approach in a broader international context. Assessing definitions and classifications in such a comparative way may highlight more sharply the reasons for the differing choices made at the national level.

In striking these comparisons, a number of issues will be critical: 1) the distinctions, if any, between "basic" and "enhanced" or "value-added services"; 2) the distinctions between "basic," and other communications services, on the one hand, and "informational," or other transaction-related services, on the other; 3) the distinctions between the provision of "facilities" and "services"; and 4) the distinctions between "telecommunications" and "cable television services." These distinctions are worthy of examination in their own right, for how they shape and demarcate market or competitive relationships. They also reveal a great deal about the basic structural and institutional arrangements that are at the core of the telecommunications and information policies of each nation. Each of the definitional groupings will be discussed separately, with a subsequent discussion on some of the more important implications of these comparisons.

A. Distinctions Between "Basic" and "Enhanced" Services

1. United States. The regulatory treatment of various combinations of computer and communications services has been the subject of regulatory attention in the U.S. for nearly two decades. In its 1971 *Computer I* proceeding, the FCC attempted to address the issues raised by the confluence of such services by focusing primarily on the boundary line between data processing services and common carriage. It devised a scheme of categorization that examined the primary thrust or nature of the activity. In the event that the offering were primarily oriented toward satisfying the subscriber's communications or message-switching requirements, common carrier regulation would attach. Where, however, services were primarily data processing or other information services, with message switching an "incidental" feature of an integrated offering, they would be classified as "hybrid data processing" and be free from regulation.

The regulatory distinctions of *Computer I* became increasingly difficult to apply as the array of terminal and other network-related services, including computer processing capabilities, grew more numerous and diverse. In this regard, the particular dilemma confronting the FCC in establishing new definitional demarcations or service categories for these services has been sketched above. *See supra* Section I.C.3. The problem for the FCC was choosing between regulating the new services as common carrier offerings or excluding AT&T from the market. Neither result was acceptable. In its *Computer II* decision, therefore, the FCC attempted to devise new criteria and standards that might allow it to avoid the regulatory dilemma.

Delineating a new line of demarcation proved to be a difficult challenge. On the one hand, the FCC did not want to establish a scheme of classification that would deprive AT&T and the then-AT&T local operating companies from utilizing advanced technologies in the network. On the other, the FCC was equally intent that the Bell system not be permitted to gain a dominant position in the provision of new services.

Given these competitive concerns, and the difficult legal questions described above, the FCC attempted to classify services on the basis of a systematic set of technological principles. In its *Computer II* decision, and subsequent orders, it stressed, for example, that the transparency of services to the user would be one of several critical criteria for determining whether a service was "basic." Where, for instance, the protocol available to a user at one end of a circuit is different from that at the other end, the service would not be considered basic. As applied, the *Computer II* distinctions have placed various voice storage services, known as Customer Calling Services II, which have "advanced calling" and "call answering" features, in the enhanced service category. Closely related call forwarding services, however, are treated as "basic." Indeed, this treatment of customer calling services is a special focus of the initial phase of the *Computer III* proceeding.

The scheme, in short, has become more difficult and controversial to apply as regulators, service providers, and users have gained experience with the categories. First, the FCC faced the problem of how the categories should be applied internationally. Many users expressed significant concern that a rigid application of the U.S. definitions to international services would be perceived as a unilateral effort to circumvent the prerogatives of other administrations in determining the terms and conditions of entry for services. The dilemma was that it was difficult to apply one set of definitions to international services and another to domestic.

What proved especially vexing was that the entire regulatory scheme rested on definitions and not on more pragmatic judgments based on economic or competitive criteria as to the terms and conditions of providing services. Consequently, the FCC was required to make the hard choice of either applying its criteria internationally or compromising the integrity and consistency of the regulatory scheme. The FCC ultimately applied the distinctions internationally, and deferred for another day the issue of whether a separate subsidiary "resale" structure would be imposed on international facilities providers. At the same time, the FCC may have limited the third-party provision of such services by leaving untouched the tariff restrictions embodying the CCITT Recommendations that restrict resale of private line facilities.

Throughout the evolution of its approach to enhanced services domestically, the FCC had never implied that the provision of enhanced services by non-carriers actually involved any "resale" of communications—any more, for example, than the provision of remote access data processing services constituted "resale." The "resale" restrictions of the tariffs, then, afforded the FCC flexibility to adapt its *Computer II* domestic policies to the international arena.

In the case of the British regulatory scheme, the relationship of "resale" of communications services to the provision of enhanced services has not been made entirely clear. In the U.K. the offering of enhanced services has been authorized without modifying existing restrictions on resale of communications.

In Canada, the CRTC has decided, in CRTC Telecom. Decision 84-18, that, although the resale of all carrier services should be permitted for the provision of enhanced services, it should not be permitted where the enhanced service has, as its primary function, the provision of a basic service.

A second major area of difficulty in applying *Computer II* distinctions has been the adjudication of an increasing number of controversies between AT&T and its competitors over the provision of new services. Now freed from the shackles of the 1956 Consent Decree, AT&T is confronted with significant dilemmas in deciding how to package and market its new services. A reluctant FCC has found itself forced to act as referee for controversies in market sectors that it has basically determined to be competitive.

The FCC has had to confront the question of how the *Computer II* scheme should affect the seven new Bell regional holding companies ("RHCs") in the provision of enhanced services. Soon after the divestiture, the FCC imposed separate subsidiary requirements on the RHCs for the offering of terminal equipment and enhanced services. It has, however, granted waivers to allow the operating companies to perform certain protocol conversion activities within the network as a "basic" service.

Application of the full panopoly of separation requirements to the operating companies' local "enhanced service" networks has been unclear. The FCC has wanted to assure that nationwide packet-switched and enhanced service providers will be able to obtain access to local distribution services. One troubling area—addressed by the *Computer III* proposal for non-structural separation requirements—could be whether the operating companies might use technological or price-bundling strategies to favor their own distribution services.

Separating AT&T from its local operating companies has significantly eliminated much of the opportunity for proscribed cross-subsidization, *i.e.*, between monopoly local exchange services and competitive offerings. In the view of its competitors, AT&T has substantial market power in providing long distance services. Nevertheless, its ability to engage in predatory behavior in all market sectors has been significantly reduced.

This diminution in market power has led AT&T to ask for a relaxation of the strictures of the *Computer II* decision. The FCC has begun a proceeding with respect to AT&T's role in the provision of terminal equipment and, in its *Computer III* Notice, the FCC is focusing anew on the provision of all services by AT&T, the operating companies, and their competitors.

The impact of the divestiture, having to wrestle with the problems of applying *Computer II* to the operating companies, and the onslaught of both technology and competition in the enhanced services and terminal equipment sectors, have caused the FCC to revisit its 1980 decision. The Notice of Proposed Rulemaking in the *Computer III* proceeding suggests that the focus of regulatory examination will be shifted from the technologically-based distinctions of *Computer II* to an analysis of the marketplace status of the particular service being considered.

To determine whether an offering by AT&T or an operating company would be subject to regulation, the FCC Notice proposes three new regulatory categories: "communications," "ancillary-to-communications," and "non-communications." For the first category, "communications," essentially equivalent to "basic" services, the regulatory status would be determined by the marketplace position of the offeror; services provided by dominant carriers would be regulated under Title II of the Communications Act and, by all others, would be unregulated.

"Non-communications" functions would be unregulated, with some minimal, non-structural, safeguards, when offered by dominant carriers. The Notice would have services that are "ancillary-to-communications," (*e.g.*, what are now "enhanced" services and the supply of customer premises equipment) be provided on an unregulated basis. Where dominant carriers offer such a service, the Notice proposes to look to whether it could be offered competitively and, if it could be so, whether it would depend on the carrier's dominance in a particular market.

The Notice specifically notes the inefficiencies that are alleged to have resulted from imposing a rigid separate subsidiary requirement on AT&T and the operating companies. Thus, the FCC Notice proposes some requirements that are short of structural separation but would prevent cross-subsidization; these might include tariff unbundling, separate cost accounting, reporting requirements, and maintaining the availability of "bottleneck" facilities and services.

The ongoing *Computer II* and *Computer III* questions of applying separation requirements to the local companies has, to a certain extent, important parallels to the European situation. In the U.S. most enhanced service vendors do not have substantial access to local services and must deal with the Bell operating companies. For Europe, where there is, as well, monopoly control over local access, the resolution of issues in the U.S. may, therefore, be relevant.

The situation in the U.S. clearly is continuing to evolve. Three observations may be pertinent. First, regulatory activity seems to have shifted from line-drawing and the construction of safeguards at the interexchange level to a focus on local services. Second, attention to boundary-line issues is increasingly economic in orientation, focusing on marketplace structure and competition rather than on technological factors. Third, there remains a basic commitment to the liberal provision of enhanced services.

In sum, the fundamental principles undergirding *Computer II* have been retained and reaffirmed. Facilities access and pricing policies at the local level are now being examined with a new intensity. The U.S. experience in assessing these issues—to be carried out in an open and transparent environment—may, in the months ahead, yield useful insights for other national policymakers wrestling with these same issues.

2. *United Kingdom.* The British are, justifiably, regarded as fast following the U.S. toward liberalization in the provision of both telecommunications facilities and a wide range of services. Nevertheless, the initial approach of U.K. policymakers toward the offering of "value-added" services differs significantly from that of *Computer II.*

The *Beesley Report,* which is widely viewed as influencing the first steps toward liberalization, urged that competition be opened in the value-added sector and that restrictions on resale be ended. The British government did agree to a liberalization of VANS. BT was concerned about "cream skimming" and possible significant revenue loss before it could rebalance rates to bring them closer to costs and, therefore, minimize incentives to arbitrage. Consequently, the government rejected the recommendation to end resale restrictions.

The first VANS license, therefore, enumerates a set of activities that could be viewed as "add-ons" to existing network services. The license was, in some sense, an extension of an attachment policy that afforded users and third-party service vendors increased flexibility to link computer and information-related equipment to the network without being regarded as infringing the telecommunications monopoly.

The rationale undergirding the VANS liberalization program was economic, not technological. It was directed at minimizing the economic impact of liberalization on BT during the transition period. There was substantial uncertainty and imprecision that surrounded the policy. For example, observers in the U.K. have varying views on whether the government intended to allow packet-switching services. Some recall the VANS licensing decision as encompassing such services; others do not.

As described above, until the government rejected the BT-IBM venture, VANS policy seemed to permit the provision of new services, but not the resale of leased lines as part of such offerings. As both remote access data processing and information services had had access to leased lines and established their own networks, the broader availability of dedicated circuits for VAN offerings remained a point of uncertainty. As a practical matter, however, leased lines were available to provide VANS because various message-switching services had been authorized.

As a result of the government's response to the BT-IBM venture, *i.e.*, that IBM should be able to offer independently its own protocol conversion networks, it became necessary to liberalize the use of leased lines for managed networks. It had also become apparent from the practices of service vendors that the government's policy of prohibiting resale could not be maintained on an airtight basis. Expansion of the concept of VAN services through marketplace challengers, and a more sophisticated approach to resale, have hastened the pace toward liberalization of network use.

The British government is now grappling with both the scope of VAN offerings and resale-related issues in two separate but closely-related proceedings. First, in mid-1985, it released a consultative document that discusses the scope of value-added services. In the DTI's Consultative

Document on the future licensing of value-added and data services, there is substantial recognition of the imprecision in the concept of a managed data network, which will provide facilities, but is not intended to function as a public telecommunications operator. The government proposes to grant individual licenses to such data network services in a manner distinct from basic transmission services and VANS.

Once the current prohibition on resale is lifted, the Consultative Document states, there will be no need to distinguish between basic services, VANS, and managed data network services; thus, it is not necessary at this point to draw precise or "artificial" boundary lines between service categories. The Consultative Document reflects the fact that defining and licensing VANS involves policymakers in making explicit choices about whether and how to open competition in particular market segments.

Second, in a related effort, the government, led by DTI (as opposed to OFTEL, the Office of Telecommunications, which has taken the lead on individual VANS issues), is deciding how to clarify or augment its policy of issuing branch licenses for corporate networks. After the VANS license was originally issued, in August 1984, the pressure of the transition to a new legal regime led both to numerous complaints about the lack of clarity in the license and to efforts by companies to obtain permission to continue existing practices. The response of the government was to issue a general amnesty for a broad range of third-party users of private lines. DTI also decided that it should not try to clarify the guidelines, but, rather, deal with them on an ad hoc basis. The difficulty with this approach is, however, that it makes it difficult to assure that equivalent conditions are available to all. Whereas a generic clarification of the license would become public and, hence, facilitate planning by service providers and users, an ad hoc appraoch will increase governmental and competitive incentives to uncover and eliminate disparities in permitted practices.

Policy in the U.K. is, therefore, likely to evolve under pressure from large corporate users. This process may well increase user flexibility to use leased lines and expand the boundary line for VAN offerings toward an opening up of general resale. Concurrently, the leased line policy itself will change in light of user and supplier needs.

One significant constraint on BT in responding to these developments is structural. It will not be able to implement tariffing policies to discourage enhanced services because that step could create significant market opportunities for Mercury, which might have a more flexible approach to making facilities available to VANS suppliers. Thus, facilities competition may be a major factor in liberalizing the VANS market.

The scope of VANS offerings will, then, be affected by the interplay of the BT and Mercury private line tariffs, Nevertheless, as the VANS boundaries expand under these pressures, it will be the government's policy on resale that will provide the chief limiting definitional line of demarcation.

3. France and the Federal Republic of Germany. It is also useful to compare the efforts in France and the Federal Republic of Germany—two countries with influential PTTs—in dealing with new value-added or "enhanced services." The French Direction generale des telecommunications ("D.G.T.") has attempted to separate its offerings on the basis of a technological classification derived from the ISO seven-layer model. By contrast, the DBP's line-drawing efforts are likely to be based on economics, *i.e.*, the impact of new services on its own offerings.

The D.G.T. emphasizes that its primary role is in providing a standardized transmission network. It carries out this role by maintaining dominance over the first three layers of the ISO protocol model. For services using layers higher than level three, the D.G.T. position is that competitive markets should be favored. To further this approach, a boundary line, based on an institutional structure, is drawn. Although the D.G.T. provides the basic transmission network, several new services, packet switching and remote access data processing, for example, are offered through its France Cables et Radio ("FCR") subsidiary.

The basis for the division of services between the D.G.T. and its FCR-related subsidiaries is not, however, entirely driven by technological considerations. Various high-speed transmission services, for example, that are offered over the Telecom-1 satellite, are provided not through the D.G.T. itself, but through its subsidiary. Indeed, the subsidiary acts as a marketing company for many of the integrated high-speed data service offerings. The principle underlying the service classifications is that competition should exist to meet, head-on, the competitive challenge from the U.S. Such competition is provided amongst the D.G.T. subsidiaries, but under its umbrella.

The D.G.T. has also taken a strong interest in standardizing terminal devices. It prescribes technical standards above layer three of the ISO model. This effort is intended to create opportunities for information service vendors by creating a common environment for terminals. The D.G.T., however, does not generally make leased lines available for networks that are not based on the higher level ISO protocols; thus, the terminal standardization policy does not readily allow for open entry or the provision of non-D.G.T. networks.

The D.G.T., in general, has attempted to encourage increased utilization of its public data networks. Although the criteria for the availability of leased lines are less formal in France than in Germany, a user in France is required to demonstrate that it cannot effectively utilize public services; restrictions on usage of leased lines may, therefore, be more important in France than in Germany and the D.G.T. policy toward access to leased lines remains rather stringent. Private lines may, in practice, however, be utilized for a wide array of uses.

By contrast, in the French July 29, 1982 Law on Audiovisual Communication, the approach toward the offering of information-based or value-added services is quite liberal. Provided that public network facilities are used, the interpretive ordinances state that a number of services, such as two-party electronic mailbox services, are permitted.

The French approach is a counterpoint to that of the DBP, which has taken a more liberal approach to the use and availability of leased lines than the D.G.T., but has been more restrictive regarding value-added services. Regarding leased line use, some observers speculate that the DBP has been less aggressive than the D.G.T. in attempting to reach agreement on higher level protocols for switched-type terminals because the linkages between the terminal equipment industry and the PTT are less close than they are in France. The absence of efforts at standardization in Germany creates incentives for developing protocol conversion-type networks that are designed to achieve an integrated environment for various computer or other terminal devices.

Moreover, current German tariffs for leased lines do allow shared use of the data network services (up to 48 Kbit/s) provided that third-party usage does not exceed 50% of the total circuit utilization. Recently-introduced 64 Kbit/s services may encourage some third-party use even though important questions relating to pricing policies and rate harmonization are not fully resolved.

Although leased lines may be made available, the DBP approach has been less flexible regarding value-added services. Until rate harmonization is implemented, to reduce the opportunities for arbitrage, the position of the DBP has been relatively restrictive, except with respect to some closed user group services. For example, the DBP has recently authorized electronic mailbox services. The third-party provision of any such service would, however, be regarded by the DBP as an infringement of its monopoly.

Although the German boundary line between basic and value-added services is not at all clearly demarcated, certainly there is less latitude in the offering of specialized networks than is now the case in France.

Nevertheless, the fundamental regulatory conditions in Germany might favor a faster expansion of enhanced services—and more rapid liberalization—than in France. This development may occur because of the less intense focus on network standardization through uniform terminal devices and the more receptive approach to private lines. Any genuine liberalization allowing "enhanced service" networks to evolve may have to await a resolution of debates over pricing policies for private lines. These debates are not only ongoing within the DBP but are part of a complicated and delicate process involving a recently-appointed governmental commission. Future line-drawing for value-added services may, therefore, be heavily influenced by a complex political and economic debate on pricing.

In France, strategy on creating definitions of services is more driven by technocratic and marketing considerations. Consequently, the D.G.T. may be able to move quickly and flexibly to permit value-added networks, largely due to the greater political insulation of the D.G.T. and its reliance on a subsidiary. By contrast, although the DBP, in theory, is more flexible in the tariffing and terminal area, it is subject to considerable political accountability based on the involvement of the Administrative Council and the DBP's administrative structure.

To extend the international comparison, the French policy on VANS is now close to that of the U.K. in the early phase of British liberalization. In that respect, the German VANS policy is more restrictive than that of the U.K. in its initial stages. Ultimately, the greater flexibility in Germany may result in opening markets on a more dramatic basis than might be possible in France under present conditions.

4. Japan. The Japanese division between Type I and Type II was originally intended to avoid what were viewed as unworkable, technologically-based distinctions between "basic" and "enhanced" services. Indeed, the Japanese viewed their scheme as more "advanced" than the U.S. approach because it was based on clear-cut distinctions between Type I "facilities offerors" and Type II "service providers." These crisp distinctions, however, have proved difficult to maintain for several reasons.

First, for any new information and enhanced services, NTT would like to avoid the rigors of rate regulation imposed on Type I entities. Therefore, it may seek to establish a Type II-like subsidiary to offer such services. To minimize any risk of cross-subsidization of competitive (*i.e.*, Type II) services by its Type I services, accounting standards, including service definitions, will have to be devised for NTT services that will be offered competitively and might be included in any NTT subsidiary. Two categories of such services—"computer communications" and "digital data transmission"—have recently been designated; significantly, these service categories do not necessarily correspond to concepts such as "enhanced services" or "value-added services."

A second reason for the absence of a sharp distinction between Type I and Type II is that Type II services are likely to be sub-classified into "voice" and "data" services. This is so because, at present, it seems that NTT will be allowed to retain its tariff restrictions on resale of voice services despite the fact that Type II authorizations are, in principle, not restricted to data services. Thus, Type II entities will not be allowed to offer voice store and forward systems utilizing NTT leased lines—a service that would be viewed in the U.S. as an "enhanced" service. (It seems that such voice mailbox services will be allowed to utilize public switched network services.)

In addition, as described below, *see infra* Part I, Section II.B. & Part II, Section II.C., the Type II category does not differentiate between "communications processing" or protocol conversion networks, on the one hand, and "hybrid data processing," or "hybrid information services," on the other. The absence of clear service-related distinctions between Type II activities—between "resale of pure transmission," "protocol conversion services," and "hybrid service," for example, is likely to complicate greatly any effort to apply Japanese domestic regulatory categories to Japanese international services.

Ultimately, the Japanese hopes of avoiding a U.S. quagmire of line-drawing seem destined to failure as the implementation of the liberalization program proceeds ahead with the restructuring of NTT and the application of domestic reforms to the international area.

5. Canada. In Canada, as noted above, the evolution of the boundary line between "basic" and "enhanced" services has closely followed the U.S. experience. This similarity follows, in part, from like regulatory approaches and from the competitive consequences of sharing a border with the U.S. Many U.S. services are available in Canada and vice-versa. As a result, Canadian corporations operating on both sides of the border have a clear interest in equivalent services in both countries.

Several factors will influence the boundary lines that control the introduction of new services. First, the current preoccupation of telecommunications policymakers is with the possible introduction of competition in switched voice services. Competition in this sector may not be welcomed by the provincial governments. One pressure point, therefore, may be in the introduction of certain "enhanced" voice store and forward services that may be a test for interconnection policies for basic switched voice services.

Moreover, if certain resale decisions of the CRTC are not challenged, the more liberal environment could encourage the emergence of value-added-type services. Concurrently, the attention being paid to rate rebalancing is also likely to lead to a less restrictive environment for the resale of services.

At present, of course, CRTC decisions in the enhanced services area are quite progressive and liberal, in contrast to the provincial approaches. It is likely that future regulatory decisions at both the federal and provincial levels will be more and more influenced by regulatory and marketplace developments in the U.S.

For the present, CRTC decisions affect only the provision of enhanced services by federally-regulated carriers, not services provided by the carriers regulated—or owned—by the provincial governments. Accordingly, enhanced services may not be as readily implemented at the provincial level. The disparities in market access between the U.S. and Canadian markets—resulting from the lack of federal-provincial coordination—may engender a significant trade dispute between those nations over the evolution of enhanced services.

Given the Canadian approach to "deregulating" enhanced services, the long-term direction of developments may be toward a two-tier regulatory scheme based on limited entry in the facilities field and rather open and unrestricted competition on the services side. In this respect, Canada is already at the point toward which, observe Japanese policymakers, their own telecommunications system is evolving, *i.e.*, with two or more facilities providers and a liberal, competitive regime for services.

6. Finland, the Benelux Countries, and Italy. No clear-cut policy toward demarcating basic from enhanced services has yet evolved in these countries. There are varying amounts of activity focused on the distinction, with attention principally being paid to the possible liberalization of the network for value-added services. The prospects for such liberalization seem to be most likely in Finland and the Netherlands. Developments in these two countries or in the others, for that matter, could be quite important in accelerating changes elsewhere, even in the larger countries of the EEC.

In Finland, the likelihood that enhanced service networks will emerge is primarily a function of the clear division of responsibility between the public and private sectors of the telecommunications industries and of a relatively unrestrictive legal regime that may create opportunities for users and third-party service providers. The stalemate between the Finnish PTT, on the one hand, and private companies, users and industry groups, on the other, generates incentives for specialized communications networks.

User pressure will play a highly important role in expanding the boundaries of permitted value-added services. First, the Finnish economy has a number of aggressive and innovative industry sectors, and a significant computer equipment sector, that are especially remarkable for such a small country. Moreover, there are close relationships between the manufacturing and services sectors that may foster an open environment in which new enhanced services, tailored to meet the needs of particular industry sectors, may develop and thrive. Furthermore, the banking industry, led by Kansallis-Osake-Pankki ("K.O.P.") and the Union Bank of Finland ("S.Y.P.") is quite aggressive, internationally-oriented, and receptive to the introduction of new technology. There is, as well, an extremely vigorous publishing industry, led by the Finnish Newspaper Publishers Association, that takes a keen interest in the marketing of electronic information services.

Given these user-driven forces for liberalization, it is not surprising that among the first signs of expansion in private offerings is the announcement of a new joint venture—Datatie ("Dataway")—between K.O.P. and the Helsinki Telephone Company, along with two other telephone companies. This venture proposes to construct and operate a private data communications network that will, at the least, link the cities of Helsinki and Tampere. The venture will compete with the PTT in both the facilities and services markets. It will undoubtedly act to exert pressure on the PTT to reduce the price of its interexchange services and to assure that its access policies for leased lines remain relatively liberal.

In Finland, then, it is user and entrepreneurial pressures—and not legal forces—that are likely to influence the future direction and delineation of service competition. Nevertheless, although Finnish legal mechanisms for policy development and regulatory control are not highly developed, discussions among interested parties and deliberations on proposed legislation could have an impact on the definition and evolution of new services. These mechanisms, however, also have the potential for producing policy deadlock, which, too, could leave fairly wide latitude for entrepreneurial initiatives.

In the Netherlands, a high-level governmental committee, the Steenbergen Commission, has, since October 1984, been studying the future structure and direction of the Dutch PTT. This Commission, which is headed by a retired executive, may well recommend a liberalization of enhanced services although it may not make precise recommendations about the scope of such services.

It is likely that the PTT monopoly on the network infrastructure and on "basic" services—telephone, telegraph, telex, and data services—will be maintained. In March 1982, however, the Swarttouw Commission, under the auspices of the Secretary for Transport and Public Works, submitted a report on the future of telecommunications in the Netherlands. After this report, in January 1984, the government submitted a policy document that stated that the PTT will be permitted to compete in the enhanced services market and that businesses may offer enchanced services over the public switched network. The Steenbergen Commission is a further response to these policy developments.

Currently, private companies in the Netherlands can offer store and forward teletex services and remote access data processing services. The government's definitional approach toward value-added services is quite like the functional approach of *Computer I*: private companies, through the public network, can provide services "in which the emphasis is on functions other than transmission," *i.e.*, in the collection, processing, or storage of information.

At present, access to leased lines is restricted to closed user groups. Resale or third-party use of leased lines is proscribed. The Steenbergen Commission may address the importance of more liberal access to leased lines; it may, however, leave open the question of how much discretion the PTT should have to reprice such services. In general, due to the population density, Dutch pricing disparities between urban and rural areas are less complex than in other European countries.

In the Netherlands, the outcome of these policy debates is dependent on political forces and is influenced by relatively intense user pressures. The users group—CIB—has pushed the PTT and the government toward liberalization and it is likely that users may have a significant role to play in expanding—as a practical matter—the scope of permissible value-added services.

In Luxembourg, there has not been much explicit public attention paid to the distinction between "basic" and "enhanced" services. Nevertheless, a bill is being drafted that might allow the government to authorize service vendors to provide services over the public switched network or leased lines. Resale will continue to be barred. In July 1985, there was a substantial parliamentary debate and motion that called for greater autonomy and a sounder commercial footing for the PTT. At present there is a parliamentary commission studying these issues; its report is expected to be released this year.

There is no study commission in Belgium comparable to those in the Netherlands and Luxembourg; nevertheless, it is clear that the Regie des Telegraphs et des Telephones ("R.T.T.") is closely watching developments in other countries, particularly in the Netherlands. The R.T.T. has followed a rather aggressive policy of interconnection with the U.S. carrier MCI to obtain significant transit traffic through its facilities to points outside Europe. Income from this arrangement contributed significantly toward reducing the operational deficits that the R.T.T. incurred in 1983.

Although the R.T.T. still has a monopoly on transmission services, there are suggestions, based on public statements by the Minister of Communications and the PTT, that it is intended that competition evolve in the value-added services sector. The Belgian users group, ABUT, is emerging in importance and meets regularly with the R.T.T. It is quite evident that a move toward liberalization of enhanced services in Belgium will meet with a quick and competitive response from the private sector.

This outcome suggests that there may be something akin to a domino effect in the smaller countries, which are anxious to expand their role as centers of trade and telecommunications. These countries are recognizing that their importance in international telecommunications may be quite large when compared with the relatively small size of their domestic markets.

In Italy, although there is no formal commission examining the future of telecommunications, in 1984 the Ministry of Posts and Telecommunications published a ten-year National Plan for Telecommunications. In April 1985, the Ministry of Industry published its own document for an industrial policy in the telecommunications sector. Hearings on the issues raised by these plans have been held before parliamentary committees. Furthermore, IRI, the Italian state holding company, has, as stated recently by high-level management, also made telecommunications central to its corporate strategy.

The significant distinctions in the Italian setting are those between "bearer," "teleservice," and "value-added" services. All "bearer" services, which correspond to the first three ISO layers, would, in the future, be provided under licensing from the Ministry of Posts and Telecommunications. For "teleservices," the carrier defines the characteristics of the terminal to guarantee user connection with the network and with other users of the service. Carriers, however, often supply these services under restrictive regulatory arrangements and with technologies that are incompatible with ISO standards; this is so, for example, with videotex. "Value-added" services may be supplied by private sector companies but they must do so by arrangement with the public network.

Resale is proscribed and private leased line networks are now limited to intra-corporate purposes, or for remote access data processing. There are quite a few such private networks, however, that can provide specialized services for industry groups. The entrance of such networks into enhanced services could influence STET policy.

This regulatory regime, although apparently quite rigid, must be juxtaposed with institutional trends. The IRI subsidiaries, which have the primary responsibility for providing bearer services and teleservices are private entities, with public ownership secured through a majority holding in shares. Moreover, cooperation in the private sector is in the tradition of IRI.

Some regulatory concerns might be diminished by entering into arrangements, such as joint ventures, with private companies for the provision of specialized services. Certain "de facto" deregulation, as well, is not new to Italy; for example, even though modems are to be provided on a monopoly basis under the regime by which bearer services are provided, a private market for modems already exists.

Future developments in Italy are difficult to foresee. They will evolve, no doubt, as a result of two opposing sets of pressures. On the one hand, there will be increased user demands and emerging private network competition in developing value-added services. On the other, STET will offer new value-added services of its own. The result might well be a series of joint ventures between STET and other groups. STET has been negotiating with IBM, Pirelli, Olivetti,and Montedison. At this point, however, it is too early to predict whether any joint ventures or other arrangements will emerge. The ultimate course of any liberalization is, therefore, unpredictable, given political and union influence on the policymaking process.

B. Distinctions Between "Basic" and Informational or Other Transactional Services

1. Introduction. Although much attention has been focused on distinctions between "basic" and "enhanced" services, other industrial sectors are of major importance. Attempts to delineate boundary lines between "communications processing" and "communications services" may obscure a spectrum of financial, information, database, and data processing services. These services, in which very substantial private enterprises are engaged in vigorous competition, are heavily dependent on telecommunications networks and facilities; however, they involve activities that are fundamentally different businesses from that of communications.

Telecommunications and computer facilities are an absolutely integral factor of production in certain service industries—banking, insurance, commodities and currency brokerage, and transportation. The telecommunications and computer elements in services for these industry sectors are not at the core of the offering. There, the offering of business information service, of an automatic trading service, of news reporting, or of a videotex service should not mean that such activities—which usually are offered by noncarriers—are subject to telecommunications regulation.

Of some significance, however, is the fact that recent efforts to establish a more liberal regime for enhanced offerings can, at once, create new uncertainties and tensions regarding the regulatory status of these service-related businesses.

Tensions can arise between suppliers and information-related service vendors in classifying such services. On the one hand, some telecommunications suppliers (AT&T, Bell Canada, and the DBP, for example) are barred by statute or judicial decree from providing information services; thus, as they do not want to be excluded from the market for information-related services, they contend that their offerings are within their jurisdictional mandate. Information vendors, on the other, offering a similar service, do not want to be considered as providing "telecommunications-related" services, which would subject them to common carrier-like regulation.

One possible consequence of this tension is that traditional boundaries between telecommunications and non-telecommunications activities could disappear entirely. Each sector eyes the other warily. Information or transactional-service suppliers worry about the potential hazards of suffering telecommunications-related regulation. Carriers are concerned that their ability to implement new financial or information services may be impaired, or that the "other" sector's specialized networks may have an adverse impact on the long-term viability of telecommunications networks.

Reaching a detente between the sectors may be one resolution of these concerns. With such an accommodation, telecommunications carriers would adopt a more liberal view toward the integration of telecommunications and information services. Concomitantly, information vendors and other financial and data processing service vendors would accept more willingly the entrance of telecommunications entities into peripheral markets, provided that they were subject to appropriate competitive safeguards. The type of competitive safeguards that might be useful in addressing concerns about intersectoral competition are addressed below. *See infra* Section III.B.3. Some of the competitive safeguards that are used for the same—telecommunications—market segments, *i.e.*, terminal equipment or enhanced services, may be relevant in dealing with the concerns posed by the rapidly blurring distinctions between the telecommunications and information- and transaction-related sectors.

Efforts to deal with these issues and problems at the national level are discussed below.

2. United States. At the time of *Computer II*, users and service vendors in the U.S. were concerned that the FCC might exercise overly broad jurisdiction over information distribution, data processing, or other transactional services. Thus, the FCC, in the *Computer II* Reconsideration Order, stressed that its exercise of jurisdiction was only over enhanced services offered by regulated carriers. It stated expressly that it was not addressing the scope of its jurisdiction over enhanced services offered by otherwise unregulated entities because there was no statutory jurisdictional nexus as to such providers. The FCC's order clarified that jurisdiction should not be exercised as to those entities because no statutory purpose would be served thereby. Despite this effort at clarification, some ambiguity as to the limits of the FCC's jurisdiction over information-related and data processing services—which use communications services—has persisted.

The Modified Final Judgment ("MFJ") that resolved the Department of Justice antitrust suit against AT&T bars AT&T or the local operating companies from offering any "information services." As a result of this proscription, there remains some degree of uncertainty about the relationship between permitted "enhanced" services and prohibited "information services." Ultimately, this question about what activities AT&T and the local Bell operating companies can offer in the future is up to Judge Greene, who has yet to be confronted with the issue of which "enhanced" services are also "information" services. The FCC's approach, in applying *Computer II* to the operating companies, is to proceed on an ad hoc basis.

In reviewing its regulatory scheme in the course of *Computer III*, the FCC may ultimately find it useful to reinstate the *Computer I* distinctions, which were based on a "primary purpose" test. Such a boundary line would make it clear that "enhanced services" (or "ancillary-to-communications" offerings) involving either protocol conversion or "communications processing" should be regarded as fundamentally different from activities that are essentially not communications but do involve incidental message switching.

3. United Kingdom. In the U.K., as elsewhere, the distinction between value-added or enhanced services and informational services has been left unclear. There remains uncertainty whether the value-added license includes information services. After the 1981 liberalization, information vendors did not need to submit any licensing documents. Under the 1981 Telecommunications Act, however, information providers may have to submit license applications for a range of services.

The government has not yet decided if a license must be issued for "hybrid" services that involve a combination of information services and message switching. No doubt such licenses will be granted on a pro forma basis. Nevertheless, the government's position on the licensing of such "hybrid services" could have an impact on the ability of U.K.-based information or other transactional service vendors to obtain services, facilities, and market access in other countries.

4. France. In France, the 1982 Law on Audiovisual Communication adopted a relatively liberal framework for information services, including those with elements of message switching. After release of interpretive documents, there are now essentially no restrictions, save for prior authorization, on the provision of such services, provided that public switched facilities are used. The French have adopted an open regime with respect to services, but not for the use of facilities on leased lines to provide services. Moreover, computer processing and database services are excluded from the prior authorization process and interactive hybrid services are left in a state of limbo.

Videotex services, however, are considered separate and are regulated by a distinct regulatory regime that is different from that for other interactive services. Although the French have more sharply demarcated information, and other transactional services, from communications services than have many administrations, the limitations on access to facilities may impede the development of such services. Moreover, as to audiovisual services, the Law may be more restrictive than had been the situation prior to its enactment. Thus, there are elements of overbreadth that result from a failure to delineate clearly the difference between communications-related and information or transactional offerings.

5. *Germany.* In Germany, the boundary line between information services and telecommunications has been drawn quite sharply because of the jurisdictional split between the Bund and the Länder. In principle, the role of the DBP is limited to the offering of transmission facilities necessary to provide information or videotex services. In practice, however, establishing the line has been a much more complex task—and the subject of controversy—because the DBP has provided the computer storage and processing facilities for Bildschirmtext, the public videotex service. The provision of concentrators and storage facilities is not deemed to be exclusively within the authority of the BDP. For example, many privately-operated information services maintain their own leased line networks, including such facilities. Thus, the provision of information-based services is now permitted outside the DBP and is free from any other regulation as well.

There has also evolved a distinction between the Bildschirmtext and various other information services that are marketed to specialized industry segments. Despite the fact that these two offerings are marketed to different market segments, there are some operational or functional similarities between them. Moreover, many European observers do not view videotex as having any independent market identity as a service offering. They would classify it as simply an information-based service that is targeted to the public at large. Nevertheless, in neither France nor Germany are these information activities, from a regulatory standpoint, perceived as similar to videotex or Bildschirmtext.

In Germany, the media-like aspects of some information-based services, have provoked some of the Länder—Baden-Württemberg, in particular—into taking an interest in their development. Some commentators on the German telecommunications scene believe that the Länder will assert a jurisdictional claim over information or transaction-related services. As a result, it is thought the Länder could play a major role in liberalizing their availability. The Länder—often through their Economics Ministries—may, at the least, seek to encourage the development of information-based industries around new "hybrid services." The Länder will, as well, certainly encourage the DBP itself to facilitate the spread and diversity of such services.

6. *Canada.* The Canadian jurisdictional situation, as applied to information services, offers an interesting contrast to that in Germany. The Canadian provincial telephone companies have been generally opposed to the marketing of information-based services over cable television systems, which form part of the broadcasting system and are, therefore, essentially subject to federal jurisdiction. Consequently, definitional boundary lines between traditional telecommunications (carriage) and cable television (content) actually determine the respective roles and powers of the federal and provincial governments. As noted above, *see supra* Section II.A.5., it is not clear what position the provinces will take regarding the provision of "enhanced services," which may—or may not—include "hybrid information services" under the Canadian scheme of regulation. They would proba-

bly encourage the provision of enhanced services over telephone company facilities, but oppose their provision over cable television facilities. Thus, provincial regulators could hinder—or encourage—the spread of new services.

As in the U.S., the line between "enhanced" and "informational services" is significant because it will, in part, determine what services the dominant carrier, Bell Canada, can offer. The July 1984 CRTC order on enhanced services contemplates that Bell Canada can offer "enhanced services." As Bell Canada is, however, barred from engaging in electronic publishing, controlling the content of messages, or creating data bases, it is precluded from offering information services. The Canadian situation is analogous to that in the U.S.; from the standpoint of the dominant carriers, there either must be a more focused effort to distinguish between "enhanced" and "information" services or the prohibitions on the provision of information services must be eliminated. As many information-based services include elements of message switching, the prohibition becomes particularly difficult to apply.

7. *Finland, the Benelux Countries, and Italy.* In several countries a laissez-faire approach to information services may evolve. In Finland, the several providers of videotex services have been able to offer both computer processing and gateway services. Early attempts at control by the PTT have faded and there is little interference from the private telephone companies. The proposed Dataway entity—the joint venture involving the Helsinki Telephone Company and the K.O.P.—is a step toward user exercise of greater control over the provision of the facilities they need to offer services.

In the Benelux countries, information services are essentially unregulated and can be provided over the public network. Interactive services are treated as, for example, remote access data processing bureaus. Generally, there is no clear definition between videotex and information services, though the PTTs are planning to enter the public videotex market in all three countries. In Belgium, the R.T.T. will manage the service; in the Netherlands, however, data base, message storing, or processing can be provided by private companies, with the PTT monopoly confined to providing the gateway function.

In Italy, some information services are regulated as teleservices. *See supra* Section II.A.6. In fact, SIP, a STET company, manages and carries the "Videotel" videotex service. The STET strategy seems aimed at providing directly, or through joint ventures with other companies, such widely-distributed services. Other information services, and interactive services, can be provided by any private company through the public network.

8. *Japan.* The Japanese effort to assess the role of computer– and telecommunications-based systems and services in the restructuring of markets has been extraordinarily intense and focused. Such networks are evolving into the new infrastructure for banking, financial services, and retail transactions. The impetus toward assuring the availability of VANs is, therefore, not so much based on the demand for new "carrier" services as it is on an effort to reorder and modernize industrial structures and relationships.

Information services themselves are considered to be excluded from Type II offerings altogether and, it is contended, may be free from regulation. Nevertheless, such services may become regulated under Type II if they are combined with message switching capability. As there is no "hybrid" information services exception to Type II, it is probable that such service providers need only comply with the notification requirements of the General Type II classification.

Thus, the Japanese approach is one of extreme liberality toward the provision of information and VAN services. Significant steps, therefore, have been taken toward market restructuring. Nevertheless, major impediments remain for the development of integrated, international, electronic marketing systems. Restrictions on international leased lines often impair the ability of multinational companies—Japan- and foreign-based alike—to institute fully integrated communications systems serving their subsidiaries and related companies.

The emergence of greater flexibility both in structuring electronically-based information and financial services and in developing markets in this way is not without its own hazards. Privately-managed networks can have substantial consequences for industry structure. They can open opportunities for more efficient services or for new entrants. Alternatively, they can exclude traditional participants in the market, or other competitors, and can create the conditions for market dominance.

The fusion of telecommunications and activities of other sectors may necessitate a new vigilance about the restructuring of markets by electronic means. Standardization can be important, not only to encourage the "universality" of telecommunications services but also to assure that competition in the interdependent markets remains vigorous. The issue of setting "protocols" for telecommunications services will, therefore, have implications beyond telecommunications and have an impact on financial, transaction, or other industrial sectors that use information or transactional services.

The differences in perspective between the Japanese Ministry of Posts and Telecommunications ("MPT") and the Ministry of International Trade and Industry ("MITI") over the MPT's proposed publication of service protocols may be an illustrative example of this aspect of developing and instituting electronic-based markets. Standardization issues historically have been a responsibility of MITI; the recent role of MPT in setting protocols is indicative of how new telecommunications technology is unsettling traditional approaches, institutional tools, and the oversight of industrial development.

A "lowest common denominator" approach to standardization is not necessarily pro-competitive because information-based businesses often compete on the relative efficiency and cost-effectiveness of their electronic systems. Such competition is impaired by imposing uniformity on services. In sum, then, standard setting in telecommunications—particularly as it affects the provision of services—can have an extraordinary effect on the quality of competition in various industry sectors.

C. Distinctions Between the Provision of "Facilities" and "Services"

One of the most significant definitional dis7tinctions currently evolving in telecommunications regulation worldwide is between the provision of "facilities," on the one hand, and of "services," on the other. In practice, the line between the two areas of activity often is not easily drawn.

1. United States. In the United States, this distinction has been played out in a variety of different contexts. The FCC early on allowed resale of private line services. It subsequently permitted the resale of public switched services. As a result, two tiers of competitors evolved: one based on the ownership and operation of communications facilities and the other predicated on the marketing of such underlying services. What has occurred is that many of the new "carriers" utilize a mix of their own facilities and facilities supplied by others.

The FCC has also allowed the sale of transponders by satellite owners. There is, consequently, a class of facilities providers who are not considered to be common carriers, although they do provide licensed radio facilities. For satellite facilities, the regulatory consequences of allowing providers to sell facilities instead of offering them to the public on a common carrier basis has not been significant, largely due to the great amount of capacity widely available. As it had concluded that the domestic, interexchange market is competitive, the FCC decided in May 1985 that a new underseas private fiber optic communications system could be offered on a non-common carrier, sale and long-term lease, basis. There is, therefore, nothing that compels suppliers of facilities to offer them to the public.

The distinction between the provision of facilities and services may turn out to be more a matter of concern in the case of cable television facilities that are provided by telephone companies. In the U.S., cable television has been provided independently of the telephone industry through separate broadband facilities. Recently, however, authorization has been granted for cable systems to be provided on facilities constructed and controlled by local telephone companies.

Such arrangements raise a number of difficult issues that have not yet been fully discussed or resolved by the FCC or the courts. For example, there is an important question of whether the telephone company is simply providing the wire facility or whether it is, in fact, installing a service. If it is only supplying a facility, it might not have any obligation to offer it to others. As a common carrier service provider, it could be obliged to provide the cable "service" to others. How should this definitional problem be resolved? A telephone company that installs a coaxial or fiber optic facility for a cable company may, realistically, be unable to refuse to offer a portion of the bandwidth to other video service providers. For example, an entity might only want to offer a single video channel or a special pay television service. The issue presented by such an entity, which may, arguably, be considered a cable television operator, is whether the telephone company should put itself in the position of enforcing municipal franchising regulations that apply to cable television operations.

In addition, in the situation where only facilities are supplied, questions may be raised regarding any limitations on the use of those facilities. The provider of the facilities may want to restrict their use for a particular purpose, *i.e.*, for cable television services, and exclude other activities, such as two-way interactive or switched voice services. Hence, the supply of facilities is usually surrounded by conditions relating to the services that can utilize the facilities. As a consequence, the boundary between "facilities" and "services" may be difficult to maintain.

2. Finland. In Finland, the new cable television legislation wrestles with these same issues. The bill seeks to distinguish between the role of the provider of facilities—*i.e.*, usually a telephone company—and the cable television operator. The bill imposes certain obligations on the service provider, the cable company, to offer services to third parties. The legislation, however, does not necessarily address whether facilities suppliers have the same obligation to offer channels or facilities to another cable operator or to another provider of video services.

3. France. In France, the distinction between facilities and services raises similar problems in the context of the new framework that has been created for the provision of cable television services. Cable facilities are to be planned, constructed, and installed by the D.G.T. Cable services, however, are to be arranged, marketed and distributed by the so-called Societe Locale d'Exploitation du Cable ("SLEC"). Ultimately, the SLECs may become quite interested in the broadband capacity available to them and begin to market interactive or other two-way data services utilizing their facilities. This interest may be driven by the long-term needs of the SLECs to seek additional markets once subscribers obtain greater control over the television services that they choose to view and rely less on the SLEC for their entertainment.

Consequently, as the SLEC seeks to exploit non-video markets, the demarcation between the provision of facilities by the D.G.T. and that of services by the SLEC will be extremely difficult to maintain. The D.G.T. will be tempted to "bypass" the SLEC and supply viewers with programming via, *e.g.*, satellite to enable them to choose what to view. The service provider, the SLEC, will have an incentive to define "service" broadly to include a comprehensive set of services—including those supplied traditionally by the D.G.T.—over the D.G.T.-supplied facilities.

The distinction between "facilities" and "services" in this circumstance will lead to several difficult competitive problems. For example, the facilities suppliers may not have an incentive to offer the service provider the same facilities, at a fair price, that it itself utilizes in marketing a service. How, in short, can equitable competition be maintained when the facilities provider and the second-tier service entity end up competing with one another?

4. Japan. At the outset of their efforts to revise their scheme of telecommunications regulation, the Japanese attempted to rely on a simple distinction between the provision of "facilities" and the provision of "services." The distinction lays the groundwork for the Type I-facilities provider/Type II-service supplier division. Such an approach was viewed as avoiding the pitfalls of other "service-based" schemes of regulation. *See supra* Section II.A.4. This attempt by the Japanese to establish a tight classification scheme has not been completely successful because some service-based line-drawing has proven necessary.

The original definitional scheme failed because it did not take into account the competitive or economic elements of the transition to a more open industry structure. For example, NTT will want to offer its own value-added or enhanced services on the same conditions as its competitors. There may, therefore, be some effort to define what services NTT might be able to offer through a subsidiary.

Moreover, the MPT or NTT has not been prepared to allow competition generally in the resale of services. Therefore, NTT—possibly with the consent of the MPT—will maintain restrictions in its leased line tariffs on the resale of circuits for voice services. Of necessity, then, there will be some service-oriented descriptions of what kind of circuit use is permissible, and what is proscribed. A scheme of regulation based solely on a distinction between services and facilities will not, without some service-based boundary lines, be ultimately successful in preventing erosion of the policy against resale of services.

5. *Canada.* In Canada, there has been an effort—both domestically and internationally—to separate the provision of facilities and the marketing of services. The Canadian case demonstrates some of the practical difficulties with such a two-tier approach to industry structure. Until very recently, Telesat Canada has not chosen to market its services independently of Telecom Canada. In response to pressure from users to offer services directly, particularly in the television market, Telesat has, since 1981, begun to diversify and engage in some direct marketing. Although Telesat has now renegotiated its agreement with Telecom Canada, and has assumed full responsibility for market research, developing, introducing, selling, and serving all domestic satellite-based telecommunications services in Canada, it is not yet clear to what extent it will have the ability to interconnect with and supply the carriers that retail the bulk of its capacity now that it will be competing with them directly.

Teleglobe Canada, unlike Comsat, its U.S. counterpart, has been confined to the wholesale "service" market. The Canadian government is now in the initial stages of privatizing Teleglobe. In this process, it must address the question of whether it should maintain a sharp distinction, between the marketing of facilities and the marketing of services, in Teleglobe's role. In the case of an international carrier such as Teleglobe, however, a move in the direction of direct marketing is bound to encourage its main customers, Canadian domestic carriers, to exert pressure to offer international services themselves.

If the regulatory wall between the marketing of facilities and services is eroded, the facilities provider will, almost certainly, be exposed to competition in the facilities area. Such competition can have substantial consequences because the main connecting carriers—the former customers—are essentially free to route their traffic around the former facilities monopolist. Concurrently, the facilities supplier, Teleglobe, if it enters the services market, will encounter vigorous and entrenched competitors, *i.e.*, the domestic telephone companies, who are experienced in selling directly to end users.

From the standpoint of competitive and regulatory policy it is difficult to maintain a policy of two-tier competition. The facilities provider can exercise substantial leverage on service-based competitors as it controls the availability and price of services for resale. However, services of a carrier's carrier tend to be priced higher than one-tier services because a Telesat-type supplier must offer a profit to a carrier and itself achieve a satisfactory return. Thus, it may be confronted with significant competitive difficulties if substitutable one-tier services exist. Moreover, and especially in the international field, once a former facilities provider is allowed to enter the service market those freed to market international services can bypass the former monopoly supplier.

6. *Germany.* In Germany the jurisdictional split between Bund and Länder is mirrored in the distinction between "facilities" and "services." By law the DBP is responsible for the telecommunications and communications network—indeed, all facilities—and the Länder, in the broadcasting and cable areas, are charged with supplying programming services. The division of responsibility has made it difficult to plan and implement coherent strategies for new technologies.

Much like the situation in France, the DBP is responsible for building and installing cable facilities and giving them to the Länder. The Länder are, at best, only involved informally in this planning process and some are reluctant to accept the cabling program as a political matter. The DBP for its part, however, does not necessarily have the best notion of what kinds of facilities might be needed because it does not have responsibility for planning or offering the services, and is concerned with not exceeding the constitutionally-imposed limits of its authority.

Such lack of coordination is evident in the use and allocation of satellite facilities. Because the DBP has control over telecommunications facilities and transmission, it argues that it can determine what programming can be "transmitted" via satellite. The Länder view the issue as one of control over "content"—a question of broadcasting services—and, hence, exclusively within their purview.

The DBP can force the issue by launching new satellites and making their capacity available. Ultimately, however, delay by the Länder can cause expensive transmission capacity to lie fallow and, essentially, waste the DBP's investment. The German experience suggests that a division between facilities and services is not necessarily prudent where its genesis is legal and political, and essentially unrelated to—or not justified by—considerations grounded in telecommunications.

7. *The Benelux Countries and Italy.* In these countries, the PTTs have monopolies on the network. In Belgium and the Netherlands, however, cable facilities are owned by, and services are provided by, cable companies franchised by the government. As is the case in France, the local cable companies are often partially owned by local governments, with the facilities themselves supplied by the PTT.

In Italy, the monopoly on the provision of network facilities is unchallenged; STET companies are, for example, also responsible for the installation of cable networks. The existing private networks, presently authorized only to provide intracorporate communication, might be the basis for some private competition with the public carriers in teleservices. How effective such competition might be, in light of a monopoly on underlying services, could raise some of the structural safeguard issues that have arisen in the U.S., with AT&T and the operating companies, and in Japan, with NTT.

D. *Distinctions Between "Telecommunications" and "Cable Television Services"*

As illustrated by the foregoing discussion of the difficulties attendant to distinguishing "facilities" and "services," separating the role of the cable television operator from that of the telecommunications provider is not always easy. Moreover, this distinction can raise very delicate issues when, as in France, Germany, and even occasionally in the U.S., the telecommunications supplier provides the facilities used for cable television services. The problem of separating "telecommunications" and "cable television" can be equally problematic when non-telecommunications entities provide the facilities.

1. *United States.* In the United States, cable systems are usually independent of telephone companies. Recently several cable systems (*e.g.*, Cox Cable) have proposed to offer two-way alarm, metering, or other interactive services or offer interconnection facilities for competitive carriers. The critical question raised by such offerings is whether cable operators, to the extent they do offer common carrier-like services, should be regulated like common carriers. State public utility commissions, concerned with the bypass threat posed by cable systems to the local telephone networks, have attempted to exert jurisdiction over such cable offerings. In August 1985, the FCC decided to preempt some state regulation of certain common carrier-like services offered over cable systems.

The fundamental question is whether regulators should take a functional view of the services that are offered and institute a regime of equivalent regulation for like offerings on cable and telephone systems. One problem, of course, with this approach would be distinguishing common carrier regulation of a particular service from regulation of the system or operator.

An alternative approach would be to have a separate regulatory policy focused on the unique characteristics of the cable television system or industry, which clearly is, at this stage, neither technologically nor economically in a position to challenge the telephone industry in common carrier offerings.

Such a separate regulatory regime might encourage the cable industry to expand its offering of two-way services. One result could be the emergence of facilities-based competition with local telephone companies. Such competition presents both risks and opportunities. The risk is, of course, that important traffic and revenue streams could be diverted from local telephone companies.

The opportunities for the cable industry lie in the increase in service options for customers and in the revision of pricing policies for local services. Competition from cable would, inevitably, mean more pressure on local rates. Consequently, there is a decreasing likelihood that access charges imposed at the local level could maintain the current price level of exchange services. These issues are, of course, the subject of a long-standing FCC docket that has grown more complicated and become controversial in light of the perceived impact of the AT&T divestiture. Thus, the question of how cable is defined or classified is intertwined in the larger economic and political context and objectives of U.S. telecommunications policy.

The Cable Communications Policy Act of 1984 makes a significant contribution toward defining the role of cable in the U.S. communications marketplace. The Act sets forth several important service definitions. It defines "cable service" as "video programming," and excludes common carrier facilities from the definition of "cable system." Interactive services such as remote access data processing and information retrieval services are not, therefore, "cable services." The Act does not, however, ultimately settle how such "non-cable" services are to be regulated. Rather it leaves that question to the FCC and state regulators, who are charged with determining cable's place in the U.S. legal and regulatory regime.

2. United Kingdom. In the United Kingdom, cable and telecommunications facilities are separate. Cable operators have, however, been encouraged to install star-configured systems that are capable of offering two-way services. They are considered to be telecommunications systems under the 1984 Telecommunications Act and can be licensed under Section 7 of the law. The responsibility for offering telecommunications-related services has essentially been vested in the two authorized facilities providers, BT and Mercury, principally because there is little more than an abstract notion that cable operators will become viable alternatives to local exchange services.

The cable licenses issued to operators require that the offering of voice services (and data services in London, Manchester, and Birmingham) over cable must be in association with either of the two facilities carriers. Nevertheless, Mercury could use the cable systems to obtain a two-way alternative to the BT local exchange network. Both BT and Mercury could have a controlling interest in a cable franchise; this possibility raises some of the same issues as are discussed in light of the distinction between "facilities" and "services." *See supra* Section II.C.1.

3. Canada. In Canada, these definitional issues are just now being addressed in the context of pressure from some provincial governments to control the offering of local telecommunications services over cable facilities. The provincial regulators, like some of their U.S. state counterparts, recognize that cable systems could threaten local telephone companies. There is, of course, some leverage to prevent such cable-telephone competition in the case of the prairie provinces because the cable facilities are provided by the telephone companies, which are owned or controlled by the provincial governments.

Under pressure, the federal government has conceded that jurisdiction over "telecommunications services" offered on cable systems is vested in the provinces. Nevertheless, the CRTC has had continuing interest in maintaining its high profile in regulating all services on cable systems, to ensure that these systems continue to fulfill their primary role as part of the broadcasting system.

4. France and Germany. As noted above, in France there may emerge incentives for SLECs to provide teleservices, such as alarm or teleshopping, that could compete with D.G.T. offerings. Over time, such competition could become more intense as the SLECs become keener to market their broadband services and seek to offer some bypass services.

In Germany, some of the Länder perceive cable systems as a vehicle for developing an alternative telecommunications infrastructure. They hope to enter the telecommunications sector with alarm, telemetry, or other related services. Despite the objections of the DBP, which argues that it has the exclusive authority to provide telecommunications services, some Länder (*e.g.*, Baden-Württemberg, to a limited extent) are using the threat of such offerings on cable both to push the DBP toward coordinated planning and innovation in services and as a political chip in other jurisdictional disputes.

5. Japan. Adoption of the Telecommunication Business Law has blurred the line between cable services and telecommunications. Although Article 2(iv) clearly excludes cable system operators from the regulations applicable to Type I and Special Type II businesses, Article 9 leaves any telecommunications business free to provide a broad array of services, including cable services—(one-way or two-way). Although the MPT may seek to keep the cable and telecommunications businesses separate, this may prove exceedingly difficult, especially with respect to two-way services; there is no clear, principled basis on which to make such a distinction. Moreover, classified as General Type II suppliers, telecommunications businesses could use broadband facilities to provide "cable service" virtually free from regulatory limitations (except the 500-line size limit).

As a result of this legal scheme, telecommunications businesses may assume greater control of two-way services—some of which have previously been provided by cable systems. The MPT has, thus far, limited the scope of two-way services available over cable. It probably cannot apply any similar limitations to telecommunications businesses (especially General Type II) functioning like two-way cable systems. This could leave competing entities subject to unequal regulatory burdens. It also could virtually foreclose cable systems from the two-way services market. Ultimately, though, it could lead to a significant deregulation of the cable market in Japan.

6. Finland. The issue of how to classify telecommunications services offered on cable systems has not been the subject of explicit attention in Finland. The cable bill has declined to focus on this question.

It is not likely that such services will emerge in the near future. For both technological and economic reasons—cable facilities are usually provided by the telephone companies—the prospect of cable bypass or other telecommunications-related competition is not great.

7. The Benelux Countries. In the Netherlands, the Director General of the PTT, in certain circumstances, may authorize the use of cable networks for non-television programming. Thus, specialized local services—*e.g.*, alarm, monitoring and telemetry—may be offered on cable systems. There is an awareness of the possible threat posed by cable to the PTT monopoly. Thus, the use of those networks for conventional telephone, telegraph, telex and data services is not permitted. Currently, however, there is an experiment in the southern part of the province of Limburg concerning interactive uses of a local cable system; the proscription on offering certain kinds of telecommunications services will be reviewed in the context of evaluating that experiment.

In both Belgium and Luxembourg, cable operators are prohibited from transmitting anything other than radio or television programming. In April 1985, a bill was introduced in Belgium that would give the government the authority to liberalize the use of cable networks for other than radio or television programming services. In Luxembourg a bill is currently pending that might allow interactive services on cable systems.

8. Italy. Cable television is possible in Italy, but only on a single channel. This restrictive factor, together with high installation costs and, above all, the expansion of commercial over-the-air television have inhibited the development of cable television. Nevertheless, cable television has been the subject of discussion in the context of the telecommunications framework set forth in the ten-year National Telecommunications Plan. In addition, SIP and other public companies, Italtel, Sirti, CSELT, and RAI, the broadcasting company, have built an experimental "optical island" at the Milan International Fair. The optical island is a small-scale communication system based on fiber-optic cables that allows the retransmission of video channels, data transmission, access to data bases, and a sample video telephone. Three other similar projects are planned for Rome-EUR, Turin, and Bari (Technopolis).

The ten-year National Plan foresees the actual operation of a broadband network, capable of carrying interactive services, by no earlier than 1990. Nevertheless, although there is much discussion about the marketing of cable and the role of private entrepreneurs, there are technological, economic, and marketing considerations that make it likely that the potential for cable systems to provide telecommunications services will not be realized until the early 1990s. These considerations include the need for broadband networks (operational by 1995) to carry a two-way interactive video signal, the high cost of installing cable when substantial investments are being made elsewhere, and the saturating effect of commercial television stations.

To summarize, how to fit cable in the grander scheme does not yet raise burning issues. Focusing on the boundary lines between cable and telecommunications is not likely to become critical until technological developments make feasible the integrated provision of telecommunications and video services. For the moment, technological-based distinctions—and the limitations of cable and telecommunications networks—make separating telecommunications and cable services an easier task for policymakers.

III. Varying National Approaches to the Structures of the Telecommunications Industry: "Competition" in Providing Facilities Versus Services

In surveying global developments in telecommunications, several distinct approaches to structuring the provision of telecommunications services can be discerned. One of the fundamental differences among the various countries involves the extent to which they permit the alternative or competitive supply of underlying transmission facilities, as opposed to the provision of services utilizing such facilities.

Some of these differing national approaches are contrasted below. Thereafter, the national responses are compared in a more detailed way in light of the issues raised in each country by its approach toward structuring the telecommunications sector.

A. National Approaches to Industry Structure

1. Open Entry in Both Facilities and Services: The United States Case. At one end of the range, of course, is the United States, which has chosen to allow basically unrestricted competition in both facilities and services. Over the years, the FCC, step-by-step, has authorized competition in dedicated private systems (in the *Above 890* decision), specialized services using leased lines, and eventually, public switched services. Over time it became difficult to maintain distinctions between specialized and switched voice services. Consequently, once one market was opened to competition, it was difficult to confine the pressures to liberalize to that sector; as a result, swiftly, and almost inevitably, competition came to characterize the entire industry.

Over the same period, the FCC authorized the resale of leased line services. Widespread resale of private lines encouraged the development of specialized packet-switching networks and certain remote access data processing services such as Tymnet and Telenet. After competition in switched voice services was permitted, the FCC permitted the resale of MTS and WATS services; this step created a "window" of market opportunity for a class of resellers of telecommunications service.

Other than encouraging the development of value-added services, the policy of liberalized resale had several important consequences. First, resale has assisted facilities-based carriers in extending their market by allowing them to "piece out" fully their network and to expand service nationwide. Second, resale facilitated entry by permitting resellers to begin marketing while facilities were being constructed. More importantly, resale generated economic incentives to rationalize rate structures and to eliminate price disparities between MTS and leased line services. The liberal resale policy was, in many respects, not popular with entities and users affected by rate revisions. Nevertheless, on balance, resale stimulated the emergence of a more cost-based, competitive environment.

In the 1970s, the focus of control over entry into facilities markets shifted from interexchange wire or microwave competition to the licensing of new radio facilities. The FCC adopted an "open skies" policy for the domestic satellite market, within the limits posed by spectrum or orbital constraints. The FCC devised procedures to curtail its intervention in the process of selecting new competitors, processing all qualified satellite applicants as a group and essentially limiting its role to assigning orbital slots and preventing interference.

With the divestiture of the Bell operating companies, the focus of attention to competitive entry and pricing issues has shifted from interexchange facilities to the provision of local facilities and services. This reorientation has been a consequence of, and a cumulation of, other policies. Cost-based pricing of interexchange facilities is induced by facilities entry, resale policies, and ultimately the AT&T divestiture process. These factors have resulted in reallocating costs and revenue burdens to local exchange services.

The end result of this process is a movement toward bypass—large users of communications services seeking alternative local loop facilities, *e.g.* DTS services, cellular radio, private microwave, or cable connections. These alternatives to local telephone company facilities are emerging in a relatively unconstrained and unplanned way, without a coordinated policy. The bypass potential will, however, create economic pressures to increase the technological efficiency of local exchange service, which may stimulate research and development in new local exchange technologies for rural and other under-served areas.

One response of the Bell operating companies to user pressure for alternatives to local service is devising innovative pricing structures. As noted elsewhere, *see supra* Section II.A.1., the operating companies' reaction to competitive pressures presents some interesting parallels to the situation faced by the European PTTs. In both the U.S. and much of Europe the prospects for competition in facilities are limited by a diverse set of economic, technological, and regulatory pressures. As well, in both cases, significant pressures to revise traditional strategies are generated by external marketplace and political forces.

The lesson from the U.S. case is that it is difficult to infuse competition into one particular sector without affecting the entire industry structure. Over time, it is anything but easy to maintain distinctions between services or sectors. As a result, the policies of allowing competition separately—in both facilities and services—have grown together and led to an entirely open industry sector.

2. Transition to Open Entry Policy: The Japanese Case. The Japanese telecommunications sector is currently in the middle of a transition in structural policies that is not unlike that undergone in the U.S. These changes are, in significant part, a product of pressures arising from trade and industrial policies. Given differences in the marketplace, and in light of the industrial and institutional context, it remains uncertain how similar, or different, the Japanese outcome will be to that of the U.S.

The new Telecommunications Business Law approaches the structural issue of allowing competition in the facilities and services sectors by creating two categories of providers. Type I suppliers will actually construct and own a backbone of facilities; Type II carriers will only utilize the transmission facilities of others.

NTT, concurrent with this liberalization, has been privatized and will be the dominant Type I carrier. There have been, however, six applicants seeking to offer Type I services; five of the six have received authorizations. Three of these—the Daini Denden, Teleway Japan (the Ministry of Construction affiliate), and Nihon Telecom (the affiliate of Japan National Railways)—have been authorized to construct terrestrial facilities.

Three other Type I carriers will utilize satellite facilities. Due to U.S. pressure to purchase U.S. equipment, each of these three ventures includes a U.S. satellite supplier (Hughes, Ford Aerospace, and RCA), and a Japanese partner (Mitsui-C. Itoh-Hughes, Mitsubishi-Ford, and RCA-Sony (the last not yet authorized)). In addition, a group formed around the Japanese Federation of Economic Organizations, Keidanren, and chaired by Taiyu Kobayashi, the Chairman of Fujitsu Computer, recently dropped plans to set up its own satellite venture. Instead, it is now proposed that Keidanren will help obtain or will provide for its members satellite capacity of the other ventures. In this way Keidanren may act as a broker or marketer of facilities constructed by others.

Originally, in June 1984, as new entry policies evolved, it appeared that the MPT might seek to limit the number of Type I applicants. By late May 1985, however, the policy had shifted and MPT ultimately granted all applications it deemed complete, thereby allowing competition to "select" among the applicants. One advantage of this policy for the Type I satellite-based applicants has been that the Japanese government essentially is removed from the process of choosing among the U.S. suppliers.

The final structure of the facilities sector in Japan is difficult to predict. Nevertheless, when compared with the emergence of facilities-based competition in the U.K., several differences may become apparent. First, it is likely that competitive facilities will be introduced more rapidly in Japan than in the U.K. Moreover, there will be more than one competitive facilities supplier. In addition, due to the great diversity of industrial interests with a stake in the outcome, NTT will have to endure more considerable governmental pressure than is the case in the U.K. Finally, and as a result of these differences, it is probable that NTT will incur greater revenue losses than has—or will—BT.

The consequences of permitting satellite-based entry in Japan are particularly difficult to assess. It is almost conventional wisdom that a Japanese domestic satellite system must also provide international services in the Pacific Basin and, potentially, serve the trans-Pacific route to the U.S. If so, economic pressures on Japanese international telecommunications policy to permit competition in international facilities will also be swifter and more acute than has been the case in the U.K.

At the local level, Type I providers can construct local loop facilities—either coaxial or fiber optic. Depending on how NTT responds to requests for access to its local facilities, therefore, head-to-head competition may emerge at the local level.

As to services competition, the perspective is also somewhat clouded. At the outset the government viewed the scope of Type II service-based competition as unlimited. Such competition, however, may be constrained because there is some question whether the MPT will permit NTT to include tariff restrictions on voice resale. These restrictions would apply to all voice services, even those having store and forward features, which could, in the U.S., be classified as an enhanced—unregulated—service.

Since June 1984, there has been virtually a complete reversal of the two-tier classification scheme for Type II providers. Most suppliers will qualify as General Type II providers and their entry will be facilitated because they need only notify the MPT of their offerings. As there are some limits on the use of lines, it is probable that Type II services will emerge from major computer manufacturers and be based on their operating systems, and may often be tied with a trading company. The pattern of services liberalization in Japan is likely to be more fragmented than in the U.S., both in terms of serving discrete industry groups and on the basis of technological diversity.

The mix of open entry for Type I and Type II suppliers will restrict the latitude that NTT might like to exercise with respect to its leased line pricing and usage policies. If NTT sought to increase leased line charges, to prevent resale of its leased lines (and in the event its tariff restrictions on resale are rejected), new facilities-based competitors will be quick to take advantage of the resulting market opening. Similarly, NTT has limited flexibility to adopt the usage-sensitive pricing structures that are being considered by the DBP. In Japan, such rate structures, used to create equivalence between switched voice and leased line rates, would, in all likelihood, be eviscerated gradually by competitive pressures from Type I providers.

NTT, therefore, has few alternatives in dealing with facilities-based competition. It can, of course, lower interexchange rates to meet the competitive challenge. The government, however, is concerned about overly abrupt rate reductions that could thwart its pro-competitive policy of encouraging the entrance of new services.

3. Limited Open Entry Policies: The British and Canadian Cases. In both the U.K. and Canada, the governments are moving in the direction of allowing limited competition in the provision of facilities in conjunction with adopting a liberal set of policies regarding service-related competition. Although the U.K. is usually held up as a case of significant liberalization—following close at hand the U.S. experience, Canada has had a limited entry policy in facilities for even longer than the U.K. In 1964, CNCP completed its own trans-Canada microwave network and it has long been allowed to provide private data and private line voice services. In 1979, it was allowed to provide competitive data and voice services through the Bell Canada public switched network.

In Canada, however, the CRTC is only now considering whether to allow CNCP to offer in three provinces the public switched interexchange voice services that Mercury has been allowed to offer in the U.K. The further extension of facilities competition in Canada is at the discretion of regulators in the provinces where the CRTC does not have jurisdiction.

Another difference between the Canadian and the U.K. situations is the presence, in Canada, of separate suppliers of domestic and international satellite services. Both Telesat and Teleglobe are potential competitors in the Canadian facilities market. The Canadian government now is considering whether and how to privatize Teleglobe or to sell its shares in Telesat. At the present time both entities essentially sell services on only a wholesale basis. The decisionmaking process, however, involves assessing whether they both might end up as retail competitors in the market.

The prospects for Telesat and Teleglobe as facilities retailers are quite different. As a retail competitor, Teleglobe could easily lose its major customers—the originators of local exchange and domestic interexchange traffic. Telesat would be confronted with an equally awkward position, of competing with its current fellow shareholders in Telecom Canada, who would have an incentive to reduce their utilization of the satellite facilities supplied by Telesat. Furthermore, neither company has any substantial experience in marketing directly to the public.

The prospects for further facilities competition are made uncertain by two difficult jurisdictional problems that face Canadian policymakers. First, provincial authorities are unlikely, absent either further clarification of their legal obligation to order interconnection or a new federal-provincial consensus, to facilitate competition in switched voice services. Second, without clear federal authority over Telecom Canada, the process of rate rebalancing—which is usually viewed as necessary to competitive entry—will be difficult to achieve. Telecom Canada handles settlements, and sets rates, for interprovincial services. Consequently, if Bell Canada or British Columbia

Telephone must lower prices, reluctance by Telecom Canada, which operates by consensus, to modify the settlements process will create serious disruptions. The Canadian scene is, therefore, confronted with a significant, and perilous, state of potential deadlock with respect to further facilities competition.

In the services sector, Canada has followed the U.S. experience in its own way. It has adopted the "basic"/"enhanced" dichotomy and left enhanced services offered by non-carriers unregulated. Nevertheless, nationwide implementation of enhanced or liberalized services is uncertain. It is not yet entirely clear how potential entrants in the enhanced services market will respond to recent CRTC decisions. Moreover, the competitive structure for the provision of such services is not certain with respect to offerings of federally-regulated carriers. Bell Canada and other telephone companies might have to remain subject to rate regulation, even though other service providers are deregulated. And, of course, the scope of such services at the provincial level is unresolved such that they cannot be offered in all parts of Canada.

Some of the jurisdictional problems facing Canadian policymakers may require legislation for resolution. If the past is prologue, however, quick action on this front does not seem too likely.

In the U.K., by contrast, there are no legal impediments to a competitive industry structure. Mercury is gaining momentum in constructing a competitive network of services. After litigation, past controversies over the provision of access are being resolved by OFTEL.

The British government seems to be navigating effectively through the narrow straits of liberalization and privatization: it had urged that BT securities be held widely, as a secure investment, and hoped, as well, to achieve the maximum return on the offering. At the same time, however, it remains the guardian of an evolving competitive market, as the BT license illustrates. The government initially has had some difficulty in squaring its representations in the BT prospectus about the future state of competition—*e.g.*, no simple resale will be allowed in the near-term—with the pragmatic pressures toward greater liberalization.

As to services offered on public telecommunications operators' facilities, in the hectic pace toward privatization and liberalization the government hastily drafted a branch system license in August 1984. The license accorded various private companies and users flexibility in using leased lines. The government soon realized, however, that many ongoing practices required adjustments in the draft. Eventually, an ad hoc approach to services using leased lines was required.

Likewise, the policy toward VANS has been subject to considerable pressure and, as described above, *see supra* Section II.A.2., has been modified in light of the BT-IBM venture. The Consultative Document on value-added services requires a unified policy toward resale because VANS depend on leased lines. One question, then, is whether the liberalization policy will deal separately with user access to leased lines and access to these same lines by VAN operators.

Liberalization in services is, however, proceeding apace under the aegis of the procedures set up in the 1984 Telecommunications Act. OFTEL is beginning to take charge of overseeing the transition process while DTI continues as a major force in formulating telecommunications policy.

4. *An Environment in Transition: The Finnish Case.* As is true for almost every other aspect of its national existence, Finland's position in the telecommunications field is unique. Due to the structure of its telecommunications sector and to its small market size, Finland presents a particularly interesting benchmark for appraising approaches to industry structure.

The Finnish mix of private local telephone companies and a very vigorous PTT, which offers international, interexchange, and some local services (especially in the less populated areas), has generated some intense competitive conflicts. Both the PTT and the private companies, for example, would like to market data services in the areas served by their competitors.

There are other actual and potential competitive relationships between the public and private sector companies. The PTT, which oversees the highly advanced mobile radio system and all radio licensing activities, could enter the market of the private companies to offer bypass services using local radio systems. Conversely, the Dataway venture of the private telephone companies and the K.O.P. bank will supply private data circuits that could compete with the PTT's long distance leased circuit offerings.

Steps toward liberalization in services are also relatively advanced. In the area of videotex, for example, the publishing industry has established an independent service, including user-owned gateways for data bases. Leased line services are also readily available for a diverse number of data processing companies.

The open legal environment creates incentives for the establishment of specialized enhanced service networks; the entry of Dataway is likely to hasten this process. Its data circuit offerings will also limit the PTT's ability to impede the entry of new services by imposing restrictive conditions on leased lines or by introducing usage-sensitive rate structures.

With an open market for terminal equipment, and a strong industrial base in the telecommunications field, Finland may be one of the most dynamic test markets for new services. Its industry and service sectors are heavily dependent on international trade and seek access to larger markets. Thus, Finland may seek to exploit the close working relationships between its tightly-knit industry sectors to develop an array of new information-based systems for export into the U.S. and Japanese markets, though it may be more interested in the markets in Western and Eastern Europe.

Faced with little in the way of political or institutional barriers to industrial innovation, Finland's situation is rare, especially as compared with the cases of Germany or Canada, which both face severe institutional and political problems in effectuating changes in pricing and general telecommunications policies. Although small in terms of market size, Finland is, as a political matter, one of the most instructive national cases examined.

5. *The European PTTs: France, Germany, Italy, and the Benelux Countries.* The European PTTs are, as described below, in a process of transition and institutional restructuring. This process is characterized by a very unreceptive stance toward liberalizing entrance into the facilities market and by a more open-minded view of the possibilities for service-oriented competition. In fact, the introduction of facilities-based competition seems unlikely anywhere in Continental Europe, at least in the foreseeable future. In France, perhaps, a shift in the political alignment in the elections of 1986 and 1988 could result in a major shift in telecommunications policy. Realistically, however, there is a consensus as to the benefits of the current structure that extends across political lines and is cemented by a core of expertise within the D.G.T.

One important development in Europe, however, is that very few, if any, of the PTTs are oriented toward preserving the status quo in the rapidly changing environment. Several innovative responses to change are either being implemented or are being studied by national commissions or political entities. These innovations are in two main areas. First, much attention has been paid to the organizational structure of the PTT itself in providing service. The focus has, particularly, been on the utilization of long-range management plans, the separation of regulatory and operational practices, and the creation of subsidiaries. Second, in several countries, policymakers are taking a hard look at liberalizing service-based competition.

Some of the most innovative and dynamic moves in response to technology and marketplace demands has been in France, where rethinking and modernizing strategy have taken place for some time. First, the D.G.T. has attempted to create a long-run business plan or charter for itself through the Charte de Gestion.

Second, and perhaps, more significantly, it has set up subsidiaries (the "filiales") through its France Cables et Radio subsidiary and under the droit prive; these filiales will offer new communications services. The new subsidiaries are, however, not facilities-based competitors; they obtain their underlying services from the D.G.T. This structural approach has several very considerable advantages. First, the subsidiaries give the D.G.T. the flexibility for financing their new ventures and, possibly, to form international joint ventures. Moreover, they provide the option of competing in the labor market for highly skilled software engineers and other technically-trained personnel. More importantly, the subsidiaries can supply services through aggressive marketing practices and be free from the constraining obligations of the PTT code against price competition, etc. Given a certain degree of substitutability among the services offered by these subsidiaries, they can act as a competitive spur to the D.G.T.

With the shift toward creating subsidiaries and management units, the D.G.T. is also isolating its regulatory activities. Such a separation will enable the D.G.T. to oversee services competition between its own subsidiaries and private sector providers.

There is no similar organizational structure within the DBP and it is probable that the monopoly on the provision of facilities will remain unchanged. Some of the organizational issues addressed in France may well be examined closely by the governmental commission set up to assess the DBP's future. Some in the DBP believe that decentralization may be one solution to the problem posed by current price structures. The DBP does have a subsidiary, DETECON, that provides international consulting services. There are, however, questions under the German Basic Law whether other subsidiaries could be created. The ability to set up subsidiaries or to separate regulatory and operational responsibilities may become central to consideration of competition in the enhanced services market.

From an outside perspective, the dominant issue facing the DBP may be service pricing. Given built-in politically-mandated pricing elements, the DBP must deal with a rate structure for interexchange services that is set well above costs. It is widely recognized that such a pricing structure makes the implementation of facilities-based or service-based competition very perilous due to the opportunities it creates for "cream-skimming" or arbitrage.

The presence of some competitive pressures—at least in international markets—creates a dilemma for German policymakers. There is, however, no consensus for tackling head-on the disruptive and politically unpopular task of revising the price structure. If the pricing issues are not addressed promptly, the DBP will face increasing competition internationally and accompanying trade-originated pressures.

The process of resolving these difficult issues will be slow. It may necessitate reorganizing the DBP. In addition, a consensus to reprice interexchange services could accelerate the pace toward services liberalization. Although its new leased lines rates caused considerable consternation among users, the DBP's policy toward leased line sharing and availability does suggest that it is receptive to the notion that specialized networks may yield innovative marketing ideas and technological standards. In this regard the DBP is potentially more receptive to the idea of diverse technical standards than is, for example, the D.G.T.

The D.G.T., as described above, *see supra* Section II.A.3., has taken an active role in attempting to achieve standardization for terminal devices such as the Minitel. The French rationale for this approach is coherent—that standardization of terminals and network systems will create more open markets in the service and software sectors. The objective, therefore, is to target particular sectors for competition and expansion. In contrast to the Japanese approach, which seeks to foster opportunities for computer and computer system manufacturers, the French place more emphasis on industries that are likely to use electronic and computer hardware.

The structural situation in Italy is quite complex and involves fragmented provision of facilities. Carriers operate under licenses from the Ministry of Posts and Telecommunications. The State Agency for Telephone Services ("ASST"), a public enterprise directly managed by the Ministry of Posts and Telecommunications, provides long-distance connections between thirty-seven telephone districts and international services to all European countries and the Mediterranean. The remaining connections are provided by companies belonging to STET, a subsidiary of IRI.

In the near future, ASST will be privatized and then transferred to the STET group. A bill with this goal has been submitted by the Minister of Posts and Telecommunications; although it has not yet been formally approved, there is an overall consensus on its objective. Thus, STET is the central actor in the structural development of telecommunications in Italy.

STET is subject to a series of governmental checks. The Ministry of Posts and Telecommunications renews its telecommunications licenses through "concessions," the last of which was signed in 1984. The Ministry also sets guidelines through planning documents and controls some cost and pricing decisions (*e.g.*, the price of teleservices). The Ministry of State Holdings, which oversees IRI, also participates in the strategic decisions of STET. Other ministries, such as the Ministry of Industry, have influence through the Interministerial Committee for Economic Planning (CIPE), which reviews major industrial and economic policy decisions, and CIP, the Interministerial Committee on Prices, which sets prices for telephone communications.

STET is the IRI holding company for telecommunications and electronics. It is regarded as well-managed and some view it as having some quasi-autonomy within IRI; IRI has given high priority to telecommunications in its investment plans. STET has financial, technical, and commercial control over its subsidiaries, which operate in three separate fields.

First, it owns and controls most transmission facilities. Through SIP it manages the urban network and the non-ASST part of the interurban network. It also owns Italcable, which administers the bulk of intercontinental telecommunications services and certain European traffic, and Telespazio, which operates earth stations for satellite transmissions. All these services are licensed by the Ministry of Posts and Telecommunications.

Second, STET is responsible for managing the electronics manufacturing industries. This sector includes Italtel, the largest Italian telecommunications manufacturing concern; Selenia-Elsag, operating civil and military systems; SGS Ates, for micro-electronics; Sirti, for plant and installation; and Siemens-data for data processing.

Third, it has interests in publishing and telematics. Seat and Sarin are providers of economic and commercial information. CSELT is a research organization.

In sum, STET acts as an integrated holding company that makes all investment, planning, and marketing decision for its services and, to an increasing extent, the overall telecommunications sector. Single organizations within the STET group do have some autonomy. SIP, for example, to enhance its planning capabilities, is presently pressing for enactment of an automatic price adjustment scheme that would be related to inflation and to variations in productivity.

The STET structure might appear to offer opportunities akin to those arising from the D.G.T.'s subsidiary-oriented structure. There are some critical differences between the Italian and French situations. First, the STET subsidiaries are not at present competitive. Furthermore, Italy lags behind France in modernizing its network; digitization will only be achieved by the early 1990s and ISDN will probably come late to Italy. Finally, there is no general industrial policy comparable to that of France, although the STET companies, and others, have developed some significant industrial capacity; in addition, Italian manufacturers would appear to have a weaker position in world markets than the French.

STET may have some comparative advantages, however. It is accustomed to operating in the market and can raise funds in both the national and international capital markets. Italian satellite technology may assist in overcoming delays in implementation of a fully digitized network.

Furthermore, the Italian structure is flexible in the terminal equipment area, with the market essentially deregulated. Italian manufacturers have strong international connections. The domestic market might favor efficient solutions; it is unlikely that the terminal equipment market will become wholly dominated by Italtel, the STET subsidiary.

In the Netherlands, at least the potential for service-based competition in enhanced services is under serious consideration by the Steenbergen Commission. If the Netherlands liberalizes in this area, the Belgian R.T.T. is likely to follow quickly. At present, however, neither the R.T.T. nor the Luxembourg PTT authorizes service-based competition, though both are exploring the possibility of liberalization in this area. If they liberalize services, both Belgium and the Netherlands, as two countries that traditionally have been critical in international trade and commerce, could exercise enormous potential leverage on policies in the larger countries in Europe—France and Germany, in particular.

B. An Appraisal of Some Consequences of "Entry Decisions"

National policies to change the competitive environment in services or facilities inevitably require more detailed policies to facilitate the implementation of liberalized or entry. These policies must deal with a range of issues, which include: (1) new systems of accounting and cost control; (2) access or interconnection; (3) establishment of subsidiaries or safeguards against cross-subsidization; (4) the treatment of "established" or "dominant" entities and new entrants; and (5) responses of the "dominant" entity. These areas are explored below to provide some texture to the prior comparison of national policies.

1. Accounting and Cost Control Procedures. Competitive entry requires that accounting and cost control principles be adopted to regulate pricing, prevent cross-subsidization, and address social and political concerns.

In the U.S., the FCC has attempted, for almost twenty-five years, to establish cost allocation systems for AT&T. These efforts have included FCC dockets 16528 and 18128, and proceedings involving the Interim Cost Allocation Manual, resulting from the AT&T divestiture, and setting access charges. For present purposes, it is not necessary to recite in detail the history of these endeavors except to note the growing despair with attempts to regulate AT&T on a service-by-service basis. Such efforts have been thwarted by problems in defining services, obtaining cost data, arranging it on a service-related basis, devising methodologies for assigning unallocable or nonattributable costs, and allocating costs between the federal and state regulatory jurisdiction.

As a result of its disillusionment with traditional rate regulation, the FCC came to rely more on entry-related strategies to control costs. With respect to AT&T, the focus gradually shifted to overseeing AT&T's business sectors—*e.g.*, terminal equipment and interexchange services—as opposed to trying to establish rates for individual services. Cost accounting efforts at the FCC, though not so much with state commissions, have tended to use this sectoral or "bulk" regulatory approach.

The sectoral approach has led the FCC to classify carriers as "dominant" or "nondominant" in their markets. Nondominant carriers—a class that originally included only non-facilities-based terrestrial resellers—now include all carriers of domestic telephone traffic, except AT&T and the Bell operating companies. As to carriers not considered "dominant"—*i.e.*, not having market power—the FCC forbears from regulating. In lieu of tariffs, which need not be filed, the FCC relies on competitive forces to "regulate" rates.

This overall approach has been expressly reaffirmed in the FCC's Notice in *Computer III*. Nevertheless, the movement from structural separation for AT&T and the operating companies that that Notice contemplates signifies that, in the future, there will be a greater reliance on accounting and costing principles as a safeguard against cross-subsidization.

The CRTC in Canada has a regulatory tradition similar to, and linked with, that of the U.S. The CRTC has just completed the final Phase III of its massive cost inquiry, similar to the separations procedure in the U.S., which is to be used as a regulatory benchmark for Bell Canada and British Columbia Telephone. This report focuses on the use of broad cost allocation categories as well as service-based distinctions. The Report rejects the Bell Canada "5–way split" methodology, which breaks down costs and revenues into service categories and into a category not causally related to a specific service. Instead, the Report selects a method based on the costing processes now used by Telecom Canada member companies in their revenue settlement plans ("RSP"). The cost allocation decision is considered of paramount importance because it is intended to enable the CRTC to identify the costs and revenues associated with the provision of broad categories of telephone company services, and to serve as a necessary predicate for rate reblancing.

One of the difficulties faced by Canadian regulators in regulating pricing is, of course, the fact that Telecom Canada is not now under CRTC jurisdiction. Consequently, the cost and rate structures of the provincial companies that supply facilities for Telecom Canada's interprovincial offerings are not subject to direct CRTC scrutiny. More importantly, the entire settlement process, which affects the price of services and the revenues of all Canadian carriers, is not presently subject to CRTC regulation. As a result, there are great structural difficulties in Canada in instituting comprehensive regulatory control over prices. The expertise for doing so, however, is present in the experience of the CRTC—which has addressed the pricing issues in a series of complex, arduous, and factually-oriented hearings. Its decision to adopt the RSP methodology should pave the way for future efforts to resolve the structural and jurisdictional difficulties.

The Canadian and U.S. experiences can be sharply contrasted with steps recently taken in the U.K. and Japan to address accounting systems for BT and NTT, the newly privatized entities. Neither BT nor NTT have had comprehensive cost accounting systems. The emergence of competition in the facilities and services sector is slowly changing that, however.

In the U.K., soon after enactment of the 1981 Telecommunications Act, BT developed its own cost allocation system based on a major reorganization of BT along functional lines. Prior to liberalization, BT had had no such accounting program. OFTEL is now attempting to "catch up" with BT's efforts and devise its own cost allocation standards and procedures. The difficulty has been that BT cannot supply separate accounts for its different business, and to allocate its capital investments.

BT, by the terms of its license, is freed from rate-of-return regulation; rather, the annual price increase from noncompetitive services is capped at some level below the retail price increase. Thus, although OFTEL need not calculate a rate-of-return, it would like to ascertain costs so that prices can be more cost-based. Its effort to implement an accounting scheme, still in an early stage, will take considerable time. With only a few members of its small staff assigned to this activity, OFTEL has a long, hard road ahead. Ultimately, regulatory controls over BT pricing practices may be maintained in a rather ad hoc or unrefined way.

In Japan, where there is no tradition of reviewing NTT pricing and costs, the MPT is well aware of the need to institute cost accounting and price controls to oversee competition. It has recently announced the formation of a Committee on Pricing to review how best to supervise NTT's pricing policies. This Committee will deal with NTT policies in three phases: the initial, transition, and fully competitive phases. It is intended that a set of auditable accounting principles be established.

The difficulty faced by the MPT is that NTT is still in the middle of the process of reorganizing itself into a structure organized around major segments of its business—local exchange, interexchange, data or information services. Until the final organizational structure is set, cost allocation schemes cannot be implemented. Nevertheless, the MPT's new approach is a more rational way of setting rates than that of past practice, where NTT rates were within Diet control.

The European PTTs are not subject to pressures from competitive entry so that any examination of cost allocation and pricing is, in a large part, driven by external pressures. In some countries, *e.g.*, Finland, there is essentially no regulation of rates. In others, *e.g.*, the Netherlands, Italy, and Germany, prices are overseen by political entities—Parliament, a governmental committee, and the Administrative Council, respectively.

In Germany, where the Administrative Council has demonstrated sensitivity to pricing policies, new services—such as 64 Kbit/s channel groups—are used for developing new pricing strategies.

In France, political control is seen as less important than the use of subsidiaries as a mechanism for reviewing and influencing costs of services.

In Italy, prices for data and teleservices are set by the Ministry of Posts and Telecommunications. As these rates should be cost-based, there is some ad hoc accounting. Some observers believe that cost-accounting of the STET group is necessary to prevent cross-subsidization inasmuch as it both supplies facilities and intends to compete in a liberalized value-added services market.

2. Access Charges. For competition to become viable, interconnection with the local exchange is necessary. Arrangements for access by new competitors inevitably raise difficult issues concerning the type, quality, and charges for access, and create pressures on existing mechanisms for cost control.

The process of establishing access arrangements in the U.S. was and continues to be one of the most complex and time-consuming aspects of the transition to competition, if not one of the most difficult regulatory problems ever to have confronted the FCC. The details of the FCC's Docket 78–72 proceeding are set out more fully in the report on U.S. developments. The central issue concerned the price and quality of access to the Bell operating companies' exchange facilities—for the new entrants—as opposed to that provided AT&T. This problem remains one of the most contested areas between the new carriers and AT&T and has been the subject of regulatory and political attention for some time. In particular, the imposition of access charges on users has raised knotty questions for Congress and the public.

Until the AT&T divestiture there were critical issues regarding the institutional process and equivalence of the mechanisms by which the new entrants and AT&T obtained and paid for access—technically, institutionally, and financially. Whereas the new entrants obtained service from the local companies by tariff, AT&T "paid" for it through an internal process known as the division of revenues. The asymmetry between the external tariff process and the internal division of revenues approach became an ongoing source of controversy. This area of contention, however, was eliminated by the divestiture, which ultimately will place AT&T and the other interexchange common carriers on essentially an equal footing for purposes of arrangements for service.

AT&T and the new entrants continue to disagree over the methodology for allocating interexchange traffic not designated by the user, to select the so-called "default carrier." Moreover, the FCC's decisions have not competely resolved disputes over intrastate interexchange access, which is within the jurisdiction of the states.

There have also been complex issues raised by the technical equivalence of the arrangements for interconnection. In particular, the new entrants have argued that their access was technically inferior and, therefore, that they should pay substantially less than AT&T. The new carriers, as well, sought to obtain interconnection on the "trunk side," as opposed to the "line side," of the local exchange switches. Indeed, the alleged continuing disparity in access has proven to be a major source of contention in this transitional period, prior to the institution of equal access nationwide—now being undertaken pursuant to the MFJ. Especially as interexchange carriers vie for customers in "equal access" areas, issues regarding points of interconnection and pricing arrangements for the new carriers remain of critical importance.

In the U.K., the access issues were early on addressed in negotiations between BT and Mercury. In late 1984, disagreements developed between the two companies. Ultimately, the controversy over the validity of the early agreement became the subject of litigation in February 1985. One question raised was whether OFTEL had jurisdiction in the face of the agreement, with BT arguing that OFTEL had no authority to prescribe the terms of interconnection. After the court declined to hold the interconnection agreements binding, a victory for Mercury, OFTEL reasserted itself to negotiate access arrangements pursuant to the conditions of the licenses.

One of the lessons of the BT and Mercury controversy may be that it is difficult to anticipate and address access issues in the abstract, prior to the operation of a new entrant. In Japan, Type I entrants are now negotiating with NTT over the terms of interconnection under the supervision of the MPT. It is not yet clear whether the MPT will insist on uniform terms of access or will intervene in the process if negotiations are not successful. In both the U.K. and Japan, discussions have focused only on the terms of access by the new entrants and not on whether such access to the local loop is equivalent to that of the established carriers. These issues will undoubtedly have to be faced.

In Canada, the entire access issue is complicated greatly by the lack of clear authority in the CRTC to exercise jurisdiction over the interconnection practices of provincial companies. Only the federally-regulated carriers are subject to the direct jurisdiction of the CRTC. Telecom Canada believes that its member companies—and not the CRTC—have "jurisdiction" over interconnection for interexchange voice services, if CNCP's application is approved. The CRTC has experience in interconnection issues, having established the terms for such with respect to Bell Canada and British

Columbia Telephone in 1979 and 1981, in connection with access for CNCP's private line/date services. CRTC will, however, certainly address the access issue in its proceeding on the CNCP application for interexchange switched voice services. In any event, if provincial authorities ever allow intraprovincial competition, a fragmented approach is probable because they will not necessarily follow the CRTC's example, set with respect to access in areas served by federally-regulated carriers.

In Finland, any access arrangements might be negotiated between the PTT and private telephone companies for new interexchange services, though there has been some controversy over the interconnection of packet-switching facilities to their respective networks. At present, the PTT and the private companies negotiate a revenue settlement agreement.

Access is not a relevant concern in the other European countries at this time because facilities-based competition is not a near-term probability. In the event "service-based" competition should emerge, a related question—over the availability and rates of leased lines for interexchange and local services—will need to be addressed.

3. Structural Safeguards. One of the mechanisms for overseeing competitive entry—and the role of service providers—has been imposing a separate subsidiary requirement on dominant carriers. Subsidiaries can, of course, as noted, be utilized as an accounting device. The relationship between a subsidiary and the parent entity can be structured, however, to include safeguards that will aid in assuring fair competition.

Especially where there is an effort to minimize or reduce service-by-service regulation of the activity provided by the new subsidiary, relationships between parent and subsidiary can become a central focus of regulatory concern. Varying degrees of separation are possible. Among the most stringent—so-called "maximum separation"—were the separation requirements adopted in *Computer II* for application to the relationship between AT&T and its enhanced services-terminal equipment subsidiary. The new subsidiary ("Baby Bell") was not allowed to use equipment or facilities of its parent. It had to hire its own personnel. There were restrictions on the flow of technical and marketing information between parent and subsidiary. A "resale structure" was imposed on AT&T such that the subsidiary had to deal with its parent at arm's-length—on the same terms and conditions as applied to similar services provided by AT&T to the subsidiary's competitors.

These particular restrictions were applied to AT&T due to its then-alleged dominance in the pre-divestiture era. The Bell operating companies are subject to a less stringent separate subsidiary requirement for the offering of enhanced services and the marketing of customer permises equipment. Other large, independent companies, such as GTE (which is the size of many PTTs) have been exempted from the separation requirements. In the aftermath of the divestiture of the local operating companies—a significant source of potential cross-subsidization—AT&T has asked that the restrictions be revisited. As noted above, *see supra* Section II.A.1., the FCC is questioning the efficiency of and need for the separate subsidiary requirements as they apply to AT&T and the operating companies in the terminal equipment and enhanced services markets.

The issue of relying on subsidiaries as a competitive safeguard is being addressed in the U.K. and Japan. In the U.K., the BT license requires it to set up a separate company for equipment supply, production, mobile radio and value-added services operation. BT's manufacturing group subsidiary, BT Fulcrum, has just been created. Although the principal safeguard lies in accounting principles, BT's efforts to establish a venture with IBM would surely have precipitated a structural debate. One issue would have been the relationship of the venture to BT and the equivalence of access offered to other carriers. Another issue would have been whether BT required an additional license to operate a VAN service, which would have afforded OFTEL the opportunity to prescribe separation requirements pursuant to the license.

In Japan, the legislation privatizing NTT specifically rejected the option of creating separate regional companies and did not mandate subsidiaries. NTT could elect to create its own subsidiaries to avoid the dilemma of having its "Type II" services more heavily regulated—due to its Type I status—than those of its Type II competitors. The reexamination and shift in the two Type II classes to facilitate entry raise questions as to what controls might apply to any NTT subsidiary. The MPT, in this regard, has adopted guidelines to guard against cross-subsidization to deal in part with this issue. The measures rely on accounting of revenues and costs, by service category, to prevent cross-subsidization. A special breakdown of two service categories which may be offered by Type I carriers in competition with Type II carriers—computer communications and digital data transmission services—is required.

NTT appears likely to collaborate with firms in the paging or construction area to create a non-affiliated resale company. It is not clear what practices will be followed by NTT with respect to providing transmission facilities to any such related company or companies.

Although NTT is reorganizing itself along functional lines, the problem of creating outright subsidiaries is complicated both from a regulatory and an institutional standpoint. Thus, it may take some time before NTT decides whether it intends to market enhanced services through its data division or through a separate entity within the company.

In Canada, the CRTC has deferred until this year the question of whether common carriers must use subsidiaries to provide enhanced or other services. The CRTC has in the past, authorized some "enhanced" services that Bell Canada could supply by obtaining—from itself—transmission capacity at tariffed rates. Other parties do not necessarily view separation as the only structural safeguard. Bell Canada has urged that the use of the subsidiary be voluntary. There are, futhermore, regulatory concerns whether CRTC jurisdiction over Bell Canada subsidiaries could be retained. Bill C–19 would give the CRTC authority to impose such a separation requirement on Bell Canada.

The D.G.T. has utilized subsidiaries with great entrepreneurial flair, more for innovation than for competitive reasons. Although arm's-length separation is not present, the D.G.T. subsidiaries do obtain services essentially on a tariffed basis. There are, however, exchanges of information and personnel among the D.G.T. and its filiales.

In Germany, one of the most difficult issues is whether, as a matter of law, a subsidiary, *i.e.*, a private law entity, could be used to offer new services. The issue of whether a structural safeguard is appropriate or lawful should the DBP enter a newly competitive market may well be explored by the governmental commission. Subsidiaries are under consideration as one possible response by the DBP to any pressure that it might feel in marketing terminal equipment.

In Italy, there is a long tradition of using subsidiaries, though not for the purpose of creating any safeguards. The STET group of subsidiaries evolved for historical reasons, with previously independent companies reorganized into a single holding company. The subsidiaries are, at present, components of an industrial strategy aimed at developing specific market segments.

In the Netherlands, the PTT is subject to a set of safeguards that begin with accounting principles and may include structural reorganizations if it chooses to provide services in a competitive services market. Alarm services provided by the PTT are provided in a separate organization—a division of the PTT. For such services a "resale" structure will be imposed so that divisions supplying competitive services will have to purchase transmission capacity at rates offered to private parties. Some users have urged that there be greater structural separation of monopoly functions in the PTT.

The Dutch PTT may, as is the case with NTT, choose to set up separate organizations when offering competitive services, to free it from burdensome regulation when competing with unregulated suppliers. Specifically, one area where the PTT may be in a less favorable competitive position vis-a-vis private competitors is with respect to the provision of valued added tax-exempt services to businesses; although private service suppliers can offset the amount of tax that they collect from their customers against the amounts that they are themselves charged, the PTT cannot, and so its rates must reflect the fact that it passes the tax on to users.

The Steenbergen Commission is likely to review the flexibility of the PTT to choose to adopt a "subsidiary" or divisional framework. It may well be, however, that the desire for safeguards will ultimately go beyond that of the Japanese situation and that some structural separation requirements will be mandated where the PTT enters competitive markets.

4. The Regulatory Treatment of "Dominant" Entities and New Entrants. One of the most important issues is how the dominant supplier is treated in a newly liberalized market. The transition from a monopoly to competitive environment raises significant concerns about preserving the advantages to the public of a sole supplier. At the same time, there is a need to allow the dominant supplier to compete fairly and on an equal footing with new entrants.

More stringent requirements are, almost uniformly, imposed on the dominant—often formerly monopoly—supplier—AT&T, BT, NTT, Bell Canada—than on its new competitors. For example, AT&T is regulated as a "dominant" carrier and has been subject to more careful review of its tariff filings than have its specialized carrier competitors, *e.g.*, resellers, MCI, GTE/Sprint, and SBS. With the emergence of competition, the FCC has moved to end all tariff and rate related oversight of the services of AT&T's competitors, but not of AT&T itself. The FCC has, as well, imposed structural separation requirements on AT&T and the operating companies and has not done so for other carriers. AT&T, for its part, has sought the ability to price its MTS services on a more flexible basis, *e.g.*, with time sensitive charges. Moreover, it argues that the structural separation has impaired its competitiveness in foreign markets, *e.g.*, for equipment.

Under pressure from AT&T to remove these disparities and permit it to compete freely with other providers of enhanced services and equipment, the FCC has initiated its *Computer III* proceeding to determine whether to maintain different regulatory standards and, if so, what they should be. At the same time, however, some of the interexchange carrier competitors are pressing for an intensive regulatory review of their relationship with AT&T. For some time to come, therefore, there will be a vigorous dialogue on the relative regulatory burdens imposed on AT&T and its new competitors.

In Japan, although there is a statutory and regulatory distinction between Type I and Type II carriers, there is no express difference between old (*i.e.*, NTT) and new Type I carriers. The MPT, however, intends to review NTT's pricing responses overseeing the extent of competition among Type I competitors. There will not necessarily be any regulatory treatment of either Type I or Type II services offered by NTT that is different from the treatment that would be applied to new Type I or Type II service suppliers. For some period of time, at least, the MPT plans to "manage" into existence a competitive environment, regardless of the underlying economic relationship between NTT and the other, new facilities suppliers.

In the U.K., Mercury's license obligates it to initiate service, exempts it from general service obligations, and permits it to raise its rates at will. BT's license contains, by contrast, several special obligations—universal service and a set of public service mandates are explicitly set forth. Moreover, BT's rate increases are limited by the license.

Although the objectives of the licenses are essentially equivalent, in practice BT may be held to a stricter standard than Mercury and VANS suppliers with respect to its competitive offerings. It does not appear, however, as if OFTEL is as likely to intervene in the BT's pricing responses to competition as the MPT appears prepared to do in Japan.

In Canada, again, any differences in regulatory treatment of carriers would be wrapped up in the jurisdictional issues. Should CNCP, for example, be allowed to offer interexchange switched voice services in areas served by federally-regulated carriers, it is unclear whether present federally- or provincially-regulated interexchange carriers would be subject to competitive constraints. A more likely scenario, especially in the case of the provincially-owned or regulated telephone companies, is that their owners or regulators would do all they could to preserve their dominant position.

As discussed above, *see supra* Section III.B.3., there may be some disparities between Bell Canada/British Columbia Telephone, and non-carriers with respect to the regulatory treatment of their enhanced offerings. The CRTC may not now be able to forbear from regulating such carrier-provided services.

There may eventually be some special treatment of Telesat if it should come to compete directly with Telecom Canada for long-haul services. The government could impose a separate subsidiary requirement on Telesat for any competitive services. Alternatively, if Telesat were to fill a CNCP-like niche market, the CRTC could order the federally-regulated companies to supply it with interconnection to the local loop.

5. Responses of the "Dominant" Entity. Faced with a regulatory environment intended to assure viable competition, the "dominant" entities have adopted a range of strategic responses that may usefully be compared.

During the early stages of introducing competition in the U.S., AT&T vigorously resisted expanding the scope of competition. This resistance was evident at each stage of liberalization—from efforts to open customer attachment policies, through AT&T-supplied "protective devices," to equipment registration; from private line competition to competition in public switched voice services. AT&T's resistance produced, in some respects, an equal and opposite legal and regulatory response. In particular, a significant governmental reaction was the antitrust suit filed against AT&T in 1974, which accompanied a spate of private antitrust litigation. By 1978-79, AT&T's strategy moved from resisting competition to focusing on obtaining reasonable terms and conditions for future competition. This shift may have been a result of the outcome in the *Execunet* case, where the U.S. Court of Appeals for the D.C. Circuit ruled that interconnection could not be denied to AT&T's competitors without an affirmative finding by the FCC that such restriction was in the public interest. The new AT&T policy emphasized that cost-based rates were needed for the pricing of interexchange services. It also focused on the need for equivalent access to new markets for the enhanced services of all providers.

In response to the government antitrust litigation, and to continuing private suits, AT&T took the bold step of settling the case by agreeing to reorganize the company to meet new competitive realities. Through the MFJ, it hoped to have the maximum amount of control over the process of restructuring itself and the industry. Ironically, this conciliatory and collaborative strategy proved to have risks of its own. Originally, the agreement was subject only to approval of the Department of Justice. The MFJ was, however, itself modified to accord Judge Greene jurisdiction over the agreement and the development and implementation of the AT&T reorganization plan. Public participation became a part of the process. AT&T's conciliatory stance proved, therefore, to be a "slippery slope." It lost control of the process and, to some extent, the competitive future of the industry is now in Judge Greene's hands.

BT has also responded vigorously to the government's decision to liberalize the telecommunications market. BT modernized its organizational structure much more rapidly and, before OFTEL emerged as an effective entity, revised its pricing strategy more aggressively than anyone cound have anticipated—or Mercury might have believed. To the great delight of major users, BT significantly reduced pricing over high density routes.

In its enthusiasm and vigor, BT perhaps moved somewhat too quickly and aggressively for its own long-term interests. BT seemingly did not expect the vehement reaction to its proposed venture with IBM from British industry and other telecommunications administrations concerned about IBM's possible dominance in Europe. By pressing the government to approve the venture on the eve of the public offering of its stock, BT may have forced a precipitous decision; realistically, the issue could not be left unresolved during the public offering. As the venture anticipated the use of leased lines, BT's haste essentially compelled the government to crystallize its theretofor ambiguous policy on VANS—as to whether they could utilize leased lines. Thus, by being assertive, BT drew OFTEL and DTI into the fray as regulatory counterweights.

Under the leadership of its Chairman, Dr. Shinto, NTT's early strategy toward meeting competition is equally illuminating. Like BT, NTT scheduled a series of price reductions in long distance service that will be implemented before formal guidelines for rate supervision are effectuated. Nevertheless, under Dr. Shinto, NTT has taken the enlightened position of encouraging and supporting the government's new pro-competitive policy. One of the top managers of Daini Denden, which promises to be NTT's major competitor in the facilities markets, was a high-ranking NTT executive. NTT has recently created a new subsidiary to provide technical and other assistance to new Type I carriers. Obviously, this pro-competition perspective is mixed with NTT's desire to be a strong competitor itself. There are also elements in NTT that find the radical transformation of NTT's role, and the impact of new policies on the technological development of future services, difficult to accept.

The D.G.T., although it has not been faced with a direct competitive challenge within France, has responded as if it had. It essentially sees itself locked in a competitive relationship with BT and, potentially, other European PTTs to obtain some of the international traffic of major industrial users. The D.G.T. sees this competitive threat as requiring measures to improve internal efficiency and maximize pricing flexibility. An essential component of its competitive strategy is the development of a structure with subsidiaries, within which there is pricing flexibility to meet international competition head-on.

Faced with a similar environment, the DBP in Germany has found it more difficult to respond quickly due to significant political constraints. At some level, the impact of international competitive pressures on domestic rate structures has not been viewed as immediately threatening. Pricing remains a central issue, however, for reasons related to the formation of an industrial and international trade policy.

In Canada, Bell Canada has reorganized itself to segregate its CRTC-regulated activities from its other businesses. In anticipation of competition, Bell Canada has pushed vigorously for rate rebalancing, so long as it occurs prior to authorizing the entrance of new competitors. With rates brought closer to costs, Bell Canada would seem prepared to meet a competitive challenge in both facilities and services. Indeed, it is as dominant in the provinces it serves as AT&T was in the U.S. pre-divestiture. Telecom Canada is the dominant force in the Canada-wide interprovincial market. It may not need to do much, at least in the short-term, to meet a switched voice challenge from CNCP, which, initially, may only be permitted to interconnect in areas served by federally-regulated carriers.

In Finland, the PTT, under the leadership of its Director General, Pekka Tarjanne, has taken several significant steps. The Director General has campaigned actively to transform the legal status of the PTT to that of a public corporation, which would enable it to retain control over investment capital and to borrow funds independently. In return for greater operational autonomy the PTT seems prepared to turn some of its regulatory responsibilities over to the Ministry of Communications.

The PTT has proposed a series of rate reductions over a five-year period for interexchange services. These rate reductions are part of a more cost-based approach toward pricing long distance services, to reduce the incentive for large users to construct private, competitive systems. All these steps—obtaining greater financial autonomy, separating regulatory and operational responsibilities, implementing more cost-based rate structures—are quite representative of the strategies of PTTs faced with domestic competitive pressures and an increasingly competitive international environment.

In Italy and the Benelux countries, there is also evidence of an entrepreneurial, independent strategy. STET is rather decentralized and some of its subsidiaries compete in value-added services. STET has also aggressively sought to create joint ventures with both Italian and multinational enterprises to exploit the opportunities generated by its diverse and integrated set of holdings.

The R.T.T.'s strategy is to make Belgium a transit center for international telecommunications. It has reached an interconnetion agreement with MCI and has obtained new revenues through transit agreements to southern Europe and South America; these equal the amount from current U.S.-Belgian traffic stream. The R.T.T. is also attempting to improve its image by creating commercial agencies and "teleboutiques" to market its products to users.

IV. Dynamics of Change: "Engines" for Change, Institutional Mechanisms, and Economic Pressures

Shifts in the substance of telecommunications policy are closely intertwined with the procedures and institutions for formulating telecommunications policy. In addition, economic pressures on the price structure of telecommunications services—that are exerted at the national and international levels—significantly influence the outcome of policy deliberations about telecommunications industry structure.

Any inquiry into the "dynamics" of changing telecommunications policies and industry arrangements is ultimately perilous. The instant discussion does not, therefore, purport to be precise in this assessment. Nevertheless, an exhaustive description of policy developments in a number of major countries—at a time when policies are changing radically and are undergoing comprehensive reexamination—necessarily leaves impressions about what is influencing or shaping change.

Policies are driven, and often subtly influenced, by a complex web of institutional processes; however, changes in policies frequently require change in the very institutions that generated them in the first place.

Beyond this, businessmen, bureaucrats, lawyers, and legislators frequently cannot direct public or private enterprises in whatever direction they wish. There often are technological and economic pressures in a complex international market that seem to sweep decisionmakers along with the current. In the end, the process of formulating national and international telecommunications policy requires decisionmakers both to "steam ahead" and to respond to outside forces.

Policymakers are more like navigators sailing on a clouded night—sometimes able to get a fix on a star, to read shifting winds and currents, and to set a course.

The discussion below is intended to illuminate some institutional mechanisms of change, institutional responses to policy shifts, and adjustments of pricing at the national and international level that affect the future direction of telecommunications policy.

The focus of the following discussion, therefore, has several aspects. First, there are many and diverse mechanisms or engines for shifting the direction of telecommunications policy. Different forces affect policy—(1) legislation; (2) internal bureaucratic processes; (3) litigation; (4) ideology or political values; (5) jurisdictional conflicts; (6) user pressures; and (7) responses to pressures from the international environment.

Second, there are specific mechanisms for controlling policy developments—some of which have evolved due to substantive policy shifts. How they are working may be useful in assessing the future course of events.

Third, there is an array of economic adjustments underway at the national level.

Fourth, international pressures also play a very significant role in affecting the national policymaking processes.

A. Engines for Changes in Policy

The mechanisms for changes in policy differ in each of the countries that have been examined. For policymakers and for businessmen it will be useful to examine the dynamics of the present in order to understand the future. Where current trends are leading cannot be foreseen with anything approximating certainty. National telecommunications policies, like a complex gear-work, are interdependent, influencing each other and the pace of change internationally.

Nevertheless, by exploring the changes of today, predicting the eventual course of events becomes a more realistic task. A hard look to the future requires a rigorous appraisal of the institutional and economic pressures on national policymakers. Some of these forces are described in the following sections.

In the U.K., the initiatives toward privatization originated at the highest levels of the British government. Even though BT had been allowed to operate without a great deal of government involvement since it was nationalized, there were still strong pressures to privatize. These were based on an ideological predilection favoring private sector investment. A further intention was to stimulate innovation in the private sector. The parliamentary process, however, essentially ratified a negotiated solution.

As a group, telecommunications users had relatively little impact on the steps toward change, though a few larger users did have some influence on the process. Some of the leaders of the British telecommunications manufacturing sector—suppliers to BT—actively opposed privatization and the liberalization of the British market largely out of concern that they would lose their most favored position as suppliers to BT to foreign enterprises. Indeed, the policies have apparently not yet developed a substantial constituency in that sector.

Although the initiatives for change came from the top, they have been executed through DTI and OFTEL. The DTI has been extremely influential in setting the pace of change. At the early stages of the transition process, DTI negotiated some of the major elements of the relationship between BT and Mercury. DTI has, of course, drafted the BT, Mercury and VANS licenses, which have been among the major legal documents shaping the competitive structure of the industry. OFTEL had a central role in the DTI decision on the BT-IBM venture and will have an increasingly more active role in overseeing the transition to a competitive industry structure, particularly in the VANS, pricing, and costing areas.

Pressure from the telecommunications industry has been substantially less vigorous in the U.K. than in Japan, where the telecommunications and computer industry has had a key role in shaping policy. This may reflect the somewhat less dynamic state of the British telecommunications industry.

Telecommunications users have recently, however, been playing a weightier role in policy, especially in influencing interpretations of the branch license and with respect to restrictions on the use of leased circuits.

The role of the government in the public offering of BT securities has had an extremely significant impact on the direction of policy in the U.K. As the offeror, the government made representations to potentially millions of shareholders about the regulatory environment in which BT would operate; thus, in some real sense, the government tied its hands in launching any radical policy initiatives. For example, although the government stated that resale of communications services would not be authorized until 1989, it has gradually and cautiously retreated from this position. It now opposes "simple resale," and not necessarily the use of leased circuits for VANS.

In Japan, the origins of the privatization and liberalization policies originated with the 1981 Second Ad Hoc Commission on Administrative Reform. This Commission was principally concerned with the role of large public corporations, such as NTT and Japan National Railways, and with their ability, as public sector entities, to cope effectively with labor-management pressures. The policies also evolved in light of the influence of MITI and its long-range perspectives on the impact of the telecommunications and information sectors on Japanese society. Concurrently, since the 1982 liberalization of leased circuits for VANS, there was some internal pressure in NTT to obtain greater flexibility in managing its operations to meet competition.

During the year preceding the enactment of the Telecommunications Business Law, MITI, as the entity most concerned with long-term industrial policy, and the MPT differed over key provisions of the new legislation. Particularly unsettled was the extent of the MPT's control over the process of approving new Type II value-added services. In addition, other entities, specifically, financial institutions and the Ministry of Finance, the Ministry of Construction, and the Ministry of Transportation (for Japan National Railways), sought to position themselves to participate in the opening of the telecommunications market. Thus, impetus for change is a product of various concerned ministries in conjunction with the industries and segments of the Diet affiliated with those ministries.

Substantial influence on the policy process has been exerted through a web of informal advisory committees affiliated with the ministries. These committees link senior advisors and industry figures, and contribute toward achieving a consensus on policy.

Industry groups in the computer and the telecommunications field have had a major stake in the success of the liberalization. Despite this interest, their actual influence is quite different from that of U.S. business interests in the U.S. regulatory process. In its dealings with the ministries, Japanese industry seems to take a more deferential and restrained approach than is so in the U.S. There is a clearer recognition in Japan than in the U.S. that the authority to set the basic parameters of industry policy is vested in the ministries.

Again in contrast to the U.S., litigation between industry members and against governmental regulatory authorities has had almost no influence or impact on telecommunications policies. The Diet took a less participatory role in shaping the telecommunications legislation than would have been the normal case in the U.S., with Congress taking the lead in decisionmaking. The basic lines of the legislation in Japan were worked out within the ministries and among the various factions of the LDP.

International forces have been significant, as well. Although the liberalization process is deeply rooted in the Japanese political process, there has been extraordinary trade pressure exerted by the U.S. government to obtain a more open telecommunications market. This pressure has succeeded in revising the MPT's proposed approach to equipment certification and the licensing of Type II VANs.

In Germany, the DBP is the dominant factor in establishing national telecommunications policy. The DBP, in part because it is essentially a government ministry and is headed by a member of the Cabinet, operates in a sensitive political context. Rate changes, budgets, and proposals for new services must be approved by the Administrative Council, which has representatives of the Bundestag and the Bundesrat, as well as of business, industry, and labor. The influence of labor unions on DBP policy is quite significant due to the sheer size of its work force and the relative weight of the DBP's national investment.

The DBP is also subject to institutional pressures within the government. The Ministries of Economics and Finance oversee budgets, rates, and charges. The Ministry of Economics, which may often reflect the views of small- or medium-sized business interests, has occasionally been a counterforce to the DBP, advocating a reduction in its role in the terminal equipment market. In addition, the Monopoly Commission urged a shift in DBP policy, and a retreat from its role as a supplier of terminal equipment. In sum, the DBP continues to be subject to pressures and constraints as it develops policies for investment in new technologies.

A very significant constraint on DBP policy is exercised by the Länder, which, under the German Basic Law, have responsibility for the media. In facilities planning, there is substantial friction as the Länder assert jurisdiction to authorize the use of new facilities that the DBP is responsible for constructing. The Länder have also claimed a broader role in participating in the implementation of services, particularly for new or hybrid services such as videotex.

Some observers, therefore, see the Länder as a pressure point for opening up opportunities for new information services. Often the Länder are interested in encouraging regional economic development; they may act on behalf of business interests to urge that the quality and flexibility of telecommunications offerings be improved. Although the Land of Baden-Württemberg had originally proposed far-reaching legislation for new cable services, the enacted law did not raise sweeping claims against the jurisdiction of the DBP. In fact, the real leverage on the DBP of the Länder is political, as they seek to influence the DBP's investment in the technology sector.

The momentum for reappraisal of the role of the DBP will, by and large, have to come from within, through the governmental commission. The members of this commission were selected after a long and careful process; they will review a set of issues on the DBP's future that are being explored with the DBP and other concerned parties.

German users and manufacturers have been divided. In general, they have not, in the past, exercised substantial leverage on the policy-formulation process. Equipment manufacturers have worked closely with the DBP. Users are, however, starting to emerge as a force in negotiating conditions for the use of leased lines and, more recently, in discussions with the DBP over the introduction of new usage-based pricing structures for leased lines. Much of the influence is ad hoc and driven by multinational enterprises.

Some litigation has, as well, been important in delineating the proper role of the DBP. In both the *Direktrufbeschluss* and the earlier *1. Rundfunkurteil* decisions, substantial latitude was accorded the DBP with respect to the limits of its authority to provide "telecommunications services." In principle, at the least, the boundary between "media" and "telecommunications" and, hence, the DBP's authority in the facilities planning area, could also be defined through litigation; the DBP's decisions to initiate private broadcasting without Länder consent might constitute a test case.

On a related front, the DBP has been pressured by the Commission of the European Communities. The Commission has challenged the DBP in its effort to control the marketing for cordless telephones; it is also attacking the DBP's control over data modems. Such European-originated pressures may have some influence over time. As significantly, it is widely predicted that pressure on the DBP from U.S. trade officials will increase significantly in the coming year in the aftermath of progress in the U.S.-Japan trade talks.

In Canada, the institutional pressures affecting telecommunications policy result from the convergence of the CRTC's steady regulatory role in cautiously opening up sectors of the Canadian market and the resistance of the provinces to many of these initiatives. In this process, the Canadian Department of Communications ("DOC") is an integral part of and oversees the Canadian telecommunications policymaking process, of which its present telecommunications policy review is the latest step. The DOC has led the effort to update and modernize Canadian telecommunications legislation and, over the years, to reach a federal-provincial accommodation. The Department has been concerned with assuring that the CRTC adequately reflects a national political consensus. Through its power to participate in any review of CRTC decisions by the Governor in Council, the DOC has the opportunity to modify the thrust of CRTC actions.

Bill C-20 will greatly extend the policymaking role of the DOC by granting to the Governor in Council the ability to issue policy directives that will be binding on the CRTC.

The Canadian courts have had a relatively minimal role in the process of liberalization, at least as compared with the impact of judicial decision-making in the U.S. The *Alberta Government Telephones* decision, however, may have truly radical significance in resolving federal-provincial jurisdictional issues. If the Court of Appeals reverses the lower court's refusal to find the province of Alberta, in its capacity as owner of the provincial telephone company, subject to federal jurisdiction, the CRTC would effectively be able to make decisions on a national basis without the need for new legislation.

In the past, users have not had a significant impact on Canadian policy. Like their brethren to the south, however, they are becoming a more potent force in the regulatory and legislative process.

To date, the Parliament has not taken an active or independent role on communications policy issues. Two bills are presently pending and, in conjunction with the DOC review, the lack of action by the Parliament might eventually change. For the moment, it is for the DOC to decide how active a role it should take in initiating legislative changes. Activism by the DOC, of course, requires tackling some of the difficult short-term consequences of change, *i.e.*, pricing adjustments. Most industry observers see these changes as inevitable and necessary if the Canadian telecommunications sector is to remain vital in close proximity to the dynamic U.S. market.

In short, the Canadian policy process cannot make rapid structural adjustments to respond to pressures for change. The moving forces are likely to be the CRTC and the courts, who are free, within limits to act independently. Although political consensus has proven difficult to achieve in the past, the current Progressive Conservative government seems intent on healing some of the divisions. Hence, the possibility of a political solution cannot be ruled out.

In France, as in Germany, the leadership of the administration—the D.G.T.—has great leverage and control over communications services. The Director General of the D.G.T. may be more independent of the political process than is the Minister of the Bundespost. The D.G.T. has a Charte de Gestion—a long-term management plan that determines the business objectives and plans of the D.G.T. for a number of years. In addition, the D.G.T. is not as exposed to pressures from such other ministries as, for example, influence the DBP, or even the MPT in Japan.

Through its Direction des affaires industrielles et internationales, the D.G.T. has a role in overseeing the French electronics industry. In carrying out this task, the D.G.T. is required to consider the industrial policy implications of its procurement decisions and the results of certain payments or subsidies to French industry. Consequently, the D.G.T. has a keen interest in standardization as it affects markets for French terminal and switching equipment.

The D.G.T. is also subject to a broader web of pressures. In August 1984, the Government raised telephone rates—a move resisted by the D.G.T. as having an adverse impact on its projections for demand and circuit utilization. The D.G.T. has maintained vigorous efforts to reinforce its autonomy. Of course, the creation of subsidiaries is consistent with that objective.

Undoubtedly, the D.G.T.'s policies are somewhat resonant of the broader political climate. The French government has recently adopted a more pragmatic, "middle-of-the-road" stance toward government ownership and industry structure than it had adhered to immediately after the 1981 election. The diversified structure of the D.G.T. and its filiales is consonant with recent French developments that have seen some publicly-owned companies offer interests in their subsidiaries to the public.

National political pressures also affect the D.G.T. institutionally. The D.G.T. civil servants are aware of the upcoming parliamentary elections in 1986 and the presidential election in 1988. The more conservative opposition has an increasingly active interest in telecommunications policies; at least one of their expert advisers would consider the feasibility of introducing facilities-based competition and a major restructuring of the D.G.T. itself.

The French administration has stressed decentralization of activities. Reliance on the SLECs reflects this focus; importantly, it is a pragmatic response by the D.G.T. to the need to diversify the sources of investment capital to fund the D.G.T.'s array of projects for upgrading the French network. These conflicting priorities become difficult to reconcile, especially when competition in the international arena is cutting into traditional profit sectors. In the long term, the SLECs, financed by the Caisse des Depots, may become more of an institutional counterweight to the D.G.T.

In Finland, a combination of factors influence the development of policy. Overriding all others, however, is that there exists a legislative and legal vacuum—resulting from the antiquated statutory framework—that makes industry negotiation and agreement critical to the policymaking process. That this approach works is largely because the group of decisionmakers is small and concentrated in Helsinki. Despite the consensual way in which decisions are made, the Finns do not hesitate to resort to litigation (*e.g.*, between the private companies and the PTT) to resolve their differences. The slow and unwieldy legislative process reinforces an environment in which telecommunications industry leaders work out their differences—or prefer to do so—with a minimum of external interference.

Underlying Finnish policy, however, is a national consensus that the success of the Finnish economy is dependent on international trade. Finnish industry is, as a result, open to innovation and understands the need to obtain access to the largest markets. To remain competitive in global markets there is close cooperation within Finnish industry and, of equal importance, with the labor unions.

In the Benelux countries, the forces that are evident elsewhere are also very much at work. Not suprisingly, the impact of developments throughout Europe serves as an impetus for reexamining telecommunications policy. An awareness of U.S., French, British, and other countries' policy shifts is driving the pace for review in the Netherlands and is encouraging a certain aggressive competitiveness in Belgium. In Luxembourg, French developments are tracked especially closely and political pressure from France—as occurred in the course of the Coronet controversy—has had a major impact.

Internal, political, and ideological pressures are important in Belgium, where the current Minister of Communications and the PTT, Mr. DeCroo, is an advocate of deregulation. Also active—and interested in the beneficial industrial policy consequences of liberalization—is the Ministry of Political Science. The Parliament is closely following the review process in the Netherlands, though the primary factor in the Belgian review is pressure from users and the business community.

In Belgium, according to some observers, the R.T.T.'s principal supplier, the Bell Telephone Manufacturing Co. ("BTMC"), a subsidiary of ITT, has been less than enthusiastic about the prospect of liberalization. BTMC, for the last twenty years, has supplied 85% of the R.T.T.'s equipment; its influence within the R.T.T., though informal, is not without substance. BTMC does not want to lose its dominant relationship with the R.T.T., which, it fears, could occur in a liberalized environment. The market for telecommunications equipment may, however, in any event, be opened to other suppliers in 1986, when the supply contracts must be renewed.

That one company can have influence in a country that is relatively compact is not surprising. It is unlikely, for example, that much of a policy initiative toward liberalization will occur in the Netherlands without the participation—or at least acquiescence—of Philips.

The Italian forces for change are a mixture of governmental, private sector, and user-originated. The central tenet of current policy is that STET is primarily responsible for network planning. The STET group is decentralized and essentially organized along facility-specific lines. Thus, where changes may be required—or seen as desirable—to respond to perceived needs or international shifts in policy, there is some flexibility within the STET organization.

The Ministry of Posts and Telecommunications coordinates planning under the supervision of CIPE. The Ministry is charged with legislative initiatives and has been at the center of formulating the National Plans for telecommunications reform. It is CIPE, however, that has approved the National Plans and, in 1982, passed an act that established new rate policies.

One important point of control over STET is the process of renewing the "concessions"—or licenses—for operation of the telephone network. The process is, at least in theory, an opportunity for the government to achieve its political ends in telecommunications policy. Although CIPE had recommended in 1982 that new agreements be struck to alter the management of services and redistribute the revenues among the services, it is not clear that there are substantive negotiations when the concessions are renewed.

User pressures on STET and ASST have been increasing in the banking and value-added sectors. Banks have, however, been engaged in essentially establishing their own telematic systems. In part, the Ministry of Industry, as is the case of MITI in Japan and the Ministry of Economics in Germany, may be urging the cause of the user-business community. The complex web of relationships between and among the private and public sectors may well create pressure points for change in the services area.

In the U.S., it is quite difficult to identify and isolate the welter of influences that have shaped and are participants in the new environment. Change is percolated into the system through litigation—the *Execunet* cases ordered interconnection; an active role by the FCC—which has, for over a decade, moved toward a competitive model in sector after sector; and pressure from new entrants—who seek to exploit new technologies (*e.g.*, satellites) and markets; and, ultimately, from users of communications services. During the pendency of the Department of Justice antitrust suit against AT&T, the FCC and Congress both attempted to restructure or recodify an industry structure to alleviate some of the concerns raised by that case. The bills introduced at that time could have had the consequence of curtailing or limiting the scope of the government's litigation. The vortex of legislative pressures made it difficult for any such complex piece of legislation to get enactment. Ultimately, the FCC's decision in *Computer II* and its implementation of the structural separation requirements significantly diminished the incentive of Congress to resolve these difficult issues.

In general, Congress has played a less significant role than the FCC; nevertheless, in its oversight capacity of the FCC, and as a forum in which policies have been articulated openly and debated, its involvement has been key. After the completion of the AT&T divestiture, Congress and the public became considerably more active and interested in telecommunications policy. In this regard, one example of legislative intervention was the decision by the FCC to postpone implementation of its access charges decision under congressional pressure. The Department of Commerce, and the National Telecommunications and Information Administration ("NTIA") within it, have not taken as active a role in charting or influencing policy; in the past year and a half, however, NTIA's role has broadened, particularly on international trade-related issues where the Department of Commerce has had the lead role in the U.S. government.

Essentially, the forces for change in the U.S. are now dominated by financial and marketplace considerations. In a post-divestiture environment, and where the FCC has basically decided to forbear from regulating all but AT&T and its former subsidiaries, the "die is cast," to a certain extent. Consequently, regulators—the FCC, Congress, Judge Greene, and state commissions—can essentially do very little to stop the momentum that is carrying the industry forward.

One significant factor that will chart the course of future competition at the local level is how local services will be priced and what will be the impact of access charges. As significantly, the development of bypass technologies and opportunities will create additional competitive pressures on the Bell operating com-panies and other exchange carriers. Despite attempts by the operating companies to expand the scope of their activities beyond exchange service, they will remain vigorous—or not—depending on technological developments, not regulatory ones.

The capacity created by competitive entry has left the facilities market in a state of uncertainty. It is likely that there will be a winnowing of competitors in the long-term. The inability of carriers in the new markets—and the success of the U.S. initiatives—will, therefore, be affected by financial considerations, by users and by Wall Street, and not by oversight entities.

Present surpluses of capacity, however, are not necessarily a sign that deregulation is not working. There may be cycles of "excess supply" and "excess demand"; ultimately, however, the financial markets are likely to do a good job of sorting out the state of the overall market and the viablity of new and established entrants.

B. New Institutional Mechanisms to Control Shifts in Policy

As telecommunications policies have evolved in Europe, Canada, Japan, and the U.S., there have, in most countries, been pressures to adopt new institutional mechanisms to control policy shifts. Not only are the substantive policies in a state of rapid flux, so, too, are these national institutions. From an internatinal perspective this development is significant because it generated new policymaking bodies and decisionmakers. As described below, national policy shifts affect the mechanisms for coordinating national and international telecommunications policies.

One of the best examples of the nexus of substantive changes and institutional developments has been in the U.K., where the 1984 Telecommunications Act created OFTEL, the Office of Telecommunications. OFTEL is an independent body, and is headed by a Director General who serves for a fixed term of years and is not subject to any administrative direction from DTI or the British Cabinet. OFTEL has certain overlapping responsibilities with the DTI in the area of licensing new telecommunications entities, but essentially there is a duopolistic regulatory structure.

Ultimately, it will be for OFTEL to resolve some of the critical issues raised by the introduction of competition in the U.K. Among these are setting the classifications and standards for VANS licensing, interpreting the branch licenses, overseeing access arrangements between BT and Mercury, supervising BT price increases, and adopting accounting standards to enable it to review BT's rates.

The intention of the British government has been to regulate with a "light touch" and not to replicate the role of the FCC in the different industrial and economic setting of the U.K. Procedures have been developed to adapt to the unique aspects of the British administrative tradition. OFTEL has utilized ad hoc procedures without the formalism of the FCC's processes. For example, in conjunction with the announcement of the BT-IBM venture, OFTEL set up a comment period for interested parties and began a process of consultation with industry.

Nevertheless, OFTEL must confront the very real problems of overseeing a licensing regime. Users are seeking case-by-case interpretations of the branch licenses. There will be pressures for achieving a uniform approach and for a more formal regime, more akin to that of the FCC, to institute rules to govern industry relationships.

Another institution set up to regulate a developing telecommunications technology is the Cable Authority, which has principal responsibility for franchising cable systems and regulating cable television services. The Authority was set up by the 1984 Cable and Broadcasting Act to operate independently of the government (*i.e.*, DTI and OFTEL) due to a desire to avoid government control over programming.

Because cable systems are telecommunications systems, approval prior to operation must be obtained from DTI (acting in consultation with OFTEL). Some of the potential for a jurisdictional conflict between the Authority and DTI/OFTEL may have been resolved in the sequential licensing process; the Authority issues a franchise and consults with DTI and OFTEL regarding the telecommunications aspects of the proposed cable offering. (OFTEL and DTI are to consult with the Authority regarding any telecommunications system proposed to be used for providing cable programming.) In any event, the Authority's grant is conditioned on the completion of a next step—the approval process—complete with comment period—under the auspices of DTI. This phase is expected to take an additional four-month period.

Thus, although only one application is required, a two-tier regulatory scheme is imposed, with essentially two sets of conditions governing the provision of cable services. Nevertheless, the flexibility of the scheme—with informal consultation between the regulatory bodies—represents an innovative solution that manages to ensure compliance with two distinct sets of regulatory requirements.

In Japan, the evolution of institutional mechanisms will be interesting from a comparative perspective. For, as the British have vowed that they will not establish a British FCC, so, too, the Japanese have emphasized that they will not create a Japanese FCC or OFTEL. This disinclination for creating a new regulatory body can, of course, be traced to the more informal, consensual approach to decisionmaking of the Japanese political culture.

Changes in the telecommunications sector and concurrent trade pressures require that the MPT develop new strategies for overseeing the industry structure as it evolves. Prior to April 1, 1985, the MPT instructed NTT on a bilateral basis as the sole player in the industry. Now, however, the MPT oversight responsibility will affect a range of participants—a half-dozen Type I providers, an array of Type II suppliers, users, other affected ministries, and international entities—both public and private.

The MPT has reorganized to adjust to the new structure. To adopt a more policy-oriented, broad-based approach it now has a Communications Policy Bureau. There is a greater recognition that its decisions will have a significant impact on an entire industry and related sectors.

In addition to participating in consensual policymaking it is inevitable that the MPT will be asked to resolve disputes involving service pricing, competitive relationships, access issues, and concerns regarding industry structure. For rate regulation, the MPT has already set up an ad hoc study committee. It has erected an innovative mechanism to deal with equipment certification issues: as a result of very considerable trade pressure from the U.S., a neutral certification process will be administered by a nonprofit entity separate from the Ministry and from representatives of Japanese industry.

Some similar ad hoc mechanism within the Ministry may be needed in other areas. Particularly with respect to inter-industry problems and issues affecting the interests of other ministries, new approaches will need to be developed. For example, the definition of and application procedures for Type II carriers were the subject of intensive discussions between the U.S. and Japan, held in the broader context of the bilateral trade imbalance. Other issues of concern—to both Japanese and foreign competitors—will emerge as the transition to a competitive environment continues. In that regard, it might be extremely useful for the MPT to formulate a set of procedures that could be used by Japanese and foreign entities alike to resolve transitional concerns. Certainly an open and accessible administrative process would seem preferable to the traditional intergovernmental negotiation process—a process that could produce tension in light of evolving competitive realities. The availability and transparency of institutional mechanisms at the national level may well be critical to creating a favorable international climate for telecommunications and information services.

In Canada, too, institutional reform is intertwined with the process of opening up and modernizing regulation of the telecommunications market. Undoubtedly, the most critical area is to create a consultative mechanism to facilitate a dialogue—if not a consensus—between the federal government and the provincial authorities. An array of issues could—and probably should—be addressed in such a forum—issues of competition, interconnection, and rates. Several recommendations for consultative bodies—between the CRTC and representatives of the provinces—have been discussed over the years; however, no informal arrangements or legislative initiatives have gotten very far.

Without legislation, or absent further judicial movement in the *Alberta Government Telephones* case toward clarifying the respective spheres of authority of the federal government and the provinces, resolving the jurisdictional disputes will be difficult. Mechanisms must be devised that will achieve consensus of the political and industry levels. For example, some of the provinces are concerned that the CRTC authority is essentially unchecked and free from political accountability. Draft legislation would, therefore, confer on the Cabinet the power to issue policy directives to the CRTC.

If no resolution of the jurisdictional issues is forthcoming, Canadian telecommunications policy may be severely impeded, or even paralyzed. Jurisdictional questions inevitably implicate the knottiest issues of market access, particularly with respect to enhanced services, where trade pressures will arise at the national level but authority to resolve disputes is vested in the provinces.

Many Canadian policymakers also believe that progress cannot be made until the CRTC has the institutional authority to deal with Telecom Canada—and the rate settlement process. Rate adjustments must be made to cope with competition, not merely from Canadian entrants, but from U.S. facilities and carriers who offer the potential to bypass Canadian networks. Without jurisdiction over the settlement process, however, there will be no effective mechanism to oversee and implement national rate rebalancing.

To address these issues, and as part of the telecommunications policy review, the Minister of Communications announced on June 20, 1985, that he was calling a conference of federal and provincial ministers to convene before the end of the year. This conference will test the ability of the new government to deal with the perplexing issues that have, hitherto, defied solutions.

In Finland, the increasingly competitive nature of the relationship between the PTT and the private companies is resulting in pressure to shift regulatory responsibility from the PTT to the Ministry of Communications. At the same time, the Cabinet has established an Ad Hoc Committee, chaired by the Minister of Justice, to consider a series of bills dealing with broadcasting, cable television, and telecommunications.

The legislative process is quite complex and deliberate—involving reviews by the Ad Hoc Committee, drafting by the Ministry of Communications, consideration by the Cabinet in informal session (the so-called "Evening School"), and, finally, parliamentary review. This process is full of pitfalls and tends to honor the Finnish tradition of private industry not being subject to direct oversight by government. The steps toward new legislation are, however, themselves influential in shaping consensus within the industry and highlighting areas for policy examination and determinations. Clearly, the active participation in this process of industry associations and users is a sign of Finland's recognition of the importance of telecommunications policy for national economic development and international trade relationships.

In France, the D.G.T. is both decentralizing and focusing more attention on separating its regulatory and entrepreneurial roles. In addition, a new body, the Haute Autorité, has been created to take the lead in decisions regarding radio and television licenses, though its role in cable is quite limited. The Ministry of Communications, however, makes the initial decisions about the content of programming on cable systems; the Haute Autorité has an advisory role with the Ministry on some of those issues. The regulation of cable is engendering new centers of influence; first among these is the Caisse des Dépôts, which has historically financed municipal developments, but now offers financial and technical assistance to the SLECs. These SLECs, with their mixed public-private status, may become a factor in diversifying control over cable. The French broadcaster,

Télédiffusion de France, is also seeking to assert greater control over cable programming and operations.

In Germany, no new mechanisms for oversight or control are contemplated. The new governmental commission may see a need to study the question of separating the DBP's roles as provider and regulator. Such a separation had been suggested in the early 1970s but was abandoned for political reasons. At the same time, clearly the Länder-Bund issues in media and planning policies may require a new or more effective mechanism of consultation. The formal Staatsvertrag process can unify the Länder, if consensus is politically possible. Where cooperation is required to facilitate facilities and services planning—*i.e.*, for utilization of cable and satellite systems—present arrangements make it difficult to reach clear-cut, timely decisions and may discourage well-formulated, efficient investment decisions.

In Italy, no new formal institutional mechanism is envisaged. Nevertheless, as may be the case regarding the DBP in Germany, there have been pressures for ASST to separate its operational functions from its regulatory authority; the restructuring of ASST to transfer its telecommunicatiaons functions to STET is in partial response to that pressure. The Ministry of Posts and Telecommunications will remain the principal planning and regulatory authority; there have, however, also been suggestions for a new body, within the Ministry, to perform coordinative and supervisory functions for the sector.

In Belgium, no steps have been taken to create new oversight mechanisms. Nevertheless, one member of the Senate has proposed the creation of a "Haute Autorite des Telecommunications," which would be responsible for investment planning, tariffs, and affording access to the network. How the proposed entity would fit into the existing framework of the Ministry and the R.T.T. is not clear.

A unique—and one of the most interesting—new institutional mechanisms being implemented to reflect policy shifts is being formed in the Netherlands. In response to the Swarttouw Commission report, the government has decided to establish a "Telecommunication Consultative Council." The Council will not have any ultimate decisionmaking power; however, it is represented that decisions on major competitive issues of structure, services, equipment, and technical requirements will not be taken by the PTT until after consultation with the Council.

Membership on the Council will include representatives of the PTT and the PTT Council, of users, suppliers, labor, and consumers, along with experts. In this way, a formal mechanism for dialogue will be established in the Netherlands—a mechanism not found in any other country structure. Although it is not clearly within the Council's charter to suggest new policies, it is likely that the process of discussion will eventually have an impact on the structure of the Dutch telecommunications sector.

In the U.S., the process of decisionmaking has been complicated by the MFJ ending the AT&T litigation, which essentially vests oversight responsibility in the Department of Justice and Judge Greene. The scope of the decree is extraordinarily far-reaching. The MFJ prescribes, among other things, the timing, terms, and conditions by which the Bell operating companies are to provide interconnection to AT&T and others; a proscription on the provision of "information" services by the operating companies and AT&T; the role of AT&T and the exchange companies in the provision of interexchange and local services.

So comprehensive is the MFJ that almost any issue affecting AT&T or the operating companies and within the jurisdiction of the FCC must concurrently be addressed, in some respect, by Judge Greene. There is, therefore, a series of difficult questions about the relationship of the FCC and the court supervising implementation of the decree. The FCC and Judge Greene have taken quite different positions with respect to the relationship of their respective spheres of authority. Conflicts in jurisdiction may eventually require the Congress to address and simplify this relationship.

In *Computer II*, the FCC went to great lengths to address the restrictive consequences of the 1956 Consent Decree that limited AT&T's ability to compete. The FCC is now confronted with a decree that is far more comprehensive in its impact on the FCC's oversight responsibility of the telecommunications industry. Unquestionably, with time, and as the FCC assumes a more active regulatory role, the institutional relationship of the FCC and the court implementing the MFJ will become a prominent topic of policy debate.

The primary focus in all these countries has been on mechanisms in which national policymakers may operate. Shifts in national approaches have brought to the fore important issues in international telecommunications policy. In this area, as is described below, *see infra* Section IV.D., the pressure of national policy changes on institutional mechanisms has been particularly acute. Yet, no country has effectively addressed the complex international policy arena with any degree of comprehensiveness.

C. National Economic Adjustments as a Response to Policy Shifts

Aside from institutional adjustments, one of the central threads of recent telecommunications developments worldwide has been a reappraisal of pricing policies for telecommunications services. The parallels among the various national pricing policies are quite striking. Cumulatively, they point toward a global trend of reducing the price of interexchange services while making offsetting adjustments in the rates of local services. These pressures on pricing structures are not confined by national boundary lines—national pricing decisions affect the policies of other administrations.

In effect, these economic interactions are a global matrix in which telecommunications are provided. This market has become increasingly more integrated than before due to the importance of communications as the backbone for new electronic services and as the electronic ganglia binding multinational entities.

The most prominent example of long-term pricing changes is the U.S., where interexchange competition and the effects of ending the separations and settlement process have dramatically altered the economic context in which services are provided. Over the years, competition from the non-AT&T carriers has reduced interexchange rates. The implementation of the divestiture, however, has had a major effect on pricing. Many observers believed that the separations and settlement process had artificially kept up the prices of AT&T's interexchange services. That process established a compensation mechanism for AT&T's use of local exchange facilities in its role as a provider of long distance services. The formula included a factor known as the "subscriber plant factor" that, arguably, had the result of compelling payments to exchange companies that were several times the actual usage of local network facilities. Over time, and with the onset of interexchange competition, AT&T has sought to revisit the methodology for calculating interconnection charges so that they become more closely related to the actual cost of their use.

In its now seven-year-old access proceeding, the FCC considered several approaches to the charges for interconnection: one approach, adopted in part, was based on collecting a "customer access line charge" ("CALC") from users. This methodology imposes on users, in an entirely cost-based way, the cost of connection of the local loop.

In simplistic terms, this methodology was viewed as an alternative to usage-based access charge. Because the cost of access did not, by and large, vary with usage, a usage-based approach was believed to create an incentive for the large users of local facilities to bypass the network. Particularly troubling to some was the possibility that bypass might occur where it is priced less than local wireline prices, but higher than wireline costs. Consequently, many participants in the access charge debate were concerned that the real economic costs of access be stated and calculated as realistically as possible, to avoid such so-called "uneconomic bypass." The FCC, after considering a host of competing methodologies, proposed a minimum flat fee CALC of $2-$6 per month for residential users and $4 for business users, with an increase permissible to take usage into account.

This step, however, generated a firestorm of congressional and public criticism; the FCC agreed to modify the access plan to reduce the residential CALC to $2 to $4 over a three-year transitional period; business users would pay $6 a month plus $25 for closed ends of private lines. After further deliberations, the FCC, having received recommendations from the Federal-State Joint Board, adopted a maximum $2 CALC for residential customers, starting June 1, 1986, with a $1 charge imposed on residential customers as of June 1, 1985.

Pressures to move access charges ever closer to costs will escalate as large users increasingly have options for bypassing local exchange facilities. This option is essentially available for all interstate interexchange service, although there is some question whether local facilities can be used to offer competitive local exchange or intrastate services. Thus, economic pressures will preclude rate stuctures that subsidize local exchange services with interexchange service revenues.

With no sector of the U.S. market closed to competition, movement of prices in the direction of costs will be inexorable. The influx of significant satellite and fiber optic capacity on facilities installed by virtually all long distance carriers will also be a major factor in lowering interexchange prices.

The Canadian pricing structure is caught up in the gravitational pull of pricing changes in the U.S. A unifying theme of telephone industry submissions to the DOC in the telecommunications policy review proceeding is the need for "rate rebalancing." Calling for "rate rebalancing" is a euphemistic way of stating that interexchange rates must be reduced—to reflect real costs—with offsetting increases in charges for lower-density routes and for local exchange services. The need for, and magnitude of, rate rebalancing changes are the subject of some considerable debate and study in Canada, as described in greater detail in the country report.

The perception that changes are needed arises from the view that the Canadian telecommunications market is already subject to competition from the U.S. Even though there is no Canadian public switched interexchange competition, large Canadian companies with business operations and telecommunications facilities in the U.S. can send their trans-Canada traffic through switching facilities in the U.S. One of the objectives of establishing Telecom Canada in 1931 was to assure that Canadian transcontinental traffic would be routed over Canadian facilities. That goal, however, is now threatened by disparities in the comparative rates and flexibility of use for U.S. and Canadian facilities.

The CRTC has recently established a new rate structure in British Columbia to reduce the economic incentives for Canadians to use a U.S. reseller marketing services in Canada from across the U.S. border. There is, however, no effective way of stopping the traffic diversion unless greater convergence of U.S. and Canadian rate levels is achieved.

There are substantial complications in making these adjustments. Some Canadian carriers that are facing the brunt of competition (*e.g.*, Bell Canada and British Columbia Telephone) might well want to lower their rates. If rates are lowered, however, there must be offsetting adjustments in the settlement pool overseen by Telecom Canada. Although unanimity would be required, it will be difficult to obtain: the provincial companies, not facing competition, do not want to agree to anything that would reduce the revenues received from the pool and that would, as a result, force them to increase provincial rates.

These differences in perspective are straining Telecom Canada at the same time that the economic pressure on the rate structure intensify. Such pressure will be enhanced if the CRTC decides to allow competition in switched voice services. The regulated companies do not want to bear directly the economic consequences of new competition. Obviously, the provincial companies—and public officials—would prefer to defer the day of reckoning with respect to rate changes. International economic pressures may make these adjustments in Canada almost inevitable.

In the U.K., BT began making a series of rate adjustments, repricing traffic on high density routes, even before Mercury had become an actual competitor. BT has continued the process of bringing prices closer to costs after liberalization, for all major charge elements. BT cannot, however, implement usage-sensitive pricing without generating a significant market opportunity for Mercury. In addition, the U.K. is a viable market for locating computer-based network facilities. This hospitable environment is a product of the branch license policies, especially the liberalization of VANS licensing, and the climate created by rejection of the BT-IBM venture.

BT has been aggressively seeking to turn the U.K. into a hub for the redistribution of traffic into Europe. In particular, competitive pressures will continue to result in liberal terms of access to leased domestic and international circuits.

Consequently, liberalization in the U.K. seems to be exercising a gravitational pull not dissimilar from that of the U.S. on Canadian pricing. It has produced an unambiguous competitive response in France, and in Belgium. The D.G.T. filiales have been given the responsibility for marketing high-speed specialized services, including Telecom-1 satellite services, to business users. The French intend to be effective and aggressive, and to tailor their services to the needs of each customer. The French approach is different from that of the U.K. and BT; there is no general revision in the rate structure, but, rather, a special sensitivity to the requirements of large users.

In response to competitive realities, the D.G.T. has focused on the importance of adjusting upward local exchange pricing. As international markets become become more competitive, and a less significant source of contribution to D.G.T. revenues, the D.G.T. will be looking to domestic markets for additional income.

The more competitive aspects of the evolving relationships among the European PTTs can be seen in the decision of the R.T.T. in Belgium. First, the R.T.T. has reduced its international tariffs to meet the new competitive posture of BT. It has implemented some usage-sensitive pricing at the local level.

Most importantly, however, the R.T.T. has opened an interconnection agreement with MCI. This agreement does not include any understanding about the R.T.T. acting as a transit point for traffic to countries neighboring Belgium. There has, in fact, been an effort within the Conference Europeene des Administrations des Postes et des Telecommunications ("CEPT") to prevent the development of such transiting agreements. The R.T.T. carries traffic outside Europe, however.

No doubt, other PTTs are eyeing the economic opportunity that new interconnection agreements present. In particular, the D.G.T. and, possibly, other PTTs, are considering striking interconnection agreements with MCI and other U.S. carriers.

In Germany, unlike France, it has been more difficult to adopt ad hoc pricing responses. The primary focus of pricing debates has been on rate-harmonization—how to achieve equivalence in the pricing of leased lines and public switched voice services. The introduction of usage-sensitive components for leased line tariffs has effectively increased their cost and caused significant protest by users. Nevertheless, there has been an intensive effort in the DBP to assess new, more cost-based, rate structures for 64 Kbit/s digital lines; there may, therefore, be attempts to create a category for high-speed digital lines that could be priced on a different basis than conventional leased lines.

For reasons described in the country report, it may be exceedingly difficult to make changes in local exchange pricing. Economic responses in Germany are limited by substantial political, social, and industrial concerns that hamper pricing flexibility.

In Finland, the PTT is not as subject to the economic pressures created by liberalization in the U.K. as other Continental European PTTs. Nevertheless, it has proposed a five-year plan of reducing long distance rates by 10% a year. This move is directed at the prospect of national interexchange competition.

The National Plan for telecommunications in Italy also considers restructuring prices to move them closer to costs. Rates for local calls have already been moved significantly upwards in large urban areas.

In Japan, the direction of price movements will follow that in the U.K. and the U.S. NTT has been reducing its long distance rates. Increasingly, these price reductions will become subject to review by the MPT—at least until the new competitors establish themselves.

Many observers of the telecommunications scene believe that the core goal of Japanese policy is to reduce drastically the prices of telecommunications services. The objective of the policy is to unleash diverse and vigorous forces for entrepreneurial activity within the manufacturing sector. There is a supply-side rationale to the strategy: one mechanism for encouraging efficiency, and generating industrial productivity, is to increase the supply and reduce the cost of telecommunications.

D. International Pressures on National Telecommunications Policies

Looking at these developments cumulatively, then, a powerful and swift economic tide is running and affecting the price of telecommunications services. Pricing changes in the U.S. have had major and far-reaching effects on the nearby Canadian market. They have broader consequences, however, because they influence national industry groups and ministries concerned with economic development. As they plan for sectoral development and investment, they must now assess the consequences of changes in U.S. pricing and structure for their impact on the global competitive posture of U.S. manufacturing and service sector industries. The effect of the U.S. case on the Japanese, for example, is clear and understandable. Analogously, liberalization in the U.K. may well have the same pull on European policy development as changes in the U.S. have had on Canada.

The effect of deregulation in the U.S., and liberalization and privatization in the U.K. and Japan, does not only have economic consequences globally. Beyond economics, there are real "emulative" and "demonstrative" effects of these changes. Decisionmakers in the U.K. studied closely the impact of the U.S. experience with deregulation. The Japanese have followed with keen interest U.S. developments and the first steps toward privatization in the U.K.

Recently, the Japanese situation has been studied with great interest in Germany, as the markets of the two countries are of equivalent size and have comparable manufacturing sectors. It is clear that the Germans must study the Japanese experience with more attention and interest insofar as the U.S. telecommunications restructuring can be viewed as a unique—and not entirely pertinent—situation.

The restructuring of telecommunications policy is scrutinized globally to assess the impact of telecommunications policies on the development of the telecommunications and computer equipment manufacturing sectors. Increasingly, however, experts in industrial policy are focusing on the stimulative effects and economic interrelationship of telecommunications and information policies in the traditional manufacturing and new services sector.

Telecommunications technologies are becoming even more critical in the management of decentralized multinational corporations and in carrying out manufacturing processes internationally. Without access to equivalent efficiency-enhancing technologies, national policymakers may fear that their industries are losing ground to U.S. and Japanese competitors.

The new service-oriented industries are also heavily dependent on computer and telecommunications technologies. In the services sectors, a high price on the use of the infrastructure, or restrictive conditions on its use, may have adverse industrial policy effects. The development of those industries at the national level may be arrested, or they may shift to neighboring countries where there may be a more hospitable climate for such services.

An interest in and concern for the implications of telecommunications and information policies are no longer restricted to government decisionmakers. Increasingly, groups of telecommunications users are taking a more active role in influencing policy. Users have been most active in the U.S.; they are becoming more involved in Canada and the U.K., as well as Belgium and the Netherlands. In Europe, the International Telecommunications Users Group ("INTUG") has become an important factor in discussions on telecommunications policy at both the national and international levels. Through INTUG, users are participating in the International Telegraph and Telephone Consultative Committee ("CCITT") of the International Telecommunications Union ("ITU"). The ITU has arranged a special forum as a basis for a new dialogue between the PTTs and the user communities.

INTUG's membership at present is quite oriented toward the multinational U.S. and U.K. companies. Many European entities have been less involved in trying to shape telecommunications policies at the national level. This may be so because they may not see that the evolution of telecommunications and information policies is critical to their future success.

The European user perspective is likely to change to a more activist stance with the increasing public visibility of the current global debate over telecommunications policies. As pressures from users intensify, they will begin to affect national and international policies. Such pressures will augment the changes resulting from the economic consequences of pricing adjustments and the industrial policy concerns raised by ministries of industry around the world.

All these factors—the adjustments of prices toward cost, the "emulative effects" of changes elsewhere, growing concerns at the governmental level about industrial policy implications, users' increased awareness of the importance of telecommunications on long-term competitiveness—will "internationalize" the debate on the future of national telecommunications and information policies.

The growing asymmetries between policies in the U.S., Japan, the U.K., and various European countries will also produce trade frictions. Trade-related pressures will come from manufacturers looking for equivalent market access elsewhere once their own national markets have been opened. The industrial sector in the U.S., for example, has argued that the divestiture created significant opportunities for Japanese equipment manufacturers; therefore, reciprocity—open markets—is demanded of the Japanese and others. Of equal importance is that multinational service-oriented enterprises will seek equivalence with respect to the terms and conditions relevant to the establishment of global networks used to provide international financial, brokerage, transactional, publishing, or information services.

What is occurring is an interlocking of the national and international telecommunications sectors. The international market is shaped by a diverse set of national policies and structures, which are, in turn, subject to national, political, economic, and institutional mechanisms of control.

To understand the structure of international markets, then, it is necessary to understand how these national mechanisms function. With such an understanding, it may be easier to forecast the direction of international policy, to foresee potential obstacles to change, and to identify areas of opportunity and innovation.

In the international environment, where there is so much at stake in gaining access to markets to provide services globally, both government and private sector representatives need to understand the points of intervention and how to calculate their individual strategies to take advantage of the likely flow of events. Understanding of the process at the national level, and how it meshes with the international arena, is a prerequisite to any decision by public officials about whether and when to intervene to influence national or international telecommunications policies. Such an understanding is equally important for the private sector if it is to make prudent and far-sighted private investment and business planning decisions.

Very often there is a tendency to evaluate national telecommunications policy in isolation, as uninfluenced by events, pressures, and developments elsewhere. For some countries, seeing the drift and flow of events will be a necessary predicate to formulating a strategy—at the business or policy level—to follow or resist the direction of changes. For countries with policies that have international influence, it is essential that they both perceive that national policies are a complex convergence of factors unique to each country and that, consequently, particular national policy solutions may be inapplicable in other settings. A clear view of the complexity and dynamic elements of each national setting is essential in bringing to international trade relationships not only a strong national perspective but also a broad appreciation of the limitations and possibilities of change and the diversity of national approaches.

Part II, therefore, is a further exploration of several key telecommunications policy issues that have an international dimension. Part III examines more closely the adequacy of existing institutional mechanisms for dealing with the expanding and complex agenda of international telecommunications policy issues.

PART II

INTERNATIONAL POLICY ISSUES

I. International Standardization and ISDN

A. Introduction

On a global basis, one of the most important activities being undertaken nationally, regionally, and internationally is the movement toward standardization of the international telecommunications network. To make international communications at all possible, there must be standards that provide for international interconnections and common operating procedures and protocols.

Equipment vendors will be able to penetrate markets worldwide only if users are able to utilize equipment and services on an international basis. Inconsistent standards would require inefficient protocol conversion and would make it difficult, if not impossible, to set up networks for electronic, financial, information, or transactional services. Thus, standard setting is critical to worldwide commercial interaction.

Standard setting, however, is a deliberative, thorough process that has been successful. Under the aegis of the CCITT, the international network has become, by and large, interconnected for basic services.

The pace of the standard setting activity—and the standards themselves—can also work to inhibit competition and the implementation of new services. A vast array of telecommunications-related equipment and services is being developed at a rate more rapid than that at which the national or international organizations (*e.g.*, CCITT) can set standards. Delay in standard setting, however, could delay the introduction of new services.

Some vendors and manufacturers, therefore, simply introduce their products without waiting for an industry standard. Many users champion their doing so. Moreover, early introduction of a new technology or product may effectively increase the pressure on the standard-setting entities to "catch up" at the same time as manufacturers hope to dominate a market to create a de facto standard.

Telecommunications carriers and others have vigorously resisted de facto market setting by manufacturers for several reasons. Not only are they concerned with the potential development of a market characterized by a web of incompatible systems and offerings, but they also want to avoid the diversion of traffic to private leased lines that might result from such inconsistent network standards. They may acknowledge that the introduction of new services can benefit the user community, but are concerned with the possibility that future growth may be stifled.

Another possible pitfall of standardization is that national or international standards may sweep too broadly, to exclude new competitors whose products are not in compliance with the criteria set by industry groups. Where standard setting is undertaken in fora where new industry participants and users are not particularly well represented (*e.g.*, CEPT), the likelihood increases that certain innovative services will be defined—or "standardized"—out of the market.

Manufacturers, however, may welcome standardization for new products and services. One example of the generic problems arising from a failure to standardize is cellular radio, where a welter of inconsistent standards has precluded introduction of a European-wide service and has impeded manufacturers that are trying to sell their products on a regional basis.

There is an extremely successful cellular network for most of Scandinavia that has enabled drivers to go from Oslo to Stockholm, or even to Helsinki, and use their mobile telephones throughout. The Dutch use the Scandinavian system, but have changed the technical specifications to render it incompatible. There is a different system in the U.K.

The French and West Germans had intended to construct a cross-border cellular network that would have entered service in 1986. The French were, however, irritated when the British chose another, U.S.-based, system. Moreover, the Franco-German plans were shelved in the last year when the parties agreed that the analogue system originally selected seemed incompatible with the plans to digitize the network.

The failure to standardize has, therefore, thwarted the introduction of a new portable European telephone service, as proposed by the Mobira subsidiary of Nokia Electronics of Finland. The lack of standardization has, in sum, not only caused the loss of a substantial business opportunity, but, more importantly, denied users, the European business community, a potentially significant new service.

As discussed below, in the European context, standardization can, therefore, be both an important and a limiting strategy for market integration. *See infra* Section IV. The debate over the Open Systems Interconnection ("OSI") model of the International Standards Organisation ("ISO model") versus IBM's SNA, outlined below, may be illuminating in this connection.

B. ISO Model Versus IBM's SNA

Concerns about single vendor domination of a market were clearly articulated in the European-wide debate over the proposed BT-IBM joint venture to provide a data network management service. The controversy—and ultimate decision—were, of course, principally focused on the anticompetitive effects of having two dominant companies join to offer services. Nevertheless, there was every bit as much concern with the possibility that IBM could come to create a de facto standard through its Systems Network Architecture ("SNA"). IBM's SNA provides a set of protocols to permit computers and terminals that use the architecture to communicate; the architecture permits interconnection with non-IBM networks, but only if the originating computer uses the IBM architecture.

IBM introduced its SNA a couple of years before the ISO developed its OSI model, which describes the relationship between services and the network features required to provide services. The ISO model is conceptual and is based on seven layers, each defined by a set of functions, to describe an aspect of a system of communication. In developing this model, the ISO and the CCITT, in its Recommendations, *see infra* Section I.C., is attempting to achieve network standardization en route to the implementation of data communications, videotex, and other new services. The Integrated Services Digital Network ("ISDN") Recommendations also reflect the ISO model.

The seven layers are: 1) physical; 2) link; 3) network; 4) transport; 5) session; 6) presentation; and 7) application. The first three—or lower-level layers—describe the control of, and interaction with, the network by terminals. These layers describe "network," rather than "service," features.

The higher layers, five to seven, describe services, *i.e.*, communications between users. Protocols contemplated by these layers can be developed and implemented independent of the network. The middle-session-layer is a bridge between the protocols that are independent of the network (higher layers) and those of the network(s).

The ISO model is a sequential set of rules that orders a particular communication between the user, terminal, network, terminal, and user. It has, however, been criticized as not providing a good "fit" to the real world; the criticism arises, in part, because service vendors and users might like to approach setting up a communication in a way that does not follow the hierarchical ISO structure.

The ISO model as a concept, however, is welcomed by telecommunications carriers, PTTs, and many vendors and users alike as being truly "open." It enables them to connect network and equipment together in any environment. In this regard, it is not necessarily the case that SNA is, as a conceptual matter, inherently inconsistent with OSI. Rather, the IBM concern is not that the world should be SNA, but that the ISO model should only define the first three levels. IBM, and others, have contended that products should define the functions described in ISO layers four through seven so that they are not subject to the risk of being defined out of the market.

IBM has not been hostile to the concept of OSI. In the context of the proposed BT-IBM venture, IBM expressed its commitment to the ISO model and to SNA compatibility at layers four and five. IBM and BT, both active participants in the standards work of ISO, emphasized that there was no inherent inconsistency between SNA and ISO. Indeed, they hoped that the venture would bridge the gap between the two; ultimately, a complete seven-layer gateway could be useful for the BT-IBM network to interconnect with other vendors' products (*e.g.*, DECNET).

Nevertheless, despite IBM's assurances that it had an economic interest in ensuring the continued development of the OSI concept, there were concerns that users would be driven toward purchasing SNA terminals. A further point of objection was that a de facto standard would be set in, and possibly for all of, Europe by a U.S. supplier. One focal point of concern, illustrative of the more widespread questions about manufacturer-developed standards, was whether IBM could modify the SNA on which the proposed network was based. If it could do so, it was argued, IBM could get a significant competitive advantage in designing terminal equipment, knowing in advance that it planned to change the network architecture that would support such terminals.

The crux of the controversy was—and is—not whether the ISO model or SNA is better. Instead, the debate is over what is perceived to be different approaches to "standardizing" a market—on the basis of consensual international agreement, on the one hand, and a proprietary technology, on the other. There seems to be no real agreement on whether SNA is a standard for structuring an entire sector, as the ISO model is perceived to be, or whether it merely represents the technical specifications of the dominant supplier in that sector.

C. ISDN: Integration of Facilities and Services

It is in the evolution of an ISDN environment where the effect of standardization will have the most significant ramifications. ISDN planning will shape future relationships among carriers, users, service vendors, and administrations. At present, planning for ISDN is occurring simultaneously at national levels as the standardization work is forging ahead in Study Group XVIII of the CCITT, the relevant organ of the ITU. ISDN planning is the most ambitious and far-reaching of attempts to achieve standardization.

At the most fundamental of levels, there is some international agreement on what is ISDN—a network that may evolve from an integrated digital telephone network ("IDN") to provide complete, end-to-end, digital connectivity (switches and paths) so that it may offer services on an integrated basis, including voice, non-voice, data, video, and other services. Current planning contemplates a limited set of multi-purpose user interfaces with the network that could accommodate a range of digital terminals and services.

Beyond this description—and promise—there is a wide spectrum of views on what should be an ISDN environment and why it is good for national and global telecommunications to move toward ISDNs.

At the international level, it is well recognized that the approach to evolve toward an ISDN environment will vary from country to country. In European countries it is generally easier to plan for the integration of services in a single network due to the centralized administrations for telecommunications. In North America, the operation of telecommunications is decentralized and planning for an ISDN structure is more complex. Thus, the standardization process at the CCITT level must contemplate implementation of an ISDN in a variety of telecommunications environments, from a single telecommunications network to a number of networks that include public data networks and long distance networks over and above the public switched network.

Given the disparity in the telecommunications environments, it is not surprising that some nations view ISDN as simply a set of protocols—a series of standards—for offering an integrated set of services. For most industrialized nations ISDN is a digital "pipe" on which integrated digital services—from narrowband to broadband—are capable of being carried. For some nations, ISDN means essentially no more than digitization of the network. For others, it contemplates pricing harmonization between services and may be seen as an overall repositioning to meet, head-on, potential competition in services. Indeed, some observers believe that ISDN may be viewed as an effective way of extending existing facilities monopolies to include "integrated" services.

There is sufficient flexibility in current ISDN planning to take into account these various views. Consequently, when there are discussions of what is an ISDN environment, and how it should evolve, there can be substantial agreement without any real, substantive meeting of the minds. The core ISDN planning question is whether there should be increased centralization of control over services offered on a single network. Some critics of the process and some users, for example, point to ISDN planning as a means of achieving control, with the PTTs aiming to provide on a primary supplier basis certain lucrative data processing segments of the market. Others view ISDN as simply a means of tying together, achieving interconnectivity of, disparate service networks.

This debate between those who see ISDN as a device for maintaining monopolies and others who view it as a force for diversity is, in part, played out in definitional gyrations. The outcome will, to a significant extent, be determined in the CCITT Recommendation process and, of particular importance, is the manner whereby the ISO seven-layer model is being used to set the parameters for ISDN planning. Indeed, the CCITT standardization work—which influences not only internetworking between national networks, but also the planning of national ISDNs themselves—is closely connected with ISO activities.

In an ISDN environment determining who will, for example, be permitted to offer data processing services has both a regulatory and an engineering component. Originally, CCITT planning documents described ISDN as supporting two types of services, "bearer" services and "telecommunications" services. It rapidly became clear that the distinction between the two did not approximate the U.S. regulatory definitions for "basic" and "enhanced" services, largely because message telephone service ("MTS") and telex, the two most common "basic" services, would be considered "telecommunications," which was otherwise composed of what would, in the U.S. regime, be classified as "enhanced" services. Subsequently, these definitional classifications were altered to accommodate more readily U.S. categories. A single overall category—"telecommunications"—was established, which was further divided into "bearer" services and "teleservices."

A "bearer" service is the basic connection service provided by the network; it "provides the capability for the transmission of signals between user-network interfaces." Recommendation I.202, Document AP VIII-97-E, Final Report to the VIIIth CCITT Plenary Assembly (Part V)(June 1984) ("I-Series of Recommendations"). A "teleservice" "provides the complete capability, including terminal equipment functions, for communication between users according to universal protocols approved by CCITT." I.203, I–Series of Recommendations.

The FCC has attempted to squeeze these definitions into the framework of the "basic"/"enhanced" dichotomy. The CCITT process has, however, ultimately been influenced by the engineers who have developed the ISO model—and not by regulators or lawyers. The CCITT I-Series describes "bearer" services and "teleservices" in an ISDN environment not by actual or contemplated services, but by certain attributes that are linked to the ISO layers. Bearer services have attributes provided by layers one to three; they are, essentially, the network transport "pipe." Teleservices have attributes of the low layers, high layers (*i.e.*, four to seven), and certain operational or commercial attributes that are largely unspecified by the I-Series.

Policy and regulatory considerations do not necessarily "map onto" the CCITT vision of an ISDN environment. The reasons for this are not surprising. Although there are some vigorous national CCITT study groups in each country, many users, the public, and even many service providers do not participate to a substantial extent in the international CCITT ISDN activities. The process is principally driven by the main carriers and administrations.

There are, then, some concerns that using the ISO model for defining some of the ISDN distinctions and services could be a major—and long-term—mistake. Although that model may be useful in a data processing world, it may not be practical for telecommunications. The FCC has pointed out in the First Report in the *ISDN Proceeding* that the hierarchical nature of the model, where each layer must be separately and sequentially traversed, may limit the flexibility of information or enhanced service providers. Others in the private sector agree that the ISO model may stifle innovation and flexibility. *See supra* Section I.B.

There is, in sum, sufficient flexibility in the ISDN Recommendations for each nation, carrier, and regulator to use ISDN as a way of achieving whatever objectives it may view as desirable. The U.S. private sector is quite actively involved in the ISDN planning process, with, especially, AT&T, IBM, GTE, the Bell regional operating companies, Bellcore, and trade associations participating at the national and international levels. The FCC, which has viewed CCITT ISDN activities as being primarily concerned with standardization, has essentially left it to industry; official U.S. representation is handled by the Department of State, which works with an advisory committee, the U.S. CCITT Organization.

The principal focus of FCC concerns is somewhat parochial, *i.e.*, that ISDN Recommendations should not impose any conditions contrary to U.S. procompetitive telecommunications policies. Of special concern is the extent to which ISDN planning by PTTs may be a "stalking horse" for centralizing the provision of both facilities and services, which could stymie U.S. service offerings abroad and thwart the domestic policy on separation of basic and enhanced services. The FCC is not primarily concerned, then with the definitions of "bearer" and "teleservices," or the ISO model, so long as basic services remain available without unnecessary overhead and are offered without economic inefficiency. Enhanced service providers may adopt the model, or not, as they choose.

Implementation of ISDN in the U.S. is moving in phases. At present, the principal focus is on digitization of the network. There are, however, a number of trial tests being undertaken this year by the Bell operating companies to ascertain user interest in digital connectivity of services.

In Japan, NTT has been the leading proponent of the Information Network System ("INS"), the Japanese equivalent of ISDN. INS development has been marked by specific milestones for digital upgrading of transmission and switching facilities, looking toward the integration of separate networks. The NTT approach historically has been more driven by technology than by services, or by user demand.

Central to the original INS concept, and to the vision of NTT's Dr. Yasusada Kitahara, was an entirely "bit-based" pricing structure that would replace the present distance and time-sensitive rates that characterize most services. The aim of bit-based pricing was, ultimately, to offer cheaper services to the user. At the same time, however, it is apparent that bit-based pricing could remove significant incentives for the establishment of ISDNs by third parties.

INS planning had, of course, evolved in a non-competitive telecommunications environment, with the assumption that NTT would operate as the sole domestic carrier in Japan. With the introduction of competition in both facilities and services, NTT has had to begin rethinking its concept of INS as a single digital network for all services. If other carriers offer digital networks, NTT will need to begin focusing on internetworking arrangements within the CCITT framework. Similarly, as NTT has established the de facto INS standard, there is some question whether other carriers will be able to compete on the same footing.

Perhaps in response to the emergence of competition, NTT is revisiting the "bit-based" pricing concept. The newer INS concept contemplates taking time and distance—as well as volume—into pricing principles. As it becomes evident that new entrants might be able to offer competitive rates not based on a national, uniform volume-sensitive tariff, NTT, too, has become more flexible in pricing policies for INS services. There are some suggestions, moreover, that the entire notion of an integrated network is being reexamined in the newly competitive environment.

In the U.K., BT has long had an ISDN policy. ISDN planning in the U.K. has proceeded in steps, concentrating on digitization of the network. Upgrading of trunk transmission and switching facilities is now almost completed, with an initial digital overlay network being extended to business users nationwide. Despite having taken the next step, the introduction of the new System X digital exchange at the local level, there still remains significant progress to be made. BT, however, is anxious to upgrade subscriber loops, which are currently underpriced, to reduce costs and facilitate tariff integration.

In light of the emergence of Mercury, there are substantial regulatory questions regarding the planning and integration of digital services by BT. The implications of a duopolistic environment for ISDN are now beginning to be addressed by OFTEL in the context of several issues—interconnection, the digitization of local facilities, and the pricing consequences of BT services.

The Canadian approach, too, has primarily focused on expansion of the integrated digital network and modernization—the first step toward ISDN. A major objective of Canadian telecommunications carriers is the evolution of the public switched network to an ISDN with complete and genuine integration of services. The evolution to a full ISDN will be accomplished in three pragmatic steps. First, there is rapid pursuit of the policy of modernizing the public switched telephone network with a digital system. Second, a Special Services Digital Network will be implemented to handle all suitable dedicated customer services during the 1985-1990 period with an all-digital network. Third, an ISDN subscriber access channel will be introduced to complement the IDN network.

There is substantial interest in the nature of user demand for integrated service offerings and in the issues of migration to ISDN from existing services. Consequently, the pricing ramifications of introducing ISDN are the subject of considerable examination. Principal goals are to increase user interest and to maintain uniformity in the pricing of traditional services.

ISDN planning in Canada partakes of both U.S. and the European paradigms. There appears, for example, to be some critical analysis of the ISO model. Concomitantly, there is a very real concern with respect to the internetworking capability with the U.S. ISDN. The advantages of access to U.S. services may, it is feared, be outweighed by the possible threat to the integrity and viability of Canadian-based services. The transborder flow of ISDN services is, therefore, a subject of concern in the DOC.

Progress toward an ISDN environment in Germany is exceptionally well-planned, with milestones for technological developments and digital upgrading foreseen well into the next decade. The DBP has been actively participating in the CCITT standardization process and has followed the ISDN I-Series Recommendations in its own planning, which contemplates digitization and eventual convergence of broadband and narrowband ISDNs.

In Germany, there are several options for pricing services. There may be special tariff structures over high-density routes designed to ease user pressure for competitive services. For pricing ISDN services, the primary benchmark for the DBP is expected to be the rate structure for telephone services. It is possible that there will be differentials for distance, usage, and peak/off-peak periods. Although the pricing may not discourage the sale of services, it is apparent that an essential component of the DBP strategy is to maintain its control over services by developing a completely integrated network to meet consumer demand.

In France, the D.G.T., as part of the "Filiere Electronique," has moved forward in digitizing the switching and transmission facilities of the public switched telephone network. Based on the experimental Biarritz optical fiber cable network, there are expectations that the D.G.T. will install high-capacity fiber optic cable for local distribution capacity. It is in the ISDN access channel—digitization of the local loop—where most French ISDN planning is concentrated. Progress, however, has been slowed by technological and economic concerns. The D.G.T. is also working with FCR to construct an overlay network. In conjunction with the cabling program, the launching of Telecom-1 is viewed as facilitating progress toward complete digitization of services. Nevertheless, the planning for the overlay and local networks does not seem closely coordinated.

In a number of other countries, ISDN planning is, essentially, focused on the installation of an integrated digital network for telephony. Digitization of the network, for example, is proceeding slowly in Finland. Given the fragmented nature of planning, however, there are some unresolved issues regarding coordination and joint investment by the PTT and the local companies.

In the Netherlands, modernization of the telephone network may be accomplished by integration of telecommunications and cable television facilities. With a single broadband link capable of carrying digitized information among all subscribers, it is hoped that an ISDN might evolve. To this end, the government has given some consideration to granting the PTT a license to install, maintain, and operate a cable television network that could offer integrated services.

Belgian progress toward digitization of transmission facilities has begun with an intercity overlay network and the installation of digital switches. Initially, a narrowband ISDN will be provided on the existing network with, at some future date, broadband services provided over fiber optic cables.

Compared with other countries, Italy appears as somewhat of a latecomer. It has begun planning for a transition to an ISDN environment and has adopted the ISO protocols to ensure compatibility and interconnectivity of services and networks. Pirelli is an important manufacturer of fiber optic cables and, in Venice, a fiber optic network is being implemented.

To prepare for an ISDN infrastructure in Italy, digitization of switching and transmission facilities will be implemented through the end of this decade, and there are plans for a fiber optic network in the 1990s. With Italsat becoming operational in 1988, and designed for integration with the digital network, it is anticipated that digital satellite capacity will be a forerunner of ISDN. Services in Italy are being described as "bearer," "teleservices," and value-added, in recognition of the CCITT efforts at standardization.

Digitization of the network to create a single "pipe" for all services is not necessarily inconsistent with providing services to third parties. One objective of ISDN planning is to facilitate transparent access by users and services to the network. Nevertheless, several issues, relating to user access, remain to be addressed in both CCITT and national ISDN planning.

Obviously, user acceptance and the diversity of service offerings using ISDNs will be a function of price and service availability. In most countries there has not been significant attention devoted to pricing issues or any substantial focus on tariffing. It is well recognized, however, that charging principles will be difficult to hammer out on a consensus basis.

Some users want tariffs that are cost-related and are independent of the type of information sent through the network. In Germany, tariff principles may reflect an effort to keep large users on the network. In other countries, perhaps Canada, for example, tariffing may be oriented toward encouraging user migration to ISDN.

One particular area of user concern is the continued existence of dedicated private line circuits, which are characterized by flat-rate charging principles, continuous availability, and no connection setup. The CCITT Recommendations had originally contemplated the notion of "permanent virtual circuits"—which were not necessarily congruent with dedicated or leased circuits. The I-Series Recommendations that were adopted in October 1984, now include a definition of "permanent circuit service," *i.e.*, channels that do not have switched capabilities and constitute private line circuits. Recommendation I.207.

Despite the apparent assurances of the most recent I-Series, there remains some anxiety among users whether the integration of services in an essentially switched digital network will allow for the offering of leased circuits. Some users want the array of services that can be provided through dedicated line services. As important to users, however, is the concept of flat-rate pricing, which may not be consonant with the usage-based tariff principles that may attach to the "permanent circuit" concept. Consequently, regardless of whether permanent circuits exist outside an integrated switched network, erosion of traditional private line tariff structures may diminish the possibility of providing services to third parties through use of leased lines.

The access of third-party service providers to ISDNs is linked to the pricing issues and is central to the planning process. If third-party access is made difficult, it will be less likely that users will migrate to ISDN services where their flexibility or choice of services might be limited.

A corollary concern that is at the core of ISDN policy is the location of the so-called user-network interface. Much of the debate over the R, S, T, and U interfaces is tied to the question of whether ISDN is a centralizing or diversifying concept. The PTTs are anxious to create an intelligent network offering the maximum number of services to the maximum number of users. Indeed, the CCITT Recommendations list the possible service offerings in detail. Recommendations I.211 and I.212.

Users and service providers—along with U.S. regulators—prefer an environment where services interface with the network, as the user chooses, and with terminal equipment provided on a competitive basis, also subject to user choice. As a result of this disparity of views on the location of certain network-terminal functions, there is a division of network functional groupings into NT1 (relating to layer one functions) and NT2 (layers one to three), the division of terminal equipment functions into TE1 and TE2, and anticipation of the use of terminal adaptors (TA) that would allow TE2 terminals to interface with the network.

How the user-network interfaces will be worked out in the real world has yet to be tested. What is apparent, however, is that the tugging and hauling between PTTs, users, and equipment suppliers is carried out in a standardization process, of defining the functions of terminals and interfaces. This drama is being played out in Germany, Japan, Italy, the U.S., and elsewhere.

There is, then, a considerable panoply of user concerns regarding the evolution and implementation of ISDN. At present, ISDN planning is emerging as a carrier initiative, and not as a response to demands of those who will actually use the network. If it is intended that an ISDN environment evolve to suit purposes broader than those of the carriers and PTTs, and if the network developed is to be utilized fully, it is critical that users be allowed—if not encouraged—to participate actively in the planning process.

The impact of CCITT and national ISDN planning may not yet be significant for service providers and users, at least beyond network upgrade and modernization. Nevertheless, planning involves choices at the national and international levels that will have a profound effect on the availability and structures of facilities and services for the transmission and processing of information.

II. Spillover of Changes in Domestic Policy to the International Arena

Implementation of significant changes in domestic telecommunications policies almost inevitably affects a country's international policies. Nevertheless, policymakers persist in thinking that domestic and international policies can be insulated from each other, believing that radical shifts can be made in domestic policy while postponing until another day changes in international policies. The following discussion highlights some of the ways and areas in which the spillovers from domestic to international policies occur.

A. *United States*

In its *Computer II* decision, the FCC had suggested in a footnote that its "basic" and "enhanced" classification scheme would apply to international services; in August 1982, it held so explicitly. Many European PTTs had, however, already reacted adversely, believing that the U.S. had decided, on a unilateral basis, to eliminate the category of a regulated telecommunications carrier. Along with the head of the CCITT, who wrote to the FCC to express his concern, the PTTs were anxious that U.S. deregulatory policy not force them to grant market access, in an unconstrained way, to a large, unregulated group of enhanced service vendors. Several PTTs, from the Nordic and Benelux countries, responded to the international application of *Computer II* by proposing that they deal on an exclusive basis with various vendors offering U.S.-European data services.

This proposal met with considerable protest by existing carriers and an admonition from the FCC that the carriers not participate in discussions as to any exclusive arrangements. Many U.S. services vendors urged the FCC to reconsider its position because they were concerned about the spillover implications of applying the dichotomy internationally. In particular, data processing companies and vendors of electronic services did not want to be swept into a web of foreign regulation by having the PTTs confuse them with entities engaged in packet switching or communications processing.

The FCC's dilemma was that "enhanced services" were defined in a way that realistically did not allow distinctions to be drawn between domestic and international services. Other considerations aside, from solely the standpoint of legal consistency, if an entity is an enhanced service provider domestically it also would be classified as such internationally. Consequently, as the definitional approach was used to remove these entities from the scope of FCC jurisdiction domestically, it was difficult to find a basis to justify regulatory control over enhanced service vendors' international dealings.

The FCC, on reconsideration, reaffirmed its earlier conclusion. It noted, however, that restrictions on resale remained—in tariffs and under the CCITT Recommendations governing private line usage. Thus, if an international enhanced service offered through the "basic" capacity of a carrier were considered "resale" by a carrier having tariff restrictions or by an administration, it might not be authorized. Essentially, the FCC preserved what it views as the status quo ante—leaving to the PTTs the decision as to whether a service vendor is authorized. Nevertheless, the implied threat of the FCC's action is to deal directly with PTTs perceived as hindering U.S. procompetitive initiatives.

In the late 1970s the FCC also extended its open entry policies into the international arena. Telenet and Tymnet were both authorized to provide service to Europe. Both carriers, however, faced extraordinary difficulties in obtaining interconnection agreements from the PTTs.

Faced with obstacles that threatened to thwart its entry policies, the FCC groped for an effective mechanism with which to address the interconnection issue with the European PTTs. Eventually, the issue of authorization of new services became intertwined in the North Atlantic consultative facilities planning process that evolved among the FCC, CEPT, and Teleglobe Canada.

Competition in the switched voice market has created additional pressures on the FCC's international policies. The FCC, having authorized new record and data services, allowed the specialized carriers—MCI, Sprint and SBS—to seek international interconnection agreements for switched voice services. These new carriers sought and obtained regulatory flexibility to compete with AT&T and, in particular, the right to select the least-cost facilities. AT&T, in turn, has been trying to free itself from North Atlantic circuit loading plans that require it to allocate a fixed portion of its traffic to higher-cost satellite facilities. Recently, AT&T was granted some flexibility to deviate gradually, and in a transitional way (by 2% a year through 1988, for growth traffic only), from the balanced loading plan. As AT&T shifts traffic to cable, increased financial stress will be placed on Comsat and Intelsat, which both depend on carrying significant segments of the AT&T switched voice traffic.

B. United Kingdom

The international policy implications of liberalization in the U.K. have also been quite significant. To expand Mercury's competitive capability in the international market, its owner, Cable & Wireless, has obtained permission from the British government to construct a new trans-Atlantic fiber optic cable, in addition to TAT-8. The cable application from Tel-Optik, Cable & Wireless' U.S. partner, has been approved by the FCC and has received a landing license from the Department of State.

The impact of this new high-capacity system on BT International's investment in the TAT-8 fiber optic cable is, as yet, unclear. The procedures followed by the British government did not require that this issue be addressed.

At the same time that policies favoring competition in construction of facilities have been extended internationally, the government has left unclear whether VANS can be provided internationally on the same basis as they can domestically. Although BT had historically taken a liberal position on interpreting CCITT guidelines, OFTEL's reluctance to address the issue has created uncertainty for companies that offer VANS domestically and internationally. Such reluctance may, in part, be a function of OFTEL's being a relative novice in international telecommunications issues. The British government will eventually need to decide whether VANS providers using internartional leased lines are to be regarded as "a customer" or a class of carrier under the CCITT Recommendations applicable to resale.

This unresolved issue—as well as Mercury's new role internationally—has required the DTI to adopt an active international posture. Formerly, it could rely on BT International to represent British interests. The creation of a new supplier, however, has complicated the representation of the U.K. in international telecommunications.

Consequently, the U.K. is in much the same position that the U.S. has been in for years, with different entities having operational and regulatory responsibilities. It has been quite difficult for the U.K.'s telecommunications partners, particularly in Europe, to adapt to this restructuring of responsibilities. In addition, the government has had to devise a new structure for participation in Intelsat; BT International is still the Intelsat representative, but the responsiblity for formulating the British position, and for consultations, are shared with Cable & Wireless.

C. *Japan*

For the past year, policymakers in Japan have recognized the international consequences of liberalization. A new committee studying these and related issues has not yet made specific recommendations about the future of Kokusai Denshin Denwa ("KDD"). Various new Type II VANs, licensed to major Japanese and U.S. interests, inevitably will want to operate internationally. Pressure for opening up the international VAN market has several implications.

In early 1985, the government took the position that VANs operating internationally would have to apply as Special Type II VAN operators and obtain MPT approval (or actually an absence of disapproval) through a registration process. Having discussed the issues with U.S. trade officials, the government subsequently simplified Type II regulation such that most VAN suppliers have applied for a General Type II license, which can be obtained merely by notification. The MPT, will no doubt, having gone through a difficult negotiation with the U.S. on the definition of "general" VANs, be less than insistent about requiring that all international VAN providers obtain MPT approval.

KDD, for its part, has been rather firm in indicating that General Type II VANs can operate internationally, but only through public switched facilities. The use of other facilities, such as leased lines, it is asserted, will require Ministry approval. In KDD's view, such approval cannot be granted because the CCITT Recommendations bar the resale of leased lines.

This contention is countered by others who argue that the CCITT guidelines are inapplicable because VANs are not "customers" but "carriers." Some VANs, as noted, do not provide carrier-like services but supply information or financial services. Moreover, if VAN operators are carriers and are accorded Recognized Private Operating Authority ("RPOA") status, how interconnection arrangements should be afforded remains an open question. Existing RPOAs operate with interconnection and revenue sharing agreements that apply to the joint responsibility of KDD and the foreign carrier to each offer a half-circuit from a fictive mid-ocean connection point; RPOAs do not use leased lines or operate end-to-end to Japan.

According VAN providers RPOA status, therefore, could mean that existing carriers either would be allowed to operate end-to-end—not likely to be an acceptable solution—or would be part of a new classification for VAN suppliers. Hence, this controversy illustrates the kind of difficult classification issue that can be created by the authorization of new service providers.

There also could be additional complications stemming from the liberalization of the Japanese domestic facilities market. For example, many observers believe that a provider of Japanese domestic satellite services could not remain economically viable unless it also provided international services. If this proves to be the case, the government will have to confront the difficult regulatory and policy issues of using a national system for international services. If the national system serves only immediately surrounding regions, *e.g.*, Korea, the impact might not be significant—or could be no more significant than the offering of U.S.-Canada transborder satellite services. It seems more likely, however, that any domestic system will seek to offer transpacific traffic as well, with the host of issues that such an offering implies.

Although domestic reform inevitably requires significant changes in international policy, it would appear that KDD, in particular, could be affected quite adversely by a radical transition in policy. KDD's hold on the market depends principally on its role as Intelsat representative, and as the holder of an investment in—and as an operator of—submarine cables. It also offers VENUS-P, an international packet-switched network, which is integrated with its International Computer Access Service to retrieve information from overseas data bases.

KDD might have difficulty protecting its position if a large number of VAN operators, including some of Japan's largest trading companies, begin to route their traffic over non-KDD facilities or offer services that compete with those of KDD. KDD, which has had no role in marketing services domestically, might have to consider staking out a position in the domestic market.

Another consequence of domestic change will be increased interest by NTT in operating internationally. NTT is in much the same position as AT&T was before the divestiture when, as originator of traffic, it could determine the viability of an international carrier. Thus, entrance of NTT into the international market could threaten KDD or any international VANS provider. (Now, of course, AT&T is itself vulnerable in the event that the Bell operating companies are ever granted a waiver under the Modified Final Judgment permitting them to originate international traffic.)

One result of these changes could be that international carriers will expand their operations to remain viable. They might integrate backward to market domestically. They also may seek to integrate forward to become involved in marketing at the other end of the circuit. Perhaps a harbinger of this development is that KDD is now involved in certain overseas marketing joint ventures through its investments in Japanese information service providers. The trend internationally may, therefore, be toward the provision of "end-to-end" carrier service, in much the same way that airline service is offered.

D. *France*

In France there are certain interesting parallels to the Japanese situation in the effort by the D.G.T. to expand its efforts internationally. The France Cables et Radio subsidiary of the D.G.T. has an important role in providing international services. FCR has, for example, a minority (20%) investment in ARGO Communications, a U.S. carrier, and will provide certain high-speed data services through this affiliate.

The FCR "filiale" structure also makes possible the provision of certain intra-European services through a joint venture of a filiale and the subsidiary of another European administration or a private company. Thus, there are several ways in which new, more flexible arrangements could develop for the provision of international services. Especially likely candidates for such ventures would appear to be in the data communications field offering services on an end-to-end international basis.

In Belgium, it is evident that the domestic needs for additional revenues have made the R.T.T. open to different, new international service arrangements. The R.T.T. agreements to provide international transiting service are notable cases in point.

E. *Canada*

Although Canada has a highly-developed telecommunications infrastructure, domestic policy decisions have only limited potential to spill over into other countries. The reverse is more often the case, with Canada, proximate to the U.S., more likely to be affected by policy changes in that country. When, for example, it is perceived that competition and deregulation benefit U.S. consumers, there is an immediate spillover in that Canadian consumers seek similar benefits.

This cross-border impact, however, can create significant problems for Canadian policymakers inasmuch as the demographic, geographic, and institutional difficulties may make U.S. approaches unworkable in Canada. The inconsistency between the U.S. and Canadian situations is made particularly evident by some of the smaller provinces; federal government proposals to introduce more competition in telecommunications, however modest, are almost invariably criticized by certain provinces as signaling "the importation of U.S.-style solutions that are inappropriate in the Canadian context."

It is imperative that Canada, as a major trading nation, retain its position at the leading edge of telecommunications technology if its industries that are dependent on efficient telecommunications services are to remain competitive internationally. Accordingly, Canadian policymakers and regulators must anticipate and react swiftly to foreign policy initiatives that may have an effect on Canadian institutions.

In particular, current initiatives to privatize Teleglobe appear to align with such a strategy. A privatized Teleglobe, free from legislative constraints imposed by its status as a Crown corporation, could be in a position to compete more effectively as and when competition is introduced in international communications markets. Similar arrangements could be made for the disposal of the government's 50% ownership of Telesat and its indirect, 50% share of CNCP.

Initiatives such as these have the added advantage that they would remove the apparent conflict of interest that occurs when the government proposes a more competitive role (and larger market share) for companies of which it is part owner. The changes that might be made are not likely to have a significant impact outside Canada. Rather, they illustrate, as does the privatization of BT in the U.K., that governments must be prepared to make fundamental policy decisions in lieu of cosmetic changes if they are to achieve domestic policy objectives and, at the same time, position their industries to meet external pressures.

F. *Italy*

In Italy, STET has often signalled that its goal of developing its domestic role must take place in international interaction. There is, then, international spillover in the implementation of its financial strategy of planning to expand the role of private shareholders and to float shares in international markets. As described above, STET companies, in an effort to upgrade their domestic position, are seeking joint venture arrangements with both national and international companies.

III. Impact of International Satellite Services on National Tariff and Service Policies

A. Europe

New satellite policies in Europe make feasible a set of new multipoint, direct access services such as data base distribution and videoconferencing. These new or unique services are suitable for satellite distribution because they involve the transmission of information from one to many points and cannot easily be offered over terrestrial facilities.

Several barriers to the marketing of new information or data base services exist, particularly at the European level. Largely this is so because the European Telecommunications Satellite Organization ("Eutelsat") operates as a facilities provider in Europe but has no role as a coordinator or marketing agent for its European satellite offerings.

Eutelsat was formed in 1977 as a consortium of European PTTs and now has twenty members; its headquarters are in Paris. It has successfully launched and begun to operate two European Communications Satellites ("ECS"); a third will be launched in August 1985. A second generation of larger, higher-power satellites is planned for late in this decade.

Although the original version of the ECS program was telecommunications, the first satellite is primarily used to beam television signals to cable head-ends. The second satellite will be used for satellite telecommunications traffic and has just inaugurated a business telecommunications service called Satellite Multiservice System ("SMS"), which is intended to offer capability for videoconferencing, remote printing of newspapers, high-speed data transmission and computer-to-computer communications; three transponders are allocated to television traffic.

The transponders on these satellites are allocated by Eutelsat to the national PTTs who have bid for them. The PTTs, in turn, have responsibility for marketing the transponder capacity and determining the rates, terms, and conditions of service that originate from their jurisdiction.

At present, Eutelsat has attempted to be a focal point for all European-wide satellite services; it has offered to acquire capacity from some of the national satellite systems and has one transponder on the French Telecom-1 satellite. There is no assurance that there will be a demand for the Eutelsat telecommunications capacity, however. Telephone usage is increasing at a slow rate in Europe. Moreover, systems are proliferating at an extraordinary rate, which will generate substantial, if not excessive, capacity. There are two Telecom-1 satellites—an Italian system, Italsat, proposed for 1988, and the German Kopernicus system, projected for 1987. In addition, there are or have been plans for direct broadcast satellite systems: the French TDF-1; the German TV-Sat, scheduled for operation in 1986; the Tele-X venture, which is led by Swedish manufacturing interests but also includes Norwegian and Finnish investments; possibly the now-dormant British Unisat (on which some telecommunications capacity originally had been planned); and, a potential project by Luxembourg.

With this diversity of capacity, Eutelsat has had a limited role in packaging or marketing new services to users. Eutelsat, on a strictly informal basis, has provided information and guidance about its facilities offerings to users; as well, it has assisted users in dealing with administrations. It is not, however, able to coordinate the packaging of satellite services that it offers—that task is carried out PTT-by-PTT.

The inability to obtain a coordinated offering from Eutelsat for a multipoint service can hamper the objectives of administrations and users alike. Although one administration may be anxious to provide an uplink service, users may be reluctant to enter into any agreements until they have worked out arrangements on a European-wide basis. This may prove vexing because there is little or no conformity in PTT practices regarding the operation of satellite services utilizing particular Eutelsat services. Some countries will allow customer ownership of receive-only devices; even so, fees will be required for the downlink service. Other administrations insist on retaining ownership of the receive-only device even when it is, or can be, located at the user's premises. To assure control over the receive-only dish, it may be operated at a site external to the user's premises, with the user paying the PTT for local access lines as part of the offering.

As is true with Intelsat multipoint service offerings, there are difficult issues regarding appropriate pricing schedules for multipoint offerings. A user arranging to lease capacity for a point-to-point service is essentially tying up the capacity of the satellite transponder; the use of that transponder for a multipoint service does not increase when additional service points are added. For the SMS service, however, agreements at the national level specify that with the addition of each additional receiving point (up to ten administrations) a downlink charge of 5% is added to the space segment.

Another problem in encouraging the development of satellite services is that, at bottom, they create significant pricing pressures on terrestrial rate structures. There may be some disincentives, therefore, for PTTs to set prices for satellite services competitively, because they then become a benchmark against which established pricing is measured. At the same time, satellites may be less welcome to the extent that they are seen as reducing substantially the ability of the PTTs to control the routing of traffic within and across terrestrial boundaries.

The vagaries of pricing, therefore, may well have stifled significantly user interest in Eutelsat services. For, although there is some rationale for increasing charges as the use of the transponder increases, it is difficult to gauge precisely the appropriateness of each stairstep. Space segment, downlink, and terrestrial charges are bundled together so that it is unclear who is, for example, paying for administration earth station charges. Furthermore, on an unbundled basis it clearly would be difficult to justify additional charges for additional downlinks. This may be the case with respect to video services to cable television systems, where the number of additional subscribers in another country can be small. In that case, where the program owner is interested in maximum dissemination, and the receive-only dishes are user-owned, the service is much like direct broadcasting. There would seem to be little reason for administrations to charge for each downlink reception of services.

A further competitive challenge to the Eutelsat services is posed by Intelsat offerings. The Intelsat Business Service ("IBS") may be an alternative—at least for U.S.-European multipoint traffic—to the Eutelsat SMS service. Although the basic rate principles of the IBS are similar to that of the SMS offering, the IBS tariffs are more fixed. Consequently, there may well be more user pressure on Eutelsat and administrations to obtain flexibility in SMS pricing. The PTTs may, however, have slightly conflicting interests in marketing both IBS and SMS services because of their Intelsat investment and role in providing terrestrial links. The intention of the distributor of a television program may be to disseminate as widely as possible an advertiser-supported program, with the minimum of interference by the local administration over the reception of the services.

It is interesting, therefore, to compare the mechanisms for the marketing of satellite services in Europe with those applicable to the U.S. satellite services. In the U.S., users may avail themselves of an extraordinary variety of options. Services can be provided under tariff by existing carriers on a service-by-service basis. Alternatively, a user can lease the entire capacity of a transponder for its own use or for the use of others. Finally, individual entities can purchase entire transponders for their own use or for the provision of service to others. As the satellite-provider is excluded from the rates charged to individual users for downlinks, these arrangements have been a significant factor in encouraging the widespread use of satellite services for video distribution services.

B. Japan

It is now too early to compare the European and U.S. situations with the satellite marketing arrangements that will evolve in Japan. It appears that there will be separate Type I carriers seeking to provide satellite and terrestrial facilities. In addition to the Type I applicants, it is possible that a group clustered around Keidanren, the industry association, will act as an agent for satellite capacity. This development would allow large companies to purchase capacity on the satellite systems of others.

In essence, then, Keidanren could act as a broker and "marketmaker" for particular satellite facilities . This approach to marketing appears intended to assure the maximum flow of benefits to industrial and service-based users. As such, it is quite consistent with what has been described above as the "supply side" rationale of Japanese telecommunications policy.

C. Finland

In Finland, the open domestic regulatory environment allows the Finnish public, and the country's cable systems, to use the many international satellite services available. This option tests the role of the PTT as a provider of international services. The PTT's position is that the reception of a satellite service is an international carrier service over which it has jurisdiction. The satellite service, however, even though it utilizes telecommunications portions of the spectrum, is structured by its owners as a broadcast service. Thus, there is a tension between the authority of the PTT to control the availability and cost of the downlink and the right of users and distributors of the signal to receive a broadcast channel. Such tension in the broadcast satellite area may, by example, have an impact on defining the relationship of users and satellite service providers in Europe.

D. Future of Satellite Services in Europe

The European approach to satellite services requires greater coordination of the PTTs in service offerings, significantly limits the role of users in developing and marketing services, and, consequently, does not encourage utilization of capacity at a time of oversupply. It may be necessary, therefore, to reexamine the tariffing practices and marketing mechanisms for services—particularly new business services—in Europe.

The first step in this direction would be to collect, in a comprehensive way, the tariffing practices of the various administrations. It might then be possible to accord Eutelsat a role in establishing a procedure for working out service arrangements with administrations and among users.

Alternatively, the administrations might create a service-marketing entity to promote and sell new business services in Europe. This company might be owned by the administrations or be franchised by them, with an obligation to pay a percentage of revenues to the PTTs.

Yet another option would be to explore the feasibility of more unstructured marketing arrangements for special classes of service. This approach might be used first with respect to video distribution or data distribution services.

How the capacity of the various satellite systems will be marketed is also of considerable importance to the evolution and viability of satellite services in Europe. Each national satellite system could be used for transborder satellite services. There may, in fact, be user requests to allow such flexibility. For example, if a large French company having plants or distribution arrangements in a neighboring country should use the Telecom-1 system, there may be pressures to offer transborder service. Users of national satellite services could then be authorized to use their capacity on a transnational basis with the cooperation of a neighboring administration.

Another development in marketing satellite services might be the evolution of transnational entrepreneurial activity by the PTTs. In France, for example, the marketing of Telecom-1 is handled by a filiale of the D.G.T; the subsidiary could form an international joint venture to market international services between countries where such activities are deemed permissible by the concerned administration. Such an arrangement might be feasible between the U.K. and France, or between France and Italy, where the STET holding company structure may allow for flexibility in marketing arrangements.

The emergence of significant excess European satellite capacity may create incentives to market in an aggressive and imaginative way. In this connection, it is interesting to speculate about the degree to which arrangements will begin to evolve for the marketing of interexchange services on a competitive basis. Viewing themselves as of the size and scale of the U.S. Bell operating companies, the PTTs may market international interexchange services.

Although the principal pressures for such services may be excess capacity and the existence of independent national systems, such satellite-based interexchange services might serve to stimulate traffic from European businesses that are dependent on telecommunications and information services. The arrangements for international services for data users might evolve into end-to-end offerings, especially as satellite services—as opposed to terrestrial services, which are based on interconnection arrangements—make the end-to-end services concept feasible.

There are at least two different approaches, in the satellite field, toward structuring marketing arrangements. One approach is essentially collaborative and rooted in the Eutelsat organization operating at a transnational level. An alternative, though not mutually exclusive, approach is to develop a structure that might be more fragmented—and ultimately more competitive—at the national level. In this way, national interests would be "integrated" at the level of an entrepreneurial venture by European-based joint ventures in which public, quasi-public, private entities, or a combination of the three, would participate.

As the experience with national satellite systems illutrates, it is difficult to confine the services to national boundaries. Thus, these approaches to marketing, which contemplate new patterns of collaboration and potential cooperation, result, in part, from the inherently multinational nature of the satellite technology itself.

E. Regional Satellite Services

Traditionally, the domestic and international sectors of the telecommunications industries were segmented and under the control of separate operating entities. The nature and capabilities of satellite technology are making it harder to preserve these sectoral boundary lines. These historical divisions persist, as described above, in Europe, where separate institutions provide national, regional, and international services. From the user's standpoint—and, ultimately, of consequence to the provider—this operational division of responsibility seems unworkable or impractical.

A classic example of such sectoral market division is in Canada, where Telesat provides Canadian domestic and transborder U.S. satellite services and Teleglobe is the international service supplier. Teleglobe, however, has gravitated toward offering U.S. services as part of its international trilateral service among points in the U.S., Europe, and Japan.

Telesat provides service on a transborder basis and has supplied facilities on the Anik-C satellite solely for U.S. use in the absence of U.S. facilities. In principle, Telesat services could be used more widely, to serve Mexico or the Caribbean. In the future, if national satellite systems have beams for transoceanic services, there will be a need to take a rigorous new look at the traditional division of responsibility between Teleglobe and Telesat.

If there is a worldwide, or at least transatlantic, move toward regional systems, Canadian satellite providers will, undoubtedly, not want to be excluded. Such regional systems will require new organizational arrangements and, to maintain a competitive stake in the market for international satellite services, may necessitate the building of national, regional, and international capacity into national systems.

The French Telecom-1 is now equipped with the technology to serve overseas departments in the Caribbean and St. Pierre and Miquelon, islands off the east coast of Canada. These beams, which are intended to serve internal French needs, nevertheless illuminate parts of Quebec, Ontario, and the eastern seaboard.

The D.G.T. has made it unmistakably clear that it intends to protect the role of Intelsat and does not plan to utilize its national system for international service. The D.G.T., however, is pragmatic and farsighted enough to anticipate the possibility that international services can and will be provided by national satellite systems.

The German Deutsche Fernmeldesatellit—Kopernikus—system will be used primarily for telecommunications but has the capability of distributing German language programs, especially to Switzerland and Austria. This programming has initially been distributed on the East Beam of the German ECS-1 transponder.

British plans for Unisat, principally a DBS system, now appear stillborn, having been much clouded by programmers' difficulty with the proposed cost of the service. Some programmers approached other administrations about obtaining access to national satellites for European-wide programming distribution. Originally, BT wanted to add telecommunications capacity to the system and even to lease an international transponder to Intelsat for transatlantic service. Although Intelsat has declined the offer, telecommunications offerings are as much in a state of doubt as the Unisat proposal itself.

In Finland, the government has agreed, as a result of intergovernmental discussions and as a matter of industrial policy, to participate in the Tele-X DBS venture, which will broadcast some Finnish-language programming.

This venture, which is now independent of Nordsat planning, is being led by Swedish manufacturing interests and will involve some subcontracting of systems to Norwegian and Finnish suppliers.

Nevertheless, despite the agreement to participate in the venture, arrangements for the use of the system are not yet resolved. The Finnish PTT has advised the Finnish government that there are other satellite capacities better suited for telecommunications users. The Finnish broadcasting corporation YLE has also been reluctant to commit to use the system. With capacity made available, however, there may be pressures in Finland and Scandinavia generally in favor of using it.

In the U.S., domestic satellite systems are used for a range of transborder services, *i.e.*, U.S.-Canada, U.S.-Mexico, and U.S.-Caribbean. A Mexico-to-U.S. service is transmitted by a U.S. domestic satellite; there is an unusual institutional arrangement in that the U.S. capacity is offered to Intelsat and Comsat to be consistent with existing international satellite marketing arrangements. Video services have been distributed by domestic satellite systems into the Caribbean for some time.

Any Japanese domestic satellite systems could include capacity to provide international services to nearby countries and to offer transpacific links as well.

IV. European Telecommunications Development: The Role of the European Commission and Implications for the Future

The international and national trends described in Part I and in the preceding sections of Part II have important implications for the future development of European telecommunications and information services. Perhaps the major factor in charting and steering the course of European developments in telecommunications is the European Commission. The role of the Commission, of Community law, and their effect on Europe is outlined below.

A. The Role of the European Commission

In recent years, the Commission of the European Communities has taken a leading role in formulating and implementing a coherent European approach to the telecommunications field. In the latest step in this endeavor, the Commission, in early 1985, requested that the Council of Ministers approve a definition phase of an ambitious program to stimulate research and development in, and the implementation of, a European-wide integrated broadband network by 1995. This program, RACE ("Research for Advanced Communications in Europe") has been developed by the Commission and high-level officials working with the Senior Officials Group for Telecommunications, a group from European ministries of economics, industry and telecommunications.

The RACE program involves three phases. In phase one, the definition phase, starting in 1985, the scope of the program will be defined. In 1986, a series of research programs in eight specific sectors (including very large integrated circuits, high complexity integrated circuits, integrated opto-electronics, broadband switching, communications software, etc.) will begin. The installation of demonstration broadband networks would follow in 1988. The trials of the networks—phase two—would begin in 1991; by 1993 broadband networks would be installed for operation in 1995. Phase three will continue to develop the technology for broadband equipment and services into the next century.

This program emerged from a carefully drawn Commission action plan submitted by the Commission to the Council of the Community in May 1984. *Progress Report on the Thinking and Work done in the field and initial Proposals for an Action Programme*, Commission of the European Communities, Com (84) 277 Final (May 18, 1984) [hereinafter "EC Report"].

The EC Report describes the telecommunications sector as one where the European position is still strong, accounting for approximately 20% of the global market and with Community firms achieving a trade surplus of approximately 1.7 billion ECU in 1982. EC Report, at 7. This situation is, however, perceived as fragile for several reasons. According to the EC Report, potential weaknesses of the Community's telecommunications sector lie in the fragmentation of the market. The EC Report speculates that compartmentalization in the Community may account for a lower level of data transmission in Europe (3% of all traffic) than in the U.S. (5%), as well as the slower growth rate of equipment markets in Europe and the U.S. (5% versus 8%). *Id.* at 8. The EC Report notes that per capita equipment purchases are $32 in the European Community versus $46 in Japan and $80 in the U.S. *Id.* at 9.

These disparities between Europe, on the one hand, and the U.S. and Japan, on the other, are seen as difficult to bridge. In a fragmented market setting, it is not easy to recover research and development expenditures. The PTTs face increasing investment burdens in a setting where significant price controls and socially- and politically-mandated public service obligations limit their borrowing and investment capacity. Moreover, PTT investments expose them to significant risks arising from long periods for recouping investments and uncertain success in the market.

At the same time, the EC Report describes Europe's competitors—in Japan and the U.S.—as seeking to expand their presence in international markets. AT&T is seen as reaching outward for new markets as a result of the deregulation and divestiture that has opened up the U.S. market to competition. NTT's strategy is seen as based on a massive investment program in the Integrated Network System project.

Based on this strategic assessment, the EC Report proposes a four-element strategy for developing the telecommunications sector in the Community. First, the EC Report focuses on the importance of a Community-wide market for telecommunications in the terminal and network components area. *Id.*

at 14. In that area it recommends steps toward uniform equipment standards and type-approval procedures.

As a follow-up to this first strategic initiative, the Commission entered into a letter agreement with CEPT in August 1984, to work together on equipment standardization issues and to formulate a European perspective on such issues. Later, on November 12, 1984, the Council of the European Communities adopted a Recommendation that member governments ensure that telecommunications administrations provide opportunities "on a non-discriminatory basis" for tenders for 1) all new telematic terminals and all conventional terminals for which there are common type-approval specifications and 2) contracts for switching and transmission apparatus and conventional terminal apparatus for which there are no common type-approval standards for at least 10% in value of their annual orders. Council Recommendation of 12 November 1984, Official Journal of the European Communities, No L 298/51 (Nov. 16, 1984).

The administrations are to report every six months on the "measures taken . . . to implement this policy, their practical effects, the problems encountered and any further action needed." The Commission is likely to submit to the Council a decision with binding rules on type-approval.

As the EC Report recognizes, however, the process of breaking down market lines will be slow under "the combined effects of demand for services, evolution of networks and increasing realization of the significance of the Community-wide dimension." EC Report, at 16.

As a second element of the Community program, the EC Report urges actions that will reduce the uncertainties of carriers and manufacturers about development strategies. *Id.* at 16. The Commission intends to encourage a joint study and consultation framework; it also intends to establish joint telecommunications infrastructure projects, including the establishment of a broadband pilot network to link decisionmaking centers in the Community. At later stages, there would be an effort to set up a second-generation transnational cellular telephone service. *Id.* at 18. The EC Report also proposes a joint investment in the main trans-Community lines for an integrated services broadband network. The RACE Project will contribute to such infrastructure investments; it is an effort to place the issue of European cooperation at a political level and remove it from the realm of technical discussions among the PTTs.

Further efforts toward standardization, to carry out this second element, were made in another November 12, 1984, Recommendation of the Council of European Communities. Recognizing the imminence of broadband and ISDN service, the Council called on administrations to consult with one another, preferably in the CEPT framework, before introducing any new service. Council Recommendation of 12 November 1984, Official Journal of the European Communities, No L 298/49 (Nov. 16, 1984). The Council wants to ensure that all services introduced from 1985 on are done so "on the basis of a common harmonized approach"; finally, digital switches ordered after 1986 should take account of Community standards.

As the third element of the program, the EC Report recommends a basic technology research program that would complement the activities of the ESPRIT program and stimulate computer technology. *Id.* As an Annex to the Report notes, there may be overlap with the ESPRIT program in the area of software technology and advanced information processing needed for telecommunications systems. Annex, Action Programme in the Field of Telecommunications, at 9. This element of the program places significant emphasis on basic research in microelectronics and basic technologies. RACE is clearly intended to stimulate research and development in critical sectors necessary to implement broadband network services.

Finally, the EC Report urges that there be efforts to assure telecommunications investment and network modernization networks in the less-developed countries of the Community. *Id.*

In addition to its role in encouraging standardization and Community-wide research and development in cooperation with the PTTs, the Commission, through its Directorate on Competition Law, has also initiated a number of complaints to encourage free and open competition in the telecommunications market. The Commission's most notable involvement was its antitrust case against IBM. This action was settled in return for commitments by IBM that it would release information about equipment standards and interfaces to the public. The Commission has been concerned that private industry standards not limit competitive opportunities for European manufacturers.

The Commission has also filed a complaint against the DBP alleging an "abuse of dominant position" under Article 86 of the Treaty of Rome. The abuses are alleged to have occurred in four areas: 1) extension of network monopoly to modems, 2) to baseband devices, 3) alleged manipulation of type-approval procedures, and 4) a forced change-over from the analogue Direktruf network to integrated data services, which will use only DBP devices. The DBP has denied that it is an "undertaking" within the meaning of Article 86 and asserts that it is acting not in an "entrepreneurial," but in its "regulatory," capacity. The case is still pending before the Commission.

The Commission also recently filed a complaint against the Federal Republic of Germany to prevent it from extending the monopoly of the DBP to cordless telephones. The complaint was filed under Article 37, which bars Member States from taking measures tending to create or extend a national monopoly of a commercial character. After the filing of the complaint, the German government decided not to make final the proposed rule.

The Commission's role in enforcing competition policy was recently given impetus by the March 20, 1985, decision of the Court of Justice of the European Communities upholding a December 1982, Commission decision in which the Commission held that British Telecom had abused its dominant position by prohibiting private message forwarding activities in the U.K. *Government of the Republic of Italy v. Commission of the European Communities*, Case 41/83, Decision, March 20, 1985. The Commission had decided that BT is an undertaking in a dominant position within the meaning of Article 86, that it had abused its position, that its measures negatively affected trade, and that BT could not avail itself of the provisions of Article 90.2, which exempts activities necessary to operate services in the general economic interest. Commission Decision on British Telecommunications, Official Journal of the European Communities, No L 360/36 (Dec. 21, 1982). Thereafter the British government decided not to pursue the case. The Italian government appealed the decision on the ground that Article 86 does not apply to PTTs because BT is not an "undertaking," that the case should have been brought against the British government, and because BT was compelled to act as it did by CCITT recommendations.

The Court of Justice rejected the argument that the Commission's competition rules did not apply to BT because, it concluded, BT was involved in an entrepreneurial activity. BT's regulatory process, held the Court, was strictly limited to overseeing prices and the terms and conditions of services, and the applicable statute did not prescribe the regulations that BT had freely decided to adopt. The Court concluded that the Commission's order had not interfered with a Member State's right, under Section 222 of the Treaty, to decide which of its activities should be reserved to the public sector, and to create national monopolies; the rules struck down by the Commission only regulated—they did not prohibit—the services of the telex forwarding agencies.

The Court also discussed the authority of the Commission to address directives to Member States under Article 90, paragraph 3, concerning their obligations under Article 90, paragraph 1 (which applies to undertakings to which Member States grant special or exclusive rights). The Court thereby explicitly acknowledged the right of the Commission, under the supervision of the Court, to ascertain a state's compliance with Article 90.

This aspect of the Court's decision could have important implications with respect to the Commission's oversight of activities of publicly-owned ventures or with respect to the regulatory activities of PTTs. Without rendering a definitive analysis of the *British Telecom* case, it should simply be pointed out that the decision may accord the Commission rather broad discretion to challenge activities or practices by PTTs that it views as impediments to competition.

The more important, longer-range implications of the decision are, however, hard to assess. First, the judicial process is not expeditious; thus, decisions to initiate enforcement actions against an administration must be taken within the overall context of Commission decisionmaking. Second, there are inherent difficulties with a strategy that, on the one hand, seeks to develop a consensus within the Community for agreements on standards and that, on the other, subjects one Member of the Community to legal challenge at the same time. Thus, a delicate balance will have to be struck between the Commission's enforcement and collaborative strategies.

There are extraordinary difficulties in legislating a comprehensive set of standards and agreements for new equipment and services. Therefore, it may be seen as easier to attempt to eliminate on an ad hoc basis—by complaint—barriers to agreements and trade. Although such a case-by-case approach could result in a consensus on the need to reach voluntary agreements, any action to eliminate barriers or address restrictions must consider the broader goals of European telecommunications policy. Hence, it is not enough that particular restrictive practices are addressed. It is critical, however, that the Commission focus on practices that truly prevent the development of European trade markets. Thus, it is essential for the Commission to formulate a comprehensive strategic view to undergird both its market integration and enforcement activities.

Such a view might take account of some of the following observations on the implications of national and international changes in telecommunications policies in Europe—and with respect to the Commission's role in formulating a strategic response to those changes.

B. Implications for Europe and the Future

One of the questions of overriding importance—for the Commission and European policymakers—is whether the development of a European-wide market, in light of the policy shifts and marketplace and technological forces described, will be centrally directed and coordinated at the political level or whether it will evolve from "channeling" strong rivalrous initiatives at the national level into European ventures at the entrepreneurial level. In addressing this question, it is important to examine the real pressures on European decisionmakers that affect the prospects for European collaboration.

There seem to be deep competitive fissures in Europe that will make market integration and stimulation by the Commission's standardization and joint investment projects difficult to achieve via a "top down" approach. European policymakers also may recognize that a strategy based upon Commission efforts to remove "bottlenecks" and barriers to interconnections has its limitations.

Such constraints may result from a fundamental resistance to collaboration—for traditional or historic reasons—as well as from competitive pressures within the European scene. As described herein, those competitive or, possibly, divisive pressures are growing due to economic forces on the PTTs, inherent difficulties in coordinating infrastructure investments, and difficulties found by PTTs in shifting to a more market-driven approach. Given these factors, a coherent strategy of achieving European sectoral and market development may have to adapt to these competitive pressures and the realities of the emerging marketplace.

In developing this strategy, the embedded fragmentation of national systems and economic pressures cannot be ignored, or necessarily be seen as a weakness. To do so would be to miss a real opportunity to "run with the tide," to exploit the diverse strengths of these centers of national initiative. By doing so, it may be more likely that market integration and a European presence in global telecommunications markets can be achieved.

It is often emphasized that the U.S. and Japanese interests in the telecommunications sectors are highly competitive with those of European manufacturers and service providers. Yet the emergence of strong telecommunications and information industries in Europe—and, therefore, a strong Europe economically—is in the long-term strategic interests of the U.S., Japan, and Europe. Europe must develop high technology industries and improve industrial efficiency through new technology if it is to remain an important international force and hold its economic position globally. Whether or not Europe succeeds will depend upon strategies that will be based on and evolve from European industrial and institutional arrangements, which differ significantly from those in the United States and Japan.

It may be useful to focus on economic realities and international pressures that must be considered in formulating an integrated set of European telecommunications policies.

First, there is now a proliferation of separate national satellite systems in Europe. *See supra* Section III.A. Many of these systems may not be fully utilized. There could well be technological and economic pressures for national systems to be used to provide international services. Such services could be offered cooperatively, through joint ventures; however, competition among the administrations in marketing such services could, instead, increase.

Second, adding to the welter of national satellite systems is pressure to install broadband fiber optic links. The RACE project is one development in this respect, to coordinate and influence the manufacturing sectors that produce these transmission capabilities. As the Council Recommendations illustrate, planning such facilities—and harmonizing services that use them—is one way of approaching standardization at the European level.

It is important to note that these activities are being driven by the Commission's industrial policy as well as by its telecommunications planning concerns. Most administrations foresee heavy investments in new facilities, such as fiber optic and digital networks, in the next decade.

Third, these investment decisions will occur in an uncertain economic environment. There are several factors operating to generate financial strains on the administrations. The market for international services, historically a source of substantial profits, is subject to competitive pressures. Competition over the heavily-trafficked North Atlantic routes should drive the price of public switched voice services closer to costs. Developments at the national level—*e.g.*, liberalization in the U.K.—have created pressures on pricing in, *e.g.*, France and throughout Europe. Increasing the price of local exchange services, as in France and elsewhere in Europe, can be difficult and controversial; in Germany, a number of years ago, local charges were set below a level many viewed as necessary to recover assigned costs.

Fourth, and exacerbating the problems of excess capacity and increasing economic pressures, is that the European market is not without risk. Demand for new services is not at all tested. The decision to make investments to develop any such new services may be more like drilling for oil than like investing in new transmission infrastructure. For this reason, the Commission has identified risk-bearing as a central issue in planning. It proposes to focus on the possibility of sharing risks among manufacturers and carriers through joint research and development programs.

At least where basic infrastructure is not involved, there may, however, be good reasons for shifting risks from the public to private institutions that may be willing to bear them in return for promises of higher investment returns. To meet the financing needs of the telecommunications sector it may be necessary, therefore, to encourage innovative mechanisms for stimulating venture capital. Venture capital activity is not yet as widespread in Europe as it is in the U.S.; hence, European telecommunications policymakers may need to think more intensively about new structures for financing and marketing securities. Indeed, to the extent that many of the conditions for venture capital investment are not present in Europe, the focal point for risk-oriented investment may have to come from venture capital groups established within large European corporations.

In short, a series of potentially severe structural and economic pressures could begin to squeeze the profitability of the European administrations, if not rock their very foundations. They are the subjects of national and Community political and industrial policy forces that may compel them to make significant and risky capital expenditures on new satellite and fiber optic facilities. At the same time, traditional sources of revenues from international services and, potentially, also from interexchange services, are beginning to dry up.

One of the core problems of European telecommunications development may, therefore, be seen not as infrastructure creation but as increasing the utilization of that infrastructure. A far-sighted European strategy might well acknowledge the overwhelming importance of increasing utilization of existing and planned capacity. There are several components to such a strategy.

First, there needs to be a more effective coalescence of facilities and utilization planning. Excessive transmission capacity is now being created by autonomous decisionmaking at the national level; such autonomy is aggravated by a separation, at the national and regional levels, between those responsible for creating capacity—*i.e.*, those with industrial policy orientations—and those with responsibility for using that capacity. Until there is a better coordination of those elements, resolving the balance of supply and demand may remain a difficult issue at the European level. However, by encouraging a unified approach to planning infrastructure development and use, it is likely that an appropriate balance will be struck.

The second component of European strategy would be to encourage research and development, as the Commission is doing, but in areas that will increase utilization of facilities. There should be a careful assessment of the extent to which collaborative or jointly-managed research projects—as opposed to more autonomous, venture-oriented activities—actually do or will stimulate innovation. There may, for instance, be differences in the most effective strategy for developing large-scale investments in infrastructure, on the one hand, and for encouraging innovation in new software and service-based systems, on the other.

Stimulating new software and electronic services may require greater autonomy and financial incentives than are possible in a centralized development activity. This may be so because application-oriented work for developing new information systems requires the exchange of resources and information among users, manufacturers, and software engineers. There should be acceptance of the fact that innovation will occur—and solutions found—on a more unstructured and ad hoc basis than is possible in a more bureaucratic setting.

A third element of the strategy to enhance utilization of the infrastructure would be for PTTs to consider a less restrictive approach to the provision of value-added or second-tier services that utilize PTT-supplied transmission capacity. Observers in some European PTTs have noted that such services can be useful in developing and refining technical standards and protocols for new offerings. Moreover, value-added service providers can explore the market potential of new areas of business without risking the scarce capital resources of a PTT.

In addition to increasing utilization of capacity, there needs to be a renewed emphasis on an open process for planning and coordinating investments in European facilities. There is, of course, substantial planning on a route-by-route basis between the major European administrations. The CEPT organization is an important unifying influence among the European PTTs. What is required, however, is a better mechanism for bringing together the diverse elements of the European telecommunications scene to formulate a strategic perspective on the future of that sector for Europe.

The participation of users in the planning process is essential if this perspective is to have any hope of illuminating or of resolving issues of European telecommunications policy. If utilization is to increase, users must be able to identify and speak candidly about some of the problems they have encountered in implementing and coordinating satellite-based services in Europe. In this connection, there should be a forum to discuss the difficulties in setting up networks on a European-wide basis for information and financial services.

As to the planning process itself, it is critical that the forum not become just a locus where administrations present facts and figures about projected investments. Rather, the need is for a mechanism to discuss and to evaluate the trends in European telecommunications services.

This forum also may be required if Europe is to achieve a better balance between traditional telecommunications and industrial policy concerns. Although telecommunications and industrial policies are not inevitably at odds with one another, there are, as described above, risks of pushing the rate of development from the "supply side" without full regard for the state of the market's needs. An open forum—with carriers, administrations, users, and the public—will contribute to development of a telecommunications policy that is more "market-oriented," though not one necessarily characterized by unrestrained competition and open entry.

Where such a dialogue could take place is not clear. The European Commission has a major role in the process of policy formulation through its activities to encourage investment and harmonization and to protect competition in the telecommunications sector. Its strategy—based on the coordination and stimulation of infrastructure and sectoral developments, and on the removal of barriers to competition, requires a broader framework for appraising the present—and future—state of telecommunications in Europe.

In developing such a framework, it is interesting, and may even be relevant, to compare how telecommunications policy is developed and coordinated within other autonomous sovereign entities. The cases of large countries, with strong traditions of federation, may be instructive in this regard. The U.S. example may well be less relevant to Europe because federal authority is used so decisively to limit the states' ability to establish independent telecommunications policies.

The Canadian experience, however, may be more revealing to European observers. Canadian policymaking has been marked by repeated efforts to achieve consensus among provinces that have diverse approaches and perspectives on telecommunications issues. That experience focuses on efforts to remove barriers to the provincial interconnection of services that are permitted to operate in some—but not all—provinces. The key to the future of Canadian telecommunications—as it might be, too, in Europe—is to strengthen mechanisms for removing barriers to market integration and to the implementation of new services.

The experience of other countries—and the circumstances of the European situation—make it appear almost inevitable that the future of telecommunications policy will emerge through a mix of collaboration and increasingly intense competition among administrations. One critical aspect of this mix is the European debate over standardization that is centered in the Commission. What is critical, however, is deciding which activities should be pressed as a matter of standardization and which should be abandoned.

On the one hand, the failure to agree on a common standard for cellular radio services has not only reduced the size of the potential market for equipment manufacturers, but also has prevented the emergence of European-wide portable telephone services that could be of great utility to European business.

On the other hand, efforts to achieve standardization with respect to certain information services—or the upper layers of the ISO model—may end up being too difficult and time consuming, given other available technological options for obtaining inter-operability and connectivity of networks. Thus, in working toward collaboration, the costs and benefits of particular initiatives to standardize must be examined critically.

Pulling in the other direction, away from collaboration, is intra-European competition among administrations. It is not realistic to think that the pressures arising from liberalization in the U.K. will abate in the next five years. Rather, there is a good chance that some other administrations, perhaps in Spain or the Netherlands, will move seriously to open competition in the area of value-added services.

Such moves, in smaller countries such as the Netherlands, with a strategic gateway position to the rest of Europe, also may prod these countries' neighbors into acting. If the Netherlands liberalizes its value-added services market, then the R.T.T. in Belgium seems likely to follow.

Moreover, the incentives for unilateral action—the decision by the R.T.T. to interconnect with MCI is one example—are likely to increase as the PTTs seek to gain financial advantages in a period of tight financial straits.

A European strategy may well have not only to recognize the inherent tension of collaboration and competition—both critical aspects of the Europe of today and tomorrow—but also to work with, not against, that dynamic. European policymakers at the national level, European users and business interests, and the European Commission might well explore mechanisms and incentives for structuring new kinds of arrangements for marketing capacity. They should encourage joint ventures at the European level to provide new services over the range of transmission facilities that are now being installed. European markets can be integrated by European multinational ventures and enterprises, and not merely through a series of intergovernmental accords.

The structural innovation in France, for example, through the establishment of subsidiaries within an administration, may be a paradigm for this approach. A strategy that is at once collaborative and competitive might encourage agreements between telecommunications entities—public and private—perhaps paralleling those that have been successful in the European aerospace field. Ultimately, the success of this approach toward European market integration will depend on the availability of innovative means of financing. Thus, how to develop new vehicles for obtaining venture capital should become a critical item on the agenda of telecommunications policymakers throughout Europe.

To shape and harmonize views on developing a strategy that takes into account this complex array of issues is a great challenge for European institutions focusing on telecommunications policies for the future. The starting point of this effort is, however, a well-defined perspective on where the sector is now and where it is going.

These observations are not intended to offer any definitive evaluation of where future developments might—or should—lead. What seems important, however, is that the Commission and administrations fully draw on the great strength and initiative in European diversity, and that they plan in that environment. Collaboration—within the complex and quickly changing European context marked by increased rivalry among national administrations—may not be the only approach toward planning for a telecommunications future. Led by the Commission, however, it can be a dynamic force for an effective European response to international competition.

V. Implications of Recent International and National Developments for Intelsat

These emerging uses of national systems for regional, and possibly international, services have important implications for the Intelsat system. Clearly, the technological capability for using national systems for international services now exists. Where such capability exists pressures will mount to make international services available.

Intelsat has reacted strongly and extremely negatively to the several U.S. proposals for private transatlantic and Latin American satellite systems. Such proposals, it is of critical importance to note, are merely one element of what is a much broader technological and economic challenge to the future of that organization.

For some time, Intelsat has faced a competitive challenge from submarine cables—both coaxial and fiber optic. These systems are constructed to serve dense traffic streams and—unlike Intelsat—can be priced without regard to obligations to provide service to all regions of the world.

There is an asymmetry in arrangements for planning global satellite and submarine cables. Satellites are coordinated on a global basis through the Intelsat Board of Governors and, ultimately, its Assembly of Parties. By contrast, cable investments are made only by an immediately concerned group of investors, usually the administrations of the landing points of the cables, and other administrations receiving the cable traffic.

The FCC has, in the past, attempted to mitigate this asymmetry through the North Atlantic consultative procedures that involved the European, Canadian, and U.S. parties in a process for planning the needs for new cable and satellite services. In this process, new cables could, at the very least, be coordinated with the plans of Intelsat because the process involved some of the most significant investors in Intelsat. Those participating in the North Atlantic planning process, it was anticipated, would attempt to influence Intelsat planning accordingly.

This kind of coordination process did, of course, occur outside the Intelsat organization; it depended on the initiative, support, and leadership of the U.S. For many reasons, not the least of which was that the locus of the process was in the FCC—and not distributed among the participating parties—the consultative process has not been entirely effective. It never, for example, involved a comparable level of planning and coordination for the Pacific Basin region.

Recently, moreover, the FCC has been downgrading the consultative process. It has, for example, excluded from the planning process the private fiber optic system being built by Cable & Wireless and Tel-Optik.

The process, of course, need not operate to require prior approval in facilities planning. There is, however, certainly some utility in a mechanism by which investors can develop a rational set of expectations about the demand for international circuits.

The Intelsat organization is, therefore, under great pressure, primarily from fiber optic systems—the currently authorized TAT-8, and the private Tel-Optik and SLC projects. Hence, the impact of private satellite systems is only likely to contribute to those pressures in an incremental way.

The recommendation of the U.S. government in favor of private satellite systems, and the subsequent authorizations by the FCC, limit them to private data and voice offerings that cannot be connected to public switched services. Although this condition is intended to minimize the impact of such systems on Intelsat's revenues, there are, of course, practical and legal problems with enforcing it. Of equal importance, however, is that the impact of fiber optic systems will not be limited in any respect. Consequently, there may well be a diversion of voice traffic from Intelsat satellites to submarine cables.

Moreover, as a result of competition among U.S. carriers in the public switched voice market, there will be pressures to eviscerate the traffic allocation formulae used by the U.S. to assure balanced loading of satellite and cable facilities. The non-AT&T carriers—MCI, Sprint, and SBS—are not bound by the loading policies. Consequently, AT&T, the only U.S. voice carrier required to comply with the current loading formula, is seeking flexibility to choose the least costly (*i.e.*, cable) facilities to meet its competition. In sum, and for all these reasons, there could be significant diversion of traffic from the existing Intelsat system.

As a result, Intelsat will inevitably be required to take steps to increase the cost effectiveness of the use of satellite circuits. It must begin repricing circuits on a route-by-route basis. Reducing rates on heavily trafficked east-west routes, to meet the challenge posed by fiber optic cable technology, could increase prices on north-south corridors.

These changes seem inexorable, and not entirely precipitated by the advent of private satellite services. One significant problem with Intelsat's present defensive posture in opposing the authorization of private systems is that it will create expectations in many quarters that price adjustments can be avoided when, in fact, they cannot. As a result, when Intelsat seeks flexibility to respond to the larger competitive pressures at work, its members may not be prepared to accept the proposition that new pricing policies are required.

Intelsat, then, must now ready itself for a different environment. It will have to look ahead with vision to determine how future services should be provided. Several steps may be appropriate or necessary.

First, Intelsat must begin to plan for new services to take greater account of competition from fiber optic cables and from potential international applications of national satellite systems. At present, Intelsat has little or no control over the planning of the former technology. Moreover, national pressures will develop that may make inevitable the offering of international services on national satellite systems.

Second, Intelsat—or other international bodies, such as the ITU—may have to try to revitalize the international facilities planning process to facilitate the exchange of information about international construction plans.

Third, Intelsat must begin to see its role in different terms, less as a provider of facilities and more as a clearinghouse for satellite capacity supplied by national and regional systems. Instead of procuring satellites from manufacturers, Intelsat could begin to influence national satellite planning by entering the market as a purchaser of satellite capacity. Concurrently, Intelsat could emerge as a carrier of last resort, filling gaps left by national or regional systems.

Fourth, Intelsat must begin to restructure its pricing over high-density routes to maintain its competitive position. Intelsat has, of course, taken the position that it lacks the authority to price services on a route-by-route basis and could only do so on the basis of operational criteria. Nevertheless, it seems likely that it could argue that operational criteria—*i.e.*, maintaining full use of main transmission paths—would justify pricing differentials over competitive routes. Intelsat has spent its energies focused on the rigidities of its position and the adverse impacts of competition. It will be necesary for Intelsat to pay greater attention in the future to how it might react flexibly to the inevitable pressures in the international satellite market.

Fifth, and as a part of this overall effort, Intelsat has a large task in explaining to its members the current pressures on the Intelsat system and why changes in prices and institutional structure will be necessary. Intelsat may require the active assistance of its members in understanding the nature and dimension of these international pressures. Unquestionably, many of its members will prefer maintenance of the status quo and will resist some of the initiatives outlined above. Nevertheless, to avoid dealing with changes in the international environment, however, will only increase the risk that Intelsat will become politicized and subject to increasingly divisive global economic and technological pressures.

PART III

INTERNATIONAL ISSUES: THE INSTITUTIONAL PERSPECTIVE

International telecommunications policy is in a state of flux and enormous change. There are challenges to substantive domestic and international policies. One profound consequence of the resulting changes in policies are challenges to the institutional arrangements in which policy is made. These international arrangements, too, must adjust to the pressures that are reshaping national telecommunications policies. Sketched out below are some observations on how present institutions for addressing international policy issues will need to change and what new mechanisms might be developed in the future.

I. Introduction: Moving Toward a Trade Model

It has been—and is—a time of almost unprecedented activity in the telecommunications field around the world. Nations historically have seemed to agree that telecommunications services could best be supplied on a monopoly basis. This common understanding facilitated the provision of international services through a process of negotiating agreements. Some countries are now moving beyond the common ground to adopt policies that differ from one another.

In the past two years, for example, the U.S. telecommunications industry has been restructured as a result of the AT&T divestiture process. New telecommunications laws, involving privatization of the dominant national service providers and liberalization for new competitive entry in services and facilities, have been enacted in the U.K. and Japan. Quite antiquated telecommunications laws in Finland and Canada are under comprehensive review and major legislative reforms are under consideration. A high-level governmental commission is studying the future of the Deutsche Bundespost. The D.G.T., in France, continues a process of technological and institutional growth. In Italy, the structure of the telecommunications system is undergoing review and reorganization. In the Netherlands, Belgium, and other smaller countries, the future of the sector is being studied carefully.

In sum, strong economic and technological currents are coursing through existing institutional arrangements at both the national and international level. How will institutions at the international level react in this time of great activity?

The shifts in competition policy, industry structure, and institutional arrangements represent a departure from the shared perspective of the past, that international services could be provided on a monopoly basis. The rapid pace of adopting and implementing divergent approaches will strain the process by which international telecommunications agreements are reached. In the past, such agreements were relatively static, and not subject to frequent renegotiation and modification. From an operational and institutional standpoint the participants in the process were known entities that did not change frequently.

Now, however, in the fields of telephony, enhanced, or valued-added services, and new electronic or financial services, there is a proliferation of emerging players in the U.S., the U.K., Japan, and Canada. There are new competitors—MCI, Mercury, Daini Denden—and, some new, governmental entities—such as DTI, OFTEL, or the Japanese MPT—that will have to be more active in structuring international service arrangements than they have in the past.

As the number and variety of choices for interconnection increases, it is inevitable that parties will seek to bargain. One result is that interconnection agreements are likely to be of shorter duration. Their terms and conditions may become subject to competitive forces. It will become more difficult to retain fixed, static, and uniform systems of settlements among service providers. Agreements in the telecommunications field are, therefore, likely to fall into the pattern of traditional trade discussions over the provision of goods and services.

If future telecommunications relations become more trade-oriented, then it will be critical to understand more about the legal and industry environment in which such discussions occur. It will be essential to document the contours of this legal framework, and how it will evolve, because there may not be complete compatibility between the flexibility and uniformity needed to implement new electronic services and the diverse and often rigid terms and conditions for the use of leased circuits available from PTTs around the world. When interconnection agreements, and their terms and conditions, did not affect trade or business relationships it was easier not to be preoccupied with them. That is all changing.

Much of the process of working out new interconnection arrangements will occur through regular business transactions and dealings. Some of these issues, however, will be difficult for individual businesses or telecommunications entities to resolve efficiently and with the requisite expertise. Issues of market access are increasingly likely to become the subject of trade discussions—as was recently the case between the U.S. and Japan, and between the European Community and Japan.

Initiating a round of trade discussions over telecommunications will impose real burdens on trade and telecommunications officials. In the past, the telecommunications experts at the national level have had little reason to be concerned with trade issues; conversely, trade officials have spent little time in developing expertise on telecommunications issues. Both sets of officials will, therefore, need to broaden their perspective. Trade officials must come to understand that changing telecommunications policies and the structure of an industry to permit market entry is a difficult and lengthy process.

These officials are accustomed to trade-oriented discussions often straining relationships and being undertaken in the context of an economic crisis. It may be useful in the trade context, however, to focus not merely on substantive policies but on procedural mechanisms that can be used to ease tensions and smooth out the process of implementing new telecommunications service arrangements.

New procedures to address these issues in a trade context may well have to be devised at the intergovernmental level. In addition, other, more informal, steps may have to be taken to stimulate dialogue between users, service providers, and policymakers in Canada, the U.S., Japan, and Europe—and ultimately create a "safety valve" to prevent excessive pressures from developing in formal trade talks. Discussed below are some procedural or institutional issues that will be important in setting up new and various services in telephony, enhanced services, and information-related activities.

II. Network Interconnection Agreements

Historically, telephone interconnections were bilateral, involving one party at each end of an international line. As a result of differing national policies and objectives, that process is greatly increasing in complexity. For example, in the U.S.-U.K. relationship there are a large number of entities on the U.S. side—AT&T, MCI, GTE/Sprint, and potentially others—and two entities on the U.K. side—BT and Mercury, both of which are authorized to engage in international service. The U.S.-Canada relationship involves an equal number of U.S. carriers and Telecom Canada on the Canadian side. CNCP has similar ties with U.S. record carriers and may soon enter the voice market.

The future pattern of the U.S.-Japan relationship is not clear. There may be connections between the U.S. carriers and service providers and the various Japanese Type I service providers domestically, regardless of whether any new entrants are authorized to compete with KDD. Any decision on that issue—whether there will be a competitor to KDD and, if so, on what terms—will further complicate the relationships.

In Europe, there will be a slightly different negotiating configuration where a number of U.S. suppliers will deal with a single European PTT.

In this new negotiating environment, several issues will need to be resolved. First, there will be a more complicated process for planning facilities. In a competitive environment the individual suppliers will have varying traffic projections that may—or may not—prove realistic. It may be necessary to share traffic projections and marketing initiatives to plan realistically for international connections, even though such information may be sensitive in a competitive environment. A set of guidelines or expectations as to what information can reasonably be regarded as confidential, and what is needed for system planning, may be required. Where a single administration negotiates with a number of international carriers it, too, may have to devise a procedural framework for sharing planning information.

Similarly, procedures may be needed for structuring ad hoc technical or economic arrangements for interconnection. Favored relationships, among administrations or between foreign carriers and an administration, may, in some instances, be viewed as pro-competitive, stimulative of competition, and fairly negotiated. In other cases, however, they may evolve into arrangements viewed as anticompetitive or collusive. Consequently, there may be an increased risk of liability under either U.S. law or foreign law—or both legal schemes—arising out of interconnection negotiations between and among U.S., European, and other carriers. Both the U.S. carriers and the foreign providers need to start articulating areas of concern—where competitive frictions might occur—regarding the new sets of interconnection relationships that are evolving.

Where there is more than one carrier on both sides there will, no doubt, have to be various types and levels of bilateral discussions with, perhaps, some joint discussions regarding plans for international transmission facilities. In all these discussions, it will be necessary to determine the appropriate sphere for participation by operational—as opposed to governmental—entities. Worked into the process might even be a structured role for neutral entities to gather traffic data and projections and to convey it to the concerned operational entities. One difficulty with implementing such new multi-tier negotiating arrangements is that public officials have traditionally tended to stay outside the area of coordinating international services. They have scant expertise in such matters, and, ultimately, may not even want to become involved. Nevertheless, during the trasitional period it may be necessary for them to be involved while new ground rules are being drawn up.

Other potential problem areas that will have to be resolved are the technical arrangements for interconnection. For the U.S.-Canadian traffic stream, for example, interconnection has generally not been handled through "gateways." With the proliferation of new carriers, that arrangement may have to be modified to take into account the additional routing complications arising from a multiple-carrier environment.

Drawing up a numbering scheme to allow for the identification of carriers internationally may create further complications. For example, with respect to calls from the U.S. into the U.K., there will be questions whether the customer will be able to designate Mercury or BT as the carrier of choice, or whether that issue will be decided solely by carrier interconnection agreements. That determination could be made by AT&T or MCI, for example, when they route their international traffic through BT International or Mercury.

If it remains for the carriers to determine such interconnection arrangements, an unresolved issue is how undesignated traffic is to be divided by an originating carrier or administration among foreign correspondent carriers at the other end of the international circuit. At present, the FCC has a uniform settlements policy, to prevent administration "whipsawing"; this policy has never been formally applied to telephony arrangements. If applied to telephone service, however, the policy would effectively prevent a

European administration from achieving a more favorable settlement arrangement with a U.S. carrier in return for increasing the outbound traffic flow over that carrier's facilities. As the international environment grows more complex and competitive, these uniform settlement rate policies will be the subject of increasing discussion, criticism, and pressures for modification in light of new market realities.

III. Enhanced Service Interconnection

The difficult problems in implementing international agreements for enhanced service entities are illustrated in a interesting way by the issues that must be faced in interconnecting Japanese Type II providers with U.S. service providers or users.

The dilemma facing the Japanese at present is how to allow Type II entities to obtain access to international circuits. The government has not decided whether to treat new Type II carriers as equivalent to KDD (as a full-fledged new international carrier), as a "hybrid" carrier with access to leased circuits, or as a "customer" required to use KDD's public switched services.

Choosing how to classify international VAN services will be difficult, particularly if the Japanese government decides on an intermediate course of action—such as according the new entities carrier status along with the ability to use KDD's leased lines. The government will, as described above, then have to decide whether RPOA status is appropriate. If so, then the questions will revolve around the type of interconnection that is sought. For example, most existing RPOAs have fictive "mid-ocean" interconnections and do not operate end-to-end, like "customers" of leased lines suppliers.

Theoretically, such end-to-end interconnection for Type II carriers would be feasible. The matter, however, is not for the Japanese government to decide on a unilateral basis. Rather, resolving these issues will necessitate discussions with the U.S. government, which must determine whether end-to-end interconnections are appropriate.

The principal difficulty, of course, is that the Japanese classification of a Type II service provider and the U.S. definition of an "enhanced service" vendor are not congruent. Therefore, U.S. officials and carriers may be troubled by policies that allow end-to-end certification of a group of Type II entities. Such arrangements could be of some concern because they might allow Type II providers to circumvent entirely the existing services of U.S. record carriers, which now provide transmission services jointly with KDD. Because the record carriers effectively offer the functional equivalent of some Type II services (*i.e.*, pure transmission services), open end-to-end interconnection policies might increase pressure on the Japanese to allow existing U.S. carriers to have a direct marketing presence in Japan—not their present limited interconnection agreements.

One related question is whether the international interconnection policies should differentiate between protocol conversion networks, which would, under the U.S. approach, be considered "enhanced services," and more "basic" transmission services, such as leased lines for voice, data, TWX, and telex. Inevitably, this debate will ensnare entities such as GE Information Services (GEISCO) and Contral Data that primarily market remote access data processing services but also make their networks available for certain protocol conversion-type services. Their data processing and other network services are intertwined so that it may be difficult to determine just how to treat such entities in interconnection discussions. One approach may be to differentiate between entities that lease services from carriers and those that provide services over circuits in which they have an ownership interest.

Undoubtedly, the current discussions between the U.S. and Japan over the interconnection of Type II services will have an important impact on the framework of arrangements between the U.S. and the U.K. and the U.S. and Canada.

The pattern of U.S.-Japan discussions—perhaps hammered out over "trade" tables—will, then, have international ramifications. Thus, determining how to "generalize" the discussions may be important. Nevertheless, keeping an eye on the real bilateral issues will be equally important because they will shed light on the practical problems of implementing enhanced service agreements in the broader international setting.

IV. Agreements for Information and Financial Service-Oriented Networks

As described above, there are many new vendors of electronic, publishing, financial, brokerage, or other informational or transactional services. They utilize communications lines, communications processing, and data processing capabilities, but are not involved in common carriage. They do not offer packet switching or "communications processing," or even data process services akin to those of a remote access time-sharing vendor. These entities cannot fairly be described as being in a telecommunications-related business; rather they are in banking or publishing.

It has traditionally been accepted that these companies can operate within the confines of foreign markets. They are subject, of course, to the normal business rules applicable to such ventures.

Nevertheless, such service providers face difficult regulatory issues that can affect their ability to engage in their lines of business. Some information services have the capability to permit subscribers to execute transactions or facilitate subscriber-to-subscriber contacts as a key element of the service. Administrations can take differing positions as to whether a telecommunications or business service is being provided. And as described above, such services can become entangled in complex discussions—on the domestic front—about how they can interconnect with facilities providers.

There are additional issues when such services are offered internationally and use lines leased from carriers. The CCITT Recommendations are a benchmark of how to treat these services, but they are not necessarily subject to uniform interpretations from country-to-country. The CCITT process itself can be useful in developing guidelines for the structuring of new services. It is less helpful in actually implementing new network services.

The process of setting up global networks is complicated by the fact that each country has a different view toward publishing regulations for the use of leased lines and, indeed, toward making such services available. The Deutsche Bundespost has a rather complicated set of regulations; the French regulations are less detailed and contemplate some flexibility in the course of business dealings. Such flexibility can, of course, be useful in dealing with situations on an ad hoc basis, but it can frustrate long-range strategic planning.

There are, then, several problem areas with the current process. One difficulty is that the process of negotiating with a carrier or administration for an interconnection or use agreement can require disclosure of confidential business plans even before they have been implemented. Thus, users and service vendors have a series of concerns with respect to the confidentiality of their plans, trusting that an administration will not inadvertently disclose them to competitors. The confidentiality is particularly problematic where the administration itself is a potential competitor, seeking to supply a similar service.

Another area of critical concern is the need for greater "transparency" in the applicable regulations and restrictions. Concurrently, administrations may have to be more open to the notion of allowing new services to use leased lines or other telecommunications circuits. Hence, one inquiry for the future is how administrations can be more responsive to the demands for specialized communications services. Another is ascertaining how telecommunications-related regulations can be altered to prevent them from regulating, de facto, the structure of electronic markets.

A further challenge is to establish a clear demarcation between telecommunications-related regulation that affects electronic market activities and the regulation of other (*e.g.*, banking or information) activities per se. As the structure of electronic markets evolves, there may well be reason to consider questions of market access, standards, or bias. Regulating electronic markets ought not to be the province of telecommunications officials. By way of example, of course, some system protocol issues have generated discussions between the MPT and MITI in Japan precisely because it is difficult to differentiate between telecommunications- and service-related regulation.

The problem, in brief, is that activities of administrations that affect standards for services, *i.e.*, for the upper levels of the ISO protocol, can grow to become substantive regulation of non-telecommunications activities. A better dialogue between telecommunications and non-telecommunications regulators over their respective roles with respect to electronic information services will certainly be necessary. Such a dialogue may be most useful in a new—non-CCITT forum—given the complexity of new electronic services and the intimate relationship of telecommunications and non-telecommunications regulation to affect activities on a cross-sectoral basis.

V. Procedures and Fora for International Agreements

New international arrangements are needed for each of the international services described above—telephony, enhanced services, and new electronic services. The failure to reach an international consensus could lead to a period of prolonged disagreement, if not chaos. As described in the preceding section, a host of challenges face policymakers as they seek to respond to technology, user needs, ideological imperatives such as competition and privatization.

The principal challenge is defining the problems that are engendered by the immense changes that are occurring globally. The traditional study group procedures of the CCITT may not be entirely adequate for delineating and addressing these new and complicated issues. Hence, it may well be necessary to create and implement a new institutional framework to evolve a new foundation for providing international services.

It may become increasingly necessary to institute regular and direct contact among the highest level policymakers. Such contacts, whether formal or informal, do take place at present in several fora—at the OECD and at various international conferences. There presently exists, however, no high-level arena where the larger issues of specific concern can be discussed and addressed based on staff papers.

Implementing a new framework for international discussions will be difficult due to differences in the responsibilities of operational entities and public officials. In some European administrations, the operational, oversight, and political roles are effectively integrated in a single decisionmaker. Elsewhere, there is a fragmentation of operational entities and divided responsibilities on the governmental side, *e.g.*, among the FCC, NTIA, and the Department of State in the U.S. Moreover, for this process to work at all effectively, it is critical that users of communications services be included.

To facilitate the international policymaking process, there must be a steadier and more reliable international flow of information about developments worldwide. A regular exchange of critical documents—papers, studies, traffic forecasts, and statutes—will go a long way toward satisfying this need. Simultaneously, various administrations must share the responsibility for interpreting these materials.

It is possible that existing institutions might be useful to develop a framework for the international discussion that is envisioned. Some have proposed that the CCITT should establish a special policy committee to deal with important international policy issues. The OECD regularly offers a forum at the international level to discuss these issues. Participation in the OECD, however, is limited in some respects because it excludes certain key countries.

Before a multilateral forum can become entirely effective, a stepped-up level of bilateral or ad hoc multilateral discussion will be needed. Such discussions may be initiated as an outgrowth of trade pressures and may lay the groundwork for a broader, multilateral forum.

There are at least five areas where the need for international discussions is likely to intensify in the months and years ahead.

First, there must be a revitalization of discussions about transoceanic services and the future planning of cable and satellite facilities. Either the ITU or Intelsat must step into this role. These institutions, in particular, must encourage the U.S., the U.K., and Japan, which have attempted to coordinate their investments in the past with CEPT and others, to take an equally active role in the future. These discussions about international facilities planning must be undertaken without necessarily requiring the participants to compromise or revise their positions on the desirability of facilities investments that are independent of Intelsat.

A need closely related to the reinvigoration of discussions on international facilities planning is that for new leadership by the industrialized countries, which must explain to officials in the Third World the realities of the present and future telecommunications environments. A new and genuinely international dialogue must openly address how to deal with some of the consequences of any repricing of international services that may be necessary.

Second, a set of additional discussions about the process for establishing interconnection relationships in specific sectors—telephony, enhanced services, and new information services—is needed.

Third, a mechanism must be created for the two groups of officials who are responsible for overseeing telecommunications and non-telecommunications activities to talk with each other about the future of new electronic market services. In this connection, there must be an effort to segregate different areas of regulatory responsibility—those affecting the telecommunications infrastructure and those affecting the nature of the electronic services or markets.

Fourth, there must be new procedures and mechanisms for defining the issues and exploring emerging problem areas. Related to this task is the gathering of information so necessary to working toward consensus. Such institutional approaches must be taken seriously to avoid having complex issues resolved in the politically-sensitive, crisis atmosphere of bilateral trade negotiations.

Fifth, policymakers must work toward a new global understanding of what should be the basis of providing international services. Regional fora for discussions of some of these issues in Europe, for example, can contribute significantly to a much broader dialogue embracing Europe, the U.S., Canada, and Japan.

In a time of changes in policy and the role of institutions, institutional innovation to address the new environment in a comprehensive way is required at the international level. To innovate, however, necessitates a comprehensive understanding of current developments. To reach such an understanding, policymakers must collect information and begin a global dialogue. There is no time to delay.

CHAPTER III
UNITED STATES

TABLE OF CONTENTS

CHAPTER III
UNITED STATES

I. INTRODUCTION TO THE REGULATORY FRAMEWORK

A. Overview

1. Telecommunications in the United States has undergone a lengthy evolutionary process. The once limited communications market now offers many alternatives, in terms of carriers, services, and technologies. The change, while significant, is far from complete.

2. Throughout this dynamic period, the federal communications legislation—the Communications Act of 1934 (the "Communications Act" or the "Act")—barely has been changed. Numerous congressional attempts to adopt a new statute—or to update it—have failed for lack of support. Consequently, a complex mixture of federal and state actions—including regulation by administrative agencies, legislation, and court decisions—has been necessary to "stretch" the Act enough to accommodate new technologies and new regulatory objectives.

3. Some of the most difficult regulatory questions that the Federal Communications Commission (the "FCC" or the "Commission") must face are ones that might seem most basic. The FCC must define—and distinguish—"common carriers," "broadcasters," "cable operators," and "private radio" services. The Act offers little guidance, although this may be a reason for its durability and resilience. Consequently, the FCC has struggled to apply these old regulatory categories to new services or activities made possible by the merger of computer and communications systems and by advances in radio transmission technology. It also has refined the boundaries between "broadcasting" and "point-to-point" non-broadcast services, between "common carrier" mobile radio and functionally similar "private radio" services, and between direct broadcast satellite ("DBS") services and other functionally similar service arrangements.

4. This broad definitional concern has been the backdrop for two of the most dramatic and complex actions in the history of U.S. communications regulation. The restructuring of the telecommunications market into "regulated" and "unregulated" activities in a ten-year FCC proceeding was followed by the divestiture of the local Bell Operating Companies ("BOCs") from the rest of the Bell System (American Telephone & Telegraph Co.) ("AT&T") in settlement of a lengthy lawsuit.

a. In the first stage of this process, the FCC devised a new regulatory distinction between "basic" and "enhanced services." The distinction not only served as a principle for reorganizing the Bell System, but also as a way of establishing the texture of regulation and deregulation for an entire industry. The proceeding that produced the *Computer I* and *II* decisions constitutes a monumental effort by the FCC to divide regulated and unregulated activities. *See generally Regulatory and Policy Problems Presented by the Interdependence of Computer and Communications Services and Facilities*, 28 F.C.C.2d 267 (1971) (Final Decision and Order) [hereinafter cited as *Computer I*]; *Amendment of Section 64.702 of the Commission's Rules and Regulations*, 77 F.C.C.2d 384 (1980) (Final Decision) [hereinafter cited as *Computer II*]. The FCC traversed difficult terrain as it moved from an attempt to distinguish between data processing and communications—and hybrid combinations of the two—to a division between "basic" and "enhanced services." This regulatory battle was waged inside of an industry where rapidly advancing technology continually blurs the lines between communications and computer services.

b. Having drawn regulatory lines in the sand, the FCC has found it difficult to maintain them in the face of changing technological and economic arrangements. The AT&T divestiture has raised significant new questions that have prompted the FCC to begin a reevaluation of the fundamental principles of the *Computer II* decision. How do the distinctions apply to the equipment marketing activities and local value-added services of the new BOCs? How do the provisions in the court's consent decreee preventing the BOCs from providing "information services" restrict the new companies' abilities to offer "enhanced services?"

c. For AT&T, there is a more fundamental question about why it still must provide enhanced services through a separate subsidiary. The divestiture was designed to preclude AT&T from cross-subsidizing "competitive" (*i.e.*, enhanced) services with the profits from local monopoly exchange services. From AT&T's perspective, the divestiture and the separation requirements are unnecessarily duplicative. Thus, AT&T has asked the FCC to consider modifying or eliminating the separation requirement that it imposed just a few short years ago. The Commission has just begun to wrestle with this problem.

d. As this report was being finalized, the Commission plunged itself into a full–scale review of its *Computer II* policies by deciding to release a Notice of Proposed Rulemaking in "*Computer III*." *See* FCC Report No. DC-166, Mimeo No. 6022 (released July 25, 1985), which is discussed below, *see infra* Section IV.G. This proceeding obviously will have a major effect on the future regulation of "enhanced services" and on the way in which AT&T and the BOCs can compete in the market for these services.

5. The FCC's definitional scheme has been tested by the evolution of technology that permits advanced processing features to be incorporated into basic communications transmission and switching facilities. These pressures have largely affected only AT&T and the BOCs, which have been required to maintain separate facilities, separate personnel, and special separation requirements for the provision of basic and enhanced services. These separation requirements impose additional costs on the companies that, in turn, increase the price of services.

6. For most carriers, the distinctions have established simply a boundary line between unregulated and regulated activities. There are,

however, more difficult issues raised in the international context. These boundaries have caused concern among all carriers because the terms "enhanced" and "basic" are not part of the international regulatory experience. Consequently, service that is unregulated within the U.S. may or may not be treated similarly outside of the country.

7. The consent decree also has required the establishment of new boundaries affecting the scope of BOC activities. Under the decree, the BOCs are required to seek court permission to engage in business outside of their exchange areas or unrelated to the provision of local exchange service. Since the effective date of the divestiture, this process has required unprecedented judicial involvement.

8. Regulatory attention during this period has been devoted particularly to establishing new, competitive economic and technical arrangements among the BOCs, AT&T, and specialized common carriers. Consideration of the mechanism for compensating carriers for gaining access to their local exchanges has produced sharp controversy. It has required a massive restructuring of local and interexchange service rates. This process represents the last step in a decade-long effort to align the prices of competitive and interexchange services more closely with costs. It also is a step toward determining whether—and to what extent—there will be competition in the provision of local exchange services. As the costs of local facilities use are reallocated among local and long-distance users, the economic incentive for the supply of alternatives to the local exchange will change. Local service competition already has raised other important definitional questions, such as when a two-way service provided by a cable television operator constitutes the provision of a regulated telecommunication service.

9. The changes in the structure of the U.S. telecommunications industry also have had effects beyond national borders. New competitors have emerged in the international record and switched voice services markets and have pressured the FCC to overhaul certain existing practices. Both new and established carriers—as well as users of international telecommunications service—have urged a restructuring of arrangments for obtaining international satellite services. They would like greater flexibility to provide alternative ground transmission connections. Ultimately, they also want to have the option of gaining direct access to Intelsat's services; they have sought elimination of the requirement that all access be provided through Comsat. As competitors have sought a greater role in providing basic international satellite transmission services, Comsat has attempted to increase its position in the resale side of the industry. The result has been a range of proposals to restructure Comsat into "wholesale" and "retail" entities and to reformulate basic inter-industry relationships.

10. Adding to the complexity of this restructuring is the challenge of new entrants who are seeking to compete with Intelsat. This development has been provoked, in part, by advances in satellite technology that allow "domestic" satellites to use "spot beams" to provide transborder

service. The development of fiber optic technology has also opened the possibility for new, high capacity cable systems to compete directly with Intelsat's satellite links. The deregulation of earth stations, which has made it attractive for businesses to install rooftop dishes, has stimulated demand in this market even further.

11. Recent regulatory developments in the U.S.—in the domestic and international sectors—are so complex and are moving so quickly that they make brief description virtually impossible. We have tried, in the discussion below, to capture much of this detail by focusing closely on major definitional controversies, the evolution of the "basic" and "enhanced" distinction, and the effect of the AT&T divestiture. We also have looked carefully at how all of the restructuring of the domestic market has caused many new tensions in the oversight of international telecommunications.

B. The Regulatory Framework: Classification by Type of Transmission

1. Introduction

The Communications Act gives the FCC regulatory power over all "interstate and foreign communication by wire or radio." 47 U.S.C. § 152(a) (1983). This general grant of power is divided into three regulatory regimes, covering common carriers, broadcasters, and—as of November, 1984—cable television operators. The Act is codified at Title 47 of the United States Code ("U.S.C."). The FCC's rules and regulations, which are promulgated under authority of the Act, are compiled in Title 47 of the Code of Federal Regulations ("C.F.R.").

a. This regulatory framework (excluding, for now, the new cable television provisions) was based upon what Congress, in 1934, viewed as the needs of the communications market. Common carriers were the monopoly telephone and telegraph operators; regulating them meant restricting the abuse of market power. This job required rate restrictions (to prevent excessive profits) and an assurance that all users would be served. In the broadcasting area—at that time radio—Congress sought to ensure the maximum use, free of interference, of the scarce electromagnetic spectrum. Congress, therefore, adopted a licensing system under which broadcast frequencies are licensed to individual operators for a term of years. The licensees are obliged to serve the non-licensed public by providing programs and services of interest to the public.

b. Section 2(b)(1) of the 1934 Act reserves for the states the exclusive power to regulate the "intrastate communication service by wire or radio of any carrier." 47 U.S.C. § 152(b)(1) (1983). This division of authority is consistent with the federalist scheme of government in the U.S. Under the Constitution, the federal government is given the exclusive power to regulate interstate commerce (which includes interstate communications). U.S. Const., art. I, § 8, cl. 3. Power over intrastate commerce (*e.g.*, intrastate communications) is not specifically delegated to the federal government; therefore, it is retained by the states. *See* U.S. Const., amend. X.

i) This arrangement essentially has left states with the job of regulating local telephone services (*i.e.*, intrastate common carriers). However, the increasing complexity of configurations has provoked significant debate about precisely what a "carrier" is and when its service is purely "intrastate."

ii) By arguing that a "local" communications service is inseparably intertwined with the interstate communications network, the FCC often has been able to assert regulatory power over that service (preempting state authority). (Under the U.S. Constitution, a federal law or policy properly adopted by the federal government prevails over a conflicting state law or regulation. U.S. Const., art. VI, cl. 2.) The FCC has argued that without this preemptive power, its policies encouraging the growth of diverse interstate communications networks would be frustrated by restrictive state actions. *See, e.g., Preemption of State Entry Regulation in the Public Land Mobile Service*, FCC No. 85-147 (reelased May 17, 1985) (Notice of Proposed Rulemaking).

iii) States, by contrast, have sought to segregate interstate and local components of a service in order to retain jurisdiction over "purely" local elements. *See, e.g., North Carolina Utility Commission v. FCC*, 537 F.2d 787 (4th Cir. 1976); *see also infra* Section VI.E.

iv) The FCC and the states also have battled over the definition of a common carrier. The FCC's authority is limited only with respect to intrastate "common carriers"—not to other types of "non-carrier" service providers. A circular statutory definition of the term "common carrier," combined with an antiquated judicial interpretation of it, have made this ongoing jurisdictional dispute particularly perplexing. *See, e.g., National Association of Regulatory Utility Commissioners v. FCC*, 525 F.2d 630 (D.C. Cir. 1976), *cert. denied*, 425 U.S. 992 (1977) (*NARUC I*); 533 F.2d 601 (D.C. Cir. 1976) (*NARUC II*); *see also infra* Section VI.E.

c. All Commission actions are supposed to uphold the public interest, convenience, and necessity. *See, e.g.*, 47 U.S.C. §§ 214 & 302 (1983). Its regulatory "mission" is "to make available, so far as possible, to all the people of the United States a rapid, efficient, nation-wide, and world-wide wire and radio communication service with adequate facilities at reasonable charges, . . ." 47 U.S.C. § 151 (1983).

2. *Common Carriers*

a. Title II of the Communications Act, 47 U.S.C. §§ 201-224 (1983), contains the FCC's authority to regulate common carriers. It was designed to ensure that the FCC could exercise effective regulatory control over AT&T. In 1934, this job essentially meant regulating the company's operation as a monopoly.

b. As noted above, determining precisely who is a common carrier has provoked both continuing scholarly debate and frequent litigation. According to the Communications Act, a common carrier is "any person who engages as a common carrier for hire." 47 U.S.C. § 153(h) (1983). The courts, applying common law concepts of common carriage (from the transportation field), have defined a common carrier to be one who holds itself out to the public for hire to transmit communications of the user's choosing. *See NARUC I*, 525 F.2d at 640-42.

c. In 1982, Congress further complicated the definition of a "common carrier" with legislation designed to clarify the FCC's jurisdiction over Specialized Mobile Radio Services ("SMRS").

i) The FCC had decided that private mobile radio services (which include SMRS) should be free of Title II regulations—to promote the growth of those services. In addition, the FCC had preempted the states from imposing certification requirements on SMRS. In *NARUC I, supra*, the court upheld this preemption. It ruled that SMRS operators would not be common carriers, since they were not likely to hold their services out to the public on an indiscriminate basis. FCC preemption, therefore, was proper; the states have power only over "carriers." 47 U.S.C. § 152(b)(1) (1983).

ii) Congress amended the Communications Act in 1982 to make clear that mobile radio services (including SMRS) are not common carriers—even if they hold their services out to the public indiscriminately. Communications Amendments Act of 1982, Pub. L. No. 97-259, § 120(a), 96 Stat. 1082, 1096-97 (1982) (codified at 47 U.S.C. § 332(c)(1) (1983)). Under § 332(c)(1)(A), Congress allowed a private mobile radio service to connect with exchange or interexchange telephone facilities without becoming a common carrier. Only if that connection were used to resell telephone services or telephone company facilities for a profit would the service provider become a common carrier. In the event of such resale, a service provider would be "engaged functionally in the provision of telephone service or facilities of a common carrier. . . ." H.R. Conf. Rep. No. 765, 97th Cong. 2d Sess. 55, *reprinted in* 1982 U.S. Code Cong. & Ad. News 2261, 2299. What Congress did was adopt a functional definition of the term "common carrier" that superseded the *NARUC I* definition in the case of mobile radio services. *See also Interconnection of Private Land Mobile Radio Systems With the Public Switched Telephone Network*, 93 F.C.C.2d 1111, 1115 (1983).

d. Under Title II, carriers must file just, reasonable, and non-discriminatory rates and terms for their services. The FCC determines the lawfulness of any tariff or service practice. It also must give prior approval to any carrier's plan to construct a new facility or to discontinue an existing service. Approval requires an application for a certificate of public convenience and necessity (or a finding that discontinuance of a service will not harm the public interest). Title II also empowers the Commission to impose rate of return and rate base regulation on carriers.

e. Although common carrier regulation has changed a great deal since 1934, Title II itself has remained virtually unchanged. A combination of FCC and court decisions has permitted Title II to accommodate recent deregulatory actions.

3. *Broadcasters*

a. Title III of the Communications Act, 47 U.S.C. §§ 301-399b (1983), gives the FCC its power over broadcasters. A major part of the Commission's responsibility is to prevent interference by allocating spectrum space to particular broadcasters. Over time, the FCC's jurisdiction has evolved to a point where it actively oversees the broadcast marketplace to ensure that individual licensees are serving the "public interest." There have been periodic attempts to restrict the FCC's scrutiny of broadcast activities. These efforts only recently have begun to meet with success, but mostly because a "deregulatory" FCC has begun to eliminate many of its own broadcast regulations.

b. The Act defines broadcasting to be the "dissemination of radio communications intended to be received by the public, directly or by the intermediary of relay stations." 47 U.S.C. § 153(o) (1983).

i) This definition contrasts both with the definition of common carriage and with the concept of point-to-point services, in which communications are distributed only to one or more specified receiving points. The Act specifically distinguishes broadcasting from common carriage, providing that "a person engaged in radio broadcasting shall not, . . . , be deemed a common carrier." 47 U.S.C. § 153(h) (1983).

ii) This definition has caused problems in efforts to regulate subscription delivery services. In 1958, the U.S. Court of Appeals for the District of Columbia Circuit ("D.C. Circuit") ruled that a subscription music service was broadcasting within the meaning of § 153(o). *Functional Music, Inc. v. FCC*, 274 F.2d 543 (D.C. Cir. 1958), *cert. denied*, 361 U.S. 813 (1959). The court decided that because the service was of interest to the *general* public, it was broadcasting; the fact that special equipment was necessary to receive the service was not considered important. The broadcaster's intent—that as many members of the public as possible subscribe to the service—was deemed dispositive.

iii) Subscription television ("STV") services, which also usually appeal to the general public, have been regulated by the FCC as broadcasting services. STV typically involves the transmission of an encoded signal that can be decoded only by subscribers who pay a fee for special receiving equipment. (Without a decoder, one sees only an unintelligible television picture.) STV arguably is not "intended to be received by the public"; it is intended only for those individuals who have purchased decoders. A number of courts have accepted this argument and have ruled that STV is not "broadcasting," as that term is used in § 705 of the Communications Act, which prohibits the unauthorized interception of radio communications that are not "broadcast" or are not intended for reception by "the general public." *See, e.g., Chartwell Communications Group v. Westbrook*, 637 F.2d 459 (6th Cir. 1980). While noting that the FCC regulates STV as broadcasting, these courts have decided that STV is not really broadcasting—for purposes of Section 705.

c. Title III requires broadcasters to hold their licenses in trust for the public; they are obliged to serve their community of license. (A broadcast "channel" essentially is licensed in a particular community; the same channel can be licensed around the country, in communities spaced far enough apart to avoid interference. The number of stations licensed in a particular community will depend upon viewer demand and interference from nearby stations. Many communities have at least three local stations, and viewers often can receive the signals of other, nearby stations.) This licensing scheme has created a system of "local broadcasting" in which licensees are obligated to provide at least some programming specifically of interest to their local viewers. Recent deregulatory moves, plus the growth of domestic satellite technology, have enhanced national transmission capabilities and diminished the emphasis on "localism." Although broadcasters continue to provide at least some local news and public affairs programming, most programming is carried nationally. Many television stations are affiliated with one of the three national programming networks—ABC, CBS, and NBC; these affiliates rely heavily on network-supplied programs. Independent (unaffiliated) stations provide mostly programming that is nationally syndicated, consisting mainly of old network shows that are sold by independent distributors.

d. Title III directs the Commission to promote a diverse array of broadcast communications. Accordingly, the FCC restricts the multiple ownership of broadcast stations and the cross-ownership of these stations by owners of other communications media. It also enforces the "Fairness Doctrine," which requires that broadcast licensees cover both sides of controversial issues of local importance. In conjunction with the Fairness Doctrine, licensees must provide political candidates with equal access to their stations on reasonable terms and must allow individuals who are attacked by a broadcast to respond.

4. *Private Radio*

The FCC has developed a specific regulatory regime for radio spectrum users who are neither broadcasters nor common carriers. These regulations are intended primarily to allocate frequencies and to control interference. Particular frequency bands are reserved for particular uses; consequently, applications for a specific use must compete for the limited number of licenses in the relevant frequency band. The Commission has defined private radio services generally to include "nationwide and international uses of radio by persons, businesses, state and local governments, and other organizations licensed to operate their own communications systems for their use as an adjunct of their primary business or other activity." 47 C.F.R. § 0.131 (1984); *see also supra* Section I.B.2. (discussing private mobile radio services).

5. *Cable Television*

a. Like private radio, cable television is a transmission system that is neither broadcasting nor common carriage—although it has some characteristics of both services. Consequently, cable communications does not fit neatly within either of the FCC's major regulatory models. During cable's early development, in the 1950s, the FCC claimed that the Communications Act did not provide it with jurisdiction over cable. In the 1960s, however, it began to regulate cable, as part of its power over interstate wire or radio communications. It justified its action as necessary to ensure that cable would not compete unfairly with free broadcast television. In 1968, the U.S. Supreme Court upheld the Commission's regulation of cable to the degree that its actions were "reasonably ancillary to the effective performance of the Commission's responsibilities for the regulation of television broadcasting." *United States v. Southwestern Cable Co.*, 392 U.S. 157, 178 (1968).

b. In the 1970s, the FCC, with the consent of the courts, vigorously expanded its regulation of cable television. However, the FCC always left to state and local authorities the task of selecting the individual franchisees who would be permitted to string their cables under local streets or along utility poles. The award, and the terms, of these franchises were left to local discretion, subject to certain federal restrictions intended to protect cable operators from excessive local restrictions, particularly those regarding program selection. The relationship between the FCC and state and local franchising authorities remains a subject of contention—and litigation. *See, e.g., infra* Section VI.E.

c. The Commission eliminated virtually all federal cable regulations by the end of 1980. The courts, and then the FCC, had concluded that marketplace conditions did not justify the imposition of most regulations. Competition eventually was seen as the best way to ensure that cable television served the public interest. *See Geller v. FCC*, 610 F.2d 973 (D.C. Cir. 1979); *Cable Television Syndicated Program Exclusivity Rules*, 79 F.C.C.2d 663 (1980), *aff'd sub nom. Malrite T.V. v. FCC*, 652 F.2d 1140 (2d Cir.), *cert. denied sub nom. National Ass'n of Broadcasters v. FCC*, 454 U.S. 1153 (1982).

d. State and local authorities filled the regulatory void left by the FCC and imposed new restrictions on cable systems. Periodically, the FCC stepped in to assert that its power over cable, although not being used, preempted state authority to regulate in certain areas. In 1984, despite the fact that there was still no federal legislation expressly giving the FCC jurisdiction over cable, the Supreme Court upheld a broad, exclusive scope of FCC power over cable. *Captial Cities Cable, Inc. v. Crisp*, ____ U.S. ____, 104 S. Ct. 2694 (1984).

e. A short time after that decision, after having failed for three years, Congress finally enacted comprehensive federal cable legislation. Cable Communications Policy Act of 1984, Pub. L. No. 98-549, 98 Stat. 2779 (1984) (codified at 47 U.S.C. §§ 601-40 and scattered sections of Title 47). This legislation, which created a new Title VI, explicitly gave the FCC exclusive jurisdiction over cable television, except to the degree that Title VI specifically reserved certain powers for states and localities (particularly in the area of franchising). Unfortunately, the Act did not completely clarify the relationship between federal, state, and local power over cable. *See, e.g., infra* Section VI.E. Some have argued that the Supreme Court's decision in *Capital Cities*, if read most broadly, gave the FCC more power over cable than it got from the legislation; however, the legislative grant of authority would appear to be more certain.

C. Hybrid Regulation: The Problems of Putting New Wine in Old Bottles

1. With the development of new transmission media, the FCC has found it difficult to fit certain systems within the established regulatory categories. Therefore, it has in recent years adopted a flexible regulatory approach under which new media are permitted to evolve relatively free of regulation. To the degree that they adopt specific characteristics of broadcasting or common carriage, they may be subjected to some—or all—of the requirements of Titles II or III. (New Title VI, covering cable television, has not yet evolved into a general regulatory model.)

2. As noted above, *see supra* Section I.B.3., subscription services have combined characteristics of broadcasting with elements of point-to-point communications. When delivered over the air, they are regulated either like a broadcast service (STV), or like a common carrier ("MDS," or microwave distribution service). If delivered by a cable system, they are considered a cable television service (and are called pay-cable). When delivered directly to subscribers from a satellite ("DBS," or direct broadcast satellite), they may be considered either a common carrier service (if the satellite operator allows third parties to provide programming), or broadcasting (if the satellite operator selects its own programming).

3. A relatively new service, multichannel MDS ("MMDS"), is a subscription service that is regulated as a common carrier, distributes an over-the-air signal and may select some of its own programming (like a broadcaster), and uses radio frequencies assigned to private radio services. To make matters worse, it commonly is referred to as "wireless cable." The FCC has indicated an intent to consider changing its regulatory treatment of MMDS. *See Amendment of Parts 2, 21, 74 and 94 of the Commission's Rules and Regulations in Regard to Frequency Allocation to the Instructional Television Fixed Service, Multipoint Distribution Service, and the Private Operational Fixed Microwave Service*, 50 Fed. Reg. 5983, 5985-86, n.17 (Feb. 13, 1985).

4. The FCC's discretion to tailor regulatory models to the technological characteristics of a new medium may be limited. A D.C. Circuit decision ruled that DBS is broadcasting—regardless of who programs the service—and that, therefore, it must be regulated under Title III of the Communications Act. *National Association of Broadcasters v. FCC,* 740 F.2d 1190 (D.C. Cir. 1984). The FCC had proposed a flexible regulatory approach. A satellite operator making its facilities available to third parties would be regulated as a common carrier under Title II. The operator's customers, who could provide either a portion of the programming or all of it, would not be regulated. The court concluded that because DBS was broadcasting the service had to be regulated under Title III. Thus, either the satellite operator or its programmer-customers had to abide by the requirements of Title III.

a. The court's decision assumes that DBS will provide a mass-appeal service—much like today's subscription television—that is intended to be received by the general public. This assumption, however, ignores the possibility that DBS might be used to provide specialized communications services. Such services would not be intended for the general public, and, according to the D.C. Circuit, would not be broadcasting. *Cf. Functional Music, Inc. v. FCC,* 274 F.2d 543 (D.C. Cir. 1958), *cert. denied,* 361 U.S. 813 (1959). Such services *could* be received by the general public; however, many, or most, viewers would not *want* to receive them. This fact should place them outside of the reasoning of *Functional Music.*

b. The danger of the court's decision is that it may use an outdated regulatory scheme to restrict the variety of new services made possible by technological change. To the degree that this decision impedes future FCC efforts to regulate new services flexibly, it may emphasize the need for a substantial revision of the Communications Act.

5. This decision could have an impact on other services that transmit point-to-point or subscription communications by means of a broadcast technology. A problem in applying the statute to such services is that Congress, in 1934, did not contemplate the possibility that a "broadcaster" might use a common carrier's facilities to communicate directly with the public (*i.e.,* engage in "broadcasting"). Thus, a "customer-user" of a common carrier facility has not traditionally been regulated; the carrier itself has been regulated under Title II.

a. The FCC has authorized radio and television licensees to use their carrier signals for both non-broadcast and subscription broadcast purposes. *See, e.g., Amendment of Parts 2 and 73 of the Commission's Rule Concerning Use of Subsidiary Communications Authorization,* 53 Rad. Reg. 2d (P&F) 1519 (1983). The Commission determined that when providing a non-broadcast service (such as one-way paging or private radio communication), the broadcast licensee either will have to seek common carrier certification or will have to notify the FCC of its intention to provide a private radio service. The proper regulatory regime will depend upon the use being made of the subcarrier. If the subcarrier is being leased to a third party, either the service provider (lessee) or the licensee (lessor) must comply with any relevant regulatory requirements. Thus, the fact that a "broadcast" technology is being used to provide a common carrier or private radio service is not viewed as an obstacle to imposing Title II, or private radio, regulation on the service.

b. However, FCC rules also say that if the broadcaster allows one or more third parties to provide a subscription service over its subcarrier, the service will not be regulated as broadcasting. The decision in *National Association of Broadcasters, supra,* may forbid this result. If, for example, a subcarrier were leased to a third party who intended to provide a data service that could be received by any properly equipped personal computer, it might, under the court's rationale, have to be regulated as a broadcast service (just like DBS). The fact that the broadcast licensee is not providing the content of the communication being transmitted in the subcarrier would not persuade the D.C. Circuit that the service is not broadcasting. Licensees could, under such a regime, evade Title III requirements by leasing—and programming—the subcarrier of another licensee's station, rather than of their own. (The court objected to this kind of an arrangement in its decision.) Title III literally applies only to licensees, and because the lessee-programmer is only a "customer-user," it does not fall within the literal language of Title III. The court has concluded, however, that such a result would contravene the intent of the Communications Act.

c. The D.C. Circuit's reasoning has a potentially expansive application that could—in the extreme—destroy the FCC's approach to regulating new media. In the FCC's view, it is unfair to impose a rigid set of statutory obligations on the many new services now being introduced. Regulating a service as a common carrier or broadcaster might unduly restrict its potential to provide innovative service arrangements that are responsive to evolving user needs.

d. The FCC also has applied the regulatory model used for subcarriers to services transmitting data in the vertical blanking interval ("VBI") of a television signal. *See Amendment of Parts 2, 73 and 76 of the Commission's Rules to Authorize the Offering of Data Transmission Services on the Vertical Blanking Interval by TV Stations,* FCC No. 84-530 (Jan. 24, 1985). A similar service, raising the same regulatory questions, would use the sideband of a satellite transmission to carry data that could be received by properly equipped personal computers.

e. This "labelling" process is further complicated by the fact that the FCC views its policies regarding any use of a broadcast medium—even to provide a common carrier service—as being part of its Title III authority. On this basis, the FCC has moved to preempt state regulation of those common carrier offerings. The Commission's argument is that such state regulation "frustrates the realization of our Title III licensing policies . . . ." *Preemption of State Entry Regulation in the Public Land Mobile Service,* FCC No. 85-147, at 4 & n.4 (released May 17, 1985).

D. Sources of Regulation in Addition to the FCC

As the preceeding discussion has suggested, telecommunications law and policy in the United States involves a complex combination of state, federal, and local authorities. There is no precise division of authority. This section offers a brief overview of some of the many participants in this regulatory process. Rather than attempting an exhaustive treatment of the subject, it provides a basic description of the major sources of law and regulation.

1. Congress

a. Congress, which created the FCC and adopted the Communications Act, can alter communications law and policy either by adopting new legislation or by exercising its power over the FCC. Although the FCC is considered an "independent" regulatory agency, it is subject to congressional oversight. Congress, which controls the FCC's budget, can have a very persuasive impact on the Commission's decisionmaking process. Since 1981 the FCC has lacked a permanent annual grant of funds; each year Congress is free to decide how much money it will provide to the FCC—and on what conditions. These appropriations are contained in legislation, to which congressmen can attach amendments to the Communications Act that otherwise might be difficult to push through the legislature. Congress also can affect regulatory actions by placing restrictions on the use of various appropriations or by instructing the FCC to use certain money in a particular way.

b. Occasionally, Congress will pass legislation to override an unfavorable FCC decision. More often, Congress will schedule hearings on controversial topics that are before the FCC in an attempt to delay Commission action or to influence the direction of any anticipated action. In addition, Congress can use the threat of legislation to sway the Commission, as it has done on a number of occasions, particularly in the past two years. As noted above, Congress has recently sought to adopt a comprehensive piece of legislation that would replace virtually all of the Communications Act with a new, updated set of laws. This effort has failed, however, and Congress has relied instead on piecemeal amendments to the Act that have encouraged deregulation gradually.

c. Individual Congressmen also may meet with FCC commissioners—or write letters to them—to express their support of, or opposition to, a particular course of action so long as the FCC is acting in its "legislative," as opposed to its "judicial," role. (When the FCC adjudicates controversies over licenses or between particular parties, it acts in a court-like capacity. The Commission's ex parte rules bar any contacts by the public or by public officials concerning a pending case in such a situation.) When these Congressmen serve on either the House or Senate Appropriations Committees, which control the Commission's purse strings, or on one of the "substantive law" committees responsible for communications legislation (such as the House Energy and Commerce Committee), their opinions may have a particularly persuasive effect on the FCC.

2. *Federal Courts*

a. A party to a proceeding (or a person with an interest affected by the outcome of a proceeding) may appeal an FCC decision to the U.S. Court of Appeals. Most often, the court's D.C. Circuit, which, like the administrative agencies, is located in the District of Columbia, will review FCC decisions.

b. Under the Administrative Procedure Act which, in part, establishes the standards for judicial review of federal administrative agency decisions, the courts are supposed to pay some deference to agency judgments. *See* 5 U.S.C. § 706 (1983). Agencies are considered to have substantial expertise in their particular fields of regulation. In reviewing an agency decision, a court is supposed to decide whether the agency has acted within its delegated authority and on the basis of a reasoned consideration of the evidence before it. *Id.* The Supreme Court has, from time to time, scolded lower courts for attempting to substitute their own judgment for the judgment of an agency. *See, e.g., Vermont Nuclear Power Corp. v. Natural Resources Defense Council, Inc.*, 435 U.S. 519, 557-58 (1978) ("Administrative decisions should be set aside . . . only for substantial procedural or substantive reasons as mandated by statute, not simply because the court is unhappy with the result reached.") Nonetheless, a court often can disguise its displeasure as an objection to an agency's decisionmaking process or to a misuse of delegated authority. Such a decision probably would withstand review by the Supreme Court.

c. The debate over the proper role of the courts in reviewing agency decisions is a continuing one. The argument against searching judicial review is that it permits activist judges to set policies—a function that Congress has delegated, by statute, to the discretion of an independent agency. In recent years, the trend toward ensuring that courts take a "hard look" at agency decisions has been undercut somewhat—in response to complaints that judges are usurping the decisionmaking powers of the agencies. Proponents of this "hard look" approach contend that courts must look carefully to ensure that agencies do not disregard the rights of individuals.

3. *Judge Greene and the Justice Department*

a. A consent decree entered in settlement of an antitrust suit against AT&T has added a new policymaking apparatus to the communications field. (The consent decree is discussed at length below, *see supra* Section III.) Judge Harold H. Greene, who presided over the AT&T case, has continued to enforce various provisions of the consent decree and to oversee the divestiture of AT&T's local telephone companies, which was required by the decree.

b. The Justice Department reviews the requests of the divested local operating companies to enter businesses other than local telephone service. It recommends that Judge Greene either approve or deny the requests. (Under the terms of the decree, the companies must have court approval to diversify.)

c. Judge Greene's continuing role in managing the affairs of the nation's dominant common carriers—AT&T and the local companies—has generated a great deal of controversy. Members of Congress, officials in the Executive Branch, and people at the FCC have questioned the propriety of this judicial foray into communications policymaking. While the decree itself may have been a proper way for a court to enforce the antitrust laws, the continuing involvement raises difficult questions about the relationship of the court and the FCC in setting national telecommunications policy. Nonetheless, Judge Greene routinely uses his enforcement powers to issue important decisions that affect the shape of competition in the telecommunications market; he even includes an occasional criticism of an FCC action that he views as contrary to the policies he incorporated into the consent decree. The Justice Department's participation has been subject to similar criticism. In part, many people see this process as a detrimental fragmentation of the national policymaking authority in the communications area. To the extent that the FCC and Judge Greene are acting incongruously, the direction of future policies can be clouded.

4. Executive Branch

a. The Commerce Department, through the National Telecommunications and Information Administration ("NTIA"), exercises a policymaking role in the communications area. The NTIA, which was once a part of the White House, conducts broad policy investigations into various areas of the communications business.

b. When international issues are involved, the State Department, which has its own communications policymaking unit, also becomes involved. (The State Department's communications activities recently were consolidated into a single office, the Bureau of International Communications and Information Policy.) Consequently, international communications issues can provoke a conflict between the Departments of State and Commerce. Such a conflict occurred recently, during the debate over whether the United States should authorize private international satellite systems. *See infra* Section IX. There has been some discussion of consolidating the policy responsibilities of the two departments into a single coordinating office, to avoid future conflicts. However, differences of view over the location of such a coordinating office—under the supervision of a particular department or in the Office of the President—has stalled any progress on the plan.

c. Ultimately, all executive authority resides in the President, who is advised by the members of his Cabinet, as well as by members of his White House staff. With respect to communications issues, the Secretaries of Commerce and State provide the most direct Cabinet advice. The Defense Department, and the Secretary of Defense, also may have significant input into any policy decisions that could affect national security or defense.

5. *States*

a. As discussed above, states have exclusive control of intrastate telephone services. This control is exercised by state utility commissions, which are regulatory agencies set up by state legislatures (similar to the way in which Congress established the FCC). A number of states also have established cable television agencies, which set statewide policies regarding franchising processes and other local aspects of cable television operation. Local authorities such as city councils or county boards frequently conduct the actual cable franchising process.

b. State courts will review decisions of these state agencies just as the federal courts review decisions by the FCC. The United States Supreme Court ultimately may review a state court decision that raises issues of federal law; otherwise, the decision of the supreme court of the particular state will be final.

c. State legislatures adopt laws regarding intrastate communications services and determine the powers of state regulatory agencies. In this regard, they function much like Congress. However, because the scope of federal power over communications is so broad, and because it preempts so much of the legislative authority concerning communications, state legislatures are left to act in a relatively small area of the market. They deal primarily with local telephone issues and with other problems of the communications business that raise peculiarly local concerns. Where these legislative actions are seen as an impediment to federal policies regarding interstate communications, they are likely to be struck down by a federal court. *See generally supra* Section I.B.

II. DEREGULATION THROUGH STRUCTURAL REMEDIES: DISMANTLING THE BELL SYSTEM

A. Overview and Background

1. *Perspective on the Divestiture*

The restructuring of the nation's telephone system that took place on January 1, 1984, when the Bell System divested its local telephone operating companies, closed a chapter in the ongoing effort to separate the competitive interexchange market from the monopolistic local market. Before the 1950s, there was little concern about such disaggregation because the competitive potential in either market was insignificant.

Chiefly as a result of technological advancement, however, the possibility of competitive interexchange service began to develop over the last twenty to thirty years.

a. The development of this competitive marketplace produced a problem in market structure that the FCC previously had not confronted. For the first time, there was a single entity—AT&T—that operated in both monopolistic and competitive service arenas—the local exchange and interexchange markets, respectively. The potential for AT&T to use its market power in the local exchange market to impede—or to prevent—competition in the interexchange market required the FCC to devise a mechanism for monitoring and, if necessary, preventing this kind of anticompetitive conduct.

b. The FCC's regulatory efforts, ultimately, were not thought to be an adequate safeguard against the possibility that AT&T would stifle marketplace competition. There was a perception that competition was evolving too slowly in the interexchange marketplace and that the reason for the delay was AT&T's continued control of the majority of the nation's local exchange facilities.

c. Using the antitrust laws, the government was able to pursue a solution that it believed would enhance competition. The government alleged a classic antitrust claim—that AT&T was using its dominance in one market (local exchange) to restrain competition in another (interexchange). Because AT&T had control over monopoly local exchange facilities, it could provide only its own long-distance lines with access to local subscriber loops. Divestiture was designed to end AT&T's ability to restrict access in this way—as well as to prevent other allegedly anticompetitive practices.

d. Perhaps the most remarkable aspect of the divestiture is that it has enabled a federal district court judge to restructure the telecommunications industry so radically. The shape of AT&T significantly affects the kinds of regulatory policies that the government will apply to the communications industry.

i) Through his review of the consent decree, his prescription of various modifications, and his continuing oversight of AT&T and of the local operating companies—with the Justice Department's help—Judge Greene has as much—or more—influence over the communications business as the Congress, the FCC, or any other governmental entity. There are conflicting appraisals of the wisdom of specific aspects of the divestiture.

ii) There also is a fundamental debate about the effect that this process has had on the communications policymaking process in the United States. In the view of some, including the powerful Chairman of the House Energy and Commerce Committee, Rep. John Dingell (D-Mich.), Judge Greene and the Justice Department have inexcusably usurped policymaking authority from the FCC. While divestiture may have been a proper way of resolving an antitrust lawsuit, the continuing oversight authority being exercised has placed the court, the Congress, the FCC, and the Justice Department in a series of potentially adversary relationships. It also has generated a great deal of controversy over whether the court has overstepped its judicial role and has assumed the guise of a quasi-regulatory agency. *See infra* Section II.D.7.

iii) A vital future issue is deciding how best to resolve this split of authority. Resolution may result in removing Judge Greene and the Justice Department from the day-to-day regulatory process. Such a move, however, could provoke a heated discussion of the respective roles of the courts, the FCC, and the Congress in developing national telecommunication policy.

2. *A Brief Early History*

a. So long as wires were the only practical transmission path for point-to-point communications, the Bell System was able to control the telephone marketplace. During the late 1800s, Bell used its patents on telephone technology to control the development of the nation's telephone system. When those patents expired, in 1893, Bell prohibited developing independent telephone companies from interconnecting with its network. This practice enabled Bell to consolidate and to expand its dominance of the nation's telephone service.

b. Competitive service was available to only a very limited degree. Independent telephone companies typically evolved in less populous areas of the country, where AT&T had not constructed facilities. Nonetheless, the industry's growth was remarkable around the turn of the century. In 1892, seventeen years after the start of telephone communication, there were 266,431 telephones operating—all of them owned by Bell. Just ten years later, Bell had 1,317,178 operating telephones, and independent companies owned 1,053,866. Gabel, *The Early Competitive Era in Telephone Communication, 1893-1920,* 34 L. & Contemp. Probs. 340, 344 (1969). During this time, rates declined dramatically, making telephone service more widely available.

c. At the start of this century, AT&T's growth became both a benefit and a threat to the telephone industry. For more than twenty years, the government and the independent telephone companies alternately supported, and then restricted, AT&T's growth.

i) In the early 1900s, AT&T changed its strategy for growth. It relied less on adding new telephones and lines and looked more toward buying existing independent systems. This allowed AT&T to expand while simultaneously eliminating its competition. In addition, this acquisition process avoided the inefficient duplication of facilities. The most remarkable of AT&T's acquisitions during this time was its purchase of the Western Union Telegraph Co., which gave it a true market presence in both telephone and telegraph services.

ii) These purchases, and the company's allegedly anticompetitive practices, brought about an increase in allegations of antitrust law violations. In 1913, the company agreed to a proposal by the U.S. attorney general that it not acquire any other competing companies and that it permit competitors to interconnect equipment meeting AT&T specifications with the company's network. This agreement was known as the Kingsbury Commitment, named after the president of AT&T at the time.

iii) Shortly after this agreement, AT&T divested itself of Western Union.

iv) Although AT&T continued to acquire noncompeting companies, competitors found that the Kingsbury Commitment prevented them from selling their assets to the one buyer capable of paying a fair price. In response, Congress adopted the Willis-Graham Act of 1921, which terminated the Kingsbury Commitment. Thereafter, AT&T resumed its aggressive acquisitions. A year later, amid growing concern over AT&T's renewed comsumptive vigor, the company agreed with the U.S. Independent Telephone Association that it would not make any further acquisitions "unless demanded for the convenience of the public or unless special reasons existed making the transaction desirable for the protection of the general public service or Bell System property." 2 FCC, Telephone Investigation 158 (1938) (Proposed Report), *quoted in* Gabel, *supra,* at 353.

d. During this period both the federal and state governments were forming administrative bodies to regulate the communications business. In 1910, Congress gave the Interstate Commerce Commission authority to regulate interstate telephone operations. Between 1910 and 1920, many states established regulatory agencies to oversee intrastate telephone activities. In 1934, federal jurisdiction over interstate telephone service was transferred to the FCC. However, because AT&T had no significant competition during these early years, federal regulation focused largely on scrutinizing the company's earnings levels and its rates. Regulators believed that the telephone business operated best as a "natural monopoly" and that the public interest warranted ensuring AT&T's continued vitality. *See* Trebing, *Common Carrier Regulation—The Silent Crisis,* 34 L. & Contemp. Probs. 299, 305-07 (1969).

e. With the introduction of microwave transmission systems and satellites, and with the integration of computer and communications facilities, the government had to change its view of the marketplace. The nature of the communications business and of the kinds of services that could be provided to users were altered by technologies that offered alternatives to wire transmission. These technologies also forced a rethinking of how services could—and should—be priced. New service opportunities generated pressure on the AT&T monopoly, eventually leading to its breakup.

B. The Courts Hasten the FCC's Movement Toward Introducing Competition into the Telephone Marketplace

In the last ten years, the once-gradual move toward a competitive telecommunications market reached a frenzied pace. The change has not involved a carefully orchestrated implementation of a master plan, but has, instead, occurred because of a complex—and sometimes unexpected—interplay between the courts and the FCC.

1. A 1977 decision by the D.C. Circuit opened the floodgates to competition in the interstate telephone marketplace. *MCI Telecommunications Corp. v. FCC*, 561 F.2d 365 (1977), *cert. denied*, 430 U.S. 1140 (1978) [hereinafter cited as *Execunet I*]. Until that decision, the FCC had been acquiescing in a gradual introduction of competition at the fringes of the telecommunications market. The agency had not, however, opened up AT&T's monopoly hold over the heart of the market—public switched services. The FCC did not assume that switched services would be provided by the newly authorized competitors. *Establishment of Policies and Procedures for Consideration of Applications to Provide Specialized Common Carrier Services in the Domestice Point-to-Point Microwave Radio Service*, 29 F.C.C.2d 870 (1971) [hereinafter cited as *Specialized Common Carriers*].

2. Even without the *Execunet I* decision, the move toward increased marketplace competition probably would have occurred; however, the court certainly forced the FCC's hand.

a. The decision prompted the FCC to reexamine its policies. In 1980, it concluded that full competition in the interstate telephone market would serve the public interest. *MTS and WATS Market Structure*, 81 F.C.C.2d 177 (1980) (Report and Third Supplemental Notice of Inquiry and Notice of Proposed Rulemaking). This conclusion allowed for a drastic restructuring of the domestic telecommunications marketplace.

b. In the wake of the divestiture, the FCC continues to struggle with restructuring the market. It now is trying to establish pricing policies that will reconcile the goals of competition and affordable universal service; a proceeding examining these issues soon will enter its eighth year. *See MTS and WATS Market Structure, supra.*

3. The roots of competition in the interstate market go back to the 1950s. Private users were seeking FCC authorization to use a portion of the radio spectrum—frequencies above 890 megacycles—for non-common-car-rier microwave communications. Carriers argued that because of the scarcity of spectrum space, this use should not be permitted; paramount common carrier needs required preserving these frequencies for future use. The FCC rejected this claim and authorized private use. *Allocation of Frequencies in the Bands Above 890 Mc.*, 27 F.C.C. 359 (1959) [hereinafter cited as *Above 890*]. After this decision, AT&T responded with a series of tariff adjustments and with major revisions in its pricing policies—particularly for private line

services. These activities plunged the FCC into an examination of rate structures that continues today as the Commission strives to develop pricing policies compatible with the post-divestiture marketplace.

4. Five years after the *Above 890* decision, Microwave Communications, Inc. (now "MCI") applied for authorization to construct a microwave system between St. Louis and Chicago. It intended to provide point-to-point, private line services. Despite the lengthy objections of such carriers as AT&T and Western Union, the FCC—after an extensive regulatory proceeding—granted the application. *Microwave Communications, Inc.*, 18 F.C.C.2d 953 (1969). It decided that the flexibility MCI would offer customers—allowing them to lease just a portion of a circuit for only part of each day and to transmit a variety of voice and data services—would provide a significant public benefit. This was particularly true because MCI proposed to price its service significantly below similar services provided by AT&T.

5. The MCI authorization touched off a flood of applications for authorization to operate various point-to-point microwave networks. As a result, the Commission instituted a broad rulemaking proceeding to formulate general policies that would govern these so-called specialized common carriers. *Specialized Common Carriers*, 24 F.C.C.2d 318 (1970).

a. A year later, the FCC determined that authorizing these new carriers would serve the public interest. *Specialized Common Carriers*, 29 F.C.C.2d 870 (1971), *aff'd sub nom. Washington Utilities and Transportation Comm'n v. FCC*, 513 F.2d 1142 (9th Cir.), *cert. denied*, 423 U.S. 836 (1975).

b. Existing carriers argued, in part, that because they could provide specialized services, the FCC must reject the competitive applications. The Commission doubted this capability and went on to decide:

> [T]here is a public need and demand for the proposed facilities and services and for new and diverse sources of supply, competition in the specialized communications field is reasonably feasible, there are grounds for a reasonable expectation that new entry will have some beneficial effects, and there is no reason to anticipate that new entry would have any adverse impact on service to the public by existing carriers such as to outweigh the consideration supporting new entry.

Id. at 920.

c. The decision established a general FCC policy favoring competition in the specialized services market. It did not, however, represent a determination that any individual applicant would further the public interest, convenience, and necessity. Nonetheless, this general decision opened the way for new carriers to enter the market. In individual cases, the Commission was left to evaluate only the applicant's legal, technical, and financial qualifications (to carry out its public interest mandate).

d. While this decision was significant because of what it did say, it ultimately became even more significant because of what it failed to say. Nowhere in the decision did the FCC define the term "specialized common carrier." It was assumed, however, that such a carrier would provide "specialized" services—services other than interstate public switched telephone service ("MTS" and "WATS"). Such services were asssumed to be reserved for AT&T. All of the applications pending before the FCC in the *Specialized Common Carrier* proceeding were for private line services. The FCC based its decision to allow competition on this implicit competitive boundary. However, its failure to make the bounds of its pro-competitive policies explicit led to a dispute that finally opened the door to full marketplace competition.

6. In 1974, MCI filed a tariff for its Execunet service, which allowed customers to make long-distance telephone calls for which they were billed on the basis of connection time. The service was similar to AT&T's long-distance telephone service. The FCC rejected this tariff in 1975, contending that MCI was authorized to offer only "private line" services and that Execunet was a "switched public message telephone service." *See* Letter from FCC to MCI (July 1, 1975), *reprinted in MCI Telecommunications Corp.*, 60 F.C.C.2d 25 app. B (1975). Two years later, the D.C. Circuit overturned this decision in the historic *Execunet I* ruling that marked the beginning of the end for AT&T's long-distance monopoly.

a. The *Execunet I* court found that absent an explicit restriction in a service authorization, the FCC always had permitted a carrier to "offer any service which could physically be provided over [its] existing systems simply by filing a tariff." *Execunet I*, 561 F.2d at 373. Once a carrier was authorized to construct and to operate a transmission line, it was presumed free to offer any service that lines could physically accommodate. To initiate a new service, the carrier needed only to file a tariff with the FCC. If the Commission explicitly decided that such a service would be contrary to the public interest, it could reject the tariff. Otherwise, assuming the tariff's terms were just and reasonable, the tariff would be approved and the service could be initiated.

b. In this case, the court found that the FCC had not imposed any restrictions on the types of services MCI could offer when it granted MCI authority to construct and to operate microwave transmission facilities. The Commission had not found, affirmatively, that MCI's offering of MTS would injure the public interest. It also had not adopted any general rules, applicable to MCI, that restricted it from offering certain classes of service (such as MTS). Thus, the FCC had no basis for rejecting the tariff.

c. The FCC argued that its *Specialized Common Carrier* decision implicitly had restricted specialized carriers to providing "private line services." The FCC argued that it had not considered the marketplace implications of opening MTS to competition; therefore, its decision could not authorize carriers to offer public switched services. The court rejected this claim, finding that nothing in the FCC's decision limited the specialized carriers to offering only certain services:

> [T]he Commission did not perhaps intend to open the field of common carrier communications generally, but its constant stress on the fact that specialized carriers would provide new, innovative, and hitherto unheard-of communications services clearly indicates that it had no very clear idea of how far or to what services the field should be opened.

561 F.2d at 379.

d. The court also pointed to the staff report prepared in that proceeding. The report considered the broad implications of AT&T's argument against authorizing specialized carriers. AT&T had argued that such carriers would divert revenues away from its system and, therefore, would raise the cost of long-distance telephone service. The court pointed out that the staff "appeared highly skeptical of the validity of AT&T's overall argument." *Id.* at 378. Finally, the court reasoned that the staff had recommended that a separate proceeding be used to consider the potentially adverse impact of services other than those directly at issue in the *Specialized Common Carrier* proceeding. This recommendation, the court believed, was strong evidence that the Commission did not make any decisions about limiting the scope of "specialized" services.

C. Efforts to Isolate the Monopoly Business of Local Exchange Service

In theory, *Execunet I* paved the way for competition in the interexchange telephone market; in reality, however, true competition faced some significant obstacles. Chief among these was the fact that AT&T owned almost all of the nation's local exchange facilities. This ownership gave it the power to decide the terms on which particular services could obtain access to most subscribers' homes, thereby enabling AT&T to limit—or to prevent—competitive interexchange service.

1. New interexchange carriers could not easily circumvent this obstacle. It was extremely expensive to construct new, often duplicative, local switches and wires. Moreover, state utility regulators, who sought to keep local telephone rates at the lowest possible level, were unlikely to permit such construction. (Duplicative facilities would raise the per subscriber cost of services—as the number of subscribers served by each local exchange diminished.) Without state authorization, these new carriers could not build their facilities—even if they had the money to finance such construction.

2. Once again the courts stepped in to open the marketplace to competition. In the wake of *Execunet I*, AT&T announced its intention to refuse to offer any new interconnections for MCI or for any other carrier providing Execunet-type service. It also sought and received a declaratory ruling from the FCC that it was not required to furnish such interconnection. *Petition of American Telephone and Telegraph Company for a Declaratory Ruling and Expedited Relief*, FCC No. 78-142 (released February 23, 1978). Two

months later, the D.C. Circuit decided that this action violated the terms of the *Execunet I* decision; it ruled that AT&T's refusal to interconnect—and the FCC's support of that refusal—were inconsistent with the obligations imposed on AT&T in *Execunet I. MCI Telecommunications Corp. v. FCC,* 580 F.2d 590 (D.C. Cir.), *cert. denied sub nom. United States Independent Telephone Ass'n v. MCI Telecommunications Corp.,* 439 U.S. 980 (1978) [hereinafter cited as *Execunet II*]. In reaching its decision in *Execunet I,* the court noted, it was assumed that AT&T was obliged to provide interconnection; absent such an obligation, MCI's right to provide long-distance service would be virtually meaningless.

3. While the Court of Appeals was clearing this obstacle from MCI's path, the government was simultaneously pursuing an antitrust suit against AT&T. That suit, in part, accused the company of using its control over local exchange facilities to prevent competition in the interexchange market. AT&T's argument against permitting interexchange competition was that new competitors would engage in "creamskimming" and would force AT&T to deaverage its service rates. Deaveraging, according to AT&T, would increase the cost of long-distance telephone service for users in more remote areas of the country. (Creamskimming is the practice of serving only high-volume, low-cost routes, where profit potential is optimal.) The FCC had for years supported rate averaging as a policy that promoted the public interest: averaging provided relatively affordable long-distance service for all telephone users.

4. This lawsuit was resolved in 1982 by court approval of a consent decree that, most notably, required AT&T to divest itself of its local operating companies. *United States v. American Telephone & Telegraph Co.,* 552 F. Supp. 131 (1982), *aff'd sub nom. Maryland v. United States,* ____ U.S. ____, 103 S. Ct. 1240 (1983).

5. The result in the antitrust suit further cleared the way for the growth of competitive MTS that the FCC had been encouraging. In 1980, most notably, the Commission had concluded directly that long-distance competition served the public interest. *MTS and WATS Market Structure, supra.* With regard to the effect that such competition would have on rates, the FCC concluded:

> . . . MTS de-averaging will not occur unless the telephone companies elect to de-average and succeed in establishing that the particular de-averaged rates they have selected are just and reasonable. The record in this proceeding does not establish that such an occurrence is very likely. Therefore, even if MTS de-averaging were deemed to be a detrimental effect, the record would not support the imposition of service restrictions in order to avoid that effect.

Id. at 195.

6. By prohibiting AT&T from refusing to interconnect competitive long-distance carriers, the FCC might have opened up the MTS

market. But the court's decision, reached with AT&T's consent, resulted in a more sudden—and more drastic—change in the telecommunications marketplace.

D. Details of the Modified Final Judgment

The settlement that ended the 1974 antitrust lawsuit against AT&T concluded more than thirty years of continuous litigation between the government and the telephone company. The decree continues to affect the restructuring of the telecommunications marketplace. Its provisions contain many rules by which the market's key players—AT&T and the newly independent local exchange carriers—must abide.

1. Background of the 1982 Settlement

a. In 1949, the government brought an antitrust suit against AT&T and its wholly-owned equipment manufacturing subsidiary, Western Electric Co., Inc. The government alleged that the defendants had monopolized the telephone market and had conspired to restrain trade in that market. The suit sought to separate AT&T from its equipment manufacturing business and its research facility (Bell Laboratories). This suit ended in 1956, with the entry of a consent decree. The terms of that decree did not include any requirement that AT&T divest itself of any of its businesses. The decree required only (1) that AT&T refrain from engaging in any business other than common carrier communications services and businesses "incidental thereto," (2) that Western Electric manufacture only equipment to be used in the Bell System, and (3) that the defendants license their patents to all applicants in return for appropriate royalty payments. The U.S. District Court for the District of New Jersey approved the decree in 1956. *United States v. Western Electric Co.*, 156 Trade Cases ¶ 68,246 (D.N.J. 1956).

b. At the end of 1974, a separate suit was brought in the U.S. District Court for the District of Columbia against AT&T, Western Electric, and Bell Labs. The government alleged that these companies had illegally sought to monopolize various telecommunications service and equipment markets. It sought the divestiture of AT&T's twenty-four local exchange companies—the Bell Operating Companies ("BOCs")—and the divestiture and dissolution of Western Electric. Discovery and pretrial activity took almost six years, and the case finally went to trial on January 15, 1981. After the government had presented its 120 witnesses, and after AT&T had called 250 witnesses (almost completing its case), the parties advised the court, in early January, 1982, that they had agreed to a proposed settlement.

c. After some procedural wrangling, a judge from the New Jersey District Court agreed to transfer jurisdiction over the 1949 case—and, thus, the 1956 consent decree—to the D.C. Court. The presiding judge in the D.C. Court, Harold H. Greene, consolidated the 1949 and 1974 suits. The proposed settlement agreement was to be treated as a modification of the final judgment in the original suit; when approved by Judge Greene, it would dissolve the 1956 consent decree. The settlement, therefore, is commonly referred to as the Modified Final Judgment ("MFJ").

2. *The Court's Standard of Review*

a. Under the Tunney Act, the D.C. Court was obligated to ensure that the proposed decree served the public interest. *See* 15 U.S.C. § 16(e) (1983). In conducting his review, Judge Greene followed an elaborate process to elicit public comment on the decree. Following the command of the Tunney Act, the proposed decree was published in the Federal Register on January 28, 1982. On February 10, the Justice Department filed a statement assessing the competitive impact that the decree would have on the telecommunications market. This statement also was published in the Federal Register. Comments by interested parties were filed with the court and with the Justice Department. There also were a series of oral arguments held, and the parties to the litigation filed numerous motions and briefs. Judge Greene's review of the proposed decree was to be based upon this voluminous amount of material.

b. Before assessing the specific provisions of the decree, the court set forth the factors it would consider in judging the effect on the public. Among these factors were (1) the decree's ability to promote free competition, (2) its capacity to prevent a recurrence of the antitrust violations that gave rise to the suit initially, and (3) its tendency to accomplish these marketplace goals while inflicting the least possible amount of harm on private individuals and on the public in general.

3. *Divestiture*

The heart of the decree is the requirement that AT&T divest itself of the twenty-two BOCs, which were wholly owned. (It also sold its interests in two other local telephone companies.) The BOCs would be grouped to form seven Regional Holding Companies ("RHCs").

a. The divestiture required that all employees, facilities, and accounting operations for local ("exchange") telecommunications be separated from AT&T. In addition, AT&T was required to transfer to the BOCs ownership of all assets necessary to permit the BOCs to operate as independent local exchange companies. AT&T was forbidden from acquiring the stock or assets of any BOC after divestiture. However, until September, 1987, some connections between the divested entities would be tolerated: in order to help the BOCs make the transition to independence, the MFJ required that AT&T, Western Electric, and Bell Labs provide the Operating Companies with a certain amount of assistance.

b. The court noted that a substantial amount of the evidence from the still-incomplete trial had pointed to AT&T's control of local exchange facilities as the key to its allegedly anticompetitive powers. The court recognized that it could not accept this evidence as definitive proof; however, it also could not ignore this evidence. For this reason, the court concluded that "the loosening of AT&T's control over telecommunications through the divestiture of the Operating Companies would entail benefits which transcend those which flow from the narrowest reading of the purpose of the antitrust laws." 552 F. Supp. at 165.

c. Divestiture was seen as a way of depriving AT&T of the ability to discriminate against competitive providers of interexchange telecommunications services. The BOCs, when providing only local services, would have no incentive to favor AT&T. Separation also would deprive AT&T of the ability to subsidize its competitive services with profits earned on monopoly local services.

d. The court discounted claims that the divestiture would raise the cost of local services and would result in less efficient service overall. Some parties claimed that the integrated Bell System was the most efficient way to provide telephone service. Judge Greene ultimately relied on the public policy favoring competition—upon which the antitrust laws are founded—to conclude that divestiture would best serve the public interest. He noted that throughout its existence, AT&T had been "neither effectively regulated nor fully subjected to true competition." *Id.* at 170. Attempts to introduce competition, through continuing regulatory oversight, had been either unsuccessful or woefully limited. Over the long run, he determined, the public would best be served by a competitive telecommunications industry. Consequently, restructuring the industry, rather than relying on continued public regulation, seemed the most effective way to produce a competitive market.

4. *Line-of-Business Restrictions on AT&T*

The 1956 consent decree had restricted AT&T to providing only common carrier communications services. Under the decree proposed in 1982, this restriction would have been dissolved, leaving AT&T free to compete in all lines of business. Judge Greene found that after the divestiture, AT&T would not have the power to exert an anticompetitive influence on other unregulated businesses. Consequently, he approved the removal of business restrictions on AT&T with one exception—electronic publishing services. These services are defined as ones in which "[AT&T] would control, or have an interest in, the content of the information being transmitted." *Id.* at 180.

a. Judge Greene concluded that AT&T's important role in the interexchange service market, coupled with the relatively undeveloped state of the electronic publishing industry, could allow the company to use its control of transmission lines to favor its own databases. AT&T could give priority to its own information or could develop transmission technologies that would exclude other information and service providers. In addition, the company could refuse to interconnect competitors' networks, thereby making it more difficult for them to reach disparate users. Thus, Judge Greene inserted into the decree a modification prohibiting AT&T from entering the electronic publishing field for seven years. This provision was also thought to be consistent with the constitutional goal of promoting diversity in the ownership of information outlets: by keeping AT&T out of the information business, the court was opening the door to the development of many new, perhaps small, information providers.

b. A number of comments filed with the court also had urged that AT&T be barred from the market for providing remote access data processing and other kinds of "enhanced services." (The effect of the *Computer II* decision on AT&T's role in these markets is discussed below, *see infra* Sections III & IV.) Largely because this market appeared to be more fully developed—and subject to significant, and increasing, user demand—Judge Greene concluded that AT&T probably could not use its control of interstate transmission lines to favor its own computer services. Competitors possessed sufficient resources to force AT&T to provide them with access to its lines. Demand also was believed to be strong enough to make it profitable for competitors to construct their own transmission facilities (should AT&T prove unreasonable). As a result, this restriction (like all other suggested restrictions on AT&T's business activities) was not incorporated into the MFJ.

5. *Line-of-Business Restrictions On the RHCs*

The proposed settlement prohibited the BOCs from using their monopoly control of the local exchanges for anticompetitive purposes. Such anticompetitive behavior would consist primarily of discriminating in favor of wholly-owned or affiliated services that require access to the local loop in order to reach individual users. AT&T, before the divestiture, had given independent competitors either unequal access, more costly access, or no access at all to the local loop. To the degree that the BOCs could use their local exchange facilities to apply anticompetitive pressures to otherwise competitive markets (or could subsidize their competitive activities with profits from monopoly services), line-of-business restrictions would appear appropriate.

a. The MFJ's basic restriction on the RHCs prevents them from providing "any product or service that is not a natural monopoly service actually regulated by tariff." *Id.* at 186. In addition, five other specific restrictions were proposed; the court adopted three of these and rejected the other two.

i) The court recognzied that, over time, market conditions might change in ways that could justify a removal of all, or some, of these restrictions. Consequently, the court modified the decree so that upon a showing that "there is no substantial possibility that an Operating Company could use its monopoly power to impede competition in the relevant market," the court would remove the contested restriction. *Id.* at 195.

ii) The court rejected a suggestion that it include a blanket waiver for RHC entry into "unrelated businesses," in which there was no possibility the company could abuse its monopoly market power. Each waiver request would have to be handled individually under the general waiver standard applicable to all RHC activities. *Id.* at 195, n.267. Since this decision, the court has spent much of its time reviewing petitions by the various RHCs for waivers of the line-of-business restrictions. This process is discussed below, *see infra* Section V.D.

b. As one would expect, the BOCs were prevented from providing interexchange telecommunications services. A ban on such interexchange activities was intended to guard against the kind of anticompetitive behavior that had led to the allegations made originally in the antitrust suit. The BOCs could use their control of the local exchanges to favor their own interexchange services. This result would undermine the court's attempt to implement an "equal access" plan by which all interexchange carriers—including AT&T—would be interconnected with the local loops on equal technological and economic terms.

c. The RHCs also were prohibited from entering the "information services" market, consisting of data processing, electronic publishing, and other related services (possibly including "enhanced" services). The court reasoned that by prohibiting the RHCs from entering these markets, the companies would be encouraged to modify their networks to accommodate the greatest number of information providers (generating the greatest amount of RHC revenues). This restriction also would prevent the RHCs from using their control over local loops to favor their own information services.

d. Finally, the court prohibited the BOCs from manufacturing telecommunications equipment; however, it allowed them to market such equipment.

e. It struck a provision that would have transferred control of the Yellow Pages from the BOCs to AT&T and would have prohibited the BOCs from engaging in any directory advertising business. The court found that giving one entity, rather than twenty-two, control of Yellow Pages operations would be anticompetitive. In addition, the revenues to be derived from the Yellow Pages were seen as a way of subsidizing local rates and thereby protecting subscribers against significant rate increases. This result, Judge Greene believed, would serve the public interest.

6. *The Equal Access Plan*

a. The MFJ requires that, by September 1, 1986, with certain limited exceptions, the BOCs must provide long distance carriers other than AT&T with "non-discriminatory" access to their local exchange facilities. *Id.* at 232 app. A. While divestiture removes much of the incentive for BOC discrimination in favor of AT&T, this provision still is necessary because of the technological inequality of current interconnections. While

AT&T's lines are connected to the "trunk side" of the local exchange, other carriers are provided only with "line side" access. Line side access means that carriers' lines are hooked into the exchange like any other customer's private line, rather than like a carrier's trunk. Such line side access provides a lower quality connection and requires the dialing of a significant number of additional digits to gain access to the carrier's network.

b. The BOCs had to begin offering equal access by September 1, 1984. BOC end offices serving at least one-third of all BOC subscribers must offer equal access by September 1, 1985. All BOC end offices must be able to offer equal access by September 1, 1986. The court approved this transition period because of the costly and time-consuming changes in switching equipment that is required to offer non-discriminatory access. *Id.* at 232-33.

c. During the period of transition to equal access, the court required that the BOCs refile tariffs reflecting any cost difference between the superior access provided to AT&T and the access given to other carriers. *Id.* at 199. The court also suggested that if there is no cost differential, it might be appropriate to increase the charges to AT&T (to account for the superior connection). The specifics of any charges were, however, left to regulators. *Id.* at 199, n.287.

d. Approval of individual tariffs was properly left with the FCC. Such approval would be given on the basis of longstanding principles of rate-of-return regulation. The court, with its approach, avoids involving itself in the process of valuing telephone services—a task for which it is admittedly ill-suited. It also stops short of invading the clear regulatory domain of the FCC.

e. The FCC addressed the access charge issue directly in 1983, with its order in *MTS and WATS Market Structure,* 93 F.C.C.2d 241 (1983) (Third Report and Order), *aff'd sub nom. National Ass'n of Regulatory Utility Commissioners v. FCC,* 737 F.2d 1095 (D.C. Cir. 1984), *cert. denied,* ____ U.S. ____, 104 S. Ct. 1224 (1985). The FCC's handling of the access charge issue is discussed below. *See infra* Section VI.D.

7. *Institutional Issues: The Court's Role as a "Policymaker"*

The AT&T lawsuit held the potential for a significant conflict between the D.C. Court and the FCC. Although the MFJ was not premised on a finding of any wrongdoing by AT&T, the resolution of the case obviously had far-reaching consequences for the nation's telecommunications marketplace. The decree itself requires a drastic change in the shape of the telecommunications market. In addition, a number of the MFJ's provisions, particularly the line-of-business restrictions, require the court to remain involved in overseeing the transformation of this market. Finally, the court has retained general enforcement authority, and oversight obligations, under the Tunney Act. *See* 552 F.2d at 215. This situation injects a court, concerned primarily with enforcing the pro-competitive aims of the antitrust laws, into the process of telecommunications policymaking. Any such division of regulatory responsibility could complicate the development of a comprehensive set of regulations intended to promote an efficient and affordable communications network.

a. *Legal and Policy Arguments in the District Court.*

i) The court sensed this potential conflict early in the course of the proceedings. It requested the FCC to submit a brief in 1975 that would address the jurisdictional issue. The FCC concluded that the court should

> take no action that will substantially alter the industry structure without initial consideration by the FCC of how such action will comport with the "public interest," as perceived by the Commission in light of its mandate under the Communications Act.

Brief for FCC, *United States v. American Telephone & Telegraph Co.*, 552 F. Supp. 131 (D.D.C. 1982), *reprinted in Satellite Business Systems*, 62 F.C.C.2d 997, 1102, 1120 (1975). The Commission claimed that it had exclusive jurisdiction over the issues of entry into the communications market, interconnection policies, and tariff approval. With regard to "other specific issues that are within or directly affect the agency's regulatory policies," *id.* at 1119-20, the Commission argued that it had "primary" jurisdiction and should be asked for an opinion before the court reached any decisions.

ii) In a 1978 opinion, Judge Greene considered the FCC's position on this jurisdictional question. *United States v. American Telephone & Telegraph Co.*, 461 F.Supp. 1314 (1978). While recognizing the FCC's obvious interest in AT&T's future, Judge Greene asserted that its regulatory responsibilities were not inconsistent with the court's power to address the antitrust implications of the issues before it.

iii) The court focused on the Commission's own admission that it had "limited authority" to dictate the structure of the telephone industry. *See* 552 F. Supp. at 212; *see also* Brief for FCC, 62 F.C.C.2d at 1117-18. This admission of "limited authority" led the court to conclude that (1) AT&T's alleged anticompetitive conduct was not immunized by a pervasive scheme of federal regulation, (2) the FCC's regulatory powers neither override the antitrust laws nor are incompatible with them, and (3) the FCC did not require or approve AT&T's alleged anticompetitive practices. 461 F. Supp. at 1322-29.

iv) The court decided that its assertion of jurisdiction was not inconsistent with federal regulatory aims and was necessary to carry out the purposes of the antitrust laws. It claimed that it was "fully prepared to refer appropriate issues to the FCC" under the primary jurisdiction doctrine. *Id.* at 1329 & n.45. Such referral, however, would not involve an abdication of court jurisdiction over the matter referred. Instead, it would allow the Commission to provide conclusions of law and fact, based upon its special expertise, that would aid the court in deciding "ultimate questions." *Id.* at 1329 n.45.

v) The court recognized the FCC's exclusive jurisdiction arguments, but it effectively dismissed them. The court concluded that by referring certain matters to the FCC for agency input, it could avoid direct conflicts between judicial powers under the antitrust laws and the FCC's scope of "exclusive jurisdiction." With respect to market entry decisions, the court noted that the FCC had admitted that its decisions do not necessarily conflict with antitrust actions; in fact, the FCC said, the antitrust laws may complement regulatory actions. The FCC also did not think that its interconnection decisions "displace[d] the antitrust laws." Finally, the court found that tariff approvals were subject to such minimal FCC scrutiny that "the courts appropriately exercise antitrust jurisdiction" over pricing issues. *Id.* at 1327.

vi) The court's resolution of these issues cleared the way for it to approve the settlement with only minimal FCC comment. The Commission expressed only its general approval of the terms of the proposed decree prior to the court's 1982 opinion. *See* 552 F. Supp. at 211. The Commission undertook a formal review of the settlement only after the decree had been modified and approved. *See Consolidated Application of American Telephone and Telegraph Company and Specified Bell System Companies for Authorization Under Sections 214 and 310(d) of the Communications Act of 1934*, 96 F.C.C.2d 18 (1983) [hereinafter cited as *Consolidated Application*]. The Communications Act required that the FCC determine whether the numerous license transfers and the massive restructuring of common carrier services would be consistent with the public interest. The FCC completed its review—and "approved" of the divestiture—just one month before the it was to take place.

vii) One could argue that the massive restructuring required by the MFJ was essentially imposed on the FCC. While the agency informed the court that implementation of the divestiture would have to await the necessary regulatory approvals, it is almost inconceivable that the FCC would have denied the necessary authorization requests. The court's resolution of an antitrust case would, in that situation, have conflicted squarely with the statutory requirement that the FCC approve the kinds of operational changes required by the MFJ.

viii) The FCC made a final attempt to preserve the primacy of its regulatory powers. It requested that the court append to the MFJ a provision stating that its regulatory powers were not affected by the terms of settlement. Such a provision had been ordered by the Supreme Court in a 1912 case where there had been some concern that a consent decree would conflict with the Interstate Commerce Commission's regulatory efforts. *See United States v. St. Louis Terminal*, 224 U.S. 383 (1912). Judge Greene refused the request, noting that such a provision would—by the FCC's own admission—have no effect on the powers of either the court or the agency. He concluded that the provision might have the effect of causing confusion more than anything else. 552 F. Supp. at 212.

ix) The court's final appraisal of the potential jurisdictional conflict was that there really was no problem: its own resolution of the issues was the one that should prevail.

> [If a conflict between the court and the FCC] arose, it appear[s] likely that, in view of the Commission's limited authority in regard to structural matters in the telecommunications industry, the judgment of an antitrust court would prevail.

Id.

x) Earlier in its opinion, the court had decided that conflicts between the decree and state regulation of intrastate telephone services represented no obstacle. The court's decision, based upon federal law, would preempt inconsistent state requirements. *Id.* at 153-60.

xi) The court gave little weight to the FCC's claim that it should be made a part of any decisions to alter the shape of the telecommunications market significantly. In the FCC's amicus brief, the agency stated that its "limited authority in this area does not mean that structural changes should occur without the participation of the expert agency." Brief for FCC, 62 F.C.C.2d at 1117-18. The Commission elaborated as follows:

> Factual issues relevant to the benefits and drawbacks of possible structural changes should be referred to the agency for its views, for the Communications Act clearly made the FCC the primary architect of communications policy. . . . [T]he FCC should be consulted before any possible remedies are seriously contemplated, either by further participation as *amicus curiae* or by exercise of the agency's primary jurisdiction as fact-finder in communications matters of national importance.

Id. at 1118. The Commission was invited to submit further comments as amicus; this was not, however, the kind of input it sought. The FCC's current General Counsel has recently stated that he disagrees with Judge Greene's determination as to who would prevail in the case of an irreconcilable conflict. J.D. Smith, *Reconciling the Antitrust Laws and the Communications Act in the AT&T Divestiture* 5 (March 20, 1985) (available from the FCC).

b. *Supreme Court Commentary on Jurisdictional Issues.*

i) Although the Supreme Court summarily affirmed Judge Green's approval of the MFJ, Justice Rehnquist, with Justice White and Chief Justice Burger concurring, filed a brief dissent. It discussed two jurisdictional questions said to be raised by both the MFJ and the court's role in reviewing it.

ii) First, Justice Rehnquist questioned whether a court could, relying on the Supremacy Clause of the Constitution, preempt state regulatory powers "by entering what is in essence a private agreement between parties to a lawsuit." *Maryland v. United States*, ____ U.S. ____, 103 S.Ct. 1240, 1241 (1983). Maryland and Illinois had brought the appeal on the ground that the MFJ impermissibly preempted certain state regulatory powers and policies. Judge Greene had, as noted above, rejected a claim that the court could not impose provisions that would conflict with state regulations.

iii) More fundamentally, the dissent doubted whether the court's public interest review of the proposed decree was a proper function of an Article III court. Justice Rehnquist quoted from a House Committee Report on the Tunney Act (the source of this "public interest" standard of review), in which a committee member had termed the "public interest" review provision an improper "transfer" of "an 'executive' question" to a court. *Id.* at 1243. Justice Rehnquist argued that there was no way for the court to evaluate what a "better" settlement of a lawsuit might be. A court could not—or had no authority to—balance the diverse elements associated with a settlement decision. These included the risk of seeking prosecution versus the certainty of a settlement, the costs of trial versus the concessions of a settlement, and the costs of delay through trial versus the need for a speedy solution of some sort. Justice Rehnquist concluded by saying that "[e]ven though Congress may by statute impose such a duty on the federal courts, they may not perform it." *Id.* Accordingly, he would have had the Supreme Court hear the appeal in order to consider the issues fully and render a formal opinion.

c. *Current Status of the Debate Between Judge Greene and the FCC.* To date, a conflict between the court and the FCC has been avoided. In situations where a clash has appeared imminent or likely, the court and the Commission have been able to resolve their differences—although not always without some degree of testiness. Nonetheless, a significant potential for conflict still remains because Judge Green continues to exercise what is, in many respects, a regulatory role with regard to AT&T and the BOCs. Under the Communications Act, the FCC could make many of the same decisions being made by Judge Green; this overlap of power keeps alive the possibility of a jurisdictional dispute.

i) A major part of this potential battlefield concerns who has the power to control carrier initiation of various services. Under its Title II authority, the FCC is authorized to prevent carriers from offering services that it finds would be contrary to the public interest. However, there is a presumption in the Communications Act that a carrier is able to offer virtually any service—in the absence of an appropriate FCC objection. *See supra* Section II.B.6. (discussing the *Execunet I* decision). Under the terms of the MFJ, the BOCs and, to a much lesser extent AT&T, must seek Judge Greene's approval before they can initiate certain services. *See infra* Sections III.C.5. & V.D. Some observers believe that this type of fragmentation of authority over the telecommunications industry—produced by judicial implementation of an antitrust remedy—is counterproductive.

ii) Judge Greene and the current General Counsel of the FCC disagree as to whose decision would prevail in the case of a conflict. Judge Greene has said that a court action implementing some provision of the MFJ would prevail over a conflicting FCC decision. Jack Smith, the FCC's General Counsel, has suggested that he believes in precisely the opposite conclusion.

> . . . [T]he FCC decisions stand as law unless reversed by a circuit court of appeals. The district court lacks jurisdiction to review or abrogate any decision of the FCC. Section 402 of the Communications Act gives the courts of appeal exclusive appellate jurisdiction over final decisions of the FCC.

J.D. Smith, *supra*, at 9. Unfortunately, Smith's argument does not really resolve the ultimate question, which is whether a court would uphold Judge Greene or the FCC in the case of a conflict.

iii) There is, not surprisingly, a difference of opinion as to whether the FCC's "public interest" finding would supplant the competitive impact scrutiny conducted by an antitrust court. Smith claims that because the Commission's public interest finding includes competition as just one of many factors, its decision must prevail over a contrary (and more narrow) antitrust law result. Smith argues that Supreme Court precedent supports his conclusion. *Id.* at 5-6. Judge Greene, obviously, disagrees, particularly because *his* action is based on the "public interest" standard of the Tunney Act.

iv) The potential for significant institutional bickering—and a concommitant disruption in telecommunications policymaking—has been most evident in the ongoing debate about access charges. At the end of 1982, the FCC adopted a plan to impose a flat monthly fee on all telephone subscribers to contribute toward the costs of non-traffic sensitive ("NTS") equipment used for both local and interexchange telephone calls. The arrangement shifts some of the burden of paying for NTS away from long-distance users (primarily businesses) and to local users (primarily residential customers). *MTS and WATS Market Structure,* 93 F.C.C.2d 241 (1983) (Third Report and Order).

v) Judge Greene had envisioned access charges as a way of "easing the burdens on the users of local telephone service." *United States v. Western Electric Co.,* 569 F. Supp. 990, 998 (D.C. Cir. 1983). Under his conception, access charges would be imposed on interexchange carriers, requiring them (and their customers) to assume the primary responsibility for paying for NTS. 552 F. Supp. at 2245 n.376. Judge Greene saw this approach as furthering the public interest in maintaining affordable local telephone service. He viewed this protection of local service users as a fundamental purpose of the MFJ, one mandated by the public interest obligations imposed on the court by the Tunney Act. (This issue is discussed in more detail below. *See infra* Section VI.D.)

vi) The FCC, by contrast, viewed as improper the longstanding practice of bundling the costs of NTS with rates for interstate toll calls, which are billed on a time-sensitive basis. This pricing structure allocated a greater proportion of NTS costs to high users of long-distance services and created the incentive for these users to find alternative technologies to bypass the nation's telephone network. Such bypass, if it became widespread, might seriously erode the public network's revenue base and could force substantial cost increases for remaining subscribers, most of whom would be small business and residential users.

vii) Judge Greene openly questioned the FCC's reasons for imposing user access charges. He rebuked the FCC for blaming the divestiture for the new access arrangements. 569 F. Supp. at 990 & n.48 ("the FCC action appears to be an effort unjustifiably to assign to the divestiture responsibility for a reallocation of charges which the Commission has decided upon for its own reasons"). He also concluded that the FCC's decision was "unfortunate," claiming it would "tend to defeat" the court's objective of protecting local ratepayers. *Id.*

viii) This controversy has gotten diffused somewhat because of congressional intervention that has resulted in a modification of the access charge plan. Most notably, the monthly fees to be imposed on local subscribers have been reduced. *See infra* Section VI.D.

8. *BOC Representation*

a. The BOCs claimed, prior to approval of the MFJ, that they had not been fairly represented in the court proceedings. It was assumed that their interests would be represented by AT&T; however, the BOCs argued that their interests—in certain respects—conflicted with the interests of AT&T.

b. Judge Greene dismissed a request by the RHCs that they be permitted to represent themselves, to protect the interests of their respective BOCs. First, he claimed that AT&T was not likely to act contrary to the interests of the RHCs. AT&T shareholders would, after the divestiture, become shareholders of the BOCs. AT&T management owed those shareholders a fiduciary duty and could be sued for a breach of that duty; thus, management could not disregard the BOCs' interests. Second, the views that the RHCs might present had—allegedly—already been placed before the court. In Judge Greene's view, "the Operating Companies would have no particular expertise that would give special value to their participation," and their "contribution was not so critical as to outweigh" the problems that would be caused by trying to afford them independent representation. *Id.* at 221.

c. The court rejected as impractical the proposals for actually giving the RHCs a separate voice. The parties had suggested either that the RHCs be divested immediately or that the court appoint a trustee to represent their interests. The court did note, however, that once the plan of reorganization had been filed, establishing the seven RHCs, the court would look to the chief operating officers of those companies for input on future proceedings.

E. FCC Evaluation of the Divestiture

1. *Context: Change in AT&T Structure*

a. Before the divestiture, AT&T, through the BOCs, provided service to eighty percent of the telephones in the forty-eight contiguous United States and the District of Columbia. Almost 1500 independent telephone companies served the remaining twenty percent of U.S. telephones. AT&T's Long Lines Department provided more than ninety percent of the interexchange connections, as well as a vast majority of the connections between the U.S. and foreign countries. The company employed more than one-million people and owned about $150 billion in assets. In 1982, AT&T earned a net income of $7.3 billion on operating revenues of $65 billion.

b. After the divestiture, AT&T was established as the corporate parent of Western Electric (manufacturing), Bell Labs (research and development), AT&T Information Systems (embedded CPE and enhanced communications systems), AT&T International (sales of equipment and services outside of the U.S.), and AT&T Communications (interexchange, basic common carrier services). The twenty-two BOCs were organized into seven RHCs. All RHCs serve roughly equal geographic areas and approximately the same number of lines. AT&T relinquished its minority interest in two local telephone companies, leaving them as wholly independent entities.

c. Under the terms of the MFJ, AT&T was required to present the court with a plan of reorganization outlining how the company would accomplish the divestiture. Divestiture required both a configuration of the territories to be served by the BOCs and a plan for distributing AT&T's assets to the BOCs. At the end of 1982, AT&T filed this plan. The Court approved the plan on August 5, 1983, after ordering that a number of modifications be made.

d. The division of facilities was to be acomplished by a fairly straightforward set of principles. Equipment used solely for communication within a single exchange area (called a "Local Access and Transport Area" or "LATA") would be owned by a BOC. All equipment used solely for interexchange communications would remain with AT&T. Equipment providing multiple functions would be allocated according to its predominant use.

e. Each BOC was to create two wholly-owned subsidiaries to hold any interexchange facilities and all CPE, respectively. Upon transferring these assets to their subsidiaries, each BOC would receive the common stock of the subsidiaries. This stock would then be distributed to AT&T (giving AT&T control of the CPE and interexchange equipment). AT&T would turn around and transfer its stock in the BOCs to the seven new RHCs. Stock in the RHCs finally would be distributed to the public, creating seven independent, publicly-owned companies that held all of the stock of the BOCs.

f. Before all of this could take place, FCC approval was required. On January 14, 1983, the FCC sent a letter to AT&T asking that by March 1, 1983, it file all of the applications necessary to complete the transfer of facilities. This consolidated application was filed on March 1. The application discussed six topics specified by the FCC as warranting Commission scrutiny:

i) Costs of divestiture already incurred and expected over the next five years.
ii) Assumptions made and methodologies used to derive these costs.
iii) Impact of these costs, if any, on ratepayers.
iv) Technical changes resulting from the divestiture, if any.
v) Plans for satisfying the equal access requirements of the MFJ.
vi) Effect of the MFJ on national security.

2. *The FCC's Decision on the Consolidated Application*

a. The Commission approached its review of the AT&T application from a broad perspective. It sought to ensure that the divestiture would not impede the availability of a rapid and efficient nationwide communications system possessing adequate facilities and charging reasonable rates. This scrutiny was to be conducted independently of the D.C. Court's review of the MFJ. While the court was concerned with promoting competition, the FCC viewed itself as having to decide whether, on balance, divestiture would benefit consumers and would promote the nation's security (by ensuring the integrity of the telephone system).

b. Despite the FCC's clear efforts to distinguish its own process from the D.C. Court's review, the conclusion reached in granting the consolidated application is quite similar to the main theme of Judge Greene's decision. The Commission reasoned that "competition . . . is likely to increase as a result of divestiture, leading to generally lower prices for ratepayers, greater technological advances, an increase in the type and number of services available, and an industry structure that is more responsive to consumer needs." *Consolidated Application*, 96 F.C.C.2d at 48.

c. The Commission viewed the MFJ as consistent with the aims of its major regulatory efforts. By lifting most of the line-of-business restrictions that had been imposed on AT&T under the 1956 decree, the MFJ followed what the FCC had done in its *Computer II* decision. *See infra* Sections III. & IV. In addition, divestiture would enhance the competitiveness of various communications markets, decreasing the need for regulatory oversight. Such deregulation would promote the objectives the FCC was seeking in various regulatory proceedings. For example, as divestiture reduced AT&T's dominance in the marketplace, the FCC might be able to extend its policy of forbearing from regulating common carriers to AT&T and, perhaps eventually, to the BOCs. *See Policy and Rules Concerning Rates for Competitive Common Carrier Services and Facilities Authorizations Therefor*, 50 Fed. Reg. 1215 (Jan. 10, 1985) (streamlining or eliminating Title II regulation for virtually all carriers). This proceeding is discussed below. *See infra* Section VII.A.

d. The FCC was most concerned about the possibility that the divestiture would force local service rates to rise. The FCC concluded, however, that any increases were not likely to be significant enough to restrict service availability. Thus, the negative effect on rates was not seen as a reason to deny the application. However, in order to ensure that customers were not burdened by costs from which they received no benefits, the FCC required that AT&T and the RHCs agree to file "semi-annual reports on the costs actually incurred to plan and implement equal access." 96 F.C.C.2d at 76. These reports must be filed from 1984 through 1994.

F. Comparison: The Acquisition of Sprint

In the wake of approval of the MFJ, GTE Corporation ("GTE"), an owner and operator of a large number of local telephone companies, announced a plan to acquire Sprint, an interexchange carrier owned by Southern Pacific Co. After the merger with Southern Pacific, GTE would have control over both local, monopoly services and competitive, long-distance services. This integration was precisely the evil that the government sought to end by breaking up the Bell System. Consequently, in May, 1983, the government filed an antitrust suit alleging that the GTE merger plan would violate the Clayton Act, 15 U.S.C. §§ 12-27 (1983). At the request of the parties, the case was assigned to Judge Greene. Before trial, however, the parties presented the court with a consent decree that was conditionally approved. *United States v. GTE Corp.*, 603 F. Supp. 730 (D.D.C. 1984).

1. The decree permitted the merger to occur, but it imposed certain restrictions on GTE and its local operating companies ("GTOCs"). It also prohibited GTE from acquiring another interexchange service provider during the next ten years. In many respects—except for the fact that GTE was permitted to retain control over both local and interexchange telephone operations—these requirements closely resembled significant parts of the MFJ.

a. A structural separation provision required that GTE keep its local, monopoly telephone operations wholly separate from its competitive, long-distance business. This provision was designed to eliminate—or to expose—cross-subsidies that might permit GTE to reduce the price of its long-distance service unfairly. Under the separation requirements, all services sold by the GTOCs to Sprint (or vice versa) had to be sold at full market value, on the same terms that such services would be made available to unaffiliated companies.

b. The GTOCs also were required to provide equal access to all interexchange carriers. Because many of the GTOC end offices lacked the necessary switching equipment to provide such access, the decree prescribes a phase-in period for equal access. In particular, the operating companies must provide an interexchange carrier with equal access no more than twelve months after that access has been requested. By September 1, 1987, two-thirds of the GTOCs' access lines must be capable of providing equal access. All lines must be so equipped by December 31, 1990. The court approved a less rigorous conversion schedule than was imposed on AT&T because the lack of advanced switching systems and the relative paucity of traffic using GTOC facilities made rapid conversion impractical.

c. The consent decree also imposed a non-discrimination requirement on the GTOCs. This provision prohibited the operating companies from providing Sprint with favored access to GTOC facilities or information. In addition, it required the dissolution of a longstanding partnership with AT&T. This partnership, which included other, independent telephone companies, had given the GTOCs an incentive to favor AT&T as an interexchange carrier. By ending this partnership, the court believed an important aspect of market discrimination would be eliminated.

d. The GTOCs were prohibited from offering interexchange services or from owning any facilities used to provide interexchange services. This restriction posed a peculiar problem in Hawaii, where GTE owned the local telephone company and provided most of the telephone service to the mainland. Such interexchange service could no longer be provided by the Hawaiian GTOC after the merger. To make matters worse, Sprint had been the major interexchange competitor in Hawaii before the merger.

i) The State of Hawaii alleged that by preventing the GTOC (Hawaiian Telephone Co.) from providing interexchange service, the court would be (1) diminishing the quality and availability of service to the mainland, and (2) removing a lucrative part of the GTOC's revenue base, which would increase local rates. The court rejected these claims, concluding that (1) other interexchange carriers would provide the needed interexchange service, and (2) charges collected from these carriers for gaining access to the local loop would bolster the local revenue base, thus protecting local rates.

ii) To ensure future competition in the Hawaiian interexchange market, the consent decree prohibited Sprint from acquiring the interexchange business relinquished by the GTOC.

2. In two very important respects, the decree departed from the solution adopted in the AT&T case. First, the court allowed GTE to own both local exchange and interexchange service providers. Second, the court agreed to let the GTOCs continue providing information services, although under certain restrictions.

a. Judge Greene relied on six distinguishing factors that he believed justified the "minimal" separation requirements imposed on GTE.

i) GTE's operations, even after the merger, were on a much smaller scale than were AT&T's. This difference in size justified differing remedies.

ii) The GTOCs, unlike the BOCs, were relatively unconcentrated, and they operated in only a small number of the markets served by Sprint.

iii) Unlike AT&T, GTE-Sprint does not have a lengthy history as a vertically integrated company. Consequently, the court thought it would be easier to enforce a minimal separation policy: it was clear, from the start, what was and was not part of the local exchange operations.

iv) This lack of integration also made any anticompetitive practices easier to detect.

v) The decree's requirement that GTE end its "partnership" with AT&T would have significant pro-competitive consequences.

vi) The merger would enhance Sprint's financial outlook, making it a stronger competitor in the future. This result, again, would have pro-competitive consequences.

b. The court rejected the argument that by allowing the merger it was endorsing reduced competition in the interexchange market. Opponents of the merger argued that GTE would have entered the interexchange market on its own, serving as an additional competitor for both AT&T and Sprint. Judge Greene termed GTE's independent entry only a "theoretical" possibility, citing the high cost of such entry. In addition, the pro-competitive provisions of the decree, coupled with the fact that Sprint was likely to benefit from its alliance with GTE, outweighed any possible detriments—in the court's estimation.

c. The court was more concerned, however, with the apparent inequity of allowing the GTOCs to provide information services while completely excluding the BOCs from that market. Yet the court concluded that because of the BOCs' greater dominance of the local exchange market, and because BOC/AT&T connections were far more numerous than would be GTOC/Sprint links, the disparity in treatment was justified.

i) The court defined information services as

> the generation, processing, and making available information which may be conveyed by telecommunications, *e.g.* [sic] videotext, some form of electronic mail, electronic publishing services, data processing services, telephone-operated burglar alarm systems, and some office management systems.

Id. at 741 n.46. This definition is similar, in all relevant respects, to the one contained in the MFJ.

ii) Thus, the court approved of a decree provision that allowed the GTOCs to provide information services through separate subsidiaries. The operating companies also had to provide access to competing information providers on a non-discriminatory basis. The information subsidiary could purchase tariffed, publicly available services from the GTOCs at the tariffed rates; information or services not generally available to competitors could be purchased only "at a price which, at a minimum, exceeds their fully allocated costs." *Id.* at 742, n.49. The information subsidiaries could not, however, obtain proprietary marketing, customer, or network engineering information from the GTOCs.

iii) The court rejected a proposal that the separation requirements expire in five years. The court found "no reasonable basis" for this expiration period. *Id.* at 743. Instead, it decided that the requirement should be lifted only upon a showing "that there is no substantial possibility that [a GTOC] could use its monopoly power to impede competition in the information services market or until a similarly situated Bell Operating Company has made such a showing and is permitted to offer information services." *Id.* In this regard, the court clearly placed all of the operating companies—BOCs and GTOCs—on an equal footing.

3. The decree supplements the various safeguards by providing that the court may, upon application of the Justice Department, order further relief, including divestiture. In order to justify such relief, the Justice Department would have to prove, by a preponderance of the evidence, "that GTE or a GTE Operating Company violated the decree either by engaging in a pattern of substantial violations or by violating the decree in a manner which materially injures competitors [a standard to be described in the final decree]." *Id.* at 741. Thus, the threat of divestiture was left in place to prompt future compliance with the standards of the court's decision.

4. Judge Greene concluded his opinion by asserting that this decree, like the MFJ, "prevent[s] the defendant compan[y] from impeding competition, by use of local telecommunications monopoly bottlenecks, in markets where such competition is technologically feasible." *Id.* at 752. The difference in remedies, though, was justified because "GTE is simply not the Bell System." *Id.* at 753.

5. The decision is interesting in that it demonstrates the latitude Judge Greene has in restructuring the telecommunications market. Rather than following the logic of the MFJ and prohibiting co-ownership of monopoly-bottleneck and competitive facilities, he opted to permit integration and to use a consent decree to create a new company that he viewed as more competitive. This conclusion conflicts somewhat with the rationale of the AT&T divestiture, which sought to end unsuccessful attempts to simulate competition through regulation by returning control to the marketplace. In the *GTE* decision, by contrast, Judge Greene seems to be saying that he can stimulate competition—using a consent decree—more effectively than can the market.

G. The IBM-MCI Deal: Implications for AT&T's Future?

1. In June, 1985, IBM announced a deal with MCI whereby it acquired an eighteen percent interest in the number two long-distance company, making it the largest single holder of MCI stock. In return, IBM turned over to MCI virtually all of the assets of its struggling long-distance telephone subsidiary, Satellite Business Systems ("SBS"). IBM has committed itself, over the next three years, to investing an additional $400 million

in MCI securities. This has led some to speculate that IBM gradually will purchase all of MCI and become an integrated computer and communications company prepared to compete head-to-head with AT&T.

2. Most immediately, the transaction will provide MCI with much-needed financial backing for its battle to gain a larger share of the long-distance telephone market. (It currently has about eight percent of the business in that market.) More importantly, however, the alliance creates a potentially potent competitive force that should be well-positioned to exploit the growing market for integrated computer and communications services.

a. IBM can add MCI's transmission network to its own computer manufacturing and marketing expertise and to other facets of the computer and communications market that it has obtained through separate acquisitions. IBM recently acquired Rolm Corp., the nation's second-largest PBX manufacturer, and it has a significant investment in Sytek Inc., the nation's largest provider of local area networks ("LANs").

b. In combination, these pieces may fit together to form an attractive and well-equipped supplier of end-to-end communications and information processing networks. This possibility may provoke AT&T to act more quickly on the speculation that it is considering the purchase of a major interest in a computer manufacturer.

3. The IBM-MCI alliance is likely to have a significant impact both on the way that the long-distance telephone market operates and on the way that it is regulated.

a. That market now is undergoing a shakeout period as AT&T reprices its services, making circuit arbitrage—the lifeblood of resellers—an increasingly less attractive, and less profitable, business. Other than MCI and GTE-Sprint, none of the new entrants into the long-distance market—all of whom rely heavily on the resale of AT&T circuits—have been very successful in garnering significant market shares.

b. Recently, GTE has led an effort by long-distance companies to convince the FCC that it must constrain AT&T in order to ensure the long-term viability of competition in the interexchange market. Without such protective regulation, it has been argued, the Commission's pro-competition policies may be doomed. GTE spearheaded this effort with a lengthy report on the long-distance market that it claimed demonstrated the bleak future for the so-called other common carriers ("OCCs") and illustrated the need for FCC action. *See* Booz, Allen and Hamilton, *Prospects for Major Facilities-Based Other Common Carriers* (March 1985). The OCCs have claimed that the FCC (1) should at least maintain the differential between the prices paid for access to local exchanges by AT&T and by its competitors and (2) should continue to monitor AT&T's long-distance service prices. Both steps would help the OCCs offer service at prices that are lower than those of AT&T, which might help them build their subscriber bases.

c. The FCC's Office of Plans and Policy released a paper that rebutted GTE's argument and claimed that GTE was attempting to improve its market position by "exploit[ing] the U.S. government's (and the citizens' it represents) affection for competition." J. Haring, *The FCC, the OCCs and the Exploitation of Affection* 11 (1985).

d. Prior to the IBM-MCI deal, it did not appear likely that the FCC would "force" further competition into the long-distance marketplace through the use of additional, drastic regulatory measures. Although the FCC clearly favors competition, it does not now look kindly toward any actions that increase the amount of regulation.

e. The IBM-MCI deal makes this remote possibility even less likely; MCI, with IBM's help, should be capable of exerting at least some competitive pressure on AT&T. This competition would allow the FCC to let the marketplace, rather than regulatory edict, determine the future shape—and price—of long-distance service.

4. The deal may have another far-reaching effect on the way that communications policy accounts for AT&T's activities. Like the GTE-Sprint arrangement, the IBM-MCI deal represents a consolidation of different parts of the communications marketplace. Whereas AT&T was broken apart in an attempt to promote competition, other companies recently have combined to promote that same competition. (The GTE-Sprint merger was, of course, approved by Judge Greene, who ordered the AT&T divestiture.) Without such consolidation, some have argued, there would be no one entity capable of competing with AT&T or the BOCs—even in their post-divestiture forms.

a. It may well be that consolidation is necessary to succeed in a marketplace that increasingly appears to require the integration of local and long-distance communications capabilities with information processing features. In this respect, IBM and MCI may be building precisely the kind of relationship that is necessary to succeed in the evolving market.

b. If such integration is necessary, AT&T and the BOCs are likely to question forcefully whether they should continue to face the separation requirements that *Computer II* imposes on their communications and "enhanced services" activities. *See infra* Sections III and IV. They will argue that the structure of *Computer II,* which seeks to divide activities along technological lines, is contrary to the demands of the current marketplace. This conflict between market-based and technology-based regulation clearly is an undercurrent of the new *Computer III* proceeding. *See infra* Section IV.G.

c. AT&T's case for relief from the restrictions of the MFJ and of *Computer II,* which has been gaining support, is likely to be helped by the IBM-MCI deal. The deal also may speed up any move to relieve the BOCs from similar restraints, despite the fact that they still enjoy a virtual monopoly in each of their local service areas.

III. DELINEATION OF COMPETITIVE MARKETS: THE MERGER OF COMMUNICATIONS AND DATA PROCESSING

A. Introduction

1. Even before the 1974 antitrust suit had been filed, the FCC had begun to grapple with the problem of avoiding the regulation of competitive services. The growth of the computer industry and the increased reliance on, and sophistication of, various forms of data processing presented the FCC with a serious regulatory dilemma. The data processing industry had never been subject to federal oversight. However, communications carriers began to incorporate computers into their transmission networks, to create new and more sophisticated communciations services. As a result, the FCC faced the prospect of having to oversee at least some portion of the data processing business—in order to carry out its responsibility to regulate the nation's communications networks.

2. In addressing this problem, the FCC faced an issue that was significantly different from the one that would be presented by the government's suit against AT&T. Instead of attempting to restructure a single carrier in order to promote competition, the FCC had to restructure the boundaries of the entire marketplace. The Commission's task was to define the limits of its regulatory authority—or to refine the way in which it used that authority—so as to leave competitive businesses free form unnecessary restrictions or obligations.

3. As it turned out, this complex task ultimately included some degree of carrier-specific regulation. Special restrictions were placed on AT&T and its local telephone companies to prevent them from using their unique position in the communications marketplace to gain an unfair advantage in the data processing and computerized information businesses. Because these restrictions on AT&T were developed in light of the company's pre-divestiture makeup, their continued need, and appropriateness, is now being reviewed. To the degree that the divestiture eliminated much of AT&T's anticompetitive power, it is argued, the additional safeguards imposed by the FCC are unnecessary and, perhaps, counterproductive. *See, e.g., supra* Section II.G.

4. The result of the FCC's examination of this issue, which spanned sixteen years, was a pair of decisions commonly referred to as *Computer I* and *Computer II*. The difficulty of the issues involved is evident in the fact that just five years after the FCC's first resolution of the problem, in 1971, it reopened the entire proceeding and ultimately opted for a drastically different approach. Now, almost twenty years after this line of inquiry began, but less than five years since the its latest decision on the issue, the Commission has again begun to question the usefulness of the distinctions that it drew.

a. Rapidly evolving technologies, the effects of the divestiture, and the structural changes occurring in the communications market have eroded the basis for significant parts of the *Computer II* rationale. However, there still are strong views—among AT&T's competitors and others— that some kind of regulation (along the lines proposed by the reasoning in *Computer II*) remains necessary.

b. The FCC gradually has reshaped the *Computer II* rules in a piecemeal fashion, stretching the boundaries set up by the decision to accommodate what it perceives as necessary marketplace changes. For the most part, these revisions have permitted carriers to incorporate greater amounts of computerized intelligence into their networks, so that they can provide users with increasingly sophisticated communciations capabilities. The Commission now has proposed abandoning this ad hoc process of adjusting the *Computer II* rules; the *Computer III* proceeding, begun in July, 1985, would adopt an entirely new regulatory framework for handling the integration of computer and communications activities. *See infra* Section IV.G.

B. Computer I: The Distinction Between Data Processing and Communications Services

1. In 1966, the FCC initiated a rulemaking proceeding designed to resolve the regulatory and policy issues created by the growing interdependence of telecommunications and data processing. *Regulatory and Policy Problems Presented by the Interdependence of Computer and Communications Services and Facilities,* 7 F.C.C.2d 11 (1966) (Notice of Inquiry) [hereinafter cited as *Computer I*]; *Computer I,* 7 F.C.C.2d 19 (1967) (Supplemental Notice of Inquiry).

a. The FCC was most concerned with the increased availabilty and use of computer systems that could provide both data processing and message switching functions. By combining these systems with communications channels linking remote locations, large corporations with excess capacity on their in-house computers could offer the general public, on a time-sharing basis, a panoply of data processing and data base services. At the same time, common carriers were making increasing use of such computers to perform message and circuit switching functions in their communications networks. It was apparent that they, too, would inevitably broaden their service offerings into the data processing field. *Computer I,* 7 F.C.C.2d at 12-14.

b. The FCC's *Computer I* proceeding was motivated by a desire to delineate clear regulatory boundaries for increasingly similar service offerings. The same services were being distributed by communications common carriers—who traditionally were subject to FCC regulation under Title II of the Communications Act of 1934—and by traditionally unregulated suppliers of data processing services.

2. The FCC's attempt to rationalize an increasingly incoherent regulatory structure was further complicated by the restrictions imposed on AT&T under the terms of its 1956 consent decree with the U.S. Department of Justice. *See supra* Section II.D.1.

a. Under the decree, AT&T had agreed not to engage in any business other than providing for "common carrier communications services" or businesses "incidental thereto." *U.S. v. Western Electric Co., Inc.*, 1956 Trade Cases ¶ 68,246, at 71,138 (D.N.J. 1956). Section II(i) of the consent decree defined common carrier communications services as

> communication services and facilities, other than message telegram service, the charges for which are subject to public regulation under the Communications Act of 1934, or any amendment thereof, or would be subject to such regulation thereunder if such a service or facility were furnished in interstate commerce.

Id. at 71,137.

b. "Incidental" services were not defined. Under a restrictive construction of the consent decree, which prevailed at the time, the FCC's decision on the extent to which it would regulate data processing service offerings also would determine the extent to which AT&T and its local subsidiaries would be permitted to enter the data processing field.

3. The FCC determined that the exercise of its regulatory authority is required only (1) where economies of scale are so great as to support the need for a regulated monopoly, or (2) where other factors create the potential for unfair practices sufficient to warrant government intervention. *Computer I*, 28 F.C.C.2d 291 (1970) (Tentative Decision). The FCC concluded, accordingly, that there was sufficient competition in the data processing industry to make it unnecessary "to assert regulatory authority whether or not such services employ communications facilities in order to link the terminals of the subscribers to centralized computers." *Id.* at 298.

4. In order to give meaning to the regulatory dichotomy between communications and data processing services, the FCC had to devise a definitional scheme to distinguish between the two.

a. In its Tentative Decision, the FCC adopted the following definitions, which were ratified in subsequent *Computer I* decisions.

> i) *Data Processing*—the use of a computer for the processing of information as distinguished from circuit or message-switching. "Processing" involves the use of the computer for operations which include, *inter alia*, the functions of storing, retrieving, sorting, merging and calculating data, according to programmed instructions.
>
> ii) *Message-Switching*—the computer-controlled transmission of messages, between two or more points, via communications facilities, wherein the content of the message remains unaltered.
>
> iii) *Local Data Processing Service*—an offering of data processing where communications facilities are not involved in serving the customer.
>
> iv) *Remote Access Data Processing Service*—an offering of data processing wherein communications facilities, linking a central computer to remote cus-

tomer terminals, provide a vehicle for the transmission of data between such computer and customer terminals.

v) *Hybrid Service*—an offering of service which combines Remote Access data processing and message-switching to form a single integrated service.

Id. at 295 (footnote omitted).

b. Under this definitional scheme, message switching services clearly would be subject to common carrier regulation. No regulation, however, would be imposed on data processing services, including remote access data services. The regulatory status of hybrid—or mixed—services remained problematical.

c. The FCC declined to adopt any bright-line rule as to when hybrid services would be subject to regulation. Instead, it decided to forbear completely from regulating services in which message switching functions were incidental to the primary application of data processing operations. By contrast, where a hybrid service was designed primarily to satisfy the communications or message-switching requirements of a subscriber, and where the data processing feature was merely incidental, the entire offering would be subject to regulation. This result was true regardless of whether or not the service provider was a common carrier.

d. The FCC said it would look to whether a hybrid service, by virtue of its message switching capability, was basically a substitute for a point-to-point service offered by a conventional common carrier. *Id.* at 304-05; *see also Computer I*, 28 F.C.C.2d 267, 277-81 (1971) (Final Decision and Order).

5. The FCC concluded that its decision to forbear from regulating data processing largely barred AT&T and its affiliates from offering such services under the terms of the 1956 decree. AT&T was, however, left free to provide data processing services incidental to communications—within the meaning of both the consent decree and the FCC's policy on hybrid services. 28 F.C.C.2d at 305 (Tentative Decision).

6. Although the FCC's decision foreclosed AT&T's direct entry into the data processing field, it permitted other common carriers to enter this market—subject to certain regulatory safeguards.

a. The FCC recognized that common carrier entry into the data processing field presented a significant number of problems. These included cross-subsidization of data processing services with revenues derived from communications service offerings and the risk that common carriers would use their control over bottleneck communications facilities to gain an unfair advantage over competitors. Nonetheless, the FCC found that the public benefits derived from increased competition and from the availability of fully integrated service offerings warranted carrier participation. *Id.* at 301.

b. To safeguard against potential abuses, the FCC adopted a "maximum separation" policy that required common carriers to offer their data processing services exclusively through newly established subsidiaries with separate officers, accounting systems, and equipment. Carriers also were barred from obtaining data processing services from their data processing subsidiary. The data processing subsidiaries were free to obtain communications services or facilities from affiliated carriers, but these arrangements could be no more favorable than those available to unaffiliated data processing entities. *Id.* at 303; *see also* 28 F.C.C.2d at 274 (Final Decision and Order). Common carriers could not engage in marketing activities on behalf of their data processing affiliates. Nor could they permit the affiliated company to use—in its name—any words or symbols contained in the carrier's name. *See* 28 F.C.C.2d at 303 (Tentative Decision); 28 F.C.C.2d at 269-71 (Final Decision and Order).

7. The FCC's maximum separation policy was challenged by a number of common carriers on appeal to the Second Circuit Court of Appeals. *See GTE Service Corp. v. FCC*, 474 F.2d 724 (2d Cir. 1973).

a. The carriers claimed that the FCC had exceeded its jurisdiction in adopting the various rules implementing this policy. The court noted the broad statutory power granted to the FCC by Section 1 of the Communications Act of 1934, 47 U.S.C. § 151 (1983) ("[To regulate] interstate and foreign commerce in communication by wire and radio so as to make available, so far as possible, to all people of the United States a rapid, efficient, Nation-wide, and world-wide wire and radio communication service with adequate facilities at reasonable charges . . ."). Courts consistently had interpreted this provision as giving the FCC expansive rulemaking authority in the new and dynamic field of electronic communications. Accordingly, the court ruled that the FCC's concerns over cross-subsidization and the potential that carriers would pass the costs of data processing on to communications service subscribers provided it with a sufficient factual predicate for its regulations. 474 F.2d at 732.

b. The court took issue, however, with the FCC's rules (1) barring use of the carrier name or symbol by the data processing affiliate and (2) prohibiting carriers from obtaining any data processing services from such an affiliate. It characterized these rules as based upon antitrust considerations—a concern that carriers would use their monopoly power over communications services to gain leverage in the market for data processing services—rather than on the potential impact on regulated communications services of carrier entry into data processing. *Id.* at 733. The court held that case law allowed the FCC to regulate on the basis of antitrust considerations only where such considerations pertain to markets over which the FCC has jurisdiction. Because the FCC had never claimed jurisdiction over data processing services, and because the court could find no statutory basis—either express or implied—for the exercise of such jursdiction, the court held these rules void as ultra vires. *Id.* at 735.

C. Computer II: The Distinction Between Basic and Enhanced Services

1. Just four years later, new developments in computer technology and inadequacies in the *Computer I* decision forced the FCC to revisit the issues it had raised. *See Amendment of Section 64.702 of the Commission's Rules and Regulations*, 61 F.C.C.2d 103 (1976) (Notice of Inquiry) [hereinafter cited as *Computer II*]; *Computer II*, 64 F.C.C.2d 771 (1977) (Supplemental Notice of Inquiry and Enlargement of Proposed Rulemaking).

a. The definitional structure adopted in *Computer I* reflected a technological environment in which subscribers' remote, "unintelligent" terminals were linked to a central, "host" computer that provided data processing services. Between the initiation of *Computer I* and *II*, however, rapid advances in large-scale integrated circuitry and microprocessor technology had permitted fabrication of mini-computers, micro-computers, and other devices capable of duplicating the data processing functions previously performed only by the host computer. These developments made it possible—and cost-beneficial—for users to distribute some of the processing power either to terminals located on the customer's premises or to facilities incorporated within the communications network itself. *See Computer II*, 77 F.C.C.2d 384, 391 (1980) (Final Decision).

b. *Computer I* failed to address the phenomenon of services that utilized these distributed processing technologies. Consequently, the FCC was forced to cope with a variety of unanticipated forms of hybrid service. It became increasingly difficult to determine whether such services were incidental to a communications offering or vice versa. These services' growing ubiquity made ad hoc determinations an administrative quagmire. *See Computer II*, 72 F.C.C.2d 358, 362-63 (1978) (Tentative Decision); 77 F.C.C.2d at 391-93 (Final Decision).

c. The legal and regulatory obstacles to AT&T's participation in the data processing field further complicated matters. Under *Computer I*, AT&T and its affiliates were barred by the 1956 consent decree from offering data processing services, except to the extent that such services were incidental to a communications offering regulated by the FCC as a hybrid service. This situation placed the FCC under increasing pressure to expand its regulation of hybrid services, which would permit AT&T more flexibility to incorporate state-of-the-art technology into a communications network. Such a result, however, was fundamentally at odds with *Computer I*'s unregulated, pro-competitive approach to data processing.

d. Finally, terminals and other types of customer premises equipment ("CPE"), offered by both the regulated carrier sector and the unregulated data processing sector, increasingly were capable of performing both communications and information processing functions. This raised new problems as to how these offerings should be classified for regulatory purposes. *See* 72 F.C.C.2d at 406-12 (Tentative Decision); 77 F.C.C.2d at 435-36 (Final Decision).

2. *Computer II* dispensed with the *Computer I* distinction between communications and data processing. Instead, it adopted a regulatory structure that distinguished between "basic services" and "enhanced services."

a. The FCC defined basic services as a carrier offering of a "pure transmission capability over a communications path that is virtually transparent in terms of its interaction with customer supplied information." 77 F.C.C.2d at 420 (Final Decision). Distinguishing "basic" from "enhanced," the FCC noted:

> [A] basic service is the offering of a "transmission pipeline" in contrast to the myriad services that are dependent upon, but different in kind from the pipeline service.

Computer II, 84 F.C.C.2d 50, 53 (1980) (Reconsideration Order).

b. Enhanced services were defined as "any service other than basic service." 77 F.C.C.2d at 386 (Final Decision). The FCC stated that an enhanced service

> combines basic service with computer processing applications that act on the format, content, code, protocol or similar aspects of the subscriber's transmitted information, or provide the subscriber additional, different, or restructured information, or involve subscriber interaction with stored information.

Id. at 387.

c. Under *Computer II*, basic transmission services were subject to Title II regulation. Enhanced services were left unregulated, although the FCC determined that when offered by a Title II carrier, they would be subject to regulation under the Commission's ancillary jurisdiction, which derives from Section 2(a) of the Communications Act, 47 U.S.C. § 152(a) (1983).

i) In the initial stages of its *Computer II* inquiry, the FCC contemplated a regulatory structure that would have required further subclassifications of enhanced services. Enhanced communications services, in which the data processing function directly related to and was for the purpose of either providing a communications service or meeting a carrier's own internal financial and operational needs, also would have been subject to Title II regulation. Enhanced data processing services, which would have been unregulated, could be provided by common carriers through a separate subsidiary on a resale basis. *See* 72 F.C.C.2d at 399-403 (Tentative Decision); 77 F.C.C.2d at 395-98 (Final Decision).

ii) The FCC ultimately recognized, however, that this division would lead to the same problems in distinguishing between communications and data processing that had caused its *Computer I* decision to unravel. Therefore, the FCC rejected the distinction. *See* 77 F.C.C.2d at 425-26 (Final Decision).

d. Although the FCC decided to forbear from regulating all enhanced sevices, it exercised its ancillary jurisdiction to require that those carriers with sufficient market power to engage in a significant degree of anti-competitive conduct or cross-subsidization abide by the maximum separation requirements of *Computer I*. *See* 77 F.C.C.2d at 468-69 (Final Decision). Both carriers and non-carriers were able to offer enhanced services, subject to this one condition.

3. The FCC also decided to deregulate CPE. It required that the charges for CPE be unbundled from those for basic transmission services; rate regulation of CPE was discontinued, and CPE was required to be sold separately from basic transmission services in a competitive market. *See* 77 F.C.C.2d at 446-47 (Final Decision). As was the case with enhanced service offerings, only those carriers with significant market power were subject to the separation requirements with respect to their CPE offerings. *Id.* at 468-70.

4. The FCC concluded that only AT&T had sufficient market power to warrant imposition of the separation requirements on its enhanced service and CPE offerings. These requirements obligated AT&T to form a separate subsidiary for such offerings. *See* 84 F.C.C.2d at 72-75 (Reconsideration Order); 77 F.C.C.2d at 466-70 (Final Decision). (In the Reconsideration Order, the FCC reversed its earlier decision to impose structural separation requirements on GTE.)

a. To avoid subjecting the subsidiary to tariff regulation, which would negate the structural separation of regulated and unregulated activities, the FCC barred the subsidiary from owning or operating its own transmission facilities. Thus, the subsidiary was required to obtain its transmission capacity from an underlying carrier pursuant to tariff. *See* 84 F.C.C.2d at 79 (Reconsideration Order).

b. The FCC also adopted the following safeguards to ensure that the subsidiary would not be cross-subsidized by AT&T and its affiliates.

i) In all transactions with its subsidiary, AT&T was required to charge the full cost of transferred goods and services on the same terms and conditions as would be available to non-affiliated purchasers.

ii) Written accounts had to be kept of all transactions that involved the transfer, either directly or indirectly, of money, personnel, resources, or anything of value between AT&T and its subsidairy. Copies of any contract, agreement, or other arrangement between AT&T and its subsidiary had to be filed with the FCC within thirty days of its execution.

iii) AT&T was prohibited from engaging in the sale or promotion of enhanced services on behalf of its subsidiary.

iv) AT&T was required to disclose network information to competitors at the same time, and under the same terms and conditions, as it was disclosed to its subsidiary.

v) AT&T was proscribed from providing its subsidiary with any customer proprietary information unless such information was public. *See* 77 F.C.C.2d 475-84 (Final Decision).

5. The FCC recognized that AT&T's 1956 consent decree with the Justice Department only could be construed definitively by the New Jersey federal court that had approved it. Nonetheless, the Commission concluded that AT&T could offer enhanced services without running afoul of the decree, despite the FCC's forbearance from exercising Title II jurisdiction over such services.

a. The FCC suggested two alternative grounds for this conclusion. First, the enhanced services were seen as "incidental to" the provision of common carrier services within the meaning of Section V of the 1956 consent decree. These enhanced services presupposed the use of common carrier facilities and, therefore, could permissibly be offered by AT&T. *See* 77 F.C.C.2d at 490-95 (Final Decision); 84 F.C.C.2d at 107-08 (Reconsideration Order).

b. Alternatively, the FCC concluded that enhanced services met the definition of common carrier services contained in Section II(i) of the decree because they were "*subject* to public regulation under the Communications Act of 1934." *U.S. v. Western Electric Co.*, 1956 Trade Cases at 71,137 (emphasis added). Although the FCC had determined that enhanced services were not subject to Title II rate regulation, it nevertheless had concluded that it had

> [ancillary] jurisdiction to regulate a carrier's participation in the provision of enhanced services under *GTE Service Corp. v. FCC*, . . . (citations omitted) . . . because these carriers' enhanced services activities "may substantially affect the provision of reasonably priced communications services."

84 F.C.C.2d at 93 (Reconsideration Order). Using its ancillary jurisdiction, the FCC had adopted its separation policy with respect to AT&T. Because Section II(i) required only that a service be subject to "public regulation" under the Communications Act of 1934—not that it be subject to Title II regulation—the FCC concluded that its exercise of ancillary jurisdiction in imposing the separation requirements brought enhanced services within the ambit of the decree's definition of services that AT&T permissibly could offer. *Id.* at 107-08.

c. The confusion that has surrounded this issue is a further example of the effect of the split of regulatory authority between Judge Greene and the FCC. *See supra* Section II.D.7.

6. In the Reconsideration Order, the FCC clarified the scope of its ancillary jurisdiction over enhanced services.

a. The Commission held that it never had decided the extent, if any, of its power over enhanced services. It had determined only that when an entity otherwise licensed under either Title II or Title III of the Act provided an enhanced service, the FCC could exercise its ancillary jurisdiction to ensure that the enhanced service activity was provided in a manner that did not frustrate other goals of the Communications Act. The imposition of the separation requirements discussed above represent the exercise of this ancillary power.

b. This jurisdicitonal ruling left undecided the issue of whether the FCC might have the power to regulate the enhanced service offerings of non-carriers. 84 F.C.C. 2d at 95-96 (Reconsideration Order). The Commission did not see a "clear nexus" between its statutory powers and these non-carrier activities, *id.* at 95; therefore, it decided not to confront this issue.

c. This undecided question has not had any practical impact on service offerings. Enhanced services provided by non-carriers—like enhanced service offerings of all carriers except AT&T and the BOCs—have been left unregulated. The question that remains, though, is whether these non-carrier activities could be regulated if the FCC so desired.

7. The *Computer II* decision was challenged on several grounds in an appeal to the D.C. Circuit. These challenges included claims that the FCC was not empowered to forbear from Title II rate regulation of all enhanced services and CPE and that the FCC exceeded its ancillary jurisdiction in imposing the separation requirements on AT&T and in ordering the unbundling of CPE. *See Computer and Communications Industry Association v. FCC*, 693 F.2d 198 (D.C. Cir. 1982), *cert. denied sub nom. Louisiana Public Service Comm'n v. FCC*, ____ U.S. ____, 103 S. Ct. 2109 (1983) [hereinafter cited as *Computer II Appeal*].

a. The court held that the FCC had acted permisssibly in forbearing from Title II regulation of enhanced services and CPE. Noting that the Communications Act of 1934 authorizes Title II regulation of common carrier services but does not itself define the term "common carrier," the court applied the test for common carriage that it had developed in prior decisions. *Id.* at 209-10; *see also NARUC I*, 525 F.2d 630 (D.C. Cir. 1976), *cert. denied*, 425 U.S. 992 (1977); *NARUC II*, 533 F.2d 601 (1976). It found that neither enhanced services nor CPE met the fundamental element of this test: a carrier's undertaking "to carry for all people indifferently." *Computer II Appeal*, 693 F.2d at 210 (quoting *NARUC I*, 525 F.2d at 640). Because both types of offerings enabled vendors to tailor their services to meet the particularized needs of individual customers, the court did not see them as within the *NARUC I* conception of "common carrier."

b. Alternatively, the court held that even if some enhanced services could be classified as common carriage, the FCC had acted properly in forbearing from regulation. The FCC's amply supported finding that it could not feasibly separate regulable from non-regulable services justified its forbearance. *Id.*

c. The court also rejected the argument that the FCC had exceeded its jurisdiction in imposing the separation requirements on AT&T and in unbundling CPE charges from basic transmission rates. It held that under § 2(a) of the Communications Act of 1934, 47 U.S.C. Section 152(a)

(1983), the FCC may exercise jurisdiction over "all interstate and foreign communication by wire or radio," even where communications activities are not within the reach of the FCC's Title II jurisdiction. 693 F.2d at 213; *see also United States v. Southwestern Cable Co.*, 392 U.S. 157 (1968). The court determined, however, that prior case law limited the FCC's jurisdiction to that which is "reasonably ancillary to the effective performance of the Commission's various responsibilities" under other sections of the Communications Act. *Computer II Appeal*, 693 F.2d at 213 (quoting *Southwestern Cable Co.*, 392 U.S. at 178). Because one of those responsibilities "is to assure a nationwide system of wire communications services at reasonable prices," and inasmuch as the FCC had demonstrated that its decision with respect to enhanced services and CPE was tailored to this purpose, the court upheld the FCC's actions. 693 F.2d at 213.

IV. THE FUTURE OF THE COMPUTER II DECISION

A. Introduction

1. Once again, just five years after its latest boundary-line decision, the Commission is considering whether—as a result of technological and marketplace changes—the regulatory scheme of *Computer II* remains an effective means of encouraging the development of new and innovative services.

2. Since 1980, the shape of the "non-competitive" market for basic services has changed significantly. In the wake of divestiture, and amid the effort to provide equal access for all interexchange competitors, the interexchange market has become more competitive. In addition, more sophisticated cable television systems and a variety of other technologies capable of bypassing the local loop have introduced very limited competition into the local exchange market. Finally, the increasing sophistication of integrated circuits, which permits the devleopment of powerful, compact, affordable computing devices, has continued to obscure the always-vague line between communications and data processing—the basis for the FCC's definitional distinctions in *Computer I* and *II*.

3. Enhanced services have developed primarily for large business users. Some contend that there is little demand for such services among individual users; others claim that residential users have suffered because of obstacles placed in the way of AT&T and the BOCs as a result of *Computer II*. It is argued that because of *Computer II* these carriers have been unable to use their vast networks to extend enhanced services to the majority of users.

4. The FCC occasionally has resorted to circuitous logic to bring a service that is fundamental to the basic transmission network, but which falls under the literal definition of an enhanced service, within the scope of its "basic services" category. The Commission also has established a waiver procedure, to allow for deviations from the *Computer II* framework

where necessary to accommodate evolving network and user needs. These evasions—and invasions—of the *Computer II* dichotomy have provoked questions about the need to revisit the decision. In recent speeches, three FCC Commissioners suggested the need for such a reexamination. Commissioner Henry M. Rivera, *Remarks Before the Law & Business, Inc. Seminar: Structural Separation for Telephone Companies?* (June 21, 1985); Commissioner Mimi Weyforth Dawson, *Remarks Before the USTA 10th Annual Seminar for Institutional Investment Analysts* (March 26, 1985); Commissioner Dennis R. Patrick, *Remarks Before the 1985 Communications Network Exposition* (Jan. 29, 1985).

a. Both Commissioners Dawson and Patrick argued that the FCC should take a more functional approach to distinguishing between competitive and non-competitive services. In addition, they both noted the importance of focusing on two separate issues: first, whether the service to be provided is subject to competition, and second, whether the carrier providing that service has the power to act in an anticompetitive manner.

b. While agreeing with his fellow Commissioners that technology has outpaced the FCC's ability to "adjust" the basic and enhanced categories, then-Commissioner Rivera (who recently left the FCC) stressed the need for the FCC to ensure that any modifications of the *Computer II* rules guarantee consumers the maximum marketplace benefits. He also emphasized a need for caution in dismantling the current regulations in order to ensure that FCC action promotes "full and fair competition." H.M. Rivera, *supra*, at 7.

5. In general, *Computer II*'s definitional approach has been criticized primarily for having proved too static. Critics claim that it has failed to accommodate the marketplace changes that the divestiture and the advent of new technologies have brought. The FCC responded to these complaints in late July by deciding to release a Notice of Proposed Rulemaking initiating the *Third Computer Inquiry—"Computer III." See* FCC Report No. CC-166, Mimeo No. 6022 (released July 25, 1985). This proceeding will consider abandoning the *Computer II* rules and adopting a more market-based approach that would regulate individual services on the basis of the actual conditions of the marketplace (*e.g.*, the dominance of the service provider, the potential for competitive offerings of the service being regulated). The *Computer III* inquiry is discussed more fully below, *see supra* Section IV.G.

6. Before it decided to undertake a complete reevaluation of the *Computer II* rules, the FCC had been working to "adjust" those rules on an ad hoc basis, in order to permit various kinds of enhanced services to be provided in reasonably economical ways. Such fine tuning has presented the Commission with a number of complex regulatory problems. These are reviewed below, in order to provide a backdrop for a discussion of the FCC's decision to initiate *Computer III*.

B. Protocol Conversion and the Separate Subsidiary Requirement

1. In Its *Computer II* decision, the FCC determined that protocol conversion operations—except for those that were wholly internal to a network—were enhanced services. This finding is consistent with the conclusion that an enhanced service is one that alters a subscriber's information or electronic signals. *See Computer II*, 77 F.C.C.2d at 420-21 (Final Decision). Protocol conversion was viewed as a competitive communications service; thus, it was left unregulated. In addition, to prevent AT&T and the BOCs from competing unfairly, the FCC required that they provide protocol conversion services only through separate subsidiaries. (While the *Computer II* decision imposed structural separation on AT&T, the FCC acted separately, in 1983, to apply the requirement to the divested BOCs. *See infra* Section IV.D.)

a. The FCC defined a protocol as "governing the rules and methods used for packaging the transmitted data in quanta, the rules for controlling the flow of information, and the format for headers and trailers surrounding the transmitted information and of separate control messages." 77 F.C.C.2d at 420 n.33.

b. Protocol conversion—of a type constituting an enhanced service—was performed when information exited the network, at its point of destination, in a different protocol from the one in which it entered the network. Processing operations often were performed to enhance the transmission capabilities of a network or to allow information to be transmitted across an intermediate network that required a specific transmission protocol. In these instances, however, the carrier's changes were wholly internal and—like a basic service—transparent to the user: before the information exited the network, it was converted back to the same protocol in which it had entered the network.

i) Protocol conversion really alters only the "control" information associated with a communication. The alteration often is necessary to permit transmission of the communication through the network. Unlike data processing, in which the carrier's interaction with a subscriber's communication frequently produces an output that is noticeably different to the subscriber, protocol conversion goes virtually unnoticed.

ii) Protocol conversion clearly is a valuable service. It allows a subscriber to use various kinds of transmission paths—such as packet-switched networks—that may be more efficient than the circuit-switched telephone system. In addition, it permits users of otherwise incompatible terminals to communicate with each other. In many instances, however, it is difficult to separate the protocol conversion operation from the basic transmission function.

c. By requiring that protocol conversion be performed outside of the basic transmission network, the FCC limited the degree to which AT&T (and the BOCs after divestiture) could modify existing circuits and switches to offer more advanced transmission services (such as packet switching). To provide a service requiring protocol conversion, these carriers had to operate through a separate subsidiary that would acquire basic transmission facilities pursuant to tariff—just like any other independent carrier. Separate staffs also had to be used to provide basic and enhanced services. By comparison, carriers not subject to the FCC's separation requirements could, after acquiring or building the necessary transmission facilities, provide both enhanced and basic services through a single network, using just one set of employees. As a result of these requirements, it was argued, the carriers subject to them were forced to segregate inherently integrated network functions unnecessarily. Inefficient loops between a central office switch and conversion equipment had to be constructed because the separation requirements prohibited such carriers from building conversion capabilities into their central office facilities. This additional wiring raised the cost of providing protocol conversion, which has dissuaded at least the BOCs from offering many services that required protocol conversion. However, the FCC legitimately was concerned with ensuring that carriers continued to offer "pure" transmission service, since many communications did not require any protocol conversion. By defining protocol conversion as a distinct, competitive service, the FCC could prevent basic carriers from bundling this processing with "basic" service and forcing all users to pay for the cost of the processing.

2. As a result of the burdens imposed by the separation requirements, the FCC instituted a proceeding to determine whether, and to what extent, protocol conversion might be treated specially. *Communications Protocols Under Section 64.702 of the Commission's Rules and Regulations*, 83 F.C.C.2d 318 (1980) (Notice of Inquiry). The primary question before the Commission was whether a dominant carrier (at that time only AT&T, since the divestiture had not yet occurred) could collocate protocol conversion and basic service equipment. Packet-switched transmission was an area of particular concern, because a number of international transmission standards that required protocol conversion had been established for packet switching. One protocol was established for communication between a subscriber and the network; another governed internetworking. There frequently was a net protocol conversion (rather than merely an internal manipulation) because individual users transmitted communications in one protocol (asynchornous), and the large mainframe computers with which they communicated received communications in a different protocol (X.25, the one used to package the communciation for packet-switched transmission). Consequently, AT&T could not provide this enhanced service as part of its basic transmission network.

3. Rather than alter its rules, the Commission "clarified" *Computer II* and adopted a set of principles under which requests for a waiver of the separation requirements would be evaluated. *Communications Protocols Under Section 64.702 of the Commission's Rules and Regulations*, 95 F.C.C.2d 584 (1983) [hereinafter cited as *1983 Protocol Order*].

a. The FCC reiterated its earlier clarification of the *Computer II* rules, which exempted internal network processing from the enhanced services category. All internal processing necessary to operate, for example, a circuit-switched network was deemed part of the network's basic service.

b. A second area of concern involved the introduction of new basic service technology. Frequently, new technology is introduced piecemeal, and appropriate conversion equipment is used within the network to maintain compatibility. A problem might arise, for example, if a call were placed by a user of equipment employing a digital interface to a user having an analog interface (with appropriate conversion equipment employed within the network). In that case, there would be a net protocol conversion within the network. The telephone call then would be considered an enhanced service, although the service itself would remain simply a switched message service. The FCC stated that it would be disposed to act favorably and expeditiously on petitions for a waiver of the *Computer II* rules—in order to avoid discouraging technological change. *Id.* at 591-92.

c. Finally, the FCC determined that the appropriate treatment of other forms of protocol conversion could not be prescribed by general rule. It did note, however, that certain structural separation requirements could result in undue inefficiency. As a result, the FCC adopted four general principles under which waiver requests would be analyzed.

i) First, the Commission indicated that it would look most favorably on waiver requests required simply to allow network interconnection. The FCC was particularly concerned, in this regard, with international services. It was likely that different national networks would use different communication protocols and that a net protocol conversion often would be required.

ii) Second, the FCC decided that it would require a carrier receiving a waiver to maintain underlying transparent transmission facilities unencumbered by protocol conversion capabilities. With this requirement the FCC sought to maintain the general availability of sufficiently versatile basic transmission services. This was necessary to meet the disparate needs of communications users and to permit third parties who could offer protocol conversion functions more efficiently than a carrier to be able to do so.

iii) Third, the FCC said it would review waiver requests carefully to ensure that only protocol conversion was being proposed, not processing which creates, deletes, or changes information, or involves subscriber interaction with stored information.

iv) Fourth, the FCC concluded that it would be inclined to act more favorably on requests for a waiver in circumstances where third-party provision of protocol processing (external to the network) was not a feasible alternative.

d. The Commission represented its decision as a reaffirmation of the principles of *Computer II*. The "adjustments" made were seen merely as clarifications necessary to avoid unintended results that could occur if the *Computer II* rules were applied in an overly literal fashion. Finally, the waiver procedure was viewed as a way of dealing with a special circumstance without eroding the *Computer II* definitions.

C. Applicability of the Separate Subsidiary Requirement to the BOCs: Local Value-Added Services

1. After the *1983 Protocol Order*, eight BOCs filed petitions seeking waivers of the structural separation requirements to provide certain types of protocol conversion within their basic networks. In a November, 1984, decision, the FCC acted only on the least controversial of the waiver requests. Action on all other requests was deferred. *Petitions for Waiver of Section 64.702 of the Commission's Rules and Regulations*, FCC No. 84-561 (released Nov. 28, 1984).

a. The FCC permitted the BOCs to provide the X.25-to-X.75 internetwork interface as part of a basic service. That interface is required to connect packet-switched facilities with high-speed, specialized, long-haul facilities. The FCC noted that such an interface could not practically be provided outside of the network. (In addition, because the X.75 interface had been adopted by the CCITT as an international standard, the FCC viewed it as necessary to allow the BOCs to provide the interface conveniently. This authorization was considered a desirable way of fostering the development of new services, since it would encourage network interconnection.)

b. In support of its decision, the Commission noted that before the divestiture, this X.25-to-X.75 conversion would have taken place wholly within the facilities of the integrated AT&T. As was clear from the *1983 Protocol Order*, such internal processing would not have been considered an enhanced service. Consequently, the FCC decided, it made no sense to impose structural separation requirements on this type of processing simply because the divestiture had separated the BOCs from AT&T.

c. The X.75 interface was permitted, without triggering separation requirements; however, it had to be provided under a separate tariff. This requirement ensured the continued availability—through unbundling—of pure transmission capacity. The FCC also authorized any other dominant carriers to provide the same interface simply by notifying the Commission, provided that a proper tariff was filed.

2. Shortly after these decisions, the Commission was beseiged with a series of new waiver petitions from the newly formed BOCs. The result of these petitions was an FCC Order that some observers—including Commissioners Patrick and Dawson—view as a tacit admission that the *Computer II* decision needs to be revisited and that the basic/enhanced line must be revised. *See Petitions for Waiver of Section 64.702 of the Commission's Rules*, FCC No. 85-101 (released March 26, 1985).

a. The BOCs sought to be allowed to build asynchronous-to-X.25 interfaces into local office wiring so that local loops could be linked directly through the local switch to existing or planned packet-switched services. Because virtually all home computers employed the asynchronous communications protocol, and because packet networks transmit information in the X.25 format, this interface was necessary to make the service attractive to microcomputer users. Value-added network ("VAN") operators already provided this interface by means of a packet assembler/disassembler device ("PAD"), which linked a VAN to the user's local telephone exchange.

b. Because of the way local telephone services were priced, VAN operators had an economic incentive to locate the PAD far from the subscriber's home. Instead of using a large number of PADs, spread among numerous local offices, these networks relied on a small number of central nodes, which linked a large number of subscribers to the VAN by means of local telephone company interoffice wiring. Users then could route their data communications over local telephone lines, for which no use-sensitive charge is imposed, to the VAN operator's central network node. In using this wiring arrangement, however, VANs required users to tie up a large number of local circuits, thereby burdening the local exchange. This configuration defeated one of the efficiencies of packet-switching, which is its ability to carry a large number of users' "bursty" data transmissions over a single circuit path without having to dedicate a line to each user. What the BOCs wanted to do, in part, was to hook users directly into a packet-switched network at a more localized level. This would reduce the demand for local circuits, since it would route data transmissions almost directly into the packet network. It also would enable the BOCs to provide local packet-switched service—between local offices; VAN services were essentially interexchange services.

c. As the FCC properly noted, the BOCs were permitted, by *Computer II*, to arrange for such services. The only constraint was that any protocol conversion services had to be provided by a separate subsidiary using equipment not located within the basic network. The BOCs wanted these separation requirements lifted. They claimed that a waiver would allow them to offer packet-switching at a lower price and in a more efficient network configuration.

d. The FCC expressed some reservations about the potential for BOC anticompetitive actions if the waivers were granted. However, it granted them—in part—subject to certain conditions.

i) The Commission waived only the collocation restriction, allowing the BOCs to install protocol processing equipment within local exchange facilities. Incidental to this waiver, the FCC also allowed BOC employees to perform the installation and maintenance of the processing equipment. The resultant packet-switched service still had to be provided by, and marketed through, a separate subsidiary. The FCC concluded that the waivers, as qualified, were faithful to the principles of the *1983 Protocol Order, supra*.

ii) To the degree the BOCs used interoffice lines to construct local packet networks, those circuits had to be made available to third parties at the same price, and on the same terms. The FCC reasoned that this requirement would extend to all service providers any cost efficiencies the BOCs realized by increasing the use of packet-switched services.

> If the BOCs are correct that lower prices [will] stimulate market growth to the benefit of the public, they will have strong incentives to promote the growth of their own packet switched services by bringing down the prices of the circuits. Because of our requirement for equal treatment of other service vendors, the benefits of this will be available to the other service vendors as well.

FCC No. 85-101, supra, at 43.

iii) The BOCs were required to unbundle circuit and interface charges so that third parties could continue to obtain X.25 lines without having to pay a portion of the BOCs' costs of installing and operating asynchronous communications ports. Third parties, as well as the separate subsidiaries, would pay a separately stated tariff charge for these "pure" transmission circuits.

iv) The BOCs also were forbidden from providing users with better access to BOC packet-switched networks than the access provided to similar networks of third parties. Thus, dialing differentials could not be used to give the BOCs a comparative advantage. In addition, the separate subsidiaries, even though they would be using a connection to end users that was located within a central office, were required to acquire that connection on a tariffed basis. The BOCs were given some flexibility in calculating the cost of this connection. The FCC observed that economies achieved by using within-office wiring—rather than external loops—appropriately could be passed along to users, even though this might give the BOCs a comparative advantage over independent service providers.

e. The FCC recognized that its waiver process—even as clarified—was highly imperfect. Therefore, it announced, in its Order, that it planned to issue a Notice of Proposed Rulemaking that would "seek to formulate general rules of future applicability to govern the treatment of protocol conversion and similar enhanced services." Id. at 7.

D. Intersection of Computer II and the MFJ: The BOCs, "Information Services," and the Enhanced Services Definition

1. In the wake of the divestiture, the FCC had to decide whether the newly formed BOCs, when offering enhanced services and CPE, would be subject to the separation requirements of *Computer II*. In principle, of course, separation would be necessary, because all carriers owning transmission facilities technically are required to create separate competitive

subsidiaries. The FCC, however, had not applied this requirement to any carrier other than AT&T.

2. The FCC also faced the question of determining whether all enhanced services, as defined by *Computer II*, were "information services" within the meaning of the MFJ. If the two definitions were identical, then the BOCs would be unable to provide any enhanced services, absent an explicit authorization from the D.C. Court.

a. Section IV(J) of the consent decree defined an "information service" as

> the offering of a capability for generating, acquiring, storing, transforming, processing, retrieving, utilizing, or making available information which may be conveyed by telecommunications, except that such service does not include any use of any such capability for the management, control, or operation of a telecommunications system or the management of a telecommunications service.

Section IV(O) of the decree defined "telecommunications" to mean

> the transmission, between or among points specified by the user, of information of the user's choosing, without change in the form or content of the information as sent and received by means of electromagnetic transmission, with or without benefit of any closed transmission medium, including all instrumentalities, facilities, apparatus, and services (including collection, storage, forwarding, switching, and delivery of such information) essential to such transmission.

b. There are, without question, ambiguities in these definitions. For example, while the "information services" definition would seem to exclude such "system operation" functions as protocol conversion, the definition of "telecommunications" excludes a "change in form," which, arguably, is the result of protocol conversion. Consequently, protocol conversion might not fit within either category. This is the same kind of problem that has plagued the basic/enhanced dichotomy: it is exceedingly difficult to define the point at which the operation of a transmisison network ends and the enhancement of it begins. While the MFJ may exclude such processing from the forbidden realm of information services, as discussed above, the FCC clearly has included it within the definition of "enhanced services" (although it has, in subsequent proceedings, chipped away at this result). Judge Greene, in his decision, did not resolve the ambiguity; he concluded that enhanced services "are essentially the equivalent of 'information services.' . . ." 552 F. Supp. at 178 n. 198.

c. To the degree that information services do not include all enhanced services, the BOCs seemingly would be permitted to offer certain enhanced services—subject to any applicable separation requirements imposed by Computer II. Yet the primary line-of-business restriction that the MFJ imposes on the BOCs—that they provide only those services regulated by tariff—would seem to preclude them from offering any enhanced service, because all such services are unregulated after Computer II.

3. To resolve these issues, the FCC issued a Notice of Proposed Rulemaking in 1983. Policy and Rules Concerning the Furnishing of Customer Premises Equipment, Enhanced Services and Cellular Communications Services by the Bell Operating Companies, 93 F.C.C.2d 722 (1983) [hereinafter cited as Computer II BOC Proceeding].

a. In its Notice, the Commission signaled its intent not to apply the structural separation requirements to the BOCs. The FCC pointed to the fragmentation of control over local bottleneck facilities caused by the divestiture and to the MFJ's prohibition on the manufacturing of CPE by the BOCs as reasons why separation might not be necessary. As a result of the divestiture, the FCC seemed to feel, the BOCs did not possess the kind of anticompetitive power that would make structural separation necessary.

b. When the Commission issued its Order in this proceeding, however, it decided to impose a modified form of structural separation on the BOCs. It also declined to address the issue of whether "information services" and "enhanced services" are the same. Computer II BOC Proceeding, 95 F.C.C.2d 1117 (1983).

i) The FCC avoided the definitional question by noting that because all enhanced services are unregulated, the only question to be answered is whether the BOCs can provide certain enhanced services. This question is one that the court would have to answer, based upon the restrictions imposed by the decree on the BOCs' permissible lines of business.

ii) The FCC said that in cases where the BOCs are permitted to offer new services, it would render case-by-case determinations as to whether those services were basic or enhanced. (This is what it did in the case of protocol conversion, as discussed above. See supra Section IV.B.)

iii) With respect to structural separation, the FCC decided that the benefits to the public of protecting against cross-subsidization and overloading of the rate base outweighed any costs that BOCs would incur by having to set up separate competitive subsidiaries. Despite its earlier intimations that the local exchange operations—as "fragmented"—might not have the necessary market power to act in an anticompetitive manner, the FCC decided that, on balance, a separation requirement would foster competition and would best serve the public interest. Thus, the Commission imposed a slightly streamlined form of separation, allowing inter alia, certain joint operations, such as billing and marketing.

4. On April 30, 1984, AT&T petitioned the FCC for removal of the separation requirements in light of the changed cirucmstances resulting from the divestiture of the BOCs. See Petition of American Telephone and Telegraph Company For Relief From Structural Separation Requirements, Dkt. No. 20828 (filed April 30, 1984). AT&T argued that the rationale for imposing the separation rules on it—control over bottleneck facilities and the potential for cross-subsidization of competitive activities with monopoly revenues at the expense of regulated ratepayers—are no longer applicable in the post-divestiture environment. At the same time, the petition argues,

the rules restrict AT&T's ability to compete with other service providers, to the detriment of the general public.

5. The FCC has proposed removing the separation requirement with respect to AT&T's provision of CPE. It has deferred consideration of the request to eliminate this requirement for enhanced services. Furnishing of Customer Premises Equipment and Enhanced Services by American Telephone & Telegraph Co., FCC No. 85-86 (released Feb. 22, 1985) (Notice of Proposed Rulemaking). The BOCs have requested that any changes in the structural separation requirements applied to AT&T should be applied to them as well. The Justice Department, which has supported AT&T's petition, has opposed the BOCs' argument. Adoption of the proposed Computer III rules largely could eliminate these problems by abolishing the separate subsidiary requirement and by eliminating or decreasing other separation requirements. See infra Section IV.G.

E. Integrated Services Digital Networks ("ISDN"): Computer II in a Global Environment

1. Regulatory Issues

a. The FCC has issued a First Report in a proceeding that assesses the role of the agency and of *Computer II*-related issues in the U.S. and international phases of the ISDN planning process. *See Integrated Services Digital Networks (ISDN)*, FCC No. 84-131 (released April 2, 1984) [hereinafter cited as *First Report*].

i) The FCC initiated the proceeding with a Notice of Inquiry, *Integrated Services Digital Networks (ISDN)*, 48 Fed. Reg. 37,404 (Aug. 18, 1983). It began by stating that it did not seek to engage actively in the planning of ISDN facilities. However, it said it would participate in and review the planning process in accordance with its statutory jurisdiction over the offering of common carrier services, the provision of facilities, and the registration of equipment to prevent harm to the network. 48 Fed. Reg. at 37,467.

ii) The FCC observed that most non-U.S. telecommunications systems are administration-owned. Some of those administrations might perceive ISDN as an extension of their centralized systems, a view not shared by the U.S., which is characterized by competition and the existence of multiple service providers. *Id.* at 37,468-69. The FCC recognized that competitive forces and the diversity of service providers in the U.S. also could result in some deviation from the uniform CCITT ISDN technical specifications. It expressed the hope that the ISDN planning process would be flexible enough to accommodate U.S. interests and policy requirements. *Id.* at 37,469-70.

iii) The FCC emphasized the importance of implementing ISDN consistently with *Computer II*. It noted that, in the U.S., there may be ISDNs that provide solely basic services (*e.g.*, those offered by BOCs) as well as ISDNs that offer both basic and enhanced services. *Id.* at 37,470. To foster its pro-competitive policies, the FCC expressed the tentative conclusion that it would have to monitor and participate in both international and domestic ISDN planning activities.

b. In the *First Report* the FCC underscored an earlier conclusion that digital network channel terminating equipment ("NCTE") is CPE, within the meaning of *Computer II*. As CPE, it is to be provided on an unregulated, competitive basis.

i) ISDN planning documents had contemplated that terminals would be required to include certain functions; however, this kind of technical specification is viewed as contrary to the FCC's CPE policies. Under its Part 68 registration program, the FCC avoids specifying any equipment standards other than those required to protect the network from harm. *See generally* 47 C.F.R. Pt. 68 (1984). This policy provides manufacturers with maximum flexibility, permitting the production of a wide variety of competitive CPE. It also avoids burdening users with possibly costly terminal capabilities that they really do not need or desire.

ii) The FCC also advocated the use of a universal network interface that would allow users to connect a wide variety of NCTE to the local loop. *First Report, supra,* at 13-18.

c. The FCC had expressed some concern in the Notice of Inquiry as to whether *Computer II*'s basic/enhanced dichotomy would be compatible with the evolving international ISDN structure. In the *First Report* the Commission said it was encouraged that a flexible approach to ISDN planning—which would acommodate U.S. policy—was developing.

i) In its planning documents, the CCITT had classified ISDN services as either "bearer services" or "telecommunications services." In its Notice of Inquiry, the FCC had observed that the bearer/telecommunications dichotomy was not analogous to the basic/enhanced distinction, largely because the most prevalent "basic" services—public switched network offerings and telex—were included in the "telecommunications" category. *See First Report, supra,* at 21. AT&T and others had urged that the *Computer II* rules be changed to reflect the classifications of an ISDN environment; however, the FCC concluded that those rules were firmly established and should, therefore, be accommodated in ISDN planning efforts. *Id.* at 23.

ii) The FCC focused on its earlier decision about protocol conversion to point out that the regulatory waiver mechanisms it had established would give ISDN service providers flexibility in designing their network operations. Using this waiver procedure, however, services could be offered within the framework of the *Computer II* dichotomy; the FCC also could ensure, by continuing to apply *Computer II*, that basic offerings were made widely available to the public. *Id.* at 23-24.

d. At the February, 1984, CCITT Study Group XVIII meeting in Brasilia, the earlier "bearer" and "telecommunications" service classifications were modified in a way that accommodated the basic/enhanced service dichotomy. The working draft of the I-Series Recommendations now establishes a single ISDN service category—"telecommunications"—with two subcategories—"bearer services" and "teleservices." "Bearer" services include such "basic" services as public switched, telex, and private line, as well as some "enhanced" protocol operations. "Teleservices" include largely protocol operations that would constitute "enhanced offerings. *See* CCITT Study Group XVIII, *Final Report to the VIIIth Plenary Assembly* 39-82 (Doc. No. AP VIII-97-8) (Report R-32) (June, 1984). The FCC views this change as significantly minimizing potential CCITT-*Computer II* conflicts because each administration or carrier, whether U.S. or non-U.S., can implement functions, or adopt interfaces, without impairing U.S. policies. *First Report, supra,* at 26-27 & n.59. U.S. carriers could provide bearer services—which are essentially "basic" services—as a pipeline ISDN offering without violating the prohibition on the collocation of equipment providing basic and enhanced services.

e. The FCC also concluded that informal or advisory participation in ISDN planning efforts was the proper approach for it to take. The FCC staff would be expected to become involved in other groups' activities as the most effective way of articulating FCC policy concerns to those directly involved in planning for and representing the U.S.

i) The FCC stated that existing groups provide adequate opportunity for participation in the development of U.S. ISDN policies. These include the U.S. CCITT Organization, an advisory committee in the U.S. Department of State; the ISDN Joint Work Party ("JWP") (which coordinates all U.S. ISDN contributions to the CCITT); and the JWP's Technical Working Group ("TWG"). The Exchange Carriers Standards Association, which has been formed to develop voluntary technical standards to govern exchange facilities, is expected to assume the TWG's functions in the near future.

ii) Policy issues, said the FCC, must be raised early on to avoid conflicts between U.S. domestic law and CCITT recommendations that are based on the different structures of various nation's telecommunications markets and systems. Nevertheless, the FCC concluded that formal rulemakings would be neither practical nor desirable, given the flexibility necessary to the ISDN design process. The FCC will seek to resolve other policy issues as they arise by issuing further reports in the ISDN proceeding.

2. *Current Developments*

a. ISDN planning in the U.S. must take into account the multiple facilities providers that characterize the telecommunications sector. The concept of ISDN that may prevail elsewhere—one network through which a plethora of services flow—is not applicable where there is no single, integrated network. ISDN activity has, therefore, concentrated on network improvements, with the stress being placed on internetwork compatibility and versatility.

b. As in many other countries, the movement toward ISDN is focused on digitization of existing networks. According to one estimate, as much as eighty percent of the local access lines and fifty percent of the interexchange switches have already been converted to digital equipment. Dorros, *The ISDN Challenge in the United States* 12 (1985). Through the end of the 1980s, it is expected that most of the digitization efforts will focus upon local switches and interexchange trunk facilities. *Id.*

c. Digital private line service, which has been available since 1974, is expected to accelerate rapidly over the next few years.

i) In part this is a result of the antiquated nature of most local loops—and the fact that little of this local plant is likely to be digitized in the near future. Consequently, business users seeking the capacity provided by digital transmission facilities need to take advantage of private line services.

ii) Users have increasingly become interested in higher-speed lines (1.544 Mbit/s). It is estimated that the number of high-speed transmission links could double annually. *Id.* Growing use of fiber optics and digital PBXs also is expected over the next three years.

d. A number of the BOCs are now beginning—or will soon introduce—various trials involving small-scale digital systems that are intended to test the equipment being used and to acquaint customers with the capabilities of an integrated network. One of the BOCs (NYNEX) recently announced its plan to introduce five new digital transmission and switching services that it views as part of the "transition to ISDN." The services will be available primarily to large business customers on a leased line basis. However, one service, called Switchway, will allow smaller users to use digital transmission capacity by pricing it on a usage-sensitive basis. Illinois Bell, Northwestern Bell, and Pacific Bell also have announced plans for ISDN trials to begin in 1986 and 1987.

e. It is anticipated that the "next step" in this process will be the deployment of various wideband services, such as bulk data transfers and video delivery services. Customer demand for these services is already high and is growing rapidly. Nevertheless, given the competitive environment, there is not much planning for the introduction of integrated "services" on a multiple-network basis.

F. Application of Computer II to International Services

1. In deciding whether to apply the *Computer II* rules to international services, the FCC had to confront how—if at all—it should take account of the policies of other countries, such as the prohibition on circuit resale that is contained in the CCITT Recommendations and is enforced strictly by many foreign administrations. The Commission has sought, in its decisionmaking, to divorce the resale issue from the question of what international services it would regulate and how it might regulate them. This separation of issues has generated considerable controversy, however, be-

cause some carriers and service providers have claimed that the application of the *Computer II* rules internationally—leaving international enhanced services unregulated—represents an implicit decision to permit U.S. carriers to resell circuits freely.

2. Despite the controversy surrounding this issue, the FCC quickly decided to apply the *Computer II* rules to all services—both domestic and international.

a. Even before the courts had affirmed the FCC's *Computer II* decision, the FCC's Common Carrier Bureau had ruled that international packet-switched services were enhanced services. A packet network, to be provided by two U.S. carriers between the United States, the United Kingdom, and Western Europe, would not, consequently, be subject to Title II regulation. The Bureau decision held that no Section 214 authorization was needed prior to facilities construction. A number of petitions were filed seeking full Commission review of the decision. The petitions alleged that the Bureau's decision was an unlawful exercise of authority because it exceeded the limits of the power delegated to the Bureau. The Commission, it was claimed, had never applied *Computer II* to international services; therefore, the Bureau's decision was improper.

b. The FCC summarily affirmed the Bureau's decision, readily finding that it was amply supported by prior Commission rulings. *GTE Telenet Communications Corp.*, 91 F.C.C.2d 232 (1982). The Commisison claimed that the basic/enhanced dichotomy had been developed to apply—on a generic basis—to all services.

i) In making its case, the FCC pointed to a single sentence in one footnote of the Reconsideration Order for a direct holding that the "basic/enhanced dichotomy is applicable to both domestic and international services provided over common carrier facilities." *Computer II*, 84 F.C.C.2d at 53, n.4. Otherwise, it relied on the fact that no other decision had distinguished between domestic and international services to argue that the basic/enhanced dichotomy applied universally.

ii) In a dissenting statement, one commissioner wrote that "[a] one line footnote which mysteriously crept into the Reconsideration Order must not be allowed to determine the course of Commission policy . . . ." *GTE Telenet*, 91 F.C.C.2d at 241. He claimed that the Commission had not sufficiently considered the complex issues presented by the international marketplace, and the precipitous action could have grave consequences.

3. The FCC also concluded that applying *Computer II* internationally would not damage a carrier's ability to negotiate operating agreements with foreign correspondents. 91 F.C.C.2d at 238 & n.8.

a. Some enhanced service providers feared that certain PTTs might view them as illegal circuit resellers or as unauthorized service providers and, therefore, would refuse to negotiate operating agreements with them.

b. Certain carriers worried that any decision by them to supply underlying transmission capacity to enhanced service providers would be viewed by PTTs as a violation of the CCITT Recommendations. In retaliation, these administrations might refuse to deal with the "reselling" carriers as well.

4. In a separate part of the *GTE Telenet* decision, the FCC decided that the separate subsidiary requirement, though technically applicable to the International Record Carriers ("IRCs"), should not be applied to them. Its application would raise directly all of the broad policy issues about international resale and shared use arrangements; therefore, the FCC concluded, the separation issue warranted isolated, comprehensive consideration.

a. Applying the separation requirements could force an IRC's competitive subsidiary to purchase transmission capacity and to resell it as part of an enhanced service. If the enhanced service were to involve activities that essentially were akin to a transmission service, making them likely to divert traffic from the public network, they could be seen as contravening the widely enforced prohibition on facilities resale. (In other countries, where a central administration enjoys monopoly control of the communications facilities, the CCITT Recommendations essentially prohibiting resale are enforced strictly to protect the government monopoly.) This result would leave U.S. policy seemingly at odds with the policies followed by many other countries. The FCC, accordingly, left this issue to a separate inquiry into international resale policy. *See Regulatory Policies Concerning Resale and Shared Use of Common Carrier International Communications Services*, 77 F.C.C.2d 831 (1980) [hereinafter cited as *International Resale*.]

b. The Notice of Proposed Rulemaking in this proceeding, which has now been out for five years, remains unresolved. Thus, the resale issue continues to cloud the international services market.

c. In its decision affirming the application of *Computer II* to international services, the Commission explicitly stated that it was not prejudging the international resale issue. Many parties claimed that the international application of *Computer II* represented a de facto endorsement of international resale. *See GTE Telenet*, 91 F.C.C.2d at 240.

5. Large users of equipment and services, two international record carriers, and an association for data processing service providers petitioned the Commission to reconsider its *GTE Telenet* decision. They argued that the FCC had acted without adequately considering the potentially adverse impact on U.S. users of international private line services. Citing CCITT Recommendations and the requirement that telecommunications be provided either by Administrations or by a Recognized Private Operating Agency ("RPOA"), the petitioners claimed that other countries might consider an unregulated user of an international private line to be violating national and international regulations by serving a third party. The petition-

ers buttressed their statements with messages from European authorities, who expressed concern about the possible ramifications of U.S. efforts to apply the *Computer II* dichotomy to international services.

a. The petitioners argued that European authorities have resisted the application of *Computer II* to international services. They highlighted a 1982 situation in which seven countries had solicited bids from U.S. carriers for exclusive operating agreements to provide U.S.-European data services. This effort was viewed as a reaction to the FCC's deregulatory activities that ultimately could thwart the FCC's pro-competitive initiatives.

b. In a September, 1982, message to FCC Chairman Mark Fowler, Leon Burtz, Director of the CCITT, expressed deep concern about the application of the basic/enhanced dichotomy to international services. Burtz feared strong reactions from foreign administrations and RPOAs that were parties to interconnection agreements with U.S. carriers.

c. In his October, 1982, response to Director Burtz, Chairman Fowler stated that the FCC had not established a new policy with respect to international resale and that carriers remained subject to existing CCITT Recommendations and to tariffs that restrict third-party facilities use.

6. In January, 1985, the Commission finally acted on these petitions when it affirmed the international application of *Computer II*. *GTE Telenet*, FCC No. 85-29 (released Feb. 22, 1985). The decision, however, continues to leave the international resale question unresolved, awaiting further action in the separate *International Resale* proceeding.

a. The FCC again ruled that the *Computer II* proceeding had contained both adequate notice of the international service issue—thereby inviting vigorous public comment—and an unambiguous application of the basic/enhanced dichotomy to all services, including international ones.

i) It pointed to a portion of the Tentative Decision in *Computer II*, 72 F.C.C.2d at 437, in which it had invited comment specifically on the issue of whether the basic/enhanced definition should be applied internationally. The FCC also had expressed some reluctance about bifurcating the regulatory process, to distinguish between domestic and international services; it thought that any such bifurcation might inhibit the expansion of enhanced services beyond U.S. borders.

ii) The FCC also expanded upon the reasoning of its earlier Order in *GTE Telenet*. It argued that *Computer II* explicitly sought to distinguish between all basic services; nothing in the decision suggested an intent to consider only domestic services. In other words, the determination was "generic." The FCC also rejected the argument that the application of the basic/enhanced dichotomy to "interstate" services clearly indicated a lack of intent to apply it to "foreign" services.

> [U]se of the term "interstate" merely establishes a jurisdictional nexus for the exercise of federal jurisdiction. . . . It serves to make clear that Section 64.702(a) applies to any service involving common carrier facilities used in interstate com-

munications, regardless of whether the end-to-end service is intrastate, interstate or foreign.

FCC No. 85-29, supra, at 23.

iii) Finally, the FCC protected itself by claiming that even if it had reserved any decision on the international application of Computer II, it would have been justified in applying Computer II internationally in the context of the GTE Telenet adjudication. "It is clear that we received adequate comments on the issue in Telenet," the FCC decided. Id. at 24.

b. Amplifying its belief that adverse consequences would not result because of the international application of Computer II, the FCC defended its decision. It termed its decision merely a ruling as to the applicability of Title II regulation to services provided in the U.S. or by a U.S. entity as part of an international service.

i) The FCC restated its contention that a decision on international resale still has not been made. It rejected the claim that by deregulating enhanced services, it has endorsed—in effect—the free resale of international facilities.

ii) A third party's ability to use a carrier's facilities is determined by the carrier's tariff, which may or may not restrict such use. The Commission, in Computer II, did not require the removal of any resale restriction that might be found in a carrier's tariffs. Such a result would be reached only if the FCC decided, in the International Resale proceeding, that such restrictions should be removed. Thus the carriers, rather than the Commission, are in the position of having to enforce resale restrictions by preventing circuit use that is viewed as inconsistent with resale prohibitions—and, hence, not authorized by applicable tariffs.

iii) Having endorsed the concept of a competitive market in international services, the FCC also committed itself to "tak[ing] whatever steps are appropriate to apprise foreign administrations of the limited effect of Computer II, . . . [including] that this Commission took no action in Computer II that contravenes or undermines international agreements or recommendations governing resale of private line facilities [,that alters] . . . the provision or deployment of enhanced services abroad." Id. at 29. It agreed to aid carriers who, while providing unregulated, enhanced services, found foreign administrations unwilling to enter into operating agreements.

iv) The issue of how to clarify the "status" of such carriers, making it clear that the U.S. has authorized numerous carriers to provide a variety of international services, is being addressed separately in another proceeding. See International Communications Policies Governing Designations of Recognized Private Operating Agencies, Grants of IRUs in International Facilities and Assignment of Data Network Identification Codes, 95 F.C.C.2d 627 (1983) (Notice of Inquiry); FCC Report No. DC-152, Mimeo No. 5791 (released July 12, 1985) (Notice of Proposed Rulemaking) [hereinafter cited as International Policies]. v) In general, foreign administrations were believed to be reluctant to deal with U.S. carriers not explicitly recognized as "official" carriers by the government. (This reluctance may represent a backlash against the structure of the U.S. market.) In his separate statement in the Notice of Inquiry, Commissioner Rivera noted that (1) such a refusal to deal had occurred just once since 1982, and (2) where necessary, the FCC would communicate directly with a foreign correspondent, as it had in that one case, to certify that U.S. law permitted the involved carrier to provide the proposed service.

vi) Nonetheless, the FCC has proposed a program whereby enhanced service providers readily could gain RPOA status. Such "official" status would not be required for a service provider to engage in international offerings; the FCC concluded that in instances where foreign administrations are willing to deal with "unofficial" service providers, the RPOA label would serve no real purpose.

7. The FCC's decision to apply Computer II internationally and to leave individual carriers with the task of enforcing their own tariff restrictions on circuit resale enables a potentially unlimited number of service providers to enter the international market—provided they can obtain the needed transmission facilities and the necessary operating agreements with foreign administrations. With its proposed rules in the International Policies proceeding, which include a requirement that carriers permit service providers to acquire equity interests in international cable facilities, the Commission is looking to enhance the opportunity for service providers to compete in the international arena. It remains to be seen whether the decision by some countries to adopt liberalized communications policies, including, in some cases, the authorization of competitive service providers, will expand further the opportunities for U.S. service providers to compete internationally.

G. Computer III: The Transition from Waivers To a New Regulatory Framework

1. It appears that the FCC finally has lost faith in the process of granting ad hoc waivers to bring service configurations within the framework of the Computer II rules. Believing that the current regulatory scheme may have delayed the introduction of new services, increased their costs, and, in some cases, prevented consumers from receiving certain services, the Commission has launched a Notice of Proposed Rulemaking that would end the basic/enhanced dichotomy. See Computer III, FCC Report No. DC-166, Mimeo 6022 (released July 25, 1985). It also would eliminate—or, at least, would reduce—the separation requirements now imposed on enhanced service and CPE offerings by AT&T and the BOCs.

2. The Notice contains two sets of proposals:

a. The first set suggests a new, comprehensive analytical framework for regulating the competitive communications offerings of "dominant" carriers (AT&T and the BOCs). All services provided by "non-dominant" carriers or by non-carriers either would be unregulated or would fall within the FCC's forbearance policies (leaving them subject to regulation, but essentially unregulated). See infra Section VII.A. Where necessary to protect against cross-subsidization, certain offerings of dominant carriers could be subjected to minimal separation requirements.

b. The second set requests public comment on four specific proposals to modify the Computer II rules—pending adoption of a broad, new regulatory regime. The modifications deal with issues that have been the subjects of debate in recent years: (1) the regulatory status of protocol conversion activities, see supra Section IV.B; (2) the rights of enhanced service providers to interconnect their technology and equipment with a dominant carrier's facilities or to collocate that technology and equipment on the carrier's premises and the impact of such policies on ISDN, see supra Sections IV.C. & E.; (3) the regulatory classification of voice message storage service; and (4) the need—if any—for regulation of network channel terminating equipment ("NCTE"), see supra Section IV.E.

c. The second set of proposals admittedly will not resolve what the FCC views as the broader problems with the Computer II regulatory scheme. However, the FCC perceives two possible benefits from the discussion of these discrete issues: (1) the comments may provide additional insight into the way in which the Computer III rules ultimately should be structured, and (2) the relatively rapid adoption of some or all of these specific proposals could provide interim relief from some of the marketplace difficulties now being caused by the Computer II rules.

3. The Commission's proposed new regulatory framework would divide the telecommunications services marketplace into three categories and would make regulatory action dependent upon the marketplace status of the particular service being considered. In determining how to treat the different services, the FCC would examine both the market power of the entity providing the service and the potential for competition in that service.

4. The three categories being proposed are "communications," "ancillary-to-communications," and "non-communications."

a. "Communications," essentially, would be what are now "basic" services. When provided by a dominant carrier, they would be subject to Title II regulation. When provided by any other entity, they basically would be unregulated. See infra Section VII.A.

b. The "ancillary-to-communications" category would include equipment and services that are subject to FCC jurisdiction but are now, primarily, unregulated. This would include, for example, CPE and activities that fall within the current "enhanced services" category. Virtually all carriers would be able to continue providing these services on an unregulated basis. However, in instances where a dominant carrier provides an "ancillary" service that (1) cannot be offered competitively and (2) depends on that carrier's dominance (e.g., is provided within a BOC's local exchange area), the FCC might impose certain separation requirements such as tariff unbundling, separate cost accounting, or continued availability of underlying transmission capacity. These partial separation requirements would replace the current separate subsidiary requirement imposed on AT&T and the BOCs. Like the separate subsidiary requirement, they would be intended to protect a dominant carrier's subscribers from cross-subsidization that would force them to pay for enhancements to the network that they do not use.

c. "Non-communications" functions of all entities would, of course, be unregulated. However, the FCC might use its ancillary jurisdiction to require that a dominant carrier, in certain instances, institute safeguards to protect subscribers against cross-subsidization.

5. The proposed regulatory scheme would change the presumption inherent in the FCC's current regulations. There would not be an expectation, subject to individual waiver requests, that AT&T and the BOCs must separate—to the greatest degree possible—all of their enhanced services from their basic services. Instead, the presumption would be that all activities except "communications" activities of dominant carriers should be unregulated. In the case of specific services, the FCC—where market conditions warrant—would impose some additional regulatory safeguards in order to minimize any perceived anticompetitive effects that could result from allowing a dominant carrier to bundle a particular activity with the basic transmission functions of its network.

6. The FCC had not, as of early August 1985, released the full text of its Notice of Proposed Rulemaking; thus, the rationale for and all the nuances of the FCC's proposed regulatory scheme are not yet fully known. What form any rules might assume remains to be seen after what is certain to be a lengthy—and lively—parade of comments from the public. The FCC's current schedule calls for an initial comment period of three-and-a-half months.

V. DEFINING THE BUSINESS OF THE RHCS: LATAS AND LINE-OF-BUSINESS WAIVERS

A. The Local Access and Transport Area ("LATA")

1. The MFJ defined the RHCs and the permissible service areas for their telephone operating companies (the BOCs). These definitions determined the primary shape of local telephone service in the post-divestiture marketplace. BOC operations reach eighty percent of the telephone subscribers in the continental United States, although the BOCs serve just 7,000 of the more than 18,000 local exchanges. The Independent Telephone Companies, which cover a much greater geographic portion of the U.S. than do the BOCs, serve many sparsely populated areas. Less than a year after the MFJ, Judge Greene reviewed and approved the blueprint for BOC operations, which now defines the way in which the companies operate. United States v. Western Electric Co., Inc., 569 F. Supp. 990 (D.D.C. 1983).

2. The term "LATA" was devised for the divestiture process to describe the area within which a BOC could provide telephone service. It is not synonomous with a "local exchange," which is the calling area within which subscribers' telephones all have the same three-digit prefix. Local telephone regulators use these exchanges to define the areas within which a subscriber can make a "local" (as opposed to "toll") telephone call. The MFJ established approxiamtely 160 LATAs; there are approximately 7000 local exchanges served by the BOCs. Consequently, a call within a single LATA may be either a local or a toll call, although it can be carried by a single BOC. The call's rate designation is determined by state regulation; it is not affected by the antitrust court's determination of LATA size and location. See 569 F. Supp. at 994-95.

3. There is significant potential for confusion between the terms "LATA" and "exchange" because the MFJ describes a BOC's service area as an "exchange area." The BOCs are forbidden, in Section IV(K) of the MFJ, from providing "interexchange telecommunication." In truth, the BOCs can provide service between exchanges; they cannot, however, provide inter-LATA telecommunication.

B. Intra-LATA Services

1. The boundary lines of the various LATAs do not determine the areas within which a BOC provides local monopoly telephone service. Monopoly service is local exchange service; AT&T and other long-distance carriers such as GTE-Sprint and MCI operate between exchanges—in the interexchange market. Consequently, a BOC and an "interexchange" carrier can compete for intra-LATA traffic. The fact that a call is a "toll" call does not mean that it must be carried by an interexchange carrier. All inter-LATA

traffic, however, must be handled by one of the long-distance (interexchange) carriers.

2. As Judge Greene noted in his decision, "the establishment of many relatively small LATAs would tend to favor the various interexchange competitors . . . , principally because among the consequences of such a choice would be a diminution in the number of points between which any particular Bell Operating Company . . . may carry telecommunications." 569 F. Supp. at 995 (footnote omitted).

3. Using its "power with respect to the Operating Companies," id. at 1005, the court required the BOCs to provide interexchange carriers with equal access for intra-LATA, as well as inter-LATA, traffic. Intra-LATA access was not required by the original terms of the MFJ. Id. at 1004-06.

a. Within a LATA, however, the court permitted an exception to the equal access concept that applied to all inter-LATA connections. The BOCs are permitted to retain a significant competitive advantage over all interexchange carriers—including AT&T—in configuring the networks to handle intra-LATA toll calls. While exchange access for all interexchange carriers must be equal, it need not be equivalent to the connections that the BOCs provide for their own wires between end offices in a single LATA (interoffice trunks). As a result, a subscriber placing an intra-LATA toll call automatically will be routed over BOC wires unless he dials a four-digit access code to select one of the interexchange carriers. Unlike the inter-LATA market, BOCs will not be required to provide for a preselection option to subscribers that allows them to select a long-distance company for which they do not have to dial an access code.

b. Judge Greene decided that the huge capital investment that preselection capacity would require the BOCs to make justified this disparity. The BOCs would have to reprogram their end office switches to accommodate user selections of as many as two carriers (one for inter-LATA and one for intra-LATA calls). He also rejected a request that users be required to dial an access code for all intra-LATA toll calls—even those handled by the BOCs. This equality requirement "would have the perverse effect of making intra-LATA, or local toll calls, more cumbersome to dial than inter-LATA, or long distance toll calls." 569 F. Supp. at 1109.

4. A current controversy over the interpretation of the MFJ concerns an RHC argument that the term "exchange telecommunications" does not restrict the company to providing intra-LATA service only within the area where its BOCs operate as the primary local telephone companies. Two of the RHCs have asked Judge Greene to "clarify" the decree and to rule that they may provide intra-LATA service ("exchange telecommunications") within any one LATA in the country. The Justice Department has opposed this motion as being contrary to the intent of the divestiture. See, e.g., Memorandum in Support of Ameritech's Motion for Clarification of the Decree Regarding Provision of Cellular Radio Services Outside the Ameritech Region, United States v. Western Electric Co., 569 F. Supp. 990

(D.D.C. 1983) (filed Jan. 22, 1985); Response of the United States to Ameritech's Motion to Provide Cellular Radio Services Outside Ameritech's Region, United States v. Western Electric Co., 569 F. Supp. 990 (D.D.C. 1983) (filed Feb. 21, 1985).

C. Principles of LATA Configuration

1. General Concepts and Limited Exceptions

a. Judge Greene sought to configure the LATAs so that they would help preserve the viability of the BOCs. He did not explicitly require large LATAs that would provide BOCs with vast service areas in which they could carry a huge number of calls. An attempt was made, however, to keep the areas large enough to generate significant service revenues and to reduce upward pressure on local service prices. The court reviewed AT&T's LATA proposals to determine whether they would provide "the most effective means of furthering the [decree's] competitive goals consistent with the Communications Act's universal service mandate." 569 F. Supp. at 1000-01.

b. Generally, LATAs were formed around individual metropolitan areas and, in most cases, did not cross state lines. There were, however, a number of exceptions that the court reviewed closely. Under the MFJ, the court had to approve, individually, any LATA that crossed state lines or encompassed more than one Standard Metropolitan Statistical Area ("SMSA"). (An SMSA is a designation used by the Commerce Department to describe an area containing a city and its associated suburbs. There were 323 SMSAs nationwide at the time of the court's decision.) In most cases, the court approved these SMSA combinations and permitted LATAs to cross state lines, in order to accommodate "established traffic patterns" among related geographic communities.

c. Another exception that the court also allowed was the so-called "limited corridor exception." This calling configuration allowed BOCs in New York, New Jersey, and Pennsylvania to carry interstate calls in a heavily used calling areas. The two corridors involved carry calls between New York City and Northern New Jersey and between Camden, New Jersey, and Philadelphia. The court noted that while these exceptions would permit the BOCs to continue serving a very lucrative calling market, that market still would be open to competition from interexchange carriers. (The corridors involve the carriage of inter-LATA traffic and, therefore, are accessible to the interexchange carriers through equal access configurations.) The court was, however, reluctant to grant the Philadelphia-New Jersey exception. It noted that "interstate carriers would be hard pressed to underprice" the BOCs, given the configuration of the lines and switches in this area. This exception, the court noted, "may be tantamount to giving the Operating Companies a monopoly over certain interstate traffic . . . ." Id. at 1023.

d. The court also permitted requests to continue Extended Area Service ("EAS") arrangements. These service configurations involve situations in which subscribers are permitted to place calls to other nearby exchanges without paying a charge in addition to the monthly service charge. In effect, EAS extends the local calling area for some subscribers. Without the exception, these calls might become inter-LATA calls and could involve potentially significant additional charges. To preserve traffic patterns and consumer expectations, the court granted the EAS exceptions wherever they were requested. Id. at 1002, n.54.

e. The court adopted a Justice Department classification for traffic carried between a LATA and an area served by one of the Independent Telephone Companies. Where such traffic was classified as inter-LATA, a BOC could not carry it from the Independent Telphone Company's territory into the contiguous LATA. In this situation, the Justice Department referred to the LATA as "not associated" with the Independent Telephone Company territory. Where the BOC was permitted to carry traffic in the Independent Telephone Company service area, the LATA was said to be "associated" with the Independent Telephone Company territory. The court summarized the classification scheme as follows:

> (1) an Operating Company LATA may not be associated with an Independent area if the latter constitutes a market of sufficient size and distance from other markets to attract multiple interexchange carrier entry; (2), if, to the contrary, the Independent area has relatively few access lines or if the distance between the Bell and Independent core communities is insubstantial, and association between the Operating Company LATA and the Independent area will be permitted. In a few instances, particularly in Oregon and Washington, traffic was classified as inter-LATA by the particular Operating Company because it elected not to serve the relatively small Independent area in question.

Id. at 1112.

2. *Relationship of LATAs to Cellular Service*

a. Under the MFJ, mobile radio services—both one-way (e.g., paging) and two-way (e.g., mobile telephone or cellular radio)—were considered to be "exchange telecommunications." This meant that BOCs could provide them within a single LATA. At the same time that the court was approving the LATA configurations, the FCC was establishing and awarding cellular radio franchises to wireline and non-wireline companies. The BOCs, which were seeking these wireline franchises, were concerned about the impact of the MFJ on their ability to provide potentially lucrative cellular services. In certain instances, the cellular franchise incorporated more than a single LATA, making cellular service "interexchange telecommunication," which the BOCs could not provide. Consequently, the BOCs petitioned Judge Greene for a ruling that would allow them to provide cellular service across LATA boundaries in nine markets (each involving a "metropolitan area"). That request was granted as a waiver of the line-of-business restriction that prohibited BOCs from providing interexchange services. United States v. Western Electric Co., Inc., 578 F. Supp. 643 (D.D.C. 1983). The waiver process generally is discussed below, see infra Section V.D.

b. Judge Greene noted that the LATA boundaries were drawn to accommodate landline telephone system configurations. Cellular markets were devised to take account of very different factors (such as automobile traffic patterns). If LATA boundaries were used to impose limits on the permissible area of a BOC's cellular service, mobile calling would be significantly inconvenienced. Callers travelling a common commuter route might find their calls being routinely disconnected because they had crossed a LATA boundary. The call would have to be redialed through the next cellular area's switching office—if the caller could decide whose LATA he had entered. Using interexchange carriers to handle traffic that crossed LATA boundaries was found to be impractical. Id. at 648, n.23.

c. Imposing LATA boundary lines on cellular services would cause other significant inefficiencies. By dividing single cellular markets into two markets—to account for LATA boundaries—the BOCs would incur substantial cost increases for providing cellular service. Judge Greene saw these consequences as imposing a significant competitive disadvantage on the BOCs. These disadvantages were not viewed as necessary to further the objectives of the MFJ.

d. Cellular connections are not seen as a substitute for landline communications—in most respects. Therefore, allowing the BOCs to provide inter-LATA cellular services does not significantly intrude on the interexchange carriers' market.

e. The possibility that the BOCs will use this waiver to discriminate against the non-wireline carriers seems small. However, this possibility is of greater concern than the potential for competing unfairly with interexchange wireline carriers for terrestrial service customers. In order to guard against the potential for discrimination, the court conditioned the grant of the waiver on three factors:

i) The BOCs must offer non-wireline carriers interconnection on the same terms as they offer their affiliated cellular companies.

ii) Affiliated cellular carriers must pay an access charge when bringing an inter-LATA service into a LATA. This charge must be the same as the charge imposed on non-wireline carriers.

iii) The BOCs must lease all inter-LATA equipment from interexchange carriers; they cannot construct their own inter-LATA facilities. The equipment must be leased on the same terms as non-wireline carriers' face.

f. With these qualifications, the court was able to conclude that there was "no substantial possibility" that the BOCs would use their power over local exchange service to compete unfairly in the cellular radio market.

D. The Business of the RHCs: Line-of-Business Waiver Requests

As discussed earlier, the MFJ severely restricts the kinds of businesses in which the RHCs can engage. Essentially, they are limited to providing local telecommunication services, termed "a natural monopoly service actually regulated by tariff." The RHCs also may petition for a waiver of these restrictions by showing that they will not be able to abuse their monopoly position in the local telephone service market to compete unfairly in another market.

1. Procedure Established by Judge Greene

a. In response to this waiver provision, the RHCs filed numerous petitions for permission to engage in businesses that are both related and unrelated to telecommunications. These businesses include equipment leasing, provision of software programs and services, entry into foreign business ventures, provision of real estate services, and participation in the provision of shared tenant services. At the request of the Justice Department, the court established a framework of procedures and a set of substantive standards under which the waiver petitions would be handled. *United States v. Western Electric Co., Inc.*, 592 F. Supp. 846 (D.D.C. 1984).

b. The court identified four areas of concern that had to be addressed in evaluating waiver petitions:

i) Preventing the opportunity for cross-subsidization through the misallocation of "common costs" (for equipment and services used in both monopoly and competitive ventures), the intracorporate transfer of assets at below cost or value, and the bundling of competitive products and services with monopoly exchange services.

ii) Preserving the "public policy" goals of the MFJ, rather than merely ensuring that the RHCs' entry into a new market will not adversely affect competition in that market.

iii) Ensuring that RHC diversification does not unduly divert managerial or financial resources from the equal access effort.

iv) Guarding against a situation in which profitable new business ventures will distract the RHCs from their basic task—to provide local exchange services.

c. The court also noted that to the degree the RHCs engage in risky new ventures, their ability to obtain low-cost capital could be adversely affected. Such a result would injure local ratepayers. The utility business always had been viewed as a very stable business for which low-cost capital was readily available.

d. Judge Greene said that any RHC diversification "will evolve only in a deliberate, cautious manner, with every step tailored to ensure that the public's telephone service does not suffer, but improves in quality and price." *Id.* at 867 (footnote omitted).

i) Judge Greene was clearly committed to preserving local service, rather than to helping the RHCs leverage their resources in numerous high-technology markets. The waiver procedure should be viewed with this bias in mind. Judge Greene's attitude is not one that is universally shared; it has been criticized as saddling the RHCs with a limited future as plain old local telephone companies. Nonetheless, the court's clear intention is to force the RHCs to concentrate on local exchange services during a time in which their development will be a crucial factor in determining the future for a competitive telecommunications market. Yet, one might ask whether limiting the RHCs' business opportunities will hinder their ability to provide state-of-the-art services.

ii) The court's position toward RHC diversification also vividly demonstrates its different views of the local and interexchange markets. In commenting on AT&T's comparative freedom to diversify, Judge Greene said, "[S]hould that company squander its resources on unprofitable non-telecommunications ventures, raise its rates, or fail to render quality service, its customers could easily take their business to one of its long distance or equipment competitors." He added, "That is not so, however, with respect to the customers of the Operating Companies." *Id.* at 874.

iii) The court sought to develop a "prophylactic" mechanism to prevent the RHCs from abusing their local monopoly position. Thus, the RHCs had the burden of demonstrating that there was "no substantial possibility" that such an abuse could occur through the requested diversification. "In the absence of such a showing, the decree presumes that the potential for harm to competition outweighs any of the claimed benefits or efficiencies that may result from diversification." *Id.* at 869 (footnote omitted).

iv) Confronting the continued claim that its participation in this process constituted the unauthorized regulation of the communications industry, the court answered that it merely was fashioning a comprehensive remedy for past, alleged antitrust violations. It also noted that its participation was demanded by the historical inadequacy of federal, state, and local regulation.

e. The court established four requirements that would be imposed on the RHCs; proposed business plans would have to satisfy these requirements.

i) New businesses will have to be conducted by a separate subsidiary.

ii) RHC assets or credit resources cannot be used to finance a new venture.

iii) The total amount of net revenues from businesses that are not "decree-related" cannot exceed ten percent of an RHC's total estimated net revenues.

iv) New businesses will be subject to the "monitoring" provisions of the MFJ, which permit the Justice Department to review business operations so that violations of provisions of the decree can be reported to the court.

f. The court then outlined a specific waiver procedure that it viewed as encouraging "negotiation and resolution," rather than protracted adversarial proceedings. All waiver petitions initially were to be referred to the Justice Department. The petitions, together with detailed business proposals, would be reviewed by the Department; discussions would be held with the RHCs and with businesses or trade groups that might be affected by a grant of the waiver. If the Department found that a petition satisfied the RHC's burden of proof, and was consistent with the principles announced by the court, it would submit a proposed order to the court granting the waiver request. Absent an objection by an "interested party," or by the court itself, that order would be entered, granting the waiver request. If the Department did not find that the petition should be granted, it would submit a proposed order to the court along with any comments and opposing materials it had received. The court then would seek "to consider the views of all interested parties." *Id.* at 873-74. It would establish a briefing schedule and, in some instances, might hold oral argument.

g. All pending waiver requests were, accordingly, referred to the Justice Department.

h. The court eliminated any possibility that requests for RHC entry into the interexchange telecommunications business would be considered.

> The Court will not even consider the merits of a waiver request seeking permission to provide interexchange services until such time as the Regional Holding Companies lose their bottleneck monopolies and there is substantial competition in local telecommunications service. That is not now.

Id. at 868 (footnote omitted). The court also reiterated its firm conviction not to permit the RHCs into the "information services and equipment manufacturing markets." *Id.*

h. One of the RHCs, U.S. West, has appealed the decision to the U.S. Court of Appeals for the D.C. Circuit. United States v. Western Electric Co., Inc., No. 84-5687 (D.C. Cir. filed Sept. 24, 1984). It has argued that Judge Greene's broad perspective in reviewing particular petitions—evaluating them in light of the principles of the MFJ rather than on the basis of the effects on competition in a particular market—is "legally irrelevant and inadequately substantiated." Brief for Appellant U.S. West, at 32-35, No. 84-5687 (D.C. Cir. filed Dec. 24, 1984). Oral argument in the case was held on February 7, 1985, and a decision still is pending. The appeal raises some of the same general questions posed by Justice Rehnquist in his dissent to the Supreme Court's summary affirmance of Judge Greene's original approval of the MFJ. See supra Section II.D.7. Once again, the proper scope of the D.C. Court's function as a judicial body is being questioned.

2. *The Waiver Procedure in Operation*

a. Less than five months after Judge Greene referred the initial waiver requests to the Justice Department, he handed down orders granting all thirteen of the waivers for which the Justice Department had issued favorable recommendations. (Two requests—by NYNEX and by Ameritech—received unfavorable recommendations and subsequently were withdrawn.) *United States v. Western Electric Co., Inc.*, No. 82-0192 (D.D.C. Dec. 14, 1984).

b. The waivers granted would allow six of the seven RHCs to enter new businesses. The waivers concerned the following ventures: equipment leasing (Bell Atlantic); foreign business ventures (Ameritech—consulting and cellular services) (Pacific Telesis, NYNEX, and U.S. West—various functions, including consulting, sale of telecommunications, computer, and software products); real estate services (U.S. West and Pacific Telesis); cellular radio service in the Gulf of Mexico (U.S. West, through its NewVector subsidiary); and, office products (NYNEX, Pacific Telesis, and BellSouth). Each grant of the requested waiver imposed additional "safeguards" on the RHC's competitive subsidiary. These safeguards provide for further assurances that the company will not act in an anticompetitive manner.

c. In March, Southwestern Bell and other RHCs were granted permission to enter the real estate, foreign business, and office equipment markets. Thus, all seven RHCs now have been authorized to engage in some degree of diversification. All of the companies continue to file additional waiver requests with the Justice Department.

d. In certain cases, the Justice Department has negotiated with the RHCs to gain various concessions. Thus, some petitions have been delayed as the company and the Justice Department argue about what restrictions are necessary to protect the new market against unfair competition and to guard the local exchange business from unwanted, detrimental effects. Delays have also been incurred because of the steady flow of petitions: three to four new ones each month.

e. Although a number of waivers have been granted, the Justice Department has vigorously opposed others. In one instance, the Department recommended against granting three waiver requests by Ameritech. It argued that a plan to provide certain shared tenant services such as traffic analysis and automatic carrier selection would involve the RHC in the provision of interexchange services—forbidden by the MFJ. It also claimed that voice storage and retrieval service for cellular customers was an "information service" within the terms of the MFJ; thus, it could not be provided. Ameritech has contested these recommendations.

f. In an interesting waiver request, the Justice Department recommended approval of Pacific Telesis' bid to enter the print media market. The company's petition specifically excluded the daily or weekly newspaper business; however, it did extend to all other parts of the industry, including writing, editing, publishing, and distributing printed materials. The court approved the waiver, as was recommended by the Justice Department. This line of business presents Pacific Telesis with an opportunity to develop marketable print products that eventually could form the basis of a successful electronic information service. When the "information service" restriction in the MFJ is removed, this experience could give Pacific Telesis a significant competitive advantage. No parties filed any formal objections to the waiver request.

g. It remains to be seen whether Congress, which—from time to time—has criticized the line-of-business restrictions, will step in and try to loosen them.

VI. COMPETITION IN LOCAL SERVICES: BYPASS—DEFINITIONS, PARTICIPANTS, PRICING CONCERNS, AND JURISDICATIONAL ISSUES

A. Introduction to Bypass: Overview and Definitions

1. The local telephone company uses a wire pair, or circuit, to connect each subscriber to one of its end offices. This circuit, called a local loop, traditionally has been the origination or termination point for all telephonic communications with a subscriber. When a user or service provider transmits information—voice, video, or data—without using this loop, the communication is said to have "bypassed" the local telephone company. Because of the way in which telephone company rates are calculated, such bypass service—should it become widespread—could increase the costs of service to telephone company subscribers. It would spread the amount of the local telephone company's recoverable fixed costs over a smaller number of subscribers, requiring a higher per-subscriber charge. For this reason, state and federal regulators have become increasingly concerned about the current use of bypass and its future potential.

2. The loop accounts for the largest portion of a local telephone company's fixed costs, *i.e.*, those that do not vary with system usage. For years, the FCC has allocated these fixed costs to both intrastate and interstate service providers—since both require access to the loop—according to a separations procedure. *See* 47 U.S.C. §§ 221(c) & 410(c) (1983).

a. AT&T had compensated the local companies through a "division of revenues" and "settlements" process. AT&T's interstate service tariffs included a charge for fixed costs that were incorporated into all long-distance service charges. Other interexchange carriers paid the local companies according to the terms of negotiated ENIFA tariffs. *See, e.g., Exchange Network Facilities for Interstate Access (ENIFA)*, 71 F.C.C.2d 440 (1979).

b. Both of these compensation methods are traffic-sensitive, meaning that frequent users of interstate services (mostly businesses) pay more toward the costs of local facilities than do infrequent users (usually residential customers). The result was that heavy users paid a disproportionate share of the fixed costs of the local plant, since those costs were not traffic sensitive. These frequent users were, consequently, subsidizing occasional users of interstate services.

c. One way for users of interstate services to escape this subsidy is to stop using the local loop. By connecting directly to an interexchange carrier—through a facility not provided by the local telephone company—the user can avoid having to pay the interstate rate component attributable to local company fixed costs.

3. Bypass services can be divided into three categories.

a. *Uneconomic bypass* occurs when a bypass facility offers call origination and termination capability at a cost that is higher than the cost to the telephone company of providing the service, but at a price to the customer that is lower because it excludes any charge for local exchange access, which otherwise would be bundled into an interstate transmission rate.

b. *Economic bypass* occurs when the cost of a bypass facility actually is less than the cost to the telephone company of providing equivalent service.

c. *Technological bypass* occurs when a bypass facility offers a service that either is not available at all, or is not readily available, from the local telephone company (such as high-speed data or video transmission service).

4. The FCC has adopted a definition of bypass that excludes technological bypass and that includes only those systems used to transmit long-distance communications. *Bypass of the Public Switched Network* (Dec. 19, 1984) (Report by the Common Carrier Bureau in CC Dkt. No. 78-72). The FCC's definition, developed after reviewing comments from many different parties, is as follows:

> Bypass is the transmission of long distance messages that do not use the facilities of local telephone companies available to the general public, but that could use such facilities.

Id. at 7. As the FCC notes in discussing its definition, the focus is placed on "the avoidance of access charges."

a. It is not clear whether a bypass service constructed by a user who either is dissatisfied with telephone company service or who thinks that the telephone company lacks sufficient capacity to accommodate its needs would come within this definition. Clearly, a user who selects an alternate system to take advantage of a transmission capability not available through the telephone company is not a "bypasser," under the FCC's definition. Such technological bypass may occur frequently under the FCC's approach; it has given a broad construction to what it considers technologies that are "not available" through local telephone companies. Its definition excludes "specialized services," such as video transmission and high-speed data, that are not easily sent over the lines used for ordinary telephone calls. Presumably, this boundary line will change as telephone companies upgrade their wires and switches to accommodate more sophisticated transmission needs.

b. The Commission also has expressed doubt about the usefulness of distinguishing between economic and uneconomic bypass. It claims that the uncertainty in establishing the precise costs of transmission makes it difficult to judge whether an alternate system is providing a cost-justified service. Consequently, the Commission has focused on the distinction between new, privately constructed networks ("private bypass") and services that use leased private lines to bypass the local loop ("public bypass"). The FCC does not consider this "public bypass" arrangement to be a real "bypass" activity because it involves the use of generally available telephone company facilities (merely substituting a private line for a connection to the local loop). See infra Section VI.C. As the definition makes clear, local networks—such as intra-office links or intracity networks—also are excluded.

c. This definition is considerably more narrow than definitions adopted by various state utility commissions. It focuses mainly on the transmission of voice communications directly to interexchange carriers which bypass the local loop.

5. The FCC, state public utility commissions, and local exchange operators have been concerned that the increasing availabilty of bypass services will cause business users to stop using the local network. Such a loss of business, as indicated above, would reduce the telephone company's rate base, forcing it to allocate non-traffic-sensitive ("NTS") costs among a smaller number of ratepayers. This result, of course, would raise the cost of local service for the remaining customers—chiefly small businesses and residential subscribers. Consequently, regulators have looked to ways of preventing this situation, either by stopping bypass or by changing the rate structure for the allocation of NTS costs to local and long-distance users.

6. Currently, there is no widespread consensus as to the gravity of the bypass issue. Indications are that the occurrence of bypass remains small. In its recent report on bypass, the FCC found that commenters were most concerned with the vast amount of revenues that were vulnerable to bypass. Bypass of the Public Switched Network, supra. Users, as one would expect, claim that the bypass question is far less serious than the telephone companies allege. They contend that bypass is frequently motivated by a need to obtain services not available from the telephone companies; this is

contrary to carriers' claims that bypass occurs to avoid the imposition of access charges.

7. Studies of bypass activity submitted to the FCC in its recent bypass proceeding included some of the following results:

a. NYNEX: A study performed by Touche Ross, surveying the company's 400 largest business users, showed that New York Telephone would lose $34 million in revenue during 1984 due to bypass; that figure was expected to rise to $146 million by 1987. Another study showed that interexchange carriers providing private lines had caused New York Telephone to lose $80 million annually. These numbers, although not insignificant, represent only a small fraction of the company's revenues.

b. Northwestern Bell: A study of twenty-two large users showed that they faced a $56/month average, per line cost for construction of a bypass system. The cost range was between $12 per line, per month and $256 per line, per month. Payback, in terms of savings on access charges, could occur in as little as one month or as much as eighteen months.

c. International Communications Association: Based upon a survey of large users, the Association concluded that most did not feel that a private communications bypass system offered a significant opportunity. To the degree that there was interest, the majority of users felt that availability of services was a more important factor in deciding whether to construct such a system—not cost savings.

B. Technologies Used to Provide Bypass Facilities

To varying extents, a number of different technologies have begun to offer the potential to provide bypass services. Those technologies that have significantly higher bandwith than the copper wire pairs used in many local loops have become particularly attractive to users seeking high-speed, high-capacity transmission facilities (*i.e.*, technological bypass). Others, which use over-the-air transmission technologies, offer significant savings in terms of installation and maintenance; these technologies may, however, be more vulnerable to atmospheric disruptions and to interception by third parties.

1. *Institutional Cable*

A large number of cable television operators—particularly in urban areas—have entered into franchise agreements by which they are required to provide an institutional cable network, or "Cable B," to serve business, government, and other institutional users. These Cable B systems generally carry low- and high-speed data transmissions on dedicated lines to and between users connected to the system. They also serve as end links for interstate message transmission. *See, e.g.*, Comments of the National Cable Television Association, Inc., 8, *in Cox Cable Communications, Inc.*, FCC File No. CCB-DFD 83-1 (filed July 1, 1983). The use of fiber optic transmission lines, which greatly expand system capacity, may further enhance the attractiveness of cable as a bypass facility.

2. Digital Transmission Systems/Digital Electronic Message Service (DTS/DEMS)

Digital Termination Systems, authorized by the FCC for use by common carriers and private entities under the Digital Electronic Message Service, provide local area microwave delivery of digital data transmissions in the 10.6 and 18 GHz bands. These systems can be utilized as the origination and termination point for both interstate and intrastate services. *See Digital Termination Systems*, 86 F.C.C.2d 360 (1981), *aff'd on reconsideration*, 90 F.C.C.2d 319 (1982), *appeal dismissed sub nom. Alascom, Inc. v. FCC*, 727 F.2d 1212 (D.C. Cir. 1984) (finding the issues on appeal were not ripe for judicial review).

3.Cellular Radio Telephone

Cellular radio telephone technology may, ultimately, offer bypass services beyond its intended use—the provision of low-cost mobile telephone service. In rural areas, at least, cellular radio could offer an alternative to local wire-line service. *See, e.g., Inquiry Into the Use of the Bands 825-845 MHz and 870-890 MHz for Cellular Communications Systems*, 86 F.C.C.2d 469 (1981), *reconsideration*, 89 F.C.C.2d 58 (1982), *further reconsideration*, 90 F.C.C.2d 571 (1982), *appeal dismissed sub nom. United States v. FCC*, Civ. No. 82-1526 (D.C. Cir. May 3, 1983).

4. FM Subsidiary Carrier Authorization (FM-SCA)

FM-SCAs—which are the sidebands to the mainchannel frequency licensed to FM stations—have now been made available by the FCC to FM licensees, or entities entering into contractual arrangements with such licensees, for paging and one-way data transmission (*e.g.*, to personal, hand-held devices or for in-store data delivery). *See Amendment of Parts 2 and 73 of the Commission's Rules Concerning Use of Subsidiary Communications Authorization*, 53 Rad. Reg. 2d (P&F) 1519 (1983).

5. Specialized Mobile Radio Service ("SMRS")

SMRS is a private mobile radio system that offers trunked service to commercial and other users in the 800 MHz band. *See Land Mobile Service Between 806 and 960 MHz*, 51 F.C.C.2d 945 (1975), *aff'd, National Ass'n of Regulatory Utility Commissioners v. FCC*, 525 F.2d 630 (D.C. Cir. 1976), *cert. denied*, 425 U.S. 992 (1977) (*NARUC I*)

6. Local Area Networks ("LANs")

Local area networks rely primarily on coaxial cable for high-speed data communication between machines. The systems operate over short distances, generally connecting computers, word processors, and other office equipment located in a single building or adjoining buildings. The FCC has excluded LANS from its own scrutiny of bypass facilities, concluding that only "long distance messages" should be considered. *See Bypass of the Public Switched Network, supra,* at 8. *But see Proceeding on Motion of the Commission as to the Provision of Telephone Service that Bypass the Local Exchange or Toll Networks,* No. 28710, slip op. at 25 (N.Y. Pub. Serv. Comm'n May 2, 1985) (recommended decision of ALJ) [hereinafter cited as *N.Y. Bypass Decision*].

7. *Shared Tenant Services*

While not strictly a "technology," this increasingly popular real estate development technique may become a widespread form of providing business customers with bypass facilities. Using a combination of technologies that may include a PBX, fiber optic links, and microwave transmission equipment, a real estate developer or office building owner can provide tenants with intra-office connections (LANs) for voice and data communications, as well as direct links to interexchange carriers. *See, e.g., N.Y. Bypass Decision, supra,* at 25-26.

8. Satellite Services: Customer Premise Earth Stations and Teleports

a. The deregulation and the declining cost of earth stations increasingly has made it feasible for users to transmit their communications directly to a satellite. The chief obstacle to the economical use of this technology is that it requires a fairly heavy traffic volume. However, for large corporate users or for offfice building tenants having the benefit of a building LAN or other interoffice wiring, the "rooftop dish" is becoming a means for bypassing both the local and the long-distance wire networks.

b. Teleports are evolving as one solution to the problem of generating enough traffic to justify satellity usage. The teleport system frequently will use a combination of technologies, including microwave, cable, and fiber optics, to bring the communications of numerous customers to a central earth station facility. Satellite links then provide the long-haul transmission capacity. In this way, the system also bypasses both local and long-distance telephone carriers.

C. Private and Public Bypass Configurations

In assessing how regulators should address the bypass issue, a significant preliminary question has been what kinds of communications systems—regardless of the technology being used—should be considered to be "bypass" facilities.

1. *Local Private Networks*

a. Subscribers with heavy calling volumes, or with special transmission needs (such as high-speed data capacity), may opt to construct their own wire or microwave links between two or more facilities. Businesses may link their local offices (such as bank branches within a particular city); a university might wire its entire campus. With the addition of a PBX to collect calls, the system also could be used to provide users with access to an interexchange carrier. The high traffic volume created by collecting all calls at a single point would make it attractive for an interexchange carrier to provide a direct connection to the PBX.

b. As noted above, the FCC, unlike certain state regulatory bodies, has decided not to focus on purely local communications networks in assessing the desirability, or lack thereof, of bypass systems. It considers long-distance connections to be of greatest concern because of the immediate rate impact that such bypass can have on local users. (For this reason, the FCC would consider the PBX/interexchange connection of a local network to be a bypass service.) Nonetheless, even the FCC has noted that local systems, often used to transmit messages between offices of a single company, can have an adverse effect on local rates. These systems carry traffic that otherwise would be carried by the local telephone company. When a local bypass network is constructed to replace existing telephone company services, it may "strand" a telephone company plant that cannot be devoted to another use. The cost of investment in this unused plant (an NTS element) then will have to be distributed among remaining local customers. *See, e.g., Bypass of the Public Switched Network, supra,* at 9-10 & n.15.

2. *Public Networks*

a. High-volume users also may lease private lines from local telephone companies. These lines provide dedicated circuits for a user's exclusive access. This private line can be used to connect a company's various offices within a local calling area. With the addition of a private circuit from an interexchange carrier, it also can connect offices in different cities. Private line services do not include a per-minute charge for local NTS costs. Instead, a fixed, monthly charge is assessed on private lines that are connected to a PBX to provide access to a local telephone company's public switched facilities. This configuration is commonly referred to as a "leaky PBX."

b. Use of a private line sometimes is referred to as "service bypass," since it bypasses only a type of service—public switched service. Construction of wholly separate communications networks, which avoid the use of any telephone company facility, is called "facility bypass."

c. The FCC increasingly has become aware of the potential for the use of private lines to bypass local exchanges. It has attributed the heightened interest to incentives created by the divestiture of AT&T. Now that AT&T has no local plant investment, it has an incentive to encourage its high-volume users to connect directly to its interexchange network through a private line.

D. The Relationship of Bypass to Telephone Rate Policies: Access Charges

The FCC's concern over bypass has been a major factor in its effort to develop a new method for compensating local exchange operators for the use of their facilities by interexchange carriers. The FCC has recognized the potential for widespread bypass to jeopardize universal telephone service by forcing significant local rate increases. *See MTS and WATS Market Structure*, 93 F.C.C.2d 241, 278 (1983) (Third Report and Order) [hereinafter cited as *Access Order*], *modified in part*, 48 Fed. Reg. 42,984 (Sept. 21, 1983), *further modification in part*, 49 Fed. Reg. 7810 (March 2, 1984), *aff'd in part, remanded in part, National Ass'n of Regulatory Utility Commissioners v. FCC*, 737 F.2d 1095 (D.C. Cir. 1984), *cert. denied*, ____ U.S. ____, 105 S. Ct. 1224 (1985). The Commission has sought to restructure its pricing policies to eliminate some of the bypass incentives and to accommodate the significant market changes brought about by the divestiture. Access charge policies have sought to promote competition in the interexchange market and to remedy continuing connection differences between AT&T and other interexchange carriers.

1. Overview of the Access Charge Proceedings

a. The FCC has sought to diminish the incentives for "uneconomic" bypass arrangements by allowing local telephone companies to recover the "interstate portion" of their NTS costs on a non-usage basis. Under a plan adopted in December, 1982, an end user ultimately would pay the NTS costs attributable to its use of the system through a flat monthly charge. The FCC believes that imposing these costs on the "cost-causer" will eliminate the cross-subsidization of local telephone service by long-distance users. This change would allow market forces, rather than the FCC's pricing policies, to determine whether bypass technologies are economically attractive. *See Access Order*, 93 F.C.C.2d at 252-54.

b. To minimize the disruption of telephone service, and to lessen the immediate impact of an access charge on end users, the *Access Order* proposed a seven-year phase-in period for the charges. In the first year of the plan, which was to begin on January 1, 1984, telephone subscribers would have paid a combination of flat and usage-based charges. Total monthly charges would have been about $4 per line, or about half of all NTS costs. Local telephone companies would have been required to assess a minimum flat monthly charge of $2 for residential subscribers and $4 for business subscribers in setting these "customer access line charges." NTS costs above $4 per customer line were to be recovered from interexchange carriers. Over the course of the transitional period, subscribers would pay an increasingly greater share of NTS costs, ultimately paying all of these costs (thereby eliminating interexchange carrier payments). *See Access Order*, 93 F.C.C.2d at 243-45.

c. Heated public debate followed the release of the *Access Order*. Congress also proposed legislation that would have guaranteed universal telephone service and effectively would have gutted the *Access Order*. As a result, the FCC was forced to modify its plan. In a Memorandum Opinion and Order released on August 22, 1983, it eliminated the usage-based component of the customer line charge and the $2 and $4 minimum flat monthly charges that were to be imposed, respectively, on residential and business subscribers. Instead, it required that multi-line business subscribers pay a $6, and that residential customers and single-line business users pay a $2, *maximum* monthly charge per line in the first year of the plan. 48 Fed. Reg. at 42,989. Higher flat monthly rates were to be phased-in over the course of the transition period; however, monthly charges for residential and single-line business customers were not to exceed $4 by 1990.

d. In a February 15, 1984, decision, the FCC deferred customer access line charges for residential and single-line business users until June 1, 1985. It also adopted the $6 monthly charge for multi-line business users. The Commission stated that it would use the time during the postponement to study, among other things, the problem of bypass and the effect of flat-rate customer charges on universal service. 49 Fed. Reg. at 7812-13. To assist it in its study, the FCC issued a Public Notice soliciting information related to bypass from government, industry, and the general public. *See* FCC Public Notice No. 3206 (released March 28, 1984). (As a result of this solicitation, the FCC prepared the bypass report discussed above, *see supra* Section VI.A.)

e. Since the February Reconsideration Order, the Commission has battled to obtain acceptable tariff filings that will implement the various aspects of the Third Report and Order, as modified. Each filing and subsequent decision has been followed by petitions for reconsideration, appeals to the courts, and pressure from Congress—in the form of proposed legislation. Both Congress and the public have sought to ensure that flat-rate subscriber charges do not jeopardize the goal of universal telephone service.

f. After the D.C. Circuit affirmed the FCC's general approach to reallocating access charges, the Commission accepted the recommendations of the Federal-State Joint Board (composed of FCC commissioners and state regulators) regarding the exact amount of subscriber-line charges. *MTS and WATS Market Structure*, FCC No. 84-637 (released Dec. 28, 1984).

i) Under the Board's recommendations, residential and single-line business users began paying a monthly charge of $1 on June 1, 1985. This charge will rise to $2 in June, 1986, and will be frozen there. In addition, in order to combat the effects of bypass, local carriers will be authorized to impose an additional surcharge of no more than $.35 per month on each subscriber line. In late 1986, at the Joint Board's recommendation, the FCC plans to issue a Further Notice of Proposed Rulemaking that will examine the effect of subscriber-line charges on universal service, bypass, economic efficiency, and interexchange competition. Subscriber-line charges will not be changed until that proceeding is complete.

ii) This decision has been appealed to the Court of Appeals in both the D.C. and the Eleventh Circuits.

g. The complex transition to a new access charge policy has included a wide variety of tariffs that seek to recover NTS costs from the many different kinds of services. These include special access tariffs, which impose a charge on private line connections (and include a surcharge on private line arrangements involving a "leaky PBX"), and carrier common line ("CCL") charges, which require interexchange carriers to pay a portion of NTS costs. The CCL charges partially mitigate the effects of imposing access charges directly on local users; they allow a portion of these costs to remain a part of long-distance service prices.

i) The CCL charges are assessed on a premium and non-premium basis. All carriers other than AT&T receive a non-premium discount to reflect the fact that they have an inferior type of connection to the local exchange. This differential will continue until true equal access is realized. *See MTS and WATS Market Structure*, FCC No. 85-149 (released April 23, 1985) (ordering that tariffs for non-premium access charges be changed from flat-rate to usage-based).

ii) On March 1, 1985, the Commission finally accepted tariffs that impose special access charges on private line users. *Investigation of Access and Divestiture Related Tariffs*, FCC No. 85-100 (released March 8, 1985). They took effect on April 1, 1985. This proceeding followed more than two years of battling over the proper method for imposing these access charges. Large users of private line services such as Western Union Telegraph Co. have argued that these charges will severely undercut their ability to use private line services. The effect of the new tariffs has been estimated as imposing a cost increase of more than sixty percent on various carriers; Western Union estimates that its service costs will rise between $60 and $210 million annually as a result of the new charges. In an effort to mitigate the effect of the new charges, the FCC will phase them in over the next year. These charges, however, also have been appealed to the courts.

2. *Effect of Access Charges on Universal Service: Congressional and FCC Responses*

a. Throughout its consideration of subscriber-line access charges, the FCC has faced a congressional threat to pass universal service legislation. The legislation is motivated principally by the fear that the access charge plan would produce substantially higher local telephone bills, which could force some subscribers to drop their service. The legislation would have restricted severely the FCC's ability to impose most end user access charges. *See, e.g.*, S. 1660, *Universal Telephone Service Preservation Act of 1983*, 98th Cong., 1st Sess. § 4 (1983); H.R. 4102, 98th Cong. 1st Sess. § 4(b) (1983). Congress' concern has prompted the FCC to pay closer attention to the effect of subscriber-line charges on universal service goals. As part of the ongoing access charge proceeding, there are still a number of out-standing inquiries into the proper means for ensuring that universal telephone service is not jeopardized.

b. The 1983 House bill sought to prevent local price increases by encouraging "uneconomic bypass." The bill would have imposed a per line charge on communications carriers—bypassers—that did not interconnect with the exchange facilities of the public network. Technological bypass would have been exempt from those charges.

c. The current Congress has again introduced "lifeline service" legislation. *See* S. 950, *Lifeline Telephone Service Act of 1985*, 99th Cong., 1st Sess. (April 17, 1985); H.R. 1632, 99th Cong., 1st Sess. (March 20, 1985) (prohibiting any subscriber-line charges); H.R. 1633, *Public Telephone System Bypass Access Charge Act*, 99th Cong., 1st Sess. (March 20, 1985) (providing for remedies similar to those contained in the 1983 legislation); and H.R. 151, *Lifeline Telephone Service Act of 1985*, 99th Cong., 1st Sess. (Jan. 3, 1985) (establishing a Lifeline Service Fund to defray NTS costs).

d. The FCC, through the Federal-State Joint Board, also has turned its attention to the issue of lifeline services. In its December, 1984, decision to accept the Board's recommended subscriber-line charges, the Commission instructed the Board to begin a study of ways to insulate low-income subscribers from the effects of increased local telephone rates. The Commission also accepted a specific Board recommendation intended to ensure that access charges do not undermine universal service. The Board recommended establishment of an optional, state-run program that would allow certain low-income subscribers (as defined by individual states) to receive a fifty percent reduction in the subscriber-line charges. To the degree that such reductions left local carriers with a shortfall in the revenues necessary to defray NTS costs, CCL charges would be adjusted to fill the gap. (This, again, would put long-distnace services in the position of subsidizing certain local services.) Implementation of this program was left to the discretion of individual states.

e. In response to the FCC's instructions, the Board has released a request for comments on four issues involved in the universal service debate. *MTS and WATS Market Structure*, FCC Release No. 3528 (released March 29, 1985).

i) The proper state and federal roles in ensuring that low-income subscribers can continue to afford basic telephone service.

ii) The criteria for determining a subscriber's eligibility for lifeline assistance.

iii) The kind of telephone service that should be made available to subscribers needing this assistance.

iv) The mechanism for funding lifeline assistance.

f. The FCC also has invited comments regarding the effect of multi-line business subscriber charges on small businesses. *MTS and WATS Market Structure*, Mimeo No. 1796 (released Jan. 9, 1985). This invitation followed a congressional expression of concern about the effect of the access charge proceeding on the nation's many small businesses. The FCC's Common Carrier Bureau previously had conducted a study in which it concluded that the access charges would not have a significant negative effect on small businesses. It saw no reason to establish a lifeline service policy for such businesses. *Further Report on the Effects of Federal Decisions on Universal Telephone Service, in MTS and WATS Market Structure*, FCC No. 84-636 (released Jan. 4, 1985). Despite this report's conclusions, the Commission has asked for comment as to whether some program should be established to help small businesses afford the access charges. Such a program might involve either a total or partial waiver of subscriber-line charges, or contributions from a lifeline service fund.

E. Jurisdictional Issues Raised by Bypass: Cable Systems

Several service offerings by cable systems, particularly data transmission that is carried on a "Cable B" network or institutional loop, resemble services that are—or can be—provided by local telephone companies. When providing such two-way services, cable systems may compete with telephone companies and may divert customers from the local rate base. State regulatory agencies, which seek to hold local telephone rates down as much as possible, have taken a dim view of this competitive foray by unregulated cable companies into the "telephone services market." Telephone companies, which are subject to strict state regulatory controls, understandably object to competing with relatively unregulated cable operators. As a result, a growing number of states have taken steps to assert common carrier jurisdiction over cable systems offering these two-way services. Such jurisdiction would allow state utility commissions to regulate these services just as telephone offerings are now regulated. It is not yet clear how the FCC's recent decision in the *Cox Cable* case to preempt Nebraska's prior certification requirement will affect these different state actions. *See infra* Section VI.E.6.

1. New York

a. On October 16, 1983, the New York Public Service Commission ("PSC") ordered Manhattan Cable Television, Inc., to apply for a certificate of public convenience and necessity to operate as a telephone corporation. Manhattan Cable, at the time, was offering data transmission services to large, institutional customers. *See Proceedings on Motion of the New York Public Service Commission as to Private Line Service Provided by Manhattan Cable TV*, No. 27091 (N.Y. Pub. Serv. Comm'n Oct. 26, 1983). At the same time, however, the PSC stayed its order pending the outcome of a general inquiry into telephone bypass. It permitted Manhattan Cable to continue offering its data transmission services.

b. On May 2, 1985, an administrative law judge released his recommended decision in the bypass proceeding. The report culminates a seventeen-month, two-phase hearing that included the testimony of more than seventy witnesses. *Proceeding on Motion of the Commission as to the Provision of Telephone Service that Bypass Local Exchange or Toll Networks*, No. 28710 (N.Y. Pub. Serv. Comm'n May 2, 1985).

i) The decision concluded that PSC jurisdiction over two-way cable services is proper:

> [W]hen any entity provides point-to-point, two-way data transmission services it is providing telecommunications services subject to the regulation of this Commission. What other business that entity may be engaged in or what other jurisdiction to which it may be subject are irrelevant. The point is that some portion of its activities are devoted to an intrastate operation subject to the exclusive jurisdiction of this Commission. That regulatory responsibility is not shared with the [state] cable commission.

Id. at 117-18. The report recognized the inequity inherent in allowing cable systems to offer two-way services subject only to the regulatory powers of the cable commission. The cable commission has no authority to apply utility-like regulations. It also determined that the FCC had not preempted state regulation of two-way cable services. Judge Thomas Matias noted that the FCC had not, at the time, acted in the Cox Cable case discussed below, see infra Section VI.E.6. He contended that even if the FCC were to preempt state regulation, which it now has to some degree, see infra Section VI.E.6., it might lack the power to do so under the Communications Act. He concluded, consequently, that "[t]his Commission should not defer action on the assertion of jurisdiction pending completion of the FCC's inquiry." *Id.* at 119.

ii) The decision also concluded that telephone company projections of lost revenues due to bypass are overstated; the chief effect of bypass, to date, has been to "slow growth" in telephone company business. Although noting that the potential for an increase in future bypass use exists, no evidence was found to support claims that this growth would have a significant impact on local telephone rates at any time in the near future. In addition, the report found that technological needs, rather than price concerns, motivated the move toward a bypass facility in most instances. Consequently, Judge Matias believed that telephone companies could regain some of this business, and could increase the growth of new business, by aggressively developing new services that are more responsive to user needs.

iii) Despite this limited view of the impact of bypass, the decision recommended that the PSC look carefully at pricing structures to devise ways of discouraging uneconomic bypass. Rate deaveraging and rate flexibility—for competitive services—was endorsed as a way of helping telephone companies compete with bypass services. Similar federal action was advocated, although the need for such action was not viewed as imminent.

iv) Judge Matias also recommended that the PSC assert jurisdiction over providers of local bypass services. They should be required to obtain certificates of public convenience and necessity. Private systems, even when used by more than one entity, were viewed as outside of PSC jurisdiction; however, when such systems make excess capacity available to the public, that offering would fall within the PSC's power over intrastate telecommunications services. It would be subject to the certification requirements.

2. New Mexico

a. The New Mexico State Corporation Commission ruled, on August 19, 1984, that the term "telephone service" included virtually every transmission service except two-way video entertainment programming. The decision requires that "any person who owns, leases, operates or constructs any facility which forms any part of a link or network for transmission of communications signals for compensation, whether as a common carrier or on a private contract basis," must obtain a certificate of public convenience and necessity from the Commission. All such persons are considered to be telephone companies "providing public telephone service."

b. The decision has been appealed to the New Mexico Supreme Court. The appellants are arguing that the FCC's exclusive power to regulate cable television as part of the system of interstate communications preempts the state's asserted regulatory power.

3. Connecticut

The Connecticut Department of Public Utilities held hearings in early 1984 concerning an institutional telecommunications network proposed by Cablevision of Connecticut, which operates cable systems in a number of cities in the state. The hearings considered whether the Commission has jurisdiction over the planned service offering and what effect Cablevision's use of its systems would have on the traditional telecommunications market (i.e., telephone companies).

4. Oregon

In 1983, the Oregon Public Service Commission began considering whether to regulate cable data transmission as a "utility service." The hearings were initiated at the request of Pacific Northwest Bell, which had sought to block a local cable operator's offering of data transmission services by refusing to permit the operator to use Bell's pole and conduit space to run its cable.

5. California

California has instituted a proceeding that addresses bypass technologies in general and their impact on universal telephone service.

6. Nebraska: State Action and FCC Response

a. In April, 1983, the Nebraska Public Service Commission ("NPSC") issued an order in which it determined that Cox Cable Communications, Inc. ("CCCI"), was engaged in offering intrastate common carrier services. It required CCCI to cease its operations until it obtained a certificate of public convenience and necessity. The services in question included both Indax, an interactive transactional service carried over CCCI's cable television system, and Commline, an institutional cable service capable of transmitting data and other business communications. Shortly before the NPSC instituted its proceedings, CCCI had announced plans to provide interstate service over Commline by connecting it to a national DTS network and by using the system to terminate MCI's long-distance voice services. See Cox Cable Communications, Inc., File No. CCB-DFD 83-1, at 2-15 (filed April 22, 1983) [hereinafter cited as Petition for Declaratory Ruling].

b. CCCI moved in federal district court for a preliminary injunction against the NPSC order. Although the court granted the injunction, thereby permitting CCCI to continue its services, it also required CCCI to seek a certificate of public convenience and necessity from the NPSC. See Cox Cable Communications, Inc. v. Simpson, 569 F. Supp. 507 (D. Neb. 1983).

c. CCCI also filed a petition for declaratory relief with the FCC, seeking a determination that the Commission has jurisdiction over two-way cable services such as those offered by Commline and that it has preempted state and local regulation of such services. See Petition for Declaratory Ruling, supra, at 1.

d. At a meeting on August 7, 1985, the FCC decided to preempt Nebraska's requirement that Cox Cable obtain a certificate from the NPSC before offering its non-video services to the public. See FCC Report No. CC-50, Mimeo No. 6282 (released August 7, 1985). It remains unclear, however, just what impact this decision will have on state regulation generally of cable services such as those offered by Commline. The Commission has not yet released its Order in the proceeding, and during the meeting there was significant disagreement among the commissioners as to how broadly the preemption decision should extend.

e. The petition for declaratory ruling in Cox Cable Communications, Inc. raised difficult and complex questions as to the scope of FCC jurisdiction over two-way cable systems that provide both intrastate and interstate services. This jurisdictional issue clearly is what continues to concern the FCC most.

i) Under the Communications Act of 1934, the FCC has no jurisdiction over the "intrastate communications by wire or radio" of any common carrier. 47 U.S.C. § 152(b)(1) (1983). The applicability of this limitation to cable depends, however, upon whether cable is properly classified as a "common carrier." Under the NARUC decisions, which are discussed above, see, e.g., Section I.B.2., a service provider will be treated as a common carrier where it transmits information of the customer's own design and choosing, holds istself out as serving all customers without discrimination, and operates as a quasi-public institution by undertaking to carry for all people indifferently. Thus, to the extent that cable service providers "make individualized decisions, in particular cases, whether and on what terms to deal," they cannot be classified as common carriers. NARUC I, 525 F.2d at 641. Hence, the statutory restriction on FCC jurisdiction over intrastate communications would be inapplicable. See Petition for Declaratory Ruling, supra, at 20-24.

ii) Even assuming that the services provided by institutional cable networks could be classified properly as common carriage, the FCC still might be able to assert jurisdiction due to the hybrid nature of cable service offerings. The FCC's jurisdiction over facilities that are, or can be, used for both intra- and interstate service on a non-segregable basis has been upheld in a variety of contexts. See, e.g., California v. FCC, 567 F.2d 84 (D.C. Cir. 1977), cert. denied, 434 U.S. 1010 (1978); North Carolina Utility Commission v. FCC, 537 F.2d 787 (4th Cir. 1976). Thus, to the extent that institutional cable providers cannot differentiate, as a practical matter, between local and interstate traffic carried by their systems, the FCC would, arguably, be free to exercise its jurisdiction over the entire systems.

iii) Finally, if institutional cable offerings are not properly classified as common carriage, they arguably still would be subject to the FCC's ancillary jurisdiction under § 2(a) of the Communications Act, which covers "all interstate and foreign communications by wire and radio." See United States v. Midwest Video Corp., 406 U.S. 469 (1972) (Midwest Video I); United States v. Southwestern Cable Co., 392 U.S. 157 (1968); 47 U.S.C. § 152(a). Congress accorded the FCC wide latitude, in coping with developing technologies, to define and to achieve national goals in the telecommunications field. Thus, inasmuch as federal regulation of institutional cable contributes to fulfillment of the Commission's responsiblity "to assure a nationwide system of wire communications services at reasonable prices," the FCC might even be able to assert jurisdiction over wholly intrastate cable service offerings. Computer and Communications Industry Ass'n v. FCC, 693 F.2d 198, 213 (D.C. Cir. 1982), cert. denied, 103 S. Ct. 2109 (1983).

iv) It appears that the FCC is struggling with the question of whether to limit any preemptive action to only those services in which the intrastate and interstate components are so intertwined that state impediments to intrastate communications also might frustrate a cable systems' provision of some element of an interstate offering. Such a result would be contrary to the federal policy favoring competition in the interstate market. The Commission might try to act more broadly so as to preempt any state prior certification requirements—or even tariffing requirements—applicable to cable facilities that transmit intrastate communications and that can be used to carry interstate communications. Under this approach, it might be argued that the cable facilities are so much a part of a single interstate communications network that state regulations tend to obstruct the federal goal of promoting vigorous interstate service competition.

v) No matter what approach the FCC's Order ultimately takes, it is likely to be challenged in the courts and also is almost certain to provoke additional attacks on other states' efforts to regulate two-way, non-video cable services. In addition, it may prompt states to deregulate some of the services offered by local telephone companies that also are available on local cable systems.

7. *Congress*

a. When it adopted federal cable television legislation in 1984, Congress chose to sidestep the controversy over the regulation of two-way cable services. Thus, the Cable Communications Policy Act of 1984 makes no contribution to the bypass debate. The only provision in the Act that addresses cable's regulatory status is Section 621(c), which says that no cable system can be regulated as a common carrier or utility because of its provision of two-way video programming (referred to as "cable services"). Cable Communications Policy Act of 1984, Pub. L. No. 98-549, § 621(c), 98 Stat. 2779, 2786 (1984) (codified at 47 U.S.C. § 621(c)).

b. The legislative history of the Act makes it clear that Congress intended to avoid the issue of non-video services completely. The House Report on the legislation specifically noted the then-pending Cox Cable case and the then-ongoing New York PSC proceeding. The Report stated that "section 621(c) has no effect on these ongoing proceedings." The Report continued:

> The Committee does not intend to resolve or even address the issues of the state or Federal treatment of non-cable communications services offered over the cable systems raised in these proceedings. The Committee intends that state and Federal authority over non-cable communications services under the status quo shall be unaffected by the provisions of Title VI. . . . While the Committee recognizes that non-cable communications services are subject to regulatory authority, the Committee does not intend to suggest that these services should be regulated or that they should be deregulated. The Committee intends to leave the decision concerning the exercise of regulatory authority over non-cable communications services to the appropriate regulatory bodies. This approach protects cable companies from unnecessary regulation, while reserving for state and Federal officials the author-

> ity they need to address the issue of competition between telephone and cable companies and the need to preserve universal telephone service.

H.R. Rep. No. 934, 98th Cong. 2d Sess. 60, reprinted in 1984 U.S. Code Cong. & Ad. News 4655, 4697.

c. Just before the FCC announced its decision in the Cox Cable case, a number of congressman wrote letters to FCC Chairman Mark Fowler generally opposing an FCC move to preempt state regulation of non-video cable services. The letters expressed concern (1) over the possibility that the FCC's decision in the Cox Cable case might be based on a two-year-old record and (2) about the effect that the Commission's decision might have on the regulatory balance between state and federal authorities that was incorporated into the overall scheme of the 1984 Cable Act. It remains to be seen how—if at all—Congress will respond to the FCC's Final Order.

VII. REGULATORY FORBEARANCE AND DOMESTIC RESALE: ADDITIONAL MEASURES TO ACCOMMODATE INCREASED COMPETITION

A. The Competitive Common Carrier Proceeding

1. Since 1979, the FCC has reduced or eliminated Title II regulation of certain carriers that it has found to be "non-dominant." (It also has reduced the regulatory burdens imposed on dominant carriers—although to a much lesser extent.) The Commission has determined that emerging competition may be frustrated by the continued imposition of strict regulatory requirements that originally were intended to contain the market abuses of a monopolist. Thus, the FCC has adopted a "new approach to reflect the nature of [competitive telecommunications] firms [that] would allow these companies to satisfy consumer demands more effectively than the undifferentiated set of rules theretofore applied." *Policy and Rules Concerning Rates for Competitive Common Carrier Services and Facilities Authorizations Therefor*, 85 F.C.C.2d 1, 5 (1980) (First Report & Order) [hereinafter cited as *Competitive Common Carriers*].

2. The FCC has distinguished between dominant and non-dominant carriers. It applies traditional Title II regulations only to dominant carriers.

a. A dominant carrier, essentially, is one that possesses "market power." This power allows it to make uneconomic decisions about facilities and services and enables it to set service prices at arbitrary levels (because there is no competition to force its pricing to an "efficient" level).

> A carrier would be labelled dominant if it has a substantial opportunity and incentive to subsidize the rates for its more competitive services with revenues obtained from its monopoly or near-monopoly services.

> . . .
>
> We will consider a carrier to be dominant if it has market power (i.e., power to control price).

Id. at 6, 10.

b. All other carriers are considered non-dominant and have been substantially deregulated. For such carriers, the FCC concluded, "the costs of continuing to regulate the service offerings . . . exceed the benefits of applying [the regulations] . . . ." Id. at 3.

c. The FCC relied on its "broad discretion in choosing how to regulate," id. at 12 (quoting American Telephone & Telegraph Co. v. FCC, 572 F.2d 17, 26 (2d Cir. 1978)), to adopt this bifurcated regulatory approach. It noted that courts have allowed it particularly wide latitude in the area of rate regulation; it also looked to its "delegated authority" to preserve the public interest by adopting policies "to permit communications services to be produced efficiently and offered at the most reasonable prices possible." Id. at 15-16.

3. AT&T (including, at the time, the local operating companies), the independent telephone companies (such as GTE), Western Union, domestic satellite carriers, resellers of domestic satellite capacity, and the so-called miscellaneous common carriers (which provide terrestrial carriage of television signals by microwave links) all originally were found to be dominant carriers. All other carriers were labelled non-dominant. Since this initial classification, the FCC has reduced significantly the number of carriers it considers to be dominant.

4. Non-dominant carriers are subject to "streamlined" regulatory requirements. They are entitled to submit tariffs on just fourteen days' notice, rather than the traditional seventy-to-ninety-day period. They also do not have to support their tariffs with extensive economic data. In addition, these carriers can add or remove circuits without requesting prior FCC approval. Section 214 facilities authorizations would give non-dominant carriers authority to operate in "the continental United States unless the applicant asks otherwise." Id. at 11. Carriers simply must notify the FCC of any expansions twice each year. Similarly, a non-dominant carrier can discontinue a service thirty days after notifying the Commission, provided that no showing is made "that a reasonable substitute service is not available." Id. at 8.

5. These changes reflect the fact that non-dominant carriers are thought to be constrained by market forces, which require them to set prices at competitive levels and to make economical service decisions based on an evaluation of marketplace demand and facilities costs. According to the FCC, the services of any non-dominant carrier can be readily replaced by the services of other carriers.

6. Since 1980, the FCC consistently has extended this

deregulatory regime to other carriers. It also has begun to forbear from all regulation of most non-dominant carriers.

a. In 1982, the Commission eliminated tariff, entry, and exit oversight of domestic, terrestrial resellers. Competitive Common Carriers, 91 F.C.C.2d 59 (1982) (Second Report and Order). This regulatory forbearance, however, did not mean that the affected carriers were exempt from Title II regulation; they remained subject to the FCC's Title II powers and still were obliged to offer their services on just, reasonable, and non-discriminatory terms. The FCC excluded resellers of domestic satellite capacity, who originally had been defined as dominant carriers. The FCC was, at the time, considering a proposal to make both satellite carriers and satellite resellers non-dominant carriers.

b. The Third Report and Order extended the principles of deregulation to "all domestic points outside of the continental United States." Competitive Common Carriers, 48 Fed. Reg. 46,791 (Oct. 14, 1983).

c. Less than a month later, the Commission extended its streamlined regulations to the miscellaneous common carriers, domestic satellite carriers, Western Union's domestic operations, international record carriers and other record carriers, and interexchange carriers affiliated with exchange telephone companies (not including interstate services provided by the BOCs under the terms of the MFJ). Resellers of domestic satellite capacity and all specialized common carriers were brought within the Commission's forbearance policy. Competitive Common Carriers, 48 Fed. Reg. 52,452 (Nov. 18, 1983) (Fourth Report and Order).

d. In 1984, the FCC decided to forbear from regulating domestic satellite carriers, the miscellaneous common carriers, and interexchange carriers affiliated with exchange telephone companies. Competitive Common Carriers, 49 Fed. Reg. 34,824 (Sept. 4, 1984) (Fifth Report and Order). Shortly after that decision, it ruled that the tariffs of all carriers subject to the Commission's forbearance policy remaining on file at the Commission would be cancelled as of August 11, 1985. Competitive Common Carriers, 50 Fed. Reg. 1215 (Jan. 10, 1985) (Sixth Report and Order). The Commission considered the tariffs to have potentially anticompetitive effects. These included fostering price collusion (since competitors could see each other's service prices) and inhibiting consumers who might believe—erroneously—that a tariff embodied all possible service configurations. The decision reflects the dramatic change in the FCC's view of Title II regulatory mechanisms: the tariff, which originally was conceived as a way of protecting consumers from the abusive market powers of monopolistic carriers, now is seen as a significant obstacle to realizing the consumer benefits of vigorous marketplace competition.

e. The Sixth Report and Order recently was overturned by the Court of Appeals, which found that the FCC lacked the statutory authority to prohibit carriers from filing tariffs. In a fairly narrow ruling, the Court pointed to Section 203(a) of the Communications Act—which says that "[e]very common carrier, . . . , shall, . . . , file [tariffs] . . ."—to hold that the FCC's latest deregulatory step simply exceeded the scope of its discretionary powers. MCI Telecommunications Corp. v. FCC, No. 85–1030 (D.C. Cir. July 9, 1985). The Court explicitly ruled that its decision did not judge the validity of other deregulatory steps in the Competitive Common Carrier proceeding. Id. at 21.

7. Despite the divestiture, the FCC continues to classify AT&T and the BOCs as dominant carriers. AT&T has argued to the Commission on numerous occasions that as a result of the divestiture it is just one of a number of competing interexchange carriers and should be subject to at least streamlined regulation. The IBM–MCI deal, see supra Section IV.G., may enhance the chances for this argument to succeed.

B. Resale and Shared Use Policies

Unlike most countries, the United States permits the unlimited resale and sharing of domestic transmission facilities. Both satellite and terrestrial facilities can be leased and resold, at a profit, to third parties. Starting with private line service in the mid-1970s, the FCC moved on to allow the resale of public switched facilities by the start of the 1980s. The progression reflected the FCC's gradual determination that competition in the public switched services market would serve the public interest.

1. The FCC Permits Resale

a. The FCC opened the door to the resale and shared use of communications services in 1976, when it held that AT&T could not prohibit these practices for services other than MTS and WATS. The Commission ruled that the AT&T tariff provisions prohibiting resale and shared use of private lines were unlawful, unjust, and discriminatory. Regulatory Policies Concerning Resale and Shared Use of Common Carrier Facilities, 60 F.C.C.2d 261 (1976), modified in part, 62 F.C.C.2d 588 (1977), aff'd sub nom. American Telephone & Telegraph Co. v. FCC, 572 F.2d 17 (2d Cir.), cert. denied, 439 U.S. 875 (1978). For the most part, this decision—and the resale decisions that have followed it—have allowed all users to enjoy the flexibility and price advantages that other carriers already were enjoying. AT&T's tariffs had permitted unrestricted use by certain carriers, such as the competing interexchange carriers. However, smaller users had been prohibited from using AT&T's lines in the same ways.

i) The Commission found that encouraging resale and shared use would promote competition and reduce the need for FCC oversight of service charges. If underlying carriers charged excessive prices for their services, resellers could undercut those prices. This arbitrage would encourage cost-based pricing. No carrier—not even AT&T—defended the tariff restrictions as lawful.

ii) In addition, resale and shared use would increase the potential for new and innovative service arrangements and would eliminate waste. Large users would now be able to resell unused service capacity rather than being forced to pay for idle circuits.

iii) The FCC also ruled that resellers are common carriers and, therefore, would be subject to Title II regulations. Sharing, by contrast, was not considered to be common carriage and so was left unregulated. The FCC viewed sharing arrangements as privately negotiated accommodations among users. They were not service offerings held out to the general public and, therefore, were not common carriage. See supra Section I.B.2. (discussing NARUC I and II). The FCC cautioned, however, that it took a functional view of the concept of sharing. If a sharing arrangement were used to earn a profit—perhaps by offering capacity to members of the public—the FCC might assert its Title II powers. The fact that the arrangement was being called "sharing" would not prevent the FCC from deciding that it was being operated as a common carrier offering. Regulation would not apply only to "bona fide" sharing arrangements. 60 F.C.C.2d at 316. This distinction, which has always been a difficult one to make, has been virtually mooted by the FCC's 1982 decision to forbear from regulating resellers. See supra Section VII.A.

b. In 1980, the FCC decided to permit resale and shared use arrangements for MTS and WATS services. Regulatory Policies Concerning Resale and Shared Use of Common Carrier Domestic Public Switched Network Services, 83 F.C.C.2d 167 (1980), recon. denied, 86 F.C.C.2d 820 (1981). The Commission's initial reluctance, in 1976, to allow such liberalized circuit use in the switched services area was based on its belief at the time that these public servies were best left solely to AT&T. In 1980, however, the FCC renounced this policy in MTS and WATS Market Structure, 81 F.C.C.2d 177 (1980) (discussed above, see supra Section II.B.). Having decided that competitive interexchange services were consistent with the public interest, the FCC soon went on to open the MTS and WATS market to resale and sharing. As it had four years earlier, the FCC found that the AT&T tariff provisions that prohibited such uses were impermissible: a carrier's unjustified refusal to serve a "reseller" was found discriminatory and unlawful.

c. A long-pending FCC Notice of Proposed Rulemaking would eliminate a remaining—and anomalous—restriction on the resale and shared use of AT&T's private lines to form MTS or WATS equivalents. Restrictions on Resale and Sharing of Private Line Services to Form Equivalents of Message Telecommunications Service and Wide Area Telecommunications Service, 47 Fed. Reg. 6303 (Feb. 11, 1982) (still pending). The restriction dates from the FCC's original distinction between specialized common carrier services and MTS and WATS service. See supra Section II.B. Like other resale restrictions, it was intended to protect AT&T's monopoly hold over public switched service. Since at least 1978, however, this "protected market" has been opened to significant competition. In 1978, the D.C. Circuit rejected the limitation on specialized carriers in the Execunet I decision, see supra Section II.B. As a result of the FCC's 1980 decision to permit MTS and WATS resale, this last remaining resale limitation has existed without much reason. Confusion and disagreement over how to impose access charges on MTS and WATS equivalents has added some complexity to this proceeding. *See infra* Section VII.B.3.

d. The FCC's 1982 decision to forbear from regulating domestic resellers, *see Competitive Common Carriers*, 91 F.C.C.2d 59 (1982) (Second Report and Order), has further enhanced competition. The FCC has recognized that competition between resellers and underlying carriers, as well as among resellers alone, creates a fairly vigorous market in which pricing and service decisions are subject to marketplace forces.

e. The marketplace impact of these decisions has been extraordinary. Circuit resale has stimulated the growth of competitive service providers in the interexchange market; companies that can afford to build only a small transmission network are able to resell AT&T's circuits in order to extend the reach of their services. Even large interexchange carriers take advantage of resale arrangements to "piece out" their networks; MCI currently is AT&T's largest WATS customer.

f. Service repricing by AT&T, along with the elimination of "unjustifiable" differentials in access charges for equivalent services, now is reducing the attractiveness of resale activities. Resellers long have depended on the ability to arbitrage the difference between MTS, which has been priced well above cost, and WATS discount rates. They also have taken advantage of access charge differentials between private lines, MTS and WATS equivalents, and traditional MTS and WATS services. These margins are being reduced by the new access charge arrangments and by new AT&T tariffs. This trend is likely to reduce the profitability—and, perhaps, the viability—of much of the resale business. The OCCs have claimed that unless these kinds of differentials are maintained, they will be unable to compete with AT&T in the interexchange market.

2. *Barriers to Resale of Intrastate Facilities*

a. The FCC has ruled that tariffs for "physically intrastate" WATS lines used to terminate interstate calls cannot restrict resale or shared use arrangements. *AT&T and BOC Restrictions on the Resale and Sharing of Switched Services Used for Completing of Interstate Communications*, 94 F.C.C.2d 1110 (1983). The Commission relied on its power to assert jurisdiction over intrastate facilities inextricably linked to the interstate communications network to prohibit this practice. *See, e.g., North Carolina Utilities Commission v. FCC*, 537 F.2d 787 (4th Cir.), *cert. denied*, 429 U.S. 1027 (1976). The Commission left it to state regulators to address any incidental resale of sharing of wholly intrastate services that might result from this decision.

b. Despite the FCC's decision, certification and entry issues for intrastate resale remain very much alive at the state level. State regulatory commissions are free to conclude that differences between interstate and intrastate resale—and the particular configuration of a state's intrastate market—justify state regulatory policies different from those at the federal level.

c. State statutes often are intended to protect existing telephone companies rather than to encourage new competitive entry. The now-amended Florida statute illustrates the legal issues that a reseller seeking certification might have to address.

i) Resellers must demonstrate that they will satisfy a "present or future public convenience and necessity" standard. Fla. Stat. § 364.33. Resellers can argue that because resale is cheap and efficient, offers the potential for ancillary services and devices, and would reduce the need for future construction (the cost of which is borne by taxpayers), this standard is met. Of course, there is no way of knowing whether such an argument would prevail.

ii) Florida's former statute did not classify service providers by the services they offered. It simply prohibited certification of a "telephone company" that would be in "competition with, or which will duplicate" another company's telephone services, unless there is a showing that the existing facilities are inadequate. Fla. Stat. § 364.335(4). Resellers faced with such a standard could—and did—argue, first, that they are not a "telephone company," within the statutory language, and, second, that the statute was intended to prevent only wasteful duplication or ruinous competition. Resale would cause neither. The Florida state commission concluded that rather than wrestle with this outdated statute, it would be more efficient to seek legislative clarification of state regulatory policies. Other jurisdictions had limited the bias in favor of existing facilities to preventing only wasteful duplication and ruinous competition. *See, e.g., Data Transmission Co. v. Corporation Comm'n*, 561 P.2d 50, 54 (Okla. 1976); *Keith v. Bay Springs Telephone Co.*, 168 So. 2d 728, 732 (Miss. 1964). These commissions concluded, therefore, that entry statutes should be narrowly construed to assure that beneficial competition is not discouraged.

iii) Florida recognized that its statute had been outpaced by technological developments. Faced with an applicant for intrastate resale, the Florida commission and legislature moved with astonishing speed to amend the statute to permit intrastate interexchange competition and to enhance regulatory flexibility to deal with resale. Laws of Florida, No. 82-51 (1982) (*codified at* Fla. Stat. § 364.335, as amended, and § 364.337). The new statute gives the Florida commission authority to classify carriers and to adopt regulations appropriate to each category of carriers.

3. *Application of Access Charges to Resale Carriers*

a. The FCC consistently has taken a practical approach to assessing a reseller's liability for access charges. Under the compensation arrangement that existed prior to the FCC's new access charge policy, "pure resellers" were not liable for interstate access charges. These resellers simply provide MTS/WATS or MTS/WATS-like services (such as those marketed by

MCI and Sprint). In this case, the underlying carriers pay the access charges, according to either the separations and division of assets/settlements process (AT&T) or the ENFIA tariff (other common carriers).

i) The FCC has rejected AT&T's argument that pure resellers are providing "MTS/WATS-type interstate services," which are within the ENFIA tariff. *American Telephone & Telegraph Co.*, 91 F.C.C.2d 568 (1982). Because the underlying carrier pays access charges, resellers need not pay the same charges; this avoids double payment. Thus, pure resellers were not considered to be within the terms of ENFIA.

ii) By contrast, a reseller that creates an MTS/WATS-type network through the resale of various leased private line circuits would not be similarly exempt from ENFIA. In that case, the underlying carrier would not pay the interstate access charge; thus, the reseller would have to pay it.

b. The FCC has decided to follow this scheme in devising its new access charge policies, which replace ENFIA and the separations and division of assets/settlements process followed by AT&T. Carrier access charges will be applied "to any private line reseller to which ENFIA would have applied." *MTS and WATS Market Structure*, 97 F.C.C.2d 682, 715 (1983) (Reconsideration of Third Report and Order). Only the local business line rates will continue to apply to pure resellers; underlying carriers will pay the access charges for facilities used by these service providers.

VIII. DOMESTIC SATELLITE POLICIES: OPENING THE SKIES TO COMPETITION

A. Introduction

1. At about the same time that the FCC was opening the telecommunications market to specialized microwave services, it was grappling with the question of whether to authorize—and how to regulate—a domestic satellite market. This potential new source of competition represented a seemingly sensible extension of international satellite service, which was already operating successfully under the terms of a multinational treaty discussed below, *see infra* Section IX.

2. In 1970, the Commission adopted an aggressive domestic satellite policy that would maximize competition and accommodate the greatest possible variety of services and service providers. Over time, the FCC has relaxed further its policies to make satellite capacity increasingly attractive to a larger number of users. Recently, the three television networks switched their program distribution arrangements from terrestrial landline and microwave networks to more sophisticated satellite links. Large corporate users also have found satellites to be a cost-effective way of bypassing both public switched circuits and increasingly costly private lines. Such a bypass arrangement is particularly attractive for high-speed, high-

capacity data communications. Technological advances in earth station design, which continue to bring down the cost and size of dishes, and the deregulation of many of these earth stations, also have added to the medium's attractiveness.

3. Despite all of these advances, there is now a significant amount of available transponder space. The excess, however, may help to reduce transmission prices over the next few years, which, in turn, may increase demand. The boom in demand during the late 1970s, which led to an explosive growth in the number of satellite authorizations, has left the industry with unused capacity. Nonetheless, companies continue to seek authorizations for new satellites, anticipating that the needs of future communications users will require the new capacity. The fact that increased transmission distances do not raise the cost of satellite transmission makes satellites a highly desirable way of sending long-distance, high-speed data and video communications. As teleconferencing and the use of sophisticated computer communications increase, this capability may prove indispensible.

B. The Open Skies Policy Introduces a Competitive Industry

1. The FCC's inquiry into domestic satellites was prompted by a 1965 application from the ABC television network. ABC requested permission to establish a satellite system to transmit network programming from earth stations in New York and California to its affiliates nationwide. The FCC returned that application, without prejudice, and asked that ABC await the outcome of a comprehensive policymaking inquiry into the numerous regulatory issues raised by domestic satellites.

2. That inquiry culminated in a 1970 Order that authorized private ownership and operation of domestic satellites ("domsats"). *Establishment of Domestic Communication-Satellite Facilities by Non-Governmental Entities,* 26 F.C.C.2d 86 (1970) (*Domsat I*). The decision was significant in that it allowed private parties, not just carriers or governmental organizations, to own and operate domsats. Such a scheme encouraged competition by permitting innovative and diverse ownership and service arrangements. It also complemented other Commission policies being developed to foster competition in the communications field.

3. The FCC initially was concerned with four basic issues:

a. Whether the Comunications Act permitted the authorization of private construction and operation of domestic satellites.

b. What impact such authorizations might have on U.S. policies, as expressed in the Communications Satellite Act of 1962 and in the then-interim INTELSAT Agreement. *See infra* Section IX.

c. The public interest implications of such authorizations, in light of a number of factors, including available spectrum space and ground facilities, the effect on carriers, and possible service benefits.

d. The technical requirements that should be established.

4. The Commission also had to determine the source of its power to authorize a communications service not expressly considered by the 1934 Act.

a. While satellites clearly were radio transmission facilities, they used space, rather than ground, facilities. Nothing in the Act gave the FCC explicit power over such a space station transmitter.

b. In addition, the private ownership scheme being considered was vigorously opposed by Comsat, the carrier established by the 1962 Satellite Act as part of the U.S. effort to establish a global satellite communications system. *See infra* Section IX. Comsat argued that it alone should be authorized to own and operate domestic satellites. The FCC, however, rejected the claim that the 1962 Act mandated such a result. According to the Commission, the 1962 Act dealt only with international services, leaving domestic radio communications (including satellite communications) wholly within the Commission's broad powers under the 1934 Act. Using these powers, the Commission noted, it had been able to adopt many novel ownership and service arrangements in order to promote the growth of a diversified and efficient nationwide communications system. *See Domsat I*, 26 F.C.C.2d at 128-33 app. C (Memorandum on Legal Issues).

5. The FCC was obligated to clarify the many uncertainties surrounding domsats, because the technology consumes valuable spectrum resources. A decision to allocate spectrum space to this service required a careful finding that the public interest would be served. Demand for the facilities and their future usefulness in providing various services was virtually unknown. However, the service had the support of all of the major carriers and of a number of large, private communications companies. In addition, domsats could complement the telephone industry's long-haul, terrestrial networks by providing economical, long-distance, point-to-multipoint transmissions (a service especially desired by the television networks). Domsats also might reduce the cost of long-distance data and record services significantly (because the cost of using satellite links is not distance-sensitive).

6. The Commission rejected suggestions to limit the types of systems and services that could be authorized. It accepted, instead, a presidential recommendation that domsats be authorized on an open-entry basis. The Commission concluded:

> [W]e will consider applications by all legally, technically, and financially qualified entities. . . . Applicants may propose the rendition of such services directly to the public on a common carrier basis or by the lease of facilities to other common carriers, or any combination of such arrangements. Applicants may also propose private ownership and use or the joint cooperative use of the system by the several owners thereof. Applicants may further propose the shared use of some facilities by different systems, or a division in the ownership of various system components (e.g., user ownership of earth stations to afford direct access to the space segment of a common carrier or cooperative system).

Id. at 93-94. Specific authorizations would be granted only on the basis of concrete proposals, which would be reviewed in light of the FCC's public interest obligations. This flexible regulatory policy, which opened the market to vigorous competition, became known as the "open skies" policy.

C. The FCC Copes With the Growth of Satellite Services

1. In response to the 1970 Order, the Commission received a large number of applications—as well as many questions about its satellite policies. Consequently, it issued a Second Report and Order in which it sought to clarify its policies before actually authorizing any particular satellite. 38 F.C.C.2d 844 (1972) (Domsat II). The Commission emphasized that while its entry policy might be "open," it was not "without any restrictions or limitations." Id. at 850.

a. In order to foster competition in the domsat market, the FCC restricted entry by AT&T and Comsat.

i) AT&T basically, was limited to providing public-switched services until it could show that there was "substantial utilization" of any satellites authorized to provide specialized services or until AT&T had been operating a satellite for three years. AT&T was entitled to petiton the Commission for removal of the service restrictions when either of those events occurred. The FCC would review the petition in light of the competitive condition of the market and the potential for AT&T to cross-subsidize competitive satellite services.

ii) The Commission also restricted Comsat's possible service configurations to prevent it from giving AT&T—which was Comsat's primary customer for international services—any undue advantages in the domestic market.

b. The Commission imposed an additional application burden on common carriers who provide public switched telephone services. These applicants had to demonstrate in their applications that the heavy investment required for starting a satellite service would not unduly burden local ratepayers.

2. The Commission summarized its primary policies as including the following intentions:

a. Maximize the opportunity to gain fast experience in the new technology.

b. Encourage multiple entries in order to demonstrate any efficiences or economies gained by using satellites to provide specialized services.

c. Accommodate the development of the technology by minimizing institutional obstacles or restraints.

d. Retain flexibility in the regulatory policies so that adjustments could be made to account for future developments.

Id. at 846-47.

3. In 1974, the FCC authorized the launch of the first domestic satellite. Western Union Telegraph Co., 46 F.C.C.2d 162 (1974). Since that time, the market has grown to include twenty-four different satellites operated by eight companies. A large number of additional satellites have been authorized or are being planned. As a result of this interest and activity, the FCC has been forced to alter and to reevaluate its policies to accommodate additional satellite traffic.

a. In 1980, the Commission issued an Order authorizing the construction and launch of replacements for the first generation of satellites. (These satellites are now reaching—or have reached—the end of their useful lives.) The Order also considered a series of new policies that were intended to increase satellite capacity. Assignment of Orbital Locations to Space Stations in the Domestic Fixed-Satellite Service, 84 F.C.C.2d 584 (1980) [hereinafter cited as Second Generation Order].

i) The FCC rejected a suggestion that it require new satellites to incorporate advanced technological designs. However, it did note that the increasing scarcity of available orbital slots might require the imposition of minimum standards in the near future. Older satellites, which had low capacity transponders, might have to be abandoned if future demand could not be satisfied.

ii) The usable orbital arc—the area of space in which domestic satellites can be positioned to serve the U.S.—expressly was left open to future adjustment. The Commission prescribed what it believed to be the outermost boundaries of this orbital space, based upon space positions that would allow reasonably priced earth stations to be used reliably. (A satellite's orbital position determines the "elevation angle" of an earth station. As that angle gets smaller—to communicate with satellites that are low in the horizon—the quality of communication degenerates, unless more expensive technology is used. Thus, earth station technology has a limiting effect on the usable orbital space.) However, the FCC emphasized its intent to remain flexible in selecting orbital slots.

iii) The FCC authorzied two satellites to operate in a new frequency band—12/14 GHz ("Ku-band"). See also GTE Satellite Corp., FCC No. 80-718 (released Jan. 30, 1981); Satellite Business Systems, FCC No. 80-717 (released Jan. 30, 1981). Prior to this time, satellites had been authorized to use only the 4/6 GHz band ("C-band"). The new frequency allowed for closer spacing between satellites (three degrees, rather than four degrees, as was required for C-band stations). The higher frequency also was free of interference from terrestrial microwave services. As a result, earth stations could be located in densely populated cities without fear of significant interference problems. iv) The Commission also decided to permit future applications for "hybrid" satellites that would use both the Ku- and C-bands.

b. The Commission's licensing procedures, which always have been somewhat unique as a result of the special characteristics of the satellite industry, see, e.g., United States v. FCC, 652 F.2d 72 (D.C. Cir. 1980), also have undergone change.

i) Initially, applications were collected by the FCC, and a number of them eventually were designated as a "processing group." This designation marked the start of the Commission's review process. Notice was given that any additional applications seeking to "compete" for any of the orbital locations requested by applicants in that processing group had to be filed within a certain number of days (called a "cut-off" period). The cut-off period allowed the FCC to consider only a fixed number of applications and to assign orbital locations to all qualified applicants. See e.g., Processing of Pending Space Station Applications in the Domestic Fixed-Satellite Service, 90 F.C.C.2d 1 (1982); 77 F.C.C.2d 956 (1980).

ii) The FCC used its discretionary licensing powers to maximize the number of applicants that could be accommodated. Rather than pick the "best" applicant for each orbital location, it would assign "competing" applicants to different, "nearby" orbital locations. In this way, all qualified applicants were authorized to operate a satellite. The market alone was then allowed to determine the success or failure of a particular satellite. To respond to unforeseen future events, however, the FCC reserved the right to reassign a satellite to a new orbital slot on thirty days' notice.

iii) Over time, the number of available slots has declined steadily. Thus, the Commission has become more rigid in its application of cut-off dates. In addition, as the availability of slots has become more limited, the licensing process has taken on more aspects of a comparative hearing procedure. Applicants seeking the same slot must be compared against each other. It has become increasingly likely that the FCC will not be able to satisfy all of the demands for orbital locations. See, e.g., Domestic Fixed Satellite Service, 54 Rad. Reg.2d 565 (1983).

iv) To improve the efficiency of licensing, the Commission reduced its authorization procedure from a multi-step to a one-step process. Under the original procedure, applicants were granted a construction permit to build a satellite. Later, as the lengthy construction period came to an end, the company would seek separate launch and operation authorizations. In 1980, the FCC collapsed all of these authorizations into a single grant. Second Generation Order, 84 F.C.C.2d at 609-10.

c. In a signifiacant supplement to its pro-growth policy, the FCC virtually eliminated its licensing requirements for receive-only satellite earth stations. Regulation of Domestic Receive-Only Satellite Earth Stations, 74 F.C.C.2d 205 (1979). Concluding that the regulation of these earth stations was not necessary to guard against interference, the Commission decided that licensing would be optional in the future. This optional procedure was retained for individuals who wanted the FCC to ensure that their stations would be protected from interference. Unlicensed stations would not receive that kind of protection.

i) This relaxation of earth station licensing requirements opened the way for the growth of the backyard "dish" industry.

Individuals were then able to erect affordable home earth stations in their back yards, to serve as satellite antennas for their televisions. The dishes allowed viewers to receive a multitude of the satellite-transmitted television signals, from a variety of programmers, for the cost of the dish alone. No subscription fee had to be paid for each service.

ii) A legal framework for this type of signal reception was established in 1984, when the 1984 Cable Act added Section 705 to the Communications Act (amending and redesignating original Section 605). Cable Communications Policy Act of 1984, Pub. L. No. 98-549, § 5, 98 Stat. 2779, 2802 (1984). Pay-television programmers, who transmit their programming by satellite, had previously argued that backyard dish use constituted signal piracy, in violation of either the Communications Act or state theft-of-services statutes. While service subscribers paid for the programming, dish owners received it for free. Cf. Movie Systems, Inc. v. Heller, 710 F.2d 492 (8th Cir. 1983) (holding that unauthorzied reception of an unscrambled, MDS transmission of Home Box Office violates the Communications Act). However, the new legislation permits the reception of unscrambled signals, unless a programmer has established a marketing program to make the signal available to dish owners. In that event, the dish owner must purchase the programming through the programmer or its marketing agent. The reception and unscrambling of a scrambled satellite signal, unless authorized by the programmer, is illegal. Cf. Air Capital Cablevision, Inc. v. Starlink Communications Group, Inc., No. 83-1997-K (D. Kan. Feb. 13, 1985) (upholding manufacturer's right under § 705 to construct and sell backyard earth stations). Changes in the programming industry, including signal scrambling and the establishment of marketing programs, are now underway. Home Box Office, Inc., the nation's largest pay programmer, recently decided to start scrambling its signal and to begin marketing descramblers to dish owners.

iii) Earth station deregulation also enhanced the potential for DBS service. In 1982, the FCC authorzied this direct-to-home satellite distribution service to operate in the 12 GHz (Ku) band. Inquiry Into the Development of Regulatory Policy in Regard to Direct Broadcast Satellites, 90 F.C.C.2d 676 (1982). Initial enthusiasm for the technology has waned. The high cost of building and operating a DBS service, combined with uncertainties about market demand, have caused a number of original DBS applicants to relinquish their authorizations. The future for DBS remains unclear, at best. Continued advances in earth station technology, which have continued to bring down the cost and size of the equipment needed to receive a DBS signal, may eventually provoke greater activity.

d. In 1983, the Commission decided to reduce the orbital spacing that would be required between satellites. This reduction allows for an increased number of orbital slots and will help accommodate further demand. Licensing of Space Stations in the Domestic Fixed-Satellite Service, 54 Rad. Reg. 2d (P&F) 577 (1983) (Orbital Spacing Order).

i) The Commission balanced the increased signal interference that reduced spacing would cause against the cost of improving equipment (to reduce noise) and the need for additional satellite facilities.

ii) The Commission settled on a plan by which C-band satellites are being spaced at 2, 2.5, or 3 degrees, with spacing moving toward two degrees as technological improvements permit. Ku-band satellites will be separated by just two degrees.

iii) Despite this change, the FCC still warned that future authorization proceedings might—for the first time—involve "comparative hearings or other administration selection procedures" in light of the steadily decreasing number of orbital slots. Id. at 600.

e. A recent decision to open the 18/30 GHz frequency band to a new generation of satellites ("Ka-band") may somewhat alleviate the pressure on the market. No Ka-band satellites have yet been authorized; some applicatons have been submitted.

f. The FCC also has recently proposed the establishment of Mobile Satellite Services, which would use frequencies in the 800 MHz band. Amendment of Parts 2, 22 and 25 of the Commission's Rules to Allocate Spectrum for, and to Establish Other Rules and Policies Pertaining to, the Use of Radio Frequencies in a Land Mobile Satellite Service for the Provision of Various Common Carrier Services, 50 Fed. Reg. 8149 (Feb. 28, 1985). The satellites would be used to provide communications to mobile ground receivers. Twelve companies have submitted applications, and the FCC will consider comments on the proposed rules at the same time that it reviews specific applications.

D. Deregulation of the Satellite Market

1. In 1982, the Commission authorized a "significant departure" from its past satellite policies by permitting licensees to sell individual transponders. *Domestic Fixed Transponder Sales*, 90 F.C.C.2d 1238 (1982), *aff'd sub nom. Wold Communications, Inc. v. FCC*, 735 F.2d 1465 (D.C. Cir. 1984). This decision created a market for transponders, which limits a carrier's ability to incorporate a significant markup into the price of complete transmission services. This result, in turn, has kept the price of satellite transmission down, enhancing the attractiveness of satellites.

a. The *Transponder Sales* decision was seen as a way of helping satellite operators raise the huge amounts of capital needed to construct a satellite. It also would spread the risks of satellite operations among both sellers and users. Sales and long-term leases could be signed before a satellite was even built. This would add to the service provider's sense of security (by ensuring at least some use of the satellite) and might present the opportunity for operators to tailor systems to the particular needs of large users. It also encouraged satellite operators to make satellites available for a wide variety of services, since seller-customer arrangements were essentially left unregulated.

b. From a regulatory perspective, the Commisison concluded that transponder sales were not common carrier services within the terms of *NARUC I*, discussed above, *see supra* Section I.B.2. They were not an indifferent "holding out to the public" of a communications service. Therefore, transponder sales are not subject to Title II regulation.

2. As part of its decision on domestic resale, the Commission also authorized large users of satellite capacity to resell unused space to others. *See Southern Satellite Systems, Inc.*, 62 F.C.C.2d 153 (1976); *Regulatory Policies Concerning Resale and Shared Use of Common Carrier Facilities*, 60 F.C.C.2d 261, 297 (1976), *modified in part*, 62 F.C.C.2d 588 (1977), *aff'd sub nom. American Telephone & Telegraph Co. v. FCC*, 572 F.2d 17 (2d Cir.), *cert. denied*, 439 U.S. 875 (1978). This resale market has reduced the cost of owning a transponder (since parts of it can be "purchased" by others) and has enabled smaller users to take advantage of satellite facilities.

3. Finally, the FCC has decided to deregulate the domsat market substantially. It has found that domsat operators and resellers are "non-dominant" carriers, meaning that they lack the market power necessary to act in an anti-competitive manner. The FCC, consequently, has decided to forbear from regulating them. *See supra* Section VII.A.

IX. INTERNATIONAL SERVICES: CONFRONTING THE PROBLEMS OF EXTENDING DOMESTIC COMPETITIVE POLICIES

A. Market Overview

1. Introduction

International communications may be carried either by satellite or by transoceanic cable. All of these facilities traditionally have been either owned or brokered by carriers; however, the FCC recently has acted to open both the satellite and the cable markets to ownership by non-carriers.

a. Initially, only radio frequencies were used to transmit voice-grade services. Record services were carried either by telegraph cable or on radio telegraph circuits. In 1956, however, AT&T introduced TAT-1, the first transatlantic, voice-grade submarine cable. This cable ended the technological division between voice and record services: it could carry both voice and record communications.

b. Despite the technological convergence of the voice and record markets, the FCC maintained a market division among services until the mid-1970s. From 1956 to 1976, AT&T was limited to providing voice-grade services; the record carriers, although not prohibited from offering voice services, never entered this market. Gradually, however, the Commission allowed AT&T to cross service boundaries, and the record carriers began to branch out. There no longer is a separation between voice and record services providers. *See infra* Section IX.B.

c. Satellite circuits were not used until the 1960s, when the U.S. began its efforts to develop a global satellite communications system. This effort eventually led to the establishment of Intelsat.

2. Satellites

a.The International Satellite Telecommunications Organization ("Intelsat") provides the vast majority of the world's transborder satellite traffic. Intelsat is a multinational organization formed and operated under the terms of an international treaty. International Telecommunications Satellite Organization, Aug. 20, 1971, 23 U.S.T. 3813, T.I.A.S. No. 7532 [hereinafter cited as Intelsat Agreement]. Plans by any of the 109 individual nations that are Intelsat members (or by groups of member-nations) to provide international satellite service independent of Intelsat are coordinated with Intelsat under the terms of this treaty.

b. The current Intelsat system provides international satellite communications service to virtually all countries in the world. It evolved from a development effort begun by the United States in the early 1960s.

c. When Congress adopted the Communications Satellite Act of 1962, Pub. L. No. 87-624, 76 Stat. 419 (codified at 47 U.S.C. §§ 701-744 (1983) (as amended)), it established the Communications Satellite Corporation (Comsat), a for-profit organization that was charged with the initial responsibility of developing a satellite communications system. 47 U.S.C. § 731 (1983). In 1964, the United States and ten other countries entered into an agreement that established Intelsat. Agreement Establishing Interim Arrangements for a Global Communications Satellite System, Aug. 20, 1964, 15 U.S.T. 1705, T.I.A.S. No. 5646. Intelsat then assumed ownership of the international satellite system, which Congress had always envisioned would be operated as part of a cooperative global effort.

d. Comsat now serves as the U.S. signatory to the current Intelsat Agreement. It participates in meetings of Intelsat's governing bodies and communicates to Intelsat U.S. views regarding international satellite communications. Voting power on Intelsat's Board of Governors is allocated according to a country's use of the Intelsat system. With Comsat demanding almost one-quarter of Intelsat's communications capacity, it controls the largest voting block on the Board—twenty– four percent. This arrangement provides the U.S. with continued influence over Intelsat. Recently, there has been extensive debate over the potential for conflict between U.S. interests and those of Comsat. As the U.S. moves forward with pro-competitive initiatives in the international satellite arena, many of which often are contrary to what Comsat would view as best for its future, this conflict is likely to intensify. New entrants into the increasingly competitive field of satellite communications have charged that Comsat cannot represent all "U.S. interests" when it is operating as one of a number of competitive U.S. entities. The debate over how to provide U.S. input into the Intelsat process is far from settled.

e. U.S. access to Intelsat circuits is provided only through Comsat. Until recently, Comsat provided these circuits solely to common carriers and to a limited group of others, who were designated "authorized users." These carriers, in turn, would provide a packaged international service to subscribers. It included domestic links to a satellite earth station and the necessary transmission links in the terminating country. Recently, Comsat was authorized to deal directly with end users. However, because Comsat remains the monopoly provider of Intelsat space segments in the U.S., the FCC required it to separate the business of providing Intelsat circuits from the competitive activity of offering end-to-end services, which include earth station services. *See Proposed Modifications of the Commission's Authorized User Policy Concerning Access to the International Satellite Services of the Communications Satellite Corporation*, 90 F.C.C.2d 1394 (1982) [hereinafter cited as *Authorized User II*], *rev'd sub nom. ITT Worldcom v. FCC*, 720 F.2d 732 (D.C. Cir. 1984). After the court's decision, the FCC again adopted this policy. *Authorized User II*, 50 Fed. Reg. 2552 (Jan. 17, 1985), *recon. denied*, FCC No. 85-323 (released June 28, 1985). This issue is discussed more fully below. *See infra* Section IX.B.7.

f. The FCC's recent decision to authorize new satellite systems to compete directly with Intelsat is likely to cause a very significant change in the satellite market. Since 1983, five applicants have sought FCC approval to provide international satellite service. A sixth applicant joined this group in May, 1985. These applications were delayed as a result of a protracted debate about what U.S. policy should be toward such competition. On July 25, however, the FCC authorized three of the six applicants to begin construction of their satellites. *See* FCC Report No. DC-163, Mimeo No. 6024 (released July 25, 1985).

g. The authorization of transatlantic satellites significantly extends the prior U.S. policy of allowing certain domestic satellites to provide a limited amount of transborder service. In 1981, for example, the FCC authorized a number of domsat operators to provide video transmission to various receiving points in North America, Central America, and Canada. *See, e.g., Transborder Satellite Video Services*, 88 F.C.C.2d 258 (1981); *see also, e.g., Satellite Business Systems*, 88 F.C.C.2d 195 (1981).

h. The applicants (and their proposed services) are Orion Satellite Corp. (video, audio, and data services between the Eastern U.S. and Western Europe); International Satellite, Inc. (video, audio, and data between the forty-eight continguous United States and Europe as far east as the Adriatic Sea); RCA American Communications, Inc. (video, data, and private line voice between the forty-eight continguous United States, Western Europe, and parts of Africa); Cygnus Satellite Corp. (various video and data services between the forty-eight contiguous United States and Western Europe, with spot beams serving Puerto Rico, the U.S. Virgin Islands, the

Carribean Basin, and parts of Central America); PanAmerican Satellite Corp. (video and audio services—particularly television—between North and South America and within South America alone); and, Financial Satellite Corp. (data services for businesses and financial institutions in the United States, Canada, Western Europe, parts of South America, the Far East, Australia, and Mexico). The systems propose to offer different service arrangements, including transponder sales, leases, and tariffed common carrier offerings.

i. The FCC has granted the applications of RCA, International Satellite, and PanAmerican Satellite; it has deferred action on the applications of Cygnus and Orion pending the submission of additional technical materials. The Financial Satellite application was not considered; it was submitted only recently, and the FCC decided that it had not yet had enough time to evaluate the application.

j. Intelsat also will be expanding its own facilities in the next five to seven years. The Intelsat VI series satellites are scheduled to begin operating in 1987. These new satellites will dramatically increase the number of available circuits. By authorizing private satellites, some have argued, the FCC will be promoting a facilities glut that will produce a fierce price war. Intelsat proponents have claimed that any such price competition could have grave consequences for Intelsat and, particularly, for the services it provides to less developed countries. The FCC's recent moves to support the introduction of new, high-capacity submarine cables have further complicated the debate over international services and facilities.

3. *Submarine Cables*

a. A group of common carriers that includes AT&T and the International Record Carriers ("IRCs") have ownership interests in transatlantic, transpacific, and regional Pacific Ocean cables. A number of these cables have gone—or are soon going—out of service. The FCC already has authorized construction of a new cable for the transatlantic route (TAT-8) and has determined that a new transpacific cable (TPC-3) will serve the public interest. The new cables will use fiber optic technology and will, therefore, offer significant capacity and service improvements over existing cable facilities. *See Inquiry Into the Policies to be Followed in the Authorization of Common Carrier Facilities to Meet North Atlantic Telecommunications Needs During the 1985-1995 Period*, FCC No. 85-176 (released April 22, 1985) (Second Notice of Proposed Rulemaking), FCC Report No. DC-184, Mimeo No. 6285 (released Aug. 7, 1985) (Second Report and Order) [hereinafter cited as *Atlantic Facilities Plan*]; *Inquiry Into the Policies to be Followed in the Authorization of Common Carrier Facilities to Meet Pacific Telecommunications Needs During the Period 1981-1995*, FCC No. 85-121 (released March 28, 1985) (Further Notice of Proposed Rulemaking), FCC Report No. DC-186, Mimeo No. 6288 (released Aug. 7, 1985) (Second Report and Order) [hereinafter cited as *Pacific Facilities Plans*].

b. U.S. carriers construct and own these cables together with one or more foreign partners ("correspondents"). The U.S. and foreign carriers sign an operating agreement under which each party provides for interconnection of the cable to its country's domestic telephone system. Operating agreements must be negotiated individually for each cable. In order to construct a cable, therefore, a U.S. carrier must find a willing correspondent in the terminating country (usually the PTT) and must gain authorization to build, land, and operate the cable, both in the U.S. and abroad. The FCC grants the authorization to operate here. A PTT, however, which serves as the correspondent, also frequently is the sole decisionmaker about international service operations in other countries. Therefore, its decision to enter into an operating agreement virtually constitutes an authorization for the cable to provide service in that country. (As countries privatize their PTTs and liberalize their facilities ownership policies, governmental units may increasingly assume this function.) Each national government also controls the landing rights in its country, although the power to grant landing rights may be delegated. In the U.S., Congress has given the president this licensing power; he, in turn, has delegated it to the FCC, which acts in consultation with the Secretary of State.

c. In March, 1985, the FCC decided to authorize its first non-common carrier applicant to operate submarine cables.

i) The Commission authorized Tel-Optik Ltd., a private U.S. company, to construct and operate two fiber optic cables between New York and the United Kingdom. Tel-Optik has signed an operating agreement with Cable & Wireless, which, through its wholly-owned subsidiary Mercury Communications, Ltd., is authorized to land and operate the cable in the United Kingdom. On May 16, 1985, the FCC granted Tel-Optik the necessary landing licenses for its cables. *Tel-Optik, Ltd.*, Mimeo No. 4618 (reelased May 17, 1985). The service will be called "Market-Link" and will consist of a northern cable (PTAT-1), to be put into service in 1989, and a southern cable (PTAT-2), to be put into service in 1992.

ii) The FCC recently authorized the second private transatlantic cable. *See Submarine Lightwave Cable Co.*, Mimeo No. 5241 (released June 19, 1985). The company will build and operate a fiber optic cable between the U.S., Canada, the U.K., Spain, and France. This cable, to be known as TAV-1, will serve primarily the international video market. The State Department also has granted SLC its cable landing license.

B. Efforts to Accommodate Competition in the International Market

1. Background: The Rise of Regulatory Oversight

In 1974, the FCC, along with a representative from the Executive Branch, entered into discussions with various European administrations to consider future plans for transatlantic cable facilities. This North

Atlantic Consultative Process ("Consultative Process") followed on the heels of the FCC's controversial 1971 denial of an application by AT&T and its foreign correspondents for a new transatlantic submarine cable, TAT-6. The process gave the FCC a comprehensive role in overseeing decisions about international facilities construction. It also brought the Commission into direct contact with foreign PTTs that, unlike the FCC, were actually systems and facilities operators.

a. The FCC's forays into this area of regulation occassionally have been viewed by some U.S. carriers and by various PTTs as an attempt to usurp an unjustifiable amount of regulatory control. They have been intended, however, as an effort to establish an international information exchange that, in the long run, will enhance relations between U.S. carriers and their foreign counterparts. (In the satellite area, by contrast, Comsat—a market participant with quasi-public, quasi-private status, and under the supervision of the Executive Branch—provides U.S. input into the Intelsat system.) In any case, this effort to coordinate multinational plans for international telecommunications represented the zenith of the FCC's oversight of international operations.

b. The Communications Act requires U.S. carriers to seek FCC authorization for the construction of any cable facilities. The FCC has been delegated, as noted, the role of granting offshore cable landing rights (which are necessary to bring an overseas cable into the United States). Consequently, the Commission has significant regulatory control of the international cable market. Overseas cables are owned according to a "half-circuit" concept: in theory, a U.S. carrier "owns" the portion of cable extending from the U.S. to some ocean-bottom midpoint, and the foreign carrier owns the other half. If the FCC does not authorize the U.S. carrier to build and operate its half, then no cable can be built.

i) Foreign PTTs have a similar regulatory hold over U.S. carriers; their participation in the construction of an international facility is obviously necessary.

ii) The half-circuit ownership arrangement, and the need to acquire a cable landing right, require multinational cooperation in the international communications marketplace. Without such cooperation, rival nations can constantly frustrate each other's plans to construct and to operate international facilities. This power is particularly significant in nations other than the U.S., where a PTT decides whether to participate in an international cable project and also controls all access to the domestic telecommunications market. Without the PTT, a U.S. carrier is not only unable to build a cable but also is unable to link it to another nation's telephone system.

c. The FCC must factor foreign nations' priorities into its own facilities decisions. To the degree that the Consultative Process and the establishment of Intelsat have provided it with a better sense of what these other nations want, it is better equipped to encourage the maximum amount of international network expansion.

d. By the end of the 1970s, rapid growth in traffic and rising demand for new services had forced the FCC to consider how best to expand international facilities. The FCC saw an international market that was substantially more competitive than it had ever been. It saw the potential to deregulate many decisions affecting international servcies—much to the consternation of PTTs in many other countries. It has not, until recently, retreated from its facilities planning role. It also has been wary about eliminating the circuit utilization guidelines it devised to redress the unequal facilities ownership policies in cable and satellite circuits. *See infra* Section IX.B.6.

2. Voice/Record Dichotomy

In 1982, the FCC decided to end its long-standing practice of protecting the IRCs from AT&T. Technological differences between voice and data transmission had originally given the FCC a logical basis for distinguishing between international voice and data services. Despite the fact that the development of submarine cables eliminated this technological barrier, the FCC explicitly prohibited AT&T from providing record services in 1964. *American Telpehone & Telegraph Co.*, 37 F.C.C. 1151 (1964) (*TAT-4 Authorization*). In the 1970s, however, the Commission gradually allowed AT&T to cross the voice/record boundary line. Finally, in 1982, the Commission eliminated all voice/record distinctions, permitting the IRCs and AT&T to compete directly in the entire international services market. *Overseas Communications Services*, 92 F.C.C.2d 641 (1982), *appeal docketed, TRT Telecommunications Corp. v. FCC*, No. 83-1193 (D.C. Cir. 1983).

3. Record Carrier Competition Act of 1981

At the same time that it was debating the elimination of the voice/record dichotomy, the FCC began an attack on the separation of domestic and international record services.

a. In 1943, Congress adopted Section 222 of the Communications Act. This amendment permitted the weakened, post-Depression domestic carriers to merge into a single surviving carrier—Western Union. However, Western Union had to divest itself of all international operations. The statute also required that Western Union use its virtual monopoly on domestic telex lines to distribute outbound international traffic equitably among the IRCs.

b. In 1979, Western Union began a service in which it routed international telex traffic directly to two foreign carriers. The FCC, relying on a lengthy analysis of the history and context of Section 222, ruled that this service did not violate the law. *Western Union Telegraph Co.*, 75 F.C.C.2d 461 (1979); *see also id.* at 483 (Attachment B). The Commission decided that because only the foreign carriers were providing foreign transmission services, Western Union was providing only a domestic service. It concluded that the statute did not require Western Union to route all outbound international traffic to the IRCs at the designated "gateway" cities. Alternatively, the FCC concluded that Section 222 did not bar Western Union from all future international service operations. The statute had merely prohibited the company from operating any of the lines it held prior to 1943. The Second Circuit vacated the FCC's decision, ruling that this arrangement violated the intent of Section 222. According to the court, Congress intended to prohibit Western Union from using its control of domestic lines to dictate the success or failure of a particular overseas carrier. *ITT World Communications v. FCC*, 635 F.2d 32 (2d Cir. 1980).

c. In response to the decision, the Congress adopted the Carrier Competition Act of 1981, which repealed old Section 222 and replaced it with legislation that opened both the international and domestic record service markets to full competition. Western Union was freed to reenter the international market, and the IRCs were authorized to operate beyond the twenty-one gateway cities in which they had previously connected to the Western Union domestic network. Under the Act, the carriers were required to interconnect their facilities with any other carrier requesting such interconnection. They also were instructed to reach agreement on the terms and conditions of interconnection, on a formula for allocating inbound international traffic that did not designate a particular domestic carrier, and on various other financial arrangements deemed necessary to promote competition. The FCC was authorized to prescribe those terms and conditions if no agreement could be reached. When the carriers were unable to agree, the FCC established the required technical and financial arrangements. *Interconnection Arrangements Between and Among the Domestic and International Record Carriers*, 89 F.C.C.2d 928 (1982), *rev'd in part, Western Union Telegraph Co. v. FCC*, 729 F.2d 811 (D.C. Cir. 1984).

d. Since the court's decision, the carriers have reached an agreement and the FCC has repealed all of its prescriptions (which would have sunset by the terms of the Act on December 29, 1984, in any case).

4. *Private International Satellites*

a. The FCC's decision to expand competition into the international satellite services market could have profound worldwide consequences. Proponents of Intelsat have argued that the establishment of U.S. satellite systems will divert traffic from Intelsat and will jeopardize that organization's ability to provide low-cost satellite services to developing nations.

b. Intelsat was developed, in part, in an effort to make satellite communications available to lesser developed countries, where low demand creates high service costs. Under the Intelsat Agreement, service prices are averaged across the entire Intelsat system. Thus, low-cost, high-traffic routes (such as the North Atlantic) are priced above cost, while less-used routes are priced below cost. This pricing policy makes Intelsat very vulnerable to price competition along heavily used (and overpriced) routes, such as the North Atlantic corridor, where the U.S. private satellite applicants plan to provide service.

c. Under Article XIV(d) of the Intelsat Agreement, member countries wishing to construct transborder systems independent of the Intelsat network are supposed to participate in a coordination process. This coordination procedure has two aims. It is designed to ensure that separate systems are technically compatible with Intelsat. It also is intended to protect Intelsat against "significant economic harm" that might result from the diversion of business away from Intelsat. Intelsat's Assembly of Parties considers proposed alternative systems and makes recommendations as to whether it believes such systems will threaten Intelsat's future.

d. To date, Intelsat has never refused to "coordinate" a separate system proposed by one or more of its member nations. Such systems have, however, been designed to carry regional traffic that either cannot be carried by Intelsat (for economic or technical reasons) or is so small that it has little effect on the Intelsat system. Intelsat now must decide how it will cope with new systems that directly threaten significant portions of its traffic, especially in the heavily travelled North Atlantic corridor.

e. Intelsat's coordination recommendations are not binding on member nations. However, the U.S. has indicated that it will "carefully consider all recommendations" in making decisions about authorizing new satellite systems. It is unlikely that Intelsat could halt construction of an independent system; it might not even try to accomplish that result. Intelsat has, in recent months, been trying to clarify just what the coordination procedure means and how it will work. Thus far, though, neither the Board of Governors nor the Assembly of Parties has been able to agree on proposals that, reportedly, would have restructured the Art. XIV(d) procedures so as to impede U.S. efforts to promote competitive satellite systems.

f. The task of clarifying national policy on the international satellite issue resulted in differences of views within the U.S. government. After a series of disagreements between the State and Commerce Departments, President Reagan finally decided that construction of new, private satellite systems would further the national interest. Presidential Determination No. 85-2 of Nov. 28, 1984, 49 Fed. Reg. 46,987 (Nov. 30, 1984). This decision, apparently, brought an end to the disagreements between the two executive departments.

g. Following the presidential decision, the FCC began its examination of the private satellite issue; under the Communications Act, the FCC has power to authorize individual systems. On January 4, 1985, it released a Notice of Inquiry and Proposed Rulemaking to consider both individual applications and general U.S. policies regarding private satellites. *Establishment of Satellite Systems Providing International Communications*, 50 Fed. Reg. 1570 (Jan. 11, 1985).

h. On July 25, the FCC decided that the authorization of private international systems, subject to certain conditions and restrictions, would serve the public interest and would not cause significant economic harm to Intelsat. *See* FCC Report No. DC-163, Mimeo No. 6024 (released July 25, 1985).

i. In reaching its decision, the FCC agreed with an earlier Executive Branch decision that had concluded that the type of services that could be provided by these satellites and the manner in which they could be offered would have to be limited. Without such limitations, it was thought, there would be little assurance that the U.S. could abide by its commitments under the Intelsat Agreement.

i) In conjunction with President Reagan's decision on the new satellites, the Secretaries of State and Commerce had instructed the FCC that two conditions would have to be imposed on new systems in order to fulfill U.S. international obligations and foreign policy objectives. First, these systems would have to be required to provide services only through the sale or the long-term lease of transponders or space segments (not through tariffed, common carrier offerings to the public) and would have to be prohibited from interconnecting with public switched networks (*i.e.*, no public telephone service). Second, the applicant would have to have at least one foreign administration that would join Comsat (as the U.S. signatory to Intelsat) in overseeing the Article XIV(d) coordination procedures for the new system. *See* Letter to Hon. Mark S. Fowler from George P. Schultz and Malcom Baldridge (Nov. 28, 1984). These restrictions were intended to protect Intelsat from significant economic harm. By imposing these limitations, it was hoped, new satellite systems could develop without destroying Intelsat's core market—international telephone services, which produce almost seventy–five percent of Intelsat's revenues.

ii) The Commission adopted these limitations. It explicitly imposed the service restrictions on all licensees, as well as on resellers and users of the new satellite systems. The FCC ruled that licensees would risk losing their authorizations if they were to fail to enforce the service restrictions through contractual or other appropriate means. Resellers also are required to impose these restrictions on their customers. Finally, the Commission determined that it would not authorize a system to begin operating until the State Department has informed it that, with respect to the particular system, U.S. obligations under the Intelsat Agreement have been fulfilled. The satisfaction of these obligations will include completion of the Article XIV(d) coordination procedure—presumably with the cooperation of at least one foreign correspondent—and a determination that the system will not cause significant economic harm to Intelsat.

iii) Consistent with the Executive Branch's recommended limitations, the FCC has imposed some additional guidelines: (1) no minimum unit of a satellite circuit must be provided, so long as all units are offered only for sale or under a long-term lease; (2) a lease must last at least one year; (3) carriers and resellers may buy or lease satellite capacity to provide any service that is not interconnected with a public switched network; and (4) the service restrictions are not subject to a "sunset" date.

iv) It is unclear whether a system that does not receive a favorable recommendation under the Article XIV(d) procedures would be licensed to operate. Presumably, the State Department could inform the FCC that such a system, nevertheless, would not be inconsistent with the terms of the Intelsat Agreement. The FCC then would be free to authorize the system to operate. A recently released Executive Branch white paper on international satellites does not really clarify how agressive the U.S. might be in promoting competitive international systems. The white paper says merely that the U.S. "will go forward only with systems it deems consistent with its obligations to Intelsat." Senior Interagency Group on International Communication and Information Policy, *A White Paper on New International Satellite Systems* 18 (Feb. 1985) [hereinafter cited as *SIG White Paper*].

j. A question raised by the Executive Branch—which will be studied carefully by both the Commerce Department and the FCC—is whether Intelsat can deaverage its prices to compete on heavily used routes.

i) It is asserted by some that the Intelsat Agreement does not permit pricing flexibility on a route-by-route basis, particularly because deaveraging could jeopardize the kind of affordable global service that is a fundamental purpose of Intelsat. Others argue that the failure to revise Intelsat's policies could have an even more detrimental impact on the organization's future. Thus, this line of inquiry must examine three related questions: (1) To what extent can Intelsat restructure its prices? (2) What will the consequence of any restructuring be for global telecommunications policy? (3) If repricing is not allowed, can Intelsat survive in a competitive marketplace?

ii) Congress recently adopted legislation that includes general support for a move by Intelsat toward cost-based pricing. One provision, however, would result in having Comsat (as the U.S. signatory to Intelsat) "ensure" that Intelsat provides "sufficient" documentation to allow for an independent determination of whether any rate changes in fact are cost-based. *See e.g.*, "Foreign Relations Authorization Act," H.R. 2068, 99th Cong., 1st Sess. § 146(c), 131 Cong. Rec. H6818 (daily ed. July 30, 1985). The legislation was accompanied by a vociferous debate as to whether U.S. support of flexibility in Intelsat pricing would demonstrate allegiance to the Intelsat concept or a betrayal of the interests of developing nations. Earlier versions of the legislation would have required Comsat to support amendments to the Intelsat Agreement that would permit flexible pricing. This language was dropped.

k. The debate over new satellite systems already has placed U.S. national goals in potential conflict with international communications objectives. Executive Branch limitations on international competition, which have gained support in Congress, *see e.g.*, H.R. 2068, *supra*, at §§ 146(a), (b) & (d), seek to avoid such a conflict. They represent a clear attempt to reconcile a pro-competitive policy with a long-standing commitment to preserving affordable global satellite service.

l. The outcome of the U.S. debate may well be a fundamental change in the structure and function of Intelsat. The organization might become more active as a coordinator of numerous regional, nationally based systems; it might reduce its role as a procurement agent for international satellite services directly from manufacturers. Intelsat also could take an active role in devising and overseeing a multinational mechanism (explicitly not using embeded rate subsidies) to subsidize satellite service to less-developed regions and less-used routes around the world. In either case, the situation offers a significant example of how U.S. domestic policy can have major international ramifications.

5. *Streamlined Regulation*

a. The Commission recently has proposed streamlining its regulation of international service providers similar to the way in which it has streamlined—or eliminated—the regulation of domestic carriers. *International Competitive Common Carrier Policies*, FCC No. 85-177 (released April 19, 1985) (Notice of Proposed Rulemaking). In its proposed action, the Commission tentatively concluded that the international services market had become sufficiently competitive to warrant a reduction of governmental oversight. To the degree that marketplace forces would protect consumer welfare, Title II regulation could be removed.

b. The Commission divided the international market into two submarkets, International Message Telephone Service ("IMTS," or switched voice service) and non-IMTS. It also determined that each foreign country constituted a separate competitive market.

i) In the IMTS market, the FCC determined that AT&T was a dominant carrier and, therefore, would remain subject to full Title II regulation. (It decided that in the non-IMTS market, however, AT&T was not a dominant carrier.) In addition, it decided that all carriers providing IMTS service between "domestic, non-contiguous points" and foreign countries were dominant carriers. All other IMTS carriers were thought to be non-dominant and could be governed by streamlined regulatory requirements.

ii) In the non-IMTS market, the FCC found that no carrier, in any geographic market, was dominant. It concluded that there was sufficient competition worldwide to make it unlikely that any one carrier could price anticompetitively. Comsat, however, was viewed as a dominant carrier in its role as a provider of Intelsat circuits and certain earth station facilities. These operations would continue to be subject to full Title II regulation. Any end-to-end services provided by Comsat's competitive subsidiary would be non-dominant offerings.

c. The streamlined procedures followed for domestic carriers would be applied, for the most part, to non-dominant international carriers. *See supra* Section VII.A. However, special regulatory requirements would be adopted to accommodate the FCC's special role in overseeing international service providers. Non-dominant carriers would be allowed to add circuits or to change services after the grant of an initial authorization to serve a particular country. However, "applications to construct, acquire or operate lines in all major facilities projects (such as the transatlantic cables) or to acquire capacity from any future private cable or satellite sources" would still have to be filed. FCC No. 85-177, *supra*, at 21. These applications, the FCC claimed, would assist its long-range facilities planning responsibilities and its participation in the consultative process. The Commission intends to continue overseeing the competitive relationship between U.S. carriers and foreign service providers.

6. *Circuit Utilization Policies*

The FCC recently announced that oversight of international facilities construction and use decisions is still necessary. "A fully competitive market does not now exist," the FCC concluded, in justifying its decision to propose a new set of guidelines for the 1985-1995 planning period. *Atlantic Facilities Plan*, FCC No. 85-176, *supra*, at 2.

a. The FCC's regulatory objective is to balance the goals of high-quality service, diverse routes, and sufficient capacity to minimize service rates. However, the FCC has long feared that facilities construction and use decisions would not be based solely on efficiency criteria such as these. Satellites and cables have not been competitive in many respects, and AT&T uses such an overwhelming proportion of the available circuits that it can influence the economic viability of existing cable or satellite investments. Cables have not been able to offer broadband services. In addition, AT&T can own interests in cable circuits, but not in satellite circuits. These disparities were seen as sources for potentially significant, distorting pressures on the international marketplace. Through its facilities planning and use decisions, which are informed by FCC participation in the Consultative Process, the FCC has structured U.S. participation in the international market to offset these pressures.

b. The FCC's main concern is AT&T, which uses almost all of the international IMTS circuits between the U.S. and the member countries of the European Conference of Postal and Telecommunications Administrations ("CEPT"). For a variety of reasons, in part because AT&T has ownership interests in cables, AT&T might shift a great deal of its traffic to cable circuits (away from Comsat and Intelsat) if FCC circuit utilization policies were abolished. Such a shift is enhanced further by the attractiveness of new fiber optic cable circuits—in which AT&T also has an ownership interest. Any such preference may be partially offset by changes—both contemplated and approved—in the relationship between users, carriers, Intelsat, and Comsat. However, the FCC apparently does not yet view the IMTS market as subject to competition. Thus, it has decided that some circuit utilization regulation must still be applied to AT&T.

i) The FCC has modified its "balanced loading" policy for AT&T, which had required that AT&T use cable and satellite circuits on approximately an equal basis. It has adopted a transitional use policy that will allow AT&T to increase the proportion of message telephone circuits it uses for U.S.-CEPT traffic on either medium by two percent a year from 1986 through 1988. However, AT&T will not be allowed to "deload" any circuit currently being used. Before the end of 1988, the FCC will review this policy and decide what, if any, utilization guidelines should apply after 1988. *See* FCC Report No. DC-184, *supra*.

ii) The Commission also has decided that all other IMTS service providers, the IRCs, and AT&T—when it is providing record services—should be free from any circuit use requirements for U.S.-CEPT traffic. *Id.*

iii) The FCC has said that it hopes the IMTS market will soon be competitive enough to permit the elimination of all circuit use policies. In addition, it has indicated that it expects changes in the satellite market to make satellite services increasingly attractive and cost-efficient over the next six years. Fiber optic cables can offer the high bandwidth services once available only on satellites at prices that are as good as or better than those provided by Intelsat. These cables are expected to compete vigorously with satellites. As these facilities compete on a more equal basis, carriers will be more likely to make economic utilization decisions (*i.e.*, based on prices). By eliminating artificial market distortions, these changes should enhance competition and overcome the need for regulation.

7. *Movement Toward Intermodal Competition: Change in Satellite Use Policies*

The FCC has considered three regulatory measures designed to heighten competition between submarine cables and international satellites ("intermodal competition"). The FCC's attention has focused on ways of changing the marketing and distribution arrangements for satellite circuits. Primarily, this has meant changing Comsat's role as an intermediate reseller of Intelsat circuits.

a. As noted above, *see supra* Section IX.A.2., Comsat traditionally has functioned as a carrier's carrier. It is the sole U.S. provider of international circuits and is permitted to lease those circuits only to "authorized users." 47 U.S.C. § 735(a)(2) (1983). The FCC defined these users to be, in essence, common carriers. The carriers, in turn, retail the circuits by leasing them directly to end users. They also provide the transmission links between a user's facility and a Comsat earth station. The FCC imposed this restrictive arrangement in the 1960s, when the IRCs were beginning to enjoy a significant growth in their leased channel business. At that time, the FCC feared that allowing Comsat to compete directly with the IRCs for leased channel revenues could threaten the IRCs' success in the market. To the degree that the IRCs lost business to Comsat, rates for public switched record services were likely to rise. Thus, allowing competition in the leased service market would benefit large users—the only ones able to lease circuits directly—at the expense of the public, which depended on the public switched services. For this reason, the FCC foreclosed Comsat from marketing directly to the public. *See Authorized Entities and Authorized Users,* 4 F.C.C.2d 421 (1966), *recon. granted in part,* 6 F.C.C.2d 593 (1967).

b. Through the late 1970s, and into the early 1980s, the FCC began to reassess this policy in light of changes in the international services market. A dramatic increase in international traffic, combined with substantial growth in the IRCs' business, made the FCC less concerned about protecting the IRCs. *Authorized User II,* 90 F.C.C.2d at 1412. In particular, the IRCs experienced brisk growth in their telex business. The share of revenue contributed by the leased circuit business declined significantly. *Id.* at 1413. Finally, the comparative costs of cable and satellite circuits varied greatly from FCC expectations. In 1966, it had been assumed that satellite circuits would cost substantially less than comparable cable circuits. However, as a result of technological advances that greatly increased the capacity of submarine cables, the per-circuit cost of these cables quickly declined. In certain instances cable can—over particular routes—be offered at a cost equal to or less than the cost of satellite facilities. *Id.* at 1414. This meant that the IRCs, if forced to compete directly with Comsat in the leased circuit market, could offer competitive cable circuits. The FCC was able to conclude, in short, that the need to protect the IRCs simply was no longer present. *Id.* at 1415.

c. As a result, the Commission decided to change its authorized user policy to permit Comsat to sell directly to the public. In addition, Comsat was permitted to establish a competitive subsidiary that could compete directly with other carriers in selling "end-to-end" services to users. Finally, the FCC made its "composite rate" policy, which had been adopted along with the original *Authorized User* decision, optional. Under this rate policy, carriers were required to file a single tariff for each service; the rate charged could not differ on the basis of whether cable or satellite circuits were being used. Thus, the composite rate had to account for overall cost savings that a carrier realized as a result of its use of satellite facilities.

d. The Court of Appeals for the District of Columbia Circuit reversed the Commission's decision. *ITT World Communications v. FCC,* 725 F.2d 732 (D.C. Cir. 1984).

i) The court's primary complaint was that the FCC had not adequately resolved the numerous competitive issues implicit in any change in the structure of the international market. In the court's view, a change in the authorized user policy would preclude Comsat and the IRCs from competing in the market to lease satellite circuits. Because Comsat could provide these circuits to users at cost, the IRCs could offer no advantage, unless they leased circuits to users at a price less than cost. In addition, the court expressed doubt that intermodal competition was actually likely. Fiber optic cables, which should be able to compete directly with satellite links, are still a number of years away. Present cable facilities were viewed as having a significant cost disadvantage. In sum, the court believed, the Commission's action might actually be contrary to the public interest. It might harm the IRCs' competitive prospects, raising the price of public exchange services.

ii) The court vacated the FCC's decision and ruled that before returning to the authorized user issue, it should resolve two related proceedings. These proceedings involve ownership of earth stations used to reach Intelsat circuits and direct access by users to Intelsat (bypassing Comsat). They could, in the court's opinion, have a significant effect on future competition in the international market. Permitting users and carriers to own their own earth stations and to acquire an ownership interest in Intelsat circuits might enhance competition between Comsat and the IRCs. The court cautioned, however, that allowing the IRCs to obtain direct interests in the satellite market could undermine the potential for intermodal competition. The IRCs would then have less incentive to develop cable facilities as a true competitive alternative to satellite links. According to the court, the FCC had to resolve these pending issues before it could judge how a change in the authorized user policy would affect the public interest.

e. The Commission concluded that its ownership policy toward international earth stations should be liberalized. Prior to making this decision, all international earth stations were owned by a consortium of carriers, including Comsat and a number of U.S. international carriers. This group is known as the Earth Station Ownership Committee ("ESOC"). Under an Agreement between ESOC members, Comsat owns fifty percent of each earth station and operates all of them; participating carriers own the remaining fifty percent. The Commission decided to allow non-ESOC members to construct and operate earth stations, concluding that this policy "would benefit users by increasing carrier and service options and creating competitive pressures on rates." *Modification of Policy on Ownership and Operation of U.S. Earth Stations that Operate With the Intelsat Global Communications Satellite System*, 97 F.C.C.2d 444 (1984), *recon denied*, FCC No. 85-352 (released July 15, 1985).

i) Limited-purpose stations—those intended only for use with Intelsat's high-speed ditigal service, International Business Service ("IBS"), or with television service, are now handled in a streamlined review process. (In effect, these earth stations have been deregulated.) Multipurpose stations, which present more complex technical, economic, and operational issues, are reviewed more closely.

ii) This deregulatory action is likely to lead to significant growth in the number of IBS earth stations. The FCC intended, with its decision, to promote the growth of IBS in the U.S.; as more users obtain cost-effective means for using IBS (such as customer premise earth stations or teleport–type sharing arrangements), the demand for the service is likely to rise. This increase could put added pressure on Intelsat to expand the availability of innovative and efficient services such as IBS.

iii) The liberalization policy brought with it further changes in the structure of Comsat. Because earth stations are now free to become a competitive business, Comsat was required to transfer its interests in the five operating international earth stations from its World Systems Division to its new competitive subsidiary. In addition, Comsat was required to unbundle its charges for space segments, which remain a monopoly good, and earth stations services, which will be provided competitively.

iv) In 1988, Comsat will cease to operate any of the five international earth stations that it now uses to link carriers to the Intelsat satellites. It recently signed a deal under which AT&T will purchase Comsat's share in three of the five international earth stations owned and operated by the ESOC. The other two stations will be retired in 1986. AT&T, which is a member of the ESOC, reportedly also is considering a buyout of the ownership interests of its fellow ESOC members. The deal will give AT&T ownership—and, hence, control—of the earth station facilities that transmit a majority of its international traffic.

f. The Commission rejected an additional liberalization measure which would have allowed parties other than Comsat to gain direct access to Intelsat space segments. *Regulatory Policies Concerning Direct Access to Intelsat Space Segment for the U.S. International Service Carriers*, 97 F.C.C.2d 296 (1984).

i) The Commission found no merit to claims that Comsat's tariffs included unjustifiable cost elements. Carriers contended that providing them with direct access to Intelsat, and requiring Comsat to unbundle the components of its space segment tariff, would reduce the price being charged for Intelsat service.

ii) Direct access was not seen as a way to stimulate competition between Comsat and other carriers seeking to offer satellite services. The Court of Appeals had claimed that direct access was the only way to stimulate such intramodal competition. The FCC, however, disagreed; it found that carriers were competing with end users—rather than with Comsat—in seeking to offer competitive satellite service. Carriers would enjoy a competitive advantage to the degree they could offer cheaper end-to-end service than a user could (by arranging for its own connections). Where carriers competed with Comsat's competitive subsidiary, which was permitted to sell end-to-end services, they would compete on equal terms. Under its *Authorized User II* decision, the Comsat subsidiary was required to purchase space segments on the same terms as were available to all other users. Thus, competition would again occur in pricing end-to-end services, since the space segment cost would be fixed (and equal).

iii) The FCC also concluded that allowing carriers to unbundle their rates (charging separately for satellite and cable transmission paths) would facilitate intermodal competition. The FCC disagreed with the Court of Appeals' conclusion that the disparity in price between cable circuits and satellite circuits made intermodal competition impossible. It said that no evidence had been offered to demonstrate that such competition, between end-to-end service offerings, could not occur.

iv) The Commission blamed the court for overemphasizing space segment charges. These charges typically represent just one-quarter of the $4,000 monthly, per channel price for end-to-end satellite service. The greatest room for price competition appeared to be in providing efficient ground services and in arranging for foreign carrier interconnection.

g. After completing these two proceedings, as required by the Court of Appeals, the FCC readopted its new authorized user policy. *Authorized User II*, 50 Fed. Reg. 2552 (Jan. 17, 1985), *recon. denied*, FCC No. 85-323 (released June 28, 1985). In doing so, the FCC undertook a fresh public interest analysis. It concluded—as it had in its earlier decision—that the change in policy would not have any significant anti-competitive effects and would, in general, benefit the public.

h. There is now renewed pressure being placed on the FCC to change its direct access policy. Proponents of direct access allege that permitting carriers and users to deal directy with Intelsat, rather than only through Comsat, would make Intelsat more competitive. The *SIG White Paper* argued that

> [t]he process by which customers obtain international satellite communications service results in end-user prices substantially above Intelsat circuit charges. The current U.S. arrangement where Comsat, in effect, functions as exclusive U.S. marketing agent for Intelsat circuits, may be ill-suited to an era of proliferating customer demands. No single entity, no matter how perceptive, can reasonably be expected to anticipate and satisfy all customer demands and needs in a market which is experiencing rapid demand-inducing and cost-reducing technological advances. Permitting expanded, direct, cost-based access to Intelsat may be the most reliable means of substantially reducing costs and ensuring valid entry signals.

SIG White paper, supra, at 32.

i. Just after the White Paper was released, the NTIA petitioned the FCC to institute a new rulemaking on the direct access issue. Petition for Rulemaking to Consider Authorizing Competitive Access by Carriers and Users to the Intelsat Space Segment for the Provision of Customized International Communications Services (Feb. 21, 1985). A large number of users and carriers have joined with the NTIA in this effort; Comsat has opposed the petition.

j. The NTIA cites four reasons for requiring a change in satellite access policy to enhance intermodal competition:

i) Improved technology and the introduction of fiber optics are making submarine cables more competitive with satellites.

ii) Carriers have ownership interests in cable facilities, but not in satellites. In addition, the FCC then was considering (and now has proposed) adoption of a policy that would allow service providers to make limited ownership investments in cables. International Communications Policies Governing Designation of Recognized Private Operating Agencies, Grants of IRUs in International Facilities and Assignment of Data Network Identification Codes, FCC No. 83-516 (released Dec. 22, 1983) (Notice of Inquiry); FCC Report No. DC-152, Mimeo No. 5791 (released July 12, 1985) (Notice of Proposed Rulemaking). This disparity creates a bias in favor of cable use.

iii) The FCC was, at the time, considering a relaxation of its facilities loading policies, which would allow carriers to make greater use of the facilities in which they have ownership interests (i.e., cables). (The FCC now has relaxed these rules. See supra Section IX.B.6.)

iv) The number of regional satellite systems that can compete with Intelsat is growing.

k. The NTIA argues that the FCC would strengthen Intelsat's ability to combat these marketplace challenges by adopting a new access policy. The NTIA suggested five possible benefits of a "competitive access" policy, which might include allowing some form of carrier investment in Intelsat.

i) Marketplace distortions, caused by unequal facilities investment policies, would be mitigated.

ii) Allowing users to pay for only those international services that they want would put downward pressure on space segment prices. Comsat no longer would be able to bundle unwanted charges into its space segment prices. (Such access also might not be needed to the degree that Comsat's prices are cost justified.)

iii) Bringing space segment rates down will discourage new entry into the international market by inefficient competitors. By closing the gap between the cost and price of Intelsat services, there will be less opportunity for cream-skimming by systems that cannot offer true cost advantages.

iv) Direct access will stimulate a competitive market in Intelsat space segments. By allowing a number of carriers to vie with each other for users' business, use of Intelsat should increase.

v) To the degree that large users can realize savings from direct access arrangements, these savings should be passed on to consumers.

l. This analysis, of course, is being offered by an Executive Branch agency, and the Executive Branch already has announced its support for the introduction of private U.S. satellite systems. To the degree that a case can be built for enhancing Intelsat's competitive potential, the Executive Branch will strengthen its case for introducing new U.S. satellites.

C. Pressures Favoring the Introduction of New Competitors

The FCC's current pro-competitive actions may be simply the

inevitable result of a move toward international competition that is already well underway. In part, the changes are responses to a variety of events taking place around the world. The international marketplace is now evolving in a way that invites further competition. Since the end of the 1970s, this movement has been visible, although its signs in the U.S. may have been obscured by the attention being paid to domestic issues—particularly the AT&T divestiture.

1. Increased Competition in Telephone Services

a. Competition in international telephone services is occurring over existing cable and satellite facilities. GTE Sprint, MCI, and other carriers that have challenged AT&T's dominance in the domestic long-distance market have recently expanded their services to include international calling. MCI has negotiated interconnection agreements with Belgium, Canada, Australia, the United Kingdom, and other countries. It expects to serve more than eighty percent of the international market by the end of 1985. GTE-Sprint has reached similar agreements with many of the same countries.

b. These new carriers are not subject to the FCC's circuit utilization policy of "balanced loading." Consequently, they can use whatever facilities configuration they deem most efficient (in terms of cost, service, or other characteristics). As these carriers expand their foothold in the international market, they will exert significant pressures on AT&T. AT&T will then, and with some justification, seek the elimination of the circuit utilization policy—so that it can compete on even terms.

c. The result—an end to all loading requirements—could bring about a migration away from satellite circuits and toward new (and less costly) fiber optic cables. This could have serious consequences for Intelsat, particularly over high-density, over-priced routes. Any move by Intelsat to reprice its services, to be competitive over the high-use routes, would have a significant impact on the debate over private international satellites. The need to protect Intelsat's position as a monopoly universal service provider would be undermined. If Intelsat begins acting as a marketplace competitor, much of the rationale for withholding competition from the international market would lose appeal.

2. Growth of Regional Satellite Systems

a. Over the past ten years, the number of regional satellite systems has increased steadily. These systems claim to have provided only services that Intelsat (and existing undersea cables) cannot readily—or economically—provide. However, they have diverted at least some traffic away from Intelsat. Systems such as Eutelsat, Arabsat, and Palapa (Indonesia) have begun to chip away at the once monolithic international satellite market. The appplicants for private systems have argued, in part, that the growth of regional systems makes competitive international satellite services a virtual certainty in the near future. Thus, they contend, the U.S. should act promptly to ensure that it can take advantage of evolving competitive opportunities.

b. Advances in satellite technology have made "spot" beams possible: these have enabled domestic and regional satellites to provide limited international service. Spot beams, which cover specific geogrpahic areas, allow satellites to provide point-to-point services. They also can be used to extend a satellite's footprint beyond its immediate transmission region. The beams give satellites an attractive flexibility because they can be shifted; submarine cables, of course, cannot be "redirected" readily once they are laid. Although these spot beams make international service technologically possible, they do not mean that satellites equipped with such capabilities will necessarily be used to provide such service. However, the availability of the technology is likely to attract some users. For example, a multinational corporation that wants to transmit its communications over just one regional or national system might find the spot beam useful for reaching its widely scattered offices.

c. European administrations may view the expansion into international service as a way of supplementing a regional system's weak revenue stream. One recent study in Japan concluded that a regional satellite system would be economically viable only if it were capable of providing Asia-Pacific service. Research Institute of Telecommunications and Economics, *A Study on the Pacific Regional Satellite Communications System* (1983).

X. CONCLUSION: FUTURE PERSPECTIVES

A. Continued Restructuring of Telecommunications Under the Modified Final Judgment

1. The verdict on the AT&T divestiture is not yet in. Although it already has brought about massive changes, the restructuring process is far from over. In the next few years, the task of clarifying the relationships among AT&T, the BOCs, the Independent Telephone Companies, and the many other competitive carriers will bring about critical changes that will further define the shape of the U.S. telecommunications market.

2. The BOCs are implementing the equal access plan. Rewiring and the installation of new switches will continue—probably throughout the rest of the decade. The result will be to place competition in the interexchange market on more of a "level playing field."

3. Telephone users already have begun to subscribe to one of the many competitive interexchange carriers. Subscription will diminish the need for access codes, which will eliminate some of AT&T's competitive advantage. This process, however, already has been filled with controversy,

including how to allocate users who do not select a specific carrier and how to ensure that the "subscription drive" is conducted fairly.

4. The process of defining the RHCs' corporate identities also will continue. Judge Greene will face many additional—and increasingly complex—line-of-business waiver requests. Congressional pressure on the Judge to reduce his oversight role also may increase.

B. Repricing of Access to the Local Exchange

1. Struggles with the access charges will proceed. Efforts to protect universal service are not likely to abate; therefore, the FCC will be encouraged to slow the rate of repricing. Arrangements to bypass the local loop, however, will require that prices be brought closer to costs. As a result, tension will build further around the issue of appropriate local service prices. Users' desire for increasingly sophisticated networks will pressure the BOCs to upgrade their transmission facilities and to become more aggressive in marketing new services.

2. State regulators will continue seeking to protect against local rate increases. Public utility commission proceedings will explore proper responses to bypass, including regulation of alternative networks, imposition of local access fees, and increased flexibility in the prices of "competitive" services offered by the local telephone companies. State actions will provoke additional calls for the FCC to preempt other attempts allegedly intended to stifle the growth of new and innovative service networks.

3. Cable television will not, for technological reasons, become a primary participant in the bypass market. However, the states will have to decide how to respond to the FCC's decision to preempt certain state regulation of cable system offerings of two-way, non-video services.

C. Competitive "Shake-Down" in Interexchange and International Markets

1. AT&T will continue to adjust its pricing, both for MTS and for private line services. Its competitors will face increased access charges as the quality of their exchange connections are made equal to those of AT&T. These moves, as well as the IBM–MCI deal, will contribute to an overall shakeout in the long-distance market. The FCC, the courts, and Congress may be required to intervene in order to protect future competition. Although it is not likely that a duopoly, such as exists in the U.K., will result, the number of competitors certainly will diminish.

2. As the market adjusts further, and as the FCC deregulates more, economic forces are certain to cause marginal carriers to fail. For some new entrants, the key to survival will be having a "deep pocket"—such as IBM—behind them. In the international arena, the glut of satellite and cable circuits will leave facilities unused. This will cause financial markets to reduce the availabiltiy of capital. In these markets, new entrants

seeking start-up money will vie with established carriers looking for loans to survive and to revitalize their operations. Some of the planned facilities may never be built. Mergers and consolidations may take place in order to eliminate unprofitable entities.

D. Computer II Reoriented for AT&T and the BOCs

As technology continues to advance, the FCC has been forced to revisit *Computer II*. A major component of the FCC's *Computer III* inquiry will be the relaxation of its separation policies, particularly with respect to AT&T. At the same time, new questions about the need for tighter competitive safeguards applicable to the BOCs' activities in the "enhanced" services market are likely to be raised. More difficult issues about which "enhanced" services can be provided by the BOCs under the MFJ—at least for now—are likely to be decided first by Judge Greene. However, any move by him to redefine the regulatory scheme envisioned by the FCC could force the Commission to examine its policies toward the BOCs and also could produce a jurisdictional confrontation with the D.C. Court.

E. U.S. Policy Toward Future of Intelsat

The U.S. decision to inject new, privately-owned satellites into the international market will have worldwide repercussions and will affect significantly Intelsat's future. It also may cause increased friction in North-South relations and between developed nations, some of whom will characterize the U.S. position as a rejection of its original commitment to lesser developed countries. Much will depend on the success of efforts to redefine Intelsat—possibly as a more competitive entity. The change in Intelsat also will affect Comsat, particularly in its role as the exclusive U.S. agent for international satellite circuits. It is possible that allowing direct access to Intelsat would reduce sharply the incentives to construct private international satellite systems. Aggressive repricing and marketing of Intelsat services also might affect significantly the structure of competition in the international telecommunications market.

F. U.S. Trade Pressures on Global Telecommunications Markets

Finally, the U.S. will continue to affect global communications policies through its trade position. Attention now focused on the Japanese market is likely to be shifted to Europe. Policies of the established PTTs could be subject to intensive efforts to open European markets to competitive U.S. manufacturers and carriers. In this way, the U.S. will continue to have a significant effect on both the domestic and the international policies of other nations.

CHAPTER IV
CANADA

TABLE OF CONTENTS

CHAPTER IV
CANADA

I. INTRODUCTION: OVERVIEW OF INDUSTRY STRUCTURE AND REGULATION

A. Structure of the Canadian Telecommunications Industry

The telecommunications industry in Canada is characterized by diversity and decentralization. No one company provides complete telephone service in all regions to all Canadians using its own facilities. With one exception—Bell Canada—no one company can even provide service on facilities that it owns beyond the boundaries of a single province. Although there were, as of 1978, 260 telephone companies, the fourteen largest account for 99% of the total plant and operating revenues. *See* TransCanada Telephone System, Submission of the TCTS in Response to the Discussion Paper of the Parliamentary Task Force on Regulatory Reform, Sept. 1980. Ownership in telecommunications providers is varied: private, public—both federal and provincial, and mixed public-private.

1. *Bell Canada*

Bell Canada (incorporated by a Special Act of Parliament, S.C. 1880, c.67 as The Bell Telephone Company of Canada) serves the provinces of Ontario and Quebec, the industrial core of Canada, and parts of the Northwest territories.

a. Bell Canada is now a wholly-owned subsidiary of Bell Canada Enterprises, Inc. ("BCE"), which is, in turn, a widely-held company. A corporate reorganization in April 1983 created BCE as a holding company with Bell Canada as the operating company. BCE also has interests in the telephone companies of the Atlantic provinces—New Brunswick Telephone Co. Ltd. (32.5%), Maritime Telegraph and Telephone Co., serving Nova Scotia and, through the Island Telephone Co. Ltd., Prince Edward Island (32.5%), and Newfoundland Telephone Co. Ltd. (54.4%). BCE also owns 100% of Telebec Ltee, serving parts of Quebec, and 99.8% of Northern Telephone Ltd., in Northern Ontario. *See* BCE, *1983 Annual Report*.

b. Bell Canada alone has 58% of all the telephones in Canada, realizes over 50% of all telecommunications operating revenues, and provides almost 60% of all the interprovincial telephone service in Canada. Dep't of Communications, *Canadian Telecommunications: An Overview of the Canadian Telecommunications Carriage Industry*, at 8, Table A2 (1982 data) (1983). BCE owns 51.9% of Northern Telecom Ltd., the second largest manufacturer of telephone equipment in North America, and from which Bell Canada purchases almost 70% of its equipment. Together, Northern

Telecom and Bell Canada own interests in a research arm, Bell-Northern Research Ltd. (30% and 70%, respectively).

2. British Columbia Telephone

Canada's second largest telephone company is British Columbia Telephone Co. ("B.C. Tel."), with approximately 11% of the telephones in Canada and a 12% share of total Canadian telecommunications operating revenues. B.C. Tel. is the primary provider of services in British Columbia. It is 51% owned by Anglo Canadian Telephone Co., a wholly-owned subsidiary of the U.S. provider GTE Corp. GTE also controls indirectly 55% of Quebec Telephone, a provider in Quebec province. B.C. Tel. owns Microtel Ltd. (an equipment manufacturer) and Microtel Pacific Research.

3. Provincial Companies

The governments of the three prairie provinces each own the principal telephone company serving their respective provinces: Alberta Government Telephones, Saskatchewan Telecommunications and the Manitoba Telephone System. These systems were established as a result of populist movements and because Bell Canada was unable to respond to government pressures to extend services into Western Canada. The company sold its assets to the provincial governments early this century and was thus effectively prevented from expanding into Western Canada and, indeed, from becoming a nationwide carrier.

4. Municipal Systems

Thunder Bay Telephone System, serving Thunder Bay, Ontario, and "edmonton telephones", Edmonton, Alberta, are owned by their respective municipalities.

5. Federal Telephone Companies

Canadian National Railways, ("CNR"), a corporation wholly owned by the Government of Canada, owns NorthwesTel (serving Northern British Columbia, the Yukon, and the western Northwest Territories) and Terra Nova Telecommunications (serving parts of Newfoundland and Labrador).

6. Telesat Canada

Telesat Canada was established by statute in 1969 to own and operate the Canadian satellite communications systems. It was created as a commercial corporation, with the idea that it was expected to make a profit, while also being charged with serving the vast reaches of Northern Canada and developing the space manufacturing industry. Telesat is 50%

owned by the federal government and 50% by fourteen telecommunications carriers (those listed in Schedule I of the Telesat Canada Act). Bell Canada has a 24.6% interest in Telesat Canada. The Telesat Canada Act originally provided for some limited equity ownership by the general public, if appropriate; the company's financial position, *see infra* Section III.A., however, has delayed any public offering. Telesat functions as a "carrier's carrier" in the domestic market, except that it is authorized to deal directly with broadcasters for full satellite channels and associated services, such as uplinks.

7. *Teleglobe Canada*

Teleglobe Canada, a crown corporation directly owned by the Government of Canada, *see infra* Section III.B., is the monopoly supplier of non-U.S. international services. Teleglobe is authorized to operate both cable and satellite facilities—the latter through its representation of Canada in Intelsat and Inmarsat—and interconnects through facilities in Montreal, Toronto, and Vancouver and, primarily for transiting traffic, with some U.S. carriers, as well.

8. *Telecom Canada*

Formerly named the TransCanada Telephone System ("TCTS"), Telecom Canada is a composite entity—an unincorporated association—of nine telephone companies and Telesat Canada; it offers coast-to-coast service using the combined facilities of its members. It was formed in 1931, when seven telephone companies, motivated by the necessity of routing Canada-Canada calls through U.S. facilities, entered into a contractual arrangement to provide such services themselves. The original seven have since become ten—Alberta Government Telephones, B.C. Tel., Bell Canada, Island Telephone, Manitoba Telephone System, Maritime Telegraph and Telephone, New Brunswick Telephone, Newfoundland Telephone, Saskatchewan Telecommunications, and, as of 1977, Telesat Canada. (Quebec Telephone has recently been added as an associate member.) Telecom Canada has virtually no facilities of its own, has one employee (its president), and is staffed by personnel seconded from the member companies.

9. *CNCP Telecommunications*

CNCP is a partnership of the federally-owned CNR and the shareholder-owned Canadian Pacific Ltd. CNCP offered the first Canadian transcontinental telegraph service in 1886 and has a nationwide microwave system. It offers private line voice, computer data, facsimile, telex and television transmission services—in competition with the telephone companies—and also operates the public telegram service on a monopoly basis. CNCP now has dial-up access interconnection with Bell Canada (1979) and B.C. Tel. (1981). On October 25, 1983 it filed an application with the federal regulatory body to enable it to compete with Bell Canada and B.C. Tel. in the provision of public long-distance telephone service. A decision on this application is expected in the second half of 1985.

B. Regulatory Overview

Jurisdiction over broadcasting rests with the federal government, with jurisdiction over telecommunications apportioned between the provincial and federal governments.

1. Federal Jurisdiction over Broadcasting

Federal jurisdiction over broadcasting has been an established fact since the 1932 decision of the Privy Council in *In re Regulation and Control of Radio Communication in Canada*, [1932] A.C. 304 [hereinafter the *Radio Reference* case]. In the area of cable television, however, the provinces have raised some jurisdictional claims. *See infra* Section II.D. The various federal Canadian Broadcasting Acts have, over time, delegated regulatory power over broadcasting to various tribunals, the current one being the Canadian Radio-television and Telecommunications Commission ("CRTC"). *See* Broadcasting Act, R.S.C. 1970, c. B-22 and Canadian Radio-television and Telecommunications Act, S.C. 1974-75-76, c. 49. The CRTC is an independent administrative tribunal, which carries out its mandate over broadcasting by creating and administering regulations and through licensing pursuant to the Broadcasting Act.

2. Jurisdiction over Telecommunications: The CRTC

Jurisdiction over telecommunications, however, is shared by the provincial and federal governments. In terms of federal jurisdiction, in 1906 the amendments to the Articles of Incorporation of the federally regulated carriers, most notably Bell Canada, extended the jurisdiction of the Board of Railway Commissioners to include telephone and telegraph companies. *See* The Railway Act, 1903, 3 Edw. VII, c. 58 and An Act to Amend the Railway Act, 1903, 6 Edw. VII, c. 42. The Board's jurisdiction with respect to telecommunications was transferred to the Canadian Transport Commission in 1967 and, in 1976, to the CRTC.

a. CRTC jurisdiction over a telecommunications carrier is dependent on two conditions precedent. First, a particular enterprise must fall within federal—and not provincial—jurisdiction. To make this determination requires an interpretation of the British North America Act, 1867, 30 & 31 Vict., c. 3 ("B.N.A. Act"), and the judicial glosses thereon. *See infra* Section IV.A. (discussing jurisdictional issue). Second, an enterprise must be a "company" within the meaning of Section 320(1) of the Railway Act:

> "[C]ompany" means a railway company or person authorized to construct or operate a railway, having authority to construct or operate a telegraph or tele-

phone system or line, and to charge telegraph or telephone tolls, and includes also telegraph and telephone companies and every company and person within the legislative authority of the Parliament of Canada having power to construct or operate a telegraph or telephone system or line and to charge telegraph or telephone tolls.

This definition has been immensely unwieldy and the source of enormous confusion and great debate over the scope of the CRTC's power to regulate telephone services. The CRTC, for example, has read the Railway Act aggressively, asserting that it has jurisdiction over all telecommunications services for which a "company" within its jurisdiction "charges."

b. Bell Canada and B.C. Tel. are regulated by the CRTC—Bell, by virtue of the interprovincial nature of its activities under the terms of Section 92(10)(a) of the B.N.A. Act, and B.C. Tel., because its federal Incorporating Act declares its works to be "works for the general advantage of Canada" and, hence, according to Section 92(10)(c) of the B.N.A. Act, within federal jurisdiction. The CRTC also exercises jurisdiction over Telesat, CNCP, and the two telephone systems operated by CNR.

c. "Company" under the Railway Act is interpreted to include any company that charges a toll for services and CRTC jurisdiction is plenary as to such "companies." CRTC's powers include authority over tariffs for exchange or toll services in areas served by the federally-regulated carriers, *i.e.*, most of Ontario, Quebec, British Columbia and the areas served by the CNR subsidiaries. However, it exercises no general jurisdiction over interprovincial services per se, aside from certain interprovincial and international services offered by the federally-regulated carriers.

d. The extent of CRTC jurisdiction over Telecom Canada is highly unsettled. Although it has jurisdiction over the participation of the federally-regulated carriers in Telecom Canada, it has not asserted direct jurisdiction over Telecom Canada; the extent of CRTC jurisdiction over Telecom Canada rates, costing principles, and the Telecom Canada Revenue Settlement Plan was addressed in a 1981 Decision by the CRTC after Bell Canada and B.C. Tel. filed applications for changes in their Telecom Canada rates. *See Bell Canada, British Columbia Telephone Company and Telesat Canada: Increases and Decreases in Rates for Services and Facilities Furnished on a Canada-Wide Basis by Members of the TransCanada Telephone System, and Related Matters,* CRTC Telecom. Decision 81-13 (July 7, 1981) [Telecom. Decision 81-13]. *See infra* Section IV.D. (discussing CRTC jurisdiction over Telecom Canada and Telecom. Decision 81-13).

e. Decisions of the CRTC greatly influence national telecommunications policy, despite the fact that the exercise of its jurisdiction over telephone companies is limited to the provinces of Ontario, Quebec, British Columbia, and parts of Newfoundland and the Northwest Territories. Nevertheless, because its decisions affect 70% of all telecommunications services, their spillover impact is nationwide.

f. There are, however, some checks on the authority of the CRTC. Section 64(1) of the National Transportation Act permits the Governor in Council—the Federal Cabinet—on its own motion or on the petition of any interested party to vary or rescind a decision or regulation of the CRTC. Thus, there is a significant political counterweight to the agency's independent regulatory function. *See* National Transportation Act, S.C. 1966-67, c. 69, Section 64(1); *infra* Section III.A.6.-8. (discussing Governor in Council variance of CRTC decisions on policy grounds).

g. The CRTC's critics not only accuse the CRTC of being "pro-competitive" but also believe that CRTC decisionmaking is piecemeal. The provincial governments perceive the CRTC as moving quickly—and without direct political accountability or control—to expand its jurisdiction. They contend, for example, that the CRTC should not set national telecommunications policy in the area of competition in public toll services and that it overstepped its bounds in the Telecom. Decision 81-13 proceeding.

h. CRTC decisionmaking is largely ad hoc because the agency essentially reacts to applications that are filed with it. *See, e.g., CNCP Telecommunications: Interconnection with Bell Canada,* CRTC Telecom. Decision 79-11 (May 17, 1979) (authorizing CNCP interconnection in Bell Canada territory) [Telecom. Decision 79-11]; *CNCP Telecommunications: Interconnection with the British Columbia Telephone Co.,* CRTC Telecom. Decision 81-24 (Nov. 24, 1981) (in B.C. Tel. service area) [Telecom. Decision 81-24]. Nevertheless, in response to the CNCP October 1983 application to offer long distance public switched services, the CRTC did institute a proceeding to focus on the broader questions of interexchange competition and related issues raised by the application. *See* CRTC Telecom. Public Notice No. 1984-6, Interexchange Competition and Related Issues, Canada Gazette Part I, Jan. 21, 1984, at 589. The CRTC has made a number of key decisions in favor of competition, having regard for the impact of technology in restructuring a monopoly environment. At the same time, the CRTC recognizes the value of regulation and of preserving the high level of service to which Canadians have become accustomed.

3. *Jurisdiction over Telecommunications: Department of Communications*

a. The federal Minister of Communications—through the Department ("DOC")—and the Cabinet are charged with various responsibilities under a number of Acts, including the Department of Communications Act, the National Transportation Act, the Teleglobe Act, the Telegraphs Act, the Telesat Canada Act, and the Radio Act. Under the Radio Act, the Minister is responsible for radio spectrum management—planning, licensing, spectrum control, and standardization. The power includes the power to issue microwave licenses. In 1982 the DOC was responsible for initiating the process leading to the licensing of cellular radio applicants. *See* Dep't of Communications, Notice No. DGTN-006-82, Cellular Mobile Radio

Policy and Call for License Applications, Canada Gazette Part I, Oct. 23, 1982, at 7800. In March 1984 the DOC imposed interconnection requirements on telephone companies—to provide access to the public network for competing non-wireline cellular businesses—as a condition of awarding cellular licenses to them. Under the Telesat Canada Act, the Minister is responsible for many of the managerial corporate decisions of Telesat. Under the Department of Communications Act, the Minister is responsible for international agreements in communications. Under the National Transportation Act, as noted above, the Federal Cabinet, usually on the recommendation of the Minister, can vary or rescind CRTC orders.

As the government does not currently have the power to issue directives, per se, to the CRTC (only to vary or rescind CRTC decisions), the DOC has traditionally exercised its role in telecommunications policy after the fact. Its involvement in cellular radio, through its powers under the Radio Act, may, however, mark a more intense level of involvement in the debate over competition. The DOC is also currently looking at the role of cable in performing telecommunications functions.

b. Further evidence of the DOC's intention to assume the lead role in policy development came on May 26, 1983, when the Minister of Communications announced that the Department would initiate a two-year review of telecommunications policy. This review promises to be the most searching inquiry into the direction of telecommunications regulation in Canada. *See* Dep't of Communications, Telecommunications Policy Review, Notice No. DGTN-001-84, Canada Gazette Part I, Jan. 14, 1984 ["Telecommunications Policy Review"]. One of the principal thrusts of the review is to stimulate innovation and competition in the telecommunications sector, while maintaining the universal availability of telephone service at reasonable rates. The review includes substantial cooperation with the provincial governments, eight of which, with the DOC, funded a study of the effect of competition in message toll and message toll substitute services on the users of telecommunications and on the industry. *See* Peat, Marwick and Partners, *Impacts of Competition in Message Toll Telephone Services* (presented to the Dep't of Communications and Provincial Governments on September 28, 1984) (in association with National Economic Research Assocs., Inc. and Telecomsyst Servs., Inc.). The DOC hopes that the review will result in draft legislation on telecommunications reform that it can propose early on in the tenure of the new government.

c. In general, the DOC, through its Telecommunications Policy Branch, has approached questions of competition cautiously. Policy decisions to introduce competition in terminal equipment, microwave licensing, cellular radio, and satellite earth station ownership, for example, were taken only after a full public consultation process. This approach takes into account the widespread public sentiment that the telecommunications system works well and that there is no compelling reason to "fix it." The DOC is, however, now moving in the direction of exploring the reasons for—and possible advantages from—change. In particular, it is focusing on the impact that the transformation to a multiple supplier environment in the U.S. may have on Canadian innovation and U.S.-Canada trade.

d. The DOC has also been very much involved in the federal-provincial "politics" of telecommunications regulation and in attempting to strike a compromise with the provinces over the jurisdictional battles that have been fought over the last decade. It has devoted significant energies to constitutional reform in the communications field and to proposing a series of legislative initiatives to respond to the reorganization of Bell Canada and to change the regulatory process. *See, e.g.*, Bills C-19, An Act Respecting Bell Canada etc., 1st Sess., 33rd Parliament, 32-33 Eliz. II, 1984-85 (Dec. 20, 1984) ["Bill C-19"] and Bill C-20, "An Act Amending CRTC etc.," 1st Sess., 33rd Parliament, 32-33 Eliz. II, 1984-1985 (Dec. 20, 1984) ["Bill C-20"]. (The Bills have both received second reading in the House of Commons, but have not yet been examined on a clause-by-clause basis by Committee. The Bills, in part, were drafted to respond to the recent reorganization of Bell Canada and the need to establish policy direction over the activities of the CRTC.

e. The DOC maintains an arm's-length relationship with the CRTC, nevertheless relations between the two bodies are good. (The DOC does not normally appear before the CRTC, due to the Federal Cabinet's statutory power to vary or rescind the Commission's decisions; however, it did, for the first time, make a submission to the CRTC—over two years ago. The issues concerned mobile radio system interconnection with the network and reminded the CRTC that the DOC is responsible for allocating spectrum.) There have been some minor differences between the CRTC and the DOC over spectrum management policy, particularly with respect to new or unconventional use of frequencies (*e.g.*, such "non-broadcast" uses of broadcast frequencies as subsidiary communication multiplex operations ("SCMO")), and over experimental services offered on cable.

f. As described above, once the CRTC decisions are made, however, the Minister of Communications is responsible for advising the Federal Cabinet in the event that a decision is appealed. In practice, the DOC usually supports the CRTC decision at the Cabinet level; for example, the decision giving CNCP network interconnection with Bell Canada for data and private line voice services (Telecom. Decision 79-11) was totally upheld by the Cabinet. Nevertheless, the distinction between directing CRTC policy and post hoc review is not always clearly demarcated; Bill C-20 delineates the lines of authority somewhat more clearly.

4. *Jurisdiction over Telecommunications: Provincial Authorities*

a. Provincial regulators—*i.e.*, public utility commissions—generally regulate the carriers not subject to CRTC jurisdiction. These include the carriers serving the Atlantic and prairie provinces. (Before 1983, the telephone company in Saskatchewan, which is an agency of the province, was not regulated by an independent regulatory agency, but it now is).

b. Provincial regulators are also responsible for approving the interprovincial rates filed by the Telecom Canada members within their regulatory jurisdictions. These filings are not scrutinized too closely, largely because Telecom Canada's rates are uniform across Canada and because the provincial regulatory bodies are disinclined to reject or question tariffs, which could affect services or regulatory agencies outside their jurisdiction.

5. Uncertainty: CRTC Jurisdiction over Provincial Companies

a. The scope of CRTC jurisdiction over the companies under provincial jurisdiction is quite unsettled. In an extremely significant and closely-followed case, a federal court trial division held last year that the CRTC did not have jurisdiction to require that Alberta Government Telephones ("AGT") provide interconnection to CNCP. *See Alberta Government Telephones v. CRTC*, Oct. 26, 1984 (Reed, J.). In a very important holding, which represented a partial victory for CNCP and the federal government, the court concluded that AGT would be subject to federal jurisdiction under the B.N.A. Act but that, as a provincial crown corporation, it had not waived its crown—sovereign—immunity so as to consent to being brought within the jurisdiction of the CRTC. Thus, absent amendment of federal law, or a successful appeal by CNCP, the CRTC cannot order AGT to provide interconnection. The case, however, has been appealed by CNCP; argument is expected in Fall 1985. The decision amply demonstrates the jurisdictional obstacles to imposing any degree of uniformity or consistency on telecommunications policy.

b. The CRTC has not attempted to assert jurisdiction over equipment attachment practices beyond those of companies directly subject to its jurisdiction.

C. Some Critical Issues

1. Resolution of Jurisdictional Issues

a. There is widespread recognition in Canada that the jurisdictional fragmentation of authority and lack of cooperation and consensus amongst the various regulatory bodies is the single most troubling issue in telecommunications policy. Not only is it impossible to set national policy—there is no single body with the power to do so—but the provider that is the most influential in creating a national "network"—Telecom Canada—is wholly outside the jurisdiction of any regulatory body. There has been an extensive series of studies, policy documents, proposals, negotiations, and discussions by and between virtually every regulatory and political body in Canada on the problems raised by the jurisdictional split—and void—in telecommunications policymaking. *See, e.g.*, Dep't of Communications, *Instant World: A Report on Telecommunications in Canada* (1971); Minister of Communications, *Proposals for a Communications Policy for Canada—A Position Paper of the Federal Government of Canada* (March 1973) [hereinafter cited as "Green Paper"]; Minister of Communications, *Communications: Some Federal Proposals* (April 1975) [hereinafter cited as "Grey Paper"]; Consultative Committee on the Implications of Telecommunications for Canadian Sovereignty, *Telecommunications and Canada* (March 1979) ["Clyne Report"]. *See generally* R. Buchan et al., *Telecommunications Regulation and the Constitution* (Montreal: The Institute for Research on Public Policy, 1982) [hereinafter cited as "*Telecommunications Regulation*"].

b. These discussions have taken place at the highest levels—between the federal prime minister and the provincial premiers—and have resulted only in a series of vague and inconclusive proposals to shift jurisdiction or to create a consultative mechanism to achieve a more coherent national telecommunications policy. *See infra* Section IV.E.,F. & G. (discussing jurisdictional issues and possible solutions).

c. The jurisdictional issues provoke questions far more profound than those implicated in telecommunications policy. They are deeply rooted in Canadian concepts of federalism and the very notion of Canadian sovereignty. They raise, then, highly complex and emotionally charged political and ideological problems. Nevertheless, before "telecommunications" issues of competition and pricing can be addressed in a comprehensive way, these jurisdictional questions will need to be resolved.

2. *Rate Rebalancing*

A central issue in Canadian telecommunications policy, and one that is under consideration in the DOC's Telecommunications Policy Review, is the perceived need to readjust the pricing of services to bring them closer to costs. In essence, rate rebalancing contemplates raising local exchange rates while reducing toll service rates. *See infra* Section V.B. (discussing reasons for moving prices closer to costs). There are several factors spurring this development.

a. First, there is exceptionally high cross-subsidization of intraprovincial exchange services by interprovincial rates. This subsidy is largely a function of the jurisdiction of the oversight mechanisms—minimal regulatory supervision of Telecom Canada's rates—and of social objectives—suppressing local exchange pricing in a vast country with high exchange costs, to make service available to all.

b. Second, cross-subsidization is generating incentives for users to use U.S. long-distance services for Canada-Canada traffic. Unless rates are brought closer to costs, more traffic could be siphoned into the United States, to the detriment of Canadian carriers and consumers. (Such diversion of traffic could have a significant adverse impact inasmuch as interprovincial toll revenues may contribute up to 45% of a company's total revenues.)

c. Third, there are discussions on the effect of local and, more seriously, long distance bypass. There is a genuine concern that bypass could diminish the flow of interprovincial revenues to Telecom Canada members.

d. Fourth, the "spillover" effect of U.S. deregulation is having an impact on the debate on competition in Canada. Before—or concurrent with—liberalizing entrance into what are now monopoly markets, existing suppliers (led by Bell Canada) are demanding that rates be "rebalanced." They want to be able to compete without being handicapped by subsidies built into their rate structures. CNCP, of course, contends that rate rebalancing issues should be separated from competitive issues, *i.e.*, its application to provide for long distance service. Most provincial governments, aware of the political consequences and, in some cases, owning their own facilities, are wary of any development that would raise the price of local service or serve as a predicate to competition. Some grudgingly accept the need for rate-rebalancing, but are adamantly opposed to competition.

3. *Competitive Entry*

There is vigorous discussion over the entrance of new providers into the market.

a. The CNCP application to provide public long distance voice service has quickened the pace of developments. The application promises that CNCP will begin by serving seven major cities in Ontario, Quebec, and British Columbia and that, within ten years, it will provide "universal service" in areas served by Bell Canada and B.C. Tel. Thus, if the application is approved, there is a genuine possibility of facilities-based competition. Such competition is vociferously opposed by most of the provinces that are currently served by non-federally-regulated carriers.

b. Competition is also likely to have an impact on the structure of—or regulatory supervision over—Telecom Canada, Bell Canada, and other providers. Competition also raises significant questions about compensation to exchange carriers—access charges—for local interconnection. Although there currently are interconnection payments by CNCP to Bell Canada and B.C. Tel. for the private line/data services that CNCP now offers, there is no readily available costing methodology for calculating an "access charge."

c. Costing and accounting procedures were examined in considerable detail in the CRTC's "Phase III - Cost Inquiry." *See* "Inquiry Into Telecommunications Carriers' Costing and Accounting Procedures: Phase III—Costing of Existing Services," June 25, 1985, Telecom. Decision CRTC 85-10.

4. The Future of Teleglobe and Telesat

There is also a significant debate over the future of the federally-owned service providers.

a. The Government has recently announced that it intends to privatize a number of companies it currently owns, including Teleglobe. Teleglobe has, in a limited way, been offering some services directly to end users and it may ultimately compete more directly with Canadian domestic carriers, with which it now has interconnection arrangements. Any such direct competition could raise questions about internal cross-subsidization of services, which would be possible to the extent that the CRTC does not regulate in that area. Canadian domestic carriers, if faced with competition from Teleglobe, might seek approval to serve overseas markets—which could leave Teleglobe itself in a difficult competitive posture with respect to end-to-end service.

b. Telesat, which is currently dependent on its membership in Telecom Canada for financial support in the revenue settlements plan, is also the subject of some discussions in the DOC. Several options for its future are being considered. Telesat's "shackles" as a "carrier's carrier" might be loosened, to allow it to compete with other carriers, or it might simply be urged to promote satellite services more heavily. In the past few years, Telesat has become increasingly dependent on Telecom Canada for financial support. In fact, in December 1984, Bell Canada, on behalf of a consortium of domestic carriers, offered to buy the government's share of the satellite carrier. Suggestions for a change in Telesat's role—to permit it to serve end users directly—would meet with opposition from Telecom Canada, its would-be competitor, and would necessitate a restructuring of the Telecom Canada-Telesat relationship and, perhaps, the ownership structure of Telesat itself.

II. CANADIAN REGULATORY POLICY: DEFINITIONAL ISSUES

A. "Enhanced" versus "Basic" Services

1. Last year, the CRTC announced that it was adopting definitions of "basic" and "enhanced" services. *See* CRTC Telecom. Decision 84-18 (July 12, 1984). [Telecom. Decision 84-18] The CRTC started from the premise that the definitions adopted by the Federal Communications Commission ("FCC") in its Final Decision, *Computer II*, 77 F.C.C.2d 384 (1980), might be appropriate in the Canadian context. Indeed, the CRTC Public Notice had set forth the FCC's definitions for comment. *See* CRTC Public Notice 1983-72 (Nov. 15, 1983). The majority of the parties that commented supported the FCC's definitional approach. Consequently, the CRTC decided to adopt definitions of "basic" and "enhanced" that, in essence, conform to their U.S. counterparts.

2. "Basic Service" is defined as "one that is limited to the offering of transmission capacity for the movement of information." A "basic service" provider "essentially offers a pure transmission capability over a communications path that is virtually transparent in terms of its interaction with subscriber supplied information." Telecom. Decision 84-18, at 12-14. "Enhanced Service" is "any offering over the telecommunications network which is more than a basic service"; it includes processing applications, and store-and-forward services. *Id.* at 14-15.

3. These definitions are rather similar to those of the U.S. and, to the extent that they may differ, such differences are not clearly demarcated. Unlike the initial FCC decision, the Canadian definition of basic services makes it clear that internal protocol conversion not manifested in the outputs of the service does not transform a service from basic to enhanced. After the Final Decision in *Computer II*, the FCC confirmed that internal protocol conversion would be part of a "basic service" offering. *First Reconsideration Order*, 84 F.C.C.2d 50, 60-61 (1980).

4. Users—data processing service organizations, information providers, businesses, bankers, the answering industry—and equipment manufacturers vigorously supported the CRTC's adopting the FCC's definitions. They noted that the FCC's proceeding had been thorough, that the categories had proven workable, and that the classification scheme would encourage the development of new services. The Director of Investigation and Research, Combines Investigation Act, also supported adoption of the FCC's definitions.

5. The carriers, however, led by Bell Canada, viewed the FCC's classification as static and not appropriate for the Canadian context, largely because it had been promulgated to define what services AT&T could offer through a separate subsidiary. Bell Canada proffered instead a flexible approach that relied on marketplace competition: an enhanced service would be one that could be provided under conditions of open market entry and exit and that uses basic services that are available to all providers. Under the Bell definition, code and protocol conversion would have been classified as "basic" offerings. B.C. Tel. offered a different approach, based on four functions—information communications, information provision, information processing and information storage and retrieval. Distinguishing between "pure" and "enhanced" services, B.C. Tel. contended that "pure" services—which do not change the meaning or content of the information—should include protocol conversion.

6. Telesat agreed with the FCC approach; it urged, however, that the enhanced service category be comprised of services that deliberately affect basic services to meet the specifications of the user. It also contended that basic service must and can only be offered by common carriers. The Government of Ontario recommended that the appropriate regulatory treatment for each type of service should be resolved separately.

7. The CRTC concluded that permitting the resale of carrier services would be necessary if competition is to develop in the enhanced

services market. Wary of the possibility that enhanced providers could, by making minimal enhancement, offer what are essentially basic services, the CRTC decided that resale should not be permitted where "the enhanced service has as its primary function the provision of a basic service." Telecom. Decision 84-18, at 23. Concurrently, the CRTC stated that restrictions on interconnection and attachment—which could inhibit the provision of enhanced services—would be inappropriate. (And, concomitantly, that any related restrictions on CNCP interconnection to Bell Canada and B.C. Tel. contained in Telecom. Decisions 79-11 and 81-24 should eventually be removed.) The carriers generally had supported the concept of allowing resale for the provision of enhanced services.

8. The CRTC concluded that it was not required to regulate enhanced service offerings provided by non-common carriers. Reading Section 320(1) of the Railway Act, which confers on the CRTC the power to regulate "companies that operate a telephone or telegraph system," the CRTC determined that it was not required by statute to regulate enhanced providers that simply make use of underlying basic services for their offerings. Telecom. Decision 84-18, at 31.

9. There was considerable debate over the terms and conditions by which common carriers could offer enhanced services. Many commenters—including users and the Government of Ontario—contended that the Bell Canada Special Act bars Bell from offering certain enhanced services. Section 5(3) of the Act states that Bell must act solely as a common carrier and cannot control the content nor influence the meaning or purpose of the message transmitted. Some users thought that the policy embodied in Section 5(3) should be applied to other common carriers. Bell responded that the Section might, in any event, only apply to certain enhanced services. B.C. Tel. argued that neither the British Columbia Telephone Company Act nor any other statute restricted its offering of an enhanced service.

10. The CRTC concluded that Bell should not be permitted to engage in electronic publishing—where it had editorial control over content—or in creating or distributing its own data bases. In this regard, Telecom. Decision 84-18 tracks the Modified Final Judgment ("MFJ") that settled the Department of Justice suit against AT&T; AT&T is barred by the MFJ from "electronic publishing" for seven years. The CRTC added that the principles of separating carriage from control over content should also be applied to other federally-regulated carriers.

11. The CRTC has postponed inquiry into whether enhanced services offered by common carriers should be through separate subsidiaries or whether some form of structural separation is appropriate. In the interim, to ensure that monopoly services are not used to cross-subsidize the provision of competitive enhanced services, the CRTC stated that carriers should be deemed to have acquired underlying basic services at tariffed rates and that carriers offering enhanced services must file rate evaluation studies for each such service. These will include costing based on tariffed rates, not

actual costs. The CRTC will eventually want aggregate rate evaluation studies; if these are feasible, it will no longer require filings for each enhanced service. As to how cost information should be supplied, the CRTC stated that it would render a decision in the broader context of Phase III of the Cost Inquiry, which it has now done.

12. The carriers contended that they should be permitted to transfer enhanced services offerings to separate affiliates to maximize their business flexibility. CNCP and others argued that such transfers should be prohibited, either pending the CRTC's decision in Phase III of the Cost Inquiry or at least until there were some assurance that monopoly services will not have subsidized the risks and costs associated with the implementation of enhanced services. The CRTC decided not to impose any restrictions on carrier transfers to a separate affiliate; it could ensure that cross-subsidization would not occur by scrutinizing the transfer price for the assets used in providing transferred services.

13. Telcom. Decision 84-18 has left unresolved many important issues involving the appropriate method for regulating enhanced services. As noted, the CRTC concluded that it was not "required" by statute to regulate enhanced services provided by other than common carriers. It is uncertain, however, whether the CRTC may, in fact, forbear from the exercise of its regulatory power. That is, although the CRTC may want to refrain from regulating, it may require Parliamentary authorization for it to do so, if the Railway Act mandates the exercise of jurisdiction once conferred. The issue turns on how broadly Sections 320 and 321 of the Railway Act can be read. If an enhanced service provider is a "company" under the Railway Act, then it appears that it must be regulated. If an enhanced service is not a "telephone toll" service, it may not fall within the CRTC's jurisdiction, regardless of the provider. Conversely, if a telephone "company" (*e.g.*, Bell Canada) offers an enhanced service that is not a "telephone toll" service, it is unclear whether or how the CRTC would regulate the service. Bill C-19 allows the CRTC to decide how to treat a "competitive activity" of Bell Canada, which effectively will confer on the agency the power to require separation, at least in the case of Bell Canada. *See* Bill C-19, Section 13(2).

14. It may be, then, that not regulating enhanced services can be accomplished most easily through establishing separate subsidiaries. If an enhanced service is not a "telephone toll service" and it is offered by a company—a newly formed subsidiary—that does not itself operate a telephone system, it could be difficult for the CRTC to exercise jurisdiction over it. Bill C-19, if passed into law, will give the CRTC the authority to order Bell Canada to create a subsidiary for any activity that is "competitive."

15. The critical question is how to allow Bell Canada to provide enhanced services—to allow full and fair competition—without subjecting it to tariff or other regulation from which its competitors would be freed. The CRTC seems not particularly anxious to erect a regulatory framework just for Bell Canada. It hopes that Bell will compete, but that there will also be mechanisms to guard against cross-subsidization. Bell had, prior to

Telecom. Decision 84-18, been given permission to offer, on a trial basis, several "enhanced" services: Envoy 100 Service (text-based messaging service on a store-and-forward basis), its Voice Message Service (store-and-forward for voice), and its TELENEWS service (offering news reports to telex subscribers). *See* CRTC Telecom. Decision 81-22 (Nov. 4, 1981); CRTC Telecom. Decision 81-10 (May 25, 1981); and CRTC Telecom. Decision 81-12 (June 18, 1981). In these decisions the CRTC had noted the advantages to the public of Bell's offering such services on an interim basis; it determined that no separate subsidiary requirement would be imposed. Underlying services, however, had to be obtained at tariffed rates.

16. Users are aware of the possibility that Bell Canada might cross-subsidize in providing enhanced services. They are anxious that Section 5(3) of the Bell Canada Special Act not become a casualty of the Bell Canada reorganization. Thus, they support Bill C-19, which contains a section preserving the requirement that Bell "act solely as a telecommunications common carrier" and stating that it "shall not control the contents or influence the meaning or purpose of messages transmitted, emitted or received." Bill C-19, Section 8. Most participants in this debate do not embrace "structural separation" as the only resolution.

17. Bell Canada has taken the position that it should not be required to use separate subsidiaries but that the choice of whether it should offer a service itself, or through an affiliate, ought to be, as is the case with its competitors, ultimately for decision by the company alone. *See* Bell Canada, "Framework for The Future," Submission to the Dep't of Communications Telecommunications Policy Review, at 25 [hereinafter cited as "Framework for the Future"]. B.C. Tel., focusing on the loss of economic efficiencies resulting from separation, which would have an especially acute impact in a territory so small and dispersed, states that separation requirements are not necessary; it also points out that the interdependency of the Telecom Canada structure would be adversely affected if members began operating through separate subsidiaries. *See* British Columbia Telephone Co., Telecommunications Policy Review, at 58-60. Other carriers contend that service, but not structural, separation is warranted. *See, e.g.*, Submission of Maritime Telegraph & Telephone, et al., Telecommunications Policy Review, at 19 (structural separation "unwarranted" and "impractical" for small carriers); Telesat, Telecommunications Policy Review, at 7-8 (obligatory structural separation unfairly burdens carriers that must compete with unregulated entities).

18. Some users and equipment manufacturers believe that stringent safeguards must be imposed to ensure full competition. They urge structural separation as the preferred approach. Their position is that other safeguards should, in any event, be regarded as mandatory: accounting and cost rules; rules regarding the sharing of personnel, facilities, information, and equipment; and rules to ensure that all enhanced service providers obtain underlying services at tariffed rates. The transitional "separation" issues raised by these concerns are unresolved—how common carrier facili-

ties can be utilized, how "separate" structural separation must be, and whether it is fair to require carriers to set enhanced rates based on underlying prices, not costs.

19. Discussions on the liberalization of the enhanced services market have taken place on the provincial, as well as the federal, levels. Each province must determine whether enhanced services provided in that province are subject to regulation. There is, at present, no consistency among the provinces on this point. Alberta, for example, has been slightly more willing to discuss the prospect of liberalization than have its fellow prairie provinces—Manitoba and Saskatchewan. After an extended inquiry on the issue of regulating enhanced services, Alberta concluded that its jurisdictional limits should extend only to the regulation of basic services. Interconnection of private and data services may follow in Alberta.

20. Unlike the situation at the federal level—where Telecom. Decision 84-18 has contributed to an understanding of the jurisdictional issues—there is a great deal of provincial uncertainty as to the scope of jurisdiction over nonbasic services. It is not clear, for example, whether the provinces can or will claim jurisdiction over remote access data processing services or over voice message forwarding. Resolution of the issues depends, in large part, on the interpretation of provincial statutes or on the perspectives of public utility commissions.

21. Important questions are raised by the capability of the provinces to deny interconnection to enhanced service providers and whether such denial would constitute discrimination. In the wake of last year's *Alberta Government Telephones* decision, it is unsettled to what extent the CRTC can require the provinces to adhere to federal statutory requirements. Thus, these issues will need to be resolved deliberately and on a province-by-province basis.

22. Enhanced services cannot, therefore, be implemented on a nationwide basis, except by Telecom Canada members. The lack of uniformity in access, even though it applies equally to Canadian domestic service providers, may become an international trade issue as U.S. enhanced service providers try to gain access to the Canadian market on a national basis. (Disparate treatment for U.S. providers in Japan has become a U.S.-Japan trade issue.) It is evident, then, that the jurisdictional turmoil in the regulation of telecommunications services could have a significant detrimental impact both on users—by restricting the availability of services, or creating incentives for them to use U.S. services—and on Canadian industry—by failing to generate opportunities or economic incentives for domestic enhanced service providers.

B. Data Processing Services

1. Companies that only offer remote access data processing services are not subject thereby to the Railway Act. Federal regulators note that the data involved in such services are transmitted, for a charge, over a

telephone line. Nevertheless, they do not interpret the statutory definition on which jurisdiction is dependent—a "company" that "charge[s] telegraph or telephone tolls"—so broadly as to include companies that offer processing services that are "incidental" to the transmission.

2. The question of carrier provision of data processing services was raised in the CRTC's discussion of the "basic"/"enhanced" dichotomy. Previously, a 1972 Department of Communications publication and a 1975 DOC and Department of Finance set of guidelines suggested that "basic" services—but not data processing—could be offered by carriers. The guidelines, which were never codified in law, would have applied only to the federally-regulated carriers. They recommended that carriers only offer transmission services for data processors, that they could perform transmission functions involving no change in message content, and that any carrier data processing offered to the public should be made available only through an "arm's-length" subsidiary. Carrier investments in such subsidiaries would be examined in the context of a rate of return analysis. The guidelines were intended to protect small Canadian computer service bureaus from undue intrusion by banks or carriers. *See* Joint Release, Dep't of Finance, Dep't of Communications, "Federally Regulated Carriers' and Chartered Banks' Participation in Commercial Data Processing," Jan. 16, 1975. The separate subsidiary "recommendation" does not seem to have much force in light of Telecom. Decision 84-18, which declined to adopt a separate subsidiary requirement.

C. Information Service Providers

1. As noted previously, *see supra* Section II.A.9. & 16., Bell Canada is prohibited by statute from exercising any control over the content of communications. This has been interpreted as an effective bar to its being involved as a vendor of certain information services.

2. Telecom. Decision 84-18 prohibited Bell Canada from engaging in electronic publishing, either controlling editorial content or in creating or distributing its own data bases. Bell and other carriers may, however, establish data bases relating to their common carrier function, *i.e.*, electronic directories and data bases for billing. Telecom. Decision 84-18, at 36.

D. Cable Services: The Boundary Line Between "Telecommunications" and "Programming"

1. Both provincial and federal regulators recognize that cable technology has some potential to offer intercity and intraprovincial telecommunications services. The jurisdictional issue between federal and provincial governments turns, in some sense, on the scope of some definitions: "broadcast" or "radiocommunication" versus "non-programming" services, and "local" versus "national" services.

2. The 1932 *Radio Reference* case firmly established federal jurisdiction over broadcasting transmitting "undertakings." There have, however, subsequently been challenges to federal authority over cable television; these challenges are primarily based on the notion that cable service is essentially local in character. Although signals are received off-the-air, and are within federal jurisdiction, it is argued that cable essentially uses local coaxial cables and acts much like a local telephone company. The courts have rebuffed such challenges, sustaining federal jurisdiction on the basis that "transmitting" and "receiving"—as components of "radiocommunication"—could not be separated. Therefore, they have concluded that the entire "cable" service, dependent as it is primarily on broadcast signals, is within federal jurisdiction. The Supreme Court of Canada resolved the issue in favor of federal authority, holding that the Province of Quebec could not require licensing of cable operators because they were "broadcast receiving" entities and, consequently, within the exclusive jurisdiction of the federal government. *See Capital Cities Communications, Inc. v. CRTC*, [1978] 2 S.C.R. 141; 81 D.L.R.(3d) 622; *La Regie des Services Publics v. Dionne* [1978] 2 S.C.R. 191; 83 D.L.R.(3d) 181.

3. In many cases, the coaxial cable network will be owned by the telephone company (owned, in turn, by the government in the case of the prairie provinces). The cable operator itself is licensed by the CRTC and leases the cable from the telephone company. The CRTC requires that its licensees control some of the facilities that comprise the system: the receiving antenna, the head-end and amplifiers, and the drop to the subscribers. In 1976, these ownership requirements conflicted squarely with the policies of the Manitoba Telephone System ("MTS"), which required telephone company ownership of the entire distribution system. The resulting dispute and attempted resolution are illustrative of how jurisdictional skirmishes—and the division of regulatory authority over facilities and services—can affect and impede the development of telecommunications policy.

4. The CRTC had invited applications for cable licenses in Manitoba and Saskatchewan; however, the applicants could not satisfy the CRTC's ownership requirements due to the policy requiring exclusive telephone company (*i.e.*, provincial) ownership of the facilities. The CRTC did ultimately award two licenses in Manitoba, however. The Government of Manitoba and MTS petitioned the Governor in Council, which set aside the CRTC award on November 10, 1976.

5. Concurrently, the federal government and Manitoba reached an agreement on cable telecommunications, broadcast programming, and hardware ownership. The agreement seemed to strike an uneasy compromise. "Programming" or "Programming service"—defined as "broadcast" programming, including pay television—would be the exclusive responsibility of the federal government. The "regulation and supervision of telecommuncations services, other than programming services" would be the responsibility of the Province. *See* Canada-Manitoba Agreement, Arts. II and III. As to the hardware that the CRTC required the

operator to control, the agreement provided that such facilities could, to the extent that they were used to provide programming services, be leased from the telephone company. The agreement also contained a provision for adjudication of disputes over terms, conditions, or rates.

6. The CRTC, however, subsequently stated that it was not legally bound by the federal government's agreement, but that it would take it into account in reviewing applications for Manitoba cable service. New applications were filed with the CRTC, which eventually did grant the licenses—to applicants different from those who had originally received the award. Thus, cable operators in Manitoba were caught squarely in the middle of a jurisdictional dispute that is not yet entirely resolved.

7. Manitoba and some other provinces believe that cable systems, as telecommunications providers, pose a potential competitive threat to telephone companies. For that reason the Manitoba-Canada agreement provides that "telecommunications services," howsoever they may be defined, are the responsibility of the Province. Another example of the perceived nature of this threat is evident in a dispute involving Greater Winnipeg Cablevision Ltd., which serves part of Winnipeg, Manitoba, and has been licensed by the CRTC to offer non-programming services such as fire and burglar alarm. Negotiations between Greater Winnipeg and MTS over whether such services can be offered have taken years. In February 1983, Manitoba enacted Sections 44.1 and 52.1 of the Manitoba Telephone Act; these provisions, in essence, provide that the approval of the Lieutenant Governor in Council is required prior to any interconnection with a telecommunication carrier or prior to the offering of any telecommunication carrier service. Those provisions have been the subject of litigation.

8. A further dispute between Manitoba and the CRTC—also involving cable operators—arose over the ownership and control of security and control devices used in connection with the offering of pay television services. The CRTC—in exercising its authority over "programming services" and pursuant to its power to regulate "broadcasting"—required that such devices—encoders, scrambling devices, and addressability equipment—be owned by the operator. CRTC Public Notice 1983-82 (April 22, 1983). Manitoba, however, has taken the position that such hardware must be owned by MTS. In furtherance of the Canada-Manitoba agreement, the Manitoba Government thereafter enacted Section 52.2 of the Manitoba Telephone Act, which required that MTS own all equipment for transmission of signals, save equipment exempted by provincial regulation. Greater Winnipeg—faced with a conflict between the CRTC and Manitoba—applied to the Manitoba Public Utilities Board, which refused to hear the matter. That decision was sustained by the courts on technical grounds. This dispute has placed negotiations over the lease agreement between Greater Winnipeg and MTS in jeopardy.

9. The potential threat posed by cable operators to existing telecommunications carriers has not received the same degree of attention elsewhere in Canada. In 1979 the CRTC authorized cable operators, on a

two-year trial basis, to provide non-programming services (*e.g.*, security, fire, and medical alarms). *See* CRTC Telecom. Decision 79-266 (March 26, 1979). Existing operators of these services had leased capacity from Bell Canada, which viewed the cable company applications as threatening its own alarm service offerings. (Bell Canada itself is prohibited from holding cable television licenses. *See* 1968 Amendments to the Bell Canada Special Act, 16-17 Eliz. II, c. 48, Section 5(27).) It opposed the applications before the CRTC on the ground that such services were not within the CRTC's jurisdiction because they were not "broadcasting" or "radiocommunication" within the meaning of the Broadcasting Act. The impact of those services on telephone company revenues, however, is so small that it cannot be measured.

10. The cable industry is not unaware that it has the potential to offer a competitive alternative to the telephone companies; it has argued that its systems are capable of supplying a panoply of services in addition to the reception and distribution of broadcast signals. The CRTC, too, in ordering telephone companies to provide pole attachments, noted that both coaxial cable and the copper pair provide services into the home and that "neither technology should be burdened with artificial barriers preventing their development in a fair and reasonable manner." CRTC Telecom. Decision 77-6, at 16 (May 27, 1977).

11. The major federal and provincial regulatory and policy differences, however, have focused on power over "national" programming services—whatever the scope of such services might be.

12. Some in the federal government, however, believe that jurisdiction over cable should have been given to the provincial authorities—save for certain paramount federal powers respecting priority carriage of "national" programming such as that of the Canadian Broadcasting Corporaton ("CBC"). If cable competition in telecommunications services should develop to the point that bypass on cable occurs—and telephone rates increase—it is thought that it will be politically easy to blame the federal government for the consequences. Not surprisingly, then, the federal-provincial discussions over the allocation of jurisdiction have included a vigorous debate over the regulation of cable services and the future of the technology. *See infra* Section IV.E.

III. DISTINCTIONS BETWEEN FACILITIES AND SERVICES: "FACILITIES-BASED" PROVIDERS

Telesat and Teleglobe essentially act as "carrier's carriers"; Teleglobe, however, does provide more than facilities (*e.g.*, it sets collection rates, manages its own network for routing, and markets some services directly to users). Both were established by acts of Parliament to fill what were perceived to be "national goals." To the extent that they may compete with private carriers, private sector providers have been concerned that the government might bestow an "undue" advantage or preferential treatment on Telesat and Teleglobe on account of their status. They are, however, presently confined to providing one service exclusively: a single technology—satellite—in the case of Telesat and a particular service area—overseas—in the case of Teleglobe.

A. Telesat Canada

1. Telesat was established in 1969 to further a variety of public policy objectives, including stimulation of the Canadian space industry and improvement of telecommunications services in the distant North. To ensure that these objectives are met, Telesat is 50% owned by the federal government and 50% by fourteen terrestrial-based companies. Although the government has not used its shareholdings overtly to influence Telesat corporate policies, there are indications that it may do so in the future, to urge the company to market its services more aggressively.

2. Telesat launched its first domestic satellite in early 1973 and today it remains the monopoly supplier of satellite transmission services to telephone companies, other carriers, and broadcasters. It was established as a "carrier's carrier" largely because only broadcasters and terrestrial common carriers would have demands sufficiently large to utilize the capacity of a single satellite channel. The government believed that terrestrial carrier ownership of Telesat would encourage carriers to use its capacity to supplement and complement their existing facilities.

3. The demand for Telesat's satellite services grew slowly from 1973 to 1976. Terrestrial carriers did not integrate their facilities with those of Telesat, partly because they were disinclined to rely too heavily on satellite services and because they had their own ample capacity, which remained cost-competitive with satellite facilities. Telesat decided, therefore, that it should become a member of TCTS (now Telecom Canada), both to facilitate integration of facilities and to obtain additional financial resources, especially for planning and building second generation 14/12 GHz satellites. In early 1976, the Government approved Telesat's joining TCTS, with the proviso that such membership be approved by the CRTC. The ensuing political and policy debate is instructive both as to the potential for future facilities-based competition—and how it might be authorized—and what it suggests as to the future role of Telesat.

4. In early 1977, pursuant to Section 320(11) of the Railway Act, Telesat filed an application for approval of the Connecting Agreement with TCTS; Section 320(11) of the Railway Act requires CRTC approval for all agreements between regulated companies and any other authorized to operate a telephone system. The Agreement focused on the financial return that Telesat would obtain from the other members of TCTS and on the future integration of satellite and terrestrial telecommunications facilities.

5. After an extensive hearing—in which some intervenors opposed the Agreement because it would mean the end of the independence of a potential competitive alternative to the telephone company—the CRTC

issued a decision not to approve the Agreement. *See* CRTC Telecom. Decision 77-10 (Aug. 24, 1977) [Telecom. Decision 77-10]. The CRTC held that the relevant test for approval is "the public interest, viewed in a broad sense." Telecom. Decision 77-10, at 276. The CRTC concluded that the Agreement would make it difficult to regulate rates, might make it likely that TCTS members would be afforded an undue preference with respect to satellite services and, significantly, that the Agreement might lessen any nascent competition between carriers. The CRTC stated that an independent Telesat could offer trans-Canada services that might be an alternative to the terrestrial TCTS system: "a potential competitive situation in long haul data, video, and other private line services may be restricted by the Agreement in the manner that does not appear to be justified." Telecom. Decision 77-10, at 56.

6. The Governor in Council, however, varied the CRTC's decision in November 1977 and approved the Agreement. The Minister of Communications stated that that action was motivated by broad public policy concerns, the consideration of which not having been within the purview of the CRTC. *See* Order-in-Council P.C. 1977-3152, Nov. 3, 1977. There were, said the government, four important benefits in permitting Telesat to join TCTS. First, significant financial resources would immediately be made available to Telesat. Second, the Agreement contemplated a system of transfer payments to Telesat in initial years and from Telesat to TCTS in subsequent years, with a guaranteed rate of return to Telesat equal to that of B.C. Tel. and Bell Canada. Third, the transfer payment system created an incentive for TCTS members to use Telesat's capacity. Fourth, membership in TCTS would give Telesat a more solid financial footing with which it could, with government support, pursue its public policy goals of serving the North and fostering the space industry. With financial commitments in place, Telesat has purchased new 14/12 GHz satellites and replacements for its first generation craft.

7. The Governor in Council decision demonstrates how the social or public policy concerns of the government can take precedence over the CRTC's interest in nurturing competitive facilities. Nevertheless, in 1981 the CRTC tried once again to make Telesat more competitive. In Telecom. Decision 81-13, the CRTC reviewed two Telesat tariffs for the provision of earth and space segment and an agreement between TCTS and the CBC. The CRTC concluded that Telesat's offering satellite services only to carriers violated the nondiscrimination provision contained in Section 265(1) of the Railway Act; thus, it ordered Telesat to strike the tariff limitation barring service to end users. Telecom. Decision 81-13, Section V.4.a. The CRTC also held that Telesat's limitation of services to those obtaining only full channel services violated the Railway Act because it effectively limited small carrier offerings and conferred an undue advantage on large carriers and, in particular, TCTS members. *Id.* at Section V.4.b.

8. In reviewing Telecom. Decision 81-13 the Governor in Council essentially endorsed the CRTC, but varied the decision so as to

maintain Telesat's "carrier's carrier" role, except to confirm that Telesat would be permitted to deal directly with broadcasters. Order-in-Council P.C. 1981-3456, Dec. 8, 1981. Undergirding this decision was the view that if Telesat had been permitted to compete directly with TCTS members by offering service to end users, it probably would have been expelled from TCTS; a "competitive" Telesat would lose TCTS financial resources and could expect diminished use by TCTS of satellite capacity.

9. Although CNCP intervened in the proceedings at the CRTC, it has not actually come to lease satellite capacity to any great extent. Similarly, even though carriers are now permitted to lease less than a full channel, CNCP has not acquired partial transponder capacity. Some observers believe that Telesat and CNCP are essentially in direct competition: for nationwide "bypass" services in particular "niche-oriented" markets. Thus, CNCP's reluctance to use satellite services may reflect its unwillingness to aid a "competitor," especially while Telesat remains allied with Telecom Canada.

10. There is a significant debate underway in Canada about the current role of Telesat and whether it should be freed to become more than a "carrier's carrier." First, Telesat has renegotiated its Agreement with the other members of Telecom Canada such that it would, subject to CRTC approval, be able to sell the full range of its services directly to customers. Accompanying the Agreement, which was filed with the CRTC on July 15, 1985, was an application in which Telesat proposes to amend the definition of "customer" in its general tariff so as to exclude no one from dealing directly with it.

11. Moreover, the pattern of CRTC decisions suggests that it believes that increasing the separation of Telesat and Telecom Canada would have competitive advantages. The DOC and the government, however, appear to believe that the current ownership structure of Telesat could generate conflict of interest concerns that might have to be resolved before effective competition would ensue. Another concern is that Telesat could not remain viable without the support of its carrier partners, unless the government itself were to provide financial support and guarantees.

12. There are several reasons offered in support of the DOC's view. First, Telesat now has substantial excess capacity problems and is, therefore, quite dependent on the undiminished flow of revenues from Telecom Canada. Moreover, it had hoped and planned to supply service on an interim basis to U.S. users, but U.S. business has not materialized to the extent anticipated, either because of low demand for services or due to regulatory obstacles. Furthermore, the government's anti-inflation "6/5" price restraint program—public companies and federally-regulated companies were not allowed to declare rate increases in excess of 6% (after September 1, 1982), 5% (after September 1, 1983) and 4% (from July 1, 1984 to June 30, 1985)—was applied to Telesat rates for 6/4 GHz service; the result was to depress earnings substantially. The CRTC has also been slow in approving new satellite-delivered programming, such as pay television and

other specialized services, a delay that has seriously affected Telesat's demand forecasts. Finally, there has been considerable delay in CRTC approval of rates for Telesat's new 14/12 GHz service. Consequently, in early 1983, Telesat had the first operating loss in its history, though earnings were up in 1984, on revenues that did grow 24% over 1983. Transfer payments from Telecom Canada to Telesat have been—and are likely to be—very high (even though it had been anticipated that, at this point, there would be payments from Telesat to Telecom Canada).

13. It may well be difficult for Telesat to compete effectively without the support—and business—of the other carriers. The long distance market that Telesat would be expected to serve if it were on its own could not be made available to it unless it received interconnection from the local telephone companies. The nature of the interconnection supplied by the members of Telecom Canada remains to be seen, at least if Telesat seeks to divert traffic from the Telecom Canada system; the CRTC could not compel such interconnection except as to the federally-regulated carriers. Moreover, it is not at all apparent how "competitive" an alternative Telesat might be. According to the DOC, even if Telesat leased all of its current and planned capacity, it would only account for less than two percent of the total domestic telecommunications market—a share hardly likely to have a major competitive impact on Telecom Canada.

14. While reviewing Telesat's role, the government has gradually eroded the scope of its original monopoly on satellite communications. From 1973 to 1979, Telesat had been the only entity licensed to own and operate earth stations for domestic services. In 1979, broadcasters and common carriers became eligible for the licensing of receive-only earth stations, and common carriers for the licensing of transmit stations for 14/12 GHz services. In March 1983, individuals and small commercial establishments were allowed to own receive-only stations without obtaining a license. On April 10, 1984 the DOC announced that restrictions on ownership of transmit earth stations—6/4 GHz as well as 14/12 GHz—would be lifted in a two-step process. *See* DOC NR-84-5265E, April 10, 1984. First, as of April 1, 1985, non-carrier business users could file applications for experimental licenses, essentially for private line services. Several applications have been filed, with the principal ones seeking authority to operate intracorporate voice and data services. Thereafter, by April 1, 1986, there would be full liberalization of earth station ownership.

15. The lifting of earth station ownership requirements was designed to increase carriers' flexibility. Both Telesat and other carriers have, however, expressed concern that liberalization of ownership will affect Telesat's revenue base. They are equally concerned that private ownership will make it possible for businesses and others to create their own networks and, possibly, compete in a limited way with regulated carriers. Thus, Bell Canada argues, for example, that new earth station ownership policies could siphon revenues from carriers and hinder integration of satellite facilities into the terrestrial network. *See* Bell Canada, "Framework for

the Future," at 43. Nevertheless, the DOC believes that liberalization—to increase earth station ownership—will bolster use of space segment and will thereby ultimately supplement Telesat revenues.

16. Telesat is also concerned about possible erosion of its monopoly on space segment services. For example, broadcasters are already permitted to resell excess leased capacity to other broadcasters. Hence, Telesat views the liberalization of earth station ownership as just another step in opening the door to broadcasters and businesses wanting to own space segment. Teleglobe, too, in offering private business satellite services, is applying some competitive pressure on Telesat by pursuing Canada-U.S. and domestic segments of its triangular international services.

17. Any inquiry into the viability of Telesat raises questions about the wisdom of confining a carrier to one technology, about the competitiveness of a "single mode" facilities supplier. Telesat has some difficulty in competing due to the technological, jurisdictional, economic, and regulatory obstacles it has had to overcome. Satellite services have some disadvantages in that direct access for businesses is more cumbersome than is the case with terrestrial offerings, which can, of course, also provide universal service. Satellite services, however, have clear advantages in providing point-to-multipoint distribution for broadcasters.

18. More generally, a carrier that relies solely on the provision of facilities has other handicaps. First, offerings on a "carrier's carrier" must necessarily include a profit for both the carrier (*e.g.*, Bell Canada) and the "carrier's carrier" (*e.g.*, Telesat). Thus, "carrier's carrier" services tend to be priced higher than competing "one tier" services. Furthermore, the return to Telesat on various facilities has not been commensurate with its proportionate investment share. It is estimated that three-quarters of Telesat's investment is in transmission facilities and only one-quarter in terminal facilities; yet, over 80% of Telesat's revenues derive from terminal equipment and just 20% from transmission. The skewing of the investment-return relationship makes it difficult to offer services that are priced in alignment with costs and, hence, that are attractive or competitive.

19. Both Telesat and its regulators are faced with a dilemma. Once staunchly opposed to competition, Telesat's managers, if not its owners, are now taking steps to free it of restraints that have stifled its growth. If others have access to space segment, Telesat argues, it should have the opportunity to offer business and other telecommunications services in competition with existing carriers. If Teleglobe is able to reach for a portion of the domestic market, then Telesat contends that it should be able to offer some international services where its facilities can be used effectively. In addition, Telesat has had a strong interest in leasing capacity to provide DBS services.

20. There has been little public discussion of what structure might be used if Telesat were permitted to offer competitive services. It is unknown, for example, whether the U.S. model for Comsat's competitive offerings would be followed, *i.e.*, whether competitive offerings would be

provided through a separate subsidiary to prevent cross-subsidization by the provider of monopoly space segment services. Establishing such a subsidiary would raise several questions. Would, for example, a subsidiary be outside the Telecom Canada structure while Telesat remains affiliated with it? Although the government is apparently reluctant to have Telesat become fully competitive in view of the constraints outlined above, it is likely that the structural issue will be the subject of further discussions in any evaluation of Telesat's role or its relationship with Telecom Canada.

B. Teleglobe Canada

Canada's overseas services are provided by Teleglobe Canada, the exclusive holder of licenses for international submarine cables and international satellite earth stations, and the Canadian signatory to the Intelsat and Inmarsat organizations. Teleglobe is a candidate for privatization; although such privatization would occur in light of the current policy framework, how the Government addresses that step—and concomitant structural and competitive issues—may also be indicative of the course of any future liberalization.

1. The present regulation of Teleglobe is somewhat diffuse. It had originally been intended that the CRTC's predecessor regulate Teleglobe's rates. However, statutory authority to undertake such regulation, though passed, never became effective. Thus, the CRTC has no jurisdiction over rates. Rather, they are set by Teleglobe after consideration of revenue settlement arrangements with foreign administrations and in consultation with Canadian domestic carriers (which then file the rates with their respective regulatory authorities).

2. Teleglobe's capital and spending budget is reviewed by the Minister of Regional and Industrial Expansion. This is because its equity is held directly by the government. Teleglobe, however, has done somewhat better than other business enterprises held by the government. By some estimates, it enjoys an after-tax rate of return of 30%, given a normalized capital structure. (In the last complete fiscal year, it was reported to have had profits of C$40 million on revenues of C$200 million; both revenues and profits increased in the first nine months of 1984 over the comparable 1983 period.)

3. Teleglobe is increasingly going after business in which it is, at least arguably, competing with other carriers with which it now has, of course, interconnection agreements. For instance, the triangular services—U.S.-Canada-overseas—are marketed both by Teleglobe and Telecom Canada, with the interconnection agreement allocating the responsibilities for marketing between them. Teleglobe is also apparently eager to pursue new private ventures in international communications (*e.g.*, private, trans-Atlantic cable ventures). In light of Teleglobe's interest in expanding its offerings in these ways, and the idealogical objective of reducing government involvement in the marketplace, it is no surprise that, on October 30, 1984, the

government announced its intention to privatize Teleglobe; the process is likely to be under way within the year. In December 1984, Bell Canada, on behalf of a consortium of the other domestic telephone companies, made an offer to buy Teleglobe at book value—C$350 million—though the eventual price may be higher—up to C$440 million. Other offers have also been received.

4. The critical issue is how such privatization will be structured. There are several options: First, if Teleglobe is given permission to sell business services directly to users, it could lose its existing customer base of domestic carriers—on which it is dependent—unless its monopoly over international services is maintained. Teleglobe is well aware of not only the size and competitive capacity of domestic carriers but, even more, that its profitability stems from its monopoly position with respect to international services. It is, therefore, anxious that this monopoly be maintained. Hence, if privatized in this way, certain mechanisms—whether accounting or structural in nature—will need to be established to prevent cross-subsidization of competitive services by monopoly services. The problem of cross-subsidization might be dealt with in the context of any CRTC regulation of a privatized Teleglobe. The example of Comsat in the U.S. might be utilized as a model for this option.

5. Another option might be to sell Teleglobe to Telecom Canada (*i.e.*, the Bell Canada proposal) or to CNCP—perhaps with a public offering as well. This option might, however, increase the dominance of the existing telephone companies, which would then be able to offer end-to-end services for overseas communications. Complete privatization—sale to the public—would, however, raise significant structural or control issues, particularly because Teleglobe is not now subject to rate regulation. The government may be unwilling, for example, to place Intelsat signatory responsibilities in the hands of a wholly private enterprise.

6. Another option would be to combine Teleglobe with Telesat and privatize the new entity. If the entity were to be sold to the public, the option would depend on the government's view of the importance of a close relationship between Telesat and Telecom Canada. A Telesat divorced from Telecom Canada and combined with Teleglobe would, however, be less attractive to investor/purchasers than Teleglobe by itself. Moreover, some observers believe that a merged entity would only make financial sense if the two were regulated as one and if cross-subsidization were permitted between overseas and domestic satellite services. Not surprisingly, existing carriers have opposed a competitive national satellite carrier. Carriers would be unwilling to route traffic to a competitor, a combined Telesat-Teleglobe; yet, for international traffic they could be forced to do so. The need to separate the competitive services of a Telesat-Teleglobe from monopoly services raises additional issues of cross-subsidization as described in the first option.

7. It is possible that the assets of Teleglobe could be divided and spun-off to create two entities to provide international services on a "duopolistic" basis (*e.g.*, British Telecom International and Mercury).

8. Although the future for Telglobe now looks promising, it will soon be forced to confront some difficult issues relating to the narrowing of its profitable monopoly. First, based on the U.S. experience, there could be, in the future, increasing pressure to liberalize earth station ownership and afford carriers direct access to international facilities. This erosion in the earth station ownership monopoly might stimulate the use of satellite services but could also have an adverse financial impact on Telesat, with similar results for Teleglobe.

9. More importantly, Teleglobe will increasingly feel the effects of deregulation in the U.S. If Intelsat's monopoly position begins to erode, Canadian users may come to use new U.S. private international services to circumvent Teleglobe entirely. The likelihood of this development, and its long-term impact on Teleglobe, are, to a certain extent dependent on changes in national policy, on whether Teleglobe would remain the sole interface for international services. Despite the interconnection agreements between Teleglobe and Canadian domestic carriers and between the latter and U.S. carriers, some Canada-Europe traffic is already being diverted to the U.S.: U.S.-Europe rates are substantially less than their Canadian counterparts.

10. Canadian domestic carriers may also have incentives to enter into arrangements with private U.S. overseas carriers for international services if and when Teleglobe becomes a private competitor. Certainly, they will argue that if Teleglobe can compete in domestic markets, they should be permitted to enter Teleglobe's current service areas. Even Intelsat, via Teleglobe, might enter the Canadian domestic markets as it expands its U.S.-Canada or Canada-international services. For its part, Teleglobe's triangular service might ultimately be used to offer Canada-Canada services. Existing carriers are opposed to Teleglobe's entry into non-international services. If that should happen, however, Teleglobe will undoubtedly be faced with vigorous competition from Canadian, U.S., and international carriers.

IV. JURISDICTIONAL BOUNDARIES IN CANADIAN TELECOMMUNICATIONS

The jurisdictional split of regulatory authority and the resulting inability to achieve a national consensus are the most critical issues in Canadian telecommunications. They are inextricably tied to the future of telecommunications policymaking because the decentralization of power makes it difficult to formulate and implement a national policy. The failure to reach a consensus has meant that the critical telecommunications issues of structure, competition, pricing, industrial policy, while addressed on a national basis by the DOC policy review, have, in the past, been only the subject of piecemeal examination.

A. Legal Premise for Split

1. The Canadian federal system is fundamentally different from that of the U.S., where the Constitution grants the federal government supremacy in areas where the states and the national government might clash. In Canada, the jurisdictional division of authority is set forth in the British North America Act, 1867 ("B.N.A. Act"). The B.N.A. Act exempts from provincial jurisdiction "Lines of Steam . . . Telegraphs, and other Works and Undertakings connecting the Province with any other or others of the Provinces, or extending beyond the Limits of the Province." Section 92(10)(a). Section 92, however, also sets forth exclusive provincial heads of power: over "local Works and Undertakings," "Property and Civil Rights in the Province." and "all Matters of a merely local or private Nature in the Province." Section 92(10), 92(13) & 92(16). The determination of whether an "undertaking" is within federal or provincial jurisdiction depends mainly, then, on whether an undertaking—the services or facilities of a carrier—extends beyond the limits of a province.

2. For purposes of dividing provincial from federal authority, the leading case interpreting the B.N.A. Act in the field of telephony is *Toronto Corp. v. Bell Telephone Co. of Canada*. [1905] A.C. 52. The Judicial Committee of the Privy Council held that Bell Canada's local and long-distance offerings were not separate and distinct undertakings for jurisdictional purposes. A.C. at 59. Thus, the Privy Council confirmed federal jurisdiction over the entirety of Bell. The *Toronto Corp.* holding would suggest that there would be federal jurisdiction over carriers where intraprovincial facilities are interconnected with extra-provincial facilities. This view has never prevailed, however.

3. The argument for federal jurisdiction over all companies that have facilities that are interconnected with interprovincial facilities has been raised from time to time. Until recently, neither the federal nor provincial authorities had sought a judicial resolution. The argument was, for example, raised, but not resolved, by the CRTC in Telecom. Decision 81-13.

4. In the *Alberta Government Telephones* decision, however, the issue was squarely addressed. Justice Reed held that AGT was a "non-local undertaking" as described in Section 92(10)(a) of the B.N.A. Act. She stated that the nature of the enterprise—not its physical facilities—was crucial. First, she found that AGT offered inter- and intraprovincial services on one interconnected system. Looking at AGT's relationship with Telecom Canada, she then noted that its facilities were integrated into the Telecom Canada network; hence, it could not withdraw itself from Telecom Canada without destroying its own system. Justice Reed concluded, therefore, that the company "operates its telecommunications undertaking as an interprovincial undertaking and not as one merely local in nature." *Alberta*

Government Telephones, Order, at 28 (Oct. 26, 1984). (Interestingly, she noted that the eighty-year-old failure of federal authorities to seek to regulate AGT was not probative: there are no "constitutional squatters rights.") Absent its "crown immunity," which arises from the fact of its ownership by the Province of Alberta, AGT would therefore be subject to the regulatory authority of the CRTC.

B. Two Jurisdictional Issues: Provincially-Regulated Companies and Telecom Canada

The jurisdictional division of authority has created significant problems in two areas of current debate: 1) control over provincially-regulated companies and 2) control over the activities and settlements process administered by Telecom Canada. Both of these areas are critical to the future direction of Canadian telecommunications policy.

C. Jurisdiction over Provincially-Regulated Companies

1. There is, at present, a jurisdictional patchwork, with different regulators and companies adopting varying positions on CNCP's access to exchange facilities and on terminal equipment. As to interconnection of CNCP services, such interconnection is currently only available in Bell Canada and B.C. Tel. territory, but is being sought elsewhere (*e.g.*, Alberta).

2. Terminal attachment policies vary widely. There appears, however, to be a trend toward liberalization that is spearheaded by the CRTC. In several provincial jurisdictions, attachment of network non-addressing equipment has been permitted. The CRTC permitted attachment of telephone and PBX equipment to Bell Canada facilities in 1980. *See Bell Canada—Interim Requirements Regarding the Attachment of Subscriber-Provided Terminal Equipment,* CRTC Telecom. Decision 80-13 (Aug. 5, 1980). Attachment was subsequently permitted for B.C. Tel. After extended hearings the CRTC concluded that its liberalized terminal attachment policy should be continued and be extended to CNCP and the two other federally-regulated carriers owned by CNR. *Attachment of Subscriber-Provided Terminal Equipment,* CRTC Telecom. Decision 82-14 (Nov. 23, 1982).

3. For provincially-regulated companies, there is little consistency in terminal attachment policies. In Prince Edward Island, the Supreme Court reversed a ruling of the Public Utilities Commission that subscriber-owned equipment could not be attached to the network. The Court held that the Commission should promulgate rules for terminal attachment because "customer-owned terminal equipment is a 'fact of life' in the telecommunications industry . . . ." *In re Garden of the Gulf Court & Motel Inc. and Island Telephone Co. Ltd.,* [1981] 126 D.L.R.(3d) 281 (P.E.I. S.C. en banc). At the other extreme, in Saskatchewan even the advertising of unauthorized customer-owned terminal equipment is prohibited. *See* Saskatchewan Telecom-

munications Act, Section 44.3. Obviously, the welter of regulation makes it difficult to market equipment on a national basis.

4. The *Alberta Government Telephones* case highlights some of the legal difficulties that have been encountered in arriving at national policies implicating provincially-regulated or owned companies. The provincial regulators, relying on the physical locus of their facilities, contend that they have exclusive jurisdiction over their own intraprovincial facilities and all services offered thereon, even if there is interconnection with the Telecom Canada network. Effectively, then, provincial authorities can regulate not only interprovincial service originating from their province, but can insist on policies that might have an impact on services in and between provinces on the other side of the continent. The only mechanism for easing any tension, or for resolving any differences, is the consensus-building—but unregulated—Telecom Canada process.

5. In one sense, then, the *Alberta Government Telephones* decision is a watershed. If sustained on appeal, the decision could bring under the jurisdiction of the CRTC all telephone company members of Telecom Canada not now subject to federal regulation—save those owned by the provinces outright. Thus, regulation of interprovincial rates, and interconnection arrangements (including any "access charges") could be within the purview of federal regulatory authorities. CNCP and others might be in a position to apply to the CRTC to order interconnection for private and data service offerings with the Atlantic, investor-owned telephone companies. Moreover, if the CNCP application for interexchange voice service is approved by the CRTC, soon thereafter there could be long-haul voice competition in all provinces except Alberta, Manitoba, and Saskatchewan. The resulting competitive pressures would, obviously, affect Telecom Canada. In time, such pressure could force the three provincial regulators to permit CNCP or others to obtain interconnection as well.

6. Despite the landmark nature of the holding in *Alberta Government Telephones*, it is not at all certain that the courts will be the principal engine of change in Canada, as they have been in the U.S. They have, however, undoubtedly played a significant role in the evolution of telecommunications policy. *See, e.g., Garden of the the Gulf Court & Motel, supra* (ordering terminal attachment in Prince Edward Island); *Bell Canada v. Challenge Communications Ltd.*, [1978] 22 N.R.1; [1978] 85 D.L.R. (3d) 351 (Fed. C.A.) (upholding a broad interpretation of the statutory authority of the CRTC). Rather, it is likely that continued provincial-federal negotiation at the ministerial level will eventually lead to a resolution of the difficulties in what CNCP terms the "balkanized telecommunications jurisdiction" that is Canada. *See* CNCP, "Crisis in Canadian Telecommunications Policy & Regulation," at 14 (n.d.).

D. Jurisdiction Over Telecom Canada

1. Telecom Canada is legally an unincorporated organization but describes itself as a "loose consortium of independent fully integrated telecommunications undertakings which work together to establish methods of planning, building plant for, and operating long distance telecommunication services within Canada in Canadian facilities." Petition to Governor-in-Council, Para. 3, July 23, 1981 (for review of Telecom. Decision 81-13). Thus, Telecom Canada functions as an "AT&T Long Lines," with responsibilities for planning, associated research, integrated network offerings, and settlement of revenues.

2. Some observers of the Canadian scene—along with Telecom Canada's would-be competitors, especially CNCP—believe that the absence of any accountability by Telecom Canada to a single regulator is the most vexing of all jurisdictional concerns. The absence of a single regulator makes it difficult to determine whether and how Telecom Canada weighs the policy objectives of encouraging national versus local services. Revenues are divided according to a complex Revenue Settlement Plan ("RSP"). The RSP provides for three classes of toll traffic: intraprovincial, adjacent province, and traffic using more than two carriers. The RSP allocates costs and reimburses carriers for costs associated with the provision of "trans-Canada" offerings on a proportionate basis. All Telecom Canada decisions must be made unanimously. (Rates for services between adjacent members are excluded from the RSP and are to be negotiated by the companies themselves; in practice, the Telecom Canada rates are used for such adjacent member services.)

3. In this scheme, long distance rates are kept high to subsidize the prices of local service. The Telecom Canada rate filings for long distance services are essentially "rubber stamped" by provincial regulators. Thus, there is no body responsible for reviewing the entire Canadian tariff structure and its relationship to social, political, economic, and industrial policy goals.

4. In the proceeding that culminated in Telecom. Decision 81-13, the CRTC, in connection with the Bell Canada and B.C. Tel. rate applications, undertook a broad-ranging and intensive review of the TCTS settlement process. The inquiry looked at whether the settlement procedures are fair and reasonable; whether the rates charged are just and reasonable; whether the terms and restrictions of facilities are reasonable and do not confer an unjust advantage on any person; whether the relative treatment of competitive and non-competitive services is just and reasonable; whether the construction program is reasonable; whether TCTS is sufficiently responsive to the demand for programming and other information services; and what should be information requirements in future TCTS rate cases. Telecom. Decision 81-13, Part I.

5. The member companies of TCTS ultimately did participate in this review, but not without CRTC subpoenas and some judicial skirmishing as to the information that was being supplied to the CRTC. (In the course of the proceeding, for instance, Alberta Government Telephones appealed a CRTC order requiring the production of financial information; however, the case was not argued or decided on jurisdictional grounds. *See Alberta Government Telephones and CRTC*, [1980] 114 D.L.R. (3d) 64.)

6. Ultimately, in Telecom. Decision 81-13 the CRTC ordered Bell Canada and B.C. Tel. to negotiate with TCTS to force a reallocation within the RSP of costs for toll and competitive services. The CRTC only had the power, however, to direct the federally-regulated carriers to report back to it on alternative methods for cost allocation. Among other conclusions, the CRTC also required that Bell and B.C. Tel. negotiate with respect to the inclusion of their intracompany and adjacent member revenues, or revenues that are derived from use of the facilities of only one member of the RSP. The CRTC deemed these practices unfair to customers of Bell and B.C. Tel. Telecom. Decision 81-13, at Part III. This decision was petitioned to the Governor in Council, which sustained the decision on most issues.

7. Bell Canada and B.C. Tel. subsequently did attempt to negotiate with the other members of TCTS with respect to these issues. They met with no success. The CRTC has now taken no action, largely because it is powerless to do so.

8. The lack of a single regulatory authority or cooperation amongst the several authorities makes it difficult to develop a uniform, nationwide system for costing and pricing services. In Telecom. Decision 81-13, the CRTC essentially approved some features of the RSP but noted that it needed information to establish cost of revenue relationships among TCTS service categories; it concluded that the Plan should be amended "to reflect more accurately [the] costs related to the resources employed in providing TCTS competitive services." Telecom. Decision 81-13, at Part III.4.b. The Report of the Inquiry Officer in the Phase III Inquiry recommended that an RSP-based, embedded cost method be developed for Bell Canada and B.C. Tel. *See* Phase III Report, at 177, 214-15. *See* Report of the Inquiry Officer with Respect to the Inquiry Into Telecommunications Carriers' Costing and Accounting Procedures: Phase III—Costing of Existing Services, April 30, 1984. The CRTC decided that an RSP-based method should be used by Bell Canada and B.C. Tel. *See* Telecom. Decision 85-10. Its success in implementing that methodology is, however, uncertain.

9. The CRTC has essentially concluded that, to the extent that the costing for competitive and non-competitive services is not disaggregated, there is some cross-subsidization of the former by monopoly services. Concurrently, a critical issue facing Bell Canada and B.C. Tel.—if not all Telecom Canada members—is how they could successfully lower rates for competitive services and still keep Telecom Canada rates reasonably uniform overall. That is, a decision to lower rates to competitive levels would reduce the revenues flowing into the settlement pool for traffic to and from

Bell Canada and B.C. Tel. territory and would, therefore, affect the revenues available for division by Telecom Canada. Thus, opening competition in some areas will effectively disrupt Telecom Canada's basic pricing principle: rates should be uniform regardless of the territory from which the call originates. At present, no regulatory body is even in a position to address whether basic exchange or toll rates should be uniform across Canada.

10. Similarly, the imposition of the government's "6/5" price restraint program has forced down the rates of Bell Canada services while identical services from other members of Telecom Canada have remained as they were. This disparity has also contributed to an anomalous rate structure. Finally, some of the provincial companies do not pay taxes, which also enables them to keep their rates down.

11. The interests of Telecom Canada members are also beginning to differ as they face—in varying degrees—the threat of competition. Although they still adhere to the principle of unanimity, movement toward rate rebalancing will make it difficult to maintain unanimous decisionmaking. Rate rebalancing to align prices more closely to costs is, for example, opposed by certain provincial companies that enjoy the subsidy from long distance services; it is, however, supported by Bell Canada. Moreover, and more significantly in the long run, rebalancing is likely to reduce the level of interprovincial revenues flowing into the settlement pool. Thus, continued progress toward the repricing of services may well create internal tensions in the Telecom Canada structure.

E. Efforts at Reaching Jurisdictional Solutions

In both of these areas—jurisdiction over provincially-regulated companies and over the Telecom Canada structure and settlements process—there have been ongoing efforts to resolve some of the outstanding issues. These efforts have principally involved shifting the jurisdictional boundary line from the locus of facilities to a distinction based on the nature or reach of the services offered.

1. Since the issuance of the 1973 Green Paper—which highlighted the fact that the planning of the national telecommunications system had largely been left to the unregulated discretion of the TCTS—there have been a series of negotiations and proposals to realign jurisdiction. The Green Paper itself suggested two approaches to the division of regulatory authority. One alternative would have been to transfer jurisdictional authority, to create a two-tier, service-oriented framework not unlike the split in the U.S. between the FCC and the states. There would be federal jurisdiction over international and interprovincial aspects of Canadian services, and provincial jurisdiction over intraprovincial offerings. The second alternative would have been to establish some formal mechanism for consultation and exchange of information between the levels of government. Both these proposals were rejected by provincial ministers.

2. The 1975 Grey Paper stated that no resolution could depend on a formal transfer of regulatory jurisdiction; instead, it offered a series of consulta-tive mechanisms, to include a federal/provincial committee and an association of regulatory bodies. After publication of the Grey Paper, there was significant discussion of that option, with substantial attention paid in particular to broadcasting and cable issues. It was in this phase that the Canada-Manitoba cable agreement was signed. *See supra* Section II.D.

3. The federal and provincial ministers met in 1977 and 1978, primarily to discuss federal telecommunications legislation. *See infra* Section VII.B.2. In February 1979, a specific proposal for the sharing of jurisdiction over cable systems was offered by the federal government. This proposal would have given both the federal and provincial governments jurisdiction over different aspects of cable television. *See* Press Release, Hon. Jeanne Sauve, Minister of Communications, Feb. 13, 1979. This proposal was the subject of a discussion by federal and provincial ministers in October 1979, after which followed an intense series of talks that eventually culminated in the much-discussed federal and provincial proposals of 1980.

4. In the 1980 round of constitutional negotiations the federal government offered a new proposal to reallocate jurisdiction between the federal and provincial governments. The federal government would have jurisdiction over national and satellite carriers (Teleglobe, Telesat, and CNCP), over interprovincial and international rates and services, over technical standards and interconnection, and over "national programme service" and non-Canadian programming on cable systems. The provincial governments would have responsibility over intraprovincial operations of provincial carriers (including Bell Canada, B.C. Tel., and Terra Nova Tel.) and exclusive responsibilty for all aspects of cable systems except those specifically granted to the federal government. The proposal was subsequently amended to include a federal-provincial joint board for interprovincial rates and services; the board would have had six members appointed by the federal government and five by the provincial governments. *See* Hon. Jean Chretien, "Federal Proposal to Ensure Efficient Telecommunication Services Between All Points in Canada," Continuing Committee of Ministers on the Constitution, Aug. 25, 1980.

5. The provincial governments rejected the federal proposal due to inefficiency, cost, and a fundamental inability to draw a new jurisdictional boundary, to effect a separation of "interprovincial" and "intraprovincial" services. (There was substantial interest in the U.S. experience, where two-tier regulation was appearing less practicable as the regulatory boundaries were being relocated from the state boundaries to the local exchange.)

6. The provinces offered a "Best Efforts Draft" by way of response to the federal proposal. This draft largely adhered to the distinctions based on the situs of facilities. It proposed that the provinces would have exclusive jurisdiction over all telecommunications works and under-

takings in the province (notwithstanding the fact of interprovincial interconnection), concurrent jurisdiction with respect to all other works and undertakings (subject to the supremacy of the provincial authority), and exclusive jurisdiction over cable, except for broadcast networks extending to four or more provinces. The federal government would have paramount jurisdiction over satellite space segment, concurrent jurisdiction over interprovincial carriers, and supremacy with respect to foreign broadcast signals and technical matters. *See* "Best Efforts Draft," Continuing Committee of Ministers on the Constitution, Aug. 26-29, 1980.

7. The Draft also contained an arbitration mechanism for Parliament to pass a law in case provincial laws happened to come into conflict. This proposal did not address the need for development of nationwide policies and demonstrated an unwillingness to recognize the role of the federal government in planning or regulating the network, resolving structural issues, or examining the place of competition in a national industrial policy. (It seems to suggest that there would not even be federal jurisdiction over Telesat, Teleglobe, or CNCP.)

8. Both proposals were and are viewed by many observers as extremely unsatisfactory, but the discussions do highlight the difficulty of resolving the jurisdictional issues. *See generally* R. Schultz, "Partners in a Game Without Masters: Reconstructing the Telecommunications Regulatory System," and R. Buchan and C.C. Johnston, "Telecommunications Regulation and the Constitution: A Lawyers' Perspective," both in R. Buchan, et al., *Telecommunications Regulation, supra*. Under the auspices of the DOC, which has been extremely involved in supporting a federal/provincial dialogue, discussions on a legislative or constitutional realignment of jurisdiction have continued. There has also been an informal agreement between the federal government and the provinces to the effect that their respective regulators should discuss current issues within the Canadian Association of Members of Public Utility Tribunals ("CAMPUT"). Despite these discussions and ongoing inter-governmental consultations, no real progress has been made to date, except that the CRTC has now been accepted as a member of CAMPUT.

9. As to the issues implicated in resolving some of the internal and external pressures that may shatter the Telecom Canada structure, there has, as well, been little progress. Within Telecom Canada itself there have been a series of proposed revisions to the RSPs that are to be implemented over the next few years. For over two years, however, Telecom Canada has been trying, without success, to alter its settlement arrangements. In Telecom Canada, therefore, there is considerable frustration and discontent, with the consensual process beginning to fray at the edges.

10. In sum, there has been a two-level discussion of the "intergovernmental" and "business/financial" issues that are confronting the telecommunications industry and regulatory agencies. These issues are interlocked, but efforts to resolve them are taking place in separate fora. Both sets of negotiations have met with little success; however, a resolution in

both sectors is essential to establishing an effective framework for future Canadian regulatory policy.

F. Deadlock in Resolving Jurisdictional Issues

1. Essentially, there is, then, a deadlock in both the government and business sectors. CNCP argues that the "balkanization" of jurisdiction has frustrated users, stifles innovation, undermines the legitimacy of the federal government, is wasteful, and, indeed, even suggests the very frailty of Canada as an economic entity or a nation-state. *See* "Crisis in Telecommunications Policy & Regulation," at 15. CNCP contends that the real problems lie in the Telecom Canada structure—with pressures being placed on members severally and together to oppose the introduction of long distance competition. Of course, CNCP does not participate in the Telecom Canada discussions on pricing of interprovincial services.

2. There are, at present, deep cleavages between the federal and provincial governments. The level of distrust has run high in the past, particularly in the early 1970s. Neither tier of government is especially willing to concede jurisdiction to the other. For example, the CRTC twice applied to join the CAMPUT consultative mechanism and the Province of Quebec has opposed its application for membership. As noted above it was only in the past year that CRTC become a member.

3. Further complicating the inter-governmental dynamic is the belief on the part of many in the provincial governments that the status quo, as unwieldy as it is, has proved workable. In their view it would, therefore, be unwise to tamper with success.

G. Suggested Solutions for Jurisdictional Problems

The solutions that have been suggested to address the jurisdictional "crisis" focus on both new procedural and institutional arrangements, and on the substantive power that must be assigned to one or the other level of government. Obviously, the viability of a particular solution depends on the vantage point of the observer. CNCP, for example, believes that no solution will be satisfactory unless it ensures that CNCP will be able to interconnect with local carriers. CNCP and others believe that no solution will work unless it reduces the level of cross-subsidization among services or incorporates rate-balancing principles.

1. One institutional option would be to create a federal-provincial joint board to address some of these issues. The amended 1980 federal proposal had suggested such a board. CNCP has advocated such a "permanent national regulator" for some time—with a permanent staff and members appointed by both the provinces and the federal government to serve for a fixed, extended term. *See* CNCP Telecommunications, "Brief on the Telecommunications Bill," at 14 (Nov. 1979), and "Crisis in Telecommunications Policy & Regulation," at 32. Although it is possible that Parlia-

ment might enact legislation creating such a tribunal, critical questions could remain unresolved, *i.e.*, the board's control over particular issues.

2. It is assumed that such a board would regulate international rates and services, interprovincial offerings, and interprovincial interconnection arrangements, including terms and "access charges." The proposal might include transferring jurisdiction over the intraprovincial offerings of the now federally-regulated "provincial" carriers to the provinces (*e.g.*, Bell Canada to Ontario and Quebec). Although this split of jurisdiction would resemble, in some sense, the unsuccessful two-tier proposal of 1980 and the 1973 Green Paper, it would, at least, acknowledge the intersection of intra- and interprovincial facilities and services.

3. One additional problem in establishing a board could be the composition of its membership. The federal proposal would have had a majority of the members appointed by the federal government. The provincial authorities are unlikely to accede unless their representatives could control the board. However, the federal government in 1980 said that it would settle for a 6-5, provincial-federal split on the board; that proposal, too, was rejected.

4. A legislative solution may be difficult to achieve, then, as the provinces do not want to cede any jurisdiction to a board that could be controlled by the federal government. Other, non-legislative, models might, however, be successful. Following the paradigm set by the Canada-Manitoba cable agreement of 1976, a system of "joint panels" involving existing regulatory bodies in consultative relationships could be established. *See* T.G. Kane, "Breaking an Impasse: A Joint Panel Proposal for Telecommunications Regulation," in R. Buchan, et al., *Telecommunications Regulation, supra*. A negotiated solution may be more possible now that the Progressive Conservative party is the party in power in the federal government and in all provinces except Manitoba, Ontario, and British Columbia.

5. Business interests may be somewhat skeptical of a "negotiated" or "joint panel" solution that excludes them from the process. They believe that the governments will try to solve the jurisdictional controversies in a political fashion—by compromise—to the detriment of suppliers, users, and what would ultimately be beneficial to Canada's competitive posture. The telephone industry is particularly wary of any "political compromise" that would effectively and necessarily restructure industry-wide financial arrangements.

6. One additional difficulty in achieving a "negotiated" solution is that the federal government does not have many political bargaining chips. The public does not perceive the need for change, especially if it leads to increased rates. Accordingly, the provinces and Telecom Canada can remain steadfast in support of the status quo and choose not to succumb to federal pressure. The ramifications of the *Alberta Government Telephones* decision may, however, increase the bargaining strength of the federal government's position over the private, provincially-regulated companies. Moreover, the federal government is not wholly without clout. For exam-

ple, cellular radio licenses will be granted to telephone companies on the condition that they afford interconnection to the "non-wireline" cellular provider. Similarly, the federal government might impose conditions on the granting of radio licenses—*e.g.*, "common carrier" microwave—as a means of compelling the provinces or the provincially-regulated companies to reach an accommodation.

7. One key question in the near-term is who has jurisdiction with respect to local interconnection. The CRTC set forth the terms and conditions of CNCP's private line/data interconnection with Bell Canada and B.C. Tel. in 1979 and 1981. Is "interconnection," however, necessarily within the jurisdiction of the CRTC? Telecom Canada believes that it is not and that the terms of interconnection, if it is ordered (either for interexchange voice with federally-regulated carriers or for private line/data outside Ontario, Quebec, and British Columbia), should be left to provincial regulators, who would provide access at "reasonable rates." The view of Telecom Canada is that if interconnection is not made available, bypass by satellite will evolve. Of course, as to switched services, satellite bypass is not a particularly attractive alternative.

8. Pursuant to its authority under the Railway Act, the CRTC could simply establish a standard for interconnection that prohibits discrimination and leaves the charges to be fixed at the provincial level. Another alternative might be for the CRTC to set the rates for interprovincial interconnection while the primary responsibility over local and intraprovincial access remains in the hands of the provincial authorities. Each of these options merits close examination. Each, it should be noted, involves jurisdictional line-drawing on the basis not of facilities, but of services, *i.e.*, whether the interconnection is for provincial or interprovincial offerings. A division of authority on the basis of the service to be regulated would be a relatively novel concept in Canadian jurisdictional disputes, but one that might provide a solution for problems that now seem to escape resolution.

V. COMPETITION, NEW ENTRY, AND INDUSTRY STRUCTURE

A. The Effect of Deregulation in the United States

1. Even without new entry by Canadian carriers into Canadian markets, there is competition from U.S. carriers in Canada-Canada services. Historically, east-west traffic in Canada was routed through the U.S. over AT&T lines. TCTS was, in fact, established in 1931 to ensure that Canada-Canada services would be routed on Canadian facilities.

2. Today, an unknown, but increasing, amount of traffic is being diverted through the U.S. Canadian users now have control over terminal and switching equipment in the most liberalized, *i.e.*, federally-

regulated, service areas. Thus, it is much easier to route traffic to the U.S. than had once been the case.

3. Telecom Canada private lines are, moreover, quite expensive; it is far cheaper to obtain a private line from, for example, Seattle to Maine, with lines running up to Vancouver and Montreal, than to lease a dedicated, wholly trans-Canada circuit. Cam-Net and Longnet are successful transborder resellers that have taken advantage of this situation. Based in British Columbia, they offer discount long distance services to the U.S. In April 1985, the CRTC approved an application by B.C. Tel. to restructure its Canada-U.S. long distance rates. *See British Columbia Telephone Company—Applications Regarding Access to U.S. Discount Long Distance Telephone Services and Rate Restructuring*, CRTC Telecom. Decision 85-7 (April 4, 1985). The CRTC granted the company's request to eliminate tariff anomalies that had encouraged users in British Columbia to avail themselves of short-haul rates that enabled them to link up with U.S. discount services at a point just beyond the border in the State of Washington. Cam-Net and Longnet have filed an appeal to the Federal Cabinet. Bell Canada filed an application similar to that of B.C. Tel. with the intent of achieving a rate rebalancing of U.S.-Canada rates. It may be that rate rebalancing will minimize the incentives to use bypass services.

4. Concerned with erosion of Canada-U.S. revenues, B.C. Tel. had earlier applied to the CRTC for authority to block calls to such services. Denying that application, however, the CRTC acknowledged the potential for revenue erosion, but concluded that the restructuring of rates would adequately address the problem. To illustrate further the severity of the problem, Telecom Canada recently inquired into the possibility of blocking U.S.-routed Canada-Canada traffic. Faced with a contrary U.S. regulatory policy, which holds that the customer should be able to use the network in the most convenient and least expensive way possible, Telecom Canada looked at other options aimed at hampering bypass services. Bell Canada has, however, recently filed a notice with the CRTC that it will start blocking calls to U.S. numbers advertised as offering Canada-U.S. and Canada-overseas bypass services.

5. Satellite carriage also makes it difficult to segment calls on the basis of national boundaries. The growth of transborder services will make it possible for Canadian users to use U.S. satellites or other facilities to route Canada-Canada traffic. Such services, at present, are, however, routed through Telesat, according to the terms of a U.S.-Canada intergovernmental agreement; the single interface policy for transborder services may make it more difficult to bypass Canadian carriers. Nevertheless, the emergence of the triangular services offered by Teleglobe may ultimately also siphon Canada-Canada traffic onto non-Canadian facilities.

6. Not all of this traffic diversion can be traced to inequalities between U.S. and Canadian pricing structures. Even if Canadian prices were brought closer to Canadian costs, there would still be substantial incentive to route traffic through the U.S. because the U.S. cost structure is itself lower.

The size of the market and the competitive environment in the U.S. have kept costs low. Consequently, even with rate rebalancing it may be quite difficult for Canadian carriers to offer competitive pricing arrangements.

7. In addition to the economic impact of neighboring on the U.S., and the resulting diversion of traffic, Canadian users are themselves acutely aware of competition and its impact. They see a U.S. market that offers services of lower price, with more variety, and equally high—if not higher—quality. Understandably, they question why Canadians cannot enjoy the same levels of service. This phenomenon of peering across national boundaries is rapidly increasing pressures in Canada for the resolution of jurisdictional disputes and the liberalization of the telecommunications structure.

8. Analogously, the "cumulative effect" of deregulation on a global scale, and not just in the U.S., has been a very significant factor in the Canadian public policy debate. Canadians are accustomed to—and rightfully proud of—the leading role that their country has taken in developing and implementing telecommunications services and equipment. They are concerned about Canada's continuing ability to maintain its stature at the forefront of the industry. There is a growing realization that competitive spurs can be beneficial and that Canada cannot maintain a sole-service supplier environment, particularly if Northern Telecom is to remain at the vanguard of equipment development. Thus, they are reviewing intensely the effect of competition both domestically—its impact on services within a particular country—and with respect to a nation's international competitive posture.

B. Issues in Introducing Competition in Canada

1. For geographic reasons, the Canadian market is difficult to serve, and the introduction of competition could cause some economic dislocations. The country has a population only one-tenth that of the United States, located in a band 5,500 kilometers long, almost 90% of the population in a corridor within 320 kilometers of the U.S. border. The remaining population is stretched out in an area reaching several thousand kilometers to the Arctic. In the context of telecommunications, this market configuration has meant that traffic to the U.S. from Canada is a full 60% of east-west Canadian traffic.

2. There has been massive subsidization of local services by long distance. According to Bell Canada's "Report on the 5-way Split Study of 1983," for each C$1.00 of revenue from non-competitive local services, the related costs were C$1.89. *See* Bell Canada, "Report on the 5-Way Split Study for 1983," at 5 (June 1984). Conversely, for non-competitive toll services, services that cost C$0.31 were priced at C$1.00. Put another way, according to Bell, for local services, there was a short-fall of costs over revenues in excess of C$1.2 billion, and, for toll services, revenues exceeded

costs by over C$1.3 billion. It is not surprising, then, that long-haul traffic is diverted to the U.S.

3. As these differentials are built into the rate structure to support intraprovincial services, competition that has the effect of raising intraprovincial rates by applying downward pressure on interprovincial prices will have significant economic ramifications. Similarly, it has long been recognized that high long distance rates have had a significant social and economic impact on Canadians. Thus, the jurisdictional debate—who has the authority to control Telecom Canada pricing—goes beyond mere political jockeying.

4. There is a recognition, at least on the part of Bell Canada and some others, that rate rebalancing will be necessary. First, repricing is inevitable as a response to competitive pressures from the U.S. It is, in the view of Bell Canada and others, the predicate to the introduction of competition in Canada. Rates are necessarily repriced when competition exists: the "5-Way Split Study for 1983" shows that relationships between costs and revenues for competitive services are much more closely aligned—it costs C$0.91 to generate C$1.00 of revenue.

5. Bell Canada has proffered several alternatives for policy-making that point to the close interdependence of the structural and pricing issues. Bell Canada, "Framework for the Future," at 12. These alternatives focus on whether there should be competition and, if so, whether it should occur without, after, or concurrent with rate rebalancing. Bell believes that howsoever the question of permitting competition is resolved, rate rebalancing should begin without delay. It adds that, preferably, the rebalancing process should be completed prior to the introduction of competition. *Id.* at 18-19. Certainly, it would seem unfair to maintain a subsidy in the face of competitive pressures. Bringing rates closer to costs, however, could be viewed as simply one way of diminishing opportunities for competitive entry. Hence, it is not at all clear whether rate rebalancing is designed to forestall competitive entry or simply to lay the groundwork for it.

6. The most urgent competitive issue now facing Canadian regulators is the CNCP application to offer public switched message service. Although CNCP seeks immediate entry, provincial regulators and the existing carriers argue for delay, urging a thorough study of such issues as the effect of repricing on local or universal service, the real impact of bypass, and the extent of any anticipated revenue loss to primary carriers.

7. CNCP has agreed to pay reasonable compensation to Bell Canada and B.C. Tel. for the actual facilities they provide for the interchange of traffic. It is also willing to pay an additional contribution similar to that set forth in the CRTC's Telecom. Decision 79-11, granting CNCP access to Bell Canada's local networks for data and private line voice services. *See* CNCP, "Application for Interchange of Traffic with Public Switched Telephone Networks," at 6-7 (filed Oct. 25, 1983). Eventually, CNCP wants trunk side interconnection, but it has requested line side connection at the outset, in order to have quick entry to the market. If its access arrangements

are of lower quality, CNCP points out, it should contribute less to recovery of local loop costs. Who should decide what charges are appropriate? The questions of interconnection type and quality, and the appropriate level of charges for access, are tied to the costing questions examined in Phase III of the Cost Inquiry. It will be difficult to address and answer those questions on a national basis before settling the jurisdictional problems themselves. As a practical matter, however, resolving the issues with respect to Bell Canada and B.C. Tel. will, to a large extent, have a major impact on national policy.

8. The issue of cross-subsidization of local services and network access—tied as it is to the competitive issue—is dealt with in the context of the Phase III Cost Inquiry. The Inquiry is similar to the cost proceedings in FCC Docket 16528, which established the separations procedure for allocating recoverable costs to the inter- and intrastate jurisdictions. Unlike in the U.S., however, there is no "separations" methodology to use in the Canadian context. The only costing methodology currently in use is Bell Canada's "5-Way Split Process," which breaks down the costs and revenues of Bell Canada's income statement into five categories: four service categories—monopoly local, monopoly toll, competitive network and competitive terminal—and a fifth category—common—which includes costs and revenues not causally related to specific service categories. Report, at 102. The Bell methodology assigns the costs of the local loop to the monopoly local service category on the theory that such costs are causally connected to providing such service.

9. The Phase III Report of the Inquiry Officer recommended that access costs should be assigned to a separate category for costing purposes. Report, at 112. This recommendation was accepted by the CRTC. Telecom. Decision 85-10, at 12. Presumably unbundling this cost would facilitate the calculation of an "access charge" in a way not possible using the current methodology. The Decision concurs with the recommendation of the Report that costs be recovered on a service basis, but calculated in relationship to a small number of broad "generic" service categories. *See* Telecom. Decision 85-10, at 38. For the terrestrial carriers (excluding CNCP), services should be disaggregated to access, monopoly local, monopoly toll, competitive network, competitive terminal, other, and common cost categories. There is, then, the expectation that cost, access and entry issues are interdependent.

10. According to the Phase III Report, auditability is the most important criterion in selecting a costing method. Auditing would be greatly facilitated by structural separation of competitive and monopoly services. Divestiture, however, on the U.S. model is not seen as an option in the near term and the question of separate subsidiaries for equipment has been postponed by the CRTC until sometime this next year. In the absence of legislation such as a generalized Bill C-19, there is still some question as to the CRTC's authority to order structural separation.

11. Competition, or at least a resolution of the jurisdictional issues, may compel a structural reorganization of Bell Canada into a "Bell

Ontario" and a "Bell Quebec." If, for example, a two-tier jurisdictional scheme is ultimately adopted, the regulation of Bell Canada might be transferred to the provincial authorities, with the governments of Ontario and Quebec having responsibility for oversight of intraprovincial services. Parenthetically, some years back, the Hon. William Davis, then Premier of Ontario, stated that the Province had little interest in regulating Bell: when telephone rates went up it was convenient to be able to blame the federal government. If Bell Canada is reorganized in this way, there would remain a question of how—by what Bell "division"—interprovincial (Ontario-Quebec) services will be provided.

12. The introduction of competition will also raise anew the issue of lack of regulatory control over Telecom Canada. Would it, for example, be equitable to regulate new interprovincial facility or even service carriers but not their existing competition? It may not be possible for Bell Canada to expand to compete in offering nationwide services. Some other carriers, particularly new service providers, however, might be created under the auspices of regulators to ensure that competitive pressures will exist to check Telecom Canada's pricing.

13. In deciding the CNCP application for interexchange services, the CRTC must decide to what extent new entrants will be permitted: whether there should be one, several, or an unlimited number of competitors. It is also possible that the CRTC might create a "super-carrier," combining Telecom Canada with Telesat in a new, regulated entity. A duopolistic model—perhaps along the lines of developments in the U.K.—might be consistent with Canadian regulatory policy. If such a duopolistic structure were created, it might, of course, be possible to divide the assets of Telesat among the two competitors by selling not entire satellites but individual satellite transponders.

14. Resale of enhanced services might be permitted on an unlimited basis and basic services on a more liberalized basis. The entry of facilities-based carriers would, however, be constrained. This would allow for significant services competition (*e.g.*, CNCP could resell Telecom Canada services) but would place a check on the possible duplication of facilities.

VI. ISDN CONCEPT IN CANADIAN TELECOMMUNICATIONS POLICY

A. ISDN: An Evolutionary Concept

1. The DOC, which has responsibility for ISDN policy planning at both the international and domestic levels, sees the development of ISDN in Canada as evolutionary. Digital technology is gradually being implemented in the domestic network. The DOC projects that by the late 1980's more than 80% of domestic traffic will be switched by digital facilities, with more than 70% of toll and intertoll trunks being carried on digital carriers.

See F. Leger, "The Prospects of Integrated Services Digital Networks in Canada: The Department Involvement," at 2 (Sept. 1984). Once an integrated digital network is achieved, an ISDN will eventually follow.

2. It is not just the federal government that is moving forward to digitalize the network. Saskatchewan Telecommunications is building a digital network to provide integrated services to over half the residents of the Province. The plans contemplate a 3,400 kilometer, province-wide fiber optics broadband network.

3. ISDN field trials will be conducted in 1986-88 with digital loop technologies. The DOC, however, is moving continuously and in cooperation with carriers in developing policies for the implementation of ISDN. First, it is concerned that technical, economic, and social issues be resolved before rapid movement toward an ISDN environment commences. In particular, there is an acute awareness of the importance of the standard setting process and a strong disinclination to set standards de facto instead of by coordinated planning.

4. The DOC conceptualizes ISDN as integrating services with facilities and not necessarily, as is the case in European planning, of an ISDN where the network itself provides services. The DOC also wants to make sure that those services meet user needs—to justify the capital expense involved in transforming the network to an ISDN. To these ends, it commissioned a study to address some of the key questions surrounding the evolution of ISDN and its impact on Canada. *See* B. A. Howley, "Final Report: A General Study on the Impact of Integrated Services Digital Network (ISDN) Implementation in the Canadian Telecommunications System" (Microtel Pacific Research Ltd.: Aug. 1, 1984) [hereinafter cited as "ISDN Final Report"]. The DOC is keenly interested in the widest participation of all parties—users, suppliers, equipment manufacturers, and existing providers—in the planning process.

B. Effect of U.S. Planning Process

1. Developments in the U.S. will have—and are having—a significant impact on ISDN planning in Canada. Certainly, deregulatory forces are affecting not only traditional telecommunications systems, but are important in the evolution of the Canadian conception of ISDN. Canadians, for example, may choose to establish an ISDN through collaboration, not competition. *See* "ISDN Final Report," at 57. The integrated North American network has influenced the evolution of the Canadian system; however, the Canadians are not so certain that they will want to follow the U.S. lead in ISDN. To the extent that the U.S. has not been the most vigorous participant in the CCITT planning process, Canada may choose one of several courses: to work with the U.S. on a North American ISDN plan, to adhere to the CEPT or international concept, or to hew its own course.

2. The unified North American numbering plan could inhibit the flexibility of a Canadian ISDN. It may be, therefore, that ISDN planning

will provide the opportunity for Canada to develop a numbering plan of its own. There is some question, moreover, whether and how an integrated ISDN numbering plan would affect the flow of ISDN traffic to the U.S. from Canada.

3. The possibility of network interworking through the connection of U.S. and Canadian ISDNs raises the likelihood that some Canadian users would use the U.S. pipe for purely Canadian services, to the detriment of Canadian providers. The "ISDN Final Report," therefore, recommends that particular attention be paid to the interworking of networks in the next CCITT Study Period. *Id.* at 58.

C. Impact of ISDN in Canada

1. The DOC is well aware of the importance of finding and developing the market for ISDN services. It is, however, believed that businesses will—if alerted to the flexibility of ISDN—create sufficient demand to warrant movement toward an ISDN environment. "ISDN Final Report," at 56.

2. There are significant questions not only with respect to the pricing of ISDN services, but also as to the effect of such pricing on basic telephone services. The tariffing issue, the subject of the next round of CCITT study, is one of the thorniest in the ISDN planning process. In the Canadian context, moreover, there is a concern that ISDN pricing could force a realignment of rates and might affect existing cost/revenue relationships.

3. At the same time, there is some interest in a flexible ISDN pricing structure, to create an incentive for widespread use of the digital services. If costs and rates for various ISDN services are unbundled, however, there may be a major impact on basic telephone rates. If basic rates remain high, users may migrate to lower-priced digital equivalents. There has not yet, however, been an extensive Canadian inquiry into ISDN pricing issues.

4. There also will be some questions with respect to the involvement of Canadian manufacturers and suppliers of equipment. The "ISDN Final Report" recommends Canadian content policies for ISDN services and equipment. *Id.* at 56.

5. If ISDN is to evolve from an existing or near-term digital telephone network, there are unanswered questions as to regulatory jurisdiction over the entire ISDN, especially with regard to rates and the terms and conditions of service. There may, for example, be an incentive for carriers to offer ISDN services first to businesses. Such a selective offering could violate the non-discrimination provisions of the Railway Act. Would these provisions be applied to carriers not subject to federal regulation?

6. The DOC sees ISDN regulation as focusing on flexibility. It is wary of defining regulatory boundaries either technologically—*i.e.*, dependent on ISO protocol layers—or as divided between "basic" and "en-

hanced" ISDN services. It is hoped that it will be left to regulators to decide what should be regulated, with a bias in favor of less regulation.

7. Additional issues arise as to whether the existing carriers or Telecom Canada will develop and operate the system. If so, the DOC might seek to exercise jurisdiction over those entities in conjunction with its responsibility for overseeing the planning phase. As the system would be "integrated," without either geographic or service-based "boundary lines," a major jurisdictional realignment might, therefore, be the inevitable consequence of an ISDN environment.

VII. ISSUES FOR THE FUTURE: MECHANISMS FOR CHANGE AND TOMORROW

A. A Sense of Urgency

1. Among Canadian policymakers, suppliers, users, and observers of the telecommunications scene there is a growing sense that action must be taken quickly to resolve what CNCP has termed the "crisis" in policy and regulation. Canadian facilities are being bypassed into the U.S., an ever more frequent occurrence in the aftermath of U.S. deregulation. There is concern that the British Columbia Cam-Net and Longnet phenomenon is just the first visible "tip" of what could be a very large "iceberg" and that economic and other steps must be taken rapidly and decisively.

2. Jurisdictional conflicts have hamstrung the ability of regulators and carriers to respond to competitive challenges. Important issues, such as rate rebalancing for Telecom Canada and nationwide interconnection for CNCP, are being decided—if at all—in an incremental way.

3. Private suppliers of national services perceive the future as fraught with risk and uncertainty. National users are becoming frustrated and carriers and regulators are somewhat beleaguered. There is a deadlock in the policy formation and implementation process.

B. Difficulty of Achieving Consensus

1. The judicial system, aside from the *Alberta Government Telephones* decision, has not played an active role in resolving some of the principle controversies. It is not likely that the jurisdictional issues, for instance, while raised by the court in that case, will ultimately be resolved through litigation. The issues are so intense, however, that the tensions between the federal and provincial governments may not be capable of resolution even politically. In the wake of the *Alberta Government Telephones* decision, however, there does seem to be some relaxation of those tensions.

2. Due to the complexities of the issues and the inherent federal/provincial implications, the Parliamentary process, however, is not itself a likely source of consensus building. For years, federal governments

have tried to enact telecommunications reform legislation, but without success. In the 1976-1978 period, several bills were introduced in Parliament to effectuate the second phase of telecommunications reform. None of the proposals even got so far as to be the subject of debate and committee consideration. Bill C-43, introduced on March 22, 1977, died on the order paper when an election was called. Bill C-24 was introduced on Janaury 26, 1978. Bill C-16 was introduced on November 9, 1978. Bill C-20 was introduced to implement specific aspects of the earlier bills—such as the power of direction over the CRTC—and to respond to the reorganization of Bell Canada. Bill C-20 also died on the order paper. The new Conservative government has reintroduced an amended version of Bill C-20, in the form of two bills—Bill C-19 deals with the Bell reorganization and Bill C-20, among other matters, with the power of direction.

3. Parliamentary committees have not participated in the debate over telecommunications policy at all, much less to the extent, for example, of the communications committees in the U.S. Senate and House of Representatives. In Canada, governmental procedural mechanisms have not been used to facilitate a legislative resolution of the jurisdictional controversies. The new Bills, C-19 and C-20, may, however, give rise to a fruitful Parliamentary debate.

4. The CRTC has traditionally approached and resolved issues on a less sweeping basis than has, for example, the FCC. It is, by and large, far less activist than its U.S. counterpart; in part this is because it has fewer resources and a more limited mandate. Its lack of jurisdiction over the principal interexchange carrier, Telecom Canada, obviously limits its reach considerably. Perhaps for this reason, the CRTC has not been particularly active on the jurisdictional front. In Telecom. Decision 81-13 it effectively dodged the question of whether it could or would attempt to regulate TCTS rates directly.

5. The CRTC recently adopted a slightly more future-oriented policy perspective by initiating the interexchange entry proceeding in connection with the CNCP application for public message switched interconnection. It may be that the CRTC will move ahead on structural or interconnection issues in light of the more expansive scope of the interexchange proceeding, and if the *Alberta Government Telephones* decision is sustained on appeal. There are, however, significant limitations in the CRTC's statutory authority. There is no assurance, for example, that it has the powers to forbear, to force structural separation and create subsidiaries, or even to compel the federally-regulated carriers to take particular positions in Telecom Canada with respect to the interprovincial rate structure.

6. The DOC has power over the issuance of radio licenses but has not, except in the case of cellular radio licensing, exercised that power to force regulatory decisions. In addition, the DOC has been quite enmeshed in media policy for some time. The DOC has attempted to lead negotiations on the jurisdictional issues between the federal and provincial governments. It has not, however, wanted a "two front" war with the provinces, over both

media and telecommunications policy. The DOC is now becoming more active in the formulation of telecommunications policy in connection with the Telecommunications Policy Review that is currently underway.

7. Users have been less active in forcing the debate or setting the agenda than has been the case in the U.S. In part, this may be because large businesses can and do make use of the "U.S. bypass option." Perhaps many users only avail themselves of the lower-priced local services and are unwilling to see that price structure disturbed.

C. Despite Difficulties, Signs of Convergence

1. The level of frustration has begun to compel the carriers to seek a resolution of the jurisdictional issues. Further incentives to resolve disputes are provided by developments in the U.S. and the perceived need to maintain usage of Canadian facilities.

2. The new Conservative government is committed to better relations with the provinces than were the Trudeau Liberal governments. And, in general, the Conservatives are expected to be much more inclined to defer to the provinces than were the Liberals. Thus, there may be more accommodation on federal-provincial issues. Moreover, the "pro-business" orientation of the new government may well lead to liberalization if not privatization of some elements of the Canadian telecommunications structure.

3. The CRTC is increasingly in a better position for resolving some major issues. Between the CNCP interexchange proceeding and the authority of the *Alberta Government Telephones* decision, it is seized with the mechanisms and tools with which to make significant progress on several troubling policy problems.

D. Areas for Resolution

1. Privatization of Telesat

As the Government appears to be moving ahead on privatizing Teleglobe, *see supra* Section III.B., it is apparently exploring the possibility of privatizing its shares of Telesat as well. If it does so, it might require that the purchaser be a federally-regulated carrier. As noted, Bell Canada has recently offered to purchase the 50% government stake in Telesat and Teleglobe, subsequently undertaking to sell parts of these carriers to the other Canadian carriers, including CNCP and, possibly, others. This arrangement would still maintain Telesat's role as a carrier's carrier. If, however, Telesat were to be pulled out of Telecom Canada and not supported directly by other carriers, there would be pressure for the restructuring of the interexchange carrier. Another alternative would be, in effect, to "condominiumize" Telesat, whereby transponders could be sold to carriers, broadcasters, or other users. Thus, the government could choose to disperse all of its assets, or Telesat could become a "space agency," charged with the task of procuring service for carriers.

2. Restructuring of Telecom Canada

There are certain pressures for a restructuring of Telecom Canada. Certainly, internal pressures—disagreements among members—and external forces—diminution in the cross-subsidy due to emerging competition—could lead to a reorganization of Telecom Canada. One possibility is the emergence of an entirely new long distance carrier. Another is that Telecom Canada could acquire IRU-like interests in the facilities of its member companies. Telecom Canada could become a "resale carrier" of its former members' services.

3. Jurisdictional Issue

Creating a new or restructured carrier to replace Telecom Canada could resolve the question of whether the CRTC has jurisdiction over interprovincial services. For, it is probable that the government, in proposing the creation of any such entity, would make certain that it would be subject to federal jurisdiction. Nevertheless, fundamental questions would remain with respect to that new carrier's relationship with the provincial companies and regulators. There are a number of alternative ways of dealing with this relationship; these need to be explored. One option would be to have the new entity obtain interconnection on a nondiscriminatory basis; however, control over the rates and terms of interconnection might remain vested in the provincial authorities. Alternatively, a joint board, the subject of discussions during the last few years, could oversee the interconnection arrangements.

4. Legislative Resolution

The legislative route, though not so successful in the past, may become more viable in light of the Parliamentary majority that the new government enjoys. It may be that the *Alberta Government Telephones* decision will serve as a stimulus for movement by legislators, perhaps even with respect to the crown immunity issue. Such a move is likely to meet with political resistance from provincial governments. A telecommunications bill could deal with issues such as the creation of a new carrier, privatization, and the jurisdictional consequences of taking such steps. For example, a bill might focus on provisions guaranteeing nondiscrimination in interconnection, or on the CRTC's flexibility with respect to forbearance or its power to enforce structural separations requirements to prevent cross-subsidization. The federal-provincial dialogue or public sector-private sector negotiations might precipitate such a bill.

VIII. CONSEQUENCES OF COMPETITION IN INTERNATIONAL SERVICES

A. Interconnection Arrangements with U.S.

1. During the last year Canadian carriers have concluded connecting agreements with the U.S. competitors of AT&T; AT&T, however, still carries the majority of U.S.-Canada traffic. MCI has been offering switched voice service from the U.S. to major Canadian metropolitan areas since 1983; now, however, it will be providing service to all of Canada for certain U.S. "equal access" customers. GTE/Sprint will offer switched voice service to Canada, serving five major areas initially before expanding in the near future. GTE/Sprint forecasts that its penetration of the switched voice market will be 10.2% by 1987. SBS will offer basic telephone service to almost anyplace in Canada, and, through an agreement with Telesat, will provide private networking capabilities to U.S. and Canadian corporations. The effect of these new entrants on Canadian carriers is unclear, though the process of negotiating interconnection arrangements and maintaining carrier control of Canada-U.S. rates and traffic may minimize their impact.

2. It is likely that the Canadian response to competition is a forerunner of the kinds of agreements that other administrations will reach. (MCI's arrangement in Belgium and elsewhere being an example.) Thus, the resolution of the issues raised in Canada may be instructive with respect to the liberalization of the market for international services elsewhere.

3. Telecom Canada has now begun to offer a discount, direct-dial service into the U.S. This "Teleplus 1022" service uses MCI to deliver U.S.-bound Canadian traffic and already has 6000 subscribers in Toronto, Ottawa, and Montreal. It would not be surprising if other services were made available to Canadain users. Together these services are, of course, intended to protect the Canadian market from the competition in the U.S.

4. The entry of multiple service providers into the international market raises a series of technical issues. First, facilities planning and circuit utilization will not be made easier as traffic forecasting is made more complicated by the multiplicity of carriers. There are also a number of questions with respect to the access arrangements that may have to be implemented in Canada. One issue is how subscribers to the Teleplus 1022 service can select a non-AT&T carrier to deliver the traffic in the U.S. There are, however, no plans in Canada to require "equal access" equivalent to the corresponding requirement in the U.S. Thus, in the short-term, Canadian customers' dial-up access to a non-AT&T service is likely to be more difficult than using AT&T.

5. The emergence of a transborder market with more than one carrier may necessitate a reconfiguration of the network, perhaps with a movement toward a "gateways" facilities structure. Unlike other international services (*e.g.*, Canada-Europe), the North American network has not

previously used gateways. Nevertheless, for purposes of routing traffic to and from U.S. carriers that customers have selected, and in the absence of equal access at Canadian local exchanges, gateway switches may be a practical solution to a difficult technical problem.

6. The coordination and facilities planning processes may also raise certain competitive issues. Will joint planning of facilities lead to antitrust problems? There are currently no adequate procedures or mechanisms for addressing the planning questions. Perhaps an informal U.S.-Canada dialogue modeled on the ongoing "Niagara" discussions might be useful. Developing such mechanisms will need to be the focus of attention in the near-term.

B. International Competition in Satellite Services

Recent or anticipated developments in international satellite services will also have an impact in Canada. Non-Canadian regional systems may evolve into competitive alternatives to Telesat or Teleglobe. A spot beam on the French satellite Telecom-1 is aimed at the islands of St. Pierre and Miquelon, but could readily serve eastern Canada; the French have disclaimed any intent to use it for such purposes, but they have done so in an environment still free from actual private international satellite systems. If the Telecom-1 satellite is used for transborder or international services, there will be issues regarding traffic routing and facilities planning. Some of these issues are addressed in current arrangements for transborder satellite services and Intelsat coordination; others raise new questions that will have to be addressed by Canadian carriers and policymakers.

CHAPTER V
JAPAN

TABLE OF CONTENTS

CHAPTER V
JAPAN

I. INTRODUCTION AND OVERVIEW

The Japanese telecommunications industry is currently undergoing the first phase of a difficult and far-reaching transformation. The country has adopted two new telecommunications laws that are likely to chart the course for change into the next century. Now the task of deciding on the details of the policies, to fit within the broad legislative framework, confronts policymakers. The early stages of this process already have shown that the laws leave ample room for change and for redirection. Thus, the future of the Japanese liberalization process resides largely within the power of those undertaking the task of implementation.

A. Problems of Implementing Competition: Transitional Issues for the Dominant Carrier

1. There is a broad consensus on the major initial objectives of the changes: to introduce competition into the domestic telecommunications market and to transform Nippon Telegraph and Telephone Corp. ("NTT") from a huge, government-owned monopolist into a more efficient, privately-owned, competitive company. However, the process of implementing the new laws—the Telecommunications Business Law and the Nippon Denshin Denwa Kabushiki Kaisha Law ("NTT Law") has raised a broad spectrum of issues and unanswered questions.

2. The Japanese situation often is viewed as only one or two years behind the pace of U.S. developments. However, the reality may differ somewhat from the common perception. Efforts to introduce competition into the U.S. telecommunications industry have been ongoing for more than two decades; in Japan, this process is just beginning. Much has been done in the United States to establish an infrastructure of dispute-resolution procedures designed to cope with the institutional and the industrial problems expected to accompany any radical market alteration. Attention also has been paid to developing accounting and cost allocation procedures to handle the restructuring of the monopolistic, dominant domestic facilities and services provider, American Telephone & Telegraph Co. ("AT&T"). Much of this infrastructure does not yet exist in Japan. However, a number of key policy disputes likely to appear in the Japanese situation already have been resolved in the American regulatory context. These policy resolutions may serve as a basis for Japan's approach to grappling with its own, similar problems.

3. NTT has embraced many of the proposed changes. They are viewed as ways of possibly revitalizing the corporation and positioning it to compete more effectively in a global market. NTT already has begun to

restructure itself along functional lines. This process, designed to enable it to market its products and services in a competitive environment, will take some time to complete. The speed of change may depend substantially on the extent to which NTT identifies important transitional issues and devises detailed procedures for resolving them in cooperation with potential competitors and with relevant governmental entities.

4. One of the major problems facing NTT is the question of how to price its services on a competitive basis. NTT will have to begin developing more structured systems of accounts as well as cost allocation procedures. Otherwise, its effort to respond to pricing changes by its new competitors will become entangled in controversy. It may be accused of engaging in cross-subsidization to keep the price of competitive services unfairly low (through the use of excess profits earned on quasi-monopolistic services, such as basic voice transmission). It also may be charged with employing other anti-competitive pricing tactics made possible by its dominant market position.

5. Some of NTT's competitors may require access to certain network-related technical information as well as to data about network traffic or service users (*i.e.*, customer lists). Without such data, it may be exceedingly difficult for new, facilities-based competitors to formulate realistic competitive strategies. Therefore, decisions will have to be made—either by NTT or by the government—about the degree to which NTT should assist a competitor, at least during the early transitional period. Sharing such information may be important to NTT if the new policies intended to give NTT greater pricing and financial independence are not to falter at the outset. NTT needs at least one potential competitor for the competitive approach inherent in the Telecommunications Business Law to be viable.

6. Another difficult issue to be resolved at the outset is the question of access charges. Japanese policymakers, both in and out of the government, undoubtedly will benefit from the U.S. experience as well as from the access arrangements now being worked out in the United Kingdom and elsewhere. There are, nevertheless, an extraordinary number of difficult issues that will have to be the subject of consultation among NTT, its new competitors, and the Ministry of Posts and Telecommunications ("MPT").

7. There also are issues relating to access to research and development and to patent information that is owned by NTT. These issues have not yet been addressed, although industry groups examining the feasibility of competition in the transmission field are reviewing them.

B. Grappling With the Effects of Liberalization

1. The degree of liberalization that the new laws would accomplish was initially the subject of significant debate. The laws left many vital issues open to resolution through MPT ordinances. Although many

questions still remain, the ordinances that the MPT drafted and put into effect on April 1, 1985 (the effective date of the new laws), have embraced an ambitious program to encourage significant competition in both the facilities and services markets. In addition, the Ministry's decision to authorize five new facilities-based competitors (rather than just one, as had initially been speculated), and its apparent commitment to liberalizing the international market, as well as the domestic one, further underscore the breadth and depth of the changes that loom ahead.

2. The complex influences involved in shaping the liberalization should not be ignored.

a. Debate among the Ministries—particularly between the MPT and the Ministry of International Trade and Industry ("MITI")—have affected both the new laws and the ordinances.

b. The concerns of both users and service providers also have influenced decisions about service availability, pricing, resale, and the degree of regulation imposed by the government.

c. Finally, international trade pressures have had a remarkable effect on the implementation process. Extensive bilateral trade talks earlier this year between the U.S. and Japan have had a major impact on the MPT's ordinances. U.S. pressure for Japan to open its telecommunications market to foreign businesses has pushed the liberalization process quite far. Most notably, the U.S. position had a significant impact on the MPT's decision to break down (almost obliterate) the legislative division between large-scale ("Special Type II") and small-scale ("General Type II") competitive service providers. With its ordinances, the Ministry has so expanded the scope of the unregulated General Type II category that there is little apparent need for new entrants to seek registration as a Special Type II business (which carries with it certain regulatory burdens). This decision has washed away initial concerns that the Ministry would use its power over Special Type II businesses to limit the amount of foreign involvement in large value-added networks ("VANs").

3. Despite all of this activity, Japan still faces a significant number of unresolved issues:

a. The MPT must decide how to coordinate the exercise of its licensing jurisdiction with the independent authority of the Ministries of Transport and Construction. These ministries decide on access to rights-of-way that will be in great demand by new telecommunications facilities builders. In one case—that of cable television—the ministries already have come into conflict. The Ministry of Construction has required cable companies to construct their networks underground (rather than allowing wires to be strung along utility poles). This requirement has imposed significant added costs on cable operators that may deter the kind of expansion of systems the MPT desired.

b. Issues of NTT structure must be resolved. Separate subsidiaries to provide services other than basic switched transmission services may be voluntarily adopted. The terms of any such subsidiary's relationship with the underlying carrier have to be regulated—or, at least, clearly defined. The MPT will assume the task of resolving these issues. In grappling with questions about NTT's future, the Ministry will have to take account of a broad spectrum of concerns. This will require it to adjust its focus. Rather than functioning as a kind of consultative unit that manages telecommunications issues in conjunction with NTT, the Ministry will need to begin establishing general policies. As competition takes hold in the Japanese market, the MPT will have to view NTT in terms of its effect on both competitors and users. Although the Japanese do not foresee any possibility that competition will cause the creation of an independent regulatory body such as the Federal Communications Commission (U.S.) or the Office of Telecommunications (U.K.), liberalization certainly will require the MPT to assume an unfamiliar role.

c. The degree to which domestic satellite services can be integrated into the working plans of new competitors needs to be determined. The government's decision to authorize two facilities–based carriers who will use U.S. satellite technology suggests that this area will undergo fast and radical changes over the next few years. Domestic satellite service may be augmented further by efforts to expand the availability of transponder capacity through either an acceleration of Japan's own, growing space program or the redeployment of satellites now serving other countries.

d. Some degree of reconciliation between international and domestic policies needs to be considered. Changes in the Japanese domestic market will have a spillover effect on transborder communications. The terms and conditions under which unregulated domestic VANs can operate internationally will require particularly careful attention. Use of international circuits by these networks may be viewed as an impermissible form of international circuit capacity resale. To the degree that these domestic VANs are prohibited from interconnecting and expanding internationally, the Japanese market for value-added services generally may suffer. This is particularly true inasmuch as Japan expects to have a significant number of foreign multinational corporations providing VANs.

II. BACKGROUND ISSUES: POLICY DEVELOPMENT

A. Introduction: Development of the Telephone System

1. Since the early 1950s, the Japanese telecommunications market has depended on the facilities and services provided by NTT (the sole domestic carrier) and by Kokusai Denshin Denwa Co., Ltd. ("KDD") (the sole international carrier). These two public corporations were established in the wake of a March, 1950, report from the Advisory Council for the Reconstruction of Telegraph and Telephone. The report recommended that telegraph and telephone services should be transferred from direct govern-

ment control to the control of newly formed public corporations. Since the turn of the century, the Ministry of Communications had operated telephone and telegraph facilities on a monopoly basis.

2. NTT was established in 1952 as a public corporation. KDD was formed in 1953 as a privately held company. The two operations assumed most of the functions formerly carried out by the Ministry of Communications. The Ministry of Postal Services assumed the remaining duties of the old Communications Ministry and was renamed the Ministry of Posts and Telecommunications ("MPT").

3. During the years of the government-run telephone and telegraph monopolies, prescribed by the Telegraph Law of 1890, anyone wishing to construct private telecommunciations lines was required to get prior permission from the Ministry of Communications. This situation continued until 1953, when the Wire Telecommunication Law of 1953 and the Public Telecommunication Law of 1953 were adopted. These two laws, which have been amended in significant ways since their adoption, were the country's primary telecommunications legislation until the adoption of the 1984 laws. The new laws have, however, drastically altered the regulatory environment. They have authorized a liberalized use of telecommunications facilities, ended the domestic telecommunications monopoly of NTT, and restructured NTT as a private corporation prepared to participate in a competitive marketplace. They also have raised the possibility of permitting significant competition with KDD in the international services market.

B. Summary of the 1953 Legislation

1. In tandem, the two 1953 telecommunications laws were designed to establish and to preserve the communications monopolies of NTT and KDD. Their purpose was to provide a set of principles from which NTT could build an efficient and reliable nationwide telephone system and from which KDD could establish a similarly dependable network for international telephone transmissions. *See* Public Telecommunication Law, at Art. 1. To promote this goal, the companies were given virtually absolute control of the relevant facilities and services—wire transmission systems. They were allowed to expand and to develop their networks without the threat of competitive pressures.

a. The destruction of telecommunications facilities during the war required Japan to undertake a major reconstruction effort.

b. Two of NTT's major achievements during this period of monopolistic control were the completion of a nationwide, automatic dialing system and the installation of customer premises equipment in all homes and businesses requesting such installation.

2. The Public Telecommunication Law gave to both NTT and KDD complete control of the facilities and services necessary to carry out the "intermediation of communications between other persons," as the law defined "public telecommunication service." *Id.* at Art. 2(3). The law de-

fined "telecommunication" broadly to mean "any emission, transmission or reception of signal codes, sounds or images by wire, radio or other electromagnetic system." *Id.* at Art. 2(1).

3. The Wire Telecommunication Law protected NTT's and KDD's monopoly control of wire transmission facilities. The law permitted private construction of wire facilities—a liberalization as compared with the policy before 1953. However, the MPT still had to authorize the construction of any such facilities that would affect the public telecommunications circuits. (Private facilities that would not in any way affect public circuits merely had to be reported to the MPT.) In this way, the Ministry was able to control the construction of wire facilities to prevent private entrepreneurs from building networks that would compete with the public telecommunications system. Private facilities were not permitted to carry third-party communications. This limitation guaranteed that NTT and KDD would operate as the sole public telecommunications service providers.

4. The laws, in effect, prohibited third parties from providing message switching services to the public. They also outlawed shared use of leased lines and prevented the interconnection of privately operated facilities to the network.

5. Because Japan is such a geographically narrow country, it has only a small number of microwave frequencies that can be used as transmission links. As a result, only NTT and KDD have been permitted to construct these links for use on a common carrier basis—except that certain governmental units (*e.g.*, Japan National Railway and the Ministry of Construction) have been able to use microwave links for private communications. This limitation is significantly different from the one imposed on wire communications, where anyone can build wire facilities.

C. Liberalization of Facilities Use: 1971-1981

1. The competitive pressures exerted by the business community, which sought to use the telecommunications network for data transmission and for facsimile communications, brought into question the efficacy of the restrictive policies surrounding the use of the public network. With an infant information processing industry seeking to expand, the narrow scope of permissible communications represented an almost insurmountable obstacle. Thus, in 1971 the MPT proposed a variety of amendments to the Public Telecommmunications Law that would permit the telephone network to accommodate some of the new business traffic.

2. Data transmission over the NTT system was authorized to take place in either of two ways: through use of a private, leased line (called a "specified circuit"), or directly through public circuits. *See* Public Telecommunication Law, at Art. 55(10). Thus, remote data processing activities could be conducted through dedicated circuits, allowing constant computer-to-terminal communications, or on a dial-up basis, with connections made through the ordinary telephone network. NTT was required to accept re-

quests for such circuit usage "within the scope of its budget." *Id.* at Arts. 55-(11), -(17).

3. Shared use of a specified circuit was permitted in two circumstances: (1) when the users have a business relationship generally and the use to be made of the circuit falls within one of the particular arrangements described in MPT ordinances, or (2) when the users have a "considerable" business relationship and the use to be made of the circuit is ruled by the MPT to pose no threat to the NTT system. *Id.* The second standard, in which users are affiliated, clearly was designed to provide more flexibility in shared-use arrangements. So long as the functions carried out by NTT were not being duplicated in a manner potentially detrimental to the public network (possibly because it would divert traffic away from NTT), shared-use plans could be approved. There was less concern about message-switching activities between closely-related users than between unaffiliated parties. The latter situation posed a greater threat of evolving into a third-party transmission service offering that would compete directly with NTT. Where users were closely affiliated, intra-corporate or industry-related traffic might be shared efficiently without fear that the private line use arrangement was providing a significant substitute for the public switched network. The position adopted reflected a clear compromise between business interests and the concerns of NTT.

4. The law further limited NTT's power to accept private line requests if the computer equipment to be connected to the circuit would damage the NTT system, if the connection would require difficult modification of the NTT system, or if the user owed, or was likely not to pay, leased circuit service charges. *Id.*

5. A private line user was prohibited from using the line to transmit third-party communications, this being a function reserved for NTT. *Id.*

6. Finally, the amendments authorized NTT to offer its own data processing services, connecting users to NTT computers by means of NTT circuits. *Id.* at Arts. 55-(19) - (22).

7. Circuit leasing also was authorized in certain circumstances where the lines would be used for services other than data processing. The general lease provisions, however, required NTT to accept a leasing request only when it (1) was not "detrimental" to the provision of public telecommunication services or (2) was not "extremely detrimental" to public telecommunications service and was "especially necessary in the public interest." *Id.* at Art. 56. Simple resale of circuit capacity still was prohibited. In addition, a lessee could not use the leased circuits to transmit third-party communications except in certain narrowly defined circumstances. These circumstances included situations in which the leased lines connected privately-held systems that were part of a single business or closely related businesses, or where the communications were carried to serve the public interest (for such things as emergency messages or police and fire communications). *Id.* at Art. 64; Wire Telecommunication Law, at Art. 9.

8. Article 106 of the Public Telecommunication Law authorized interconnection of privately owned wires to the NTT network. This connection could be made to link the wires to a private branch exchange or to leased circuits. Interconnection also could be made where it was "necessary for the public interest." Public Telecommunication Law, at Art. 106. Other provisions of the Public Telecommunication Law that prohibited the use of leased circuits or of private branch equipment for the purpose of transmitting or switching third-party messages prevented this interconnection from becoming a means for bypassing the NTT network.

9. A significant omission from the 1971 amendments was any authorization for the provision of value-added services by third parties. Restrictions on the use of leased circuits to *transmit* third-party communications prevented users of the NTT system from offering their data processing capacity to other individuals or businesses, except when connections were made over public circuits. In addition, there were no provisions permitting private circuit users to offer these circuits to third parties as message transmission services that included such value-added enhancements as packet switching.

10. NTT, which was authorized to provide data processing functions using its circuits, could offer users certain computer services over dedicated lines. There was no private competition, however, to spark innovation and to expand the variety of service offerings. In 1979, NTT also began to offer circuit switching and packet switching over its digital data exchange ("DDX") data network. It also made available to users a facsimile communications network. This expansion of the scope of NTT's business raised questions about the degree to which a monopolist should be permitted to diversify, particularly into areas other than basic transmission services.

D. Liberalization of Facilities: 1981-1984

1. On October 23, 1982, the Public Telecommunication Law was again revised, and an MPT ordinance was issued under the authority of Art. 55-(13) of the Public Telecommunication Law. These actions significantly liberalized third-party use of NTT circuits.

2. The amendments authorized the interconnection of leased circuits in a wide range of configurations, even including interconnection to the NTT network. The restrictive conditions of Article 106 were practically eliminated. The MPT still was required, however, to approve interconnection of leased lines that joined the NTT system at both ends. This approval requirement permitted the MPT to prevent leasing arrangements that allowed third parties to provide a circuit resale service offering only basic transmission services, including message switching. Such functions still were preserved solely for NTT. In addition, restrictions were imposed on any interconnection arrangements that permitted one of the parties to perform simple message switching functions for another user's communications.

3. Shared use restrictions were reduced significantly. NTT was permitted to allow any shared use of leased data circuits if (1) no computer involved in the network conducted message-switching (other than incidental switching required to use the computer), or if (2) no user switched otherwise unprocessed data from another user. The degree of merely "incidental" message switching was not clearly defined.

4. In tandem, these requirements ensured that a sharing arrangement did not involve a user in the business of simple data transmission and switching. If, however, the users sharing a circuit had a "close business relationship," they could share a leased circuit even to perform only simple switching activities. This "close relationship" was defined to mean long-term business arrangements, such as contracts or sales arrangements, in which the parties have a clear common interest. *See* NTT, *New Data Communications Circuit Utilization Conditions in Japan* (Pub. No. 32-2) (1982) [hereinafter cited as NTT, *New Circuit Utilization*].

5. The ministerial ordinance adopted in accordance with the 1982 reforms brought the first authorization of privately-offered VAN services. These services were permitted to use NTT circuits to link closely affiliated groups of small or medium-sized users. It was expected that much of the Japanese attention to developing VANs would involve the incorporation of data processing operations, rather than the enhancement of transmission capabilities. Although VANs were limited to smaller groups of affiliated users, it still was expected that much of the country's demand for VANs would be satisfied. Essential links between manufacturers, wholesalers, and retailers—thought to be the greatest immediate market for value-added services—would be permitted by the terms of the revised ordinance. *See* KDD, *Second Stage in Liberalization of Data Communications and VAN Service* (1983) (unpublished).

6. The number of participants in a VAN was defined by industry category. Retailers or service providers with capital of up to 10 million yen and with fifty or fewer employees, wholesalers with capital of up to 30 million yen and with 100 or fewer employees, and other industries with capital of up to 100 million yen and with 300 or fewer employees, all were permitted to participate in value-added service offerings. All the participants in a service had to share a business affiliation equivalent to a parent-subsidiary, joint venture, or retailer-wholesaler-manufacturer relationship.

7. Basic communications services that were not permitted as VAN offerings included circuit switching, packet switching, facsimile services, and "others, which are already offered by NTT on an experimental basis. . . ." Telephone, telex, telegram, and circuit leasing services were not permissible VAN applications: these services represented the primary activities of NTT. Before offering a VAN, the offeror had to notify the MPT of the services to be offered, the facilities to be used, the privacy protections to be

afforded, and the expected users (including their respective sizes and their relationship to each other). The MPT could order modifications in a planned service as it thought necessary. NTT, *New Circuit Utilization, supra,* at 27-28.

8. One reason given for the decision to permit value-added services to be offered to smaller business units was a claim made by MITI—and apparently believed by certain politicians. MITI had argued that if all VANs were to remain prohibited, a chasm would develop between those firms large enough to install their own computers and smaller companies not able to do so. By allowing value-added services to be distributed through the NTT network, smaller companies could take advantage of the computer system capabilities of organizations willing to provide third-party services.

9. With this liberalization, NTT's only monopoly markets were basic telephone services, telex, and telegram. (The telex and telegram markets, however, were subject to erosion from intra-corporate VANs and from other enhanced service operations beginning to develop in the wake of the 1982 liberalization.) Unlike the monopoly carrier in the United States, though, NTT was able to provide data processing services, a market open to competition.

10. A debate arose in the Japanese business community as to whether NTT should be permitted to operate outside of the area of basic transmission services. While some people believed that NTT should be confined to these basic services, NTT sought to move into new telecommunications fields, to take advantage of the potentially lucrative new services. A reconsideration of NTT's monopoly status and its scope of authorized services seemed in order.

11. The new telecommunications laws represent the government's decisions about to how to resolve the situation in which NTT is caught in the middle of a transitional period. The Japanese telecommunications market is moving from an era in which traditional phone service needed to be the focus to one in which the value-added service markets, providing services primarily for data processing operations, demand greater attention. This change in emphasis required that NTT be given some flexibility to adjust its own operational focus. The MPT recognized that the time for requiring an NTT monopoly to spend most of its effort ensuring that Japan had a nationwide, efficient telephone and telegraph system had passed.

E. Institutional Impacts on Policy Development

1. In the telecommunications field, a large number of ministries have been involved in the policymaking process. This is because of the great scope and diversity of interests affected. The Japanese Information Processing Development Center ("JIPDEC"), for example, had prepared a list of approximately 100 related laws that required amendment in connection with adoption of the new telecommunications legislation.

2. The MPT is the ministry most directly involved. With the increased convergence of computers and communications, the scope of

MPT's interests has widened and has infringed, to some degree, upon MITI's traditional interest in the development of the computer and electronics industries.

a. The MPT recently has been reorganized to assume the new responsibilities conferrred on it by the new laws. The Ministry now has three bureaus—Communications, Telecommunications Policy, and Broadcasting.

b. Once primarily the overseer of NTT, the Ministry now is being forced to evolve into a more generalized, policymaking unit. Its power over NTT has been increased, and it now also must supervise NTT's relationship with its new competitors. As a result, the MPT no longer can function in a purely consultative fashion, dealing with NTT on a bilateral basis. It must look more broadly at the marketplace and make generalized policy judgments.

c. A significant new responsibility for the MPT is the oversight of NTT tariffs. The new laws have transferred this rate-setting power from the Diet to the MPT. While this change is likely to depoliticize the tariffing process, it also will burden the Ministry with the job of devising some sort of rate formulas under which it can evaluate NTT pricing policies. Once again, these judgments will require decisions made in light of overall market considerations. The interests of NTT—and its customers—alone cannot be the determinants of what is and is not proper.

d. Finally, the Ministry also must grapple with deciding how best to apply the liberalization policies of the new laws to KDD and to the international services market. This involves some exceedingly complex and difficult judgments and is discussed fully below. *See infra* Section VIII.

3. MITI also has been reorganized. The Electronic Policy Division of the Machinery and Information Industries Bureau of MITI is the key decisionmaking entity.

a. MITI's basic concern has been to assure that the new telecommunications laws provide for a competitively viable marketplace and that regulatory control over the computer industry and related businesses is minimized. A dispute with the MPT has developed over recently proposed communications protocols. MITI contends that such standard-setting has always, and is still, within its "jurisdiction." It has criticized the standards proposed by the MPT and has sought to develop its own.

b. MITI also has taken an interest in the question of which entities will be able to enter the new market for the provision of telecommunications transmission services. At one time there had been some discussion of having MITI assume a significant role in managing the new competitive market; however, the MPT has the major responsibility for this job.

4. The Ministry of Transport also is involved in this process because of its oversight of Japan National Railways ("JNR"). JNR, like NTT, is a public corporation that may be privatized. However, unlike NTT, JNR has, over the years, been an exceedingly unprofitable entity. Yet, JNR also

has been one of the few entities authorized to maintain and to operate microwave facilities independently of NTT. Therefore, it has a group of experienced radio engineers who would be in a position to install and to operate additional microwave facilities.

a. It has decided, however, to construct a fiber optic network along its rights-of-way that would provide basic transmission services in competition with NTT. The company formed to undertake this project is called Nihon Telecom.

b. JNR rejected requests from Kyocera, the world's largest manufacturer of ceramic integrated circuits, to establish a joint operating company to compete with NTT. Kyocera is, nonetheless, organizing what it hopes will be a formidable competitor to NTT. *See infra* Section III.C.1.

5. The Ministry of Construction ("MOC") has been involved in two aspects of evolving telecommunications developments.

a. First, it has expressed interest in the installation of fiber optic facilities along the rights-of-way of public highways. However, unlike the Ministry of Transport or JNR, the MOC has little or no experience or expertise in the telecommunications field. Nonetheless, its interest has prompted the Japan Public Highway Corp., which manages the country's highways, to form Teleway Japan. The new venture, which includes companies such as Toyota and Nissan, which are closely tied to the MOC, will install these fiber optic facilities along the highways. Kyocera and Mitsui also are involved in the project.

b. The MOC also has responsibility for control of the poles in local areas along which cable television facilities would have to be installed. In the middle of June, 1984, the MOC issued a policy declaration that cable television facilities would have to be installed underground, instead of being attached to poles. This step was viewed as very detrimental to the future of the cable television industry. However, some observers viewed it as an effort to gain leverage in negotiations with the MPT—or with the entities that would be authorized to compete with NTT.

6. The Ministry of Finance ("MOF") has a role in this process through ordinances that affect the nature of the transactions and other services that financial institutions can offer. The MOF essentially reserves the right to oversee or to approve the fees for any bank-related transaction.

a. Under regulations adopted by the MOF, an official funds transfer network and a private data network run by a number of banks have begun to operate. NTT has a role in this latter network, which is called the Zengin System. This system handles electronic messages regarding many domestic exchange transactions and also operates as an electronic account settlement system. Virtually all of Japan's banks participate, and the system is coordinated by the Tokyo Bankers Association, Inc. The Bank of Japan serves as the settlement bank, and NTT provides and manages the data processing and transmission equipment and services. A data communications center in Tokyo is linked by NTT leased lines to Zengin terminals in all member banks. *See The Zengin System: A Nationwide Data Communications*

System for Financial Institutions, 59 Japan Computer Quarterly 27 (1984) (formerly JIPDEC Report).

b. Because of the overlay of MOF regulations, some financial institutions have established separate corporations through which data processing and other information-related services are operated. It is not clear how any MOF regulations may have a bearing on the operation by banks of various new VAN services authorized by the new legislation.

7. Overall, there are a number of ministries involved in the policy process; however, there also is no clear-cut mechanism for telecommunications policy coordination. The autonomy and independence of the various ministries run deep. Each ministry has close ties with key members of the Diet, some of whom once served as vice-ministers and maintain a focus on the issues of concern to that ministry. Former ministers also remain active in the private sector, further complicating the web of influence that can affect ministry decisionmaking. There is a Cabinet-level council which often resolves procedural disputes among the different ministries. There is, however, no routine process for integrating the different threads essential to a national telecommunications policy.

F. The MPT Report: Telecommunications Policy Objectives

In order to study the changes taking place in the telecommunications market and the implications that these changes had for Japan's future, the Telecommunications Policy Bureau of the MPT established the Telecommunications Advisory Council in October, 1980. This twenty-four-member ministerial council, with representatives from academic institutions as well as from the telecommunications industry, assisted by the Research Institute of Telecommunications and Economics, conducted a comprehensive examination of the industry and released a report in August, 1981. The document, *A Vision of Telecommunications Policy in the '80s* (1981), sets out a series of fundamental policy issues that the Japanese must face as a result of the growth of data processing and the increasingly competitive opportunities in the communications market. The report is divided into three parts: the first examines fundamental issues in telecommunications policy, the second looks at the social implications of the changing information marketplace, and the third reviews significant technological developments.

1. Introduction

The report identifies the "more sophisticated and diversified" needs of telecommunications users, in conjunction with the development of the telephone system in Japan and "rapid technological progress," as the reasons for change in the marketplace requiring a reassessment of regulatory policy. *Id.* at 5. The report also identifies society's growing dependence on information as a catalyst for change. This dependence has prompted a need to reconsider privacy issues, to pay increased attention to the reliability of transmission networks, and to plan some degree of coordination among various nations—to be certain that one country's policies do not impose a harmful, external effect on another's.

2. *Basic Considerations*

The report identifies regulatory flexibility as a vital goal of Japanese telecommunications policymaking. It states that existing concepts should not be unduly relied upon, and that the move away from public sector monopolization must be embraced, in order to exploit private sector innovation. As telecommunications also is seen as intimately involved with the Japanese economy and culture, the report suggests that the formation of a national consensus to harmonize "the interests of those receiving services and those providing them" be sought. *Id.* at 15.

3. *Toward a Market System*

The report perceives a need to integrate regulatory regimes that previously had been segregated along facilities-based and technological lines. The convergence of wired and wireless media, along with the overlapping functions of such media as cable television, telephone services, and broadcast stations, favors consideration of a new regulatory structure. This structure would take account of all of these media in light of a comprehensive communications policy. With the introduction of competition, distinctions between monopoly and competitive services may have to be drawn. The report suggests that basic telephone and telegraph services remain suitable for monopoly operations, but that other markets should be made competitive. A major concern of this market restructuring is the effect it might have on rates. The report suggests that rates must be high enough to cover costs but low enough to make basic services affordable to all users. In this regard, the report says that for the basic transmission service providers, "a fixed amount of internal capital must be held in reserve and a proper surplus must be added to the proper costs in order to arrive at the rate levels." *Id.* at 22. Priority also is placed on the deregulation of data transmission markets, particularly with regard to limitations on circuit use for data processing. The report claims that NTT and KDD should provide data circuits, to allow maximum use of existing facilities. It also urges a liberal allowance of privately developed data transmission networks. To promote these dual aims, the report stresses the need for careful attention to the way in which NTT and KDD are allowed to compete with the private sector.

4. *Public Operators in the New Market*

The report specifies that NTT must cooperate with the private sector if private innovation is to be encouraged. Attention must be devoted to implementing accounting systems that identify revenues clearly and so allow for the prevention of undesirable cross-subsidization. A need to set rates "geared to promoting fair competition" also is urged. *Id.* at 29. Attention must be devoted to the carrier's management systems, which the report says require streamlining and revision to accommodate the transition from public monopoly to a private, competitive enterprise that still will bear public obligation burdens. With respect to KDD, special attention needs to be paid to the affect on other countries, and on Japan, of its business policies. International cooperation and coordination are seen as vital.

5. *The Move Toward Integration*

The report specifies a number of technological advancements that are necessary to the development of an integrated market system and transmission network.

a. Installation of digital transmission and switching capacity will permit a single network to carry a wider array of communications and will accommodate a bit-based tariff structure. The use of satellite links will promote economy and reduce distance-sensitive transmission costs.

b. The report points to standardization as a major concern in the development of an advanced network. Taking account of user, manufacturer, and network operator demands, as well as of international activities, uniform equipment and transmission standards need to be developed. The report calls this effort "urgent." *Id.* at 41.

c. Development of a new integrated network will enable the Japanese market to accommodate a variety of services now in their early stages of evolution. Databases, for example, would be available for widespread access. The report identifies their development as a highly desirable goal, both to promote the advancement of the scientific and technological fields that make use of them and to provide Japan with a domestic information storehouse that will decrease its dependency on data assembled by other countries, such as the United States. Formation of such databases, however, poses several significant problems, including simple organizational measures as well as more complex issues of privacy, intellectual property protection, and transborder data flow. The report calls for governmental support of the database expansion effort. To facilitate further the growth of this industry, the report suggests that the following steps be taken: (1) expand the public data network and permit its interconnection to the public telephone system, (2) standardize database access procedures, (3) promote technological advances that will ensure reliability of use and the protection of intellectual property, and (4) work toward achieving integration of the transmission network.

d. The establishment of a satellite communications system is given a high priority in both the development of advanced communications services and the implementation of a single, integrated network. The report suggests careful consideration of an overall policy framework for the introduction and use of satellites, including decisions about how such satellites should be used, by whom, and at what rates their use should be billed. The report notes that satellites should provide both new communications services and traditional telephone services (as a supplement to the terrestrial network).

6. *Adjusting to New Problems*

A chief concern of the move toward a sophisticated and comprehensive communications network is the degree to which society will become dependent upon the network's operations and the damage that could be caused, as a result, by the network's failure to operate properly. The report identifies a number of areas of particular concern: (1) prevention of information theft, (2) improvement of the reliability of the transmission system, (3) protection of user privacy, (4) introduction of measures that allow for a more individualized control of the massive amounts of information flowing through the network (including installation of user-controlled systems), and (5) automatic delivery of relevant daily information directly to individual users (so that they will not have to sift through vast amounts of irrelevant data). The report stresses that individual system operators cannot be left to assume the primary responsibility for initiating these protections; thus, governmental oversight and coordination are seen as crucial.

7. *International Considerations*

The report stresses Japan's need to be sensitive to international trends in communications policymaking, to cooperate in efforts to coordinate international regulatory efforts, and to assume a leadership role in developing policies carefully crafted to meet the demands of the information age. In order to accomplish these objectives, the report specifies a need to strengthen the consultation process with other countries, to organize programs to provide technical and financial exchanges with other nations, and to develop telecommunications systems that will assist developing nations. NTT's vast resources are seen as a significant potential contributor to these efforts.

8. *Reexamination of Issues*

The diversification of telecommunications services and facilites is expected to prompt a need for a general reassessment of Japanese policies. The report establishes a three–tiered priority system for categorizing issues that require reexamination: "emergency"—applying to issues involving the use of data communications circuits; "urgent"—referring to issues of satellite communications, rate setting, and means for improving network reliability; and, "continuous reexamination"—encompassing issues such as the role of public telecommunications operators, research and development programs, and international concerns, which require less immediate and more long-term evaluation.

G. Recommendations of the Ad Hoc Commission on Administrative Reform: NTT Structure

1. Of primary concern to the Japanese is the future structure of NTT and its participation in a competitive telecommunications marketplace. Because NTT is a publicly owned corporation, it has been subject to periodic review by governmental commissions established to evaluate administrative performance. The First Ad Hoc Commission on Administrative Reform turned its attention toward NTT a number of times during its tenure, from 1961 to 1964. It recommended such changes as removing Diet control of the NTT budget, abolishing the limitations on the number of NTT employees and on their salaries, and relaxing the rate control imposed by law on NTT telecommunications services. These reforms were not carried out. In 1981, however, the Second Ad Hoc Commission was established, once again to study the efficiency of governmental systems; it conducted an evaluation of NTT.

2. The thrust of the Commission's recommendations was that NTT should be released from government control and should be allowed to make autonomous decisions about both its management structure and the scope of its operations. The eventual aim was to convert NTT into a privately owned company that would be able to compete effectively in a liberalized telecommunications marketplace.

3. The Commission's suggested approach involved a two-step process. First, NTT would be organized as a special company owned in full by the government. During this first phase, the Commission recommended that drastic improvements be made in certain NTT services, such as repair and maintenance, and that certain operations be divested, including customer premises equipment and data communications. In the second phase, to be completed within five years of the initial reform, the company would be separated into a main operating company that handled trunk services and several local companies responsible for handling local telephone service operations (following the model of AT&T). The government would own all of the shares of the trunk services company, which, in turn, would own all of the shares of the local companies. In time, these shares would be sold to the public.

4. These changes in NTT's structure were to be accompanied by a government-supervised introduction of competition to the trunk services market, a general deregulation of other telecommunications mar-

kets, and authorizations allowing NTT to expand its scope of business so long as new ventures continue to serve the public interest.

5. These recommendations met with general government approval. The Cabinet, in 1982, drafted a document that stated that a bill should be proposed to take account of the Commission's recommendations. No bill was introduced before the Diet, however, during its 98th session, which ended in May, 1983. Thereafter, the Cabinet renewed its call for legislation. This legislation eventually was adopted and is now the NTT Law. The law leaves NTT as a single operating unit, without any obligation to divest itself of particular operations. However, it requires government study of NTT's operations over the next five years and authorizes the formulation of "any measures that may be necessary as a result of such study." NTT Law, at Art. 2 (Supplementary Provisions).

6. Although the Liberal Democratic Party supported these recommendations, the minority Socialist and Communist Parties did not. The National Telecommunications Workers Union also opposed the plans to privatize and to reorganize NTT. The Union would have preferred the establishment of a new company jointly funded by the government and by service users. The union contended that the MPT's plan to reorganize NTT was designed to limit workers' rights further—particularly the right to strike. The Japanese press generally voiced editorial support for the Commission's proposals.

7. The Commission's recommendations were based upon a series of committee reports prepared by members of the Commission. These committee reports reflect a general dissatisfaction with publicly owned companies. They claim that the intervention of both political considerations and regulatory constraints frustrate corporate efficiency and hamper a company's ability to compete effectively. A specific concern is that top management tends not to undertake aggressive and innovative actions because its decisions are subject to subsequent review and to possible veto by politicians and bureaucrats. In addition, government control of the number of workers the company may hire and of the salaries they may receive has been cited as a cause of labor-management strains. Japanese laws prohibit public company employees from striking, leaving the unions that represent public workers with less effective means for promoting improved working conditions. This contributes to poor worker morale and has resulted in unlawful strikes.

8. With particular regard to NTT, the committee reports note that the company's expenses for providing telephone services (which account for almost ninety percent of NTT's revenues) have risen sharply as a percentage of revenues, largely as a result of a failure to trim the workforce despite substantial equipment upgrades and the installation of automated systems. The committee also noted that the telecommunications market was undergoing rapid and significant change and that Japan needed to benefit

from a wise use of NTT's resources if it was to remain internationally competitive. Thus, it concluded, autonomous decisionmaking power was particularly important for NTT.

9. With respect to the liberalization of the telecommunications market, the committee was careful to stress that government supervision of the trunk services market was essential to ensure that universal service goals and unprofitable public services (such as emergency and disaster communications) are maintained. For this reason, it was recommended that new entrants into the trunk services market be considered public telecommunications operators, responsible for protecting individual privacy and for providing public services. The government would retain control over the newly organized NTT trunk services company until such time as it was determined that this market was subject to effective competition. To promote competitive aims, the local service companies would be required to provide interconnection for all new trunk line companies on the same terms as the interconnection provided to NTT.

III. THE NEW TELECOMMUNICATIONS LAWS: OVERVIEW

A. Introduction

1. The Japanese Diet adopted the two new telecommunications laws on December 25, 1984; they took effect on April 1, 1985. The new laws substantially liberalize the telecommunications marketplace in Japan. They have ended the NTT monopoly on domestic facilities operation and have opened the VAN services market to significant private investment. The laws are designed to facilitate greater interconnection between computers and transmission circuits, which will encourage the increased integration of the information processing and telecommunications industries.

2. Both laws provide the MPT with a great deal of discretionary power, covering both the way in which the newly privatized NTT will operate and the manner in which competition will be introduced into the telecommunications marketplace. The MPT, for example, is required to approve plans by carriers to construct telecommunications facilities and must register certain large-scale telecommunications service operations.

B. NTT Law: Synopsis

1. The NTT Law establishes a new corporation, Nippon Telegraph and Telephone Company, Ltd. ("NTT"), initially wholly owned by the government. Over time, however, the government will be able to sell up to two-thirds of the NTT stock. NTT Law, at Art. 4(2). None of the stock may be held by foreign persons, foreign corporations, or foreign governments. Art. 4(1). Sale of NTT shares must receive prior approval by the Diet, which can limit the size of any proposed sale. A committee—appointed by the MPT—

established the company and prepared the articles of incorporation after consultating with the MPT. *See* Art. 3 (Supplementary Provisions).

2. The company is required to manage the "domestic telecommunications business" and "business activities incidental thereto. . . ." The MPT is required to approve NTT's involvement in "other activities necessary to achieve" this purpose. Art. 1. Article 12(2) (Supplementary Provisions) states that all current NTT activities not falling within the definition of the "domestic telecommunications business" are to be considered as approved by the MPT. The term "telecommunications business" is defined in the new Telecommunications Business Law, discussed below. *See infra* Sections III.C. & IV. Thus, NTT will not be forced out of any of its present services. The more interesting issue, however, is what new service areas the mandate of Article 1 will be construed to permit NTT to enter.

3. The new NTT is charged with "con- tribut[ing] to the securement of provision of stable nationwide telephone services through Japan such as are indispensible to the people's life at appropriate conditions and impartiality." Art. 2. This requirement implicates some universal service obligations. NTT's other business activities remain undefined. It must, however, submit an annual business plan for the MPT's approval. It also must submit any subsequent changes made in that plan. Art. 11. The MPT also must approve the appointment or the dismissal of the company's executive officers or auditors, further involving it in company governance. Art. 9. The broadest provision regarding the MPT's authority states that the Minister will supervise the company and may order it to act in a particular way "if he determines it to be especially necessary in enforcing this Law." Art. 15(2).

4. The law lifts restrictions on the company's ability to issue corporate bonds. This gives NTT some increased financial flexibility and, presumably, a greater variety of resources from which to draw in seeking to meet the challenges posed by new competitors. Art. 7. Its power to issue additional NTT shares is subject to prior MPT approval, Art. 4(3), which can be given only after consultation with the Minister of Finance. Art. 17. Thus it is clear that the financial health of NTT remains of significant concern to the government. The MPT retains broad supervisory powers over NTT to ensure that it does not go too heavily into debt or become subject to outside control that could steer it in ways not believed by the government to be in the country's best interests.

5. In combination, these provisions provide the Ministry with wide-ranging power to supervise and to shape the direction of NTT's activities in the new competitive environment. It is, perhaps, surprising that the government would retain this degree of control over the company. The Ad Hoc Commission—on whose recommendations the new laws largely were based—had recommended strongly that NTT be freed of most government intervention. Government oversight was thought to have inhibited NTT's innovation and its efficiency as a public company.

C. Telecommunications Business Law: Synopsis

1. Regulation of Facilities Owners: Type I Businesses

a. The mere fact that the new law approaches its mission as providing for "business" legislation, rather than a "public telecommunication law," suggests the shift in emphasis contained in the new legal framework. The telecommunciations market is no longer viewed as requiring regulation to ensure the construction and operation of simple telephone services that will interconnect the entire nation. The new law reflects a perceived need to privatize the market to a great degree. This privatization will promote innovation and competition that will produce more diverse service offerings at prices and on terms that will benefit consumers most. This change in emphasis reflects the fact that Japan is satisfied with its basic telephone services and now is looking to construct new capabilities that will meet the increasingly sophisticated needs of its citizens and its business organizations.

b. For this reason, the provision of services largely is left open to unregulated competition. The construction of telecommunications facilities, however, remains subject to prior approval by the MPT. Art. 9.

i) Article 94 of the Telecommunications Business Law, however, provides for the establishment of a Deliberative Council, to be formed under government ordinance. In making certain licensing decisions and in approving particular tariffs, the MPT is supposed to defer to this council and to respect its decisions.

ii) The relationship between the council and the MPT is not yet clear. The council could function either as an independent unit or merely as a part of the Ministry.

c. Immediately following adoption of the new laws, six groups formed to seek the MPT's approval as basic facilities operators (called Type I Telecommunications Businesses). The MPT has granted licenses to five of the six groups. The Ministry withheld any final decision on the sixth applicant's future pending the submission of a completed application from that group (which is headed by Sony and RCA).

d. Three groups propose terrestrial facilities, and three plan to operate satellite-based networks. All of the satellite competitors plan to use U.S.-built space stations and have signed agreements with U.S. partners. (They have kept U.S. interests at less than thirty percent to remain within the new law's restriction on foreign ownership of Type I businesses.)

i) The largest new entrant calls itself Daini Denden, which translates, roughly, to"number two phone company." Five major Japanese corporations, led by Kyocera, own sixty percent of the venture, which plans to install a microwave network. The other primary participants are Sony, Ushio (an optical equipment manufacturer), Secom (maker of security systems), and Mitsubishi. As many as 20 other groups, including banks and trading companies, hold at least some interest in this business.

ii) Japan National Railways has formed Nihon Telecom to operate a fiber optic network that will use the rights-of-way along bullet-train tracks.

iii) A joint venture among companies with affiliations to the Ministry of Construction have formed Teleway Japan, which plans to install fiber optic lines alongside of Japan's highways. Japan Public Highway Corp., Toyota, Nissan, Mitsui, Sumitomo, Kyocera, and others are involved.

v) Japan Communications Satellite Co., Ltd., is a joint venture between Hughes Communications, Inc.; C. Itoh & Co., Ltd.; and, Mitsui & Co., Ltd. The system will use two Ku-band satellites estimated to cost more than $300 million. The first of the two satellites is expected to become operational early in 1988. (Japanese satellites have traditionally used the Ka-band (18/30 GHz) because the Ku-band (12/14 GHz) is used by terrestrial microwave.)

v) Mitsubishi Corp. and Mitsubishi Electric Corp. have signed an agreement with Ford Aerospace to use Ford's satellites for a Type I business.

vi) Sony has joined with five other companies to form Satellite Japan Corp. The new firm plans to construct its network with satellites built by RCA. The satellites will have thirty transponders and be capable of handling both Ka- and Ku-band transmissions.

vii) Initially, Keidanren, the Federation of Japanese Economic Organizations, had planned to organize its own satellite-based competitor. However, Keidanren members, which include the nation's most influential manufacturers, could not reach a consensus on whether the organization—as a business association—should be involved as an entrepreneurial venture. Nonetheless, Keidanren and its members are expected to have a significant impact on the future of new Type I businesses. The organization had performed an extensive feasibility study of a satellite-based network and has significant expertise on pricing and service issues. It is likely that Keidanren members, led by Taiyu Kobayashi, chairman of Fujitsu Limited, will draw upon this knowledge in the future and might collatorate to negotiate for and buy satellite transmission capacity for corporate communications needs. Acting together in this way, Keidanren members could well determine who will succeed or fail as a new Type I business.

viii) An additional interesting aspect of the scramble to enter the Type I business category is the way in which associations have formed. Trading companies and banks have been heavily involved. Companies also have contributed money and expertise to more than one group. Kyocera, Mitsui, Sony, C. Itoh, and Sumitomo, for example, each are affiliated with at least two potential competitors. This overlap may reflect a reaction to the initial speculation that the MPT planned to authorize only one Type I competitor for NTT; apparently some companies wanted to be sure that they were able to enter the new market. Finally, companies with close affiliations to some of the government ministries have banded together. It is not clear how such groups will operate, but they may provide ministries other than the MPT with at least an indirect influence on future telecommunications policies.

2. *General and Special Type II Businesses: The Distinctions Between Service Providers Disappears*

a. In addition to Type I businesses, which generally include any telecommunications business that owns its own transmission facilities, the law provides for the operation of Type II businesses. These businesses consist of telecommunications operations in which services are provided on leased facilities. The law does not expressly limit the scope of these services. Art. 21. A Special Type II business provides these services to a group of "many and unspecific persons," employing equipment on a scale that exceeds standards set by the MPT. Type II businesses are all other telecommunications businesses not falling within the other categories. Art. 22. The MPT's implementation of this definition, by ordinance, has virtually obliterated the distinction between Special and General Type II businesses. Under the Ministry's ordinances, virtually any business can operate within the General Type II classification.

i) The Special/General distinction had been intended to classify a telecommunications business on the basis of either users served or circuits operated. There had been some speculation that a Special Type II business would be one involving 500 or more lines. This distinction still exists, but the MPT's ordinances have made the distinction virtually meaningless—in practical terms. Largely as a result of U.S. pressure to open the Japanese telecommunications market to foreign businesses, the Ministry's ordinances permit virtually anyone to operate as a General Type II business. This is significant because the MPT is not required to approve such General businesses; thus, there is little chance for it to keep out foreign companies.

ii) The Ministry has defined "many and unspecific"—the key to the Special Type II category—to include four criteria: (1) the conditions of the business' tariff are made public, (2) there is no variation among customers for services or rates, (3) the business must serve all users who request such service, and (4) the service can be accessed through the public telephone network. In order to be classified as Special Type II, a business must satisfy *all four* of these criteria. Thus, a business can avoid a Special Type II classification simply by leaving its rates open to individual negotiation or by refusing to serve all users who request such service. The Ministry's ordinances have turned the statutory scheme "inside out." Type II businesses essentially are free to operate as General businesses unless they choose to be Special Type II entities. In view of the regulatory requirements imposed on Special Type II businesses—and the ease of avoiding Special Type II classification—it is unclear why anyone would seek to register as a Special Type II business.

iii) Any business with more than 500 exchange access lines (connecting a processing node or data facility to a local telephone exchange) is to be classified as Special Type II. Originally, this limit had been expected to apply to services reaching more than 500 *users*. However, the Ministry does not take subscriber lines into account in calculating the size of a business; only trunk lines (leased by the carrier) are counted. Since each carrier line can provide service to many users through connections to a local switch, a service with 500 access lines will be able to reach thousands of end users. Thus, this limit poses little practical restriction on the size of a General Type II business.

iv) During trade negotiations, the U.S. had sought to have the Japanese amend the Telecommunications Business Law to eliminate all regulation of Type II businesses. The Japanese refused to take this step. However, the ordinances that were adopted have almost accomplished the same result within the existing legislative framework.

v) Article 2 of the Business Telecommunications Law (Supplementary Provisions) requires the government to review the implementation of the new law in three years and to take any measures viewed as necessary to improve the telecommunications system at that time. During the recent trade negotiations, the Japanese government expressed its expectation that all Type II businesses might be unregulated in the near future. This change may come in 1988, when the government conducts its review.

b. Telecommunications businesses that "provide telecommunications facilities designed for communications between Japan and foreign points for the use of communications of others" also were originally expected to be Special Type II businesses. Once again, however, as a result of bilateral trade talks between the U.S. and Japan, the Ministry has agreed that no company will be classified as a Special Type II business "solely on the basis of international links." Thus, the international service marketplace has been opened—at least technically—to unregulated competition.

c. The dynamics of this remarkable implementation of the new law should not be overlooked. Through its ordinances, the MPT has been able virtually to eliminate virtually an entire, legislatively imposed service classification—Special Type II. If nothing else, the result underscores the discretionary power held by the Ministry. It clearly is capable of altering drastically the contours of the telecommunications market, even within the "fixed" framework of the new laws.

3. *Procedures for Commencement of Operations: Approval Standards*

a. Article 22 provides that a General Type II business simply can notify the MPT of specific information in order to begin operating. For example, the applicants' names and addresses must be submitted along with the "category of telecommunications service according to the classification stipulated in the applicable ordinance of the Ministry of Posts and Telecommunications." Art. 22(1).

i) The ministerial ordinance sets forth four service categories: voice, image, data, and other composite services.

ii) Further notification is required if the business is transferred to a new person. Art. 23.

iii) The statute makes no provision for the rejection or revocation of any approval. The Ministry has said that General Type II notifications will be simple and will be accepted immediately if properly completed.

b. Article 24, by contrast, states that Special Type II entities "must receive the registration" of the MPT.

i) Registration proceeds on a disapproval basis. A business is considered to be registered twenty days after submitting its application if it is not notified by the MPT of an objection within fifteen days.

ii) Under Article 26, the MPT must reject a Special Type II application if the proposed registrant (1) is someone who has been convicted of violating the Telecommunications Business Law, the Wire Telecommunication Law, or the Radio Law within the last two years, (2) is someone who has had a Special Type II registration revoked within the last two years, (3) is a corporation or organization with a director who falls within either of the first two categories, or (4) is not financially or technically qualified to conduct the proposed business.

c. The law does not identify the criteria upon which Special Type II applications will be considered or the specific circumstances for approval. There had been much talk about the fact that the Japanese value-added services market cannot sustain an unlimited number of competitors. Therefore, questions had arisen as to whether the MPT would establish a de facto benchmark for the number of new entrants. Recently, however, the MPT has decided not to adopt any such limitations on entry. In addition, the substantial broadening of the General Type II category has made it possible for virtually any VAN operator to enter the market under the notification procedure. Thus, Ministry restrictions are clearly no longer a concern.

d. Type I approval procedures, as outlined by the statute, explicitly provide the MPT with significant discretionary authority to withhold approval. The MPT must find that a Type I operation, as proposed, (1) will conform to the demands of the area to be served, (2) will not result in a "significant excess" of circuit facilities to be used by the business, (3) is operating under a "reliable and feasible" business plan, (4) is submitted by a financially and technically qualified applicant, and (5) is "appropriate for the sound development of telecommunications in general." Art. 10.

i) These standards clearly provide the MPT with power to determine the contours of the facilities market. It can decide who will be permitted to operate as a Type I business and how many competitors will be approved—in light of almost any overall goals that the government may have.

ii) Initial concern about the MPT's broad discretion appears to have been mitigated by the Ministry's decision to approve five new Type I businesses. What appears to be an "open-door" policy has saved the Ministry from having to choose among U.S. companies, which are involved in all of the plans for satellite-based Type I businesses.

e. Type I businesses are prohibited from having more than one-third of their directors be aliens or from having more than one-third alien ownership. *See* Art. 11. There are no comparable alien-ownership restrictions on Type II businesses. This difference is the result of significant political pressure applied by a variety of countries, particularly the United States, which were anxious to open the Japanese market to foreign service providers. A ban on foreign control of VANs would have precluded foreign multinationals from operating their own networks. These companies, then, would have been required to employ a third-party Japanese service provider—a potentially troublesome and expensive proposition. Open entry also will help U.S. companies do more business with Japan, which will alleviate the current trade imbalance between the two countries. This was a primary goal of the recent U.S.-Japan trade negotiations.

4. *The MPT's Other Supervisory Powers*

a. The MPT's general supervisory powers over both Type I and Special Type II businesses are rather broad. The MPT can specify a time by which a Type I business must begin operating. The Ministry also may extend this time period or may apply it differently to different kinds of services or different service areas. Art. 12. Prior to beginning its operation, a Type I business must obtain the MPT's "confirmation . . . that the telecommunications facilities . . . conform to the technical standards" prescribed by the MPT, in accordance with Art. 41. *See* Art. 12(4). These standards must include assurances that (1) change or failure of the facilities will not "significantly hinder telecommunications," (2) service will be of "adequate quality," (3) "secrecy of communications will not be violated," (4) interconnection with other networks will not damage or impair these networks, and (5) the responsibilities of the business' facilities are "clearly stipulated." Art. 41(2).

i) Any changes in a Type I operation or a Special Type II registration that alter the services or equipment to be offered (and, in the case of a Type I business, the geographic area to be served) must be approved by the MPT. Arts. 14 & 27.

ii) In addition, the assignment, transfer, merger, or takeover of a Type I business must receive the prior approval of the MPT. Arts. 15 & 16. The MPT must approve an assignment of a Type I business only if it determines that the assignment is "necessary" to provide the involved telecommunications services effectively and that the assignee is an "appropriate person" to carry out the involved business. Art. 15(2).

iii) One who inherits a Type I business must apply to the MPT for a new approval within sixty days of inheritance or risk losing the status of a Type I business. The approval standards for an inheritance are the same as for an original application. Art. 17.

b. The MPT also is empowered to scrutinize the tariffs under which telecommunications services are provided. A Type I business must obtain the MPT's prior approval for its service charges. These fees will be approved only if they are "fair and reasonable in consideration of proper costs under the efficient management," and if the "calculating methods of charges [are] . . . properly and clearly stipulated." Art. 31(2). The tariff also may not "unreasonably restrict" the use of the telecommunications circuits (preventing the operator from inhibiting use of non-affiliated circuits or products), and may not "unfairly discriminate against any person." *Id.* A Special Type II business must notify the MPT of its tariffs prior to enforcing them; there is no requirement that these tariffs receive the MPT's approval. Arts. 31(5) & (6).

c. To allow the MPT to supervise rates, the law requires that Type I businesses must conform their accounting procedures to standards prescribed by the MPT. Art. 33. The MPT has sought, through its ordinance, to prevent cross-subsidization and to establish accounting procedures that will allow it to detect such cross-subsidization.

i) The Ministry has required that separate accounts of costs and revenues be kept for individual service categories. Particular attention will be given to services expected to be subject to heavy competition from Type II businesses. These services are defined as "computer communications" and "digital data transmission."

ii) In determining service charges, the MPT has said that it will provide for the recovery of costs "plus normal profits" for each service category. This approach essentially imposes a rate-of-return regulatory structure on Type I businesses. It is not clear how this rate regulation will fare as new competitors begin to operate and try to undercut NTT's rates. The approval process may impose significant obstacles to the use of prices as a competitive weapon. However, the Ministry views regulation as necessary to ensure that NTT does not abuse its market position unfairly to undercut the prices of new competitors. The MPT plans to form a Telecommunications Rules Research Council to study pricing policies. Over the next year, the Ministry will develop specific rate standards on the basis of the Research Council's recommendations. These standards then will be reviewed by the Deliberative Council established by the Telecommunications Business Law. The Deliberative Council originally suggested this form of rate regulation to the Ministry.

5. Public Welfare Obligations of Telecommunications Businesses

a. A Type I business, although privately owned, must assume certain obligations imposed on it to serve the public welfare.

i) Article 34 requires that such a business "shall not, without due reason, refuse to provide telecommunications service [to anyone] within its service territory."

ii) When the MPT determines that a Type I business' fees or other service conditions "have come to be significantly improper as a result of changes in the social or economic circumstances and to impair the interests of users," it may order the business to seek approval of an amended tariff. Art. 36(1).

iii) The MPT can order Type II businesses to improve their operations when necessary to guard against damage to the interests of users or of Type I facilities. Art. 37.

iv) The MPT can order any changes in all telecommunications businesses that are necessary to protect the secrecy of communications carried by those businesses. Arts. 36 & 37.

b. Article 38 requires the MPT to approve the interconnection of the facilities operated by different Type I businesses when such interconnection would promote the public interest. One of the parties seeking interconnection may ask the MPT to order such interconnection when an agreement cannot be reached and when the connection is "especially necessary and appropriate to promote the public interest." Art. 39(1). The MPT is empowered to arbitrate fees to be charged for such interconnection. Arts. 39(2)-(8).

c. To guarantee "the reliable and stable provision of telecommunications service," Type I and Special Type II businesses must establish regulations for the control and use of the telecommunications equipment that is part of their businesses. Art. 43(1). The MPT, by ordinance, specifies the focus of these regulations. *Id.*

d. The law gives Type I businesses a certain degree of power to require land owners to allow use of their land for the construction of telecommunications facilities. These businesses have power to use and to enter upon private land, to cut down vegetation that obstructs or may damage lines, and to use public "water surfaces" to lay underwater lines. Mechanisms are set up to protect owners from unreasonable interference with their right to use their property and to ensure compensation for any loss of use. Arts. 73-88.

6. *Transitional Provisions*

a. The law provides that both NTT and KDD shall be considered, as of the date of enactment, approved Type I businesses. Art. 4 (Supplementary Provisions). These companies' telegraph businesses will be considered telecommunications services under the definition given by the law, *see infra* Section IV., and will be operated as such exclusively by NTT and KDD. To encourage competition, no Ministry approval is needed before either company assigns any part of its telegraph operations to other companies. Art. 5 (Supplementary Provisions); *contra* Arts. 15 & 16.

b. VAN operations conducted under the 1982 amendments to the Public Telecommunication Law are deemed to have notified the MPT of their operation as General Type II businesses, as is required by Article 22(1). Telecommunications Business Law, at Art. 6 (Supplementary Provisions). All current VANs probably qualify as General Type II businesses. This transitional provision will permit them to continue operating under the new law, without having to seek registration from the MPT.

IV. DEFINITIONAL ISSUES RAISED BY THE TELECOMMUNICATIONS BUSINESS LAW

A. Introduction: "Horizontal" Versus "Vertical" Distinctions

1. As a general matter, the law's basic structure involves a clear-cut distinction between the provision of "facilities" by one type of business (Type I) and the provision of "services" by a second type (Type II). Japanese policy analysts sometimes describe this scheme as involving a "horizontal" division between classes of activities. It avoids the difficulties of having to create a definitional scheme for distinguishing between services on a "vertical" basis (*i.e.*, between "basic" and "enhanced" services or "information processing" and "communications").

2. The boundary line approach of the Japanese legislation is thus described as "more advanced" than the approach underlying either the *Computer I* or *Computer II* decisions in the United States. A number of difficult definitional issues still are raised by the new legislation and unavoidably involve the demarcation of service distinctions on a "vertical" basis.

B. Broad Definition of a "Telecommunications Service"

1. The definition of a "telecommunications service," Article 2(iii) of the Telecommunications Business Law, is far reaching. It includes "intermediating communications of others through the use of telecommunications facilities, or any other acts of providing telecommunications facilities for the use of communications of others." "Telecommunications facilities" includes a variety of devices used "for the operation of telecommunications," which Article 2(i) defines as "transmitting, conveying, or receiving codes, sounds or images by wire, radio, or any other electromagnetic method."

2. Without any limiting provisions, this language encompasses a wide range of activities, including remote access data processing, the provision of data bases to third parties, and various communications processing (*e.g.*, value-added services) and basic transmission services.

3. There are a number of exclusions from the scope of a "telecommunications service." For example, Article 2(iv) defines a "tele-

communications business'' as one providing ''telecommunications service,'' with the exception of various activities subject to the cable television laws. Despite this explicit exclusion, a number of concerns arise due to the relationship of the legal regime for cable television and the new Telecommunications Business Law. These are discussed below. *See infra* Section IX.

4. Article 90 provides for a number of additional exceptions to the provisions of the Telecommunications Bill. Article 90(1)(i) excludes telecommunications businesses that provide telecommunications service ''to a single person (not being a telecommunications carrier).'' Article 90(1)(ii) excludes those entities that provide services to third parties that are located ''on the same premises'' or are ''below in scale the standards stipulated in the applicable ordinance of the Ministry of Posts and Telecommunications.''

C. Boundary Line Between ''Telecommunications Service'' and Data Processing and Data Services

1. The most significant exclusion from the category of a ''telecommunications service'' would, however, appear to be contained in Article 90(1)(iii). This exception applies to ''any Type II telecommunications business which provides telecommunications service other than telecommunications service which intermediate communications of others provided by telecommunications facilities.'' The scope of this exclusion is obscured by ambiguous drafting. However, the intention is to exclude both remote access data processing services and data services.

2. It is not entirely clear whether remote access data processing operations would be excluded from the provisions of the law by the definitions in Article 2 alone, without the exception in Article 90(1)(iii).

3. The fact that ''pure'' data processing or information services are excluded from regulation is less important than the fact that, when combined with any message switching or third-party service, these activities are subject to regulation as Type II businesses. Thus, the new law does not contain any exclusion, such as was involved in the *Computer I* proceeding in the United States, for services where message switching is merely ancillary or incidental to data processing or data services. Those activities not within the scope of the Article 90 exemption are fully subject to the provisions applicable to Type II business. This fact has become less significant in view of the Ministry's decision to open the General Type II category to virtually any business.

4. Under this definition, however, those companies involved in remote access data processing and in information provision—so long as they also employ some degree of message transmission—technically would be considered together with those companies engaged in ''communications processing'' (or pure value-added services) in the licensing procedures of Articles 21-30. The implementing ordinances do not establish any distinc-

tions among Type II businesses that primarily engage in data processing activities as opposed to communications processing services.

5. For practical purposes, many of the concerns raised by this statutory framework may have been alleviated by a decision to exclude from all regulation data processing and information services that include incidental or ancillary message switching capabilities. It remains to be seen, however, whether the terms "incidental" or "ancillary" will be applied broadly or narrowly.

6. There also is some doubt about the feasibility of distinguishing between remote access data processing businesses and VANs. In the view of some, these two activities are closely intertwined. In the U.S. market, for example, Tymnet, GE, and Telenet all offer both services. In practice, however, these companies have segmented their own business—from a marketing standpoint—even though the same licensed transmission facilities and computer networks are being used for both "communications processing" and "data processing." The law does not resolve (nor even address) the boundary line between computer processing that constitutes a mere communications enhancement function and computer use that rises to the level of "information processing"—to which message transmission is merely incidental.

7. However, this lack of a clear division between the services will not have a detrimental impact on information providers and data processing businesses within Japan. All such operations should be able to escape regulation by operating as General Type II businesses. Other than ensuring the confidentiality of users' communications and requiring reports on the service providers operations, General Type II businesses are free from substantial regulation.

8. It remains to be seen whether the absence of a distinction between "hybrid" information services and value-added "communications processing" services will have any adverse impact on such service providers in their business activities outside of Japan. To the extent that such entities are regarded as being involved in communications services subject to regulation in Japan, the Japanese regulatory scheme may increase the likelihood that they will be regulated—or prohibited—in countries that do not adhere to entry policies that are as liberal as those in Japan, the U.K., or the U.S.

V. THE ORGANIZATION AND REGULATION OF NTT AS A COMPETITIVE CARRIER

A. NTT Before Privatization: Corporate Overview

1. In its last year as a public company, NTT was extremely successful. It posted a $1.59 billion profit in fiscal 1983 (April 1, 1983 to March 31, 1984), four percent higher than the prior year's total. The company had expected an erosion of revenues from telephone services—the

major component of NTT's revenues; however, in the wake of recent rate reductions, telephone use soared, providing the company with 87.5% of its total revenues for the year.

2. A major focus of the company's current efforts is the eventual implementation of its Information Network System ("INS"). NTT has been engaged in the process of digitizing its transmission network, installing both fiber optic cables and digital exchanges to permit the simultaneous carriage and switching of huge amounts of data, including such broadband services as video. The company also has begun to use satellite links that can provide an INS operation with an effective means for transmitting information over long distances at costs that are not so distance-sensitive.

a. In October, 1984, NTT launched the first phase of its INS program in Tokyo with the opening of a thirty-month test of a model INS network. The $80 million project involves the use of 2000 home and business terminals linked to a digital network that includes a fiber optic transmission system reported to be 150 kilometers long. The system provides teleshopping, electronic banking, security services, and a variety of video services. The test was expanded in March, 1985, with the addition of new users, services, and information providers.

b. INS is all part of NTT's plan to invest more than $50 billion to construct a nationwide fiber optic system over the course of the next decade. Plans call for a conversion to digital transmission in stages, with the first stage to include Tokyo, Osaka, and Nagoya (initially using some remaining copper wire links). Other cities are expected to be digitized during 1986, with nationwide optical circuitry installed by 1988. This digital network, including digital exchanges, will be used to provide high speed facsimile and data services at significantly reduced prices. These services are expected to become available, starting in 1986, in Tokyo, Nagoya, and Osaka. *See infra* Section VI.

3. NTT has no manufacturing division, so that it must purchase its equipment completely from outside suppliers. It has spent approximately $2.5 billion a year recently on equipment purchases. The company's procurement policies have been the subject of some controversy, particularly with respect to the United States. For years American suppliers were basically ignored, as NTT focused its purchasing attention on four Japanese companies, Fujitsu Ltd., NEC Corp., Hitachi Ltd., and Oki Electric Industry Co. In 1983, however, NTT spent $140 million to purchase American goods, an increase of almost 200% from 1982. The two countries now have signed a three-year agreement and have agreed to a series of changes in the company's procurement policies made in 1983, including an agreement to accept applications in its European and United States offices and to provide English applications. These moves are designed to permit Japanese and foreign suppliers to compete on a non-discriminatory basis.

4. The company's primary business remains telephone service, which continues to account for the vast majority of its revenues. In anticipation of an expected decline in the demand for telephone service, the

company has lowered rates, including those charged for push-button telephones and long-distance services (which, in 1983, were dropped for the fourth time in five years). To supplement the basic telephone service market, NTT has expanded its operations in the mobile phone, pocket paging, and facsimile services areas. Mobile phone service is now available not only in individual automobiles, but also on public trains and on ships. Facsimile network services were extended nationwide in 1982. The company also provides telegram and telex services. In 1982, however, NTT found that its telex services were being used less frequently as companies switched to alternative communications systems to send high-speed transmissions.

5. NTT also leases transmission circuits both for traditional message carriage and for data transmission functions. In the area of data services, the company provides circuits on both a private-leased and shared-use (public) basis. NTT offers its own complete data processing operations, allowing users to take advantage of an integrated transmission and data processing network. NTT's existing data processing operations include both public and private systems such as a network for bank transactions, a cash-dispensing service that allows users of member banks to receive cash in more than 200 locations nationwide, an on-line pension management service, a data service for the Ministry of Labor, and a meteorological data collection network.

6. NTT also operates the CAPTAIN videotex system, developed jointly with the MPT. CAPTAIN stands for Character and Pattern Telephone Access Information Network; it was run on a trial basis in Tokyo between 1979 and 1984.

a. A recent trial, which ended in March, 1983, involved the use of 2,000 monitors drawing on a database of 200,000 information frames. The monitors have been placed in homes, offices, and in the CAPTAIN Center (where the database computers are located). Information is input using special terminals that can accept text (alphanumeric and ideographic), illustrations, and photographs. Almost 300 information providers participated in this trial. Particular interest came from the finance, insurance, and manufacturing industries, as well as from public utilities, which all supplied information for the system.

b. The final CAPTAIN test ended in July, 1984, and involved more than 350 information providers. During the first two tests, usage figures showed that the overwhelming majority of users spent most of their time on CAPTAIN with entertainment and hobby services.

c. CAPTAIN has been operating as a commercial service since November 30, 1984. It is available in Tokyo, Osaka, Kyoto, Kobe, and certain surrounding areas. CAPTAIN Service Co., formed in February, 1984, manages the system.

d. The CAPTAIN system, technologically, is probably one of the world's most advanced. It is capable of handling not only standard alphanumeric characters and common special symbols, but also the 3,000 Chinese ideographs, as well as Katakana and Hiragana—the Japanese script and block characters. Particularly high resolution, as well as the capability to allow users to move through information screens line-by-line, character-by-character, or on a continuous scrolling basis, make the system quite expensive.

e. CAPTAIN uses the public telephone network to link users to videotex communications processing equipment ("VCP"), which in turn switches users to the appropriate information centers and sets up all necessary circuit connections. The VCP handles all communications processing. The information centers, including the main CAPTAIN Information Center, perform data processing operations.

f. The system imposes on users a one-time contract charge (approximately $30), information charges (which vary, depending upon the information providers), and communications charges (approximately $.10 for three minutes). It operates from 6:00 a.m. to 1:00 a.m. daily. As of December 21, 1984, there were more than 500 information providers for the system and more than 3000 users. Average access time was ten minutes, during which time an average of forty pages would be viewed. The system expects to reach 500,000 to 700,000 subscribers by 1990.

g. Both one-way and two-way services are available over CAPTAIN. Current services include news, travel information and reservations, teleshopping, telebanking, telesoftware, games, quizzes and contests, exchange rate information, stock prices, medical and financial information, and computational programs (taxes, loans, and interest on savings). The technology also can be used to create various private videotex networks that are useful for businesses.

h. Growth should be helped by an expected drop in the price of a CAPTAIN terminal, to $400 by 1986. Software also is being developed to permit personal computers to be used as CAPTAIN terminals.

i. The CCITT recently recognized CAPTAIN as one of three international videotex standards. (The other two are the European CEPT system and the North American NAPLPS.) Although the three systems are incompatible, work is being done to establish protocol conversion mechanisms that would allow for compatibility. A program to convert CAPTAIN to the NAPLPS format has been written, and work continues on perfecting a reverse conversion.

j. A recently announced joint venture between Sony and the Japan Cable Network will use the NAPLPS standard to provide a videotex service in the Tokyo area that will compete with CAPTAIN. Because it uses the North American standard, this system would permit data exchange with North America—perhaps a significant advantage. A number of the companies, including the Nichimen Corp. and a joint venture by Mitsui & Co., Ltd., and Nippon Univac, also have obtained rights to market NAPLPS systems in Japan. These last two ventures will use the Canadian version of NAPLPS, called Telidon.

B. NTT's Reorganization

1. To prepare itself for competition, NTT has begun to reorganize itself. It has adopted a more functional form of organization and has divided itself into three basic components: interexchange services, local exchange operations (with eleven regional headquarters), and product marketing units (which are designed to sell particular equipment and services). The company's emphasis has been placed on marketing its various products—an activity that was less important when there was no competition. One of its new marketing units, for example, the Integrated Communications Systems Division, was created especially to provide consulting services to customers regarding data processing and communications systems needs.

a. This reorganization currently is being finalized. It has been a slow, deliberate process. The Japanese approach to collegial decisionmaking—based on longstanding working relationships—will make it more difficult to reorganize than it would be in an organization with a more hierarchical structure. NTT will have to create new decisionmaking "clusters" and procedures.

b. The reorganization obviously will affect accounting and costing procedures. It is expected that the revision of NTT's antequated accounting system will lag behind its corporate reorganization by at least two years.

2. An important aspect of the company's new organization is its reliance on a strong central management and the establishment of a centralized strategic planning unit. NTT has not, over the years, had such a corporate group. It has been managed from the "bottom up" through advice and consultation from the various functional divisions within the company. In a period of change and transition, it may be especially necessary to steer NTT from the top. The strategic planning unit will focus on both corporate innovation and engineering issues. The planning process is expected to provide the company with an overall sense of purpose as it undergoes the disruption of internal reorganization and confronts a rapidly evolving, uncertain economic and regulatory environment.

3. Dr. Hisashi Shinto remains the president of the company, having served in that position for the last four years of NTT's existence as a public company. Shinto has expressed his support of the restructuring and has supported competition, viewing it as in the best, long-term interests of the country. He has played a critical role in achieving a consensus within the company about the benefits of a new competitive era, particularly among those who believed that NTT had done its job exceedingly well as a monopoly. Many still remain unconvinced that the technological benefits of integrated digital networks can be fully realized in a fragmented competitive market.

4. A major question facing the company will be whether to spin off one or more competitive subsidiaries to provide services on an

unregulated basis, in competition with Type II businesses. An engineering joint venture with ten other companies has been announced. However, plans for any other subsidiaries, such as one to provide VANs, remain uncertain.

a. There are three divisions within NTT that have an active interest in new information-based or enhanced services. One is the Data Communications Bureau, which manages NTT's data processing operations. The other two are its INS unit and the consulting division, Integrated Communications Systems.

b. Because the NTT law does not require the company to provide certain services through a separate subsidiary, any such move would be voluntary. It could, however, help NTT compete with unregulated service providers (General Type II businesses), since all services provided by NTT (a Type I business) are subject to rate regulation and tariff approval.

c. The relationship of a subsidiary to the parent would also be a significant issue that could raise a multitude of regulatory concerns. These are discussed below.

d. The engineering business—being run as a joint venture—is called Sogo Tsushin Engineering Co. It will provide consulting, technology transfer, and survey services for new telecommunications businesses. NTT owns fifty percent, and ten other companies, including Fuji Bank and Nippon Steel Corp., own five percent each. Interestingly enough, the venture will be working for some of NTT's future competitors, such as Daini Denden.

5. Seven companies have formed the Japan Communications Network Co., which will resell NTT private data lines between Tokyo and Osaka. Three of the participating companies, which have affiliations with NTT, currently sell NTT paging equipment; four are involved in inside wiring. The precise relationship between this new company and NTT is unclear. Depending on the details of the "affiliation" between the companies, additional regulatory concerns could be raised.

C. Service Restrictions Applied to Type I Businesses

1. Type I businesses are required to seek prior approval from the MPT for the rates and terms of services. Special and General Type II businesses do not need to obtain such approval. (Special Type II businesses must notify the MPT of their tariffs before enforcing them; General Type II businesses do not even have to file tariffs.) *See supra* Section III.C.3. This disparity undoubtedly will create certain pressures to specify precisely the situations in which Type I carriers are subject to the full range of rate regulation. For example, NTT, as a Type I business, will be faced with a certain dilemma in its efforts to compete with Type II businesses in the provision of value-added or other "competitive" services. NTT will be required to obtain approval for the service terms of its value-added offerings, whereas its essentially unregulated Type II competitors will be free to charge

prices subject only to marketplace restraints. NTT's tariffs could be delayed, in a review process, for some period of time.

2. This situation may prompt NTT to seek—voluntarily—to establish a separate subsidiary to provide value-added services as a Type II business. The subsidiary would be subject to fewer regulatory requirements. Yet, even if it does take this step, a number of difficult issues could arise. For example, there is the question of what services should be provided by the subsidiary. The subsidiary's offerings might be limited to certain protocol-shifting functions, or they might include some of NTT's data processing services. Enhanced voice services and information-related services also could be moved to the control of the new subsidiary. Each of these activities also might be segregated into separate divisions. At the very least, it will be necessary, in setting up a new subsidiary, to establish certain "service demarcations."

3. NTT's role with respect to information services, or to other operations where it can exercise control over the content of the transmission, raises another area of concern.

a. It is not clear to what extent the new statutes prevent NTT and its Type I competitors—operating primarily as carriers for third-party messages—from providing the content transmitted by information services. Article 4 of the Public Telecommunication Law of 1953 prohibited NTT from exercising any censorship over communications handled for others. Moreover, NTT's mandate was limited to providing "public telecommunications services." Article 2(3) defined these as "a service of intermediation of communications of *other persons* by using the telecommuncations plant for the use by other persons in their telecommunications activities." Article 5(2) also, apparently, limited NTT to "public telecommunications business affairs."

b. By contrast, Article 1 of the NTT Law provides that "[t]he Company may, besides [managing domestic telecommunications business], engage in business activities incidental thereto and, subject to the authorization of the Minister of Posts and Telecommunications, other business activities necessary to achieve the purpose [of managing domestic telecommunications business]." This language could be interpreted as broadening the corporation's mandate to extend its business affairs into related sectors—particularly cable televison or information-related services. (At the present time, NTT's role in the CAPTAIN videotex service—an information offering—is limited to ownership of a third of the stock of a separate subsidiary. Information found in the system is provided, edited, and updated by unaffiliated businesses.)

c. Consequently, there may be an incentive to define those related, but non-telecommunications, businesses in which NTT may engage. It should be noted, of course, that NTT's remote access data processing has been specifically defined to be included within the scope of a telecommunications service provided for a third party. *See supra* Section III.B.

D. Restrictions on Relationships Between Type I Carriers and Their Subsidiaries Engaged in Type II Services

1. If NTT or any of its new Type I competitors establishes one or more separate subsidiaries, a need would arise to adopt rules defining the relationship between the Type I business and the Type II activities of a subsidiary. There are many difficult issues that could be faced in this area. The choices ultimately made will depend upon basic public policy judgments regarding the degree of autonomy that should exist between a parent and its subsidiary. A fundamental question is whether such "relational rules" will apply equally to NTT and to its new competitors. The Telecommunications Business Law does not distinguish between NTT and new entrants.

2. NTT has decided how it will handle certain aspects of this issue. A subsidiary will have to have only its own switching facilities. It will not need to maintain its own transmission lines. NTT will make tariffed services available on a nondiscriminatory basis to both affiliated and non-affiliated subsidiaries. Non-affiliated competitors will have access to the same facilities and services—at the same rates and conditions—as the affiliated subsidiary.

3. Questions that relate to the pricing structure applicable to use arrangements remain unresolved. If services are available or are priced on the basis of bit-rate capacity, then some of the incentive to develop competitive, Type II businesses could be significantly reduced.

4. Other basic concerns involve the sharing and costing procedures for any joint arrangements between a Type I parent and its subsidiary for personnel, overhead, or other common assets. Attention also must be devoted to determining a subsidiary's degree of access to network-related technical information, to customer lists, to pricing data, and to research and development work performed by the parent.

5. The resolution of all of these issues will involve an assessment of the potential market influence of the new Type I businesses. It certainly is true that Type II businesses may not, for some period of time, have access to network transmission facilities other than those owned and operated by NTT. Moreover, concerns about preventing cross-subsidization between competitive services and those services with respect to which there is no realistic market alternative—such as basic transmission services—also will affect the way in which any parent/subsidiary relationships are regulated.

VI. Reconciling Competitive Goals with Advanced Service Capabilities: The INS Experiment

A. Introduction: The INS Concept

1. The expanded digitization of transmission lines and switches allows a single network to begin carrying a wide variety of communications, including voice, video, and data. The goal of unifying the network in this way is to allow users to access a broad variety of services through a single network, using an integrated terminal. This integrated network is commonly referred to as ISDN; in Japan it is known as INS.

2. The Japanese aggressively have sought to explore the potentially revolutionary impact of INS. As discussed above, *see supra* Section V.A., NTT already has conducted an INS experiment in the Tokyo suburbs. Japan's intensive, progressive interest in INS has enabled it to assume a leading role worldwide in the process of evaluating the integrated network concept.

3. Japan appears to view INS primarily as a technical proposition. The goal being sought is the expansion of a single network's transmission capabilities and the reduction of distance and time sensitivity in network usage charges. Digitization of the transmission network is the first step toward these goals. Network integration and the maturity of INS as a functioning entity will follow.

4. A question raised by interest in INS is the degree to which it will conflict with the Japanese goal of promoting competition among facilities providers. As NTT, particularly, moves deeply into INS experiments and continues to upgrade its network, the company becomes better able to provide comprehensive telecommunications services for all users. INS could dissuade new service providers from entering into the VAN market and could significantly undercut the attractiveness of the Type II service category.

5. Nonetheless, the potential for an advanced technological network that could reduce service prices and dramatically expand service availability cannot be ignored. INS could do, on a large scale, what many small VAN could do in particular parts of the country. Consequently, the future of the communications market in Japan is likely to involve a careful weighing of the costs and benefits of INS and of a competitive, multi-network structure.

6. The Japanese also are acutely aware of the potential that INS holds to alter daily life, as well as social and cultural customs. Concerns about privacy, patterns of commerce, and the effects of having ready access to massive amounts of information and varied communications capabilities are being carefully considered in the Japanese evaluation of INS. INS represents a new era in the "informatization" of society. It has a vast potential to enhance both national and global flows of information. It also poses a threat

because it invites increased reliance on a unified network; the misuse or malfunction of that network could have a catastrophic effect on all parts of society.

B. The Japanese Experience with INS

1. *Introduction*

a. INS is seen as the next evolutionary step in the advancement of communications systems, providing the ultimate integration of communications systems, providing the ultimate integration of computers and transmission facilities. The Japanese view INS as a socio-cultural phenomenon that will make possible the development of an Advanced Information Society and will satisfy the increased and more complex information needs of individuals and of businesses. *See* Y. Kitahara, *Information Network System* (1983).

b. Currently, NTT provides separate transmission paths for voice, data, facsimile, and video carriage. With the increased use of fiber optic cables and satellite links, facilitating a vastly increased transmission capacity and reducing the distance sensitivities of transmission costs, it is expected that movement toward a single operating system, carrying all communications according to a unified tariff (based primarily on the amount of information transmitted, rather than on the distance over which the information is carried), will become feasible. A single digital user terminal will be capable of transmitting a variety of data in different forms.

c. Current network improvements have allowed for more economical and efficient forms of transmission. The DDX networks have been introduced by NTT to provide packet-switched data communications. Using the store-and-forward packet technology, which removes the need for establishment of a dedicated transmission path each time communication between two terminals is desired (as is required in circuit-switched network), this data network reduces the distance sensitivity of transmission costs. In addition, because all information is transmitted in bit form, and is later assembled into addressed packets, all communications can be charged according to a uniform, bit-based tariff.

d. The improvement in communications brought about by the DDX networks is significant; however, the changes are miniscule when compared with the potential revolution that INS would cause.

2. *NTT's INS Experiment*

a. The INS Model System has been operating in the Tokyo suburbs since September 28, 1984. It will continue through early 1987. It also has been connected to the Den Den INS Pavillion at Tsukaba Expo '85, which is connected with satellite halls around Japan to demonstrate the network to users and information providers.

i) The INS includes digital telephone service, which permits the display of call charges; voice and message store and forward service; multi-media, circuit-switched, and packet-switched data transmission services; analog and digital videotex; video conferencing; one-way and two-way motion picture distribution services; high-definition television; and, digital, color, and ultra-high-speed facsimile service.

ii) An expansion in March, 1985, included the addition of a number of broadband services and the opening of "INS Model Offices" that allow people who live outside of the experiment area to see INS in operation. The system now includes more than 500 users and more than 300 information providers.

b. NTT's objectives are to determine the technological feasibility of providing INS, users' opinions about the services being offered, the effect of INS on the local community, the proper rate structure to operate INS profitably.

c. The Model System includes the following components: 450 digital telephones, 1050 digital facsimile units, digital videotex terminals, video conference terminals, and 200 CAPTAIN (analog videotex) terminals. The INS network is connected to the main NTT network, and to CAPTAIN information centers, through various processing facilities.

d. Subscriber lines consist of both metallic cables and fiber optic links. This configuration permits simultaneous use of more than one service or communication with more than one person at a time. It also allows the system to provide basic telecommunications services at a 64 kbit/sec. transmission rate as well as to carry high-speed digital services and various broadband communications.

e. NTT has discovered valuable information about the expectations of users of INS. These include improvement of the quality of life through access to more information sources, increased free time, and a broader diversity of experiences. Users also had some concerns, including the potential for stratifying society based on differences in users' abilities to absorb the available information, increased chaos in daily life patterns, and threats to personal privacy.

f. NTT also has gathered information about users' reactions to the early stages of the experiment. There was some disappointment expressed about the limited sources of information available during the experiment's early days. NTT has since expanded the base of information providers and services. Users also wanted smaller terminal equipment that would be easier to operate.

g. A February, 1985, survey of users regarding the CAPTAIN system revealed that directory-type services (train and airline information, weather forecasts, and movie and theater guides) were the most used, along with quizzes and horoscopes. These services were also said to contain the most useful information. Three percent of the users rated CAPTAIN "very useful" or "useful," while one-quarter called it "not very useful" or "not useful." Users said that database-type services would be a good addition to CAPTAIN. They requested "little known" or "difficult-to-obtain" information as well as information "useful for work or study."

h. Information providers to the Video Response System ("VRS"), which provides database information including full-action video, viewed cost reductions and a need to provide more desirable information as important to ensuring the future success of the system. Two-thirds of the information providers rated the technology "attractive" or "very attractive" in their responses to the February, 1985, survey.

i. Some of the current uses of the Model INS include the following:

i) Fifteen department stores and supermarkets are operating a home shopping service.

ii) Thirty-three organizations are participating in a home banking trial service that includes the ability to perform various account functions and to pay bills.

iii) One company has used INS to provide improved intracorporate communications, using a variety of media.

iv) A number of companies are planning to provide new kinds of client services using the network.

v) The city of Mitaka offers a variety of public services including events directories and various administrative information. An ultra-high-speed facsimile service is being used to provide "immediate transfer service for resident certification documents." A consumer group in Mitaka also is supplying consumer information, and a commercial organization is providing information about town merchants and their services.

vi) Doctors and teachers also are experimenting with ways of using the network for medical and educational purposes.

j. The future for commercial INS remains unclear. However, the continued digitization of the NTT network represents an important move toward the establishment of an infrastructure that could be used to bring commercial INS service to Japan. The digital network then would have to be used to integrate existing separate networks so that users would ultimately have universal access through a single terminal or set of integrated terminals.

C. Implementing INS While Liberalizing Service Opportunities

1. There may be some fundamental incompatibility between traditional views of INS and the new competitive market structure that the new Japanese telecommunications laws are designed to promote. If competition in the facilities area results in the development of at least two suppliers of basic transmission services, some mechanism will have to be adopted to assure compatibility of these two systems. Standardization of formats and protocols will permit the interconnection of the networks to form a unified

transmission path. The fact of separate ownership will then be "invisible" to users.

2. There is also a question as to how the structure of different Type II VANs will mesh with the concept of an NTT-based INS. It is not clear whether the various options for different systems for protocol, speed, and format capability will be external to the backbone network or internal to it. If the functions are to be internal to an advanced, integrated NTT network, competitive service suppliers may be unable to produce any advantages or achieve much innovation. If, on the other hand, these capabilities are external, a single network would be unable to offer the full range of services that INS is intended to achieve. How far the analysis of this apparent (or potential) conflict in objectives has been pursued within NTT or the MPT seems somewhat unclear.

3. In Europe, the focus of network integration has been on achieving uniformity at the lower layers of the ISO standard. Differences among services providers, which create incompatibilities, have been recognized and left in place—at least for the present time. Creation of a single, comprehensive network has not been the primary aim of integrated services plans. In the higher protocol levels of the ISO standard, for example, there may well be diversity in the approaches taken by various service providers. The effort to differentiate among various applications-related services may, therefore, result in a more definite separation of basic and other services in Japan, with only the "basic" services becoming part of the integrated network.

4. Unless compatibility can be achieved among various competing systems, competition will be focused on Type I businesses that can construct their own integrated facilities, which will include VANs. Without this compatibility, Type II businesses will be unable to provide value-added services to a great number of otherwise incompatible end users. The development and adoption of systems software, which permits communication between incompatible terminals, has to be a high priority if disparate VANs are to compete and to offer valuable communications services. Without such enhanced compatibility, the business that can offer the integrated facilities, with the necessary terminal equipment, will enjoy a significant competitive advantage. In the short-term, NTT will enjoy the greatest advantage: it has begun to assemble such an integrated network, through its INS objectives. It will have a substantial lead over other potential Type I businesses, which will need time to begin installing their own facilities.

5. As a greater variety of services are introduced, further clarification of the INS concept will become necessary. Some early explanations of INS focused on the fact that the offering was both a technological concept and a set of rate principles. In the former respect, INS involves the installation of a backbone of high-capacity, fiber optic cables and extensive digital-switching facilities. In the latter respect, INS is touted as a strategy for pricing communications capacity on a bit-rate basis. This would harmonize the pricing of voice, data, and video services. The price of transmission

would depend only on the volume—not the kind—of information being carried. If this bit-based tariff structure is pursued, it may remove much of the incentive for establishing value-added networks.

6. The precise meaning of the INS concept has not yet been resolved, and it is now under reexamination.

VII. INFORMATION PROCESSING AND VANS

A. Information Processing: Contours of the Industry

1. Probably the most difficult aspect of describing the information processing industry lies in trying to define its components. In Japan, as in many countries, there is some disagreement as to the true boundaries of the industry.

a. A 1983 report prepared by the Japan Information Processing Development Center ("JIPDEC") adopts a definition that is also used by MITI. It defines the industry as containing three sub-industries: the information processing industry, which makes computing services available to the public; the software industry, which develops and sells software; and the database service industry, which provides information through data retrieval operations. *See* JIPDEC, *Information Services Japan '83* (No. 56) (1983) [hereinafter cited as JIPDEC, *Report No. 56*]; *see also* JIPDEC, *Computer White Paper* (1984). These three components constitute an industry that is separable from, though closely related to, the computer industry.

b. It is estimated that in 1982 the information processing industry included 1300 businesses and total revenues of 911.9 billion yen. Although the Japanese information processing industry has grown rapidly over the past four years, its size remains miniscule as compared with the more developed information processing industry in the United States.

2. JIPDEC identifies three types of companies in the information processing industry. The first type is an integrated service company, which provides data processing functions accessed by means of its own nationwide networks. Type two companies serve local governments in major population centers of Japan's more remote areas. These companies have experienced strong competition from the nationwide network companies and so have begun to diversify, offering small business computers. The third type of company is the small data processing center found in numerous locations throughout major metropolitan areas in Japan. Due to the increased popularity of office and home computer systems, these companies have begun to look to software development and to the sale of turnkey systems to supplement their businesses.

3. The software industry divides the majority of its business between developing packages for computer manufacturers and designing systems for private businesses. High demand for custom-designed software has slowed the development of pre-packaged products.

4. In the database services area, Japan has been slow to develop. Most database services are provided by companies that offer it as only a small part of their total business operations. Only one company, Quotation Information Center K.K., the eleventh largest firm in the information processing industry, operates solely as a database service company. The database service industry serves a market that is about one-sixth the size of the U.S. market and about one-third the size of the European market.

5. JIPDEC noted that of the 456 databases available in Japan as of September, 1982, only about one-fourth were constructed in Japan. By type, the databases available in Japan were primarily textual (65%), rather than numerical (22%), precisely the opposite of the worldwide mix. JIPDEC, *Report No. 56, supra,* at 20. The numerous foreign databases were available to Japanese users through domestic distributors or through leased and public international telecommunications circuits.

6. Scientific and technical data are requested by the greatest number of database users. Newspaper and magazine articles, world patent information, and chemical and pharmaceutical services all draw a slightly smaller number of users.

7. JIPDEC identifies domestic database creation as a high priority for the growth and development of the information processing industry generally. One recommendation offered to help accomplish this goal is that the government make its vast data resources more readily available to the public. *Id.* at 28-29. The Report also suggests that to attain more pronounced growth, the industry needs to develop better methods for computer recognition of Japanese-language keywords. Systems capable of providing automatic translations from English into Japanese, and vice versa, are also necessary.

8. Database security poses another major concern for the developing industry. MITI has established security standards both for computer systems and for data processing centers. It has imposed a rigorous set of certification criteria covering both facilities and systems operations. MITI conducts inspections of both facilities and services to ensure compliance with the criteria. The high cost of complying with the security measures (running into the tens or hundreds of millions of yen) is seen as a reason for the slow growth of processing centers. There were just thirty-eight centers open as of the end of 1983.

9. The liberalization of NTT circuit use, which permits the interconnection of databases to form distributed networks, should provide a major stimulus for growth in the database industry. In 1981, the Science and Technology Agency began one such networking project—expected to take five years to complete—which permits users to access a variety of different scientific databases through a single network. Growth of complex sharing arrangements in a single network will bring about the need to develop more advanced database management systems. Search techniques and retrieval commands also will have to be standardized, to permit the optimal use of shared facilities.

10. Industry development also will raise concerns about systems of copyright protection to guard against the misappropriation of database resources and about transborder data flow issues. These transborder concerns include the international standardization of transmission technologies, tax and tariff policies regarding data, privacy and data protection regimes, and the problems caused by information disparities between developing and developed nations.

B. Development of VANs

1. Overview

a. The expansion of the General Type II category should stimulate an explosion of VANs in Japan. Early indications suggest that the race to enter—and conquer—the newly competitive market will be both fast and furious.

b. The number of existing and potential value-added service providers has grown rapidly since the 1982 liberalization, which permitted entities other than NTT to offer value-added services. The emphasis of the recent development work has been on systems software, which allows communications among otherwise incompatible computers. Such networking capability will be particularly important to the successful growth of VANs as the new liberalization policies permit expansion into inter-corporate, rather than merely intra-corporate, communications systems.

c. Value-added service activity has been spread among more than 10,000 network services, provided by a wide variety of industry participants. Perhaps the greatest degree of activity has involved wholesalers and retailers, who have been part of a wide array of VANs that provide them with a variety of enhanced communications services. Two pharmaceutical companies have combined to provide a VAN that carries product supply information for pharmacists. A conglomerate of thirty companies has begun to explore a VAN that would use cable television and teletext technologies to provide a network video mail-order service, operating like an on-line catalog.

d. With the new laws having taken effect, the Japanese market is seeing the start of a new wave of VANs. By mid-April, five new Special Type II VANs had applied for registration with the MPT. The choice of seeking Special Type II registration is somewhat surprising, in view of the government's substantial expansion of the General Type II category. *See supra* Section III.C.2. However, all of these companies plan very large scale operations, which could exceed the 500-line limit imposed on General Type II businesses. In addition, it has been speculated that Special Type II businesses might gain some sort of advantage as the MPT sorts out the treatment of international VANs. The complex international situation is discussed below. *See infra* Section VIII.D.

2. VANs Being Planned for Introduction

a. IBM Japan has announced plans for a large-scale, nationwide data processing network, called Information Network. IBM also will be involved in a smaller-scale VAN through a joint venture with Mitsubishi and Cosmo 80. This venture, called AST, will use IBM's systems software, System Network Architecture ("SNA") to integrate small-scale VANs into a communications network. SNA represents a formidable competitor for NTT's Data Communications Network Architecture, which is being developed and is in use in NTT's inter-bank data network. *See supra* Section II.E.

b. AT&T has joined a sixteen-company consortium, led by Mitsui & Co., the Industrial Bank of Japan, Sony, Nippon Steel, and Toyota to provide a large-scale VAN that will use AT&T's Net 1000 technology. This systems software will provide users with a network capable of linking computers of various makes and of offering massive data storage and processing capacity. The network also is expected to offer users access to certain applications software. The companies have established a joint venture called Japan ENS Corp. Full operation is scheduled to begin in 1986.

c. Mainframe manufacturer Fujitsu registered to provide a three-stage VAN. The first phase will involve installation of an in-house digital information network linking its headquarters in Tokyo with its Osaka office and the company's factories and laboratories. Early in 1986, phase two will add all of the company's sales branches to the network. The final phase would integrate all Fujitsu subsidiaries, twenty-four affiliated software houses, and 108 computer service companies. Fujitsu FIP Co., one of those subsidiaries, was one of the first private VAN operators following the 1982 liberalization. It offers one of the largest VANS operations currently in place, linking 400 supermarkets nationwide.

d. Hitachi, another mainframe manufacturer, has already established a wholly-owned subsidiary, Hitachi Ltd., which is working on a nationwide packet-switching network to be used by four Hitachi subsidiaries. The system, called Hinet, eventually is supposed to reach nine major Japanese cities and will be available to a variety of Hitachi-affiliated companies. Hitachi has also registered for an international VAN called Hitachi Information Network. It will link Hinet with the U.S. Tymnet service to provide international packet switching, information processing, and access to economic and financial databases.

e. NEC Information Service (NEIS) now operates NEISNET, a nationwide VAN. Under the restrictions of the 1982 laws, it was available only to smaller users. It has now been registered, however, and will be expanded. NEC also is considering an international VAN that would link NEISNET to the 600-city General Electric network in the U.S. NEC's network is not compatible with IBM hardware, setting up the potential for a battle between the two computer companies—now that IBM appears ready to enter the VAN market.

f. Intec has registered to provide data transmission, facsimile, and voice services over its VAN. The company also is considering an international VAN linking its services to the GTE-Telnet system in the U.S.

g. Japan Information Services has registered to provide a large-scale VAN offering data transmission.

h. General Electric Information Services Co., a GE subsidiary, has formed a joint venture with Dentsu, the world's largest advertising agency. Called Information Services International-Dentsu, the business will build upon GE's current Japanese VAN to offer international protocol conversion and database access. The venture is the second international business being planned by both parties. (GE is discussing plans for a network with NEC, and Dentsu is part of the ENS group.)

i. The growth of VANs is expected to bring the development of more extensive electronic mail networks and a variety of private conferencing links for video, audio, and computer hookups. It is estimated that these systems will carry as much as fifty percent of the nation's intra-corporate communications by the end of the decade. The development of increasingly intelligent and complex computers, plus the expansion of the digitized fiber optic transmission network, should help the number of VANs accelerate rapidly under the liberalized legal regime.

VIII. INTERNATIONAL IMPLICATIONS OF TELECOMMUNICATIONS LAW REVISION

A. Introduction

1. The Telecommunications Business Law and the MPT ordinances adopted to implement it inevitably may require the introduction of competition into the international telecommunications field. This would bring about a significant change in KDD's long dominant role in the market. The Ministry apparently intends to open and to liberalize the international market. However, KDD intends to have an active role in identifying and in shaping the hard choices that must be made about the future structure of the Japanese international telecommunications industry. These choices will require decisions about whether there will be new facilities providers (*e.g.*, through regional satellite systems) and about how to structure the relationship between KDD and the Type II VANs. The ultimate resolution of these issues is now far from clear.

2. There is nothing in the Telecommunications Business Law that limits its application to domestic services. Article 6 defines a Type I business to be one that "provides telecommunications service by establishing telecommunications circuit facilities." A Type II business is any other telecommunications business. In addition, the MPT ordinance that apparently permits international VANs to operate as General Type II businesses would allow for fierce, unregulated competition among international ser-

vice providers. For now, however, KDD continues as the sole provider of international communications links.

B. KDD: Corporate Overview

1. KDD is a privately owned company that operates as a monopolist in the international services market. NTT owns approximately ten percent of its stock.

2. The company has come under increasing scrutiny, with the MPT now apparently debating the extent to which KDD will be permitted to maintain its past monopoly.

a. Before he was replaced in a Cabinet reorganization on November 1, 1984, Posts & Telecommunciations Minister Keiwa Okuda requested a study of how competition could be introduced in the international market. The report, which was presented in April, 1985, did not really address the questions of whether the KDD monopoly should be ended or what the future structure of the international telecommunications monopoly should be. It looked more generally at issues involving the future of the International Telecommunications Union ("ITU") and other international organizations such as Intelsat. It also considered the state of the North-South dialogue on communications. It appears that the issue of KDD's future will be resolved separately over the next year.

b. Perhaps anticipating the introduction of international competition, KDD has entered into discussions with MCI about forming a second international telephone service that would compete directly with the service AT&T now offers with KDD. It appears that KDD, although seeking to protect its monopoly, also is moving to solidify its market base.

3. Recently, KDD has begun a significant facilities upgrade to accommodate increased demands for international data transmission and for high-speed, low-cost communications.

4. In 1980, the company introduced its International Computer Access Service ("ICAS"), which permits Japanese users to access foreign databases. Originally connected only to the United States, the service was later expanded to cover a number of countries in Europe and Canada.

5. In April, 1982, the company introduced an international packet-switched data transfer service called VENUS-P. This network is also connected to the NTT domestic packet-switched network, allowing users of NTT's packet-switched service (called DDX-P) to gain access to high-quality, international data transmission networks. ICAS was absorbed into VENUS-P in July, 1983. In May, 1984, the MPT approved a KDD agreement with AT&T to provide leased circuits for data communications between Japan and the United States.

6. The company plans to invest more than $1 billion in facilities expansion and in new construction through 1987, including construction of a fiber optic submarine cable, Transpacific Cable No. 3 ("TPC-3"), that would link Japan and Hawaii. This fiber optic cable, to be built in

cooperation with AT&T and several PTTs, has provided the stimulus for intense research efforts into the development of fiber optic cables that can withstand the water pressure exerted on lines laid along the ocean's bottom. One such cable was tested in 1982 and was found to provide satisfactory transmission results.

7. The growing demand for international telephone service has caused KDD to expand direct-dialing services to more than half of the 200-plus total areas it serves worldwide. The vast majority of KDD's international traffic (more than seventy percent) is handled by existing direct-dial services. In addition, KDD has reduced international service rates and has instituted a nighttime and Sunday rate differential.

8. Although international telex service has continued to increase, international telegram use has declined. Facsimile (bureaufax) use, however, has grown at a phenomenal pace. In 1982 it more than doubled, as KDD expanded the number of areas served to twenty, up from the original eleven. This facsimile service could face competition from an international electronic mail service now being operated by the Postal Ministry. The Ministry has said it is considering setting prices for electronic mail below the levels charged by KDD for its facsimile (bureaufax) services.

9. Increased demand for international satellite service has prompted KDD to construct a fourth earth station in its Ibaraki communications center. A third station in the Yamaguchi center was completed in 1984. Satellite services generally are expected to receive a significant boost with the continued development of Japan's own satellite-launching capabilities, a result of new investment in the Japanese space program. Japan is working on developing a rocket capable of launching heavier payloads that would be useful for carrying advanced communications satellites. The introduction of U.S. satellite technology, *see supra* Section III.C.1., also could significantly expand satellite traffic.

10. The growing use of international services has helped KDD enjoy an increase in its operating revenues, which reached $710 million in fiscal 1982, up 3.4% from the previous year. Net income of $56 million was down slightly from the prior year, as a result of an increase in operating expenses of almost six percent. Approximately fifty-five percent of KDD's revenues were attributable to telephone services; thirty percent came from telex operations, and the remaining fifteen percent was contributed by all other services.

C. The Potential for Expanded International Satellite Service

1. One major question facing the government is whether to permit one or more facilities-based competitors for KDD. It is possible that an entity might be able to purchase an interest in a transoceanic cable. More likely, however, any such competition would come from the use of new

satellite facilities. In either case, it is not clear that the government would approve such an international Type I business.

2. KDD currently provides service over both satellite and cable facilities. It relies upon international satellite circuits leased from Intelsat and upon a number of transoceanic submarine cables in which it holds ownership interests. The satellite area, however, is where it may be more open to facilities-based competition.

a. The Research Institute of Telecommunications and Economics ("RITE") prepared a study that examined the feasibility of a regional satellite system in the Pacific region. *A Study of the Pacific Regional Satellite Telecommunications System* (1983). The report outlined a system for using a Pacific satellite to augment the inadequate communications facilities of remote areas and isolated islands. The system would enhance the transmission capacity that now links them to major cities and would provide them with video and facsimile opportunities. The satellite also would provide metropolitan areas with a low-cost, high-speed, digital data, facsimile, voice, and video transmission network.

b. The Japanese government is taking a cautious approach to any plans for third-party ownership and operation of international telecommunications services. It has not endorsed the conclusions of the RITE study. Developments in the United States regarding proposals to establish transatlantic satellite networks that compete with INTELSAT are likely to have a significant impact on Japanese policymakers. (Japan, like the U.S., is an INTELSAT member and is under similar treaty obligations to avoid causing significant economic harm to the INTELSAT system.)

c. Japanese entrepreneurial interests undoubtedly will take a keen interest in investing in a specialized regional satellite system. In addition, it is possible that regional satellite facilities might be used to provide domestic satellite services within Japan.

3. There are a number of possible linkages between domestic and international satellite policies in Japan. The Japanese national market may be too small to support a single dedicated system. Thus, there could be interest in regional services from the spillover of the satellite's beam or through the use of a spot beam. Conversely, if a regional system gains momentum independently, some of its capacity might be used for domestic services.

4. The attention to satellite issues undoubtedly has been heightened by the government's decision to permit the development of two new Type I businesses that will use U.S. satellite technology. A desire for more advanced space stations makes U.S. technology, which can provide the added sophistication, particularly appealing. Current plans to upgrade the country's relatively new domestic satellite facilities should provoke additional interest in this area.

a. The first generation of Japanese satellites, CS-2, was put into orbit last year. The two satellites, CS-2a and CS-2b, each have a 4,000-circuit capacity, and they are used primarily for communications with remote islands. The CS-3 series, set for a 1988 launch, will have twelve transponders and a 6,000-circuit capacity. It is intended to serve as a basic facility for Type II businesses, including VANs.

b. The MPT has announced plans for a $600 million space development project to begin in 1984. The project will include the launch of a new generation of satellites, called Super-CS, housing sixty to seventy transponders and capable of handling 100,000 telephone circuits. The major use of the circuits will be data communications, including VANs. Projected launch would be in 1991, with a second launch in 1994. The two-ton satellite will require the development of a new rocket booster for launching. The government plans to share investment expenses with the private sector.

D. The Impact of Competition Among VANs

1. Despite the fact that the MPT has not taken any steps toward introducing international, facilities-based competition, it clearly has recognized that competition in VAN services will not be confined to the Japanese domestic market. These VANs will, therefore, be engaged in service-based competition with KDD. A major question, however, is how all these Japanese-based VAN services can offer international service in light of KDD's current role and responsibilities.

2. KDD's VENUS-P is a packet-switched service based on a usage-sensitive pricing scheme that differs significantly from the tariff structure applied to basic leased private line offerings. KDD, no doubt, would prefer that all of the new domestic Type II networks be permitted to interconnect internationally only through its packet network. However, in some oberers' views, that outcome is not practical, given the diversity of protocols and economic interests underlying the various services. Thus, it might be expected that several packet services will become available to VAN providers. It is not clear, however, whether this number will be equivalent to the number of domestic Type II businesses. If not all Type II businesses are qualified automatically to provide international packet services, there will be a significant and difficult set of procedures for determining which entities will be permitted to operate internationally.

3. KDD's own approach to competition from new services differs in significant respects from that of NTT.

a. KDD has a number of well-focused concerns about the economic impact of competition on certain profitable sectors of its international business and about the relative vulnerability of its position as an exclusive supplier of international satellite services. KDD's exclusivity depends not on ownership and control of these facilities, which are in fact internationally owned and controlled, but on KDD's role as the designated representative to Intelsat.

b. KDD has taken the position that international VANs would have the status of "customers" under its tariff regulations and would be engaged in resale of communications services. In its view, use by VAN suppliers of leased international circuits would be inconsistent with CCITT Recommendations proscribing resale. Therefore, Type II services, according to KDD, must rely on the services of authorized U.S. international carriers and its own VENUS-P offering.

4. KDD does make leased circuits for private data network services—but not for "enhanced" transmission services—available to companies such as GE Mark III and Control Data. It considers those operators to be engaged in remote access data processing, which is permitted under the Recommendations, and not in the carriage of communications. To the extent that those entities are "customers," their offerings are not resale because their users use the line in a manner consistent with the business of the "customer" of the line, *i.e.*, for remote access data processing. These activities are, therefore, de facto differentiated by KDD from VANs, thereby establishing—as a matter of practice—a distinction between VAN and data processing services. It may well be necessary to make explicit this service-related distinction in light of conflicting and uncertain interpretations of what is and is not a permissible international third-party service. To the degree that such distinctions are left unclear and embedded in the KDD's practices (based on relevant CCITT Recommendations), the pressure to liberalize the international VANs market could well result in new restrictions being imposed on information-related or data processing services—limitations that could seriously impede the transborder flow of data and international business operations.

5. Particularly difficult issues are involved where existing remote access data processing services and information services are offered with elements of message switching. The "hybrid" or combination services clearly do not constitute "core" communications-related services. However, KDD has been inclined to consider such services as third-party offerings inconsistent with the existing terms of availability applicable to international private business line services. It will be important to observe how such past restrictive interpretations evolve in a climate where pressures are increasing for greater flexibility for international VAN services. It is not certain whether such services—even though bundled into a Type II category domestically—will be considered internationally as a category separate from "communications processing" and activities.

6. The failure to distinguish between "hybrid" data processing, information, or VAN services and "communications processing" activities could have broader adverse international implications. Any international application of the Japanese domestic Type II category could create the same uncertainty for multinational users that many viewed as resulting from the international application of the "enhanced" service concept of the *Computer II* proceeding. For example, providers of unregulated information or data processing services might agree to operate in Japan as General Type II businesses because this classification would not impose any regulatory burdens on operations within Japan. However, other countries,

with more restrictive regulatory regimes, might then view these information services as indistinguishable from entities actually in the "communications" sector. All General Type II businesses—whether or not a VAN or a hybrid information service—might then be subjected to telecommunications-related entry (and other) restrictions by foreign governments.

7. The potential international spillover effects of Japanese regulation are greater than in the U.S. case. That is because the Type II category actually could include companies involved in "basic transmission" services that are exactly comparable to the international telex services of KDD or the U.S. record carriers. Thus, policymakers will have to create international service distinctions unless the practical effect of liberalization in the Japanese domestic market is, effectively, a complete deregulation of the international resale market. The impact of Japanese domestic developments on the international arena—as was the case in the aftermath of liberalization in the U.S.—is evidence of the close relationship between domestic and international policy issues.

8. The MPT also faces the difficult task of trying to align a liberalized domestic resale policy that frees leased line usage with KDD's restrictive approach to resale of international circuits. It will not be the first time that this domestic/international interconnection issue has been confronted. In fact, until recently NTT's DDX-P network was incompatible with KDD's VENUS-P system. The two carriers had used different versions of the X.25 transmission protocol; and, until recently, a gateway between domestic and international packet services did not exist. Now, the government is likely to feel significant pressure from users, both foreign and domestic, who want not only the flexibility of access to international VAN services, but also greater ability to connect domestic and international private leased lines. Such users might include financial information services—*e.g.*, relaying information on global stock market trading activity—or operators serving the transportation sectors. Joint ventures involving Japanese and U.S. companies will want to link up their leased line networks.

9. The Japanese government already has faced U.S. pressure on the domestic VANs issue during the recent trade negotiations. International competition was a high priority for U.S. trade negotiators; U.S. pressure may have contributed to the MPT's decision to include in its ordinances a provision permitting General Type II businesses to extend services internationally. The MPT now must formulate a uniform means of classifying international VANs and leased line services so that effective arrangements for international services can be established. The international issues are much more complex than the domestic ones; both Japanese and U.S. policymakers are likely to have some difficulty in working out the parameters of the relationship between Japanese domestic liberalization and the international telecommunications service market.

IX. CABLE TELEVISION SERVICES

A. Jurisdictional Issues

1. A difficult issue presented by the Telecommunications Business Law is the exact relationship between "telecommunications services" and cable television services. Article 2(iv) defines "telecommunications business" to exclude various cable television services subject to the different laws relating to cable radio, Law to Regulate the Operation of the Cable Sound Broadcasting Service, Law No. 135 of 1951, and cable television broadcast services, Cable Television Broadcast Law, Law No. 114 of 1972. Nevertheless, under the terms of Article 9, either NTT or a new Type I business other than NTT could install local coaxial or fiber optic cables to carry cable television services (one-way or two-way, voice-related or non-voice).

a. The objective of the new telecommunications law seems to be to maintain a separate authorization for such services. However, to the extent that the basic wire transmission plant could be used for a wide variety of services, any Type I business could be authorized to offer cable television services.

b. A Type II business also could provide these services, using the wires of a Type I business.

2. The MPT presumably will use its supervisory powers over Type I and Special Type II businesses to limit the degree to which they can provide services thought to be within the domain of cable broadcasting service. (The Ministry cannot, of course, regulate a General Type II business.) Yet without some clear concept of a division between cable services and telecommunications—which seems almost impossible to make in the area of two-way offerings—any such regulatory restraints would be purely arbitrary. Moreover, creating divisions between cable services and telecommunications offerings would appear contrary to the INS principle—to the degree such separation promotes development of distinct, incompatible transmission networks.

3. In May, 1983, the MPT decided to permit cable systems to offer two-way services, despite the fact that the current cable television law authorizes only one-way transmissions. The scope of two-way services is limited, however, by the MPT's requirement that such services be "limited to the existing network." This means that services can involve communications between the cable station and subscriber homes. This precludes the use of remote access databases or the interconnection of the cable network to other transmission systems, such as the telephone system or private data links.

4. The MPT has indicated that the cable law will be revised to permit a wider variety of two-way services to be offered (such as home banking or data transmission). It is unclear, though, how any limitations on

cable service will be enforced with respect to Type I carriers who operate networks that can carry a variety of cable services. The new laws, along with changes in technology, may hasten the convergence of the now-separate legal regimes for cable television and telecommunications services. If telecommunications businesses are able to monopolize two-way services, cable facilities will be left to provide primarily broadcast retransmission. The future of cable television then might rely almost exclusively on the development of a Japanese satellite distribution network that could provide cable systems with new programming.

5. Potential cable/telephone service competition has already developed with the announcement by Japan Cable Television Company that it will market a videotex service with Sony Corp. to its 18,000 subscribers in Tokyo. This system will compete with NTT's CAPTAIN service, which is discussed above. *See supra* Section V.A.

B. The Current Cable Television Market

1. Under the legal framework established by the 1972 Cable Television Broadcast Law, approximately 35,000 separate systems have evolved to serve 3.6 million subscribers. The primary focus of these systems' activities has been providing retransmission of local broadcast channels. Under Article 3, the MPT, in cooperation with its Cable Broadcast Council (formed under the 1972 law), licenses the construction and the operation of cable television broadcast facilities. The MPT is given broad discretion in licensing decisions. The law requires the MPT to grant a license only if the facilities plan "is reasonable and its practicability is ensured," if the operator is technically and financially qualified to establish and to operate the facilities, and if construction of the system is "needful and appropriate in the light of natural, social and cultural conditions" of the area to be served. Cable Television Broadcast Law, at Art. 4(1). The MPT also is instructed to consult with the prefectures to be served by the proposed cable facilities. *Id.* Art. 4(2). Clearly, the MPT retains a rather free hand in deciding whether to permit the installation of new facilities. Any change in facilities must be approved by the MPT. *Id.* Art. 7.

2. The cable law distinguishes between the facilities licensee (the person approved to construct the actual cables) and the service provider (the person who actually provides cable services). *See id.* at Art. 2(2) & (4). Of course, a single person or entity may both build the system and operate it. Although a facilities builder must receive prior authorization from the MPT, *id.* at Art. 3, a service provider need only notify the MPT, *id.* at Art. 12.

3. Article 13 obligates a cable facilities licensee to retransmit—intact—all local television broadcast signals. No other television broadcast signals can be retransmitted without the consent of the broadcaster. Local retransmission must be carried out according to the terms of a contract to be approved by the MPT. This contract is to include a "reason-

able'' charge for the retransmission—to be viewed in comparison with the costs of retransmission. *Id.* at Art. 15.

4. Cable television broadcasting services also may include original one-way transmissions, *id.* at Arts. 2(1) & 17, and, under the terms of the 1983 MPT ordinance, certain two-way services. A cable facilities licensee may not refuse to provide services in its service area ''unless there is a justifiable reason.'' *Id.* at Art. 16.

5. In December, 1983, Japan's first cable television network, Japan Cable Network, was formed with plans to serve 150,000 subscribers nationwide. Testing of the network began January 1, 1984.

C. Cable's Future Potential: A Crossroads

1. The direction of cable development appears uncertain. On the one hand, cable systems have been urged to coordinate some form of satellite delivery capacity that would allow Japanese cable systems to receive and to carry nationwide programming such as the satellite services now common in the United States (*e.g.*, Home Box Office, MTV, ESPN). The Seibu Group of Retail Companies announced in January, 1984, plans to establish a joint venture with American Television and Communications Corp., the cable system operator owned by Time, Inc. One goal of that venture was to be the possible introduction of Home Box Office (''HBO'') programming in Japan. (HBO also is owned by Time, Inc.) However, a significant obstacle to introducing such services are the current costs of domestic satellite services in Japan.

2. A spur to the development of satellite distribution may come from the announcement of a joint venture to provide the first pay-cable service in Japan to show Japanese-language films. (JC TV, another pay service, runs films in English.) Called Premiere International, the service will use microwave facilities and hand delivery of videocassettes to distribute its programming. The Japanese partners (Dentsu, Sochiko, Toho, and Tokyo Broadcasting Co.) own fifty-two percent of the company. The American and British partners (Columbia Pictures, Thorn/EMI, Twentieth Century Fox, Warner Brothers, Home Box Office, and Showtime/The Movie Channel) own the remaining forty-eight percent. Service is planned for early 1986. It will use films made by all of the partners (dubbed when necessary).

3. There are significant disincentives being placed in the way of new cable system growth in Japan.

a. Development of DBS—now stalled by the lack of usable transponder space—and the potentially less expensive construction of various SMATV systems around Japan have raised questions about the prospects for cable's future.

b. In addition, a recent decision by the Ministry of Construction to prohibit cable facilities licensees from stringing their wires along utility poles, requiring instead that cables be installed underground, has burdened the fledgling industry with a massive new expense. (The

Ministry can impose this requirement as a condition for use of roadside rights-of-way, which it controls.) One planned new cable venture, the International Cable Network ("ICN"), led by the Odakyu Electric Railway, was halted temporarily as a result of the drastically increased costs imposed by the underground construction requirement.

c. It remains uncertain as to whether the additional financial burdens, as well as the expansion of alternative delivery systems, will obstruct cable's development significantly.

4. Cable also appears to face a significant price barrier. A recent survey in Machida, near Tokyo, revealed that most residents could not afford to subscribe to the sophisticated two-way system being operated by ICN. Only seven percent said they could pay the $200 initial subscription fee and the monthly charge of $8-$12. People said they would be willing (and able) to pay about $40 for the initial charge and $4-$6 each month. The addition of new program services, which would supplement the eight retransmitted local broadcast stations available in most major cities, could increase the attractiveness of cable.

CHAPTER VI
UNITED KINGDOM

TABLE OF CONTENTS

CHAPTER VI
UNITED KINGDOM

I. INTRODUCTION: A SERIES OF CONFLICTING OBJECTIVES

A. Overview: Conflicts in the Pursuit of Competition

1. The U.K. government has adopted two broad strategies in its effort to inject competition into the telecommunications marketplace.

a. First, it has committed itself to promoting a diversification of service providers and offerings in order to stimulate increased marketplace activity. The government has ended the monopoly formerly held by British Telecommunications ("BT") and has permitted a new service provider, Mercury Communications Ltd. ("Mercury"), to construct new communications facilities. It is hoped that this facilities-based competition will encourage innovation that will accommodate the increasingly sophisticated communications needs of individuals and of businesses. The government also has taken steps to liberalize the use of communications circuits available to users. It has not, however, authorized "simple resale" of such services.

b. Second, the government has pursued an ideological commitment to dismantling public (government-owned) companies. It has chosen to convert them into private-sector businesses that can operate more independently of government supervision and can become more aggressive, competitive organizations.

2. This ideology has led to the privatization of BT, a long-time, government-owned, telecommunications monopoly, which was separated from the British Post Office in 1981. The government sold 50.8% of BT's stock in December, 1984, in a highly successful public offering. BT now is in the process of adjusting to the pressure of competition and the new freedoms of operating as a private company.

3. A major issue raised by the simultaneous pursuit of these two goals is the degree to which they may conflict. Any government effort to ensure the success of the newly privatized BT could frustrate the goal of introducing competition into the British telecommunications market. In addition, the particular regulatory measures adopted to pursue these broad objectives involve their own series of potentially conflicting goals: (1) preserving "universal service" or creating a competitive market that allows a more liberal use of communications services, (2) regulating with a "light hand" or assuring an effective transition to a new competitive environment through close regulatoy supervision, and (3) successfully privatizing BT or effectively establishing a new facilities competitor.

4. The government cannot avoid having to choose between these objectives during the coming months. The fact that the government's

policies may frustrate each other means that the ultimate outcome of new British telecommunications policies is surrounded with great uncertainty.

B. Preserving Limited Participation in Basic Service Operations

1. The government faces the delicate task of trying to subject BT to competition without emasculating it. The government seeks to retain BT as the backbone provider of nationwide basic telephone services. While adopting a general plan to liberalize the use of BT circuits, the government has decided not to permit the pure resale of transmission capacity—at least until July, 1989. This prohibition will prevent third-party service providers from competing directly with BT's basic service—public switched transmission services (*i.e.*, basic telephone and telex service). This restriction provides some degree of protection for BT in the short run (helping to maintain its continued, profitable operation as a public telecommunications service provider). New competitors will be stopped from diverting high-volume users—with the lure of lower prices. Such diversion could jeopardize BT's ability to furnish telephone service to all residents of the U.K. BT argues that such competition also could hamper its ability to provide a variety of costly public services, such as emergency calling and public call boxes.

2. In order to ensure that BT does not languish in this protected basic services market, the government has licensed one alternative basic carrier, Mercury. Thus far, Mercury has posed only a limited competitive threat to BT. The time and money necessary to develop the basic Mercury transmission network have required that the company grow gradually. However, much of the initial work is now being completed, and Mercury appears ready to assume an aggressive competitive position. Nonetheless, there remains some doubt as to whether the government's reliance on a single competitor ultimately will prove successful. In this regard, the government's expectations as to how fast Mercury could develop as a competitor to BT may have been unrealistic. Mercury has been further hindered by the evolution of pro-competition policies and by an ongoing dispute with BT about its right to interconnect with the BT network.

3. At the fringes of this basic services market, the government has approved certain liberalized circuit users and other potential alternative facilities operators. All of these evolving services are provoking BT to innovate. In addition, they are expected to compete among themselves to provide consumers with a wide array of diverse communications services. The government has authorized the interconnection of private circuits and private branch systems that are designed to foster a certain degree of third-party transmission activity. Regulatory limits, however, prevent these new service providers from establishing extensive switched networks that could drain significant amounts of traffic away from the BT and Mercury facilities.

4. Developing cellular and mobile radio networks, advanced, interactive cable television systems, and managed data networks eventually

may provide some transmission competition for BT's local exchange network. However, a number of significant obstacles appear likely to limit the competitive effects of these technologies.

a. Regulatory, technological, and financial obstacles have hindered cable system development. The government required cable systems to install advanced, interactive capacity that is suitable for providing the kind of public switched services offered by BT and Mercury. However, cable system operators have chosen not to build more sophisticated switched star networks due to increased costs and complexity, as well as the entertainment-oriented backgrounds of most operators. This has left cable with a technological obligation that is out of step with its likely service demands. Moreover, the required technology is not only expensive, but also relies upon the manufacturing capacities of a limited number of equipment suppliers (many of whom have now withdrawn from the U.K. market).

b. The U.K.'s attempt to promote the rapid development of cable technology may have resulted in the formation of a medium that lacks an overriding purpose. The aspirations for its market impact, the requirements for system configuration, and the actual use of its capabilities are not clearly coordinated. Recognizing the disjunction of regulatory objectives and marketplace realities, the government has now relaxed the technological requirements for new franchises.

c. In addition, BT has gained a significant degree of involvement in both technologies. It is a partner in one of the two cellular radio ventures. The cable television laws also require that the cable system operator must work in conjunction with either BT or Mercury to provide two-way voice services anywhere in the U.K. or data services in London, Birmingham, or Manchester. Consequently, it is not at all clear that these alternative transmission paths will impose significant competitive pressures on BT.

d. The future of managed data networks, a service category that the government only recently proposed in a consultative document assessing the future licensing of value-added services, is highly uncertain. These transmission networks, which would operate as limited exceptions to the prohibition on circuit resale, could become the most significant competitors of basic service providers—at least in the area of data carriage. *See infra* Sections III.A., G. & I.

C. Seeking to Avoid an Explosion of Supervisory Institutions

1. The liberalization process will require careful government attention to ensure that new competitive relationships promote the development of varied and competitively priced telecommunications services. The variety of technologies involved in the transmission and processing of both information and communications implicate a wide range of regulatory interests. The government's approach to supervising the liberalized market

seems intended to develop a degree of expertise, which might help to ensure that the complex telecommunications market is intelligently supervised. Such a result would be contrary to the Thatcher Government's antipathy toward large public institutions. Nonetheless, the liberalization scheme being pursued may demand more extensive regulatory oversight than the government would ordinarily be inclined to permit. A dislike for large bureaucracies could leave the newly created Office of Telecommunications ("OFTEL") continually understaffed and always struggling to keep abreast of marketplace developments.

2. The goal of avoiding a complex regulatory scheme seems threatened by the many difficult issues inherent in the transition from a monopolistic to a competitive service market. Decisions about how BT's services should be priced, as well as the task of supervising its accounting changes to guard against cross-subsidization, will require close involvement by OFTEL. Producing clear and understandable BT accounts will require a massive overhaul of BT's historical practices, which include a noticeable lack of any systematic accounting procedures. These tasks are likely to strain OFTEL's capacities; they will require substantial commitments of time and money and may demand the attention of a more elaborate, formalized regulatory institution than the government has intended.

3. Part of the need for close government involvement is a result of the legal definitions adopted by the Telecommunications Act of 1984. The Act defines "telecommunications services" broadly and leaves the task of deciding precisely what services will be permitted to the Secretary of State of Trade and Industry, or by delegation to OFTEL. Service providers must be licensed, and only the terms of these licenses, which are set by the Secretary of State, after consultation with the Director General of OFTEL, will dictate the limits of a service provider's activities.

4. The government already has demonstrated that it cannot avoid involvement in the process of introducing competitive telecommunications services. As part of the licensing process, it has denied a request by BT and IBM to operate a joint venture that would have provided a managed data network. The proposal was characterized by the public and by OFTEL as potentially anticompetitive. The objectionable aspect of the proposal was its structure, which combined two dominant companies into a powerful joint venture. The government's competition policies demanded that BT and IBM diversify individually—to compete with each other.

5. The government also has decided to refer BT's plan to acquire fifty-one percent of Mitel, a Canadian PBX manufacturer, to the Monopolies and Mergers Commission. This decision, which was supported by the Director General of OFTEL, further illustrates the government's concern over the potential for BT to exert significant anti-competitive pressure on the U.K. market in telecommunications services and equipment. In this case, it was feared that BT's acquisition plans would cause it to stop

buying PBX equipment from unaffiliated U.K. manufacturers, which would reduce drastically the demand for their products. BT then might use its affiliation with Mitel to monopolize the PBX market in the U.K.

D. Conflict Between the Government's Interest in BT and in a Liberalized Marketplace

1. A major component of the liberalization movement has been the privatization of BT, authorized by the Telecommunications Act, 1984, ch. 12, §§ 60-69 (1984). Privatization and liberalization may, however, conflict in certain situations. For example, the government, as the offeror of BT stock and as a major shareholder, has a significant interest in seeing that BT continues as a successful company. By contrast, as a regulator pursuing liberalization policies that either subject BT to increased competition or restrict it from using its dominant position in certain markets, the government may frustrate the quest for maximum profitability. If a too-lenient regulatory regime is implemented, BT shareholders will benefit. That approach could be detrimental to the emergence of effective competition and of an environment that will benefit users of communications services.

2. Any regulatory policies that would adversely affect BT's future face the burden of overcoming the Thatcher Government's unabashed commitment to privatization. Recent disappointments in the sale of Britoil and Enterprise Oil stock, which left underwriters with a significant number of unsold shares, along with the magnitude of the BT sale, put significant pressure on the government to ensure that the BT offering succeeded. The remarkably positive market response to the offering may have bolstered confidence in the government's privatization program. (The success of the BT offering also may prove an ironic benchmark by which subsequent privatization efforts will be measured). However, BT's future success—beyond the offering—may be crucial to ensuring the continued viability of the privatization strategy.

II. BACKGROUND DEVELOPMENTS ON TELECOMMUNICATIONS POLICIES AND THE INDUSTRY

A. The Government Leads the Move Toward Competition

1. Reasons for Change

a. The move toward liberalization and the privatization of BT represent a government-led initiative, undertaken largely on the basis of political motives and the recommendations of analytical papers examining the marketplace. This course has not, however, generated enthusiasm from all parts of the telecommunications industry. Nonetheless, as a result of the Thatcher Government's commitment to the ideals of free-market competition, both goals have been pursued. The government's intent is to install market forces as the primary regulators of the telecommunications industry.

b. A major factor in moving the government in the direction of liberalization was a report prepared in 1981 by Michael Beesley, an economics professor at the London Graduate School of Business Studies. M. Beesley, *Liberalisation of the Use of British Telecommunications Network* (1981) [hereinafter cited as *Beesley Report*].

i) The *Beesley Report* argued that pure resale would stimulate competition sufficiently to offset any revenue loss to BT that might result from the diversion of traffic away from the BT network. Such diversion raised concerns about BT's continued ability to provide reasonably priced, universal service and other unprofitable services like public call boxes. *Id.* at ch. III.

ii) By looking to the U.S. experience, Beesley was led to conclude that the development of value-added network services ("VANS") probably would increase as did the availability of BT circuits for transmission of third-party communications. In Beesley's view, the most liberal market—allowing pure resale—produces the greatest variety of services. *Id.*

iii) The government, despite opposition to much of the *Beesley Report* by BT and by the Post Office Engineering Union ("POEU," which represents almost ninety-five percent of BT's employees) accepted many of its conclusions in shaping the Telecommunications Acts of 1981 and 1984. It did not, however, opt to permit pure circuit resale—at least not immediately.

c. The government also sought to remove BT from the process of overseeing entry into the telecommunications market. With the 1984 Act, the government eliminated the provision of the 1981 Act that had left BT with a consultative role in the licensing process. The 1981 provision had permitted BT to protect itself from competition.

2. *The Process of Transition*

a. The government's plan for stimulating increased competition in the telecommunications industry initially drew significant opposition from British equipment suppliers. They specifically objected to the planned privatization of BT, believing that the company would use its monopoly position to eliminate competitors.

i) Manufacturers claimed that BT was able to remain in the equipment supply business while losing £60 million in 1982 because it could subsidize such losses from profits in other areas of its business. They argued that this cross-subsidization would make true competition impossible.

ii) The manufacturers fought for severe restrictions on BT's ability to supply and to manufacture equipment.

b. A 1977 report by the Post Office Review Committee ("Carter Report") had recommended separating the Post Office's postal and telecommunications functions—to increase efficiency and to generate greater innovation. Support for opening the telecommunications market to competition soon developed in various sectors of British industry, which generally was dissatisfied with the Post Office's performance.

c. In July, 1980, Sir Keith Joseph told the House of Commons that the Thatcher Government planned to phase out BT's monopoly in the telecommunications market. The Department of Trade and Industry ("DTI") then commissioned the *Beesley Report*. The report was released in April, 1981, and the Thatcher Government announced its enthusiastic support for most of the report's conclusions—with the notable exception of pure resale of basic transmission services.

d. The British Telecommunications Act of 1981 embodied the government's position at the time. That Act created BT as a separate public corporation, distinct from the Post Office. It also provided for a process whereby the Secretary of State, after consultation with BT, could license telecommunications systems.

i) Pursuant to this power, in February of 1982, the government licensed the Mercury consortium to provide basic switched services in direct competition with BT. In 1983, the government expanded the scope of Mercury's activities by allowing it to compete in the international services market, as well as in the domestic market.

ii) A general license for VANS also was granted, clearing the way for the introduction of a broad variety of applications designed to meet particular users' special communications needs.

e. The Act was quickly outmoded. The aims of liberalization—along with the government's commitment to privatize various industries—prompted the development of legislation that eventually became the 1984 Act. In July, 1982, the Secretary of State for Industry, Patrick Jenkin, told the House of Commons that the government's attempts to further consumer choice in the telecommunications market required the privatization of BT. His statement was later released as a White Paper.

i) Jenkin pointed to the way in which public ownership limited BT's borrowing capacity. BT's borrowing counted against public spending limits, which were, in turn, severely limited by anti-inflation legislation. He also claimed that BT's public ownership had hampered the company's efficiency and had dulled its desire to innovate. Dep't of Industry, *The Future of Telecommunications in Britain* (1982).

ii) The government ended BT's consultative role in the licensing process and eliminated its exclusive privilege to provide telecommunications services. It also created OFTEL, which would work with the Secretary of State to ensure fair competition and to promote the liberalization process. These moves, it was thought, would open the way for a dramatic upswing in the number of competitive communications services.

f. The bill that was introduced in November, 1982, eventually emerged as the 1984 Act. It embraced the goals that Jenkin had outlined more than two years earlier.

B. The Privatization of BT

1. Sale of BT Stock

a. The October, 1981, separation of BT from the Post Office marked the first major step toward injecting competition into the telecommunications market formerly monopolized by BT. The 1981 Act permitted the licensing of competitive services. This has been followed by the 1984 Act's removal of BT's exclusive privilege to provide telecommunications services. As a result of the December, 1984, public offering of BT stock, the company now operates as a privately owned (fifty-one percent), licensed telecommunications systems operator. It remains the dominant services carrier, particularly in the area of basic switched services. Mercury is its chief competitor.

b. BT's public stock offering was greeted by spectacular enthusiasm. The three billion shares offered were greatly oversubscribed. Europhoric initial shareholders found that their holdings commanded a premium of eighty-five to ninty percent the day after the public offering. This surge brought charges in Parliament that the Conservative government had deliberately underpriced BT stock, which was sold at £1.30 per share, in order to ensure the viability of the privatization program.

c. What investors got was part of a company that posted a £1.5 billion pre-tax profit for the fiscal year ended March 31, 1985, up £490 million from the prior year. BT's total assets are valued at more than $13.5 billion. However, the company is faced with inadequate accounting and management systems. These make it quite difficult to document revenue streams that would allow for efficient cost allocations. BT also operates one of Europe's older wire networks, although the company has recently focused on a swift upgrading of its transmission and switching facilities. Finally, the highest ratio of employees-per-customer-served of any major nation's dominant phone company burdens the payroll and makes cost-effective operation a major business challenge. To prepare for the transition to private ownership, however, and to position itself for the public stock offering, BT has undergone a drastic internal reorganization. It has attempted to project the image of an aggressive, technology-minded information conglomerate ready to tackle a competitive marketplace.

i) The BT offering involved almost £3.9 billion ($4.6 billion) of stock, more than three times larger than the largest prior stock offering (that of AT&T). Its magnitude was so great that financial observers had questioned whether there would be enough demand to support the sale of all of the shares. The government, which was worried about a shortfall, spent £107 million to carry on a worldwide promotion effort. This amount is almost ten times more than the next highest cost of a prior privatization effort by the British government (Britoil, which raised £549 million).

ii) The government prohibited any single investor from acquiring more than fifteen percent of the BT stock. This restriction was intended to prevent the type of situation that developed in the Enterprise Oil sale, where the government had to step in at the last minute to prevent one company from purchasing forty-nine percent of the stock. Such a large acquisition was of particular concern in the BT sale, where there had been reports that some large British telecommunications manufacturers were planning to purchase significant amounts of BT stock.

iii) The offering was so drastically oversubscribed that only those investors who applied for the minimum number of shares—200 to 400 shares each—received all the stock they requested. More than 7,000 applicants who applied for more than 100,000 shares each were completely turned down in the allocations process. Large institutions, which failed to get significant holdings intially, were actively buying stock at premium prices immediately after the offering. The fifteen percent limit, however, restricted these investors' purchases.

iv) The offering involved complex international arrangements in which 415 million shares were allocated to markets in the U.S., Canada, and Japan. These offerings were coordinated by various underwriting syndicates. There are provisions for bonus shares—providing a one-share bonus for every ten held—to be issued to purchasers of the original offering who hold their stock for at least three years. Shareholders in the U.K., as an alternative to bonus shares, can, over the next three years, get vouchers from the government that can be used to pay BT phone bills.

2. *Corporate Structure*

a. A major focus of BT's reorganization—in preparation for the privatization—has been to decentralize its decisionmaking apparatus. It has created smaller profit centers that manage more narrowly defined service obligations.

i) BT was split into four divisions in 1981. The Inland Division operated telephone service within the U.K. The International Division oversaw all international communications. Major Systems purchased the switching and transmission system and took responsibility for research and development. BT Enterprises managed customer premises equipment and service.

ii) Last year another reorganization took place, creating the five divisions that now make up BT: Local Communications Services ("LCS"), National Networks, BT International, BT Enterprises, and Development and Procurement. The recently announced plan to purchase a majority interest in Mitel, a Canadian PBX manufacturer with international operations, would further enhance the company's diversity. BT would gain its first significant foothold in the international equipment market—particularly in the U.S., where Mitel products are well distributed.

b. LCS contributes the greatest amount of BT's revenues (almost fifty percent), the largest share of its problems, and more than eighty percent of its workforce. The division operates the local telephone networks and distributes and maintains BT's consumer products and services. Its 6,300 exchanges and twenty million lines carry an average of sixty million local calls each day. They provide local access for ten million long distance and 600,000 international calls. In the first six months of 1984, local traffic increased seven percent.

i) A major concern for this division is its outmoded network facilities. The bulk of the local exchange equipment consists of outdated electro-mechanical switching facilities.

ii) The company is in the process of installing its System X exchanges, which use a digital transmission system that can handle high-speed voice and data communications. Four local digital exchanges have already been installed. However, the company has experienced numerous delays in bringing the new exchanges into service. The company hopes to have seventy-five percent of its local lines using digital technology by the mid-1990s. It also has ordered an alternative exchange known as System Y.

iii) LCS also will operate (for BT) five of the first eleven cable franchises under the 1984 Act. It has operated six other cable systems in the past and will continue to do so.

iv) LCS shoulders the burdens of BT's unprofitable public services, including public call boxes, emergency calling, and directory assistance.

c. National Networks, BT's long distance division, manages the long distance trunk network and services the specialized services needs of business customers. In operation, it functions as two separate units, Trunk Services and Specialized Services.

i) The division generated £2.1 billion in revenues in fiscal 1983, almost one-fourth of BT's operating revenues. This total will rise again, as long-distance calling for the first six months of fiscal 1984 showed a nine percent increase.

ii) The National Networks division has focused on installing optical fiber trunk lines to replace the old copper wires. It is hoped that this move will help to prepare BT for the introduction of fierce competition that will attempt to divert the company's business customers to specialized service networks. Plans call for fifty percent of the trunk network to consist of optical fibers by 1988. In 1983, just three percent of trunk traffic was carried over optical fibers.

iii) The Specialized Services unit manages telex operations, private circuit leasing, and X-Stream services.

iv) Telex remains the country's dominant text transmission service. In fiscal 1983, domestic telexes carried by BT numbered 95,000, up 2.7% over the prior year. By the end of 1984, BT plans to introduce—gradually—stored program control telex exchanges. These will permit telex storage, multiple address transmission, message recording (for callers), and message redirection.

v) More than half of this unit's business in 1983 came from leased circuit revenues.

vi) The X-Stream business has diversified to provide KiloStream and MegaStream (private high-speed, digital networks for business users' data transmission needs), Packet SwitchStream (a specialized packet-switched data network), an automated-payment clearing system in London that uses Packet SwitchStream, VideoStream (a videoconference service), and SatStream (a satellite business service designed primarily for international transmission). SatStream also is capable of providing business users with private line capacity and point-to-multipoint services.

vii) This division is the one expected to see the most intense and most immediate competition as a result of the country's liberalization process. Consequently, modernization and innovation are top priorities.

d. BT International has become a profitable source of international business traffic revenues. It benefits from Britain's low-cost international transmission rates—as compared with most other European countries.

i) Business customers account for more than seventy percent of the international traffic revenues. The division's private line leases account for almost fifty-five percent of the approximately 10,000 private circuits that currently operate between Europe and North America.

ii) Britain's popularity as a center for international traffic links also contributes to the division's success. The country claimed eleven percent of the world's satellite telecommunications in 1983, and eight percent of its cable-carried service. Sixty percent of American multinational corporations use Britain as their European communications centers.

iii) The division also operates the company's maritime communications operations and its submarine cable facilities. In 1988, it is scheduled to begin operating the first transatlantic fiber optic cable linking France, the U.K., and the U.S. The cable will be competing, however, with two owned by Cable & Wireless, Mercury's parent company. These cables, being operated in conjunction with Tel-Optik, Ltd., a U.S. company, will provide U.S.-U.K. transatlantic services and will begin operating in 1989 and the early '90s, respectively.

iv) International telex traffic last year continued to grow, allowing BT to carry 500,000,000 paid minutes. International telephone calls, however, continued to be the greatest growth market; volume increased twelve percent in the first six months of fiscal 1984.

e. Development and Procurement has focused its research efforts on fiber optics, microwave radio service, speech synthesis and recognition technology, microelectronics, software engineering, and network development.

i) The focus of its procurement efforts has been on System X, which it is installing in both the local and trunk exchanges.

ii) BT invested a total of £179 million in research and development efforts in its 1983 fiscal year. It spent £39 million on System X in fiscal 1983 and is expected to spend almost £60 million in fiscal 1984.

iii) BT's plans for a competitor to System X—called System Y—recently drew criticism from the French. The Director General of the D.G.T. rebuked BT for failing to include any EEC company in its list of potential System Y suppliers. BT was considering bids from Northern Telecom of Canada, AT&T-Phillips, and Thorn Ericsson. Apparently, no EEC company was able to meet BT's technical specifications. BT recently decided to use Thorn-Ericsson as its supplier. OFTEL has decided to investigate BT's decision in the wake of complaints that System Y would harm British manufacturers.

iv) BT's recently announced plans to purchase fifty-one percent of Mitel, a Canadian manufacturer of PBX equipment, for £180 million, should have a significant effect on its manufacturing operations. The purchase will give BT an instant international equipment presence: there are more than 35,000 Mitel PBX owners in the U.S. Mitel also has manufacturing plants around the world. The deal also will give BT substantial leverage over its other PBX suppliers, such as General Electric Co. ("GEC"), Plessey Co., and Standard Telephones & Cables ("STC"). The potential anti-competitive effects have caused the government to refer the proposed transaction to the Monopolies and Mergers Commission.

f. BT Enterprises has invested heavily in the £3 billion office automation market (through its Merlin unit). It also has moved into mobile communications and a variety of VANS ventures, seeking to capitalize on the development of competitive, unregulated services.

i) BT Enterprises manages BT's fifty-one percent interest in the Telecom Securicor Cellular Radio Ltd. venture with Securicor. The service is called Cellnet.

ii) Its Merlin unit, marketing business products and systems, has moved aggressively into the PBX field. BT's Mitel acquisition could alter drastically its current reliance on three PBX suppliers, Plessey, GEC, and STC.

iii) Its VANS include the Prestel system (the world's first public viewdata network, which began operating in 1979) and BT Gold (electronic mail services). Services provided by third parties on Prestel include such interactive offerings as Skytrack (an airline reservation system) and Homelink (a home banking service). BT also recently purchased a twenty-five percent interest in Micronet 800, a home computer database that is claimed to be the world's largest residential user network. The service, offered on Prestel, has 15,500 subscribers. Prestel is now adding about 1200 subscribers each month. (Slow initial acceptance of Prestel left the system with just 43,000 subscribers after five years of operation). As of mid-1983, a large proportion of the world's viewdata and teletext systems were using the British standard pioneered for Prestel.

iv) BT Enterprises also provides Yellow Pages, which in 1983 drew 200,000 advertisers to the twenty-two million copies distributed free to telephone users. These figures make it the U.K.'s largest advertising vehicle.

g. BT is looking to move toward establishment of an integrated services digital network ("ISDN") as it brings digital switches into service. The company brought a model ISDN into operation during 1985.

i) It seems unlikely that a single integrated network will serve all users or provide all telecommunications services. The proliferation of private and public systems under the U.K. liberalization program make the prospects for such wholesale integration appear doubtful. However, standardization of protocols, transmission speeds, and various other interconnection factors may lead toward increased compatability between systems, thereby leading toward an ISDN ideal.

ii) BT's ISDN aspirations reflect a desire to integrate voice and non-voice services into a single, continuous network with uniform, bit-based pricing. BT already has said, however, that some data communications, which are best transmitted in packet form, would require a separate packet-switched network. One goal, however, is to make this packet network accessible through the single ISDN terminal.

h. The company also has announced plans for its first significant foray into computer manufacturing. Earlier this year it released details of a project to build its own computers, based on a design by Bleasdale Computers, a small British company. The units initially will be used internally but are expected to be sold to the public in the near future. BT battled to win manufacturing authority in its license.

3. *Overview of the BT License*

a. All of this growth is designed to help compensate for the various restrictions placed on BT by its new operating license. *See infra* Section III.D. These burdens include requirements to provide universal services, emergency services, public call boxes, and mandatory interconnection for other telecommunications systems. BT also is prohibited from cross-subsidizing its VANS, mobile radio, manufacturing, and equipment supply operations, where the greatest competition is expected to develop in the near future. In addition, the limitation on price increases—applied to trunk and local calls—will inhibit BT somewhat (in the interest of preserving affordable service during the early transition period).

b. In BT's favor, the limitation of basic service competitors to just Mercury, at least until November, 1990, and the ban on pure resale of BT circuits, at least until July, 1989, will protect its market to some degree. In addition, the requirement that cable systems use either BT or

Mercury to provide certain data transmission and switched voice services also provides a measure of protection. The question that remains is how BT will function as a private company, especially amid allegations that it will use its monopoly power in more damaging ways.

c. Privatization seems certain to heighten the tension between profit-maximization and public-service objectives. This is a tension with which OFTEL will have to cope.

4. *The Relationship Between BT and the Government*

a. One of the more complex aspects of BT's future is the nature of its continuing relationship with the U.K. government, which remains its major shareholder. After the public offering, the government holds 49.2% of BT's outstanding voting stock. In addition, it holds all 750,000,000 shares of the non-voting, cumulative, redeemable, preferred stock (11.95% dividend). The government also possesses a "Special Share," which only the government can hold and which entitles the government to appoint or to nominate (and to remove) two special directors of the corporation. These two directors cannot hold any executive office, but they can vote on matters of interest to the Crown that come before the Board. The Special Share carries no voting rights, but it entitles the government to receive notice of all general shareholder meetings and to speak at these meetings.

b. The Secretary of State is required to fix a target investment for the government that may not increase the government's proportion of voting stock. This limit can be revised, from time to time; however, each such limit must decrease the government's proportion of voting shares. *See* Telecommunications Act, 1984, ch. 12, § 65 (1984).

c. The government has promised not to sell any of its voting stock before April 9, 1988. After that date, it is free to sell its stock, although it has promised to confer with the BT directors before any sale is made. It also has promised to consult with the directors before selling any of its preferred stock.

d. In a letter to the chairman of BT, the Secretary of State indicated that the government intended to observe its standard policy of not intruding into the affairs of a new private entity. The government also has said that it does not expect to vote on general resolutions introduced at shareholder meetings, although it retains the power to do so.

C. Mercury: BT's Competition for the Future

1. *Background*

a. Mercury has developed gradually since its birth in February, 1982, but is now gaining momentum at a steady pace. In the wake of the adoption of the Telecommunications Act of 1981, Mercury was licensed by the Secretary of State, using his newly created power to authorize telecommunications systems that would compete with BT.

b. In the early stages, there was doubt about whether Mercury would survive at all. The POEU moved to block Mercury's growth by threatening to prevent its interconnection with the BT network and by threatening job actions against potential Mercury customers. At one point, Mercury alleged that these actions had cost it between £500,000 and £1.5 million in annual business. Network growth also was delayed by many factors, including the requirement that Mercury pay a development land tax before laying its wires.

c. Originally a consortium owned by Cable & Wireless (forty percent), British Petroleum (forty percent), and Barclays Bank (twenty percent), Mercury is now wholly owned by Cable & Wireless.

i) In Cable & Wireless, Mercury has an aggressive, growing, financially stable parent company. Strong growth in its Pacific and Far East operations have helped Cable & Wireless earn a £22 million increase in profits for the first half of fiscal 1984, to £109 million. In those six months, profits for the lucrative Far East operations were up thirty-four percent, to £74 million. In February, 1984, the company increased its ownership of Hong Kong Telephone Co. from thirty-five percent to seventy-nine percent. It also has signed lucrative agreements to lay fiber optic cables along U.S. railroad rights-of-way.

ii) In 1984, there had been speculation that Pacific Telesis, one of the seven regional phone companies produced by the breakup of AT&T, and Reuters, the international news and business information organization, were considering making significant investments in Mercury. Those plans, however, have been dropped. Mercury is now moving forward on its own in an effort to become a formidable competitor to BT.

d. It is estimated that Mercury will be capable of providing full switched voice services sometime in 1985.

2. *Current and Planned Operations*

a. Mercury began service by offering leased, point-to-point capacity designed for business users with the need to transmit large amounts of information over a high-speed data network.

b. It now also is using microwave transmission links to provide inter-city services in London, Birmingham, and Manchester. The microwave links are being supplemented with fiber optic cables as quickly as Mercury can upgrade its network. Mercury has acquired the rights-of-way for its fiber optic network from British Rail. By the end of 1986, Mercury will have completed both a southern and a northern loop, which will allow it to carry transmissions throughout the nation. *See generally* Comm. for Information, Computer and Communications Policy, *Background Report: United Kingdom* (Doc. No. DSTI/ICCP/82.33/17) (1982) [hereinafter cited as *OECD Background Report*]. The company still faces the task of overcoming customers' reluctance to choose Mercury over BT. As it builds a customer base, this obstacle should recede.

c. Mercury's future seems to have been helped by the government's August, 1983, decision to allow the new carrier to compete in the market for international switched services. It has already begun offering discount-rate, leased-line service between the U.K. and the U.S., working together with Western Union. Mercury's parent, Cable & Wireless, is involved in a $600 million venture with Tel-Optik, Ltd., a U.S. firm, to operate two transatlantic, fiber optic cables. Tel-Optik recently was granted cable landing rights in the U.S. Plans to put the first cable into service by 1989 are now moving forward. In the U.K., Cable & Wireless will use installation and service rights owned by Mercury as part of its international communications operating authority. The service, called Market-Link, is expected to provide significant discounts from rates now charged for other transatlantic services.

d. There still are some who question whether Mercury will be able to attract a sufficient number of customers to fuel its growth and development. Some believe that the country cannot support two parallel communications networks.

e. The government's guarantee that Mercury will have to compete only against BT in the basic service area, until at least November, 1990, provides some further security for Mercury. This restriction eliminates the possibility that new, aggressive competitors will emerge to fragment the market foothold share that Mercury has been able to gain.

f. In recognition of Mercury's competitive position, its license does not contain all of the public-service obligations imposed on BT, such as universal and emergency service requirements and price-increase limitations. *See infra* Section III.E.

3. *The Battle Over Access to the BT Network*

a. Mercury's ability to be interconnected to BT's nationwide network is vital to the company's future success as a provider of basic switched services. While Mercury trunk lines will link major U.K. cities, it depends on interconnection to BT's circuits for most of its local calling links.

b. The interconnection issue is now being investigated by OFTEL. The two companies were unable to reach agreement on an interconnection arrangement, and after a brief courtroom skirmish, the dispute was placed before OFTEL.

c. BT's operating license imposes interconnection obligations on it. *See infra* Section III.D. However, BT contended that a "heads of agreement" reached with Mercury in June, 1984, outlined all of of its interconnection obligations with Mercury. By contrast, Mercury claimed that the heads of agreement was merely an interim document—without legal status—intended to guide negotiations between the two companies. It argued that BT's interconnection obligations are imposed by the BT license, which was granted in August, 1984, after the signing of the intercorporate agreement. Mercury asked OFTEL to step in to set the terms of interconnection, using its power to enforce the terms of the BT license granted under the 1984 Telecommunications Act. BT contended that OFTEL lacked jurisdiction over the matter.

d. On March 10, 1985, Mercury won the first round of its battle with BT when the High Court ruled that the heads of agreement was not legally binding. After BT announced that it would not appeal the decision, OFTEL stepped in to resolve the controversy. OFTEL is expected shortly to conclude its investigation into technical and economic issues.

e. Mercury is seeking unrestricted use of the BT network; any restrictions placed on that use will have a significant impact on the shape of Mercury's future operations and its ability to compete with BT.

III. THE BRITISH APPROACH TO SERVICE DEFINITIONS AND CATEGORIES

A. Introduction: The Spectrum of Service Categories

There is a tendency to view the British regulatory scene only in terms of the competitive relationship between a dominant established carrier (BT) and a new entrant (Mercury). In fact, the structure of competitive relationships that now are evolving is far more complex, particularly in light of the government's recently announced intention to license managed data network services ("MDNS") individually as distinct from either the basic transmission services provided by BT and Mercury or VANS. *See generally* Dep't. of Trade and Industry, *Government Proposal for the Future Licensing of Value Added and Data Services: A Consultative Document* (1985) [hereinafter cited as *VANS Consultative Document*]. These relationships are demarcated by a series of different categories of services and service arrangements.

1. Public Telecommunications Operators ("PTOs")

Each PTO has a mandate to provide a full spectrum of services, but each also has a different set of obligations imposed through individually negotiated licenses. The scope of the services that can be provided by a PTO is strictly defined by the PTO's license. Whether or not cable television operators will be classified as PTOs is not yet resolved, nor are the regulatory implications of such a classification.

2. VANS

a. VANS are intended to involve an "enhancement" of the basic service offerings of BT. However, the scope of such a value-added service never has been precisely defined. The government has, however, adopted a "working" definition of a "basic" service that would appear to include such transmission-related activities as packet-switching. The term "VANS" is left to encompass all non-basic services. *See MDNS Consultative*

Document, supra, at 16. It remains to be seen whether the government will try to draw a precise line between "basic" services and the "remainder" value–added category. The *Consultative Document* suggests that such precision is unnecessary.

b. The government presently has a relatively liberal policy toward the establishment of VANS. Under the proposed new class license, which would be issued to replace the existing general license, this policy would be liberalized further—except to the extent that the government will license managed data networks under a separate, more stringent regime.

3. MDNS

a. The government has suggested that an MDNS, which would not be covered by a new VANS class license, but would require a separate license for each proposed system, would be "authorized to provide telecommunications services comprising basic conveyance and non-voice directory information services, . . ." *Id.* at 23. Third-party service providers (other than the MDNS operator) would be able to use an MDNS to provide VANS, and the MDNS license strictly would prohibit data network operators from providing switched voice telephone services. The *Consultative Document* describes an MDNS as a "high quality basic conveyance service." *Id.* at 15.

b. In its *Consultative Document,* the government has acknowledged that the concept of a managed data network is "insufficiently precise." *Id.* at 23. It is clear, however, that an MDNS will exist as a limited exception to the policy of prohibiting any entities other than BT, Mercury, Hull, the two cellular radio operators, and cable operators working in association with either BT or Mercury from providing basic conveyance services. The MDNS category also constitutes a liberalization of the government's policy against circuit resale.

c. It is not yet clear how many managed data networks the government may be prepared to license. The *Consultative Document* proposes that an MDNS (1) "should provide significant facilities which are not normally available from (or which compliment the facilities provided by)" PTOs, (2) should not be intended—or likely—to divert "traffic revenue" from PTOs, and (3) should involve a licensee that has "the technical and financial resources to install and operate the systems necessary to provide such services." *Id.* at 22-23.

d. The government also has suggested that initially it would be reluctant to license managed data networks to "operators whose primary business in running the MDNS system would be to provide services to persons outside their own group." *Id.* at 23. Although this limitation is vague, it clearly is intended to minimize the degree to which an MDNS would divert traffic from either Mercury or BT by providing switched services to unaffiliated third parties.

4. *Information and Data Processing Services*

These services never were regulated prior to recent steps toward liberalization. They now may fall within the VANS general license or, in some instances, be subject to the more restrictive MDNS licensing process. The unresolved question is when "ancillary" transmission or message-switching functions associated with these services will cause them to fit within the government's still undefined concept of an MDNS. Such a result would subject these services—for the first time—to a prior approval requirement.

5. *Shared Use and Limited Resale Networks*

a. The government recently has begun to issue licenses under the 1984 Act to systems involved in some degree of shared use or resale service to a closed group of users.

b. Government efforts to clarify the amount of permissible resale—through the adoption of a new general license—have been dropped. Instead, ad hoc decisions will be made as particular service plans are presented; some of these services might fall within the MDNS category. This procedure has the obvious disadvantage of making it difficult for entities with similar service plans to determine whether or not they will be violating the goverment's limits on resale.

6. *Cable Television and Cellular Radio*

Both cable television and cellular radio services are emerging as possible alternatives to BT's local loop facilities. Their regulatory status is likely to become the focus of increased attention.

B. Licensing Process Determines Services That May Be Provided

1. The Telecommunications Act of 1984 applies a facilities-based definition to require the licensing of all telecommunications systems. *See* Telecommunications Act, 1984, ch. 12, §§ 4 & 5 (1984). The division of services among various entities is determined in the course of issuing the licenses necessary to operate telecommunications systems. This avoids the need for devising generic service categories in a comprehensive piece of legislation; however, it makes the licensing process both cumbersome and complex.

2. A "telecommunications system," as that term is used in the Act, encompasses any "electrical, magnetic, electro-magnetic, electro-chemical, or electro-mechanical" transmission system. If a system uses any of these technologies to convey voice, music, visual images, other sounds, any

matter not otherwise audible or visible, or machine-control commands, it falls within the definition of a "telecommunications system." *Id.* at §§4(1), (7).

3. The Act excepts broadcast transmissions, Section 6(1) (conveyed by wireless telegraphy); semaphore communications that use light flashes, Section 6(2)(a); and communications systems contained on a single premise, or under one individual's control, or for communications solely within a single business, Sections 6(2)(b) & (c), (3). Private branch systems do not come within this exemption, as the exemption does not apply to a system that is connected to another telecommunications system.

4. Transmitting and receiving apparatus connected to, but not part of, a domestic telecommunications system also must be separately licensed as a telecommunications system. *Id.* at § 4(2)(a).

5. If the operator of a telecommunications system transmits, switches, or receives any of the variety of matter specified in Section 4(1), provides directory services, or installs, repairs, or removes apparatus, he engages in the provision of a telecommunications service. *Id.* at § 4(3).

6. This facilities-based legislative approach creates jurisdictional overlaps, because additional regulatory requirements may be imposed on the basis of the services a system provides. Thus, for example, a cable television system must be licensed to operate as a telecommunications system under the Telecommunciations Act, *id.* at § 7, and to provide cable program service, under the Cable and Broadcasting Act, 1984, ch. 46, §§ 2 & 3 (1984). *See* Dep't of Industry, *The Development of Cable Systems and Services* 68-73 (1983) [hereinafter cited as *Cable White Paper*].

C. Public Telecommunications Operators: Generally

1. The backbone of the nation's telecommunications facilities is provided by PTOs, which are licensed telecommunications systems operators designated by the Secretary of State to undertake certain service obligations. Telecommunications Act, 1984, ch. 12, § 9 (1984). A PTO provides basic switched service to individual system users. To further the goals of universal service and the provision of certain public telecommunications services such as emergency calling features, the Act deviates from its general technology-based approach and applies particular service requirements to a PTO.

2. The only two "conventional" carriers licensed as PTOs are British Telecom and Mercury. (There also is a small public system that the City Council of Kingston-Upon-Hull operates, but it is a distinct and special situation not posing a competitive threat in the marketplace.) Cellular radio operators also are licensed as PTOs, but they do not yet compete directly with either BT or Mercury. The British Government has said that it will not license any other PTOs before November, 1990; however, cable systems may be classified as PTOs within their franchise areas. The obligations imposed on them will take into consideration the fact that they are local networks

and are not serving primarily as providers of switched, two-way voice services.

3. Designation as a PTO brings with it both benefits and burdens. The chief benefit is that the PTO is given the right to install wiring underneath both public and private lands. *See id.* at §§ 34-41; *see also id.* at § 10(2) (applying to PTOs the Telecommunications Code now contained in Schedule 2 to the Act, which saves the operator from the need to seek individual permits for any land use that installation of the wired network entails).

4. Enjoyment of these powers, however, comes at the expense of having to provide both liberal interconnection to the public telecommunications system—according to published tariffs—and non-discriminatory service. *Id.* at § 8.

D. The BT License Defines Its Scope of Operations as a PTO

1. Introduction

In licensing a PTO, the government can impose service conditions that require such actions as interconnection, which is designed to further competition and the policies of liberalization. The Telecommunications Act provides only broad directives as to the types of conditions to be placed on the PTO licensee. *See, e.g., id.* In the case of BT, the dominant switched-services carrier, the licensing process has been used to retain the BT facility as the basis for universal switched services. It also has opened to competition a variety of markets that require, at some point, the use of the switched network. In large part, this objective has meant preventing BT from using its dominance as a carrier to monopolize the peripheral services and equipment markets.

2. Authorized System

BT's license to act as a PTO took effect on August 5, 1984. The license itself is actually just three paragraphs long. It gives BT permission to operate a telecommunications system, as that system is defined in Appendix A to the license. It also confers on BT—for the purpose of operating the system—the power to install underground wiring on privately owned land; it specifies the license term to be twenty-five years, with revocation thereafter on at least ten years' notice. The fifty-three conditions attached to the license specify the variety of obligations and restrictions to be applied to BT. These conditions are what actually define the contours of BT's operations.

a. The license defines the authorized system as one used only to "convey" messages, with "convey" having the meaning given to it in the Act. Reading the license in conjunction with Section 4(7) of the Act, which defines "convey" as transmission, switching, and reception, it would appear that BT's license authorizes only basic switched service operations. The precise scope of a "basic" service may be clarified by the definitional scheme that the government has proposed in the *VANS Consultative Document, supra,* at 16. The government, in that paper, suggests that a "basic conveyance service" includes:

> The conveyance of a message by means of a telecommunications system to a single destination which may be derived from an address contained in or associated with the message so that it is delivered by the system in the same form that it was received without any additional services having been provided in respect of the message in the course of conveyance except such services as permit or facilitate its conveyance to its destination in an accurate, reliable and economical manner.

This definition would appear to include packet switching services, but it would not include any protocol conversion operations in which the transmitted data undergoes a net protocol conversion (*e.g.*, from asynchronous to X.25).

b. BT's value-added service activities are to be authorized by a separate license. The terms of such a license will be vital to determining the scope of BT's competitive activities in the liberalized market.

c. BT's cellular radio venture with Securicor already is operated under a separate license.

3. Universal Service Obligations

Pursuant to Section 3 of the Act, the Secretary has imposed on BT a universal service obligation, particularly with respect to rural areas (but excluding the area served by the Kingston-upon-Hull City Council). Condition 2 permits the Director General of OFTEL to relieve BT of this obligation in areas where he finds that adequate service is already being provided. BT is also obliged to provide various other public services. These include directory information service, maintenance service, emergency call service, public call boxes, and maritime services. *Licence Granted by the Secretary of State for Trade and Industry to British Telecom Under Section 7 of the Telecommunications Act, 1984*, at Conditions 1-12 [hereinafter cited as *BT Licence*] (1984).

4. Access Charges

Section 3(1)(b) of the Act instructs the Secretary to ensure that the public-service obligations imposed on BT are adequately funded. Condition 19 permits BT to impose access charges on connecting carriers, but only to the extent that such charges are needed to fund losses incurred in providing the various public services imposed on BT. These charges must be uniform for all carriers. *Id.* at Condition 19.2(a). BT must contribute on an equal basis to the pool of funds collected. *Id.* at Condition 19.2(c)(i). The Director General must approve all such charges. *Id.* at Condition 19.2(b).

5. Interconnection

a. Individually licensed systems (*i.e.*, not those operated under a class license) serving the public can require that BT provide them with interconnection. Condition 13 obliges BT to reach agreement with a system operator seeking interconnection. This agreement may impose connection charges, the terms of services, and other matters that the Director General believes should be accounted for in any particular case. *Id.* at Condition 13.4.

b. If the parties fail to reach such an agreement, the Director General may impose the terms of interconnection. *Id.* at Condition 13.5. As noted above, *see supra* Section II.C.3., OFTEL now is moving to set the terms of Mercury's interconnection with BT under this provision of the license.

c. Condition 14 obliges BT to connect other systems not within Condition 13 and to connect approved apparatus. Interconnection that would damage the BT system, or require modification of the BT system, or be impracticable, is not required. *Id.* at Conditions 13.2, 14.2-.3.

d. Where interconnection involves a system that operates lines more than fifty kilometers long—such as Mercury—the connection must allow customers to select (to the extent practicable) the degree to which their messages are carried by BT and by non-BT facilities. This provision protects a competitive carrier's ability to take advantage of its own facilities, which may provide economies that allow for significant service price differences.

6. Ban on Cross-Subsidies

The Director General has power to prevent BT from cross-subsidizing its equipment supply and production operations, its mobile radio service, or any value-added services. By April 1, 1987, or sooner to the degree practicable, BT is required to record transfers between any parts of its business at the full value of the transfer. *Id.* at Condition 18. This cross-subsidy prohibition does not prevent BT from subsidizing services that the license otherwise permits it to subsidize (*i.e.*, the non-competitive services such as emergency services). BT also must offer its services pursuant to published tariffs, *id.* at Condition 16, and must not discriminate in its provision of service, *id.* at Condition 17.

7. Promoting Competition

Competition is further sought through a variety of separation requirements applied to BT and through the imposition of regulations designed to prohibit the use of market dominance.

a. Condition 20 requires, no later than April 1, 1987, separate accounting procedures for BT's systems business and its equipment supply business. Any equipment production business must be placed in a separate subsidiary by April 1, 1986, and that subsidiary cannot engage in the systems business. Various procedures also are set forth to help the Director General ensure that BT does not favor its equipment production subsidiary in its equipment purchasing decisions.

b. Condition 22 requires that when BT bundles equipment and services, it must make available to competing equipment suppliers telecommunications services offered on equivalent terms. This requirement is designed to ensure that users receive comparable services, regardless of whose equipment they use.

c. Condition 35 further prohibits tying arrangements by which BT would require that certain equipment be purchased along with any purchase of certain services, other equipment, or interconnection arrangements. In addition, where BT provides services and equipment as a bundle, it must state the charges for each separately. This obligation, however, does not take effect until BT has been able to separate its accounting procedures—although in no case later than July 1, 1987. *Id.* at Condition 37.

d. BT cannot engage in exclusive dealing arrangements, subject to the consent of the Director General. *Id.* at Condition 36.

e. Condition 39 prohibits the anti-competitive use of patents and copyrights.

f. Condition 42 prohibits BT from installing integrated wiring after December 31, 1985. This prevents BT from limiting competition in non-exchange services through the monopolization of a premise's wires.

8. *Rate Regulation*

a. Condition 24 limits BT's power to raise the prices of a range of services (line rental, trunk and local exchange calls). The annual price increase for this "basket" of services—taken together and weighted according to the proportion of BT revenues for which each service accounts—is restricted to three percentage points less than the increase in the year's retail price index. These price-controlled services account for more than half of BT's business.

b. It is significant that the government has not chosen to impose a rate-of-return formula on BT's tariffs. Such a formula would limit BT to a particular level of profits, expressed as a percentage of total assets. A report prepared for the government, *see* S.C. Littlechild, *Regulation of British Telecommunications' Profitability* (1983) [hereinafter cited as *Littlechild Report*], rejected this traditional regulatory measure for supervising monopoly tariffs. Avoiding rate-of-return regulation was seen as a way of evading a significant regulatory burden that might discourage BT's innovation. The *Littlechild Report* also criticized rate-of-return regulation as ineffective in controlling the charges levied for monoply services, because rate-of-return schemes are applied business-wide. Regulation that specifically seeks to control the price of monopoly services was seen as a more desirable alternative. A question that remains, however, is whether this averaged limit on price increases will prove an effective way of preventing BT from raising local service prices faster than long-distance prices. Using such a strategy, BT could remain within the three-point limit, but could reduce the financial burden of traditionally unprofitable local services. BT contends that such "rebalancing" of rates is necessary to ensure its competitive future.

c. BT's November, 1984, price adjustment, its first under the new license, has met with the approval of OFTEL Director General Bryan Carsberg. Carsberg said that increases in exchange line rentals had been offset by reductions in long distance service prices. The result was a proper balance, as required by Condition 24.

d. OFTEL now is turning its attention to the price of individual service elements. In response to complaints about the prices of services outside the scope of Condition 24 (particularly concerning drastically increased charges for some leased lines), Carsberg has begun a general investigation. Should price changes be found contrary to the public interest, Carsberg has said he would take "appropriate action." Just how OFTEL will go about this process is uncertain, largely because the scope of its "investigatory" authority over individual service prices is not clear. Its supervisory role also is complicated by BT's still-garbled accounting procedures. The company's historic practice of not reflecting individual cost and revenue figures for particular services makes the job of judging service prices particularly difficult.

e. The ultimate objective is to see that prices are brought into line with costs. BT's attempts to do this are most evident in its reduction of service prices over high-density routes, which it made quickly, in anticipation of competition with Mercury.

9. Ban on Resale

a. Although BT must provide liberal interconnection to its system, it is required, under Condition 46, to prevent interconnection that would result in allowing the connecting system to offer simple resale services. This condition enforces the government's resolve to limit the number of carriers providing basic switched service. Competition may then be structured around a duopolistic switched network.

b. Until 1989, the ban on simple resale prevents the arbitrage of BT circuits that would take advantage of above-cost pricing. As BT's prices are brought into line with its costs, this resale prohibition is likely to be relaxed—or possibly eliminated.

10. Supervising New Ventures

BT is required to give the Director General prior notice of any plans to participate in the formation of a new corporation, partnership, or joint venture that will operate a telecommunications system, provide telecommunications services, or produce or supply equipment in a way that would lead to monopolization of the equipment market. *Id.* at Condition 49. Under this provision, OFTEL is now evaluating BT's plan to purchase fifty-one percent of Mitel, which is discussed above. *See supra* Section II.B.2.

11. Qualification

All of these conditions are qualified by the provision allowing BT to avoid doing anything that is impracticable, unreasonable, or prevented by uncontrollable circumstances. *Id.* at Condition 53.

E. Mercury's License Reflects Its Position as a Non-Dominant Carrier

1. The license for Mercury to operate as a PTO, which was approved in early November, 1984, is in many respects very similar to the one granted to BT. The most significant difference is that Mercury would not be required—nor even permitted—to provide public services such as emergency calling, public call boxes, and maritime communications. These non-competitive areas are left to BT, which already possesses the infrastructure necessary to provide them. A requirement that Mercury provide unprofitable public services could frustrate the attempt to have Mercury develop as an alternative switched-services carrier. Most of the other differences in the two licenses similarly account for Mercury's less dominant market position. *See generally Licence Granted by the Secretary of State for Trade and Industry to Mercury Communications Ltd. Under Section 7 of the Telecommunications Act, 1984* (1984) [hereinafter cited as *Mercury Licence*].

2. Mercury's ability to increase the prices of its services is in no way restricted. *Compare BT Licence, supra,* at Condition 24.

3. As a result of Mercury's smaller size, the government has required it to respond more quickly to separation objectives, including changes in its accounting procedures, *see Mercury Licence, supra,* at Condition 18, and the valuation of intracorporate transfers, *see id.* at Conditions 33 (separating charges for bundled equipment and services) and 37 (ceasing installation of integrated wiring).

4. In general, however, the license still is designed to prevent Mercury from exploiting its privileged position as one of just two facilities providers for switched services. The adjustments made seek either to relieve Mercury from the burdensome obligations that BT can absorb by virtue of its market dominance or to eliminate restrictions that are inapplicable to Mercury because it cannot abuse a dominant market position.

F. British Approach to VANS

Competition among service providers is likely to be most aggressive in the area of VANS. This competition, which already has mushroomed since adoption of the 1984 Act, can be expected to accelerate further if the additional liberalization proposed in the government's *VANS Consultative Document* eventually is adopted.

1. Background

a. The Telecommunications Act, 1981, ch. 38, § 15(1)(a) (1981), empowered the Secretary of State for Industry, after consultation with BT, to grant licenses for any telecommunications services specified in the license. Alternatively, the Secretary could delegate to BT the power to grant licenses. *Id.* at § 15(1)(b). In actual practice, this provided BT with an opportunity to determine which services merited introduction, thereby allowing it to protect particular markets. Absent a specific license, any telecommunications service provided by someone other than BT violated the company's exclusive privilege to operate telecommunications systems. *Id.* at §§ 12 & 15. The Secretary reached judgments about licensing with the help of a committee that included Bryan Carsberg, now the Director General of OFTEL.

b. Technically, the 1981 Act permitted the use of leased BT circuits for any third-party service offering for which a license was issued. The official government policy, however, was to permit third-party operators to offer only those services that provided "substantial elements additional to the basic network facilities . . . ." Statement Before Parliament of Kenneth Baker, Minister of Industry and Information Technology (July 30, 1981). Authorizations to provide VANS were designed to permit service competition while protecting the BT monopoly in the basic services market—by prohibiting pure circuit resale.

c. Under the 1981 Act, the government issued a general license for the provision of VANS that prohibited (1) interconnection of value-added networks ("VANs"), except through BT or Mercury, and (2) message conveyance unless an additional service was provided. *See General Licence Under Section 15(1) for Telecommunications Systems Used in Providing Value Added Network Services* ¶¶ 2(1) & (2) (1982) [hereinafter cited as *1982 VANS Licence*].

d. An explanatory note to the license specified sixteen services that were intended to be covered. These included automatic ticket reservation and issuing, conference calls, customer data bases, deferred transmisison, long-term archiving, mailbox, multi-address routing, protocol conversion, secure delivery services, speed and code conversion, store and retrieve message systems, telephone answering using voice retrieval systems, telesoftware storage and retrieval, text editing, user management packages, viewdata, and word processor/facsimile interfacing.

e. Since the issuance of the *1982 VANS Licence,* 140 companies have registered to provide more than 600 services. More than seventy of these services involve either message store and forward or protocol conversion capabilities.

f. With the adoption of the 1984 Act, the Secretary of State no longer is required to consult with BT before issuing a new system license. Telecommunications Act, 1984, ch. 12, § 7 (1984). This removes BT's power to exert direct control over the introduction of competitive VANS. BT must even cooperate with the expansion of new services, because its license requires it to connect all licensed systems—absent extenuating circumstances.

2. *Proposed Terms of the New VANS Class License*

a. Existing VANS will continue to operate under the terms of the general license that grandfathered systems in operation before August 5, 1984. *See Licence for the Running of Certain Telecommunications Systems First Run Before 5 August 1984 Granted by the Secretary of State for Trade and Industry Under Section 7 of the Telecommunications Act, 1984* (1984). However, a new VANS license will have to be issued before August 5, 1986, (the end of the "transitional period" of the Act). The precise terms of this license will provide a significant indication of how far the government is prepared to go in permitting competition with BT.

b. The latest indication of the government's position regarding VANS is found in the recently released *VANS Consultative Document. See supra* Section III.A. In discussing its regulatory scheme, the government has reaffirmed its commitment to prohibiting "pure" resale of circuits until, at least, July, 1989, and to leaving VANS relatively undefined. A value-added service would be virtually anything other than a "basic" service. The *Consultative Document* notes that after the resale prohibition is lifted, it will become unnecessary to distinguish between basic services, VANS, and MDNS; therefore, the task of drawing precise and admittedly "artificial" boundary distinctions among the different service categories is not viewed as worthwhile. *VANS Consultative Document, supra,* at 13-14.

c. The government proposes granting a new class license for VANS that would liberalize the value-added services market by eliminating the current registration and fee requirements for VANS. The license would apply to any service that provides something "*additional* to the service of basic conveyance." *Id.* at 17 (emphasis in original). The document does not attempt to decide what degree of enhancement is necessary for a service to qualify as value-added.

d. PTOs and MDNS operators would be required to obtain individual licenses to provide VANS. This limitation on the scope of the class license is intended to guard against the potential anti-competitive effects of having basic service providers use their networks to favor their own (or affiliated) value-added services. In considering requests for these individual licenses, the government would pay close attention to the possible anti–competitive effects of each authorization.

e. As discussed above, *see supra* Section III.D.2., packet-switching and protocol conversion operations that do not involve a net conversion would appear to fall within the proposed definition of a "basic" service.

G. Relationship Among VANS, MDNS, and Information Services

1. There is some dispute as to whether information services, including the transmission of news and financial reports, constitute a "telecommunications service" subject to licensing under the broad definition of that term in the 1984 Act. Under the 1981 Act, no licenses were thought necessary for information-related services. The possibility that information providers would have to seek government approval for their operations obviously is of concern. It appears that the delineation between telecommunications and information services will have to be clarified as the process of issuing new licenses under the Act and replacing the former BT licenses proceeds.

2. The Act does not appear to distinguish between primary communications functions and those that are ancillary to an information or data processing operation. So long as there is a conveyance of some information unit—as broadly defined in Section 4(1) of the Act—a telecommunications system, requiring a license, exists. The definition of a "basic" service, as used in the *VANS Consultative Document, supra*, at 16, would appear to exclude any service that includes more than transmission capabilities. *See supra* Section III.D.2. However, this does not mean that information or data processing services will escape licensing. The proposed MDNS category, which will require governmental licensing, does not distinguish between non–dedicated services that provide transmission capacity for a wide variety of data from unspecified third parties and networks that are dedicated to providing the ancillary transmission capabilities necessary for access to and use of an information or data processing service. These very different kinds of systems are technologically indistinguishable, and the *Consultative Document* appears to sweep them both within the MDNS category. Such a result would have the consequence — perhaps unintended—of requiring that both types of services be licensed. Both also might be required to obtain individual VANS licenses; under the scheme proposed by the *Consultative Document*, the VANS class license would not cover an MDNS operator providing a value-added service over its own data network. *See supra* Section III.F.2.

3. The British approach to MDNS could have the effect of subjecting information and data processing services to a more restrictive regulatory regime in the U.K. than in Japan. Moreover, this grouping of processing and communications activities into one licensed category, which

is similar to what the General Type II business category may provoke in Japan, could have serious consequences internationally. In countries with more restrictive regulatory regimes, these licensed "communications" services might have trouble arguing that they are not, in fact, communications activities. As a result, information services could be regulated (or prohibited) in some of these countries.

4. In the *Consultative Document* itself, the government indicates that it is uncertain about what practical effects its proposed licensing scheme might have. The paper includes a request for information from any companies now operating under the VANS general license that believe they would be "unable to continue their present operations under the proposed licensing arrangments." *VANS Consultative Document, supra*, at 31. It remains to be seen whether the providers of information and data processing services will comment on the potentially inhibitive effects of the government's proposal.

H. Distinctions Between Permissible Private Branch Systems And Third-Party Networking

1. Third-party service providers have been authorized, under a liberal general license, to develop a significant amount of private exchange service—including the interconnection of a limited number of private branch systems. This authorization will permit expanded use of the public telecommunications system and will enable large users to enjoy substantial conveniences and economies. As an alternative to pure resale, this option reflects a compromise that can open up a competitive market without eroding the financial viability of either BT or Mercury. To protect against erosion, the branch systems license restricts interconnection to ensure that private networks cannot engage in functions that directly compete with the public systems.

2. The branch systems license permits a variety of interconnection arrangements among branch exchanges, although it prohibits such interconnection to be used to transmit messages to a third party. Thus, company A could have its branch system tied to those of both companies B and C and could communicate with either. Company B could not, however, send a message to company C, using company A as a transmission link. *See Licence for the Running of Branch Telecommunications Systems by the Secretary for Trade and Industry Under Section 7 of the Telecommunications Act, 1984*, Condition 13 [hereinafter cited as *Branch Systems Licence*]; Statement Before Parliament of Kenneth Baker, Minister of Industry and Information Technology (July 17, 1984). One private branch also cannot serve as a switching point between the public telecommunications system and a second branch exchange. *See* Branch Systems Licence, *supra*, at Conditions 14 & 15.

3. The government has expressed a willingness to grant individual licenses "to individual applicants whose proposals for the use of private circuits significantly enhance the economic performance of the mu-

tual business interests of a defined but closed group of users [even if the number of connections proposed exceeds the number permitted under the general branch systems license]." Statement of Kenneth Baker, *supra.*

4. The government appears to believe that its proposal to establish the MDNS category will accomplish this objective in the area of data transmisison. However, in the absence of defined standards for an "acceptable" data network, resale arrangements will remain subject to ad hoc consideration by the DTI.

5. In proposing the new VANS class license, the government has suggested an additional safeguard against resale. The limitation would protect against the possibility that a third party could connect its telecommunication system to private circuits and offer—as a "value-added service"—what is essentially a switched voice service for unaffiliated parties. To discourage this kind of circuit arbitrage, the new VANS license would require that the charge for such a "live speech" service "be greater than the lowest available public switched telephone network tariff for the basic conveyance of the same message over the same route." *VANS Consultative Document, supra* at 19.

I. Combination of Limited Resale and VANS: The Case of the BT-IBM Venture and "Enhanced Services"

1. The rejected BT–IBM joint venture offers an example of how confusing it can be to fit new services within the structure created by the 1984 Act. The venture was intended to provide users with data networking facilities and with network management services, including potential expansion to accommodate a variety of VANS. The British government refused to license the venture, viewing it as potentially anticompetitive.

a. IBM and BT were viewed as potential competitors. Their combination would not only have eliminated the possibility of having them compete with each other, but also would have created a new business that could overwhelm others. The government, in opposing the venture, indicated that there would be no obstacle to having each company provide the proposed services independently.

b. The proposed network's potential as a major carrier of the country's data communications could well have enhanced the dominant market positions of both IBM and BT. Perhaps more importantly, it would have provided the two companies with an opportunity to introduce other VANS: the network would have delivered ready access to a huge number of potential value-added service users.

c. The attractiveness of an advanced data communications network, which could have enhanced both the data processing and the general VANS marketplace, was an obvious benefit of the venture. However, the network would have introduced a new, potentially overwhelming, entity into the telecommunications market. The U.K. government would then have faced the additional task of ensuring that this product of liberalization did not monopolize the market for enhanced telecommunications services and facilities.

d. It is ironic that BT's first significant attempt to engage in an innovative, competitive service offering, was rejected for fear that it would prove *too* competitive. The incident highlights the tension between encouraging BT to diversify and preventing it from dominating markets still in their early stages of development. It also demonstrates the government's intention to evaluate BT's partnerships and new ventures in light of their potential imact on competitors. BT clearly will have only limited competitive freedom during the early stages of the liberalization process.

2. BT would have used its leased lines to provide the venture's services. This configuration would have involved simple resale of BT circuits. The amount of "resale" activity, however, would have been no more significant than what occurs when a data processing service provides users with remote access capabilities over a private, leased network.

3. The leased line capacity, combined with the network management services, probably would bring a service like the BT–IBM venture within the scope of the proposed MDNS category; it is unclear whether such a service also would require the separate grant of a VANS license.

4. To the degree that BT would have been involved on both sides of the deal, serious questions about whether interconnection and circuit leasing arrangements could be negotiated at arm's length would have been raised. Similar concerns about IBM's detachment, given its dominance of the world computer market, also were present.

5. The British computer industry believed that the venture posed potentially disastrous consequences for the future of a competitive market in this area. The proposed network was to use IBM's Systems Network Architecture ("SNA"), which permits the attachment of both IBM and non-IBM equipment. It was claimed that SNA would accept many of the protocols supported by the ISO standards and would, therefore, accommodate the interconnection of numerous types of user terminals. Although SNA apparently allows for compatibility among a variety of protocols, in many instances—particularly for non-IBM equipment users—compatibility requires an intermediate connection to provide communication with the network through acceptable protocols. This requirement gives IBM equipment users a significant benefit.

6. The fact that the government would have permitted IBM to provide the same enhanced services independently of BT suggests some softening of the government's position on third-party use of BT circuits. Prior restrictions on resale might have been seen as prohibiting the formation of such an enhanced service network.

J. The Regulatory Status of Cable Television Services: A Competitive Alternative to the Local Wire Loop

1. *Overview of the British Concept of Cable Service*

a. Cable television systems are licensed both as systems and as service providers. The system, as a transmission technology, falls within the Telecommunications Act's definition of a telecommunications system. Telecommunications Act, 1984, ch. 12, § 4(1) (1984). Accordingly, it must be licensed under Section 7. A separate license from the newly created Cable Authority is required, however, to allow the system to provide cable program services, as defined by the Cable and Broadcasting Act, 1984, ch. 46, § 2(1) (1984). The Cable Authority also determines the system's franchise area.

b. The dual licensing requirement reflects the government's vision of cable as both a carrier of telecommunications services and a distributor of broadcast-style programming. To permit this use, the government has required that cable systems either be built with switching capacity or be capable of swift upgrade to a switched network. *See Cable White Paper, supra,* at ch. 2.

c. The government's commitment to two-way technology relies on a theoretical notion that advanced network design will best serve the nation's communications needs. A realistic assessment of what the market and the technology can sustain probably would not support that theory. There are strong indications that two-way systems will not readily prove viable. This is particularly true because it appears that cable systems that provide two-way, switched voice services will be burdened with some of the obligations of a PTO. These PTO obligations could dissuade many cable operators from providing these two-way transmission services. This could jeopardize the government's plan to use cable technology as an alternative transmission path for local exchange services.

d. In addition, the government's plans may be frustrated by a lack of available switching technology. Jerrold and GEC have announced their withdrawal from a plan to manufacture the switches necessary for much of cable's planned advanced networking capability. Scientific-Atlanta and Plessey also have ended a plan to manufacture the sophisticated head-end switch needed for the switched-star configuration preferred by the government for two-way cable services. (Three of eleven new cable franchisees had planned to use the Plessey switch.) This equipment shortage has added to doubts about cable's future, because systems are required to provide—or to prepare to provide—switching capacity.

e. Were this two-way technological capability to become widely available, it could prove particularly useful, for example, in helping Mercury evolve into a developed alternative service carrier. Two-way cable networks could provide Mercury with a non-BT local exchange network.

f. The dual nature of cable technology is reflected in the definition of a cable system contained in the license giving BT authority to operate such a system. The license defines the system to include all equipment used to convey "messages" (defined to mean any of the various things contained in Section 4(1) of the Telecommunications Act of 1984) from a broadcast station, or a broadcast receiving antenna, or some telecommunications apparatus, to an individual customer's receiving apparatus. *Licence Granted to British Telecommunications for the Running of Certain Cabled Systems Under Section 7 of the Telecommunications Act, 1984*, at app. A (1984).

i) The receiving apparatus is not limited to a television set, making it clear that data services or basic phone services could be received by means of a telephone, a computer, or a facsimile machine.

ii) The origination point for "messages" can be apparatus used either in wireless telegraphy or in wired telecommunications systems, making possible the carriage of both broadcast and telecommunications services.

g. The license authorizing carriage of cable program services permits reception of both broadcast and satellite-fed programming, which are transmitted by wireless telegraphy. Such reception was separately licensed under the Wireless Telegraphy Act, 1949, § 1 (1949) (broadcast programs), and the Post Office Act, 1969, § 89 (1969) (non-broadcast services). It is now authorized by the single license issued pursuant to Section 4 of the Cable and Broadcasting Act of 1984.

h. This diversification of cable technology represents the result of the government's concerted effort to upgrade cable systems as part of the country's plan for future communciations needs.

i) Until 1981, cable service consisted primarily of retransmission of the four broadcast television signals.

ii) In 1981, a series of two-year experimental licenses were issued to seven operators, permitting them to provide a feature film pay-television service tier.

iii) Some expect, however, that the real revolution will come as a result of the government's newly announced effort to bring cable technology into the mainstream of modern communications systems. *See Cable White Paper, supra*. In the initial licensing process, the government basically ignored operators who did not pay close attention to cable's function as a potential provider of interactive services.

i. The government sought to promote the growth of cable through marketplace competition and private investment. For this reason, plans to assign the task of cable installation to Mercury and BT were abandoned. While these companies had the technological expertise, their assumption of the entire nation's cable plant would have had an obviously stifling effect on British liberalization ideals. The requirement that two-way voice services be provided in association with either BT or Mercury represents an accommodation of the belief that these two companies can and should make a significant contribution to cable technology.

i) The emphasis of state-of-the-art technology has imposed a significant financial burden that may discourage private investment. This poses a formidable obstacle to the government's privatization policies. It also has slowed the spread of cable service: technological requirements have caused initial system construction to lag way behind schedule.

ii) The prospects for private investment have been further clouded by the government's decision to deny operators full tax write-offs for the cost of underground system construction.

j. One recent study of cable's economics—taking into account the technological requirements and recent industry and regulatory developments—now suggests that an operator should not expect to break even until the ninth year of operation. This kind of pessimism may explain why the two largest cable system operators in the U.K.—Rediffusion and Visionhire—have announced plans to sell their assets and to leave the cable business.

2. The License and the Licensing Process

a. According to the Cable Authority, a successful applicant will be one "who appears best placed to exploit the potential of cable and to deliver the benefits it offers." Cable Authority, *Guide to Franchise Applicant* 1 (unpublished, undated). The Authority will consider entertainment and non-entertainment service plans, the technology to be used, and the management and marketing skills of the applicant in evaluating the applications.

b. The dual licensing requirement is coordinated by the Cable Authority. Applicants submit their applications to the Authority, which then institutes consultations with OFTEL and the DTI. Under the Telecommunications Act, the Secretary of State or the Director General of OFTEL is required to consult with the Cable Authority before granting or revoking a cable operator's license to operate a telecommunications system. Telecommunications Act, 1984, ch. 12, §§ 7(10A) & (10B) (1984).

c. While the Authority's cable licensing power is exclusive, it consults with the public, DTI, OFTEL, and all local authorities who would be affected by the grant of the cable license. All Cable Authority licenses are also conditioned on the satisfactory outcome of an operator's application for a telecommunications system license.

d. The telecommunications license imposes on the system operator a variety of service and technical requirements. These requirements may include certain obligations of a PTO—if the operator chooses to provide two-way switched voice services.

i) The telecommunications license will require cable systems to provide "telecommunications services (other than voice telephone services) to anyone who requests them in an area where the cable system has been installed." *Licenses to be Granted by the Secretary of State for*

Trade and Industry to Westminster Cable Co., Ltd., and Broadband Ventures, Ltd., at Condition 1 (1985).

ii) OFTEL will monitor installation of the system.

iii) The License requires the system operator to engage in various interconnection arrangements. The system operator must seek an interconnection agreement with either BT or Mercury whenever a customer requests a service requiring such interconnection. (Mercury and BT have similar interconnection obligations in their licenses.) This requirement need not be satisfied if such interconnection would be impractical and if the Director General of OFTEL has not otherwise required that the requested service be provided. *Id.* at Condition 2. Under Conditions 8 and 9, the system operator is obligated to interconnect with other telecommunications systems when requested by the operator of such a system. The Director General is authorized to set the terms of interconnection if the parties cannot agree independently. There also are various exemptions from this obligation, such as if interconnection would be unsafe. Under Condition 19, the cable operator can levy an access charge on interconnected systems.

iv) These interconnection arrangements are vital to the government's vision of cable as a two-way service network. However, the commercial impracticalities of such internetworking could force the government to retreat from its position. A decision to relax interconnection obligations would further jeopardize cable's potential as a two-way service provider.

v) The cable system is required to be capable of (1) providing data services at a minimum transmission speed of 64 Kbit/s, (2) carrying switched communications to and from the public switched telephone network, and (3) offering a return video capacity. *Id.* at Condition 13.

vi) Licenses are granted for a period of fifteen years—twenty-three years for star-switched systems. If an operator commits to upgrading its system within five years of being licensed, and if that upgrade is completed within two years of making that commitment, the license can be extended to a twenty-three-year term.

3. *Initial Results of the Franchising Effort: Looking Ahead*

a. Although the Cable Authority has completed the process of awarding its first round of franchises, most observers agree that the effort has not been terribly successful. Delays in arranging financing and in obtaining telecommunications licenses have slowed the process of bringing systems into operation. One franchisee, Windsor Television, has been forced to shut down system construction, at least temporarily. Windsor needed an estimated $45 million to continue building, and its ability to obtain the financing had been called into question. Windsor's potential failure is seen as a significant setback for the nation's cable policies. The franchise was thought to involve a good service area, experienced management, and a commitment to the kind of advanced technology that the government intended to promote.

b. Nonetheless, the Cable Authority has moved into the second round of the franchising process. Plans call for franchises to be granted at the rate of twenty per year—five every three months. The Cable Authority sent initial inquiries of interest to forty companies. Between thirty and thirty-five responded positively, but only half indicated a desire to undertake immediate construction. According to the Cable Authority, many of the replies expressed a more general, long-term interest.

c. To combat the malaise, the Cable Authority has relaxed its technology requirements. It has told second round applicants that "the application of advanced technology, although remaining a factor . . . , will not represent the central issue . . . ." While this flexibility may help to attract new operators and to enhance the likelihood of system construction, it will obviously undermine the government's plea for cable to function as a sophisticated communications network.

d. Of the eleven franchises granted initially, only one—Aberdeen—has gone into operation. Although the Aberdeen system was significantly behind schedule in beginning its service, it met with an enthusiastic response during the opening days of its first subscription drive. Seventy-four of the 120 homes visited signed up for service. Aberdeen serves a franchise area with 97,000 homes. The system is being built by BT and will cost between £25 and £30 million. Aberdeen is paying BT £6 per month for each subscriber. Service consists of fifteen channels at a cost of £16 per month; four of those channels are the British broadcast stations.

e. Two early, heavy investors in cable technology, BT and Thorn EMI, have announced plans to "review" their investments before committing additional funds to cable. Thorn EMI spent approximately £2 million to upgrade the old Swindon system to a broadband network. Its current annual operating costs in Swindon are near £1 million, and the system has been struggling to sign up subscribers. Just 300 of the 2,600 homes in the franchise area—eleven percent—had ordered the company's fifteen-channel service as of April, 1985.

f. Cable's future in Britain is highly uncertain. The potential for it to operate as a broadband, switched communications network seems particularly unlikely. The Information Technology Advisory Panel, which advises the Prime Minister on information technology, has begun a review of the cable industry to assess the numerous problems that it faces. The Panel recommended the initial pro-cable movement to the government.

K. Cellular Radio Services: Another Alternative to the Local Wire Loop

1. The government has authorized two groups to provide cellular radio services. In January, 1985, they both began operations, two months ahead of schedule. Racal (eighty percent), Millicom (fifteen per-

cent), and Hambros Bank (five percent) have combined to form Racal-Vodafone. BT and Securicor have joined to form Telecom Securicor Cellular Radio Ltd. ("Cellnet"). Both groups have been granted licenses under the 1981 Act, which required that they begin operating by March 31, 1985. *Licence Granted to Telecom Securicor Cellular Radio Limited Under Section 15(1) of the British Telecommunications Act, 1981* (1984); *Licence Granted to Racal-Millicom Limited Under Section 15(1) of the British Telecommunications Act, 1981* (1983).

2. The cellular systems are interconnected with the public telecommunications systems, allowing users to make both domestic and international calls. The systems also will provide value-added services. Vodafone has announced plans for a unit that will allow mobile radio communications with computers, telex, electronic mailboxes, and viewdata services.

3. Both systems are considered public telecommunications systems, requiring that, among other things, they seek to provide universal service. Under the terms of the license, they must serve ninety percent of the U.K. population by 1990. The license also requires that service be offered according to published tariffs, and that no charge be imposed for emergency calls. At present, cellular service reaches approximately forty cities and claims 12,000 subscribers. In effect, the systems will serve as wireless extensions of the wired, switched network, permitting mobile apparatus (which the service licensees cannot provide) to be hooked into the basic telephone network.

4. As the licenses permit cellular systems to interconnect with networks other than public telecommunications systems, the cellular systems could carry a variety of value-added services. The cellular license permits carriage of "speech, music, and other sounds, visual images and signals."

5. Cellular systems that are linked into both value-added networks and the BT and Mercury systems will permit bypass of the wired PTOs' local exchanges. The degree to which cellular service will exert competitive pressures on BT and Mercury, as a result of this capability, remains to be seen.

6. Policymakers in the DTI believe that the cellular radio, like cable technology, will help to check any long-term efforts by BT to shift costs from interexchange to local exchange services. The likely impact of such services on BT's ability and incentives to cross-subsidize is very questionable. As noted above, the emergence of cable as even a one-way distribution system is quite clouded; its development of two-way switching capabilities for data or voice transmission is even more remote. Cellular radio facilities are not, moreover, well adapted at this time to function as an alternative local loop for interexchange services. Therefore, it will be necessary—in the interim—to rely on traditional regulatory, as opposed to market-oriented, restraints on cross-subsidization.

IV. INSTITUTIONAL ARRANGEMENTS

A. The Proliferation of Supervisory Institutions

1. The liberalization of the telecommunications market has brought with it a proliferation of institutional concerns, many of which center on jurisdictional issues. The new legislation has added two governmental bodies—OFTEL and the Cable Authority—who must now work in conjunction with the DTI and the Home Office, both of whom retain supervisory powers. This multiplicity of institutions could frustrate liberalization more than encourage it. Tension may be particularly acute because OFTEL has close ties with the DTI and because the Cable Authority is selected by the Home Office. The DTI and the Home Office may seek to extend their particular policy goals by shaping the characteristics of the new institutions.

2. It was originally thought that a cable system would need to obtain four licenses from three different sources: the DTI would license it as a telecommunications system, the Home Office would authorize it to receive broadcast programming and to distribute off-air programming, and the Cable Authority would approve its cable program operations (as well as define its franchise area). In addition, OFTEL and the Mergers and Monopolies Commission would be responsible for license enforcement and for handling license modification requests. The Cable and Broadcasting Act of 1984 streamlined this process somewhat by consolidating the licensing procedure into two steps: the DTI approves operation as a telecommunications system, and the Cable Authority licenses all other functions. *See Cable White Paper, supra,* at 26-28 (1983).

3. The proliferation of supervisory authorities is contrary to the government's dislike of complex regulatory processes. The government has not commented favorably on the way in which the United States—through the interaction of courts, administrative agencies, the Congress, and the executive branch—has restructured AT&T and the U.S. telecommunications market. *See, e.g., Beesley Report, supra,* at ch. VIII; *Littlechild Report, supra,* at 8. The privatization of BT is intended to turn the process of regulation over to market forces; however, maintaining BT as a regulated quasi-monopoly will require the government's continued oversight of BT's interaction with its competitors. Nonetheless, the government views regulation as a makeshift construct designed to "hold the fort" until true competition exists. *Littlechild Report, supra,* at 7.

4. The new regulatory order is generally guided by the licensing process, which determines what services a particular entity may offer. The Secretary of State, assisted by the Director General of OFTEL, have the primary responsibility for licensing. The Telecommunications Act directs them to promote a number of policies—many of which involve contradictory aims and strategies. These goals are enumerated in Section 3 of the Act:

a. Provide universal service to satisfy all reasonable demands by the public.

b. Ensure financial security for any entity required to provide unprofitable services demanded by the universal service objective.

c. Protect consumers' interests in the variety and affordability of services (particularly the interests of the elderly and the handicapped).

d. Promote competition.

e. Expand international service offerings.

f. Attract large users of telecommunications services into the country.

g. Enable domestic service and equipment providers to compete effectively in the international market.

B. The Department of Trade and Industry

1. The DTI long has functioned as the primary supervisor of telecommunications policies. It drafted much of the new legislation that has restructured the telephone and cable communications markets.

2. As a result of the Telecommunications Act of 1984, it retains a major role, because the Secretary of State for Trade and Industry has been given primary responsibility for the licensing of all telecommunications systems. He may delegate that authority to the Director General of OFTEL. It appears that the Secretary of State will continue to grant the initial licenses, which will set precedent and involve sensitive policy choices. Over time, however, this responsibility is likely to be delegated more fully to the Director General.

3. The DTI increasingly will be joined by OFTEL and, to a lesser degree, by the Cable Authority in making major decisions about the future course of liberalization. In certain instances, the DTI actually will relinquish its role as a primary regulator; the 1984 legislation has given—and transferred—significant responsibility to OFTEL, particularly.

a. For example, the Director General, in conjunction with the Monopolies and Mergers Commission, is responsible for overseeing license modifications. He also is obligated to guard against anticompetitive activities and to ensure that licensees comply with the terms of their licenses.

b. Reliance on OFTEL is not, however, complete. The Secretary of State may, for example, order the Director General not to grant a license modification under certain circumstances. Telecommunications Act, 1984, ch. 12 §§ 12(5) and (6) (1984).

4. The DTI also has gained a significant new responsibility. It has taken over the task of assigning broadcast frequencies, a job once performed by the Home Office. The Home Office continues to oversee broadcast operations generally; however, the DTI now manages all technical aspects of broadcasting. Despite recent attempts to consolidate authority in

the DTI, the Home Office has succeeded in retaining its jurisdiction—largely in an effort to prevent diminution of its scope of authority and a corresponding loss of influence and prestige.

5. A major question that remains is the degree to which the DTI will continue to function as the primary licensor of telecommunications systems. This would seem a particular concern as OFTEL gains experience and begins to shape the market, chiefly through its power to enforce the terms of licenses granted under the Telecommunications Act. The potential exists for a conflict to develop between the DTI's licensing activities and the general oversight and enforcement work done by OFTEL.

C. Role of the Newly Created OFTEL

1. A major feature of the 1984 Act was the creation of OFTEL as an independent office. This may permit the development of a concentrated source of expertise on telecommunications issues that is largely insulated from political pressures.

2. OFTEL is headed by a Director General, appointed by the Secretary of State for a term of up to five years, which can be renewed. The Director General serves as an independent Officer of the Crown, Telecommunications Act, 1984, ch. 12, § 1 (1984), although he can be removed from office by the Secretary of State for "incapacity or misbehaviour," *id.*

a. Bryan Carsberg, an accounting professor from the London School of Economics, is serving as the first Director General, for a three-year term.

b. The OFTEL staff, appointed by the Director General, was expected to number about fifty. The complexity of the liberalization process, however, already has required OFTEL to hire at least 70-80 employees; it expects to exceed 100 in the near future. All staff members are civil servants.

3. OFTEL's general responsibilities include licensing (as delegated by the Secretary of State), enforcement of license provisions, monitoring of the telecommunications marketplace to police anticompetitive practices and the abuse of monopoly power, advising the Secretary of State and the government generally on telecommunications matters, and prosecuting—when necessary—those who run unlicensed telecommunications systems or who violate consumer protection provisions regarding equipment. The Director General also is required to consider user complaints about telecommunications services and equipment. Approximately 800 complaints are now being submitted to OFTEL each month. *Id.* at § 49.

a. The breadth of this jurisdictional grant hardly can be overstated. As the general policing office of the telecommunications market, OFTEL is responsible for overseeing all licensees. It must pay particular attention to the activities of the newly privatized BT. This oversight requires decisions about accounting and separations policies, service and equipment activities in light of the controlling license terms, resale activities, and individual business ventures (such as BT–IBM and BT-Mitel).

b. The variety of issues confronting the office raises an immediate problem in terms of priorities. Initially, the licensing process will require a great deal of attention. (A major aim of the liberalization policy is to authorize—as quickly as possible—a variety of competitive services.) However, licensing cannot come at the expense of ignoring such vital concerns as BT's accounting practices or its satisfaction of interconnection obligations. Controversies about resale issues also seem likely to arise. This is particularly true with regard to branch exchange operations in which there is a fine line between a permissible service and the impermissible resale of transmission capacity. Finally, the sudden appearance of emergencies, such as the BT–IBM venture that demanded close attention, is likely to divert OFTEL's resources in unexpected directions. The enormity of the office's task already requires that some decisions be made as to what matters will receive the greatest attention.

4. With the privatization of BT, the Postal Office Users' National Council and its Country Councils no longer are concerned with telecommunications issues. Therefore, the Director General has assumed the duties of considering consumer complaints about telecommunications services and equipment. Given his power over license terms and license enforcement, he will have the ability to act quickly to correct the sources of complaints. He may modify licenses or order compliance with license provisions when necessary.

5. Although the Director General has the power to make modifications in the terms of a license, the process requires the involvement of both the Secretary of State and the Monopolies and Mergers Commission. Such modifications can be made either on the initiative of the Director or at the request of a licensee or a third party.

a. Modifications can be made only after public notice of the proposed change has been given. At least twenty-eight days must be provided for public comment.

b. For the Director to make a modification on his own initiative, the licensee must consent. Before the modification of a class license can take effect, there may not be any outstanding objections from any person authorized to operate a telecommunications system under the license. Telecommunications Act, 1984, ch. 12, § 12(4) (1984).

c. A modification will be referred to the Monopolies and Mergers Commission if a licensee objects to the proposed modification, or if the Director General seeks outside advice, or if the Secretary of State orders the referral. *Id.* at § 13. The Commission is directed to determine whether the situation threatens to harm the public interest and whether a license modification might rectify or alleviate that harm. The Commission must make the details of any matter before it public, unless the Secretary of State directs that they be kept confidential (for reasons of national security or foreign relations). *Id.*

d. If the Commission finds that a license modification could avert a threatened public harm, it can instruct the Director General to modify the license in a particular manner. The modification must be published, to allow for public comment. The Secretary of State can order that the modification not be made public (for national security or for foreign relations reasons). *Id.* at § 15.

e. The Director General is required to publish the details of the Commission's investigation, unless the Secretary of State directs him to withhold certain matters (to protect the public interest or the private commercial interests of an individual). *Id.* at § 14.

6. To avoid a jurisdictional conflict in the area of monitoring anticompetitive commercial practices, the Telecommunications Act assigns some of the responsibilities previously committed to the Director General of Fair Trading to the Director General of Telecommunications. As a result, the Director General of Telecommunications must review all commercial activity in the telecommunications field and must investigate and refer any monopolistic or anticompetitive practices to the Monopolies and Mergers Commission. The Director General of Fair Trading retains investigative power in the telecommunications industry only over mergers and restrictive trade agreements. OFTEL has no power over these two commercial practices. *Id.* at § 50. This division of authority consolidates OFTEL's power over the telecommunications field. Without the separation, the competitive practices of telecommunications businesses would have been subject to duplicative scrutiny.

7. Under Section 55 of the 1984 Act, the Director General is required to submit an annual report on telecommunications matters in the U.K. to the Secretary of State.

a. In compliance with that requirement, Professor Carsberg recently delivered his first report. OFTEL, *Report of the Director General of Telecommunications to the Secretary of State* (April 1985) (released July 3, 1985). As required by the 1984 Act, the report discusses the activities of the Director General and the progress of matters referred by him to the Monopolies and Mergers Commission. It covers developments between August 5, 1984, and December 31, 1984—the first five months under the new Act.

b. In the report, Carsberg emphasizes his general belief that that the promotion of consumer welfare is the key to his responsibilities. He notes that he is "required to promote competition because this is an important means—in many cases the best available means—of bringing benefits to consumers: . . . ." *Id.* at 7. Most of the discussion in the report, consequently, focuses on issues such as interconnection arrangements, service pricing, consumer satisfaction with carrier performance, and the need to improve the complaints process.

D. Duties Delegated to the New Cable Authority

1. The Cable Authority, created by the Cable and Broadcasting Act of 1984, operates independently of the government. This independence reflects the government's desire to avoid involving itself in decisions affecting the content of communications. The Cable Authority grants franchises and supervises the provision of cable program services, pursuant to licenses that it grants. It oversees such things as program decency standards and political impartiality. Unlike the Independent Broadcasting Authority ("IBA") or the British Broadcasting Company ("BBC"), the Cable Authority is not responsible for actual program transmission or for direct content control: its role is merely supervisory. The Authority can, however, prevent a cable operator from showing a particular program at an unsuitable time.

a. Because of this potential involvement in the area of program oversight, the government decided not to have OFTEL—which is made up of civil servants—supervise cable services. *See Cable White Paper, supra,* at 23, 59-60 (1983). (The involvement of the DTI and OFTEL in licensing cable systems as telecommunications systems relates only to cable's role as a transmission network. Program content concerns are not implicated.)

b. The government also felt that cable policies should be formulated at a national level (with only limited local input). Therefore, local authorities were not given power to supervise cable. *Id.* at 22. *But see supra* Section III.J.2.

2. The government recognized that the Cable Authority was yet another regulatory body that would have to work with OFTEL, the IBA, the BBC, and the Monopolies and Mergers Commission in supervising cable's development. It chose, however, to create an organization that could serve as the principal coordinator of the country's cable policies. *Id.* at 23-24.

3. The Authority is responsible for supervising video services. *See* Cable and Broadcasting Act, 1984, ch. 46, §§ 1-4 (1984) (regarding the licensing of cable program services). The DTI and OFTEL supervise cable's role in providing non-video services, such as voice and data transmission, which fall under the provisions of the Telecommunications Act. This division appears to avoid any serious jurisdictional conflict.

a. The broad definition of a telecommunications system found in the Telecommunications Act encompasses a cable system, regardless of what service it provides. Thus, simply to operate, a cable system must be licensed under that Act.

b. Provision of a "cable programme service," requires a license from the Cable Authority. Such a service is defined to mean the transmission of "sounds or visual images"—not by wireless telegraphy—for reception either in more than one place or in a place of public reception. *Id.* at § 1.

c. To provide voice or data transmission services, which are not cable program services, the cable system must be licensed separately under the Telecommunications Act. The Cable Authority cannot authorize the provision of these telecommunications services.

d. OFTEL is further involved in this process to the degree that the cable operator provides data services in London, Birmingham, or Manchester, or switched voice services anywhere in the country. Such services can only be provided in conjunction with BT or Mercury. Under the terms of those companies' licenses, the Director General must approve any joint business arrangements in advance.

e. If either Mercury or BT operates a cable system, it must be licensed under the Telecommunications Act to operate that system. It also would have to get the Cable Authority's approval to provide cable program services. In addition, it would have to seek a franchise from the Cable Authority.

f. Although the division in services may be clear enough to avoid jurisdictional problems, the mere fact that regulatory authority is divided may pose problems. The Cable Authority's mandate to promote the growth and the development of cable service may not always align itself with OFTEL's goals. If, for example, voice and data services become a crucial factor in assuring the financial viability of cable systems, the Cable Authority would want to see that systems are permitted to provide such services. However, OFTEL might, for some reason, find that result contrary to the best interests of the public (in receiving telecommunications services generally). If OFTEL were to believe that voice and data traffic over cable networks was diverting significant amounts of traffic from BT or Mercury, thereby threating these companies' ability to provide affordable nationwide telephone service, it might not want to grant the licenses necessary for cable systems to provide telecommunications services.

V. INTERNATIONAL SERVICES: THE U.K.'S ROLE AS A TRANSATLANTIC HUB

A. The Transatlantic Price War

1. Britain's domestic policies have opened the way for an international services war. Mercury has been permitted to offer international service in competition with BT International, which has allowed foreign carriers to take advantage of competition between the two British carriers. That is not to suggest, however, that Mercury and BT are unwilling pawns in a battle among foreign carriers. The two companies view the chance to expand their international service arrangements as potentially effective ways of competing with each other.

2. In addition, the country's aggressive liberalization policy makes it an attractive link between the United States and Western Europe.

The plethora of competitive U.S. carriers now racing into the international market have found Mercury and BT to be more willing correspondents than many of the Western European PTTs, which still take a dim view of open competition in basic transmission services.

3. International service traditionally has been a BT mainstay. It has for years been the company's most profitable service and continues to show a high profit margin. Nonetheless, international services from the U.K. have remained relatively inexpensive—particularly when compared with the rates of many Western European nations. From BT's perspective, the aggressive pursuit of multiple international service arrangements allows it to take traffic away from both Mercury and the European PTTs.

a. This competitive edge is particularly important to BT now, because Mercury is just beginning its network's operation. To the degree that BT can use its past role as the monopoly service provider in the U.K. to forge relationships with a variety of new carriers, it may be able to limit Mercury's ability to gain an effective presence in the market.

b. The U.K. is operating as a transatlantic telecommunications hub. Attractive rates between the U.K. and the U.S. have made it cheaper for multinational companies to route their calls through London than directly from Europe to the United States. As a result, almost one-third of the multinationals in Europe route their telecommunications traffic through the U.K. Because of this traffic pattern, calls between the U.S. and the U.K. now account for almost half of the $700 million transatlantic telephone market.

c. In response to this interest from foreign companies, both BT and Mercury have looked closely at providing innovative transmission systems that can accommodate high-speed data services. Such services are expected to appeal to companies that increasingly rely on computer communications to link their offices. They particularly will attract the banking and finance communities, which rely on the prompt transmission of vast amounts of computerized information.

4. Competition should expand even further as new service arrangements involve the construction of more efficient and innovative facilities. The Market Link cables to be built by Tel-Optik and Cable & Wireless are expected to afford users with a dramatic savings in transatlantic services. An agreement between Western Union and Mercury to offer shared private line services between the U.K. and the U.S. also should offer significant price reductions. Initially, this service will only permit a closed user group in one country to contact a single subscriber in another country. Eventually, the network will implement a more flexible sharing arrangement that will increase a user's calling options. However, the companies face long-standing, and often adamant, European and international restrictions on resale and shared use of private line circuits. Both Mercury and Western Union have contended that by using "closed user groups" they can work within CCITT and CEPT guidelines.

5. This vigorous British activity has not gone without European response. While some PTTs continue to reject offers to deal with new U.S. carriers such as MCI and GTE-Sprint, others have openly welcomed—and encouraged—the new business. MCI has reached agreements with Argentina, Belgium, Brazil, East Germany, Greece, Spain, and the United Arab Emirates to provide discount-rate telephone service to and from the United States. It also has announced plans for a worldwide electronic mail service that will network through Belgium. GTE-Sprint has announced many similar service agreements.

6. The result of this British activity may be a loosening of worldwide restrictions on international correspondent agreements. Competition is likely to face continued opposition from PTTs, which still subsidize unprofitable services (such as postal delivery) with the profits earned on basic communications services. Because competition tends to force service rates down, the PTTs view it as a threat to their cost structures. Nonetheless, as a larger number of countries reprice their services and accept competitive carriers, pressure will grow either to enter the market or to face losing substantial amounts of international business. In this regard, Britain's liberalization has had a significant transborder effect.

7. An ironic result of the new international competition in the U.K. may be the injection of government oversight into the facilities and services decisionmaking process. The DTI increasingly is being urged, by both domestic and foreign groups, to exercise its jurisdiction over international services and to manage the explosive growth now occurring in the U.K. Any such move by the DTI would mark an extraordinary departure from the traditional arrangement in which BT International has essentially managed its own service decisions. However, with the introduction of Mercury, the increased activity of new U.S. international characters, and the volatility of the current international satellite market, *see infra* Section V.B., it now may be necessary for the government to step in. As is the case in the domestic market, the introduction of competition may require at least some regulatory oversight of the competitors.

B. A Future for International Satellite Service?

1. Britain's plans for a domestic satellite industry appear to have collapsed after a series of disagreements about the viability of a British DBS service.

a. A twenty-one-member consortium formed to bring DBS to the U.K. first rejected the government's plan to use satellites supplied by United Satellites ("Unisat") and then decided to abandon altogether any plans for DBS.

b. Unisat was formed by British Aerospace, BT, and GEC-Marconi. The £500 million Unisat project was considered too expensive, particularly in light of plans by a competitor, Britsat, to offer the same two-satellite system—using American satellites built by RCA—for just £379 million.

2. The consortium's decision is just the latest in a long series of battles about whether British DBS service can be provided at an affordable price. DBS initially was supposed to be the sole province of the BBC. However, when the BBC complained that it could not fund the project on its own, the government brought together the current consortium in an attempt to save the satellite plans.

3. If DBS cannot provoke the launch of a British statellite, it is not clear when a space station will begin operating. Lately there has been talk in the U.K. about using capacity on the Eutelsat ECS system to provide British viewers with DBS. However, plans for the launch of an Irish satellite that would use Ku-band frequencies for medium-power television transmission and telecommunications may provoke the U.K. to get some kind of British satellite into operation. The problem facing the U.K. is to determine precisely what such a satellite would do.

a. Unisat originally was conceived as a system to provide both DBS and telecommunications services. However, after the BBC was joined by other companies to form the DBS consortium, additional DBS channels were added to the project—at the expense of the transponder space originally intended for telecommunications service.

b. It is not clear whether a satellite will prove economical if devoted purely to DBS or completely to telecommunications service. There are continued doubts about whether a large enough number of British viewers will pay a sufficient price to support a DBS system. The viability of any future DBS system may be sinking fast as Sky Channel, the satellite-to-cable program service of Australian media magnate Rupert Murdoch, gains popularity across Europe. In addition, the Independent Television Companies Association ("ITV") has announced its plan to consider a competitive programming service using the ECS satellite. It seems even more unlikely that domestic telecommunications needs could fill the capacity of a British satellite system. The country's relatively small geographic area does not place a high demand on the advantages of satellite distribution, which offers long-distance transmission at a much lower cost than do terrestrial facilities.

4. It may well be that the future for British satellites will depend on whether they can offer transborder and transatlantic services. If Britain were permitted to use domestic satellite facilities to enter the lucrative transatlantic market—in competition with Intelsat—the attractiveness of the satellites would grow tremendously.

5. In this regard, it is interesting that the U.K. has supported certain aspects of the United States' basic position on private international satellites. At the Intelsat Board of Governors' meeting in March, 1985, both the U.S. and the U.K. criticized proposals by Intelsat Director General Richard Colino regarding the Article XIV(d) coordination procedure (for non-Intelsat satellites). The U.K. did not take as extreme a position as the U.S. However, it did argue that Intelsat should not seek to prevent all future

competition and that it should judge each competing system on its own merits, rather than in terms of the net competitive effect of all such systems on Intelsat. This position may foreshadow a desire to enter a future competitive, international satellite market. Private satellites obviously would be an attractive supplement to the U.K.'s existing, vigorous business in transatlantic cable services.

VI. FUTURE ISSUES

A. Introduction

The evolution of new regulatory and industrial policies for the telecommunications market will present some of the U.K.'s major participants with significant new challenges and dilemmas. The future course of the U.K.'s liberalization process will depend greatly on the responses of Mercury, BT, the British government, and users.

B. Mercury's Perspective

1. For Mercury, the most difficult question may be whether it can construct its system quickly enough to become a viable competitive alternative before BT preempts its market opportunities. BT was able to reduce its pricing over high-volume routes before any effective regulatory mechanism was put in place to oversee the pricing changes. Although OFTEL appears satisfied that at least part of this rate adjustment was not unfair or anticompetitive, the speed of BT's reaction demonstrates that Mercury will face a determined—and obviously powerful—competitor.

2. The competitive relationship between Mercury and BT differs decidedly from the relationship between AT&T and long-distance service competitors in the U.S. In the U.S., the FCC had existing cost allocation guidelines in place and was able to apply them on numerous occasions. It was ready to intervene and to require modification of pricing moves made by AT&T to respond to competitive offerings of companies such as MCI. OFTEL is working from a much more uncertain position in trying to control BT. It is a new governmental unit lacking the background of years of trying to control the actions of a dominant communications carrier.

3. Mercury is now wholly owned by Cable & Wireless, an entity with great experience in the telecommunications field and one that is no doubt prepared to bear the costs and burdens of a new venture. Thus, it appears more likely than ever that Mercury will be able to withstand the initial difficulties of breaking into the market. In addition, it seems unlikely that the British government can stand idly by and allow Mercury to fail. Even though the British government has a great stake in the financial success of the BT offering, it appears to have at least an equivalent interest in seeing its policy of encouraging competition succeed. The key to achieving

some degree of effective long-term competition is Mercury's ability to construct an alternative transmission network. Nevertheless, there are some in the British government who undoubtedly viewed Mercury's primary role as a prod to BT. From this perspective, the collapse of Mercury might not necessarily be seen as evidence of policy failure; many believe that Mercury's mere formation already has resulted in BT's becoming more innovative and efficient.

4. The British government is encouraging OFTEL to promote competition while simultaneously preserving a duopolistic competitive relationship—at least in the near term. A test of that resolve may arise as the government continues to work out its licensing policies, which require it to confront the question of whether, and to what extent, it should allow the resale of telecommunications transmission services. Initially, the government had taken a firm stance against resale. This position apparently was taken to limit new competition that could undercut Mercury. It is not clear, however, whether Mercury or BT benefits more from resale restrictions. Mercury might well find it useful to be able to lease capacity from BT to "piece out" its network and extend its services throughout Britain.

a. In the U.S., MCI found resale of AT&T facilities immensely important in its efforts to extend services on a universal basis. Moreover, smaller intercity competitors in the U.S. are trying to gain ground on the early market entrants by constructing some of their own facilities and reselling other carriers' services to fill out a transmission network. Resale in the U.S. also ended up being an extremely important mechanism to thwart price discrimination in AT&T tariffs that retained larger customers "as willing captives" in preferential rate structures. The U.K. apparently believes that resale should await the readjustment of BT's rates—so that prices will more closely reflect costs. However, one could argue that by allowing resale quickly the government would force BT to adjust its rates more rapidly. Of course, such swift, marketplace repricing might have other, less desirable, effects on some of BT's less profitable, public services.

b. More flexibility on the resale issue would appear to be to Mercury's advantage. However, it is not clear that the government will be able to retreat significantly from its present position on this issue. The government may have locked itself into maintaining the status quo because of its prior policy statements and because of the need to add stability to the regulatory environment. Any fundamental shift in the regulatory requirements applicable to BT might be viewed as undermining the government's credibility, in light of "representations" made to BT shareholders prior to the public offering of BT stock.

c. Thus, it may be necessary to work within the confines of the government's policy against resale by allowing an increased number of exceptions to that policy. The government already refers more and more frequently to a policy prohibiting "simple resale" (*i.e.*, a restriction on only the resale of message toll services). One result of the rejection of the BT–IBM joint venture has been a policy statement that IBM and others could independently enter the market to provide "enhanced services." The creation of a separate service category for data networks, as proposed in the *VANS Consultative Document*, appears, at least in part, to be an additional outgrowth of the BT-IBM proposal. These actions may bode well for Mercury, which could benefit from more flexibility in the government's resale policy.

C. British Telecom's Perspective

1. BT would seem to be facing a bright future, having made swift moves to rejuvenate its organization and to reprice its services. Nevertheless, it still confronts the problem of deciding how to deal with a new competitor and a new regulatory process without appearing to exploit its dominant market position unfairly. The dilemma that BT will face is one that AT&T has had to deal with—and continues to confront—and that NTT and other dominant forces in newly competitive markets will be facing.

2. The question is simply one of how to position its competitive responses. BT could simply storm the market and await the resistance of its competitor or of the government. However, if it acts in this way, it might provoke a strong regulatory response that will further liberalize the market and further restrain BT. It is at least arguable that AT&T provided a great deal of the impetus for the opening of the American market because of the intensity of its resistance to competition in the early years of its competitive struggle with MCI.

3. BT's joint venture with IBM may have been a similar case of trying to reach for too much too soon. The venture presented obvious threats to the future of competition, and its timing raised a challenge for OFTEL—in its first days—that could hardly have been ignored. BT's recent plan to purchase a majority interest in Mitel suggests that it is still inclined to favor dramatic, swift competitive actions. Once again, it appears, the government may resist BT's plans.

4. A more cautious approach by BT might not have produced these consequences. Indeed, BT—for the first time confronted with a regulatory apparatus—may be experiencing what might be seen as a "Newtonian law" of the regulatory process. That is, for every aggressive initiative by a dominant carrier in a deliberately balanced competitive and regulatory environment there may be an equal—and sometimes greater—regulatory response.

5. There also is a danger in an approach based on caution, in which BT takes an "enlightened" competitive stance. Were BT to suggest a "moderate position" that allows for a "fair" degree of competition and offers a "fair" amount of self-restraint, it could find that its position is taken as only the starting point in the regulatory dialogue. The naturally contentious regulatory process will view BT's position as an extreme one, not as its honest assessment of a fair market arrangement. The adversarial nature of the regulatory process inevitably builds in an expectation that competitors

will suggest unrealistically favorable solutions in order to get an eventual compromise that favors their own interests most closely.

6. The question is whether it is possible to create a more cooperative environment in which to develop regulatory policy. The litigious tradition of the U.S. regulatory process encourages the participants to adopt extreme positions that eventually will be reconciled through compromise. Where, as in Britain, there is no comparable tradition of litigation, and where the regulatory entity has relatively limited resources, it may be possible—and desirable—to adopt different mechanisms for policy formulation and for dispute resolution. Such mechanisms would rely on having the parties to the process put forward their best foot first—not only after extensive wrangling. Yet, the initial phase of BT's battle with Mercury over network interconnection suggests that such a conciliatory approach is not likely. Both companies have adopted extreme positions and have required a court decision to resolve a heated dispute. OFTEL now must settle the controversy; the process has all the makings of a traditional, adversarial regulatory fight.

7. BT's actions in the early phases of the industrial and regulatory transition can exert a remarkable amount of influence on the future direction and role of the regulatory process. It is not yet clear what approach BT will choose to adopt.

D. The Government's Perspective

1. The British government faces a set of enormous challenges in implementing its new telecommunications policy. As noted above, it must be able to revise its policies on an ongoing basis without jilting the new BT shareholders that it so successfully courted.

2. It must assure that OFTEL emerges as an effective regulatory body. For OFTEL, the primary challenge is to establish a set of priorities and to allocate its limited resources to the most critical areas of regulatory concern. Even a cursory review of the U.S. and Canadian experiences with cost accounting schemes reveals what a complex and difficult task OFTEL faces in this area.

3. The burden on the regulatory process—as a referee of price competition—may be increased because some key elements of the government's policy do not seem likely to work efficiently. It had been the view of some decisionmakers in the DTI that the development of cable and of cellular radio systems could provide an alternative to BT's local transmission facilities. As a result, it was thought, BT would be reluctant to shift charges from its interexchange to its less profitable local exchange services. It seems likely, however, the neither cable nor cellular radio will provide realistic alternative facilities.

4. In a related issue, the government will have to determine whether its cable television policy is based on realistic technological and economic assumptions. The view of some in the telecommunications indus-

try is that cable systems can be constructed to satisfy the need of Mercury and of other large users for transmission facilities to bypass BT's local network. There is, however, a real question about whether this view is a correct one. Whatever is finally decided about the merits of this issue, the government should ultimately determine how important it is to its overall telecommunications policy to see that two-way cable facilities are, in fact, constructed. The Cable Authority's recent decision to relax technological requirements for future franchises may indicate a government vote for cable *television,* rather than cable *communications*—at least for now.

5. The government also must continue to sort out its policy on the implementation of enhanced services in the aftermath of its rejection of the BT–IBM joint venture. The *VANS Consultative Document* is not a definitive answer to the numerous problems that accompany the line-drawing process inherent in determining the scope of permissible services for entities other than BT and Mercury. The questions that must be faced include whether BT and Mercury will be required to make leased lines available to enhanced service vendors and what will be the pricing arrangements and terms and conditions of use for these facilities.

6. The government is confronted with the extremely difficult task of supervising a mechanism to ensure the continued viability of costly universal and emergency service goals. It has chosen to achieve this objective by allowing BT to impose charges on other carriers for access to its network. However, no mechanism for using these charges has been established. It is difficult to decide what subsidies should be made available to BT—which is responsible for providing these services. BT's outmoded accounting policies still obscure the costs that it faces in supplying particular services.

7. Undoubtedly, debate over the use of the access charges again will focus on the economic and political consequences of the pricing of services. Some concern about the effect of repricing on regional development surfaced during the debate on the 1984 Telecommunications Bill. Questions are likely to emerge in sharper relief after some of the consequences of competitive entry become more concrete and apparent. A heated debate over access charges—in political terms—could have a significant impact on the vigor with which the government implements its new regulatory policies.

8. The government faces the task of assessing the international consequences of its recent changes in domestic telecommunications policy. The government must put in place better mechanisms for representation on international bodies. It may even have to manage some of the competition beginning to complicate the international service markets.

9. The government will have to decide what its position on standards for ISDN services will be, given its present commitment to a duopolistic market structure. Moreover, it will need to decide to what extent its procompetitive domestic policies should influence its approach to the

provision—on a competitive basis—of international satellite and fiber optic facilities.

10. At the present time, the European PTTs view British telecommunications policy as increasingly divergent from their own national priorities. They see Britain drifting away from Europe and toward the U.S. The British government must carefully evaluate the consequences of moving away from a European orientation toward an international telecommunications policy. Once the major aspects of the privatization of BT are in place, the government will have to turn to these international issues as ones of pressing importance.

E. The Users' Perspective

1. The central question for users of telecommunications services is how all of the recent developments—particularly the entry of Mercury and the privatization of BT—will affect the price, quality, terms, and conditions upon which services are available to large and small users.

2. For large users of communications services, there is the concern that the privatization of BT will work against their desire for a more liberalized regulatory regime. The government's complex, continuing interest in BT's future involves, in part, concerns about its role as both the major supplier of domestic communications services and facilities and the country's primary entrant in the international telecmmunications market.

3. With BT now operating as a private company in a competitive market, both the DTI and OFTEL must grapple with the task of balancing the many interests that affect telecommunications policies. BT's interests, like those of users, are just part of the equation. Although users may favor rapid liberalization, in order to promote innovation and change through competition, the government may find it necessary to moderate the pace—partially to avoid subjecting BT to overly "traumatic" new conditions.

4. Some continental observers believe that, over time, the consequence of all of the recent activity might be a return to the status quo ante—with the most notable shift being BT's transformation from a public to a private monopoly. Many European observers see this as the inevitable consequence of privatization.

5. The test for British telecommunications policy, in the years ahead, will be to see if it is possible both to privatize BT and to create effective, lasting competition. The government's goal is to keep BT on its toes and to keep users satisfied with the quality, price, and variety of communications services available to them.

6. In this process, Mercury, as a new facilities provider, has a pivotal role to play. In the new competitive setting, Mercury's success essentially is in its own hands, dependent primarily upon Cable & Wireless' considerable expertise, revenues, and ability to project Mercury effectively and quickly into the domestic and international markets. The government

increasingly recognizes that it has an important role to play in creating an effective, competitive market. Although BT is a determined competitor, neither Mercury nor OFTEL seems prepared to assume that the only result of recent British developments will be the successful privatization of BT. Rather, they appear committed to seeing that a viable, tough, long-term, competitive market benefitting British users will be the outcome of the 1984 Telecommunications Act.

CHAPTER VII
FINLAND

TABLE OF CONTENTS

CHAPTER VII
FINLAND

I. Overview: Industry and Policy Developments

A. Statutory and Legal Vacuum

Finland has an extremely innovative and efficient, but fairly complex, telecommunications industry. This industry has developed in the context of a completely antiquated legislative framework. The basic charter for the telecommunications industry is an 1886 czarist decree, a 1919 telegraphy statute, and a 1927 Radio Act. Consequently, new developments occur in a legal environment in which the critical question is whether the old statutory requirements apply at all. In general, it has been presumed that there is a "legal vacuum." Although there are ongoing discussions about new legislation, recent industrial developments—influenced by negotiations among concerned parties and sometimes by litigation—have tended to generate support for the absence of current restrictions.

B. Industry Composition

1. The structure of the Finnish telecommunications industry is characterized by a tightly-drawn balance between the public and the private sectors. The PTT, a state-owned business enterprise subordinate to the Ministry of Transport and Communications ("Ministry of Communications"), provides all international and long-distance services. It also provides local services to about one-quarter of the Finnish households. Local service is provided in the remaining seventy-five percent of the households by fifty-eight private telephone companies, the largest of which, the Helsinki Telephone Company ("HTC"), serves the Capital Area.

2. At one level, the industry may be characterized as a conglomeration of territorial monopolies: local service in each region is provided either by the PTT or by one local telephone company. At another level, though, the division of the marketplace is based on a number of service distinctions that are essentially undisputed. For example, the PTT alone is responsible for long-distance voice telephone service and for telegraphy and telex services. The basis for the latter monopoly is the 1919 telegraphy statute.

3. Beyond these areas, however, the division of responsibility is complex and is subject to intense controversy. Claims of "territorial monopoly" and arguments over the legal scope of the "telegraphy" monopoly (as interpreted by the PTT) provide the bases for disputes. The PTT and the local companies have had disagreements over their respective roles in providing circuit-switched data services and packet switching services. This controversy has generated what one observer described as a "telecommuni-

cations war"—characterized by an intense legal battle over the PTT's authority to define the scope of the local companies' service responsibilities.

4. The controversy has, however, generated new concepts of both "joint service provision" and new approaches to "service-based competition." Under these arrangements, both the PTT and the local companies offer the same service, either through competitive or through collaboratively-provided facilities. In the absence of a settlement dividing responsibility definitively between the PTT and the local companies, traditional notions of territorial monopoly and traditional service monopolies might be undermined by telecommunications technologies and services. For example, Finland has a very sophisticated cellular mobile system that is provided by the PTT in all of the local companies' service areas and could be used to bypass the companies' wire facilities. The PTT also has responsibility for all radio services, and it could siphon off the traffic of large network users through other radio-based microwave services.

5. Recently, Finland's largest bank, Kansallis-Osake-Pankki ("K.O.P."), the HTC, and other private telephone companies formed a joint venture to establish a network linking the largest cities in Finland. It will use fiber optic transmission lines and will bypass the PTT's trunk service facilities. This new venture seems likely to have an impact on the PTT's approach to pricing leased line services. It also may generate new, active involvement by Finnish manufacturers and service providers in developing enhanced data services.

6. Finland has a strong and diverse telecommunications and computer equipment industry. The industry leader, Nokia Corporation, could spearhead efforts to develop specialized information-oriented networks for one or more Finnish industry sectors. These networks and their related software systems eventually could provide companies like Nokia with an important source of technology exports. Because there are essentially none of the barriers to service innovations in the Finnish market that exist in other European markets, Finnish industry could experiment extensively with those networks. As European markets open up in the future, this experimentation could pay off in the form of tested turnkey systems that would be ready for installation overseas. There also might be excellent opportunities for joint ventures with European companies.

C. Other Wired Services

Services like cable television and videotex also are developing based on complex relationships between the provision of "facilities" and the provision of "services." Generally, cable and videotex services are not directly marketed by either the PTT or the local companies. However, the telecommunications facilities needed for these activities often are provided by telephone companies. The lines of responsibility are being established on the basis of a distinction between control over transmission facilities and control over content. Such a distinction frequently is not, however, neat or clearly observed. For example, in the case of a videotex service, the videotex provider—a non-telephone company—also can provide facilities for data storage and even a data switch or a gateway.

D. Broadcasting

The relationship between the public and the private sectors is equally complex and interesting in the broadcast field. There is no provision in the Finnish legislation for a broadcasting monopoly. Both radio and television were started as private enterprises, and a private television program company (MTV) still exists. However, the public sector now has de facto monopoly control of all broadcast facilities. Private programmers see alternative distribution technologies as a way of escaping dependence on the public network. In addition, a perceived need for greater local and regional programming has forced YLE, the Finnish Public Broadcasting Company, to begin instituting more local and regional services in its predominantly national monopoly broadcast network. Local radio services are beginning to operate and are stimulating new activity by YLE.

E. International Issues

Overall, Finland is subject to extraordinary international market pressures. Its telecommunications equipment markets are generally open to outside suppliers. Its own, very progressive manufacturing industry is heavily dependent on opportunities for international trade. Finland not only is influenced by the availability of Western European satellite services, but also is under some pressure—because of its unique geopolitical situation—to use Soviet bloc satellite services.

F. Mixture of Regulatory Approaches

Finland involves a complex blend of private ownership and control with a more traditional European PTT approach to telecommunications. Its unique position—in which it is subject to international economic and geopolitical pressures—makes Finland a fascinating counterpoint to the policy developments in larger industrialized countries.

II. BASIC STRUCTURE OF THE FACILITIES INDUSTRY: PUBLIC AND PRIVATE OWNERSHIP

A. Introduction

Basic telephone service in Finland originated in the late 1800s with the development of local, privately-owned telephone companies organized to provide commercial service—primarily in Helsinki and certain other cities. More than 700 such companies were formed before the government entered the market after the 1917 independence. The government assumed control of the telegraph and certain long-distance operations formerly run by the Russian imperial government. After acquiring a private long-distance company in 1934, the PTT grew to assume monopoly control of both long-distance and international circuits as well as telex and telegraph networks. The PTT also operates some local exchange facilities, although this market continues to be dominated by a broad variety of private companies. *See* Howkins, *Communications in Finland,* Intermedia, July/Sept. 1982, at 46.

B. The PTT: Structure and Facilities

1. The PTT is responsible for both postal and telecommunications activities. It is divided into two primary operational units, the Central Administration and the Line Administration. The Line Administration is made up of separate regional organizations that provide both postal and telecommunications services. There are ten such regional groupings, which serve as the country's ten telecommunications districts. They all are supervised by the Regional Administration, a subdivision of the Line Administration. Local operations are further subdivided into thirty-seven telecommunications areas, all of which are under the control of the Local Administration of the Line Administration. There are both district and area offices in each of these subdivisions. *See Telecommunications in the P.T.T. of Finland* 3-4 (1982).

2. The PTT employs almost 13,000 people, just ten percent of whom are involved in the Central Administration—primarily in the general telecommunications and radio departments.

3. The PTT is headed by a Director General. The telecommunications operations are headed by a Deputy Director General—one of four PTT deputy directors—who has jurisdiction over two telecommunications departments, as well as over the radio department and a division responsible for the inspection of telephone companies.

4. Under the present law, the PTT's radio department has responsibility for assigning frequencies to radio communications services, including the radio services of the privately-owned telephone companies. There have been disputes over the assignment, for example, of radio paging

services to such companies. This controversy is discussed below. *See infra* Section E. The PTT also has claimed authority to define the scope of the local companies' franchises. The attempt by the PTT to assume broad supervisory powers over the nation's wire networks has generated litigation. Significant pressure to redefine the PTT's role in the policymaking area has developed. Private telephone companies have expressed a preference to be licensed directly by the Ministry of Communications, rather than by the PTT, which is both a governmental authority and—in many areas—a competitor. The conflict between the public and the private sectors has become most acute in the attempts to determine who will control more advanced communications services and how the marketplace should develop in the future. The PTT has argued in favor of an integrated, monopoly network; the private companies have opposed this as contrary to the nation's best interests (if not their own). *Telecommunications in the P.T.T. of Finland, supra*, at 3-4.

5. Income for the PTT amounted to 4.4 billion FM in 1982, a 17.4% increase over 1981. Expenses were 4.05 billion FM, yielding a surplus of 35 million FM. PTT, *Report on Operations* 4 (1982). The total revenues of the PTT equal 1.9% of the Finnish GNP. *Id.* at 12.

6. The Ministry of Communications controls the budget of the PTT. Surplus revenues are available for capital outlays in telecommunications services, subject only to the influence of the political process.

a. In this regard, the Finnish PTT differs from Televerket (the Swedish PTT) and the French D.G.T., which appear to have a greater financial autonomy that provides them with the ability to finance their expansion needs more easily. As a result, PTT Director General Pekka Tarjanne has suggested that the PTT might be converted into a public corporation, freeing it from the constraints inherent in its affiliation with the government. *Id.* at 18. This recommendation to modify the structure of the PTT has recently been addressed by a high–level state commission, the Rekola Commission. It issued a report in February, 1985, concerning the future status of the PTT, the state railway, and other state-owned companies.

b. In most respects, however, it appears, the industry is generally satisfied with maintaining the status quo.

7. The basic telecommunications network is divided into three main levels: international, long-distance, and netgroup (or local). *Telecommunications in the P.T.T. of Finland, supra*, at 5 (diagram). For traffic to make its way from international circuits to the local level, it must flow (1) through an international exchange, (2) over trunk circuits to a transit trunk exchange, (3) to a trunk exchange, (4) to a netgroup exchange, and (5) finally to a group exchange, which connects subscriber lines and terminals.

8. Finland has been divided into seventy-eight numbering areas, which are called netgroups. Each netgroup functions as a separate local traffic area, with traffic between netgroups being carried by trunk circuits. Within each netgroup, a star configuration of exchanges carries local traffic. From each netgroup exchange, circuits connect to group exchanges, which join terminal exchanges, all of which radiate out from each

other in a star pattern. The netgroup exchange, and its associated circuits and exchanges, correspond roughly to an area encompassed by a single municipality. The average size of a netgroup is 4500 sq. kilometers. Of the 2500 terminal exchanges, less than one-quarter can accommodate 120 or more lines, with the majority handling forty to eighty subscribers. *Id.* at 5-6.

9. There are eighty-six trunk exchanges in Finland. Most of the exchanges are register controlled, but more advanced SPC exchanges—the first of which were introduced in 1974—are being installed. Automation of the trunk network, begun in 1958, was completed in 1980. At the same time that the last manual exchange was taken out of service, the first digital switching facility was activated. *See id.* at 9; Rauhala & Vainamo, *Digitalisation of Finland's Telecommunications Network*, Teletiedotuksia '83, at 3.

10. The PTT has plans for the digitization and upgrading of network facilities through the year 2000—which is the goal for the network to reach full digitization. Network trunk switching and transmission capacity is to be installed over all major routes by 1990. Five digital trunk exchanges are now in operation. Between 1983 and 1985, it is expected that more than forty local telephone companies will begin installing digital exchanges. Digital lines also are being installed, although most exchanges initially will work with analog circuits. Long-haul digital facilities are being installed over a number of routes, and fiber optic systems are planned for operation in 1987. *Id.* at 6. In the local networks, it is estimated that the percentage of digital connections will reach nine percent by 1985 and twenty-four percent by 1990. This coverage will affect forty percent of Finland's seventy-eight netgroups. *Id.* at 7.

C. Local Telephone Companies

1. There are fifty-eight user-owned telephone companies, which are served by a central organization known as the Association of Telephone Companies in Finland. The Association was formed in 1921 to coordinate the companies' common interests in the areas of both operations and policymaking. Ass'n of Telephone Companies, *Telephone Companies in Finland* 1 (1982).

2. Local companies serve only one-quarter of the geographic area of Finland, but that area contains more than two-thirds of the population. They provide three-quarters of the country's telephones, eighty percent of the modems necessary for data transmission, and eighty percent of the facsimile equipment. *See* Howkins, *supra*, at 46-47.

3. In 1982, the total billings of the local companies were 2.5 billion FM, of which forty-five percent was turned over to the PTT to pay for long-distance charges. *Telephone Companies in Finland*, *supra*, at 3; *see also infra* Section II.D.

4. Of the private companies,the HTC is by far the largest. It has 730,710 telephones in place, or 37.3% of the two million telephones installed by private companies and 27.6% of the country-wide total of 2.6

million. When a subscriber joins the HTC, he receives a share certificate in return for a capital contribution, which constitutes the annual connection fee. This certificate is negotiable, similar to stock in a corporation. Unlike a corporation, however, there is no set limit on the number of shares that the HTC may issue. Members of the company have voting rights proportional to the number of shares held, with no single member being permitted more than twenty votes. Such local subscriber participation, which frequently includes the power to elect local company directors and board members, is the basis for organization of the private segment of Finland's telephone market. The next largest private companies are Tampere, a cooperative, and Turku, which is managed by a municipality, with 150,000 and 115,000 telephones, respectively. *See Telephone Companies in Finland, supra*, at 18-21; *see also* Ass'n of Telephone Companies, *Telephone Statistics 1982* 14-16 (1983); Howkins, *supra*, at 46-47.

5. Beyond the largest companies, many of the private companies are quite small, cover large areas, and are severely undercapitalized. Some observers stress that increased investment in basic plant facilities is vital to the future of these companies. Although the development of new services remains important, these observers warn that substantial investment in the basic transmission facilities still are necessary in order to accomplish modernization and digitization of the plant by the year 2000.

D. Overall Relationships of the PTT and Local Companies

1. The PTT issues franchises and carries out technical inspections of the local companies, as noted above. In addition, the Association of Telephone Companies and the PTT participate in a Joint Telecommunications Committee that is chaired by a senior civil servant in the Ministry of Communications. The Joint Committee has a number of Working Groups through which many of the operational details involved in the joint provision of services are worked out. *See* Comm. for Information, Computer and Communications Policy, *Background Report: Finland* (Doc. No. DSTI/ICCP/82.33/22) 11-14 (1982) [hereinafter cited as *OECD Background Report*].

2. The PTT typically has established—by individual contractual agreement—a method for dividing the revenues collected by local companies for long-distance services. Collections are handled on the basis of an aggregate charge generated by toll counters or registers that are located on the toll switches. (In most exchange areas, there are no individualized call billing data, but only a total cost of charges for services.)

3. Recently, local companies have begun to investigate other ways of settling accounts with the PTT. The possibility of instituting an access charge that would be assessed by the local companies for the use of their facilities to provide the termination points for long-distance services is now being investigated.

E. Relationship of Local Companies and the PTT in the Data Communications Field

1. The 1919 telegraphy statute generally is viewed as granting the PTT a "monopoly over telegram services." However, the scope and definition of this monopoly has been the subject of many recent disputes between the PTT and local companies, especially as the growth of data processing has led to an increased need for data transmission networks. Such networks have never been clearly allocated as the service responsibility of any particular entity. The PTT, however, in its role as the governmental unit responsible for telecommunications issues, has addressed this issue by reserving for itself the primary task of providing data services. This result has provoked considerable friction with the local companies.

2. As a matter of custom and practice, however, the PTT's role in providing telex services has never really been disputed. Telex service is based around a network of seven group exchanges, each of which connects three to six terminal exchanges. Helsinki is the location of the largest telex exchange, which serves not only as a group exchange, but also as an international trunk services gateway. *Telecommunications in the P.T.T. of Finland, supra,* at 12-13.

3. Data services have been provided since 1981 through a high-speed, specialized, circuit-switched public data network provided in conjunction with Denmark, Norway, and Sweden. Plans call for packet-switched services to be introduced in this network. *Id.* at 14; Howkins, *supra,* at 47. Both the PTT and the local companies also provide data transmission services over the public switched network, with transmission rates ranging up to 4800 bps. For faster transmission speeds, up to 9600 bps, circuits can be leased from either public or private operators. In 1972, the PTT and the local companies worked out an arrangement relating to the use of data circuits. Under this agreement, both the local companies and the PTT can be involved in providing modern, local circuits, multiplexers, and local network terminal or data circuit-terminating equipment. All such equipment must, however, satisfy PTT technical standards. This equipment-supply role is exclusive to the PTT with respect to telex services. *OECD Background Report, supra,* at 2.

4. Expansion and development of data networks has been hindered significantly by disagreements between the PTT and the local companies. A major area of dispute has been whether a local company can offer a concentrator for data traffic as part of its network. To date, the PTT has insisted that all of the concentrator equipment be included in the PTT's switching facilities. Thus, there has been no movement toward any joint provision of facilities for the circuit-switched Datex services. The sale and advertising of the data service also have been concerns of the individual companies.

5. Recently, the local companies and the PTT have begun to develop packet-switching systems. The PTT constructed a packet-switching center within the territory of the privately owned Helsinki Telephone Company. Interconnection of this facility to the local exchange of the HTC was denied, apparently as an outgrowth of the dispute between the PTT and the local companies concerning concentrator placement and connection. Not to be outdone, the PTT has not allowed the connection of the HTC's packet-switching facilities to its network, although access to the HTC switch can be obtained through the direct-dial network.

6. The major question that needs to be resolved in order to permit a more aggressive development of Finland's data network is whether joint provision of services on a cooperative basis will be undertaken or whether a form of duopolistic competition will emerge, with both the private companies and the PTT marketing separate network services to the public.

F. Litigation Between the PTT and the Local Companies

1. Although there have been ongoing discussions between the PTT and the Association of Telephone Companies, the past five years have been marked by substantial open controversy. Most of the controversy has been the result of the PTT's role as both a provider of services and an entity with regulatory responsibility for radio licensing and the franchising of local telephone companies.

2. In a particularly bitter dispute, the question of applying the 1919 telegraphy statute to the provision of new services brought the PTT and the local companies before the Supreme Administrative Court. At the end of 1981, the PTT had granted the request of local companies for new franchises, but it had placed limitations on the scope of their activities and had obligated them to turn over lines for new telecommunications services to be provided by the PTT. *Telephone Companies in Finland, supra,* at 15. The local companies claimed that the PTT was seeking to assume monopoly control of all data transmission services—even in the franchise areas of local companies. The court issued two decisions in related cases on July 5, 1982, and November 8, 1982, respectively. The local telephone companies claim that these decisions clearly indicate that the 1919 telegraphy statute does not apply to new services. The court found, in part, that regulations for constructing telephone networks did not condone the exercise of the PTT's franchising authority to restrict the activities of private telephone companies in this way. According to the local companies, the PTT was incorrect in trying to divide service authority—between the local company and the PTT—on the basis of the services being provided. They claim that the nationwide network must be operated jointly by the PTT and the local companies on the basis of geographical divisions, with each entity having full freedom of service provision in the area in which it owns the network facilities.

3. The PTT clearly was attempting to assume complete responsibility for "enhanced" services such as data transmission. Rejection of this position means that the local companies will continue—at least for the immediate future—to have some leverage and control over the provision of data services. The long-term division of such services essentially must be worked out on the basis of negotiations between the private companies and the PTT. Such negotiations already have begun and are continuing. *Id.* at 17.

G. Future Relationships of the PTT and the Private Companies

1. Efforts to restructure the relationship between the PTT and the local companies by legislation seem to have stalled. It now appears that there is a truce—albeit an uneasy one—between the PTT and the private companies. In the summer of 1984, however, the HTC indicated that it might begin to compete outside of its own territory, marketing terminal equipment in the service areas of the PTT and of other private companies. However, the HTC's new marketing subsidiary, Heltel, has moved slowly to implement its plans.

2. Despite the difficulties between the PTT and the local companies over data services, it does not appear likely—at this time—that competition will spread into the voice telephone area. For example, the private companies are not likely to operate their own microwave or satellite networks to link together the various privately owned telephone systems and bypass the PTT's trunk services network. Any development of this bypass capability would have a significant impact on the PTT.

3. However, the joint venture between the K.O.P. (as a twenty percent owner), the HTC, and other private telephone companies, *see supra* Section I.B., could have a more immediate impact on the PTT. The venture, which will be known as Datatie ("Dataway"), believes that the 1886 czarist decree authorizes the Ministry of Communications to exercise power only over "telephone lines." By using fiber optic lines for its "data services," the venture contends, it avoids having to seek prior approval from the Ministry.

4. The new venture plans to offer shares to other private companies and bears a striking parallel to the U.K.'s Mercury Communications Ltd. Mercury included both Cable & Wireless and Barclay's Bank as early investors. The future network structure also has interesting parallels with new Type I (facilities-based) business applicants in Japan. These businesses plan to construct new lines to reduce or to control their transmission costs and to stimulate new business.

5. Whatever its eventual competitive impact, Dataway is likely to encourage the PTT to keep its leased line charges within reason. In

addition, the potential entry of this private line carrier should prevent the PTT from adopting overly restrictive regulations for the use of leased lines or from establishing usage-sensitive charges for its facilities.

6. Some observers also believe that the possibility of interexchange competition from the private companies will be a factor in negotiations over a proposed telecommunications bill now being considered by the Ad Hoc Cabinet Committee on Communications.

7. Developing technologies also make possible an erosion of the traditional territorial division of responsibilities. For example, the PTT has, since 1970, operated an interconnected mobile radio-telephone system in areas served by the local companies. There are 150 base stations, each with a service area of thirty kilometers, to cover the country. These stations are connected to the regional telephone exchanges. Service through Scandinavia is made possible by participation in the Nordic Mobile Telephone ("NMT") system, which connects Finland with Sweden, Norway, and Denmark. It serves 32,000 subscribers and was first introduced in Finland in March, 1982. *See* Makkonen, Merontausta & Tapiola, *Land Mobile Telephony Finland*, Teletiedotuksia '83, at 31, 31-33; *see also* Howkins, *supra*, at 48. The system is to cover the whole country by 1990. It offers services more sophisticated than those available in the fixed telephone network, including speed-dialing and call-forwarding. Makkonen, *et al.*, *supra*, at 34. There are no specific plans to bypass local telephone facilities, and economic factors may work against such a development. Nevertheless, the threat of bypass exists.

8. Local radio facilities, as well as satellite transmission links, also may be used to establish services without the need for the facilities of local telephone companies. Such "bypass" of local facilities now occurs, but it is increasingly likely that the potential for bypass could become a significant factor in the future negotiations between the PTT and the local companies.

9. All of these technological opportunities are likely to undermine the traditional territorial division-of-service concept. The potential for the private companies to enter the PTT's market and for the PTT to enter the local companies' markets continues to expand. Continuing technological development will affect the future course of negotiations between the PTT and the private companies.

H. The Future Role of the PTT

1. The Director General of the PTT has, as noted above, *see supra* Section II.B., been a leading advocate of converting the PTT from a state-owned business administration into a "public corporation." In February, 1985, a high-level state commission, the Rekola Commission, recommended that the PTT be given broader control over day-to-day activities and that it be overseen by a Board of Directors from the public and private sectors. (The Commission's Chairman is one of Finland's most distinguished

senior-level civil servants.) In general, the Commission's report has received favorable reviews. However, it has been severely criticized by the unions, particularly the railway unions. Ultimately, the recommendations would have to be embedded in legislation, and this process is likely to be a lengthy one. Nevertheless, the PTT's Director General regards the report as an extremely important first step.

2. Status as a public corporation would afford the PTT the capacity to borrow independently of the state in financial markets. This is viewed as very advantageous to the PTT; Finland's overall credit standing is very high in world financial markets, and telecommunications is considered to be an attractive investment sector. In addition, as a public corporation the PTT would have greater control over its cash flow. At the present time, the Ministry of Finance controls the PTT's budget.

3. The PTT has been working to structure itself more like a competitive private business. It also has proposed an annual ten percent reduction in long– distance charges, to be carried out over a five-year period.

a. The PTT's long–distance rates have been the subject of some criticism over the years; they currently are not unbundled from local charges. Rate reductions are intended to bring the price of services more into line with costs. This repricing undoubtedly will undercut incentives by private telephone companies or by business users to make substantial investments in new interexchange facilities.

b. The PTT has, in the past, tried to announce its rate reduction plans in advance, to encourage telecommunications and data communications managers to plan ahead for expanded use of PTT services. The PTT believes that any lost revenues resulting from rate reductions essentially can be offset by the stimulating effect that repricing has on network demand.

c. Repricing was reluctantly supported by the Ministry of Finance, which has an obvious interest in maintaining the PTT's revenue level. Eventually, however, the Ministry viewed the reductions as a useful step in implementing the government's anti-inflationary program.

4. Bringing rates more in line with cost also is seen as a step toward easing competitive tensions between the PTT and the private companies. A more cost-based rate structure would, in principle, leave the PTT with less ability to cross-subsidize competitive forays into the territories of private companies.

5. The Director General of the PTT is attempting to adopt a long-range perspective on the role of the PTT and its relationship with the private companies. There is less concern about the potential entry of specialized competitors such as the new Dataway venture than about a more general breakdown of the lines of competition. A private line competitor like Dataway is considered less of a threat to the PTT than one authorized to compete generally for switched voice service traffic. The emergence of a

competitive intruder in the Finnish market might underscore the PTT's argument that it needs to be permitted to operate on a new, more competitive basis as a public corporation.

I. New Legislation: Restructuring the Finnish Telecommunications Industry?

1. There is a strong tradition in Finland of reaching decisions by consensus and of avoiding legislative intervention. However, the various struggles between the PTT and the private companies have focused attention on the possibility of adopting new legislation to resolve these disputes. It is unclear, though, whether actual legislation will be the result of this effort. The legislative process in Finland often functions as a forum for ironing out differences and working toward consensus.

2. Because of the attention focused on cable television legislation, *see infra* Section III., an Ad Hoc Cabinet Committee on Communications did not begin to draft a telecommunications bill until May, 1985.

a. A number of areas do not seem subject to dispute, such as a proposal to liberalize the procedures for terminal attachment. The proposed legislation would create a neutral decisionmaking body to certify equipment. However, most observers believe that this procedure would have little practical impact on a market that already is essentially open.

b. The bill also would liberalize substantially the resale of communications services and would differentiate between "special" and "common" networks. Special networks could be operated to serve the needs of particular users or groups of users. They would be under no obligation to deal with third parties. Under the proposed law, the Ministry of Communications would be responsible for determining that a special network did not have an adverse impact on the public telephone companies (which operate "common" networks). The proposed Dataway venture is likely to have some impact on the Ad Hoc Committee's consideration of proposals for such special network services.

c. There is as yet no agreement about how or whether the bill should deal with the broader questions of the relationship between the PTT and the private telephone companies. Ultimately, there may be a standoff—and then a consensus—among the parties that a continuation of the present ambiguous relationship is preferable to a more rigid, institutional solution. It also appears unlikely at the present time that a legislative package would include a resolution of the broader structural issues regarding government business administrations, which were examined by the Rekola Commission. It would seem both logical and desirable for the issue of the PTT's competitive relationship with the private telephone companies to be linked more broadly to the question of its future organizational structure. However, the only structural issue now before the Ad Hoc Committee concerns whether the PTT should continue to have regulatory responsibilities affecting the private telephone companies.

III. THE ROLE OF CABLE TELEVISION IN THE EVOLVING INDUSTRY STRUCTURE

A. Introduction: Legislative Vacuum

1. Cable's role in Finland's changing telecommunications market appears likely to be moving in a different direction from the one being taken in either the United States, Canada, or the United Kingdom, where cable operators will install a physically discrete cable network.

2. The future prospects for the expansion of the cable industry are unclear; its growth may be slowed by the rapid expansion of home videocassette recorders ("VCRs") in Finland. Initially, VCRs sold poorly, with a total of just 15,000 having been sold through 1981. However, in 1982 an additional 20,000 VCRs were purchased; by 1985 there were approximately 250,000 VCRs in operation. Conditions in Finland generally appear ripe for a home video explosion, with a small domestic film industry leaving potential moviegoers dissatisfied and with an apparent cultural preference for home entertainment providing a ready audience for the technology. *See* Howkins, *supra*, at 59.

3. Finnish cable systems were the second ones in the world (after those in the U.S.) to receive distant program services delivered by satellite. The signal of Satellite Television ("Sky Channel"), from London, was carried as early as February, 1982, when it was transmitted on the Operational Test Satellite ("OTS"). The signal now is received on the European Communications Satellite ("ECS"). Huuhka & Torikka, *Television Programme Transmission Experiment via Orbital Satellite*, Teletiedotuksia '83, at 26, 27. The Helsinki cable system also carries programming from French TV5 and from the London-based service known as Music Box. Both services are delivered over the ECS.

4. There is no existing legal or regulatory system regarding the reception and distribution of distant signals. Therefore, absent legislation, it is likely that cable systems will begin carrying the growing number of new program services available on the ECS or on other European national satellite systems (TV-SAT, from the Federal Republic of Germany, available 1985; TDF-l, from France, available 1986; L-SAT, from the European Space Agency, available 1986; and Tele-X, from Sweden, available 1987), as well as those transmitted by Nordic satellite services. Kuitunen, *Wideband Networks and Services*, Teletiedotuksia '83, at 21.

B. Current Operations

1. Helsinki Television ("HTV"), the cable system serving the Capital Area, and the largest system in the country, has proven quite successful, with 100,000 of the area's households (a majority) having subscribed. It was formed in 1973 by three non-profit groups who offered partnerships to

broadcast operators YLE and MTV, as well as to the Sanoma Corporation and other major publishers. The offers all were turned down as too "politically contentious." *See* Howkins, *supra*, at 54. After the system experienced a series of financial crises in the late 1970s, Sanoma purchased eighty percent of the HTV stock in January, 1981. Pay-television hookups amount to approximately 23,000 subscribers, or twenty-three percent, of the connected households. HTV, *Cable Television Services and Their Regulation: The Finnish Model* 4-6 (1984) [hereinafter cited as HTV, *The Finnish Model*].

2. The Helsinki system was unprofitable for its first decade. It produced a profit for the first time only in 1983. The system, which began test transmissions in 1975, is a limited-capacity, one-way, twelve-channel system—although an upgrading to thirty-eight channels was begun in 1983 in some areas. The system carries the two Finnish national broadcast stations, programming from the U.S.S.R., a pay-television channel (HTV's Entertainment Channel), an information channel, and the Helsinki Channel (a commercial, advertiser-supported station operated by HTV). *Id.* at 6.

3. The Helsinki Telephone Company plays a role in operating the Helsinki cable system. The HTC installed some of the trial facilities. The telephone company is not, however, a dominant—or controlling—force. Parts of the system, such as local access lines, often are owned on a cooperative basis by system users. There are, at present, no plans to install two-way capacity in the system.

4. At least half of the 1.7 million television sets in Finland are connected to some type of antenna system, either a community cable system or a smaller MATV hookup. Most cable systems are rather small. Although there are more than 40,000 systems, just 100 of them have 300 or more subscribers. Ass'n of Telephone Companies, *Cable Television and Broadband Services in Finland* 1 (1983). Most systems provide just six channels of programming, although newer systems are building capacities that range from twelve to twenty channels. All systems use two channels to carry TV-1 and TV-2, the national network programming of YLE (the Finnish Broadcasting Company). In the southwestern part of the country, two channels also are used to distribute Swedish programming to the large Swedish-speaking population in that area.

5. The few relatively large community systems exist in the following places: Turku (17,000), Rovaniemi (8000), Tampere (ll,000), Oulu (3000), Laitila (1200), and Pori (1000). HTV, *Cable Television in Finland* 1 (1983). The Tampere system was intended to be among the country's most advanced, offering two-way transmission capability; however, those plans are being reassessed. It also carries the same pay-television services as are carried by HTV. *Id.* at 2. HTV is now expanding to transmit programming to suburban areas in Espoo and Tapiola by means of microwave links. A third microwave hookup also is being planned. *Id.*

6. Cable services are offered to the public essentially free from any special regulation.

C. Prospects for the Future

1. The long-term potential for cable system expansion in Finland would seem to be relatively modest because of the advanced age of many of the largest cable systems and the small size of systems in other markets. The largest cable system, HTV, is being operated on a very pragmatic basis. Excessive expenditures on staff and on local origination activities were eliminated. The company plans to upgrade trunk capacity and to improve the capabilities for addressable pay TV services, but it does not believe that two-way cable is as cost-effective as utilizing telephone lines for two-way services.

2. HTV has attempted to establish some regulation of cable technology on the basis of the regulatory model applied to the print media. The essence of HTV's approach involves a separation of control between programming and transmission functions. Its proposal includes the following elements as part of a so-called "Finnish model." *See* HTV, *The Finnish Model*, *supra*, at 1-2.

a. Cable system operations are divided into four functions: the facilities owner, the system operator, the program providers, and the program producers. It is unclear to what degree these functions must be performed by separate persons or organizations. A commentary to the model, however, indicates that some regulation may be necessary to ensure that a system operator acting as a program provider does not unduly favor its own programs and exclude the programs of others. The commentary says simply, "Companies or corporations acting in several different functions in cable TV operations shall naturally be subject to the appropriate regulations for each function." *Id.* at 3.

b. The owner of the cable system facilities will be subject to municipal restrictions on access to the streets and possibly to technical regulation regarding network specifications. However, centralized review of facilities construction by the PTT or by other national bodies would not seem to be required. Housing corporations will remain the owners of any master antenna facilities installed in apartment buildings. The trunk and branch wiring could be owned by a specially formed cable company, by the local telephone company, or by some form of neighborhood cooperative.

c. The cable operator would have a de facto monopoly in each geographic area and would have full control over the provision of services. As the sole wideband network facilities provider in each area, the cable operator would, however, have obligations to lease capacity on a first-come, first-serve basis, according to a non-discriminatory price scheme. There would be no formal regulatory control over pricing, leaving the marketplace as the sole regulator; however, complaints could be brought to the Competition Ombudsman. Practices for the fair allocation of channels in circumstances of scarcity might have to be adopted. The model does not specify whether the operator also can be a program provider. It does, however, say that the operator may not "influence the content of programmes transmitted on his network." Accordingly, the operator is not to be held responsible for the content of this programming if it violates such standards as the obscenity prohibitions.

d. Program providers would be responsible for the content of particular programs. They would exercise this control primarily through the process of selecting the programs to be distributed. Each program provider would have a program director, who would be given unfettered editorial control of program content and would enjoy the kind of protections now given to print editors under the Act on the Freedom of the Press. There would be no restriction on the amount or the type of advertising and no limitations on the national origin of programming. Although, in principle, the model advocates no restrictions on program content, a prohibition on violent or obscene programming would be permitted. The model also suggests that the State Film Censor should be invited to give advice on close disputes about permissible programs and should be asked to provide norms to guide programmers.

e. Program producers would create and would sell programs free of any regulatory restraints. The model does not specify whether program providers also may act as program producers.

3. The Finnish government had a parliamentary committee on radio and television, which reviewed this and other proposals for regulating cable for the past year.

a. An Ad Hoc Cabinet Committee under the chairmanship of the Minister of Justice, Christoffer Taxell, a member of the Swedish Party, has met about twenty times since 1984 to address the regulatory issues raised by cable. It now has formulated a bill that has been reviewed within the Cabinet. That bill is undergoing legal review in the Ministry of Justice and could be submitted to the Parliament in the near future. One proposal would impose licensing requirements on public and private companies, as well as on municipalities, seeking to provide cable service.

b. One of the difficulties faced by the committee was that there are a large number of different forms of ownership of the underlying cable facilities. These ownership arrangements are being worked out in most major cities at the same time as the legislative process reviews the regulatory options. This legislative review, however, is being outpaced easily by commercial dealings.

4. The licensing proposal being considered by the government would, as part of the license, limit the amount of advertising to eleven percent of the time available airtime (a structure similar to that applicable to broadcast television). It also would require that a certain amount of programming be of Finnish origin. The licensee would be obligated to provide a diversity of programs and to pay special attention to the particular interests of the local community—especially if there are communities with special language needs (such as the Swedish-speaking community found in the southwestern part of the country). The difficulty with proposals to limit the

amount of advertising and to control the content of cable programming is that they are likely to reduce the potential revenues and to increase the costs of cable system operations. They, therefore, could make it less likely that cable would gain a substantial foothold in the telecommunications industry. Because cable is not now being held back by any regulatory requirements, the cable and newspaper industries may strongly favor the continuation of the current legal vacuum.

5. The proposals for regulating foreign programs are difficult and controversial because they create, for the first time, a program review authority in the Ministry of Communications. This would be a new and unaccustomed regulatory role for the Ministry; many in the cable industry would like to avoid any such approval mechanism. (The foreign content restrictions also are viewed as quite difficult to enforce.) Some in the industry would prefer to see the government consider tax incentives to encourage new Finnish productions. Alternatively, the government has been urged to advocate the issuance of a compulsory license that would allow cable systems to use the programming contained in the inventories of YLE and MTV. (Advertising limits also are seen as worrisome problems; however, cable's limited role as an advertising medium suggests that the proposed limitations might not significantly affect the industry's future.)

6. Another difficult issue is whether to impose the obligation to provide access to cable facilities on the facilities owner or on the cable operator. This issue has been the subject of extensive discussion within the Ad Hoc Committee. The proposed legislation imposes access obligations on a cable operator, who uses the system of a facilities provider (under the structure being considered for application to the cable industry). However, the draft does not prescribe clearly the relationship between the facilities provider and the cable operator. It also does not address the provider's obligations to make capacity for video services available to other operators or users. This situation raises, in Finland, the general problems that accompany a scheme in which a "cable operator" must rely on leased capacity, rather than on its own wire. The "cable operator" is not clearly distinguishable from other potential lessees of the provider's facilities. Yet, "cable television" has special access obligations not imposed on other leased channel services made available to the public.

7. The cable bill could face significant hurdles if and when it is submitted to the Parliament. Some believe that it should be reviewed concurrently with the telecommunications legislation that is still at an early stage of consideration. There also is a question about whether the bill violates the Finnish Constitution. Questions about the bill's constitutionality could create serious procedural obstacles in the Parliament.

a. Article 10 of the Constitution protects freedom of the "word"; Article 6 provides for the protection of property. The access obligations might be viewed as infringing on these constitutional rights. The

Minister of Justice believes that the bill does not raise constitutional concerns; ultimately, however, that question must be decided by the Constitutional Committee of the Parliament.

b. If the bill is viewed as involving potential constitutional questions, then a five-sixths majority would be needed to save the legislation from a vote for deferral to a subsequent session of the Parliament.

c. There are many observers who believe that the cable bill will not pass during the current session because of concerns raised by members of the Conservative Party.

8. Most Finnish cable systems are small and without two-way capacity. As a result, there has been no need to confront the question of whether, or to what extent, certain two-way services should be classified—for regulatory purposes—as cable services or as telecommunications services. The cable bill proposed by the parliamentary committee declined to address the question of whether such two-way services could be provided by cable systems. Thus, it is possible in principle—but not likely in economic reality—that a new generation of high-capacity, fiber optic cable systems could be installed to provide value-added network services ("VANS") and could later be used for other services. The PTT has discussed the feasibility of installing such facilities. It initiated these kinds of experimental networks in Lapreenranta and Rovaniemi in 1980, as well as in a number of other cities. Kuitunen, *supra*, at 23. However, the efforts are being conducted on an extremely small scale, and it is acknowledged that the installation of star-switched networks—equivalent to the present telephone network—"will be difficult and expensive." *Id.* at 25.

9. The involvement of the PTT at all in providing cable services or facilities may prove the subject of some controversy. Sanoma has proposed that the PTT (or local telephone companies) be permitted to build cable networks but that they then be required to lease these networks to independent operators on a long-term basis. Cable's separation from other communications media has generally been a topic of some dispute. The parliamentary committee's proposed legislation suggested, for example, that YLE be allowed to provide cable services under the terms of its existing license, while requiring all other operators to seek separate licenses. This suggestion was heavily criticized. Howkins, *supra*, at 55.

10. The planning of integrated digital telecommunications services (with the upgrading of switching and transmission facilities) appears to be quite divorced from the planning of wideband video networks. It does not appear likely that such integrated services will evolve in the near future. Consequently, there probably will not be a significant need to address how two-way cable services, which might constitute a part of such an integrated network, should be regulated. Instead, it appears likely that the fragmented and ad hoc regulatory approach will continue for some time. If anything, such an approach will leave cable operators free to explore the addition of new ancillary services without becoming concerned about the applicability of regulatory restraints.

IV. REGULATORY STATUS OF VIDEOTEX SERVICES

A. Regulatory Posture

Videotex services in Finland, as elsewhere in the world, present rather novel questions about their regulatory status. Videotex has not yet gained a significant foothold in the worldwide telecommunications market, so that in many instances it has not become subject to specific, specially designed regulatory regimes. Some observers do not believe that, from a regulatory perspective, videotex can be differentiated realistically from database services oriented to more specialized business users and distributed by means of the telephone network. (Videotex services generally involve a database geared toward mass-market users.)

B. Videotex in Finland

1. By mid-1983, there were some 30,000 text-equipped television receivers in Finland, or two percent of the total number of television receivers. The total number of videotex users at that time was approximately 1250. Ass'n of Telephone Companies, *Videotex in Finland* 1 (1983). Based on this level of penetration, well-informed Finnish observers are not necessarily optimistic about the future of videotex services in the country.

2. Early in the development of such services, the PTT took the position that videotex provided over the telephone network, rather than by broadcast frequencies (*i.e.*, viewdata, rather than teletext), was a "telegraphy" service and, therefore, within the scope of its monopoly. There was debate about this claim, and the PTT ultimately did not persist in its opposition to competitive videotex offerings. The PTT eventually formed its own viewdata service company, choosing (as had the West German Bundespost and British Telecom) to take an active role as an information provider in order to see that viewdata service was initiated.

3. The major viewdata service supplier is not the PTT, but a joint venture company known as Helsinki Telset, formed by the Helsinki Telephone Company, Sanoma Corporation, and Nokia Electronics. Each of the major partners contributed assets or expertise—as was appropriate to its own area of specialization. Sanoma was responsible for the provision of information for the database. Nokia produced editing terminals and other equipment. The Helsinki Telephone Company had, of course, a significant role as a provider of telecommunications services.

4. Telset initially functioned primarily as a common carrier, providing indices, a user's guide, and information about Telset, in addition to the communications network. After a two-year test, the company began commercial operations in April, 1980. Recently, however, the partners have begun to reevaluate the structure of Telset. Increasingly, Sanoma has exercised a major role as a vendor of information. As a result, service charges

that once were oriented toward exacting a fee for the provision of access capabilities to third-party databases now are being revised to impose costs for the actual use of information. In so doing, Telset has become involved in recasting the nature of its service in order to demonstrate how it is possible to redefine the boundary between being in the business of conveying information and of vending information. *Id.* at 2.

5. Newspaper and telephone company interest in videotex has resulted in the formation of twelve companies to provide videotex services, four of which were operational in 1983. Howkins, *supra*, at 48. Videotex is not subject to PTT licensing requirements. This is unusual because in many European countries the PTTs have either a legal or practical monopoly on viewdata operations.

6. YLE provides broadcast teletext service, which it began offering in December, 1981. About 120 pages of news, weather, sports results, television schedules, and recipies are transmitted in the vertical blanking interval of both YLE and MTV transmissions. *See infra* Section VII. (discussing the relationship of YLE to MTV). Pages can be received either by special television sets or by sets with teletext adapters. A point of controversy is YLE's practice of placing teletext information in the MTV signals. MTV contends that its programming is its own property, which YLE cannot use without permission. This dispute remains unresolved. Howkins, *supra*, at 54.

C. Regulatory Issues

1. A significant regulatory question is whether videotex services should be regulated as information services, as enhanced telecommunications businesses, or as some combination of the two. In other countries, a major question has arisen about whether a videotex operator who simply provides a transparent link—a gateway—to third-party databases is providing a communications service or transmission function that is merely ancillary to—and necessarily a part of—an information service. In Finland, where Telset has engaged both in gateway operations and in the actual generation of its own databases, this issue is unresolved.

2. The conceptual problem involves trying to establish a distinction between telecommunications services—which, presumably, would be subject to regulation—and non-telecommunications activities—which, as in the case of information provision, have traditionally been unregulated. Gateway services might be considered enhanced communications functions, to be provided separately from information services. This vertical market division could require third-party service providers to compile information for public distribution—on an unregulated basis—that would have to be accessed through a regulated, telecommunications gateway service.

3. Alternatively, regulators might choose to permit vertical integration. Videotex service as a whole—access operations as well as

database compilation—might be viewed as a distinct, non-telecommunications service, distinguishable from other telecommunications activities. In this model, a single service provider would perform both the access and the information provision functions. Thus, the decision about how to categorize videotex services will determine whether a single entity can provide all of the components of the service or whether it must join with other parties to create a usable system.

D. Videotex's Future in Finland

1. The current situation in Finland makes it difficult to predict the future direction of the market. Without specific regulatory direction as to how the different aspects of videotex service are to be allocated among the various competitors in the market, Telset has been able to evolve freely. It has gone from being a gateway communications company to being a form of hybrid operator, providing both gateway and integrated videotex (access and database) services. It is interesting to note, of course, that Telset, not the Helsinki Telephone Company, is the entity now responsible for providing gateway functions. This may suggest that other third-party service providers can enter the market and offer integrated videotex services, operating as both transmission networks and information providers.

2. A model of joint ownership for viewdata seems to have worked in Finland, with newspapers and other publishers joining telephone operators to provide service. This cooperative effort includes both the local telephone companies and the PTT. In Turku and Tampere, ventures with the local telephone operators are already underway. In Kouvola, a videotex service with the PTT, aimed at business subscribers, is being examined. Howkins, *supra*, at 49. It appears that for the present time, the marketplace alone will decide the shape of Finland's videotex services.

3. In the teletext area, clarification of the institutional relationships will have to await some resolution of the unsettled situation between YLE and MTV, as well as of the future status of YLE's transmission monopoly.

V. REMOTE ACCESS DATA PROCESSING AND "ENHANCED SERVICES"

A. Finland is rapidly developing an active database and data processing industry. The country's dynamic publishing industry has taken a leading role in developing electronic information services. In addition, the remote access data processing industry has been relatively open to outside suppliers such as GE Mark III. A major issue raised by the industry's expansion is the impact it will have on the data networking capabilities of the current transmission systems and on the development of value-added networks that will make remote access operations more useful to a wider array of terminal devices.

B. Many of these electronic publishing and data processing companies have been working to establish networks that take account of the different user protocols of various terminal devices. For example, the Central Statistical Information Bureau has created a network capable of adjusting for the various protocols of terminals that seek access to its system. However, publishers have become impatient with the continued strained relationship between the PTT and the private companies that impedes the establishment of a nationwide information network. Thus, the publishers have forced discussions about such future services with both the PTT and the private companies. If agreements cannot be reached, these users may formulate their own user-controlled network that essentially imposes a collaborative structure (an "overlay" network) on the transmission facilities of the PTT and the private companies. In this way, the division in industry structure between the public and private sectors may stimulate the evolution of a "second tier" of service providers.

C. The relatively open, competitive environment in Finland also is likely to encourage the emergence of "enhanced" service vendors who, among other services, will look to provide networks that allow communications between otherwise incompatible terminals. In this way, remote access data processing, and the associated growth of computer use, are likely to stimulate the development of enhanced service networks. There are no such specialized services yet; however, some observers clearly see the need for some system to permit the interconnection of various personal computer devices.

D. The IBM personal computer is becoming a de facto standard in Finland as elsewhere in the world. The highly successful existing generation of Luxor personal computers, however, which is made in Sweden (now as part of the operations of Nokia Electronics), is not compatible with the IBM System Network Architecture ("SNA") standard for protocol conversion and networking. Some well-informed Finnish policy observers have expressed grave concerns about efforts to establish rigid networking specifications. Thus, for example, there is some doubt about how Europe, in general, and Finland, in particular, should react to efforts by IBM to entrench the SNA standard through such activities as its proposed (and rejected) joint venture with British Telecom.

E. The current Finnish telecommunications environment would appear to contain some elements that could be favorable to the long-term development of enhanced services. Under existing PTT regulations, data processing providers are allowed to lease circuits to provide their customers with data processing terminals. This is viewed as "serving the proper business of the user." *OECD Background Report, supra,* at 7. In addition, there is some leeway in existing regulations to allow customers to share the use of leased circuits, so long as circuit ordering and billing responsibility is vested in the hands of a single user. *Id.* The resale of telex and of circuit-switched sevices, however, appears to be restricted. *Id.*

F. Generally, private companies appear to favor the relaxation of existing restrictions on resale. The Rekola Commission has accepted the concept of resale, and it could well be embedded in any new telecommunications legislation—if and when it is adopted by the Parliament. Even if such legislation is not enacted immediately, the existence of a legislative recommendation in favor of resale may assist in opening up an even more flexible environment for users.

G. Two other significant factors have stimulated the emergence of "enhanced services" and the pressure for an even more liberal and open environment in Finland.

1. The proposal for a the Dataway private line network is likely to encourage users to take a more active role in developing specialized services. As a "potential entrant," Dataway may encourage the PTT to offer more flexibility for enhanced services. As noted above, *see supra* Section II.G., it will curb any tendency by the PTT to propose restrictive rate structures and conditions on leased lines. Because the venture may be limited to offering data circuits, it may become a facilities-based competitor that will serve as a testing ground for new information-based services.

2. The other factor that could influence the development of those networks is the potential impact of a diversified, nationally-based supplier such as Nokia Corporation. Subsidiaries of Nokia now are using leased lines for remote access data processing services. The company has developed information systems for the banking industry in Finland that incorporate a significant amount of advanced information processing capability. In addition, as a supplier of switching equipment and computers, Nokia is ideally positioned to develop information-based network services that require flexible communications systems. Close ties within the Finnish industrial sector may provide a unique opportunity for an industrial partnership to develop new advanced networking services. If Nokia can apply its engineering expertise to meet the particular networking needs of various parts of the industrial sector, a Finnish partnership also might be able to develop highly useful networks that would prove valuable in the export market.

H. Considerations about data processing and enhanced service needs are injected into the policymaking process from a number of sources. A group known as the Data Delegation has a telecommunications subcommittee that actively follows data network developments. A cooperative group concerned with computer communications also has been formed to represent the interests of telecommunications users, manufacturers, and service providers. The Association of Automatic Data Processing Service Providers functions as a voice for ADP telecommunications users. Finally, the Central Chamber of Commerce follows the development of data transmission services. *Id.* at 13.

VI. INSTITUTIONAL MECHANISMS FOR CONTROL OF TELECOMMUNICATIONS AND INFORMATION POLICY

A. Existing Statutes

1. Communications statutes now offer little effective guidance for the resolution of communications policy issues. The relevant legal norm or standard is that any activity not expressly prohibited is permitted. Thus, there are effectively no requirements that impose restraints on the development of cable television services, videotex, or enhanced services.

2. It is reported that Matti Puhakka, a former Minister of Communications, once had said that the 1886 czarist decree was "hopelessly out of date." However, others do not necessarily agree that new legislation is required. They see the legal vacuum that exists as a "state of nature"—the ultimate liberalized environment in which telecommunications can evolve. Negotiation, as well as the impact of domestic and international technological and economic pressures, are seen as the forces that will be used to shape the telecommunications market.

3. There is much evidence that the system adjusts effectively to change and that high-quality services are now being provided, despite the dearth of legislative direction.

B. Litigation

Despite the obvious importance attached to negotiation among concerned parties, litigation has played an important role in the recent evolution of Finnish telecommunications policy. Ironically, though, the outcome of this litigation has been indecisive, merely reinforcing the need for extensive negotiation. For example, the 1982 Supreme Court decisions nullifying changes in the PTT's franchising procedure for local telephone companies largely have strengthened the forces favoring the legislative status quo, requiring that adjustments be made through negotiation.

C. Users of Communications Services

1. Users of communications services have not yet been active in the process of formulating telecommunications policy. The potential exists, however, for business users to become more actively involved in showing policymakers a broader view of telecommunications issues. There are signs that this increased activity may soon begin.

2. The Confederation of Finnish Industries and the Finnish Employers' Association represent industry interests. This division of responsibility is quite unique; it is unlike the situation of the Keidanren in Japan or of the Chamber of Commerce in the U.S.—where a single association serves all business interests. The Confederation focuses broadly on industry issues

and represents industry views to the government. The Employers' Association, by contrast, concentrates on industrial relationships with the trade unions. These unions are extremely influential, from both an industrial and a political standpoint. The Employers' Association has taken a leading role in explaining to unions the importance of various business policies. It has emphasized the impact of these policies on industrial efficiency and on Finland's international trade position. This activity has tended to reduce friction between industry and the trade unions. It also has helped to achieve a consensus on many policies necessary to maintaining the Finnish economy's high level of performance.

3. Both industry associations can have an important impact on Finnish telecommunications policy. They appear to be taking a new interest in this subject. They also may try to encourage user involvement in telecommunications issues elsewhere in Europe (in order to enhance the Finnish international trade position). Such broader activity will be necessary to open new market opportunities for both equipment and information-based services.

D. Administrative Control

There is little in the way of effective administrative contr(under existing statutory authority. The Ministry of Transport and Communications can exercise control over the PTT by imposing budgetary guidelines. However, the direct radio licensing and wire franchising powers continue to reside—as delineated by recent court decisions—in the hands of the PTT, not of the Ministry. The major mechanism for influencing policy is the Joint Telecommunications Committee, which acts as a cooperative body including representatives from the Ministry, the PTT, and the local telephone companies (through the Association of Telephone Companies).

E. New Legislation

1. The process of trying to develop new communications legislation has proved highly complex and lengthy. A commission set up by a former Minister of Communications did recommend certain shifts in policy that were criticized harshly by the privately owned local telephone companies. They argued that the recommendations would have augmented the authority of the PTT. The Rekola Commission recently has developed a more neutral set of recommendations that deal essentially with two issues: (1) the division of responsibility between the PTT and the private companies, and (2) the licensing of telecommunications.

2. The Ad Hoc Cabinet Committee on Communications has formulated a bill concerning cable television as part of its mandate to deal with broadcasting and cable television policy issues. *See supra* Section III.C. The committee has representatives from each of the major parties in the

government and is intended to reflect a broad policy view on communications issues.

3. The Cabinet consideration of legislation is being exposed to the diverse influences of the various parties that are now part of a coalition controlling the Finnish government. The Ministry of Communications has for years been in the hands of the Social Democratic Party, which historically did not favor free enterprise. After a disastrous experiment with a massive program of public investment in the electronics sector, however, the Social Democrats recently have adopted more of a free-market approach. The Swedish Party has been concerned about the right of the Swedish minority in Finland with respect to broadcast and cultural issues. The Centre and Conservative Parties have heavily favored private enterprise. Also represented in the coalition until recently has been a significant Communist Party minority. The juxtaposition of the right- and left-wing parties in the government has tended to neutralize efforts to make drastic revisions in telecommunications policy. However, it now appears that some consensus is forming around the need to rely, to a greater extent, on free-market principles. Thus, it is not likely that significant inroads will be made on the influence of the private telephone companies. It also seems likely that there will be an effort to place the PTT under greater public control, by reorganizing the PTT as a public corporation.

4. If there is inertia in the legislative process with respect to communications issues, it is often because fundamental interests favor a slow process of negotiation that does not upset either internal political checks and balances or the external, geopolitical positioning of Finland—between the East and the West. That latter relationship might be unsettled by a sharp realignment of the Finnish industrial structure away from a mixed public/private approach. Thus, there is a healthy regard in the Finnish political process for the need for wide-ranging and careful consultation with all concerned groups about pending legislative proposals.

5. The same policy considerations that have affected telecommunications issues also influence the development of media policy. However, in Finland, unlike the Federal Republic of Germany, for example, the PTT has no control over telecommunications facilities that are used for broadcasting. YLE, the Finnish Broadcasting Company, controls the microwave network that is used to distribute television programming throughout the country. YLE also exercises responsibility for satellite receiving equipment used for television transmission. In this regard, the Finnish and the French models usefully can be compared. In France, the D.G.T. has had no direct control over the facilities used for mass media distribution. Supervision of such facilities is undertaken by Telediffusion de France ("TDF"), an entity subject to supervision by both the D.G.T. and the Minister of Communications.

VII. BROADCASTING: INDUSTRY STRUCTURE AND POLICY

A. Development of the Industry

1. Since 1964, YLE, the Finnish Broadcasting Company, has been the only licensed television broadcaster in the country, although there is no legal monopoly in the broadcast market. The 1927 Radio Act authorizes the Council of State to license an unlimited number of broadcasters, but since 1964 it has licensed only YLE. The current YLE license runs through 1985.

2. Originally formed in 1926 to produce and to transmit radio programs in both Swedish and Finnish, YLE went on to conduct regular test television transmissions with MTV (Mainos TV), a commercial broadcasting company founded in 1957. At the time, Helsinki's private Tesvisio and Tampere's Tamvisio were licensed by the PTT to provide broadcast television programming. In 1958, YLE and MTV began commercial operation. YLE went on, in 1964, to purchase all of the stock of Tesvisio and Tamvisio and took over their licensed channels to form TV-2. TV-1 was later begun, and these two services now provide the country with all of its nationally broadcast programming. The channels are networked, but there is no local or regional program insertion, as occurs in the United States, where local affiliated outlets carry nationwide network programming as part of their local program schedules. *See* Howkins, *supra*, at 52.

3. The public/private dichotomy found in the telephone market is carried through to the broadcast market in the current relationship between MTV and YLE. In this instance, however, the public entity—YLE—is, by far, the dominant one. YLE owns all of the transmission facilities throughout Finland. Under a negotiated agreement with MTV, though, approximately twenty percent of the programming for TV-1 and TV-2 is provided by MTV. In 1982, MTV paid YLE sixty percent of its revenues from advertisement sales for the opportunity to program the YLE channels. *Id.* at 53. This leaves Finland with a broadcast system that is almost completely under public control, although private programmers—and foreign producers—have contributed an increasing amount of material to the television transmissions.

B. MTV

1. MTV is a private corporation owned by advertisers, financial institutions, and retailers. No more than five percent of its stock can be owned by any one entity.

2. MTV has been subject to tight programming restrictions based on the limited availability of broadcast time. Recently, though, MTV has been able to expand into a new and desirable program area—news. In 1981, YLE's Administrative Council (selected by Parliament) agreed to per-

mit MTV to provide a twenty-minute news broadcast on weekend nights for a trial period. This marked the first time that YLE had relinquished exclusive control of television news programming. On January 20, 1984, the Administrative Council agreed to make the MTV newscasts a permanent program offering.

3. In 1983, MTV programmed a total of 543 hours, 31 minutes, on TV-1 and 294 hours, 25 minutes, on TV-2, for a total of 837 hours, 56 minutes, overall. MTV produced 44.7% of the programs it provided; 5.4% originated with Finnish producers, and another 49.9% were of foreign origin. MTV, *Annual Report, 1983* 11 (1984).

4. The turnover of MTV was equal to 395,450,065 FM in 1983, or an increase of 16.47% over 1982. The profit equalled 2,449,834 FM. Under an agreement signed for 1983, MTV must pay YLE 219,643,000 FM for programming and advertising time and for advertising sold in connection with sports programs. *Id.* at 29. MTV is permitted to sell fifteen percent of its time for advertising (about twenty minutes each day). Advertisements must be approved by MTV; alcohol and tobacco advertising are prohibited, and certain other advertising subjects are strictly regulated (*i.e.*, lotteries, medicines).

C. YLE

1. YLE operates primarily as a government-owned company, although it also has some private stockholders. A senior official of the Ministry of Communications attends all Board meetings, and the Parliament elects all twenty-one members of YLE's Administrative Council. The government must hold at least ninety percent of YLE's stock. Currently it holds 99.9%, with sixty businesses and educational groups sharing the remainder.

2. YLE is heavily dependent on fees paid for television set licenses, with rates being set by the Council of State. These fees accounted for 76.3% of YLE's 1983 total income, with payments by MTV constituting an additional 22%. Turnover for 1983 totalled 908,536,288 FM, an increase of 14.2% from 1982. Profit equalled 29,852,974 FM. YLE, *Annual Report, 1983* 8-9 (1984).

3. YLE views its apparent "monopoly" position in the broadcasting field as a rather narrow one. It notes that MTV is the sole broadcaster authorized to accept advertising and that only newspapers provide comprehensive regional and local information (because YLE's broadcasts are all national in scope). YLE has presented this view of the country's media marketplace to counter suggestions that unless it relinquishes control of the broadcast facilities, free speech and a diversity of ideas will not be possible in Finland. *See id.* at 16-19.

D. Relationship Between MTV and YLE

1. Traditionally, the relationship between YLE and MTV has been highly competitive. With the spread of cable television service and with the increased availability of imported signals, however, there may be a new basis for cooperation in order to increase the level of Finnish production for television. Both MTV and YLE have expressed a strong interest in using their programming for cable and for videocassette distribution. Both are confronted with new satellite-based competition and may, therefore, see it as in their common interest to stimulate new Finnish television productions.

2. YLE has tried to exercise control over MTV's operations. Recently, though, MTV secured the right to operate its own receive-only satellite station.

3. MTV and YLE still see their relationship from differing perspectives. YLE views MTV as a programmer that "assists" YLE in the operation of TV-1 and TV-2. *See YLE Operating License* 1 (1980); *see also* Howkins, *supra*, at 52. MTV, on the other hand, sees itself as a private, independent programmer that merely leases channel space from YLE. *Id.* YLE is publicly viewed as a source of reliable, political, factual, complex programming, whereas MTV is seen as the supplier of enjoyble commercial programs. *See* M. Oksanen, *YLE in Focus* (1982).

E. Local Radio Services

1. One of the more interesting recent developments is the spread of private radio services. Thirty-two local stations are scheduled to be started on an experimental basis, and there are as many as 500 available frequencies. There are now questions about the ultimate ownership of private radio channels—especially whether newspapers should be involved.

2. Many of the experimental companies are joint ventures of highly diverse groups (*e.g.*, political parties and businesses). The first local radio station on the air in Helsinki—Radio City—is operated by a youth organization and has begun to fill a significant gap in the area of popular music programming. The station is off to a good start in garnering advertising revenues, and it has begun to influence the programming practices of the public radio services operated by YLE. Later in the fall of 1985, Radio l, a joint venture of newspaper companies, will begin competing with Radio City for the same audience. It remains to be seen how this competitive relationship will evolve.

3. The new local radio services are typically Finnish in their innovation and their entrepreneurial approach. Radio City had begun to launch a "public offering" of shares in the venture while the Ministry of Communications was still in the process of considering the various possible financing options for local radio service.

4. It will be interesting to see whether the new private radio companies seek access to the license fees imposed on receiving equipment. These fees have historically been set aside completely for YLE. However, Finnish law does not require that the fees be given exclusively to YLE (just as it does not confer an explicit monopoly on the company). The law establishes only that an eligible recipient must be a radio licensee. (MTV, as a program company, has never been deemed eligible for these funds.)

5. YLE operates the national radio broadcasting facilities, providing nationwide Swedish and Finnish programming. It has begun local radio service in Turku and Tampere, with experimental regional broadcasts in Lapland and Ostrobothnia. YLE has identified the expansion of local radio service as an important part of its effort to extend local and regional public broadcasting beyond simply news and information programming. *See* YLE, *The Role and Function of Public Broadcasting in the 1980s* 8-9 (1981) (unpublished).

F. New Legislation

Government reports on radio and television were submitted for comment in January and February, 1984. They have been criticized, however, for not taking enough of a farsighted view of the future of broadcasting in Finland. *See* MTV, *Annual Report, 1983* 1 (1984). They appear to ignore the need to address concerns raised by the proliferation of technology and are satisfied to leave institutional responsibilities in basically the current state of organization.

VIII. INTERNATIONAL CONSIDERATIONS

A. Overview

1. Finland has been an extremely open market and has been heavily dependent on international trade developments and opportunities. The legal vacuum in telecommunications policy has tended to result in procurement issues being driven by market forces and by competition between the private companies and the PTT.

2. For a number of reasons, the Finnish telecommunications manufacturing and service sectors have obtained a uniquely strong international position. The often tightly balanced relationship between the public and private sectors in Finland has produced a very self-reliant and independent entrepreneurial spirit. Finnish manufacturers prefer autonomy to the risk of the kind of potentially stifling embrace that accompanied past government efforts to promote an "industrial policy."

3. The Finnish market also has historically been open to outside suppliers. This competition, as well as the competition between public and private purchasers of telecommunications equipment, has promoted innovation and rapid development.

4. The Finnish economy, because of its small size, traditionally has been geared to reaching out to international markets. Current developments within Finland may enhance further the opportunity for expanded international marketing of the country's telecommunications products and services. *See supra* Section V.

5. The PTT and the local telephone companies, along with a consulting company and a state-owned utility, have formed Telecon, an independent telecommunications consultant intended to export Finnish telecommunications expertise into the worldwide market. *See* Rauhala, *Telecon Exports Finnish Telecommunications Know How*, Teletiedotuksia '83, at 54-55. Greater international cooperation, however, remains a somewhat elusive goal. The failure to reach standardization agreements on cellular radio service, for example, has crippled the ability of Nokia Electronics to market a portable telephone service on a European-wide basis.

B. Satellite Services

1. The impact of international satellite services in Finland is highly uncertain. In the area of broadcasting, satellites may promote a new degree of cooperation between YLE and MTV by making possible the growth of alternative delivery technologies such as cable television. To the degree that satellite links can provide cable systems with foreign programming, both YLE and MTV may have a strong incentive to join forces to build a more dynamic Finnish program production industry. *See supra* Section VII.

2. Conversely, satellites may prove a means for provoking greater competition between MTV and YLE. The availability of direct access to subscribers through satellite transmission links—making obsolete MTV's reliance on YLE's transmission facilities—may tend to make MTV more independent of the public broadcasting network.

3. In the area of telecommunications, it appears rather unlikely that international satellite transponders will be used to upgrade domestic telecommunications facilities or to provide a significant means for bypassing the PTT's trunk network. However, direct access to Intelsat or to Eutelsat might become the basis for competition between the PTT and the local telephone companies in the area of specialized service offerings. The role that the private companies will play in Nordic data services, or in international private line services such as videoconferencing, remains unclear.

4. The use by Finnish cable systems of satellite-delivered programming services has raised a number of very interesting questions about the pricing of access to these services.

a. These services are intended for general distribution; however, they are offered through the PTT over non-broadcast (*i.e.*, point-to-point or point-to-multipoint) satellite facilities. Thus, the PTT has taken the position that it can reasonably assess "down-link" charges for such programs. The basis for the PTT's charges are just beginning to be explored in Finland. The appropriateness of these charges may be questionable where it is the program supplier's intention that they be directly received as a broadcast-like service.

b. Finland's open legal environment has permitted the development of a conflict over the pricing of downlinks for video services that could have broader significance in other parts of Europe. The resolution of this issue—without the effect of particular (and peculiar) laws and regulations—will be of interest to others around the world.

5. Finland's involvement in Scandinavian satellite services is complex. The development of Nordsat does not appear promising at the moment. There is no evident desire on the part of YLE to pay the costs of the system. The counterpart to Nordsat is the Tele-X system that has been pushed forward as an industrial development activity. Finland will have to pay a significant price to obtain limited economic participation. In the spring of 1985, the Finnish government decided, for industrial policy reasons, to make a four-to-five percent investment in the Tele-X venture. It is not clear, however, who will bear the operational costs of the system. Neither YLE nor the PTT has committed itself to using the capacity that will be made available.

6. This gap between industrial policy and telecommunications policy planning is an interesting and significant one. The Tele-X situation is not dissimilar from developments elsewhere in Europe, where there are pressures to create new transmission capacity and no effective coordination for the use of the service.

7. Finland also must consider the pressure to participate in the Eastern Bloc communications satellite program. In this regard, geopolitical considerations clearly may figure into the telecommunications policy equation.

C. Pricing Issues

The gradual shift in pricing policies toward cost-based pricing on a global basis is creating significant opportunities for Finnish manufacturers that have developed techniques for serving remote geographical areas at lower costs. Finland has done substantial research on the problems of serving such remote areas. The technology might prove particularly useful in the U.S. or in Canada, where the economic pressures of deregulation may be most acute. The increased need for cost-saving and innovative technologies will be accentuated by repricing strategies that raise service prices in sparsely populated or geographically remote areas. As costs become more closely aligned with prices, low-cost transmission technology will become increasingly attractive.

IX. CONCLUSION: FUTURE ISSUES

A. A major question facing the Finnish telecommunications market is whether new legislation will be adopted to fill the current legal void. The overwhelmingly distinctive characteristic of Finland's telecommunications and broadcasting markets is the lack of legal guidance for the myriad of problems raised by new technologies and innovative service configurations. There is, understandably, a fairly strong feeling that the system, which has worked well for almost an entire century, should simply be left alone. However, the interesting complexity of facilities and service relationships, such as those raised by the offering of information services or cable television, might be seen to require legislation to resolve at least some of the conflicts. Of course, a legislative "solution" poses the same hazards for Finland as it does anywhere else in the world: broad legislative proclamations may prove either too vague to improve the current situation or so inadequate that they will merely disrupt the status quo—without establishing a new order. New laws, inevitably, raise new questions. These concerns have lent support to those who prefer to operate within the current legal vacuum.

B. The unusual public/private structure of the communications sector in Finland also is the subject of legislative attention. In the telecommunications area, it appears likely that the PTT's relationship with the private telephone companies will continue to evolve. Although the PTT may lose its regulatory control over these companies, it is not clear how that change will affect the competitive situation.

1. Such a change would, of course, prevent the PTT from adversely affecting the private telephone companies through governmental fiat. However, even without the PTT's restrictive influence, it is not clear that the telephone companies would depart significantly from the general contours of the current market structure. Bypass of PTT facilities may occur, but it is unlikely that a significant duplication of basic transmission facilities will take place.

2. It is perhaps more likely that any bypass activity will take advantage of new transmission technologies such as satellite links and fiber optic lines for new data services. These high-capacity, broadband transmission paths will permit price reductions and the further development of new high-speed data transmission services. The planned Dataway venture is probably a good indication of where the emphasis on future network development will be placed.

3. PTT efforts to digitize the existing transmission network and to reprice transmission services will affect significantly these new facili-

ties plans. The PTT also may respond to facilities-based competition by encouraging the resale of its enhanced transmission facilities—to allow third parties to develop value-added network services. (It also, of course, could provide such enhanced services on its own.) In the absence of any regulatory controls, tension is likely to evolve between the construction of alternative transmission networks and the provision of various services through an integrated—and digitized—PTT network.

4. The most remarkable result of any change in Finnish law might be the emergence of a new regulatory entity within the Ministry of Communications to oversee the relationship between the PTT, the private telephone companies, and any new competitors. This entity would face the same kinds of issues now perplexing regulators in other countries that are pursuing liberalization policies: interconnection disputes among competitive carriers, access charge concerns, repricing questions, and difficulties in reconciling general competitive goals with the desire to preserve a unified national telephone system. These kinds of issues now are handled through negotiations coordinated by the Ministry of Communications' Joint Telecommunications Committee. The process would be dramatically different if the Ministry were mediating a competitive battle between a privatized (or "de-publicized") PTT and other private companies. The PTT would no longer be able to fall back on its regulatory powers to shape the industry; it would have to rely more on its competitive strength. As a consequence, competition might become more intense and negotiation more difficult.

C. Negotiation and accommodation work well in Finland because the market now possesses a delicate balance. The PTT deals, of course, from a position of strength: it has a dominant network and the powers of a public authority behind it. However, it is keenly aware that new, private competitors can challenge its position. The lack of legal prohibition means that innovation is rarely forbidden.

D. A remarkable aspect of the Finnish situation is that it has produced innovation and growth despite industry structures that have been blamed for stifling progress elsewhere in the world. The country has developed full-fledged, nationwide broadcast and wire communications networks. It has one of the world's more extensive—if not sophisticated—cable networks. It also has an extremely progressive equipment manufacturing industry. Changes in technology, however, which have enabled various companies to diversify across traditional boundary lines, have produced discord. As a result, the country is considering a new resort to legislative line-drawing. The question the country faces is whether it would do as well with fixed rules and established categories as it has done in a completely fluid environment.

CHAPTER VIII
FRANCE

TABLE OF CONTENTS

CHAPTER VIII
FRANCE

I. INTRODUCTION AND OVERVIEW

A. The French telecommunications network has undergone a radical transformation in the past decade and is now one of the most modern in the world. The Direction générale des télécommunications ("D.G.T.") is continuing to improve the network through a major development program. It is installing digital switching (35% of total main lines in 1984) and transmission facilities, implementing a universal network of data terminals useful for electronic directory and any other videotex services, and planning to build switched fiber optic cable networks throughout the country.

B. The core of the French regulatory approach is to ensure that there are modern, low cost, standardized infrastructure facilities. These, it is believed, will stimulate investment and new entrepreneurial activity in software, value-added services, and other telecommunications-related sectors.

C. The D.G.T. is acutely aware of the new economic and competitive conditions that are a result of deregulation in the United States and elsewhere. Its objective is to assure the competitive parity in the global market of French services—in terms of both price and quality. To achieve its goal, the D.G.T. has engaged in a creative strategy of establishing a web of affiliated entities, each of which operates as a "société d'économie mixte"—a company organized under private law (de droit prive), but owned primarily, if not exclusively, by the State. This approach is intended to encourage the development of new services and to enhance flexibility, with an eye toward reducing the rigidity that might otherwise encumber a large organization. In particular, the D.G.T. expects that by adopting this approach, it will better be able to recruit personnel to market and to manage new services. Along with creativity in management, there is substantial flexibility to price services innovatively and to tailor them to the unique needs of users, loosening the constraints imposed by the PTT Code. In this way, the D.G.T. intends to match the competitive environment that is evolving in the U.K. or the U.S. without a structural shift to a competitive market structure. Its intent, then, is to establish an internal set of competitive spurs to guide the interrelationship of the subsidiaries and the D.G.T.

D. In addition to relying on subsidiaries, there is an important emphasis placed, in general, on "decentralization" of management—an overall thrust of the current French Government. Consequently, the various operational units of the D.G.T. have been accorded more operational flexibility. Moreover, in each locality cable television services will be provided through a new entity, a Société Locale d'Exploitation du Câble ("SLEC") (local cable service company, which the cable laws refer to as Société d'Economie Mixte Locale). A SLEC must be under the direction of municipal officials, but will have important working agreements with the D.G.T. (as the owner and provider of network services). The long-term impact of this movement toward decentralization is as yet unclear.

E. Overall, the D.G.T. is wrestling with the tension between its dual roles as an "administration" and as a commercial and industrial enterprise. During the past few years it has sought to reinforce its entrepreneurial "center of gravity" by developing a multi-year management plan agreed to with the government. This autonomy has, however, recently been tested in a controversy over basic telephone rates. The government decided unilaterally, and contrary to the wishes of the D.G.T., to increase the basic unit rate from 64.5 centimes to 75 centimes on August 1, 1984. Nevertheless, the D.G.T. is still attempting to separate its entrepreneurial activities more completely from its supervisory role. The move toward establishing subsidiaries is one aspect of this effort.

F. Like other administrations around the world, the D.G.T. is beginning to grapple with the critical problem of pricing telecommunications services. Increased competition in international markets—and among national providers of domestic telecommunications services—is likely to result in pricing changes that are intended to tie prices more closely to costs. To this end, the D.G.T. is involved in an effort at encouraging usage-sensitive pricing at the local level. This repricing will, as it has in other countries, intensify political scrutiny of the D.G.T. It appears that the D.G.T. is attempting to make these difficult decisions from a long-term perspective, based on an appraisal of economic and technological realities. In this regard, the D.G.T. may be adapting to new marketplace realities more effectively than some other administrations. The D.G.T. seems to have a strategic vision—and the institutional, technological, and pricing policies to implement it.

II. OVERVIEW OF THE STRUCTURE OF THE FRENCH TELECOMMUNICATIONS INDUSTRY

A. The Ministry of the PTT and the Direction Générale des Télécommunications

1. The Ministry of the PTT ("Ministère des Postes, des Télécommunications et de la Télédiffusion") has 480,000 employees. It is organized into two major general directorates: the D.G.T., with 160,000 employees, and the Direction générale de la poste ("D.G.P.") with 320,000 employees. P. Lemoine, *Les Technologies d'Information, Enjeu Stratégique pour la modernisation économique et sociale, Rapport au Premier Ministre,* Annexe 2, at 181 (La Documentation Française: Paris, 1982) [hereinafter cited as *Les Technologies*]. In addition, the Ministry's central administration includes two functional directorates that serve both the D.G.T. and the D.G.P.: the Direction du personnel et des affaires sociales ("DIPAS") and the Direction du budget et de la comptabilité ("DBC"), which oversees, among other things,

preparation of the budget. *See* Ministère des PTT, *Les Télécommunications Françaises* (Ministry: Paris, 1982).

2. The PTT budget, including the posts and telecommunications operations, is not included in the general state budget. It is an annexed budget in which expenses must be balanced by revenues. The budget estimate for revenues in 1985 is FFr 162.7 billion, and expenditures are expected to total FFr 154.8 billion. The corresponding figures for 1984 were FFr 143.6 billion and FFr 139.6 billion, respectively. *See Sénat, Rapport Général fait au nom de la commission des Finances, du Contrôle Budgétaire et des Comptes Economiques de la Nation sur le projet de loi de finances pour 1985*, adopté par l'Assemblée Nationale, TOME III, Annexe No. 42 (1985). Capital expenditures for 1985 are projected at FFr 33.7 billion. This will include FFr 32.2 billion for capital projects ("autorisations de programmes") and FFr 7.5 billion in contributions to the electronics industry and to the space agency (Centre National d'Etudes Spatiales). Almost FFr 30 billion will be invested in telecommunications equipment and almost FFr 3 billion in postal equipment and facilities.

3. The D.G.T.'s operating budget for 1985 projects FFr 89.2 billion in revenues and FFr 81.6 billion in expenditures, leaving a positive balance of FFR 7.6 billion. The corresponding figures for 1984 were FFr 72 billion in revenues, FFr 65.4 billion in expenditures and a surplus of FFr 6.4 billion. These revenues put the D.G.T. among the ten largest enterprises in France. In 1983, its value to the economy, on the order of FFr 55 billion, represented 1.4% of the Production Intérieure Brute of France; its employees represented .78% of the total French work force. *See* Ministère des PTT, Direction Générale des Télécommunications, *Rapport d'activité 1983* [hereinafter cited as *Rapport*]. The total staff of 165,000 has a per capita productivity of about FFr 500,000.

4. The D.G.T., as a profitable organization, has recently been called upon to subsidize the postal service as well as to contribute to the electronics industry, the space agency, and the nation's general budget (in what is the equivalent of an income tax). Contribution to the electronics industry will more than double in 1985, to almost FFr 7.5 billion. *See* Eric le Boucher, *La Hausse du téléphone représente pour plus de la moitié—un impôt déguisé*, Le Monde, September 19, 1984.

B. Structure of the Direction Générale des Télécommunications

1. The D.G.T. is organized into a number of intermediate level directorates: the Direction de la production ("DPR"), Direction des affaires commerciales et télématiques ("DACT"), Direction des affaires industrielles et internationales ("DAII"), and Le service du personnel ("SPEL").

2. Under the DPR is the Direction des télécommunications du réseau national ("DTRN"), which has responsibility for the intercity network. There are five operational directorates within DTRN, at Toulouse, Paris, Lyons, Nantes, and Metz.

3. Also within the DPR are twenty-two regional telecommunications directorates ("DRT"), which are responsible for facilities planning, attachments for subscribers, maintenance, and customer relations. In 1973, the larger DRT units were subdivided into small operational directorates ("directions opérationnelles des télécommunications" or "DOT"). There are forty-eight such operational units at the present time; they are responsible for the use of equipment and services. Since 1981, there has been an effort to increase decentralization in providing service by allowing the DOTs to set objectives and the means of achieving them, and to oversee the results.

4. The main role of the DAII is coordinating international policy developments with the activities of the telecommunications industry. The Direction des télécommunications des réseaux extérieurs ("DTRE"), which oversees the development of the international network, operates within the general policy determined by the DAII. Since January 1, 1984, the DAII has been accorded several additional areas of responsibility to assure that there is synergy between the telecommunications and industrial sectors. It oversees the procurement of informatic services in the French government.

a. The DAII also oversees two nationalized industries, CMB (Bull) and the Compagnie générale de constructions téléphoniques ("CGCT"). The impact of the D.G.T. on the telecommunications sector is significant inasmuch as nearly FFr 20 billion are invested in the electronics industry annually. *Rapport, supra*, at 35. Globally, these investments represent 18-20% of the total investment in the French electronics industry, which was, in 1983, in excess of FFr 100 billion. *Id.*

b. The DAII also plays a major role in the D.G.T.'s relationships with international institutions, such as the International Telecommunications Union and the Commission of the European Communities. It supervises research activities and applications research by the Centre national d'études des télécommunications ("CNET"). *See Les Télécommunications Françaises, supra*, at 73. The CNET is a major research organization that performs fundamental and applied research, as well as development work, in the telecommunications field and in related areas. The CNET provides expert advice and assistance to outside companies and organizations and employs a staff of approximately 4300. *See* Jean Voge, *Survey of French Regulatory Policy* (March 1984) (paper presented at Research Workshop on Economic Policy Towards Telecommunications and Media Activities in Industrialized Countries) (Preliminary Draft).

C. "Filiales" (The Affiliates) of the D.G.T.

1. The D.G.T. works with two groups of affiliated entities. The first are involved in financing the telecommunications system. Created in 1967, the Caisse Nationale des Télécommunications ("CNT") assists in raising capital on national and international financial markets. In 1983, the CNT raised FFr 10.9 billion, of which 59% originated in foreign capital markets. *Rapport, supra,* at 34. The CNT is complemented by five finance companies, Finextel, Codetel, Agritel, Creditel, and Francetel—which contributed FFr 3.2 billion in the form of lease-back financing.

2. More important are the affiliates that are organized under France Câbles et Radio ("FCR"). FCR is a "société d'économie mixte a capitaux publics." This means that it is a private company in which the state is the sole shareholder. As a group it employs approximately 2700 people; it had revenues of about FFr 2 billion in 1983. This amount is estimated to grow to approximately FFr 2.5 billion in 1985. *See generally* Groupe France Câbles et Radio, Report 1983 (1984) [hereinafter cited as *FCR Report*].

3. In 1984, the stock of the Transpac system, the French public packet-switching system, was shifted and placed under the control of FCR. In addition, FCR has responsibility for marketing various digital services, including the Telecom-1 satellite, through an operational group within FCR. (For a fuller discussion of FCR, *see infra* Section V.A.)

4. The FCR group also includes five French subsidiaries, two of which are particularly important. Entreprise Générale de Télécommunications ("EGT") is involved in marketing peripheral equipment, pagers, telecopiers, and radio telephone equipment. *FCR Report, supra,* at 22. Télésystemes operates through a number of groups to offer software and assistance in the establishment, management, and operation of information networks. Télésystèmes Eurodial has been involved in commercializing the electronic message service Mercure and a system of teleconferencing by computer. Télésystèmes Questel is involved in the creation, management, and distribution of data bases. Other subsidiaries are involved in developing network software and application software for mini, micro, and large-scale computers. *FCR Report, supra,* at 19-21.

5. The FCR group consists of a group of foreign subsidiaries that are minority-owned by FCR and are located in former French colonies. (In a number of other countries, *e.q.*, the Ivory Coast, Senegal, and Cameroon, the FCR no longer holds an ownership interest, but it provides technical assistance in the management of telecommunications systems.) In a number of countries, FCR also has ownership interests in corporate entities involved in the construction of underseas cable.

6. FCR's holdings in all of these subsidiaries will soon be transferred to a new holding group. FCR will then become one of a series of affiliated entities that will be overseen and managed by the holding group.

7. FCR is overseen by a board consisting of representatives of the D.G.T. and the Treasury. Moreover, it has a network of operational relationships with the various groups within the D.G.T. Many of the key executives of FCR originally worked in the D.G.T.

8. In general, the D.G.T. has utilized the FCR subsidiaries to develop and to introduce innovative new services. It is apparently the D.G.T.'s view that subsidiaries have greater flexibility in planning, managing, and pricing new services. The subsidiaries have complex relationships with the operational groups in the D.G.T. that are marked both by cooperation and competition. The rationale for the use of subsidiaries is discussed more fully below. *See infra* Sections III. & IV.

D. French Telecommunications Industry

1. A primary characteristic of the French telecommunications industry is the predominant role played by the State. This accounts for the industry's highly regulated status. The State is the major purchaser of the country's telecommunications products, making almost three-quarters of the French purchases and half of the purchases worldwide. CNET contributes technological expertise to enhance the industry's competitiveness. For example, it helped to make CIT a leader in France's telecommunications industry by assisting it in the development of an electronic time division multiplexing switch. *See* P. Duran, *Règlementation/Déreglementation des télécommunications en France*, 11 (December, 1984) (Rapport de Synthese réalisé pour le compte d'ASCOM—France) [hereinafter cited as *ASCOM Report*]. Between 1960 and 1981 the PTT invested more than FFr 150 billion in the telephone equipment program alone. *Id.* at 12.

2. Through its nationalization program the State became the major stockholder in the industry. It owns 100% of the two largest telecommunications groups, Thomson-Brandt and Compagnie générale d'électricité ("CGE"). In addition, the State has obtained majority control (51%) of Matra and CII-Honeywell Bull. It also owns all of the CGCT, which was previously under the control of ITT. *See* J.M. Iacino, *The French Audiovisual Revolution: The Case of Telematics*, International Trade Practice and Law 380 (1984) [hereinafter cited as *French Audiovisual Revolution*].

a. In 1984, Thomson became principally involved in manufacturing components and consumer electronics. Thomson's communication interests were grouped in a new company, Thomson-Télécommunications, which, in 1985, was taken over by CIT-Alcatel under the name Alcatel-Thomson. In 1984, Alcatel-Thomson International, a joint export subsidiary, was set up.

b. The nationalization program was part of the five-year "Filière Electronique" action plan that was adopted by the Government on July 28, 1982. This plan was prepared by the Direction des Industries Electroniques et de l'Information ("DIELI"), a department of the Ministry of Industry. It calls for FFr 50-60 billion in government spending to integrate and systematically organize an entire industrial sector under the aegis of the national government. The plan is to achieve what the State views as the optimal allocation and use of all resources, research and development, production and distribution facilities to reduce France's dependence on imports, to increase its exports, and to develop new products and services. Telecommunications is one of the eleven sectors within the "Filière Electronique," which also includes electronic components, software industries, and consumer and professional electronics. *Id.* at 378.

3. The telecommunications industry in France employs 80,000 people. In 1984, its revenues were about FFr 30 billion before taxes, of which 27% was earned in the export market and 73% in the domestic market.

a. The manufacturers' association, Syndicat des Industries du Téléphone du Télégraphe et de leurs Applications Télématiques, ("S.I.3T") calculated global revenues of FFr 19.8 billion in 1983. This association encompasses the French telecommunication equipment manufacturers (not including the equipment related to the radio frequency spectrum and telephone cables) and software producers for that equipment. *See* S.I.3T, Rapport d'activité (1984). Projections for 1984 were FFr 22 billion.

b. In 1983, the industries of the "Filière Electronique" realized global revenues of FFr 135 billion and employed approximately 300,000 people. The balance of trade for the "Filière Electronique" industries showed a deficit of FFr 11 billion, up from FFr 5.3 billion in 1983. Forty-five percent of the domestic market was supplied by imports, and 35% of the national production was exported. *ASCOM Report, supra,* at 24.

4. There are approximately forty companies manufacturing telecommunications equipment. About 90% of the production is attributable to five large companies: Alcatel-Thomson, G3S (SAT and SAGEM), CGCT (formerly the ITT group), Télécommunications Radioélectriques et Téléphoniques ("TRT") (a subsidiary of Philips) and LTT (formerly in the Thomson group). *See Les Télécommunications Françaises, supra,* at 89. Three of these companies are owned entirely by the State. *See supra* Section II.D.2.

5. After the nationalization program, the government reorganized the different companies to increase each one's specialization. CGE, along with its subsidiary CIT-Alcatel, is increasing its activity in the telecommunication sector. It manufactures the E10 and MT20/25 electronic time division multiplexing switches, digital pulse code modulation transmission systems, private branch exchanges ("PBXs"), and telephone systems. CIT-Alcatel itself has four affiliates: Alcatel Electronique, SESA (engaged in developing packet-switching systems), TELIC (terminal equipment), and Câble de Lyons (France's largest manufacturer of telecommunication cables).

III. FRENCH PERSPECTIVES ON BOUNDARY LINE ISSUES: AN INTRODUCTION

A. At the core of French telecommunications policy is the establishment of a boundary line between the provision of an infrastructure for telecommunications services—which is within the exclusive province of the D.G.T.—and the provision of services—where it is intended that there be competition.

B. Within the telecommunications services infrastructure, the D.G.T. has carved out key sectors or areas of activities (*e.g.*, data transmission services) to be provided through one or more subsidiaries. These subsidiaries are managed by the holding company, FCR, but essentially function as private entities. They have more flexibility in terms of pricing and management practices. It is important to focus on the internal lines for dividing services between the D.G.T. and its subsidiaries.

C. The actual line of demarcation between the D.G.T.'s infrastructure activities and the service sector has been sharply established in principle. In practical or in technological terms, however, it is more difficult to delineate. The D.G.T. sometimes defines the boundary line in technological terms by focusing on its responsibility to offer the capabilities included in the first three levels of protocols in the ISO standard. The remaining layers, including the capability for protocol conversion, are viewed as outside the D.G.T.'s basic monopoly.

D. The D.G.T. does not, however, believe that its area of activities is necessarily confined to the provision of transmission services. It believes that it can and should participate in the provision of new services on a nonexclusive basis. Thus, the D.G.T. has had an active role in stimulating the development of telematic services for residential as well as business use. In this regard, it develops a set of service "labels," including high level protocols (Télétel for videotex, Teletext, electronic mail, etc.) within a coherent scheme (ARCHITEL), and promotes their usage by independent service suppliers. Moreover, it is involved in remote access data processing through the Télésystèmes subsidiary of FCR. The D.G.T. emphasizes that these subsidiaries—which are engaged in areas outside its monopoly—must deal with the transmission services divisions of the D.G.T. on an arm's-length basis. The D.G.T. has placed great emphasis on software and service development to stimulate the utilization of the network infrastructure.

E. To implement the Law on Audiovisual Communication ("La Loi sur la Communication Audiovisuelle"), which was enacted by the French Parliament on July 29, 1982, boundary lines between various information services are now being established. The Audiovisual Law requires that certain information services be authorized, but it contains a series of exclusions for internal information services or services intertwined with transaction-oriented capabilities. *See infra* Section V.C. In the evolving French scheme there is significant regulatory forbearance with respect to third-party transaction services that might—in other national contexts—be viewed as third-party or message switching activities.

F. Intertwined as they are with information services provided over the D.G.T.'s public network facilities, these third-party services do not seem to be subject to any significant regulation. Thus, in a little-noted way—but de facto—the Audiovisual Law created a category of "value-added services" that are provided under what is essentially a liberalized or unregulated regime. This category might roughly correspond with what were viewed as hybrid data processing services under the *Computer I* regime in the U.S.; it does not, however, include complex value-added or enhanced services that have developed.

G. There has been substantial recent activity in France to define the nature and role of cable television services. Cable services will be offered at the local level by new entities, the so-called SLECs. These entities will be open to investment by the private and public sectors. They will be responsible for managing the day-to-day aspects of cable television services (*i.e.*, billing customers, marketing the service, selecting programming). The basic cable facilities—fiber optic cable in a switched star configuration—will be owned and operated by the D.G.T. The facilities for reception and distribution of programming to the local cable system will be provided by Télédiffusion de France ("TDF"). TDF provides and manages the transmitters and intercity transmission for the French radio and television broadcasting systems. The division of responsibility between the D.G.T., TDF, and the SLEC reveals the unique manner in which cable television services are "defined" in France and are given an institutional setting.

H. In Section V., *infra*, there will be a more-detailed examination of some of these evolving boundary lines in French telecommunications policy. First, it is necessary to focus on the telecommunications infrastructure of the D.G.T.

IV. TELECOMMUNICATIONS INFRASTRUCTURE AND THE D.G.T.

A. Modernization in the 1970's

1. The French telecommunications infrastructure underwent a massive modernization in the 1970's. At the beginning of the decade, the French network was antiquated, with significant delays in installation and services. Overall, France's telecommunications system was not as modern or efficient as the systems in many of the major industrialized countries.

2. In 1985, France has one of the most modern telecommunications sectors among the industrialized countries. The number of subscriber lines has increased more than five-fold since 1971, from 4.6 million lines to 22.05 million lines in 1984. Expectations are that in 1985 this total will reach 23.1 million lines. The density of lines per 100 inhabitants (40%) is

now superior to that of the U.K. and Japan, and comparable to that in the Federal Republic of Germany. *Rapport, supra,* at 5. More than 85% of France's households now have a telephone. *See* J. Dondoux, *The French Telecommunications Network and the Introduction of New Services* (May 1984).

3. Moreover, in the mid-1970's, the level of self-financing was approximately 40%, whereas, in 1983, that level had increased to 74.6%. Ministère des PTT, Direction générale des télécommunications, *Statistiques & Finances 1983,* at 38. This significant increase reveals the extent to which the D.G.T. has itself been able to mobilize the resources necessary to modernize the French network.

4. The relative price of telephone service is approximately one-half that of fifteen years ago. Increasing the demand for and expanding the use of the infrastructure will boost efficiency and reduce the relative cost of network facilities.

B. The Digitization of Network Facilities

1. In 1970, the D.G.T. installed the first time division switch; such switching equipment now represents 35% of the switching equipment in the national network. By 1986, half of the switches are expected to be digital. By 1990, almost three-quarters of the French subscribers (approximately 29 million) are expected to be connected to an electronic switching system. *See* J. Dondoux, *supra.*

2. In 1985, the D.G.T. introduced a 64 Kbit/s switched digital service that is a first step in the direction of an ISDN service (Le Réseau Numérique a Ìntégration de Services). This process will commence with the digitization of transmission elements. In 1984, of 26,000,000 circuits installed, over 35% were digital. In 1983, approximately 10,000 kilometers of optical fiber facilities were ordered. *Rapport, supra,* at 23. In addition, high-capacity digital coaxial cable links are being put into service. The Telecom-1 satellite, *see infra* Section IV.E., will increase enormously the digital link capacity available.

3. In the second phase, in 1986-1987, the network interface for ISDN services will be standardized, and software for ISDN services will be developed. There will be an experimental ISDN program, known as Project Renan, in region Lannion. *See Rapport, supra,* at 48-49. By 1986, as part of the Project Renan, the telephone network will be further enhanced with the introduction of connection units for digital subscriber lines, providing ISDN services in accordance with CCITT Recommendations.

4. Network digitization permitted five new services to be introduced in 1983: itemized billing, call waiting tone, conference calls, call forwarding, and freephone numbers (called the "green number" service). By the end of 1985 any subscriber anywhere in France will be able to request any of these services. *See* J. Dondoux, *supra.*

C. The Expansion of the Network of Electronic Terminals (Videotex)

1. The D.G.T. has pressed forward aggressively with a plan to develop a network of terminals for an electronic telephone directory. By mid-1985 there were more than one million switched terminals (called the "Minitel") in place, and it is expected that, by the end of 1986, there will be three million terminals. *See* D.G.T., *Resultats 1984 (1985)* [hereinafter cited as *Resultats 1984*]. This expansion is intended to replace paper with electronic directories on the assumption that the annual cost of a paper directory is equivalent to the annual amortization cost of a switched terminal. The D.G.T. is not the exclusive provider of the Minitel; it can be purchased from certified equipment vendors.

2. The electronic directories program was initiated in February, 1983, in Brittany. Service was implemented thereafter in Ile-de-France, Picardie, and Marseille. *Rapport, supra,* at 8. To date all French regions have requested the service, and the D.G.T. has developed a plan to introduce the service throughout France by 1987. *See* J. Dondoux, *supra*. France has the world's largest, operational videotex system as well as a successful electronic directory service.

3. The objective of the electronic directory program is to encourage the expansion of videotex services generally by developing a much lower cost terminal (by a factor of two to four times) than has been available in other countries. *Rapport, supra,* at 16. It is expected that the existence of the web of switched terminals will stimulate demand for new electronic mailbox, electronic information (transaction-related services), and, ultimately, the D.G.T.'s transmission services. Today, over 500 videotex services are offered by independent entities, including banks, industrial firms, administrative agencies, and associations. Indeed, the growth of information services and the widespread penetration of the Minitel terminals has been so successful that it has strained the D.G.T.'s data transmission network, Transpac.

4. To facilitate these services, switches providing the interface between the telephone network, the packet-switched network, and the service providers, called Point d'Accès Videotex (PAVI) were implemented. The D.G.T. has devised three types of access arrangements for information services. First, the user pays only for local access; the service providers pay for the use of the packet-switching network. Second, the user pays the entire access fee based on two minutes of usage independent of distance. This option is intended for use where information providers want to disseminate information broadly but do not want to pay the transport charges. Third, in 1984, the D.G.T. introduced the "kiosk" in which the user can pay for both the access charges and the information requested. *Rapport, supra,* at 16. These rate structures reflect an effort by the D.G.T. to develop new information services by tailoring the price and availability of transmission services.

To this end, the D.G.T. has expanded the number of access gateways for its information services from 405 in 1982 to 821 in 1983. *Rapport, supra,* at 25.

5. The D.G.T. has made a considerable effort to develop a "carte à mémoire" to facilitate transaction-related services. In 1984, it published a set of specifications for a memory card to be used in banking services; it has been developing a card reader that could be tied into the switched terminals. *Rapport, supra,* at 48. The delicate role for the D.G.T. is to establish protocols and standards that facilitate universal access but do not intrude significantly into the activities of the banking sector. This process—of standard-setting without affecting another industry—warrants closer examination. The active role of the D.G.T. in this area reflects its desire and commitment to expand the utility of the telecommunications infrastructure.

6. By February 1985, after months of wrangling over financial and technical problems, the French banks were expected to have decided to place the first large-scale order for the card, leading eventually to a nationwide cashless banking system.

D. The Transpac Network

The D.G.T. has had an active role in developing Transpac, a public packet-switching network. With 22,000 direct subscribers it is now one of the largest such networks in the world. Transpac's rates are insensitive to distance; its services are intended to stimulate investment in the software, database, and computer processing industry. Its revenues were FFr 250 million in 1983, up 93% in one year. With the introduction of new data services and the spread of electronic terminals, the number of subscribers in 1984 increased by about 70% over the previous year. *See Resultats 1984.* The network is expected to have 50,000 customers by 1987.

E. Telecom-1 Satellite System

1. Telecom-1 is a sophisticated new digital satellite system that will allow the introduction of high-speed links for broadband and wide area digital services, and videoconferencing. The project grew out of extensive coordination and joint planning between the D.G.T., equipment manufacturers, and data service users. The satellite, however, is fully owned and operated by the D.G.T.

2. The Telecom-1A satellite was launched in early August 1984, and became operational on December 1, 1984. One transponder is dedicated to European digital communications, one is leased to the Deutsche Bundespost, three are dedicated for French domestic use, and the remaining transponder is dedicated to analog videoconferencing. The D.G.T. has set up a specific organization, the digital service department, to operate this satellite. The department will seek to offer global digital transmission services using the most appropriate transmission path for each job (*e.g.,* satellite, cable, microwave). FCR is in charge of marketing the service.

3. The satellite covers not only adjacent European countries, but also overseas French departments in the Caribbean and islands off Eastern Canada. French authorities have consistently argued that they have no intention of using this coverage to divert transatlantic traffic and have expressed continued support for retention of the Intelsat monopoly.

F. Broadband Videonetworks

1. The D.G.T. has committed itself to an extremely ambitious program of recabling France with broadband, switched network facilities that can be used for cable television and other services. The cabling plan is intended to stimulate both the manufacturing and the cultural sectors of the French economy. F. Gerin and N. de Tavernost, *From the Biarritz Project to the French Videocommunications,* (1984) (presented at the Advanced Wired Cities Forum, Washington, D.C.). As of the middle of 1984, 160 communities, with a population of more than 14,000,000 people, had expressed an interest in the program. *Id.* at 8.

2. The wiring plan calls for the use of a star-switched network containing fiber optic transmission lines. In 1983, the first orders of cable for the networks were placed. These cables will be used in areas of Paris and Montpellier. *See Rapport, supra,* at 46. It appears, however, that fiber optic cables are still much more expensive than coaxial cables, and some have questioned the choice of an "all optical" design—at least in initial stages. Nevertheless, after lengthy debate, the fiber optic network decision has been reaffirmed, largely due to the greater capacity and versatility that fiber optics will provide.

3. The considerable cost of the operation has required the D.G.T. to seek outside financial investments in the new network facilities. Investors will include the Caisse des Dépôts et Consignations, the public television companies, independent producers, and local actors. *See* T. Vedel, *Local Wiring Policies in France: From Biarritz to Paris,* 12 (1984) (paper presented at the Advanced Wired Cities Forum, Washington D.C.).

G. Future Developments in Infrastructure and Services

1. Concomitantly, the D.G.T. has underway a series of activities to upgrade both local and interexchange network facilities. A substantial part of the strategy is to stimulate the development of the service sectors ancillary to the telecommunications network, rather than to generate competition in the provision of the infrastructure itself. The D.G.T.'s view is that fragmentation of the telecommunications infrastructure will generate divergent standards and diminish access—which will stifle the emergence of important ancillary markets. There is a well-formed, coherent strategy that undergirds the D.G.T.'s approach; it is in contrast to the U.S. or Japanese strategies, which are predicated on directly stimulating the hardware, switching, and network services sectors.

2. Despite the monopoly on the telecommunications infrastructure, the D.G.T. has not decided to market or to develop all network services in the same way. It has, in effect, singled out certain service categories (*i.e.*, packet-switching and digital services) for marketing through its subsidiaries.

3. Value-added services are all (except for the electronic directory service) provided by entities independent of the D.G.T. using the public switched network. To further its policy of promoting a coherent network that requires little coordination of fragmented parts, the D.G.T. tries to minimize the use of leased lines. In general, leased lines are provided only for highly specialized applications and only if the public network cannot offer satisfactory service. Resale of services and third-party use of leased lines are not permitted.

V. SERVICE-BASED BOUNDARY LINES: THE D.G.T. AND OTHER PROVIDERS

A. Lines of Demarcation Between the D.G.T. and its Subsidiaries

1. As discussed above, the D.G.T. is divided into several operating entities. *See supra* Section II.B. The D.G.T. also has affiliates, or "filiales," which are engaged in providing specific telecommunications services and facilities; they are generally in the form of "société d'économie mixte." *See supra* Section II.C.

2. FCR, the major filiale of the D.G.T, is subject to two separate lines of control. Its stock is held by the Treasury, and its financial operations are subject to control by this Ministry. Technical and operational oversight of FCR is, however, the responsibility of the D.G.T. These varying influences are brought to bear on FCR through its Board, which consists of representatives of the D.G.T. and the Treasury, as well as outside directors.

3. In 1984, two steps were taken by the D.G.T. and FCR with respect to packet-switching and digital services. Transpac services had been provided through a société d'économie mixte that had been two-thirds owned by D.G.T. and one-third by private companies that had been involved in the development of the services. In the spring of 1984, however, the interests of the private entities were acquired by the government, and Transpac was placed under the aegis of FCR.

4. In a related move, the D.G.T. has defined a package of digital services that include Transfix (a data transfer service on specialized lines, which includes the former Transmic service), Transcom (a 64 Kbit/s data transfer service on the standard switched telephone network), and Transdyn (a high-speed data transfer service that includes Telecom-1 services). The assets and networks for these services belong to the D.G.T.; however, the responsibility for marketing these services, and for some net-

work planning activities, is to be vested in FCR. FCR pays the D.G.T. for switching and transmission services but is itself the billing agent for the service. The FCR staff is recruited separately; they are not civil servants on the D.G.T. payroll. They will, however, work closely with the DOTs. In essence, the FCR group will function as a "reseller" of D.G.T. services within the D.G.T. structure.

5. It is significant that current plans do not call for an integration of the Transpac packet-switching services with the other new digital services being marketed. The reasons for this may be complex. Transpac is a service with a widely-established customer base; it must operate in light of these relationships. By contrast, the new high-speed digital services are oriented to a small, but emerging, business sector. They will, in large part, be directed at major customers.

6. FCR is striving to create separate centers for innovation, marketing, and the recruitment of skilled personnel. It may have greater flexibility in offering services that cannot or will not be provided by the D.G.T. due to its status as a public entity. The private subsidiaries may not be so rigidly covered by the PTT Code; thus it may be easier for them to tailor service offerings to specific industrial customers.

7. In essence, the goal is to be flexible—or to "deregulate"—within the structure of the D.G.T. This flexibility is seen as being necessary if the French are to compete vigorously for the business of not only domestic multinationals, but also users of international communications services. A competitive advantage of marketing services through FCR is that the value-added taxes on them can be deducted by business users.

8. Within this framework, FCR cooperates closely with DTRE on international arrangements. DTRE enters into general interconnection agreements with foreign administrations or carriers. Thereafter, FCR or its subsidiaries work out the details of the operational arrangements. For other—domestic—services, cooperation between FCR and the D.G.T. may occur at the local DOT level.

9. Service distinctions are being established by the D.G.T. on the basis of market sectors. Lines are being drawn to target certain new services for businesses, with a special focus on services for the largest users.

10. The pricing of digital services is a sensitive and critical matter. If prices are set too high, demand might not emerge and the new services could lose money. If, however, prices are set too low, there is a risk of having digital services "cream-skim" the D.G.T.'s own business base by drawing customers away from the switched network (or even Transpac services). To this extent, then, the service distinctions represent a series of mechanisms that both create and control some competition within the D.G.T. structure, with separate marketing organizations utilizing common network facilities.

11. There is also a technological underpinning for some of the service distinctions. Digital switching is being used in the construction of an overlay network in D.G.T. facilities; it could become the basis for ISDN

service. For example, there are now approximately twenty ISDN-like exchanges offering multiple service access; about fifty such exchanges are planned for 1985. These exchange facilities will be used as concentrators for the 64 Kbit/s service. Part of the service will involve PABX connections to the network using 2 Mbit/s and 512 Kbit/s digital links. Thus, the D.G.T. will have an institutional vehicle for introducing high-speed services at attractive rates to a class of customers who will be particularly sensitive to economic pressures in the international market.

12. Assessing whether FCR will use its flexibility in areas other than pricing raises some interesting issues. For example, it is not clear what use restrictions might be placed on groups of users that subscribe to large channel configurations. There are a spectrum of such users, ranging from unaffiliated corporate entities and affiliated industry groups, to entities interested in providing a service to users (*i.e.*, data processing or protocol conversion). It is likely that FCR will look extremely closely at any "group" activity that might significantly divert traffic or revenues from D.G.T. services. A certain modest competitive relationship, however, is inherent in the "institutional resale" relationship that has been created. It will, therefore, be interesting to see what latitude the FCR group will have in negotiating specialized arrangements with multinationals to set up transborder networks. For example, an entity could be established to market transborder service on Telecom-1, an activity not previously engaged in by the D.G.T. To date, capacity on Telecom-1 has only been formally offered to Eutelsat for marketing at a European level.

B. Establishing "Fences" Between the "Telecommunications Infrastructure" and "Services"

1. The D.G.T. repeatedly emphasizes its commitment to establishing a "fence" between the "telecommunications infrastructure" and "services." The D.G.T. attempts to distinguish "infrastructure" from "services," to focus attention on its principal concern: establishing an agreement on "transparent" transmission services. By separating transmission functions from other "services," the D.G.T. is seeking to achieve an international consensus on network transmission and interfacing standards. It is also attempting to forestall the acceptance of norms established by an industry or by a single dominant firm. For that reason, the D.G.T. was alarmed by the proposed venture between British Telecom ("BT") and IBM. It was believed that that arrangement could have significantly delayed the prospects in Europe and elsewhere for an agreed-upon interface between transmission and related services.

2. One of the practical difficulties in defining the network/services interface is that the concept of separating "telecommunications," as a transmission function, from "services" on the basis of ISO protocol levels is relatively new. In fact, the concept can be described generally; the distinction may only be meaningful, however, in the context of

specific cases. For example, it might be useful to examine the issue of standard setting in the context of the memory card. What might be the impact of "telecommunications" standards on the higher level protocols that are critical to service delivery by banks and other institutions?

3. Some observers have focused on the issue of where the "nexus" point—for access to the network—should or will be established. One question is whether third parties can perform protocol conversion functions through their terminal equipment or whether some of these functions are to be carried out through "overlay" in the basic transmission network. The D.G.T. does not object to "mailbox" or protocol conversion activities that are performed by a user on behalf of third parties so long as these activities are carried out utilizing the public switched network facilities. The D.G.T. will not, however, currently provide leased lines to establish a network service that offers protocol conversion to third parties.

4. Another important issue is the way in which policies on user access to the service provider are set forth. French regulatory policies in this area have been stated clearly—in principle. Their application in practice, however, has not been delineated in a detailed way in published rules and regulations. In this respect, the practice of the D.G.T. differs significantly from that of the Deutsche Bundespost, which maintains a detailed set of rules and regulations. The absence of comparable documentation in France has its advantages and disadvantages. The French approach may be more receptive to interpretations of use that are flexible or are evolving, within the context of rather firmly worded principles about the permissible boundaries. The degree of institutional innovation within the D.G.T. structure, however (through the use of FCR and other affiliates), implies that existing administrative practices may not be rigidly applied. There are quasi-independent centers of decisionmaking that can and do propose unconventional or ad hoc arrangements regarding the use of basic transmission services.

5. The absence of current statements on user access may, however, leave the policy of the D.G.T. shrouded in some uncertainty. Such ambiguity may be an impediment to users who would otherwise want to innovate in using the network infrastructure.

6. As noted earlier, *see supra* Section III., the boundary line that defines the limit of D.G.T. "monopoly" services is critical not only to outsiders, but also to the D.G.T. itself. The D.G.T. has taken the position that it may engage in certain competitive activities—such as data processing or software activities—through Télesystèmes, which is owned and controlled by FCR.

7. Télésystèmes is allegedly structured to conduct business on an arm's-length basis with the D.G.T.—or in some cases with sister affiliates, such as Transpac. Like its competitors, Télésystèmes obtains services on a tariffed basis. There is, however, an exchange of personnel among Télésystèmes and the other D.G.T.-related entities. The company is making some serious marketing efforts in what is a highly competitive sector. Entities that compete directly with Télésystèmes are not, however, completely

convinced that its pricing practices involve no cross-subsidies or that its relationships are adequately "arm's length."

8. In addition to data processing, the D.G.T. has indicated that certain teleservice activities (*i.e.*, alarm services) can be provided on cable, can be offered by D.G.T. directly, or even by others acting on D.G.T.'s behalf. The protocols and procedures for providing facilities to third parties have not been completely established. They also have not been settled with regard to the provision of similar services to D.G.T. and to its affiliates. If cable telecommunications systems are ever to be in a position to market services other than broadband television, these protocol issues will need to be addressed.

C. Boundary Lines for Information-Related Services

1. Under the July 29, 1982, Law on Audiovisual Communication, users of telecommunications services can freely offer certain transaction-related services. A review of the law and related interpretive material suggests that French policy essentially has established an unregulated zone for certain services. Some of these unregulated services may, in traditional terms, be viewed as third-party or message switching services within the telecommunications monopoly. Others, however, such as information services, may be both outside the terms of the Audiovisual Law and also apparently not within the boundaries of traditional monopoly services. The treatment of these "unregulated" services is left uncertain by the law: they may be freely permitted or absolutely prohibited.

2. The Audiovisual Law establishes that the audiovisual communications (by cable or broadcasting), to the public of writing, sounds, images, documents, or messages of any kind shall be free. N. Canile and A. Dunley, *Audiovisual Law of July 29, 1982: An Interpretation* (1982).

a. Article 8 provides that the State establishes—or authorizes—transmission facilities for broadcasting and audiovisual communication, and applies to facilities that cross private property.

b. Article 3 states that the provision of audiovisual communication services to the public is subject either to filing a declaration or to obtaining an authorization under Articles 77 and 78.

c. Article 78 refers to broadcast services (*i.e.*, any service that is not interactive, such as teletext,) and the cinematographic services. These are subject to prior authorization.

d. Article 77 applies to interactive services. It provides that the provision of services to the public or to categories of the public whereby a user asks for writings, sounds, audiovisual images or documents or messages and only receives in return the information demanded is subject to prior declaration. This article also provides that, as a transitional measure, these services will be subject to prior authorization until a certain date, to be fixed by Decree, which may not be later than January 1, 1986.

3. A threshold question—necessary to defining the purview of Article 77—is what the law means by distribution "to the public." Neither the explicit terms of the law nor any subject clauses clarify to what extent the prior registration requirement applies to specialized databases distributed to narrow classes of users or closed user groups.

4. A significant period of time elapsed between the time of the Law's passage and the release of interpretive guidance regarding its provisions. In January 1983, a Commission du Suivi des Expériences Télématiques Destinées au Public (Monitoring Commission) issued an Interim Report which proposed that regulatory measures be adopted to complete and to clarify the Audiovisual Law. *See French Audiovisual Revolution, supra,* at 423-24. More significantly, however, a number of decrees and an administrative circular were issued in January 1984; they have established substantive criteria for the application of the law as well as administrative procedures.

a. Decree No. 84-58, issued January 17, 1984, establishes an Advisory Commission consisting of representatives from the PTT, the Secretary of State for Communications, the Ministry of the Interior and Decentralization, two deputies, two Senators, a representive of the municipalities, the written press, representatives of consumers and labor, and audiovisual experts. The chairman of this Commission, which began work in June 1984, is a member of the Conseil d'Etat. The Commission is to be consulted before any prior authorization issued under Articles 77 or 78 is refused or is granted on conditions. It is also to be consulted before any prior authorization is withdrawn. The Commission is intended to offer general advice on the authorization of interactive services.

b. Decree No. 84-59 provides that the actual demand under Article 77 is to be filed with the Commissaires de la République of the Départment where the applicant has its registered office. The authorization is granted by the Secretary of State for Communications. The procedure is intended to be pro forma. The local officials have a month to indicate whether the application is complete. Once a file is complete, the application is deemed granted if no reply is received within a two-month period. The deliberative period can be extended to four months when the Advisory Commission is consulted. The Commission must act within a specified period of time. *Circulaire d'application du décret No. 84-59,* Journal Officiel, Jan. 17, 1984.

5. The entire prior authorization procedure is, as mentioned earlier, interim. This interim procedure is generally viewed as establishing a window within which the written press can adapt to the impact of the new information services. For, during the transition period only the written press and press agencies can offer videotex services, which are to include classified advertisements. *The French Audiovisual Revolution, supra,* at 425.

6. Administrative interpretations of the law have also sought to clarify the scope of some excluded services. Article 1 of Decree No. 84-59 excludes from the purview of Article 77 interactive services that have the

character of private correspondence or are wholly within a single organization, administration, professional organization, or enterprise. These services are not subject to the prior declaration requirement because they are not considered to be services "to the public or to categories of the public". The circulaire d'application discussed above also clarifies the types of service that are excluded from Article 77. *See also The French Audiovisual Revolution, supra,* at 930; J. Huet, *Droit de l'informatique: le régime juridique de la télématique interactive* (1984). There are three categories of interactive communication services that are excluded from the purview of the law. J. Huet, *supra,* at 16:

a. *Personal communications.* These are electronic mail transfer services between two or more users, or services whereby the user produces for its own use original information, such as videogames or computer assisted design. Where, however, messages are not specifically directed to an addressee, the line of exclusion is unclear. In particular, there is some ambiguity with respect to closed user groups.

b. *Communications inside an organization.* These include messages inside a company, administration, or professional organization, as well as external computer-processing services performed for the needs of the organization.

c. *Services with a commercial character allowing the user to perform different transactions.* These include personal transactional services such as placing an order, making a travel reservation, or engaging in personal banking transactions.

7. The law does not make it clear how to treat "hybrid services," which include data, information as well as transactions. It would appear that a primary or principal purpose test is evolving to minimize the scope of prior authorization. At least one interpretation, however, contends that such a test will not be applied. Under this view, a service including any component that is within the scope of Article 77 will be considered subject to the law. *See The French Audiovisual Revolution, supra,* at 435.

8. The issues raised by the interpretation of the Audiovisual Law require considerable attention. There is already a significant body of existing interpretative material. *See, e.g.,* J. Huet, *Droit de l'informatique: le régime juridique de la télématique interactive,* 3147 Semaine Juridique (1984); J. Huet, *La modification du droit sous l'influence de l'informatique: aspects de droit privé,* 3095 Semaine Juridique (1983); D. Trucher, *Une loi de la dernière chance? La loi du 29 juillet 1982 sur la communication audiovisuelle,* 3120 Semaine Juridique (1983). This brief discussion is intended to provide only an overview of the major issues.

9. There is also a question as to how one-way teletext services fit into the structure of the Audiovisual Law. (The French teletext service, ANTIOPE, is transmitted over broadcast or cable television. Developed by TDF, it can be received on a standard television set by using a decoder.) Decree No. 84-60 provides that "services de vidéographie diffusée" are subject to prior authorization by the Secretary of State for Communications. At the threshold, it is not clear what services, if any, might be considered

private service offerings and, hence, be excluded from the scope of videotex services. The Cahier des Charges Type attached to the Decree, however, prescribed some of the basic terms applicable to videotex services. The furnishing of service must be authorized by the Secretary of State for Communications, who has jurisdiction over cable carriage, not the Haute Autorité. The service is, however, subject to agreement with the providers of broadcast or cable service. These agreements can define the condition of distribution; it is not certain just how the agreements can have definitive regulatory consequences. In this respect, videotex services differ from interactive telecommunications services. With respect to the latter services, the provider of the underlying transmission service would appear to have little or no influence over the terms and conditions of provision of service.

10. Article 4 of the Cahier des Charges limits the ability to furnish services supported by classified advertisements to press entities alone. With respect to such services, revenues from advertisements cannot exceed 80% of total financing. Article 12, Cahier des Charges.

11. The Audiovisual Law creates for interactive videotex services a regime for prior authorization that is more restrictive than the status quo ante—even though it was the general intent of the Law to create a more open, insulated regulatory environment for broadcasting services. Audiovisual services have been tossed into the mix; many observers believe that a careful reevaluation of this regulatory scheme is warranted when the interim authorization procedures expire on January 1, 1986.

12. The French regulatory scheme has aspects of overbreadth that are characteristic of efforts in other countries to create a more liberal regime for new communications services. The failure to distinguish between "information-" and "communications-related" services means that information services that would largely be free of any regulatory control, when provided on a print basis, instead become entangled in a web of regulation and licensing. It is difficult to separate the dissemination of information by electronic means from its use as part of a transaction-related service. It may, therefore, be useful to establish lines of demarcation that prevent regulatory "spillover" into the area of pure "information" services.

13. At a more fundamental level, it is important to define and to clarify the economic relationships between the print and new electronic media. The primary public policy concern would appear to be the role of new media in advertising. It is not evident, however, that the new media represent any basic threat to the existing advertising base of print publications. Even if they did, it is not clear that regulatory control over the new media—and their potential service to the public—is in the best interests of consumers.

14. Clearly, regulatory and legal policies in this area are in a state of evolution. The French government is about to issue a new set of policy guidelines that will affect the provision of full channel or broadband information services on cable.

15. Current regulatory policy allows significant latitude for the provision of new media and transaction-related services independent of telecommunications-related regulation. This flexibility, however, may now be somewhat constrained by a licensing regime that will shape the role of new electronic media services and, in particular, their relationship to the print, broadcast, and cable media.

D. Definition of Cable Television Services

1. Cable television services in France will be developed through novel local institutional structures, the so-called Société Locale d'Exploitation du Câble ("SLEC"). The role of the SLEC, however, is sandwiched between that of the D.G.T. and TDF. The discussion that follows briefly examines the role of the SLEC and focuses on some areas where policy is still in a state of evolution.

2. The SLEC's role is as an intermediary—to arrange for subscribers, to market, and to arrange programming. On August 1, 1984, Loi No. 84-783 was enacted to clarify a number of aspects relating to the management of the SLEC. Journal Officiel, Aug. 2, 1984. The chairman of the managing board must be a representative of the local community. The representative of the State in the local department, however, is responsible for ensuring that the SLEC conforms to its cahier des charges. This official is empowered to force a reconsideration of any decision taken by the SLEC.

3. The SLEC is to operate with a certain amount of private financing; the largest source of such financing will be from public entities, such as the Caisse des Dépôts et Consignations and the Lyon Water Company. These entities traditionally have financed investments in local infrastructures (*i.e.*, sewers and other local developments). Now they are being involved in financing a local communications infrastructure. Although these entities will be offering financing, they will not have direct control over the local facilities. Generally, funds are being provided to cities as reimbursable advances to capitalize local cable development. Notwithstanding the insulation of financing and control, many observers believe that institutions such as the Caisse des Dépôts will play a significant role in the development of new local communications systems.

4. Private companies cannot, according to Article 80 of the Audiovisual Law, participate in the financing of more than one cable operating company or other radio or television company. An amendment has been submitted to the House to raise this limit to five.

5. The Caisse des Dépôts plans to offer management advisory service to cable operators and, through its subsidiaries, it will be in a position to offer software and systems for interactive services. As an investor, the Caisse will take an interest in expanding the base of service sufficient to assure a return on investment. For its part, the D.G.T. will be wary of losing

control over the mechanism for providing new information services. Lacan, *Le Savoir-faire de la Caisse des Dépôts*, Le Monde, March 22, 1984; Lacan, *Les Enjeux politiques*, Le Monde, May 2, 1984.

6. The D.G.T. will be responsible for installing and planning the new cable communications networks. It is now in the process of negotiating the general terms of the agreements with local municipalities. These agreements will specify the price to be paid by the SLEC to the D.G.T.; they will generally require payment on a per subscriber basis based on projections as to the penetration of the cable system. Thus, the SLEC and the D.G.T. will be negotiating a formula to share the risks of developing cable.

a. One of the more important issues to be addressed deals with the price for each cable connection. The current design of the system involves drop lines from a switching center that will, despite the broadband capacity of the fiber optic trunks, only be able to transport, at the initial stage, one television signal at a time. At a later stage, the drop line will be able to carry at least two signals by using the "wavelength multiplexing process." The advantage of this system is that the network can be upgraded without reengineering the trunk system.

b. Another important pricing and service-related issue concerns the charges to the SLEC for the provision of ancillary or interactive services. These arrangements and contractual provisions will determine the scope of the SLEC's activity and the likelihood that it can develop income from non-broadcast-related activities.

7. Pressuring the SLEC from another direction is TDF, which is responsible for local and intercity transmission of broadcast programming. An outstanding issue between the SLEC and TDF is whether TDF will own and operate the cable head-end or merely the satellite receiving capability. In either case, TDF will be responsible for setting up the receiving site of the head-end station. It also will operate the cable system—if the SLEC so requests.

a. It should be noted, however, that the D.G.T. reserves for itself the right to lease the antennas for receiving point-to-point satellite transmissions, which are part of the telecommunications monopoly. DBS reception, by contrast, is free.

b. Furthermore, as part of the operation of the distribution network, the D.G.T. will provide the long-distance transport of programs from any part of France and programs of European origin. This service, limited to five programs, is included in the price paid by the SLEC to the D.G.T. If more programs are desired (and are allowed by the Haute Autorité or the government), the SLEC would have to pay an additional price.

8. On May 31, 1983, a protocol was signed between TDF and D.G.T. relating to their respective roles in providing cable television services. TDF and D.G.T., however, have, in other areas, been in a position of conflict over, *e.g.*, the future role of the TDF broadcasting satellite, TDF-1, and whether a second satellite would be constructed. TDF itself operates in a

complex web of relationships. It is responsible to the Secretary of State for Communications, who is responsible for authorizing the signals that may be carried on cable systems. TDF also takes technical direction from the D.G.T. with respect to many aspect of its operations, although TDF's role was to establish a line of separation between broadcasting and telecommunications. Thus, the emergence of new media technologies, such as cable and other satellites, has placed strains on these old boundary lines. At the same time, cable television is caught between two rival institutions, each wanting to provide transmission services for the new service.

9. The SLEC, therefore, will have to operate in a complicated set of legal and institutional relationships.

a. It will have a significant financial and advisory relationship with the Caisse des Dépôts.

b. It will be licensed by the D.G.T. to operate the network exclusively. In addition, the D.G.T. will grant it nonexclusive rights to operate interactive services, such as teletext, teleshopping, and telealarm, on a potentially competitive basis.

c. The SLEC must also develop a relationship with TDF that will establish the terms and conditions of the program distribution services.

d. The SLEC must obtain from the Secretary of State for Communications the authorization to install the audiovisual communication equipment (under Article 8 of the Audiovisual Law).

e. The SLEC must obtain an authorization from the Haute Autorité to provide local (*i.e.*, within a radius of 30 kilometers) radio and television services. For services extending beyond this area, an authorization from the Secretary of State for Communications must be requested.

f. The Audiovisual Law and the decrees of January 17, 1984 provide, as discussed above, *see supra*, Section V.D., a system of authorization or of prior declaration for videotex and teletext services.

g. The SLEC, thus, has three important contractual relationships—with the D.G.T., the Caisse des Dépôts, and TDF—and requires four separate regulatory authorizations. Its position in the French regulatory scene is, therefore, unique.

10. A "cahier des charges générales" for cable radio and television services contains various obligations. Thus, the SLEC must devote at least 15% of its television capacity to programs that it produces; only 30% of the radio and television capacity can be used for programs coming from foreign organizations. A compulsory time schedule is provided regarding the distribution of cinematographic works as well as a minimum quota of films coming from Community countries (70%) and a minimum quota of original French-speaking films (50%).

11. Given the unique posture of the SLEC, some speculation about its future role and evolution is warranted. Some observers believe that the SLEC's role is antiquated and will disappear with time. In an era with capability for "on demand" selection of programming by users, they see no

need for an intermediary or an editor selecting video and audiovisual programming. These appraisals may overlook the ongoing problems of marketing cable services and the likelihood that selection of programming by an intermediary can actually be eliminated in the future. Another scenario suggests that the SLEC might become an independent force in the marketing and development of local services. As an investor in the new local plant, the SLEC might demand more control; with the participation of technically competent entities—such as the Caisse de Dépôts—it might seek wider latitude to market new local information services utilizing the local plant.

12. The potential for reselling wideband channels licensed by the SLEC may generate another problematic issue. Of course, existing policies with respect to channel use and the role of the D.G.T. would preclude such practices. It may be relevant, however, to speculate whether decentralization through the creation of the SLEC might not eventually create pressure for more diverse marketing control over local network services. It may be difficult, in short, to confine the SLEC to cable service when broadband capacity can be utilized for voice and data services. In an ironic way, the emergence of broadband networks might not reinforce the influence of the traditional service providers but might permit more diversified structures of control over the service.

VI. INSTITUTIONAL ASPECTS OF FRENCH TELECOMMUNICATIONS POLICY

A. Introduction

The institutional relationships for developing French telecommunications policy are complex. The D.G.T., however, retains a rather central and autonomous role within the structure of the French government. The central element of that autonomy derives from the Charte de Gestion (the Management Charter) that the D.G.T. concludes with the Council of Ministers. In addition to the Charte, some of the other important influences on telecommunications policy are described below.

B. Key Institutional Relationships

1. Charte de Gestion

a. This agreement is essentially a long-term management charter that establishes the rules for management as well as the benchmarks and objectives for the D.G.T. for the period between 1983 and 1986. The current plan was executed on February 2, 1980; it was incorporated into the "Deuxième loi de développement économique, social, et culturel 1984-1988," the Ninth Plan that was approved by the Parliament on December 24, 1983.

b. The plan establishes a goal of preventing telecommunications prices from increasing in excess of the overall economic price level. As discussed above, however, *see supra* Section I.E., the Government, despite the plan, increased the telephone rates on August 1, 1984 by more than 10% (following an earlier, more limited, rate increase). The plan also establishes a ceiling on external financing.

c. In terms of service objectives, the plan establishes a goal of 24.5 million lines by 1986 (versus 19.5 million in 1983); 50% of subscribers on digital switches by 1986 (versus 15% in 1982); 3 million videotex terminals in 1986 (versus almost none in 1982); two million cable subscribers by 1985 as well as other goals. In essence, the plan is a multi-year agreement that is intended to establish the overall relationship between the budget of the D.G.T. and the general budget of the State.

2. Cabinet Relationships

a. Under the cabinet arrangements of the Fabius government, the Minister of the PTT, Louis Mexandeau, reports through the Minister of Industrial Redeployment and Foreign Trade, Edith Cresson. Within the Ministry of Industry is DIELI, on whose initiative the government adopted the five-year "Filière Electronique." As significant as is the "Filière Electronique" in terms of its impact on the structure of the French electronics and computer industry, neither it nor the Minister of Industry has exercised significant influence on the evolution of telecommunications policy. In this respect, the French structure is similar and dissimilar to that of the Japanese. There is no substantial evidence that the Ministry of Industry has been pressing for significant change in telecommunications policy, as was the case in Japan. On the contrary, there is a tradition of autonomy among the various Ministries, which tend to operate in separate spheres of influence. In this regard it is interesting that, in 1983, the DAII in the D.G.T. was awarded significant new authority to oversee and supervise developments in the French telecommunications and computer industry. Hence, the D.G.T. retains the authority to focus French telecommunications policy on industrial policy objectives.

b. The Minister of the PTT and the Secretary of State for Communications have established relatively independent areas of influence and do not seem to be in significant conflict. The jurisdiction of the Secretary of State for Communications is over issues concerning the content of communications—such as the carriage of distant signals by cable systems and the authorization of one-way videotex services on cable. By contrast, the PTT has responsibility for the development of the telecommunications infrastructure for cable and other services.

c. A main point of conflict regards the role of TDF, which is overseen both by the Secretary of State for Communications, in his capacity as having responsibility for the content of communications, and by the D.G.T., with respect to technical matters. The controversy between the D.G.T. and TDF has intensified over the construction of the TDF-1 and 2 broadcast satellites; ultimately, there were efforts to mediate the dispute through an advisory report of the former Director General of the D.G.T., Gerard Théry. *See* Rohde, *La Voix Médiane de M. Théry*, Le Monde, March 14, 1984.

d. As far as the development of cable television services are concerned, an interministerial committee, La Mission TV Cable, has been established. *See* Le Décret, Dec. 19, 1983, sur le développement des services de communication audiovisuelle diffusés par câble. This entity is charged with attempting to develop programming resources for cable and assist the cities in the development of cable telecommunications services.

e. There exist, as well, mechanisms for the resolution of interministerial disputes through advisers in the office of the Prime Minister or the Conseil d'Etat.

3. *Haute Autorité*

a. The High Authority was established by the Audiovisual Law to issue licenses to, and oversee the operation of, radio and television stations. It will have a role in approving the provision of local video program services. Its role in cable development has been severely restricted. It will not decide what distant television signals are to be carried or even license full channel videotex services. These responsibilities are vested with the Secretary of State for Communications. As noted above, the request for prior authorization of interactive services must be filed with local authorities under the oversight of the Advisory Commission, *see supra* Section V.C.4., with the power to grant such authorization vested in the Secretary of State for Communications.

b. Recently, the Haute Autorité has become enmeshed in a controversy over the appointment of the head of one of the French television networks. In the view of many observers, its influence is significantly on the wane.

4. *Local Authorities*

Despite recent initiatives in the direction of decentralization, France has, historically, been an extremely centralized state. France has, therefore, not been beset with the jurisdictional issues that have complicated telecommunications decisionmaking in Germany, Canada, and, to a lesser extent, the U.S. Local officials will have only limited control over cable television developments although, as noted above, it is possible that the influence of the SLECs may grow in the future.

5. *A Look Toward the Future*

a. The dynamic center of French telecommunications policy is very much the D.G.T. There are no major competing centers of influence, a situation that is not likely to change unless telecommunications policy becomes a central tenet of economic planning of the present or a new government. Even in that event the French civil service does not have a strong tradition of combative interrelationships among the Ministries. It is, of course, possible that telecommunications policy—along with decentralization and deregulation—could become a major theme of the position of the opposition. If the opposition should prevail in the 1986 parliamentary election, the legislature might increasingly become a focal point of debate on telecommunications policy. The impact of legislative developments on telecommunications policy, however, would depend on the relationship between the French Presidency and the legislature in the event that these two sectors of power were under separate control.

b. If the legislature were to emerge as a policymaking organ, there would be increased pressure on telecommunications policy from other institutional centers of influence. Those centers, as noted before, would seem to include the banking sector, institutions such as the Caisse des Dépôts, and, through the SLECs, local municipalities. These institutional pressures are likely to be augmented by the business community and user sectors, which might want to expand from manufacturing into service sectors. At the present time these pressures do not exist because those economic sectors operate within a relatively managed environment.

VII. INTERNATIONAL IMPLICATIONS

A. The D.G.T. has had a leading role in developing a European-wide perspective on telecommunications policy issues. It has promoted the integration of European markets through standardization activities and has urged a European focus to industrial policy in the telecommunications area. The Director General of the D.G.T., Jacques Dondoux, has forcefully articulated his concern that recent ventures linking European and U.S. companies would undermine a truly European approach. *See* J. Dondoux, *Towards a European Telecommunications Market,* (presented at World Telecommunication Conference, London) (Dec. 11, 1984).

B. The D.G.T. has focused, in particular, on how European PTTs should respond to the efforts by U.S. carriers to open new interconnection agreements. It has attempted to prevent the various PTTs from being set against one another through unrestricted "transiting" of services from one European country to another. In the aftermath of the agreement by the Belgian R.T.T. to interconnect with MCI, the D.G.T. hopes to encourage an orderly structure for negotiations with the new carriers.

C. Promoting maximum commonality in technical transmission and equipment standards is another important prong of French international telecommunications policy. The French view is that international standards should work to open markets to European service providers and manufacturers and should encourage industrial developments in Europe. For this reason, the French voiced strong opposition to the proposed BT-IBM venture, which would have promoted IBM's network transmission standards—not the ISO standard favored by European PTTs. It is a key tenet of French policy that standards should be determined in the public arena and tied to French national and European policy goals, and not flow from the marketplace influence of a dominant supplier. This policy is viewed as promoting competition and creating a wider range of choices and options for users. The French are supportive of the European Community's establishment of common infrastructure projects in Europe as one means of promoting standardization and stimulating European industry.

D. The D.G.T. has been extremely critical of other European countries that have restricted procurement to their domestic markets. BT's exclusion of all Community suppliers from its short list for production of a new digital switch triggered vigorous protests in France. The D.G.T. has also pressed the European Commission and the Deutsche Bundespost directly for a more open approach to procurement and network interconnection practices.

E. French industrial and international policies are closely linked through the activities of the DAII. The D.G.T. has been extremely aggressive and effective in marketing its presence, not only in the major industrial markets, but in the developing world as well. Alcatel-Thomson has sold its electronic switches to more than fifty countries worldwide, totaling 17 million lines operational or on order. Thomson-CSF has sold "intelligent" telephones to U.S. companies. The list of marketing achievements is lengthy and is evidence of how to marshal effectively an international effort.

F. In addition to its focus on European integration, France has been extremely sensitive to the impact of the telecommunications policies of the industrialized nations on trade and telecommunications relations with the Third World. This global perspective stems from the French interest in international affairs generally; it is, however, also significant in terms of advancing French trade and industrial interests. Perhaps more effectively than their trading partners in Europe or the U.S., the French have demonstrated an ability to link an international telecommunications policy with an international business strategy. Thus, the strategic perspective that underlies the French approach has a strong dose of pragmatism.

G. In this regard, the D.G.T. avails itself of new market opportunities whenever possible, responding aggressively to pricing changes and other competitive developments in the international market. In response to rate reductions by MCI and GTE/Sprint on their international links—particularly between the U.S. and the U.K.—the D.G.T. has reduced its own prices for transatlantic service, to avoid the siphoning of traffic to the U.K. FCR is participating in the installation of the SEA-ME-WE (South East Asia, Middle East, Western Europe) undersea link. The D.G.T. also has a 20% ownership interest in ARGO, a U.S. company that is marketing services in the U.S. and will offer certain high-speed data services in conjunction with the D.G.T. The D.G.T. has a wholly-owned subsidiary in the U.S. and is, thereby, developing market opportunities and experience.

H. In the satellite area, France is the first European country to operate its own domestic communications satellite—Telecom-1. With TDF, it also will have its own DBS satellite. France has now unequivocally committed itself to maintaining the integrity of the Intelsat system. At the same time, the increasing international presence of the D.G.T. allows it to respond to changing international conditions. Consequently, should Intelsat acquiesce in the effort to establish private, competitive satellite systems (or should it succumb to pressure from member countries), France would be well-positioned to participate in the new market in light of the experience in the satellite business that it has gained with Telecom-1. It also seems possible that Telecom-1 could be the basis for imaginative European joint ventures to market transborder information services.

VIII. THE FRENCH PERSPECTIVE ON ISSUES OF STRUCTURE AND COMPETITION

A. Introduction

The formulation of French telecommunications policy involves a coherent and carefully crafted set of perspectives on issues of institutional and industry structure as well as competitive relationships. The key elements of that strategy are briefly delineated below.

B. Central Policy Tenets

1. Development of the Network Infrastructure

The D.G.T. has engaged in an extensive effort over the past decade to modernize and upgrade the telecommunications infrastructure. It has focused on making available a network with a set of protocols that will facilitate the development of new services. It has, therefore, disfavored policies or initiatives that would disrupt centralized network planning or lead to a diversity of standards for the interconnection of equipment.

2. Focus on Competition in the "Service" or Software Sectors

The D.G.T. has deemphasized the concept of competition in the provision of backbone or switching facilities, forsaking the spur that such competition might generate in the hardware manufacturing sector. Instead, it has attempted to encourage investment in the software sector by investment in a network of terminals or in the expansion of Transpac services, which are priced on a basis insensitive to distances.

3. Establishment of Internal, Competitive Relationships

The D.G.T. has utilized imaginatively a group of affiliated sociétés d'économie mixte to provide new services on a flexible basis. These entities can be managed and operated as if they were profit-making businesses in the private sector, often recruiting special staff who could not be attracted, adequately compensated, or promoted in the civil service. Using a private entity also allows greater capability to make special service arrangements or set prices in relationship to marketplace developments. More importantly, the separate subsidiary structure can exercise some competitive influence in the ranks of the D.G.T. itself. As noted above, *see supra* Section V.A.11., the pricing of high-speed data services is a delicate matter. If prices are set too high, services will not develop and the new subsidiaries will be business failures. If too low, the subsidiaries will attract traffic from existing D.G.T. services. In this respect, the subsidiaries may operate as an internal competitive spur to the D.G.T., much as Mercury has operated as an external prod to British Telecom.

4. *Establishing a Core Management Strategy*

a. For the past decade the D.G.T. has increasingly emphasized the entrepreneurial aspect of its dual role as an administration and as an enterprise of an industrial or entrepreneurial character. *See Les Télécommunications Française, supra,* at 64.

b. Thus, it has taken steps to reorganize FCR as a small holding company that is responsible for developing an entrepreneurial strategy for the various companies that it owns and operates. FCR has been given more latitude to function under the direction of its board through relationships at the local operational level of the D.G.T.

c. At the same time there has been an effort to segregate D.G.T.'s role as the regulator of industry relationships. Thus, it may be more independent, and able to arbitrate issues involving its subsidiaries in business sectors outside the area of its telecommunications monopoly.

d. Equally important, the D.G.T. has attempted to maintain some degree of autonomy and control over its investment strategy through a long-term management plan. There was, therefore, considerable concern in mid-1984, when the government unilaterally increased the telephone rates in order to raise revenues. This increase had the effect of disrupting various D.G.T. management projections based on assumptions about the pricing of services.

e. The D.G.T. also desires a greater degree of autonomy in managing and pricing services. It is the view of many that the D.G.T., in the coming years, will have to take steps to reprice local and interexchange services. The international market, where profit margins are being squeezed by competition, is the source of some of the pressure to reprice. A loss of profits in that market requires revenue adjustments in other services. There is additional pressure due to the D.G.T.'s sensitivity to the pricing of domestic services in France as compared with that in other countries. Multinational entities are looking at the cost of operations as a major factor in decisions about where to locate switching and other facilities. The steps to market Telecom-1 services aggressively through a subsidiary clearly reflect the D.G.T.'s intention to respond to this international competition.

5. *Repricing Services*

The D.G.T.'s efforts to construct an overlay ISDN network are also a response to the need to be flexible, both in pricing and in offering specially tailored service to major business users. At the same time, the D.G.T. is moving to implement usage-sensitive charging for local services. J. Damlamian, "Monopole et dérèglemention: le point de vue français," (Nov. 11, 1983).

6. *Diversifying Financing for the Network*

The D.G.T. has been very effective in raising its level of self-financing over the past decade. Now, however, it is facing increasingly difficult challenges in financing an array of new and potentially risky projects, such as the cabling of France and the digitization of the network. Thus, it has sought outside financing for cable through the SLECs; the question might well be whether these entities, with their role in system financing, might exercise a liberalizing influence on the D.G.T. The same assessment might be made of the role of the "filiales" in the management structure. These entities may seek to move somewhat autonomously by virtue of their separate status. It is also possible, however, that they might begin to seek outside financing through investment or joint venture arrangements.

C. Other Perspectives on Structural Issues

1. Telecommunications policy issues are becoming an increasingly important part of a national political dialogue on economic policy. *See* P. Mentre, Le Monde, Nov. 13, 1984. Deregulation of telecommunications is becoming intertwined in a broader dialogue about loosening economic controls on the French economy.

2. What is interesting about recent developments at the D.G.T. is that they represent a flexible and pragmatic approach toward industry structure. As such, they may seem in line with the views of Prime Minister Fabius who, in his previous position as Minister of Industry, had had oversight responsibility for the PTT. The D.G.T. approach certainly does not reflect a doctrinaire vision of providing services through a public administration.

3. As the parliamentary election approaches in 1986, the views of key members of the opposition party might have some bearing on future telecommunications policy developments.

4. The exact contours of opposing views have only begun to crystalize. *See* "Des schémas opposès," Le Monde, May 16, 1984. Some believe that the D.G.T. should be restricted to its monopoly services alone, and that value-added services should be offered on a competitive basis. *Id.* Some policy analysts stress the need to undertake a basic reexamination of the structure of the D.G.T. They would focus, for example, on proposals to separate the post and telecommunications roles—a position that had been explored but not implemented during the previous government. The opposition might well consider continuing the trend toward establishing subsidiaries by spinning off some of the activities of FCR or, at least, by allowing increased levels of private investment in such entities. There are even some who urge a careful review of the U.K. approach of authorizing a new long-haul transmission service. These ideas are, however, still very much tenta-

tive and exploratory, and, of course, irrelevant to the realities of day-to-day decisionmaking within the D.G.T.

IX. CONCLUSION

A. Using a decentralized organizational structure, the D.G.T. has worked to inject innovation into its monopoly over the nation's transmission infrastructure. The D.G.T.'s subsidiaries add greater sophistication and diversity to its services and spur the D.G.T. to be as efficient as possible. It may be increasingly difficult and important, however, to delineate the lines of separation between the subsidiaries' activities and the core infrastructure of the D.G.T. It is also essential that rules of engagement between the subsidiaries' activities and those of the private sector be established in the information services and equipment field.

B. The increasing sophistication of services, which invariably makes it more difficult to separate communications and processing, will add to the complexity of defining the outer limits of the "transmission" monopoly. As the D.G.T. seeks to achieve a "universal" transmission infrastructure for new electronic services, it may find its interests and those of other business sectors—in banking and transactional services, for example—in potential conflict as technical or network standards restructure those sectors.

C. The difficulties in applying the Audiovisual Law to hybrid information transaction services suggest some problems of categorization in the competitive services market. As these definitional issues are confronted, though, the D.G.T. will use its unique approach to organizing a monopoly communications administration to enhance the capabilities of the French network.

D. The D.G.T. has promoted an aggressive and well-developed French telecommunications industry that competes actively with the liberalized regimes in the U.S., the U.K., and Japan. The French have a tough, pragmatic, and market-oriented view of developments on the international telecommunications scene. On the basis of that view, they have defined a strategic response that focuses on the development of the European market and is extremely attentive to the impact of telecommunications developments in the industrialized countries on developing nations—both from the standpoint of the broader national interest and French industrial policy concerns.

E. The French experience is an instructive example of a flexible, coordinated, and innovative response by a public telecommunications entity to the challenges of a new era in the telecommunications field.

CHAPTER IX
FEDERAL REPUBLIC OF GERMANY

TABLE OF CONTENTS

CHAPTER IX
FEDERAL REPUBLIC OF GERMANY

I. INTRODUCTION AND OVERVIEW

A. The Deutsche Bundespost

1. The Deutsche Bundespost ("DBP") is, by most measures, not only the largest entity in Germany—the largest investor and one of the biggest employers—but also the largest in all of Europe. The DBP, which clearly is one of the most important telecommunications organizations in the world, now is faced with change and with uncertainty in the European and the international telecommunications markets.

2. The size and the prominence of the DBP, and its firm adherence to maintaining the technical integrity and the economic effficiency of the German network, have made it the subject of great scrutiny, and often of criticism, within Germany, Europe, and the international community. Indeed, over the past ten years, the DBP may have been one of the most studied institutions in Germany—having been reviewed by the KtK Commission from 1973-1976, and having been the subject of a 1980 report of the Conference of Länder Economics Ministers, a 1981 study by the Monopoly Commission, and a 1981 report of the Enquete Commission. *See infra* Section II. These commissions examined the role of the DBP in providing telecommunications equipment, and some recommended that the DBP be excluded from that market entirely.

3. Through this review process, the DBP has marshaled the arguments for its continued presence in the market—expanding consumer choice and providing smaller manufacturers with another distribution channel. In the end, despite the studies, little has changed for the DBP except that less attention is focused on the quality of its services and that enhanced flexibility exists with respect to the use of leased line networks.

4. In May, 1985, a new governmental commission convened to study the future of the DBP. Many of the controversies of the past will be reviewed again. There are, however, changes in the international environment that may require the commission—and the DBP—to take a hard, new look at its future. Among the changes likely to be of significance are the further progress of deregulation in the United States and liberalization in the United Kingdom, along with the restructuring of the telecommunications market in Japan. Both the U.S. and U.K. examples could be viewed as unique. By contrast, German policymakers may well want to pay careful attention to the Japanese situation in light of the comparable sizes, and industrial development, of the two markets and the historic similarity of their approaches to the provision of telecommunications services.

B. Issues For the Future

1. The policy changes in the U.S., the U.K., and Japan are significant not only because of their "demonstration effects" for Germany, but also because they have real economic consequences for the German approach to pricing telecommunications services. Competition will draw international rates closer to costs. As a result, a significant profit center for the DBP, and for other PTTs, will be eliminated.

2. In countries where these changes are occurring, inter-exchange rates also will be moving quickly toward costs. Under the influence of these competitive pressures, the French, with their traditions still intact, will be moving in the same direction. The DBP, however, has an historic pricing scheme that reduces the flexibility to reprice domestic services; DBP pricing is intended to generate revenues to support important social objectives, *i.e.*, postal services, universal service obligations, low residential rates. Not addressing these pricing matters on a priority basis may have real costs; nevertheless, it is now widely accepted in Germany that moving prices toward costs is not politically possible. Consequently, "second best" solutions must be explored.

3. These "second best solutions"—which involve liberalizing leased line use and adopting usage-sensitive rate structures—have serious drawbacks. They are unpopular with large users, who have options to route traffic so as to minimize involvement with the DBP or who may locate new electronic services in regulatory environments more open and more receptive than Germany. Such "solutions" may, as well, discourage the implementation of new enhanced services, which may be easier to offer in the U.K., or in Germany's smaller neighbors, such as the Netherlands, if events there take an expected course.

4. Thus, the new commission may have to evaluate what options might be available for allowing new enhanced or hybrid information services to enter the market without significantly jeopardizing existing rate policies. There may be several strategies for defining value-added services so as to minimize any adverse economic consequences for existing "public switched services."

5. In addition, the new international environment may require that the commission examine issues relating to the future structure and organization of the DBP. For example, if the DBP does decide to allow certain value-added services onto the network, it may want to explore the possible advantages of segregating its operational and regulatory responsibilities. Another potential area for examination is whether, or to what extent, the DBP could set up subsidiaries under the private law, as has the French administration, to offer new services both domestically and internationally. These issues of PTT structure are being examined elsewhere in Europe, such as in France and Finland, even where there is no decision to institute a competitive regime.

6. The issues of pricing, development of a competition policy for enhanced services, and organizational structure probably are among the most important and difficult facing the DBP. Of increasing importance, however, is the division of responsibility between the Bund and the Länder. As telecommunications facilities and media services have become closely intertwined, it has become increasingly necessary to assure effective coordination between the planning and construction of telecommunications facilities—for satellite distribution services, cable, and DBS services—and the planning and implementation of media services. There have been, however, considerable difficulties in achieving agreements in this area. As a result, the implementation of new services has been delayed.

II. TELECOMMUNICATIONS POLICY STUDIES IN GERMANY

A. Early Studies Raise Key Issues

1. In 1973, the Government created the Kommission für den Ausbau des technischen Kommunikationssystems ("KtK") (Commission on the Expansion of the Technical Communications System). In January, 1976, a massive nine volume report—*Telekommunikationsbericht*—was released. The report focused on technical issues and suggested new services, such as broadband communications and teletext, that eventually were implemented. It advocated, by 1980, the installation of copper coaxial cable, and not fiber optic cable, which was viewed as unprofitable in the short-run. It did not focus on the possibility of changing the DBP structure or on the control of new telecommunications technologies.

2. Professor Eberhard Witte, an economist at the University of Munich, supervised the study. Although the Ministry for Posts and Telecommunications issued the report, it dates from a period when that Ministry and the Ministry for Research and Technology were headed by the same man, Horst Ehmke; the Research Ministry has had a significant role in stimulating new services in conjunction with its view that the DBP should contribute to the development of an overall industrial policy.

3. Some observers believe that the KtK report was focused too narrowly on technical issues; they are wary that the new commission similarly will be reluctant to examine some of the broader structural issues.

4. In January 1979 the Wirtschaftsminister- konferenz ("WMK") (Conference of Economics Ministers of the Länder) set up a working group on the DBP and the telecommunications monopoly. The final report, issued in February, 1980, asked that the Länder be more involved in decisionmaking on the introduction of new telecommunications technologies. In particular, by focusing on the lack of DBP consultations with respect to new services, the report highlighted the friction between the Bund and the Länder.

5. The report called for requiring the consent of the Bundesrat (the upper house of the German Parliament in which the Länder are represented) prior to a DBP decision on services and terminal equipment and for full participation in the process by both the Minister of Commerce and the Länder.

6. The DBP prepared a reply to this report in which it reiterated its important position in facilitating the participation of smaller firms in the equipment market and, therefore, its role in stimulating competition and specialized services.

B. The Monopoly Commission Reports: Functional Separation—Monopoly on Network Services and DBP Role in Terminal Equipment

1. The report with probably the greatest impact on discussions about telecommunications policy and structure was issued by the federal Monopolkommission (Monopoly Commission) in February, 1981. The Monopoly Commission, a standing body of five members focusing on issues of concentration in German industry, examined the role of the DBP from the perspective that competition should be encouraged and with a keen eye on U.S. deregulatory initiatives—which were a significant force in the Commission's discussion.

2. The final report, *Die Rolle der Deutschen Bundespost im Fernmeldewesen* (*The Role of the Deutsche Bundepost in Telecommunications)*, ultimately recommended—at least provisionally—the continuation of the DBP monopoly's providing of network services. The Commission called for the licensing of "specialized networks" and for some licensing of resale.

3. The Commission concluded that the DBP should not be permitted to provide terminal equipment, at least in the near future; the sole exception was that the DBP should provide the main station connection on an exclusive basis. The report added that the DBP should continue to approve equipment, but it opined that it might be less than optimal to vest approval and supply powers in the same body.

4. Various industry associations and companies submitted comments to the Commission. The DBP asserted that the U.S. context made it difficult to transplant the U.S. experience to Germany. Further, the DBP stated, any value-added networks should, in fact, not be allowed to cream-skim. Rather, to the extent that they are allowed, they actually should be of value to the user beyond that of the underlying service. The DBP also expressed concern with respect to its position as the supplier of the main station. Most equipment manufacturers, not surprisingly, argued for liberalization of the terminal equipment market.

5. The Commission also relied on three reports that it had commissioned: one by a U.S. firm of consultants, one analyzing DBP pro-

curement policy, and the third—and most influential—prepared by three German economists, Günter Knieps, Jürgen Müller, and Carl Christian von Weizsäcker.

6. This third report—*Die Rolle des Wettbewerbs im Fernmeldebereich* (*The Role of Competition in the Telecommunications Sector)* [hereinafter cited as *The Role of Competition*]—focused on both economic theory and data on competition in markets characterized either as natural monopolies—where principles of economies of scale or economies of scope (*i.e.*, where a multiproduct firm enjoys cost advantages over an arrangement relying on a number of different firms to supply products) may govern. *The Role of Competition* also examined the environment elsewhere, especially in the U.S.

7. *The Role of Competition* initially distinguishes among the various functions of the DBP—as network operator and provider, servicer of terminal equipment, purchaser of network equipment, employer, and network planner. It focuses separately on the possibility of competition in the network as distinct from that in terminal equipment. The report concludes that competition in the network could be beneficial but that, pending study of the U.S. experience, a country should move cautiously in this area. However, the report recommended that, for the time being, competition should not be implemented.

8. Once having made the separation between network and terminal equipment, the report concludes that terminal equipment should be liberalized as much as possible. The report recommends an open consumer choice policy for equipment coupled with minimum certification standards.

9. Turning to the role of the DBP in a liberalized terminal equipment market, the report analyzes the arguments both for and against its participation. In a recommendation not followed by the Monopoly Commission, the report concluded that the DBP should be allowed to participate in the market—especially because there may be economic benefits from its role as network supplier to the consumer. The report stated that it would be illogical to deprive the market of the DBP's competitive participation; however, it noted that German antitrust law should be amended to cover the activities of public enterprises such as the DBP, if it should abuse its dominant market position.

10. *The Role of Competition* recommended a separation of the DBP's equipment licensing function from that of the competitive enterprise; the report noted U.S. proposals to set up separate subsidiaries or to institute accounting methodologies to forestall predatory pricing behavior. The Monopoly Commission did not adopt the suggestion made in *The Role of Competition* that imposing accounting standards on the DBP could be useful.

11. The report also recognized the industrial and trade policy aspects of deregulation: the competitiveness of German exports could be hampered if developments in the telecommunications sector elsewhere (*e.g.*, in the U.S. and the U.K.) are not reviewed in the context of allowing competition in Germany.

12. Soon after the publication of the Monopoly Commission report, the DBP issued a short release commenting on that report. The DBP was pleased with the Commission's recognition of its function in operating the network and in supplying the main station equipment. The DBP disagreed with the conclusion that it should be excluded from the market for terminal equipment and argued that it should compete in all such equipment markets. It emphasized that its continued participation in the market increases the options of consumers and especially benefits smaller manufacturers with limited distribution outlets. As to value-added services and resale, the DBP accepted the principle that these ultimately should be permitted. It contended, however, that tariffs first should be tied more closely to costs and then should have disparities between public switched and leased circuits eliminated.

C. Backdrop for Study by the New Commission

1. In April, 1981, the Enquete Commission, a special inquiry of the Bundestag, published its Interim Report entitled *Neue Informations und Kommunikationstechniken* (*New Information and Communications Technology*). This Commission, composed of politicians, experts, and industry representatives, was charged with analyzing telecommunications policy. Although media issues were to be excluded from the inquiry, the Commission was drawn into political debate during the change in Government and became entangled in the highly controversial issues surrounding the future of television. These issues ultimately overshadowed the telecommunications "focus" of the inquiry. No final report was issued or is expected; the Enquete experience demonstrates the extent to which telecommunications and media policies are tied together, to the detriment of resolving pure "telecommunications" issues. In brief, the report focused on the introduction of cable and the choice between fiber and coaxial technologies. It also addressed how such technologies should be implemented and how they can affect industry sectors and social attitudes.

2. Against the backdrop of these and other studies, the government has created a new commission to examine telecommunications structures in Germany. After a lengthy period of deliberation over the issues to be discussed and the commission's composition, Professor Witte, who chaired the KtK Commission, was designated as Chairman of the new commission. The commission held its first session in May, 1985, and is expected to conclude its work in 1987.

3. The report from this commission is likely to examine the U.S. and Japanese experiences and the impact of telecommunications on industrial policy, trade, and global competitive positioning. The Ministry of Economics has played a role in the debate, as had the Ministry of Research; the latter, under Minister Riesenhuber, sees itself as a German version of Japan's Ministry of International Trade and Industry ("MITI"), promoting the telecommunications sector for broader industrial purposes. Neither Min-

istry, however, has the same comprehensive portfolio as does MITI in Japan.

4. Among the issues that are likely to be examined are (a) the role of the DBP in the supply of terminal equipment, where the DBP and the Ministry of Research are in some agreement; (b) value-added networks, with the underlying definitional issues (*i.e.*, "basic" versus "enhanced" services) having been the subject of intense study in the DBP during the late summer and early autumn of 1985; and (c) pricing issues, which are the subject of greatest political controversy. It is improbable that the new commission will focus in any significant way on possible competition in facilities.

III. THE STRUCTURE OF THE DEUTSCHE BUNDESPOST

A. The Ministry of Posts and Telecommunications and Political Control of the DBP

1. The Ministry of Posts and Telecommunications is authorized to exercise jurisdiction over telecommunications. The Fernmeldeanlagengesetz of 1928 (Telecommunications Installation Act) ("FAG") sets forth the responsibilities of the monopoly of the DBP and the Postverwaltungsgesetz ("PostVwG") (Postal Administration Law) of 1953 contains the details of organization, responsibilities, limits, and duties. The Minister sets the overall policy direction for the DBP; currently, the Minister is Dr. Christian Schwarz-Schilling, a member of the conservative Christlich-Demokratische Union Deutschlands ("CDU") (Christian Democratic Union) party.

2. Administrative guidance comes from the Administrative Council, which also has certain supervisory functions and has been compared to a board of directors. At present the council is headed by Walter Hesselbach, who has some ties to the Sozialdemokratische Partei Deutschlands ("SPD") (Social Democratic Party). The Council approves the budget and tariffs and decides on the introduction of new services. The Council does not give administrative guidance, but mainly reacts to proposals submitted to it. Nevertheless, it must approve any pricing plans or internal arrangements and thus could exercise potentially substantial influence on the DBP's future plans.

3. The Administrative Council is comprised of representatives from the Bundestag (lower house of Parliament), the Bundesrat (upper house, with representatives from the Länder), commercial interests, trade unions (who are strong in the DBP and oppose liberalization), and financial and communications experts. Thus, it is the mechanism for tying DBP policy to political or to union interests. Nominations to the Council are made by the Houses of Parliaments, commercial associations, the unions, and the Minister (and, in the case of the financial expert, with the Minister of Finance). The Federal Cabinet selects the appointees from the nominations.

Differences between the Minister and the Council could be resolved by the Federal Cabinet. (Some observers believe that the relationship between the Minister and the Council is, at present, subject to some strains and tensions.)

B. DBP Relationship with Other Ministries

1. The DBP has a budget independent from that of the remainder of the Federal Government; it receives no subsidies or capital from the Government so that its financing must be generated internally or through borrowing on the open market. Nevertheless, the Minister of Finance has to agree to the budget of the DBP, and the Minister of Economics must assent to rates and charges.

2. The DBP is tied to the general budget by its payment of ten percent of its annual operating income to the Government (raised from 6.67% in 1981). This payment has equalled about DM 4 billion; thus, there is a strong institutional interest—especially on the part of the Ministry of Finance—in increasing revenues and enhancing the DBP's operating efficiency. The DBP provides a DM 2 billion annual subsidy for postal services from telecommunications revenues.

3. The Ministry of Research is interested in research policy and has taken a more collaborative approach to the DBP than has the Ministry of Economics. The Ministry of Research and Technology supports research and development in the German computer industry (*e.g.*, Nixdorf and Siemens). The Ministry of Economics is involved in industry structure, particularly for "sick" industries undergoing a period of transition. It has taken an active interest in competition policy.

C. Internal Organization: From Minister to Local Offices

1. At the ministerial level, media policy issues compete for attention with telecommunications policy issues. Assisting the Minister is the Parlamentarischer Staatssekretär (Parliamentary State Secretary), currently Wilhelm Rawe, who is the Ministry's liaison to the Parliment on DBP policymaking. The Staatssekretär (State Secretary), Dr. Winfried Florian, has direct line authority to the operating divisions of the DBP. Dr. Schwarz-Schilling has been interested in media policy as well as in telecommunications and has questioned vigorously the monopoly held by the broadcast media. In addition, he has pushed forward a plan to cable Germany with coaxial technology, to the chagrin of the SPD, which believes that cabling should be delayed until fiber optic technology has matured. (This debate always has been politicized, but has become more so in the last two years: the SPD sees cable as a threat to traditional public broadcasting institutions and as opening the door to the commercialization of the mass media—to which they have, until recently, been solidly opposed. As discussions have proceeded, however, the SPD has adopted a more open stance toward cable, at least in some of the Länder.)

2. With the change in Government in 1982, it was expected that liberalization would be accelerated because the parties of the new Government—the CDU and the Freie Demokratische Partei ("FDP") (Free Democratic Party)—always had argued for such. Until now, this has not happened to the extent anticipated. The reasons for this are complex but seem to be Dr. Schwarz-Schilling's focus on private broadcasting and media issues generally, and his greater sympathy for the current monopoly structure in telecommunications. A lack of pressure from users and intense political pressures that are tied up in difficult pricing and cross-subsidization issues also have contributed to this dynamic.

3. Within the Ministry, Postal and Telecommunications functions are separated. There are two operating divisions for Telecommunications: Telecommunications Networks (currently headed by Mr. Waldemar Haist) and Telecommunications Services (by Mr. Helmut Schön). There is a degree of responsiveness to political changes that extends to this and to the next tier. For example, Franz Arnold, who was tied to the SPD, was replaced as head of Telecommunications Services by Mr. Schön. Supporting the operating divisions are divisions for personnel; finances; building construction and real property; press, public relations, and market; and central matters.

4. The Fernmeldetechnisches Zentralamt ("FTZ") (Central Technical Office for Telecommunications), located in Darmstadt, has a 2700-person staff working on research questions, practice codes, management studies, central procurement, pricing conditions, and the development of standards for new services (*e.g.*, new "130" service for toll-free calls, akin to "In-WATS" in the U.S.). The FTZ used to handle terminal equipment certification. In response to the Monopoly Commission report, which had suggested separation of the private equipment approval function from the approval of equipment supplied to the DBP, several people involved in private equipment approval were transferred to the newly established Zentralstelle für Zulassung im Fernmeldewesen ("ZZF") (Central Approval Office for Telecommunications) in Saarbrücken. Hence, the ZZF now has responsibility for equipment certification.

5. There apparently has been some friction between the FTZ and the ZZF. The FTZ has a separate line of authority to the Minister parallel to the other operating divisions; this could create some tension with the Network and Services divisions and, in the view of some, has made it difficult for the divisions to cooperate in the introduction of new services.

6. Below the federal level, there are seventeen regional post office directorates and the Landespostdirektion Berlin, similar in structure to the DBP and with their own telecommunications divisions. These do not have substantial operating independence; rather, they manage, coordinate, and consult at the regional level and are responsible for implementing policy and services at the local level. There are 107 local offices performing general, specialized, or supply functions.

D. Decentralization: A Model for the Future?

1. This structure suggests that decentralization—along the lines pursued by the D.G.T. in France—has not been relied on by the DBP. Nor is there common use of subsidiaries. In 1977 the DBP did set up on subsidiary—the Deutsche Telepost Consulting Ltd. (DETECON)—to offer consulting services to administrations and firms of other countries in posts and telecommunications. DETECON is set up under private law and may operate in Germany so long as it does so within the sphere of the DBP's monopoly. The DBP holds the largest percentage of shares (30%) in DETECON and supplies personnel; large banking concerns also have a significant interest.

2. Some staff in the DBP have looked at the success of DETECON and are interested in the notion of further decentralization through subsidiaries. Decentralization may be a way of recognizing regional differences and of adjusting prices accordingly, to move them closer to costs. However, it is not known, for example, whether the newly-established governmental commission will focus on structural reorganization of the DBP as a means of addressing pricing issues that would minimize the immediate political consequences of a more direct approach to rate realignment.

E. Impact of Relationship with Länder on DBP Structure

1. Among the difficult issues facing the DBP is its relationship with the Länder. *See infra* Section VII. The relationship is both politicized (*e.g.*, SPD Länder governments versus the CDU) and marked by significant debate over the new services. To a very significant extent these ideological discussions can tie up introduction of such services, with the Länder arguing that new DBP services require their consent and the DBP responding that the Länder are intruding into areas of exclusive Bund competence. These difficulties can—at least in part—be aired through Länder representation on the DBP Administrative Council. Indeed, the Administrative Council stopped the introduction of telemetry exchange services on the ground that certain data protection issues must be resolved by the Länder; the Länder, through their data protection commissioners, conceded that the service—essentially meter reading—was "telecommunications" but contended that their consent still was required prior to introduction.

2. A factor toward mitigating the tension may be the CDU Government, which is perceived in some quarters as being more sympathetic to the concerns of the Länder than was the previous SPD government. Finally, some informal discussions, by correspondence or otherwise, do take place between the Länder and the DBP.

3. The DBP also may supply some technical guidance (it did so, for example, with respect to agreements "Rundfunkreferenten"—

Länder officials responsible for broadcasting questions); in so doing, however, the DBP has cautioned that it does not consent to the exercise of Länder jurisdiction over areas that it asserts are reserved to the DBP.

F. Structural Options for the Bundespost

The governmental commission, which is examining the future of the DBP, may consider a range of views involving the organizational structure of the DBP and its role in the German telecommunications market.

1. Threshold questions about the DBP's present structure arise from the Basic Law (Grundgesetz). Certain structural changes, therefore, would require amending the Basic Law, which could occur only by a two-thirds vote of the Bundestag; this occurrence is quite unlikely, given the controversy that probably would be generated by a proposed change in the status quo.

2. The DBP is the only German ministry mentioned in the Basic Law, and it is referred to therein as providing posts and telecommunications. Some have argued that this linkage—between "posts" and "telecommunications"—precludes their separation in the Ministry. The Basic Law does not, however, mandate that the two activities be financially intertwined. It is not likely that the current subsidy of postal services by telecommunications can be ended by separate accounting for separate activities.

3. Article 87 of the Basic Law states that the DBP is administered by the Bund, the federal government. The DBP interprets this provision to mean that it could not be "privatized" or, in any essential way, be removed from public control. The Article also has been interpreted as meaning that the DBP could not carry out its responsibilities by relying exclusively on a regulatory role, but, rather, that it also must provide services. It is not, however, necessarily asserted that Article 87 confers a monopoly on the DBP. This last legal view implies, therefore, that some competitive entry might be consistent with the DBP's obligations, but that the DBP must retain a significant market share of telecommunications services.

4. The interpretation of the Basic Law also must take into account Section 1 of the FAG of 1928, which states that the right to install and to run telecommunications facilities belongs exclusively to the Bund. Some argue that the fact of legislative intervention—passage of the FAG—to affirm statutorily the DBP monopoly suggests that the Basic Law itself does not confer unequivocally such a monopoly. Section 2 of the FAG confers the right to install and run telecommunications facilities for specific lines or districts. The provision does not necessarily grant the DBP broad authority to license others to provide comprehensive services; nevertheless, it may imply a somewhat more restricted licensing authority. By implication, Section 2 could be modified to confer licensing authority, without conflicting with the Basic Law, so long as the DBP retains regulatory authority to "administer" the telecommunications system. The countervailing view, however, is that Article 87 requires the DBP to be involved directly in

providing service, and not through a licensing scheme. The constitutional question might focus on whether licensing, with the DBP permitted to provide services, would result in a sharply reduced market position for the DBP.

5. Licensing of private entities by the DBP could raise the question of whether or how to separate its regulatory and operational responsibilities. At the present time, the Minister is both the chief regulatory official and the chief executive officer for the DBP's operations. In the early 1970s, a plan was proposed that would have separated the regulatory and operational responsibilities to a greater degree. The plan failed on account of differences over possible labor union representation on the DBP's proposed new board of directors. The proposal called for fifty percent labor representation and was supported by the SPD; however, their then-partners, the FDP, objected to this representative structure, and the plan died.

6. Recently, one small example of segregating regulatory and operational responsibilities within the DBP has been the shift in equipment type-approval procedures from the FTZ to an independent group under the Minister, the ZZF.

7. If the DBP ever were to decide to authorize value-added networks, it might adopt a similar separation of regulatory and operational roles. It might, at the very least, be desirable to create some separation between the DBP as facilities provider and as offeror of new value-added services. This separation might contemplate establishing some "relational rules" between the DBP and its subsidiary that could "parallel" the relationship of the DBP to unaffiliated service providers.

8. Whether, as a legal matter, the DBP can operate through subsidiaries under private law raises a difficult question of constitutional law, *i.e.*, whether the DBP could carry out its responsibilities under Article 87 through contractual or stock ownership arrangements with its subsidiary. There is, at present, a subsidiary that offers international consulting services. *See supra* Section III.D. If, however, the DBP could "license" unaffiliated entities to offer services, it would seem to follow that it could "license" affiliated entities to carry out similar responsibilities. Resolving this issue may be important for the DBP because flexibility could increase the options available to it, to enter into joint ventures and marketing arrangements, as has the French PTT.

9. One possible difficulty with the DBP taking steps toward entering new activities is that its presence in new sectors may open up a debate with the Ministry of Economics over whether the DBP should have any role at all in those fields. These differences have sharply characterized the dialogue between the DBP and the Ministry of Economics over the DBP's position in the terminal equipment market, as to which the DBP has argued that its presence benefits users and smaller manufacturers.

10. Finally, any argument over the future role of the DBP must focus on how "telecommunications"—that which is within the DBP's jurisdiction—is defined in Article 73 of the Basic Law. As discussed below, the

term has, in litigation over the years, been subject to some interpretation. *See infra* Section VI.A. In the most recent case, the 1977 *Direktrufbeschluss* decision, the Federal Constitutional Court adopted a rather flexible approach to the boundaries of the DBP's authority. Such an important "definitional" term places the DBP in somewhat the same dilemma as that faced by AT&T in the 1956 Consent Decree. As telecommunications and computer technologies and markets converge, a failure to define what constitutes "telecommunications" could expose the DBP to the risk of being precluded altogether from entry into the sector. Conversely, if the term "telecommunications" is defined broadly, it may create the specter of an ever-expanding monopoly. Thus, it may be prudent for the DBP to mitigate that impression by adopting a more flexible approach to the "hybrid" services that are a product of the new technological convergence.

11. Thus, the governmental commission may have to address a provocative set of organizational questions: (1) Does the Basic Law confer a monopoly on the DBP? (2) If not, how can the powers of Section 2 of the FAG be exercised to license third-party service providers (such as enhanced service vendors) consistently with the DBP's responsibilities under Article 86 of the Basic Law? (3) Does licensing of third parties require separation of the regulatory and operational roles of the DBP, and would such separation be consistent with the Basic Law in light of past precedent? (4) Does the DBP have the flexibility to restructure itself as a corporate entity under private law? (5) How does the definition of "telecommunications" in the Basic Law affect—either restrict or expand—the future role of the DBP?

IV. BACKGROUND: PRICING ISSUES IN TELECOMMUNICATIONS POLICY

The "definitional" issues involved in the introduction of—or jurisdiction over—new services are tied quite closely to pricing and tariff issues. The pricing question appears to be the most discussed issue in DBP telecommunications policy. Indeed, the DBP is faced with significant pressure to liberalize—to allow third-party use, or resale, of its services; the DBP's response to these pressures is to minimize tariff discrepancies through rate harmonization. Harmonization of such discrepancies is presented by the DBP as an interim alternative to cost-based pricing: a fundamental element of DBP policy is to ameliorate pressures toward permitting competition by structural realignment of the tariffs.

A. The DBP Tariff Structure and Internal Subsidies

1. The DBP's tariffs for telecommunications are viewed as being in the upper tier of European service suppliers. Several explanations are offered for this tariff structure. First, telecommunications services cross-subsidize postal services. The subsidy, in the past, has ranged between DM 3

and 4 billion; it is now approximately DM 2 million. Dr. Karl-Heinz Neumann has calculated that if telecommunications services simply had to cover their own costs, rates could be approximately fifteen percent lower than at present. *See* K-H Neumann, *Economic Policy Toward Telecommunications, Information and Media in West Germany* 15 (Preliminary Draft, April 1984) (Research Workshop on Economic Policy Toward Telecommunications, Information, and Media Activities in Industrialized Countries) [hereinafter cited as *Economic Policy*].

2. Second, the DBP subsidizes the federal budget through the payment of ten percent of its annual operating revenues (the DM 4.074 billion payment in 1982 represented about 1.5% of the federal budget). Dr. Neumann concludes that such payments are higher than would be the case if the DBP were taxed as a private firm.

3. Finally, the tariff rate structure for local and long-distance services does not reflect accurately cost differentials based on distance, peak load pricing, and differences between the provision of local and rural services. The telecommunications tariff structure currently works to favor residential and low-income users over business and high-income users, given the current structure of demand.

4. The DBP recognizes that the cross-subsidies and pricing uniformity makes it impossible for tariffs to reflect costs. However, the DBP accepts the fact that the Ministry is led by a member of the federal cabinet and must be responsive to political groups and pressures, making it quite difficult to introduce cost-based rates. There also is pressure from the press and from parcel industries to maintain the postal subsidy. However, due, in part, to pressure from the Ministry of Finance—which would like to see an increase in the annual payment of the DBP—at some point there may be greater structural separation of postal and telecommunications services, to diminish the impact of the postal subsidy that reduces the net overall revenues on which the payment is calculated.

5. In 1980, the DBP attempted to redress some of the pricing problems by introducing local call timing to revise its local service rate structure, which had long been based on calling units. The DBP had advocated a local rate based on three-minute units but, under political pressure, was forced to base charges on eight- and twelve-minute units. At the same time, sixteen to eighteen local calling areas were combined to create large local calling areas. The current tariff is twenty-three pfennig for eight local minutes, a rate that does not reflect adequately the real economic value of the service or its cost.

6. The political pressures cause tariff structures to diverge from pricing that would minimize welfare losses. Divergence from optimal pricing, estimates Dr. Neumann, causes a loss of DM 1 billion. Based on 1979 figures, he concludes that optimal pricing, given the profit level in 1979, would have increased the price of local service by ninety-three percent, with a reduction in toll service pricing by twenty-seven percent.
K-H Neumann, *Economic Policy*, *supra*, at 23.

B. Tariff "Harmonization" as "Second-Best" Solution

Given the political infeasibility of moving prices closer to costs, at least in the near term, the DBP has been discussing actively principles of tariff harmonization: bringing closer together the pricing of services capable of substitution. The DBP's approach to tariff restructuring is that tariff harmonization, where alignment with costs is not politically possible, is almost imperative as a "second best" solution to liberalize and to protect the current rate structure at the same time. There are several factors behind this development:

1. Dr. Neumann and Professor von Weizsäcker describe the resale of services to third parties as a preliminary form of competition. They call this Stage I competition. Stage II competition would be based on an alternative network—which would drive prices closer to costs but is a development unlikely in the German context. *See* K-H Neumann and C.C. von Weizsäcker, "Tariff Policy for Leased Circuits and Private Branch Exchanges from the Economic Point of View," in *Harmonization of the Tariffs for Fixed Connections in the Public Telecommunications Networks* 248 (reprint from *Jahrbuch der Deutschen Bundespost* 1982) [hereinafter cited as *Tariff Policy*]. *The Role of Competition* and the Monopoly Commission had urged that Stage I competition be permitted: as a predicate thereto, the DBP has, therefore, moved toward harmonization.

2. Leased circuits had been charged on a monthly flat-rate; the DBP argued that permitting resale of such circuits in that environment would siphon traffic from the public switched network, lead to "uneconomic cream-skimming," and, as a result, inevitably decrease DBP revenues. K-H Neumann and C.C. von Weizsäcker, *Tariff Policy, supra*, at 249. And, as a political matter (fueled largely by the internal subsidy of postal services), the DBP cannot afford to allow arbitrage that would significantly diminish its income stream. There was—and is—a real concern throughout the DBP that resale-qua-"cream-skimming" poses a significant threat to network viability and could subordinate the more advantageous consequences of allowing resale (*e.g.*, the development of innovative or more affordable service offerings). The DBP views resale in the U.S. and bypass technologies as not necessarily the most economic means of achieving competition.

3. Looking ahead to an ISDN environment, current network tariffs must be harmonized. That is, with digitization of voice, text, data, and video services, a failure to harmonize will lead to tariff avoidance or to arbitrage by users who will migrate toward the lowest tariff.

C. Usage-Based Pricing for Leased Circuits: DBP Movement and User Reaction

The DBP response to pressures to liberalize—movement toward a harmonized tariff structure that would lessen opportunities for arbitrage and cream-skimming—led to the introduction of usage-based pricing for leased circuits. Undergirding this development was the notion that leased circuit pricing must be more closely aligned with that of the switched network; the switched network is used more heavily, and it would be economically imprudent to align its tariffs with the flat-rate pricing of leased circuits.

1. Usage-based tariffs for fixed connections (and a system surcharge for PBXs) were introduced by the Administrative Council in September, 1981, in the Seventeenth Order Amending the Telecommunications Regulations, Federal Law Gazette I, at 977 (Sept. 26, 1981) [hereinafter cited as 17th Amendment Order]. The 17th Amendment Order came into force January 1, 1983; it dropped regulatory provisions that stated that there was no entitlement to be leased or to receive fixed connections in the public networks. There remains no obligation for the DBP to lease fixed connections for private installations.

2. In the 19th Amendment Order, adopted by the Administrative Council on February 25, 1982, and put into force on January 1, 1983, the tariff model of the 17th Amendment Order was applied to higher volume lines with digital interfaces for transmission at 64 Kbit/s, 2 Mbit/s, and 34 Mbit/s. Federal Law Gazette I, at 284 (March 10, 1982). The DBP views the 19th Amendment Order as making possible the offering of new services and as laying the predicate for the introduction of ISDN. Pricing of these connections is based on 64 Kbit/s; the broader bands—2 Mbit/s and 34 Mbit/s—reduced to 64 Kbs equivalents can be used to permit the simultaneous transmission of thirty and 480 calls respectively. This pricing offers substantial flexibility to users and was designed to encourage shifting to digital services. It is possible for a customer to divide channels to achieve either multiple use of circuits or simultaneous transmission of voice and data. Clearly, given the 64 Kbit/s basis for ISDN, there is a close nexus between current pricing strategies and preparation for transformation to ISDN.

3. The 24th Amendment Order, adopted December 19, 1983, restructured datex tariffs; it became effective January 1, 1984. *See* Federal Law Gazette I, at 1825 (December, 1983). This tariff—with the 19th Amendment Order—represents a further movement toward an "ISDN-like" tariff. Indeed, the DBP's provision of 64 Kbit/s terminations in its Datex-L ("model network"), which began this year, is intended to encourage utilization of high-speed data transmission technology, with an eye toward a transition to ISDN.

4. The last and most controversial amendment was the 25th Amendment Order of June 24, 1984. It involved a restructuring of usage tariffs for packet-switched (Datex-P) and circuit-switched (Datex-L) services. Arguing that it was losing 35-39% on Datex services, the DBP increased Datex-P rates by up to 100% in two- or three-step increments; Datex-L would be increased by twenty percent. The 25th Amendment Order has been the subject of many meetings between users—represented by twenty-eight individual organizations—the Ministry of the Interior and the DBP; these industry representatives expressed doubt over the claim of a DBP deficit. Adding to user concerns was the fact that the Order alone was lengthy and very difficult to interpret.

5. Users have objected to the new basic charge for fixed connections—which is based on a minimum monthly usage of eighty hours. Usage will be recorded only for public or private network calls beyond the local area and for data installations. Users also are concerned about threefold price increases—prorated over a decade—based on unrealistic usage predictions. Moreover, users view the DBP as simply having increased prices for leased circuits without having provided better service or having offered any additional value in return.

6. Although the 64 Kbit/s pricing would seem to be relatively attractive—especially for data/voice calls—users are not now flocking to the new services. This reluctance seems, in part, to be based on corporate cost-orientation and on a certain unfamiliarity with non-traditional pricing structures. Users, however, attribute the lack of demand for the newly-priced services to a failure by the DBP to identify a market, to market the services to likely users, and to forecasting that is neither accurate nor precise. Some industry spokesmen contend that the rate hikes of the 25th Amendment Order threaten the viability of such new services as teletex (a teletypewriter service).

7. More significantly, users are awaiting the liberalization that the DBP implicitly promised by introducing harmonized tariffs as a "predicate" for Stage I competition.

8. The users have responded to these tariff restructurings by reviewing their use of the network with an eye to reducing costs. For example, to the extent use of fixed connections for data transmission is uneconomic, users are likely to change the mix of data processing and telecommunications services; they will move from centralized processing dependent on substantial use of transmission services to a model based on decentralized data processing with reduced transmission utilization. The DBP tariff structure, therefore, may lead to user efforts to reorganize or to minimize the use of DBP services.

9. Users' choice of the mix of data processing and telecommunications services based on sensitivity to DBP pricing may have certain industrial policy implications. Companies may be inclined to localize processing activity when—from an organizational standpoint—centralized processing is more efficient or suitable to the enterprise's goals. If compa-

nies prefer decentralization—but DBP transmission costs are too high—they may choose a telecommunications environment that offers services more in line with corporate objectives, expectations, and budgets.

10. The DBP has looked at the question of whether introducing usage-based tariffs for domestic leased circuits while retaining a non-usage based structure for international circuits might have such an adverse effect on industrial policy. *See* K-H Neumann and C.C. von Weizsäcker, *Tariff Policy, supra*, at 278-80. Neumann and von Weizsäcker look to developments in Europe and the U.S. and are hopeful that the example of tariff harmonization set by the DBP may be followed elsewhere in Europe. Thus, any differential in tariff structure, they assume, will result in only a short-term disparity. They recognize, however, that the lower international tariffs in the U.S. may cause corporations to set up their computer centers there. Hence, they call for further discussion, in international fora and among PTTs, of harmonization of international switched- and leased-circuit pricing. They note that there are some usage-based tariffs for data networks (*e.g.*, SWIFT and Reuters information network) and that the principle of usage-based pricing eventually could be applied to voice networks. They conclude, therefore, that the DBP and Germany will suffer no significant loss of competitive posture through the introduction of usage-based tariffs.

D. German Pricing Policy and the International Arena: The Key to the Future

Usage-sensitive pricing schemes have been referred to as a "second best" solution because the "first-best" solution, a more cost-based pricing system, is not politically feasible. It is widely accepted in Germany that the existing balances and equities in the pricing system—averaging prices between regions, and using business services to subsidize residential services—cannot be disturbed. The price for maintaining the status quo on pricing—and not striving for the "first-best solution"—may be very high.

1. The main difficulty is that German pricing policy cannot take only domestic German factors into account. The economic consequences of not making certain adjustments are increasing, even though the pricing decisions themselves are clearly within the DBP's sovereign authority. For example, users, unsettled by usage-sensitive charges, may be motivated to construct networks that bypass Germany or minimize any economic contact with Germany. The effect of avoiding the German network may be lost jobs and a reduction of economic oppportunities to participate in the development of new electronic services. Other countries—first the U.K., and then France—are reducing their interexchange rates; unless Germany responds, it may be more isolated in Europe, as new international services are based elsewhere. In addition, Germany's smaller neighbors, such as the Netherlands, may liberalize their policies toward enhanced service vendors, further increasing international pressure on German domestic rate policies.

2. Rate restructuring is, for many reasons, a difficult task. It is, of course, hard to develop politically palatable explanations as to why freedom of action is limited on domestic pricing issues. Looking to the future, however, it may be critical to establish the principle that change is necessary in the long run. Pricing policy may be the most important issue currently confronting the DBP. Thus, whether and how the governmental commission addresses these questions may affect significantly the future vitality of the DBP.

V. ISDN: POLICY PLANNING ACTIVITIES

The DBP has been involved actively in planning for the introduction of ISDN—both in the international (CCITT) planning process and in methodically moving toward an ISDN environment in Germany. On March 26, 1982, the DBP announced its intention with respect to introducing ISDN in Germany and, to that end, toward digitizing the network as rapidly as possible.

A. Digitization of the Network as a First Step

1. The first step in the process is the introduction of digital 64 Kbit/s switching and transmission capacity into the existing analog network. The DBP decided to give priority to digitization in 1979. Having done extensive testing in the last year or so, through a presentation procedure for both long-distance and local switching, the DBP has decided to install the first local digital exchanges by the end of the year. As of mid-1984, forty percent of long-distance exchanges terminated digital line paths. *See* H. Schön, *The Deutsche Bundespost on its Way Toward the ISDN* 14 (June 1984) [hereinafter cited as *Toward the ISDN*]. These switches will be manufactured by Siemens (EWSD) and by ITT's Standard Elektrik Lorenz subsidiary ("SEL") (System 12).

2. Since 1982, the DBP has purchased only digital transmission systems for its regional networks. The transition to the introduction of ISDN—currently projected for two local digital exchanges in 1988—will be gradual: modernization, which focused initially on installing fiber optic capacity, now centers on digitization of trunk exchanges and gradually will move down the network to local switches, beginning with the most heavily used switches. (The Hamburg-Munich corridor has the highest traffic and will be upgraded; the eight largest cities in Germany form eight nodes that will also be the first to be digitized.) Local network-upgrade will be slower, using concentrators; digital microwave will be used for long-distance service and soon will be used for local networks as well.

3. It is expected that, by 1990, one-quarter of all trunk exchanges will be digitized and that the network will be completely digitized by 2020, at the latest. *Id.* at 16. CCITT common channel signaling system

No. 7, for signalling between digital telephone exchanges, will be applied in 1986.

4. Initially, the DBP forecasts connectivity at 64 Kbit/s transmission, with evolution to higher bit rates for such services as moving pictures. Still under discussion are the appropriate bit rates for services such as video conferencing; the options include 2 Mbit/s, 34 Mbit/s, and 140 Mbit/s. Decisions as to pricing and the means of ultimately integrating broadband services will affect the outcome of these discussions.

B. Technical Issues: Plant and Equipment

1. The basic subscriber access to the network will be multiple use of the copper pair—already installed and usable in the period prior to total digitization and the installation of fiber optic technology. For signalling between the subscriber's terminal equipment and the exchange, the special 16 Kbit/s "D" Channel will be utilized. Thus, for local services, the copper pair—for two basic 64 Kbit/s channels—plus a 16 Kbit/s signalling capacity (144 Kbit/s total), is deemed adequate.

2. To test the components of the ISDN under operational conditions, a pilot project, planned for 1986, will be carried out in Mannheim and Stuttgart. Scheduled to last two years, the project contemplates about 400 ISDN basic accesses to test the performance of the network, the operation of terminal equipment, and the signalling systems. (This pilot is distinguished from the broadband project ongoing in seven cities. *See infra* Section V.E.)

3. There has not yet been a resolution of who should supply the terminal attachment and network interface. This question may be quite difficult to resolve; it may be that a different policy will pertain to ISDN interfacing equipment than to other equipment. In any event, the issues certainly will be tied to the older questions surrounding the DBP's involvement in supplying terminal equipment.

4. Fiber optic technology probably will not be used in the short run—at least at the local level. (However, in West Berlin there have been technical tests of optical fiber technology for some six years.) There is, however, a recognition that fiber optics eventually will be widespread and a belief that the French moved too quickly to adopt the new technology. There is some testing of fiber optic technology in the experimental BIGFON project, *see infra* Section V.E., which is being conducted at the local level. The DBP already has installed the first fiber optic cables in a long-distance network, which will allow it to offer integrated broadband services for individual communications.

5. The reluctance to embrace fiber optic technology at the exchange level may illustrate once again the interdependence of media and telecommunications policy in Germany and the way in which the former affects the latter. Because Minister Schwarz-Schilling is committed to using coaxial rather than fiber technology for cable—on the ground that the latter

is still in a state of evolution and is too expensive for cable television networks—there has been an almost inevitable spillover into ISDN planning. The widespread installation of fiber technology in Germany has been postponed until, it would seem, the political decision is made that fiber—whatever its use—is a practical alternative at the local level to existing technologies.

C. ISDN Environment: Regulatory Distinctions and Pricing Consequences

There is, therefore, active planning by the DBP for developing an "intelligent" network by adding common channel signalling and the "D" channel protocol. Hence, there may well be a reluctance to distinguish "basic" from "enhanced" services.

1. It is hoped that all services will develop from 64 Kbit/s offerings—so that there is no need to distinguish one service from the other—and that the "intelligent" network ultimately will be able to handle them all. The DBP will consider marketing certain individual service features as "supplementary" or as a subset of the "basic" service. "Basic" service will be the minimum service configuration—subscriber termination and circuit type. *See* H. Schön, *Toward the ISDN, supra,* at 20. A variety of "supplementary" services will be made available—station features, connection features, and information features. *Id.* Thus, it seems that services will not be isolated completely or necessarily offered separately; this represents a slight difference in perspective from the Japanese and U.S. ISDN models.

2. ISDN activities in Germany also can be seen as an effort to cope with the possibility that alternative or other value-added networks might emerge: the DBP describes ISDN as "obviat[ing] the need for uneconomical special networks for different services." H. Schön, *Toward the ISDN, supra,* at 18.

3. Although most of the discussion in Germany has focused on technological issues, critical to the impetus for movement toward ISDN is the opportunity for restructuring prices. There appears, however, not to have been much of a focus on pricing issues. It is, of course, expected that businesses will be the initial customers, especially for data, text, and voice services; eventually, residential use of ISDN will increase. The movement toward ISDN represents one way of eventually integrating the two networks—telephone, and data/text, which is already "integrated" in the sense that the digitized 64 Kbit/s service affords substantial flexibility to users and makes possible a wealth of services. ISDN creates the opportunity for digitizing all leased circuits and for moving pricing for those circuits closer to telephone tariffs.

4. The DBP is now examining the possibility that ISDN telephone services will not deviate substantially from telephone tariffs. Given the impossibility of changing telephone tariffs, and the unwillingness to risk the integrity of the all-important telephone tariff structure, it will be the

ISDN tariff that will move to meet telephony pricing. Non-voice ISDN services, however, will be offered at a more favorable tariff than is possible at present; it is anticipated that demand for such services will, therefore, increase.

5. Consequently, although the DBP looks upon ISDN as affording it tremendous oportunities to supplement its revenues, ISDN may, in fact, lead to price discrimination between "like" services. Moreover, it will be difficult to implement pricing structures—and monitor customer use—based on "services" (*e.g.*, "telephone" versus "data") when users will readily be able to use the network for a variety of applications that are technically indistinguishable to the ISDN operator. Conversely, new definitional issues will be raised if the DBP must rely on distinctions between services to determine applicable tariffs.

6. Nevertheless, an undercurrent in German planning for ISDN is the attempt to eliminate some "definitional" distinctions and to rely instead on technical or engineering criteria or standards when describing ISDN capabilities or offerings. There is a focus on using the standards of the International Standards Organisation ("ISO") and the CCITT in implementing ISDN; as only the first three—of the seven—levels are yet specified by the ISO, the DBP views ISDN as a significant opportunity for PTTs, the European Community, manufacturers, and users to develop global standards. There is both a conceptual approach and a definitional approach to analyzing ISDN.

7. The ISO model is a "conceptual" one that focuses on the sevices that are provided. It describes ISDN in seven layers: (1) physical (mechanical and procedural characteristics between termination and exchange; (2) data link (error control, frame management); (3) network (signalling and clearing); (4) transport (end-to-end control terminal-to-terminal); (5) session (establishes, maintains, terminates connections for transfer between processes); (6) presentation (data format and information); and (7) application (data source, services offered).

8. The CCITT I-Series Recommendations create a class of telecommunications services under which there are two subclasses, "bearer" services and "teleservices." "Bearer" services provide the capability for information transfer by the network (layers 1 to 3). Teleservices include layers 1 to 3 and also provide support at the higher levels, for services that enable users or terminals to communicate. The DBP engineering staff would prefer to focus on bit rate or switched versus fixed connections, and not to linger over distinctions between "bearer" and "teleservices." The DBP's objective is both to allow the user to enjoy maximum flexibility and to work toward obtaining international standards that will help it meet this goal. Hence, it does not want international standardization to stop at "bearer" circuits, but urges all industry sectors and administrations to do their utmost to allow compatibility.

D. Consequences of the Standardization "Choice"

1. The DBP staff expresses an affinity for the ISO model over IBM's Systems Network Architecture ("SNA") standard. A long-lasting, reliable standard is perceived as mandatory; there is considerable skepticism whether it would be prudent to rely on SNA, a standard developed—and subject to change—by one manufacturer. Nevertheless, despite the DBP's rejection of SNA, and in the aftermath of the U.K. rejection of the proposed venture between British Telecom and IBM, there still is some significant debate about the impact of SNA on achieving standardization in Europe.

2. The DBP's staff believes that there is some risk that manufacturer standards will develop too soon, prior to a full understanding of the direction of ISDN. The DBP also is concerned with the risk that international standards could develop in ways that may not be optimal. The outcome of the standardization debate in Europe is not clear. Moreover, there is perception that the U.S. is outside the international framework and is working on ISDN somewhat in isolation. It is hoped in the DBP that the U.S. can be brought back into the international planning process and that it will acknowledge the near-term viability of ISDN.

3. A failure to standardize—or a premature agreement on standards—could create opportunities for the development of specialized networks. There may be a need to create new services to link together—or to achieve compatibility—between divergent "ISDNs." The DBP's vigorous participation in the international planning process is an attempt to forestall this eventuality—one that could stymie development of an integrated network and could threaten the monopoly offered by the DBP. For its part, the DBP has described such separate special networks as being incapable of profitable operation. H. Schön, *Toward the ISDN, supra*, at 24.

E. The BIGFON Project

1. As part of promoting the development of ISDN, the DBP's experiments with narrowband technology have been supplemented by the trial tests of optical fiber, local broadband transmission: the BIGFON Project (*B*reitbandiges *I*ntegriertes *G*lasfaser-*F*ernmelde-*O*rts*n*etz, or Broadband Integrated Optical Fiber Local Telecommunications Network). BIGFON trials began in late 1983 in seven German cities: Munich, Stuttgart, Nuremberg, Düsseldorf, Hanover, Hamburg, and West Berlin.

2. The DBP is testing the technical feasibility of a network in which all present and future telecommunications services (from telephone and telex to videoconferencing and TV phone) are to be transmitted on one subscriber line using optical fiber technology. In West Berlin, the three BIGFON networks will be connected by optical fiber; there will be some capability to connect with cable television networks. The trial phase will end in 1986.

3. Corning Glass, a U.S. firm, is supplying the fiber optic wiring. Philips, Siemens, and SEL are helping to establish the seven-city trial network.

4. Once having established the viability of optical broadband technology, the DBP intends to expand ISDN to incorporate broadband facilities and to integrate narrowband and broadband services. This step is planned for 1990 and beyond.

5. Once broadband technology is integrated into an ISDN, television and radio services could be distributed over the network. Current planning calls for the integration of such distribution services after 1992.

VI. THE DEFINITIONAL ISSUES: A GERMAN PERSPECTIVE

A. "Network" and "Transmission": The Extent of the Boundaries of the DBP Monopoly

1. The debate over what is part of the "network" and within the jurisdictional ambit of the DBP was invigorated by the 1977 *Direktrufbeschluss*, a decision of the Federal Constitutional Court. BVerfGE 46, 120. In that decision, involving leased lines for digital transmission, the Court held that the legal concept of "telecommunications networks" must be construed dynamically; the thrust of the decision is that "telecommunications" is a word that defines an area ever in evolution. Hence, it cannot be a static term. "Telecommunications" must be read to embody not only existing—but also future—developments. The packet-switching component of the "transmission" service did require some storage and forward capability; nevertheless, the Court held, the DBP could provide it consistently with the *1. Rundfunkurteil*. *See infra* Section VI.A.3. (The Court, however, also confirmed the limitation on the DBP's jurisdiction that it had enunciated in the *1. Rundfunkurteil*, BVerfGE 46, 151-52.)

2. The *Direktrufbeschluss* raises, by implication, the definitional issue of what is "like" or "unlike" telephone or telecommunications services that may, therefore, be provided by the Bund. This reading of the decision sheds some light on whether new statutory authorization is required for the introduction of new services. If a service is within the ambit of the DBP's jurisdiction over "telecommunications networks," no law or other parliamentary action will be required; conversely, if the service is not "like" services that were within the contemplation of drafters of the legislation, it might be subject to Länder regulation or necessitate an amendment of the statutory scheme that now delimits the powers of the DBP.

3. A 1961 decision of the Federal Constitutional Court, *1. Rundfunkurteil*, BVerfGE 12, 205, held that the DBP's mandate over "telecommunications" ("Fernmeldewesen") is confined to "transmission" (übermittlung), at 226-27, and the technical aspects of the construction of the network, at 237-39. Chancellor Adenauer had wanted to create a federal

broadcasting organization (nicknamed "Adenauerfernsehen"), and the Länder brought suit; the Court determined that the Bund was limited to technical areas and transmission while the Länder were responsible for programming and content. One interpretation of this decision is that the Bund cannot do anything to—*i.e.*, "process"—information that it receives except to transmit and to deliver it to the intended recipient.

4. Thus, as issues arise as to the scope of the DBP's monopoly, the decision may be read as establishing one boundary line, limiting the DBP to "transmission" and reserving "content" to the Länder. The decision further reinforces the inclination to meld telecommunications and media policies: that which involves selection of "content" for media or for mass distribution would seem to be without the jurisdiction of the DBP. This limitation is not entirely dissimilar to the permissible role of AT&T under the 1956 consent decree.

5. Based on this decision, Dr. Joachim Scherer of Johann Wolfgang Goethe-Universtät argues for a tightly-drawn definition of "telecommunications services" that limits the DBP to "transmission" and would place any additional functions within the jurisdiction of the Länder. Dr. Scherer contends that the DBP is, therefore, barred from offering any services that involve altering content—including data processing, protocol conversion, or offering an "enhanced" service, which are all reserved to the Länder. *See* J. Scherer, *Neue Komminikationssysteme zwischen Fernmelderecht und Medienrecht—Das Beispiel des Bildschirmtextsystems*, DVR Beiheft 16 [hereinafter cited as DVR Beiheft 16]. This jurisdictional contention is, of course, rejected by the DBP.

6. As to such services as Bildschirmtext ("Btx"), which require storage and transmission, Dr. Scherer's position is that the only storage function that the DBP is permitted to perform is that which is necessarily contained in network transmission. Dr. Scherer believes that other storage, such as that in Btx, would be exclusively within the province of the Länder.

7. The *1. Rundfunkurteil* and Dr. Scherer's analysis raise a substantial question with respect to what is part of the network transmission services—*i.e.*, transport—that the DBP may provide. First, the DBP has no involvement in remote access data processing activity. This is in contrast to the remote access data processing activities being undertaken by NTT and the D.G.T. The only exception to this principle has been the DBP's provision of central processing as part of Btx services; the DBP processes some frames for users, but its involvement in this activity has not been without controversy. *See infra* Section VII.E.13-14.

8. The introduction of Btx raised the conceptual issue of whether the computer is part of the network—and therefore reserved to the DBP—or is part of the service and within the Länder jurisdiction. The DBP was compelled to argue vigorously—and, ultimately, successfully—for its right to provide central processing facilities for Btx. The Ministry of Economics (led by a member of the more conservative FDP), which had an interest in fighting the DBP monopoly and was keen to leave some aspects of

Btx to the private sector, contended that the computer facilities were not part of the network.

9. There also are significant consequences of drawing this "transmission" boundary line with respect to the provision of terminal equipment by the DBP and, in particular, the attachment of data processing equipment to the network. The DBP generally has trod carefully in the area of providing new terminal equipment to avoid risking an unfavorable outcome on this issue. Nevertheless, the introduction of each new service provokes a discussion about whether the DBP legally can provide terminal equipment therefor. The governing principles are set out in the FAG of 1928, which gives the DBP the right to operate and to construct all "telecommunications" equipment—the network, switches, and all equipment that is "allied" to the network.

10. To preserve its theoretical power and to preserve the network, the DBP maintains that it should have the right to provide—or, at least, to regulate—all terminal equipment, including that which has substantial, if not complete, data processing capabilities. In practice, the DBP avoids complications by entering the terminal equipment market in only a limited way. Although it has a monopoly on the main stations and modems, it only has a market share of about fifteen percent in PBXs, ten percent in telefax, and zero percent in mobile radio, teletext, paging, and telex.

11. With respect to ISDN terminals, the DBP policy seems to be that it will have complete technical and operational responsibility for the network termination unit. The subscriber should, however, have some flexibility with regard to the terminal device used. The DBP position is that it should not be excluded from the terminal markets; if it has experience with terminal equipment, it can more readily engage in discussions aimed at standardization of network services, which it views as critical to achieving international compatibility in services. *See* H. Schön, *Toward the ISDN, supra*, at 21-22.

B. The Distinction Between "Facilities" and "Services"—A Predicate for Liberalization?

This statutory and jurisprudential framework appears to have generated—at least by inference—a distinction between "facilities" and "services." The DBP's primary responsibility for providing the technical infrastructure ("technik") implies that services using the networks can be offered separately. Thus, the limitations on the DBP's authority may lay the predicate for the proposition that other entities might be permitted to offer services that are not subject to the direct control of the DBP.

1. The line between "facilities" and "services" is capable of significant erosion, however, where, for example, a particular "service" function is integrated into the network or the hardware. If the DBP is, by way of example, barred from providing "enhanced" services, to what extent can it "process" data through data concentrators? At one end of the spec-

trum, it appears that the DBP cannot offer complete remote access data processing to subscribers; at the other, it provides central computing capacity to users of Btx services.

2. It may be that the distinctions turn on to whom the "service" is offered or how it is marketed. If, for example, it is a service capable of being marketed separately—and is of immediate use—to subscribers, it may not be within the jurisdiction of the DBP. If, however, it is a "service" inseparably tied to the "transmission" function, it is likely to be reserved to the DBP. These pure "definitional" issues will have to be confronted as such by the DBP, by German policy makers, and, most probably, by the new governmental commission.

3. In this connection, the new commission will examine value-added services and how they should be defined. Currently, private company value-added networks offering third-party services to the general public are not permitted. One point of departure for the commission's analysis may focus on the existing distinction between "basic," or network-related services, and all others. It is likely that the commission will scrutinize the potential for engaging in "resale"—Stage I competition—that adds value to the underlying transmission and is not simply "arbitrage." The new 64 Kbit/s digital tariffs offer opportunities for private data services that will collect traffic and use data concentrators. Hence, private routing of data will, in some cases, be cheaper than use of a subscriber's own leased circuit. Voice resale, by contrast, is not a likely candidate for liberalization.

4. The DBP does permit some shared use of the public fixed data connection network for lower speed transmission. Indeed, the degree of flexibility and availability of leased private lines—compared with some other major European countries—is often overlooked. Although the scope of private line use is limited, third-party users are permitted where there is a common business interest. In 1974, the DBP published regulations on the use of the public data network for fixed connections for the transmission of digital information. Typically, the DBP leases a modem with the fixed circuit; the primary restriction on use is that data terminal equipment—concentrators, processors, etc.—may not be used "exclusively" ("ausschliesslich") or "predominantly" ("überwiegend") for the purpose of transmitting information for third parties. *See* Article 6, para. 6 of Regulations. Hence, some limited third-party use is permitted as long as it does not exceed fifty percent of the use of the circuit. This limitation was the subject of a complaint before the Federal Constitutional Court. In 1977, the Court held that because private data transmission would reduce DBP revenues, the restriction could remain—at least until the development of usage-based charges. *See Urteil vom 12.10.1977 zur Verfassungsbeschwerde gegen die Direktrufverordnung*, 1 BvR 217/75, 1 BvR 216/75. (Decision on the Constitutional Complaint re: Fixed Connection Regulation).

5. Some users hope that the DBP's introduction of usage-based pricing, in accordance with the decision of the Court, will be the predicate for the elimination of these shared and third-party use limitations.

There is, however, in general, great resistance to the usage-sensitive rate structures being proposed in Germany.

6. As of 1984, the DBP has itself begun offering a "telebox" service—a "value-added" service with public switched message delivery and store and forward features. Subscribers will need to supply their own terminals and will have access via the public switched or Datex-L and Datex-P networks. The central computer will be operated by the DBP. In West Berlin and Bayern, bills have been proposed to regulate this service under the guise of "data protection." The DBP has responded that the service is within the jurisdiction of the Bund and not the Länder; any amendment to data protection laws should, therefore, be initiated by the DBP. The Länder reply that they do not want to assert regulatory jurisdiction over the entire service, but just with respect to the data protection aspects.

7. The Länder also are involved in the issue of defining new services: some are now moving forward to regulate "enhanced" services on cable systems that, they contend, are not within the exclusive province of the Bund. In particular, the Land of Baden-Württemberg has drafted a statute on telecommunications that asserts jurisdiction over new telecommunications/media services such as Btx and other text communication. *See* Gesetzüber die Neuen Medien-Landesmediengesetz Baden-Württemberg (Entwurf) (July 1983). Subsequently, the draft was revised to relate more closely to media policy issues.

8. Aside from strict limitations on third-party provision of services, there are some extremely limited opportunities for alternative facilities. Private long-distance systems may be set up by public entities (*e.g.*, the federal agencies charged with responsibility for railways, shipping, and roads, and the utility companies.) Private firms are allowed to construct their own facilities, on their own premises, or to connect buildings located not more than 25 km apart. Private, intra-firm long-distance services require obtaining DBP permission; in no circumstance is third-party use of such systems allowed. It appears that a private network has, on occasion, been interconnected with the DBP network.

C. German Pricing Policy and "Enhanced Service Networks"

1. As described above, *see supra* Section IV., the DBP is extremely concerned that unrestricted liberalization of leased line use would encourage widespread "cream-skimming" and arbitrage due to the rate differentials between leased lines and public switched voice services. The DBP also has recognized that leased line services, when connected to PBXs, or to the public switched network, are not always a direct substitute for public switched services. In some cases, such leased line services can even stimulate network utilization of public switched services.

2. In analyzing certain value-added services, for example, Dr. Neumann and Prof. von Weizsäcker have noted that some such services

actually can develop market opportunities that subsequently can be exploited by the DBP. K-H Neumann and C.C. von Weizsäcker, *Tariff Policy, supra*, at 254. Such networks are recognized as possibly assisting in the effort to standardize subsequently-developed DBP networks. Thus, there is some recognition that autonomous development in services can yield benefits to the DBP. Activities that truly are innovative are, moreover, not substitutes for existing services and they are, therefore, unlikely to divert DBP revenues.

3. Usage-sensitive rate structures are implemented to permit liberalized use of leased lines while minimizing the risk of an adverse impact on public switched services. Such rate structures, intended to reduce incentives for pure resale and arbitrage, may be overbroad and may stifle the development of innovative services. To avoid this result, one approach may be to create categories comprised of special service vendors that can be authorized outside of the potentially inhibiting usage-sensitive rate structure. Concurrently, a usage-sensitive rate element could be used to reduce incentives for services that involve "pure resale" and as to which there are fewer benefits—and more detrimental consequences—than there are from value-added services.

4. The linchpin of German policy on leased lines has been economic and pricing related. Therefore, it seems likely that the DBP approach to defining permitted "value-added" services also would focus on the economic aspects of such services, *i.e.*, the substitutability with existing services, rather than, as was the case in the U.S., on technological criteria.

5. Where the criteria of economic consequences are difficult to quantify, establishing clear-cut administrative benchmarks will be troublesome. One approach, of course, would be to exclude altogether categories of activity, such as pure resale of leased lines for the provision of switched voice services. This classification scheme is the basis for the U.K. policy of proscribing "simple" or "pure" resale. In adopting this policy, however, the British faced the problem that their ban on resale was overbroad; they retreated into a more flexible approach through a branch license authorizing various uses of private line services.

6. Usage-sensitive charges, or a prohibition on third-party operation of message-switching-like activities, may hamper the development of new types of transactional, brokerage, or information services; for such services the communications or message-switching elements may be quite incidental to the clearly unregulated components, *e.g.*, data processing or electronic publishing. Such limitations on leased line usage may dampen innovation in the electronic service sector without any appreciable advantage for the public switched services. Therefore, one categorical methodology would be to include these new electronic services in a class of activities that are not likely to serve as substitutes for switched services. It may be useful to begin a liberalization process with a special category of "hybrid"

data processing" or "hybrid informational service," as was recognized in such dissimilar regulatory settings as the *Computer I* proceeding in the U.S. and the July, 1982, French Law on Audiovisual Communication.

7. As to services between pure resale and "hybrid services," one relevant test might be to weigh the benefits of increased network utilization from such services against the potential impact on public services. One drawback of this benchmark, of course, is that the rationale for allowing new services becomes attentuated once the DBP makes its own equivalent offering. Obviously, a test for "market entry" that depends on whether the dominant entity offers the service is not desirable; for, if the dominant entity does so, there is a competitive rationale for its setting tariffs so as to discourage the entry—or to impair the viability—of a would-be or actual competitor.

8. Some observers of the German telecommunications scene believe that adopting a tariff-based "economic effects" test to determine the entry of enhanced service providers is a difficult proposition. One way of limiting the potential for an adverse impact on the public network is to do as the Japanese did with respect to classifying Type II carriers, *i.e.*, restricting the number of lines that can be provided. The recent experience in Japan, however, suggests that a limitation on lines is subject to interpretations that can generate competitive alternatives. Another policy toward enhanced services could focus on authorizing certain industry sectors to set up specialized networks. A value-added network oriented toward serving a significant industry could, however, have a more detrimental economic effect on public switched services than might a network offering service to the general public.

9. The German policy on value-added networks ultimately may focus on the adoption of a more cost-based pricing scheme for public switched services. Steps toward such a scheme would reduce the actual or perceived cost of liberalizing the use of the network.

VII. JURISDICTIONAL ISSUES AND THE FEDERAL SCHEME: SKIRMISHES ON THE BOUNDARY BETWEEN BUND AND LÄNDER

A. Introduction: Tensions Between Bund and Länder, Among the Länder

The division of responsibility between the Bund—telecommunications (including transmission facilities) and telecommunications services—and the Länder—media issues and content regulation of all non-point-to-point communications—can produce deadlock and considerable confusion in efforts to establish telecommunications policy.

1. At the least, the separation has made the introduction of new services extraordinarily difficult. The Länder argue that even telecom-

munications offerings cannot be initiated without their consent; the DBP asserts its exclusive jurisdiction. The tension between the Bund and the Länder is compounded by political and ideological give-and-take. The four Länder that now are controlled by SPD governments (Nordrhein-Westfalen, Hessen, Hamburg, and Bremen) are reluctant to acquiesce in CDU initiatives taken at the Bund level: they may block services for ideological or partisan purposes, not on the basis of some pragmatic view.

2. Further, compounding the problem is that, for some services (*e.g.*, Btx, DBS, satellite-to-cable, private broadcasting), all eleven Länder must reach an agreement—a "Staatsvertrag"—on how the service should be provided or regulated. The Staatsvertrag process, in dealing with private broadcasting issues, is made difficult by partisan disagreements between the four SPD and the seven CDU Länder governments. Moreover, a decided lack of organizational or procedural structure among the Länder—and of real depth in expertise in any one Land—can be a further roadblock to any agreement. Deadlock on achieving a Staatsvertrag can jeopardize or delay the introduction of new services.

B. Planning for "Facilities" versus Responsibility for "Services": An Example from Broadcasting

Separating responsibility for the provision of facilities, on the one hand, and services, on the other, can, therefore, be a major roadblock in telecommunications and media planning. A further distinction between "telecommunications" and "media" services—or between "individual" communications and "mass" communication—raises complex questions about the way authority is divided between the Bund and the Länder. One example of the problems that arise from the jurisdictional division that results from the distinction between "facilities" and "services" may serve as an introduction to some of the themes that recur throughout the German experience:

1. The primary broadcasting organizations in Germany are two television networks, the ARD and the ZDF, both of which are within the control of the Länder. *See infra* Section VII.H.2. The Länder broadcasting organizations pay the DBP for its operation of the transmitter networks. There also are two federal broadcasting organizations: the Deutsche Welle ("DW") and the Deutschlandfunk ("DLF"). DW is a shortwave service for the international audience. The DLF is a medium frequency service directed at East Germany and elsewhere in Europe; it is not generally received in West Germany, except in Bonn, where it uses a high frequency signal. The authority of the Bund to provide the DW and the DLF service is based on the federal power to conduct foreign policy.

2. There have been several discussions between the Bund and the Länder with respect to the inauguration of a European-wide broadcasting service. The Ministry of the Interior—which has responsibility for media issues at the federal level—has claimed that such a service should be

offered by the DW and the DLF. The Länder, however, argue that the Bund has limited competence in broadcasting and that primary responsibility for the production of programming is vested in Länder broadcasting organizations and not in the DW or the DLF.

3. The struggle over which level of government should provide a service has now spilled over into facilities planning and the assignment and allocation of frequencies. The DBP represents German broadcasting organizations at ITU conferences; thus, Länder stations must file their claims for new frequencies with the Bund. The DLF, however, now claims that it should receive high frequency assignments so that it can supply the new service. The Prime Ministers of the Länder ("Ministerpräsidenten") contend, conversely, that Länder claims should have priority. Concerned with the Bund control over frequency assignment—and the potential for giving the DLF the authorization to provide a service based on such authority—the Länder now have taken the position that they should have the power over assignment and allocation. Prior to assigning certain frequencies to the DLF, they continue, Länder consent must be obtained.

4. The DBP responds that all technical issues, such as tower height and allocation, are within its exclusive competence. The issue is joined because the Länder claim primary competence in the field of broadcasting and argue that the Bund's competence in the provision of service is limited to that necessary to carry out foreign affairs (*i.e.*, there is no reason why DLF transmissions should be directed at a domestic audience.)

5. The struggle arises because it is difficult to distinguish control over facilities from services. There is no clean demarcation as regards the Länder's control over providing services that ultimately are dependent on facilities provided by the Bund. This dispute may need to be decided by the Federal Constitutional Court.

C. German "Videotex": The Line Separating "Broadcasting" and "Press" for an Information Service

Teletext services (or "videotex" in German), which use the vertical blanking interval, provide another field on which the Länder and the Bund have done battle: the definitional distinction in this dispute is between "broadcasting" and the "press."

1. The Länder—and Länder broadcasting organizations—argued that videotex is a "broadcast" text service because it constitutes the mass distribution of information to the entire broadcast audience. Furthermore, they contended that videotex, as a technical matter, is an integral part of the television broadcast signal. The Länder concluded, therefore, that their competence over broadcasting extended to videotex and that the Bund had no jurisdiction over the service.

2. The Bund's cudgel was taken up by the print publishers. They argued that videotex services were "press" services, a distinction with jurisdictional consequences. The Bund has some "skeletal"—and essentially

unused—power to regulate the press inasmuch as the Fifth Article of the Basic Law protects freedom of expression and freedom of the press. The Länder are barred from regulating or controlling the press. Thus, if Article 5 were applicable, it was argued that broadcasters could not deny publishers of their "right" to publish by, for example, denying them access to vidotex facilities. The Ministry of the Interior, which has competence over press matters, also pressed for jurisdiction over videotex services.

3. There was no clear understanding of how, should this argument have prevailed, the publishers would be afforded access to a technology fundamentally within the technical control of the broadcasters. The publishers had wanted to create a common editorial staff to generate the text and urged that the broadcasters simply make transmission capacity available to them. The publishers wanted the Ministry of the Interior to "license" access to the videotex facilities even though it was not evident how such a scheme would work in practice (*i.e.*, how responsibility for the service would be shared). The Ministry, however, planned to propose "model" legislation to the Länder to enable them to enact uniform legislation without overt Bund involvement. (The Ministry has been reluctant to exercise its power over the press; hence, an outright "licensing" scheme would seem to be an improbable development.)

4. The controversy between the Länder and the Bund—through their respective broadcasting and publisher surrogates—lasted from 1979 to 1981. A compromise was struck in the nature of an agreement—a two-year "Videotex Vertrag" between the public broadcasting organizations and the publishers' association. This agreement is being implemented in an extended videotex pilot project in which the broadcasters and the publishers are information providers in a four-to-one ratio. During this experiment, it is likely that the Länder will decide how to regulate videotex. Ultimately, additional capacity may be made available to the publishers.

5. Because the dispute over videotex was not resolved in a Staatsvertrag, the controversy is not yet over. It appears likely to become active again soon. The dispute illustrates how the tension between the two levels of the federal structure can be fought on definitional bases that classify services—as either "broadcast" or "press"—and on technical grounds that operational control by the Länder broadcasting organizations over broadcast facilities necessarily implies control over services. Interestingly, the fact that the DBP has ultimate control over transmission facilities for broadcasting apparently was not prominent in the argument that the Bund should have jurisdiction to license videotex providers.

D. "Broadcasting": Jurisdiction over "Transmission" Services

Similar questions, over the broadcasters' use of their facilities to provide services that are not traditional "broadcasting," have not yet arisen in Germany. In the United States, for example, FM stations are permitted to use their subcarrier capacity to offer data, paging, or other common carrier services. Although subcarriers in Germany are used by FM broadcasters for stereo sound, there apparently has been no suggestion that those facilities can be made available for other kinds of services. Should such issues ever surface, it seems certain that, with respect to common carrier offerings, the DBP would not want the Länder broadcasting organizations to provide such "transmission" services without contesting their competence to do so. Without an adequate procedural mechanism for dealing with the jurisdictional dispute, it is likely that subcarrier services could not be initiated quickly.

E. Bildschirmtext: Problems in Classifying a Multifaceted, Hybrid Service

The controversy over the introduction and regulation of Bildschirmtext ("Btx") (interactive videotex or viewdata) has presented an array of complex definitional—hence, jurisdictional—questions. The struggle between the Länder and the DBP over the initiation of Btx—both wanted to introduce the service—has been waged on the turf of classification. Is Btx a "private" or "individual" communication offering, within the scope of the DBP's competence, or is it a "mass" communications service, for the Länder? *See* J. Scherer, DVR Beiheft 16, *supra*.

1. In the mid-1970's, the Länder argued that Btx was a new form of media and that, therefore, the general legal principle that there is no competence in the Bund unless explicitly conferred should apply. The DBP was primarily concerned that it would not be denied resonsibility for the underlying transmission or operation of the central computers, which, it claimed, were "telecommunications" equipment that were inseparable from the network. (The Btx system now relies on one IBM central computer.) The DBP, however, also vigorously claimed jurisdiction over that aspect of Btx that could be defined as an "individual" communications service, such as a mailbox service. The Länder responded that the DBP should have no responsibility for Btx programming or content. The Länder and the DBP, however, agree on one thing: Btx should be introduced.

2. From 1980 to 1983 the DBP conducted two pilot projects for Btx in West Berlin and Düsseldorf/Neuss. The two Länder involved in these tests—Nordrhein-Westfalen and Berlin—did cooperate with the DBP and drafted pilot laws on, for example, data protection. Despite such cooperation, there were some disputes over the respective competences of the Bund and the Länder. The DBP was anxious to prove that the service would

be successful; the Länder, however, were quite concerned with the negative aspects of Btx services, *i.e.*, the impact on children and families, the effect of advertising, and the nature of consumer protection guarantees, especially with regard to adhesion contracts. The DBP's position was that questions of consumer protection and data protection are matters for the Bund. (Specifically, the DBP took the position that the Länder had ceded jurisdiction over some data protection by their participation in the Bundesrat; some Länder legislation in this area is, however, permissible.)

3. The issue of data protection arose from a concern that mass or individual patterns of Btx usage might be conveyed to third parties. The Länder data protection commissioners had been active participants in this debate. The DBP contended that the Länder had no jurisdiction over data protection because data protection issues are implicated primarily when "individual" communications are involved. The DBP said that it could not, in any event, be obligated by Länder legislation to protect personal data in the computer. Rather, it contended, it had the primary obligation for secrecy under both Article 10 of the FAG and Article 10 of the Basic Law, which obligates the Bund to protect data.

4. Other legal problems highlight the jurisdictional complexity of Btx service offerings and may explain why it was so difficult to achieve an agreement on a legal framework prior to introduction of Btx. Services such as telebanking or teleshopping involve contract law—areas not within the competence of the Länder but subject to civil law principles. There also were discussions involving the role of the DBP as billing collector; there was some question whether the DBP should work for private companies in this capacity or, indeed, whether the massive DBP should compete with private debt collection agencies at all. It was clear, however, that the relationship between the DBP and the information provider is governed by the DBP's regulations.

5. There also was a significant debate on the role of the press in offering Btx. On the one hand, there was some question whether Btx would threaten the viability of the press, whose status is protected by Article 5 of the Basic Law. On the other, the press is within an exception to the data protection laws: data stored by the press for press purposes is not subject to the control of the data protection organizations. This exception, which eventually was embodied in the Staatsvertrag, raises the question of whether Btx information providers are "press" for data protection purposes. If so, it seems that the data protection laws would have little effect on much of the information collected by Btx providers.

6. Finally, there has been some concern that the mass media opportunities of Btx could lead to a concentrated information market that is controlled by a handful of large print or broadcast organizations. With respect to this last concern, the *Freie Rundfunk Aktiengesellschaft Gründung (FRAG)*, BVerfGE 57, 295, decision of the Federal Constitutional Court, *see infra* Section VII.H.12., may shed some light on the Land's responsibility to ensure that diversity in the media is preserved.

7. In the course of the pilot projects, the DBP pointed to three categories of use for Btx: (1) information distributed to everyone, (2) information for closed user groups, and (3) individual or mailbox communications. It took the position that the latter two categories were "telecommunications" and that, with respect to the first, classification was dependent on the content of the information being distributed. That is, if the "mass" communication is cultural, or akin to the press, it would be within the Länder's jurisdiction; if, however, it is like a catalogue—teleshopping—and merely offers products for sale, it is not a "mass media" service and, consequently, would be outside the competence of the Länder. The Länder replied that contents cannot be classified by type. The Länder also contended that they alone should should control the access of information providers to the systems.

8. Consequently, the two "trial" Länder passed laws that conditioned providers' access to the system on the following: whether they (1) were in Germany, (2) were capable of holding public office, (3) were capable of contracting, and (4) would be held responsible for full criminal liability. The DBP contended that questions of access must be resolved exclusively by federal law, that it would be obliged to give all users access, and that it would not be confined to users sanctioned by the Länder. The Länder position was that only Länder approval—in accordance with these conditions—would be required.

9. The discussions on resolving these issues were not completely public, largely because it was believed that extended and vociferous public debate could delay introduction of the service. Faced with DBP pressure—that it would introduce Btx services on its own by September 1, 1983—the Länder struck a compromise: they would enter into a Staatsvertrag that would attempt to resolve some of these jurisdictional issues and would hedge on others. Both sides appeared desirous of having a legal framework prior to introduction of Btx, and the major questions was whether the Staatsvertrag would be signed in time. Nevertheless, this compromise did frustrate the public because of its exclusion from effective participation in the process.

10. As this dispute illustrates, there are significant problems when a service has facets that require a "Solomon-like" splitting of the baby to resolve jurisdictional disputes. Btx services do straddle the boundary lines that separate the Länder and Bund competences. They include data processing, access to third-party data bases, and individual and closed user group communications. Thus, Btx has many characteristics of a communications system, within the jurisdiction of the Bund. Moreover, Btx also resembles a "press" service, for which competence also is vested in the Bund. However, to the extent that Btx is like broadcasting it falls within the purview of the Länder. Even if it were to be classified as "broadcasting" the Länder could not act without constraint: Article 5 of the Basic Law, which explicitly includes broadcasting, still would have an impact on *how* the Länder would or could regulate Btx as a "broadcasting" technology. Many organizations

desiring to offer Btx tried to sidestep Länder control by arguing that the new service was not in fact broadcasting.

11. There was little guidance in decisional or statutory law as to how these jurisdictional skirmishes might be resolved. The *1. Rundfunkurteil* of the Federal Constitutional Court only framed rules and guidelines for traditional broadcasting services. There was no precedent for how the efforts to classify Btx for jurisdictional purposes might proceed. There was ample opportunity, therefore, to draw lines and to apply different standards for different aspects of the service. The procedures, however, for reaching a jurisdictional accommodation were far from regularized: a key lesson from the Btx experience is that it is difficult to achieve the level of coordination that is required for introducing a technology that offers a complex array of services and that falls within two jurisdictions. Indeed, Dr. Scherer has criticized the agreement between the Bund and Länder for failing to comport with constitutional standards for procedural regularity. *See* J. Scherer, DVR Beiheft 16, *supra*.

12. In March, 1983, the Länder ultimately concluded the Staatsvertrag on Btx. The Staatsvertrag starts from the premise that Btx is a medium for which there is no Bund jurisdiction. For a general discussion of the issues raised by the Staatsvertrag and the questions of jurisdiction implicated in the various broadcast, press, and telecommunications aspects of Btx, see J. Scherer, *Rechtsprobleme des Staatsvertrags über Bildschirmtext*, Neue Juristische Wochenschrift, August 17, 1983, Heft 33, at 1832. Cognizant of the nature of and circumstances surrounding the "compromise" with the Bund, the Länder Staatsvertrag has only minimal regulations with respect to the "point-to-point" aspect of Btx communications. The DBP adopted implementing regulations for the technical infrastructure and for other issues (*i.e.*, tariffs) in the 22nd Amendment Order, Federal Law Gazette I, at 783 (issued May 6, 1983).

13. Despite the accommodation with the DBP represented by the Staatsvertrag, the DBP itself is nowhere mentioned in the agreement. Certain processing or store and forward functions are performed by the Bildschirmtext Zentrale (Central Computer), but the Staatsvertrag supposes that the installations need not necessarily be owned by the DBP. Thus, the DBP's functions in this area are referred to only as those of the "carrier" ("Betreiber"), thus leaving open the possibility for private organizations to operate the central processing services. *See* Article 1, Staatsvertrag über Bildschirmtext.

14. The exact scope of the DBP's role in Btx remains, therefore, unresolved. Who, for example, controls implementation of data protection statutes with respect to the central computing facilities? The DBP maintains that the responsibility lies in federal officials because the facilities are within the DBP's jurisdiction. To this end, the DBP has implemented data protection provisions in its own regulations. The Länder data protection controllers claim primary responsibility for ensuring that Btx services adhere to data protection laws. The DBP views these Länder officials as unjustifiably

endeavoring to broaden their jurisdictional reach: a maneuver by the Länder to regulate fields that are within the competence of the Bund. The issue is now stalemated because the DBP, in refusing to acknowledge Länder authority, has refused to allow their data protection controllers to enter the DBP central computing facilities.

F. Private Cable Television: Tensions Between Bund—"Telecommunications" and "Facilities"—and Länder—"Broadcasting" and "Content"

The controversy over private cable television illustrates how media and telecommunications policies have become intertwined, how politics plays a role in setting those policies, and where the DBP and Länder are testing the limits of their respective jurisdictions.

1. For more than a decade there have been discussions of cabling Germany, primarily to allow the introduction of private cable programming. Since the 1950's there has been cabling in several areas, largely to improve broadcast reception of the three normal television channels and assorted radio stations. Nevertheless, as the density of transmitters in Germany obviated the need for cable retransmission in most areas, there was no reason to proceed with a nationwide cabling program. (In West Berlin, however, the geographic and political situation has contributed to a high rate of cable penetration; it was expected that sixty percent of all households would be passed by cable by the end of 1984.)

2. Cable television was the subject of some discussion in the KtK report. In 1976, pilot projects were discussed. After five years of preparation, on January 1, 1984, the first of four cable television projects began in Ludwigshafen. Service began in Munich on April 1, 1984, and is planned for June, 1985, in Dortmund and for September, 1985, in West Berlin.

3. Before the change in government, the Länder wanted to install coaxial cable—under their auspices—to forestall rapid movement toward private broadcasting. The DBP attempted to fight the initiative, largely to preserve its own jurisdictional authority. With the change to a CDU government, the DBP now has become much more committed to cabling Germany. To a certain extent this commitment appears to be connected to partisan perceptions of who controls the broadcasting organizations. The CDU claims that the public broadcasters are biased against it; concomitantly, Dr. Schwarz-Schilling is committed to cabling Germany and to the implementation of commercial television. Dr. Schwarz-Schilling points out that only two percent of German households received cable connections in 1982 whereas other European nations had a 50-90% penetration level.

4. The SPD is—at both the federal and Länder levels—reluctant to embrace the cabling project. (The anti-technology Grüen (Green Party) is opposed to spending any money at all on cable). It has believed that private broadcasting threatens the viability of public television; but that

position is now softening somewhat. Given the rather severe limits on the availability of over-the-air frequencies in Germany, cable is the most practicable way of introducing private broadcasting. Thus, the previous—SPD—federal government had a rather reserved approach toward cable.

5. This partisan dispute—based on ideological principles—has had an impact on the planning and construction of cable facilities—facilities that will be used to extend the telecommunications network. The CDU vigorously pushes the construction of coaxial cable as the quickest way of generating additional capacity for commercial broadcasting. At the same time, the CDU views immediate cabling as a means of providing significant opportunities for employment and stimulating the economy. The DBP now is investing DM 1 billion/year on installing coaxial cable and expects a profitable return in the next seven or eight years.

6. Although the SPD now favors cable—at least in principle—it disagrees with this strategy, urging that cabling be delayed for some years. It is skeptical about the positive economic impact of cable and is concerned about the effect of the new technologies on families, children and the marketplace. The SPD contends that it makes little technological sense to construct a coaxial system at this time when much more advanced and efficient fiber optic cable will soon be available.

7. The DBP replies that broadband technology is not yet mature enough for local distribution services. These issues are obviously wrapped up in the larger issue of private broadcasting. *See infra* Section VII.H. It is, however, not at all clear that the parties have focused on the impact of the coaxial/fiber optic decision on the potential for using cable to expand telecommunications services.

8. With cable—as much else in Germany—jurisdiction is split among several entities, and the absence of a single responsible regulator can make implementation of the technology difficult. The DBP constructs the network and installs cable and equipment. Private parties have responsibilities for inside wiring and final hook-ups, and they may, in certain circumstances, invest in DBP cable construction projects. Finally, the Länder are responsible for programming—deciding what gets sent through the cable.

9. This split has several consequences. First, as a technical matter, dividing installation responsibility between the DBP and private concerns, it is asserted by some in the Länder, might lead to inconsistent standards of workmanship and could increase costs; this claim, however, is disputed by the DBP.

10. Moreover, the distinction between cable facilities and cable programming can be an obstacle to coherent planning. The DBP gives cable facilities to the Länder and allows them to allocate the use of the facilities. The DBP is reluctant to go any further—to do anything that would bespeak the setting of media policy—lest it find itself before the Federal Constitutional Court. Länder involvement in the facilities planning process might be extremely useful. Some cooperation between the Länder and the

DBP obviously is required because the profitability of cable to the DBP depends on the services offered. Such cooperation is extensive—at least informally—between the DBP and the Office of the Berlin Senator of Culture, who is responsible for selecting programming in that region. Nevertheless, the DBP's decisions to build facilities or to establish services are neither regulated nor formalized. There is no opportunity for public participation nor is there a mechanism for the Länder to offer their perspective on the facilities that will be turned over to them. *See* J. Scherer, DVR Beiheft 16, *supra*. The inability to participate—not to say the division of responsibility between facilities construction and system planning—could be, for example, a significant hindrance when a local operator wants to expand the system more rapidly than the DBP's pace of construction might permit.

11. The Länder are setting up quasi-governmental entities to decide which programmers should have access to the system and what public access channels should be made available (and on what terms). These entities also will market the service, hire personnel, and negotiate with program suppliers for rights. The operator of the Ludwigshafen project is the Anstalt für Kabel-Kommunikation ("AKK"), which has involved local community groups. AKK has licensed Kommunal Bau as the operator to provide a link between the DBP and the subscriber. For Munich, the operator is the Münchner Pilotgesellschaft für Kabelkommunikation mbH ("MPK"), which rapidly is trying to expand plant to meet customer demand. Investors in MPK include the Land of Bayern, the city of Munich, the Chamber for Industry and Business, the newspaper and magazine publishers association, the ZDF, Bayerischer Rundfunk (Bavarian Broadcasting), and a "new media syndicate." Kabelsignal has the exclusive license to act as a commercial operator for MPK; it argues that it has had difficulty in coordinating efforts with the DBP and, consequently, that subscription levels are low.

12. Despite the primary responsibility of the Länder and the local operators for marketing the service and for selecting the programming, the DBP can play an active role by setting the price of a subscriber cable attachment. The hook-up had, until recently, cost households DM 400. Dr. Schwarz-Schilling, however, recently dropped the price for multi-dwelling houses to DM 20 in an attempt to increase subscription levels. The SPD and the Greens protested this move. Although the Ludwigshafen and Munich projects charge an additional monthly fee, it is obvious that the DBP can influence significantly the level of interest in cable services.

13. Even among the Länder there ultimately may be different criteria with respect to the level of commercialization, how and if private broadcasting should be allowed, and how transponder capacity should be allocated. The Länder have been trying for many months to work out a Staatsvertrag to develop a uniform set of programming standards (*e.g.*, limits on foreign-originated programs or advertising)—or, at least, to work out a mechanism for accommodating inter-Länder differences.

14. The DBP's satellite transmission of signals for cable transmission (*See infra* Section VII.G.) is a further example of how the distinction

between facilities and services can lead to confusion and can constitute a potential impediment to the harmonious introduction of cable services. More particularly, it raises the question of how to distinguish a point-to-multipoint transmission service from a broadcast service, and what might be the jurisdictional consequences therefor.

15. The DBP takes the position that it operates the two transponders allocated to Germany on the Eutelsat European Communications Satellite ("ECS") and, therefore, has primary responsibility for determining which programming is uplinked. The DBP also contends that downlinking is a "transmission" service. Hence, Dr. Schwarz-Schilling argues that because the DBP paid for both satellite and cable facilities, it, therefore, can not only place programming on the ECS at its discretion, but also downlink it to the Länder. Although it is questionable whether a producer would pay for transponder capacity without any assurance that the Länder would feed the signal into its cable system, Dr. Schwarz-Schilling contends that if only one Land agrees to take the program, it can be downlinked to all Länder. (The SPD is about to bring a case before the Federal Constitutional Court as to whether one Land can, in essence, force other Länder to adopt a particular policy or receive programming without consent.) Of course, the Länder could not be compelled to use the feed, so that the ability to transmit is, at least economically, tied to Länder decisions on content selection.

16. The Länder, however, take the legal position that the DBP, in downlinking signals, is not simply operating a telecommunications/transmission facility, but that its distribution makes it a "broadcasting" organization operating a network. Because such transmissions are like "broadcasting," the Länder contention is that deciding what signals can emanate from the ECS-1 transponders is subject to Länder approval. The DBP, of course, does not regard itself as providing a broadcasting service.

17. Starting January 1, 1985, Sat-1 began beaming an unscrambled signal to Germany's cable headends (except in West Berlin) from the ECS-1 satellite. Program consortia have developed to provide programming for Sat-1. Programming sixty percent of the Sat-1 schedule is the Programmgesellschaft für Kabel und Satellitenrundfunk ("PKS") (Program Company for Cable and Satellite Broadcasting), financed and principally owned by DG Bank in Frankfurt; it has links with the Beta-Taurus publishing group. There are many other program suppliers for Sat-1; some news and public affairs programming is supplied by Actuelle Press Fernsehen ("APF"), a consortium of 165 newspaper publishers that is dominated by the Axel Springer group, which has a thirty-five percent share. Additional news programming is supplied by Tele-Faz, a division of the *Frankfurter Allgemeine Zeitung* newspaper.

18. The DBP had reserved the two transponders on the ECS-1 satellite for the Länder's use in cable programming. The Länder, however, could not agree on how to allocate the capacity. The four Länder governed by the SPD held up agreement because they objected to private broadcasting. The Prime Ministers met three times and finally, in March, 1984, a protocol

was reached. The SPD Länder acceded to the following: the two transponders were to be given to the ZDF public broadcasting organization (East Beam) and a private consortium comprised of the PKS group and powerful German publishers, including the Burda group and Axel Springer (West Beam). The West Beam now transmits Sat-1. Since January 1, 1985, the East Beam has transmitted 3-Sat, a service of three German language networks: ZDF, Austria's ORF, and Switzerland's SRG. Programming on the East Beam is advertisement-free and is beamed to Ludwigshafen and Munich, with West Berlin cable subscribers due to receive the signal in the fall. The publishers had been concerned that private television could siphon revenues from the advertising income of the print media. Hence, involving the publishers in the ad-supported West Beam service may have been a way of defusing the threat of active print media opposition to private television. Once the Länder reached an agreement, the DBP moved ahead with its plan for private cable services.

G. Confusion in Television and Telecommunications Satellite Planning

The planning process for satellite services also has been marked by jurisdictional confusion arising from the facilities/services split. As the discussion on implementation of cable offerings on ECS-1 suggests (*see supra* Section VII.F.14.-16), the DBP's control over satellite transmission facilities coupled with the Länder's responsibility for broadcast services, can lead to some jurisdictional sparring. There are several areas that have the potential for raising similar issues.

1. The German TV-Sat project, with TV-Sat 1, now scheduled for launch in 1986, will be one of the first European DBS satellites in orbit. TV-Sat is currently being constructed by Eurosatellite Gmbh—a consortium of AEG-Telefunken and MBB of Germany, Aerospatiale and Thomson-CSF of France—and ETCA of Belgium. (The consortium, a product of an April, 1980, memorandum of cooperation between France and Germany, also is building the French Satellite, TDF-1.) According to a compromise among the Länder that now may have fallen apart, TV-Sat will have one transponder each for the two public broadcasters and a third for sixteen stereo radio services. (Although TV-Sat 1 has five transponders, only three can be operated simultaneously. On TV-Sat 2 the public broadcasters will be allocated four channels.) TV-Sat 2 will be available in 1987 or 1988.

2. Allocating the channels on TV-Sat had been difficult; the Federal Association of German Newspaper Publishers and the Federation of German Magazine Publishers had pushed hard to obtain the television channel allocations. Looking ahead to the utilization of TV-Sat, the DBP, at the end of 1982, asked the Länder to reach an agreement on the use of the satellite to enable the DBP to plan the scope of its investment. Specifically, the DBP wanted to know whether the Länder would even allow DBS services and, therefore, whether there would be users to justify building the satellite.

The DBP set a deadline on Länder agreement for the close of 1983 but preferred that they resolve the issue before that time. (Having assembled the construction personnel, it would have been easier to configure the satellite to fit the contours of the services that the Länder would permit instead of having the crew disband.)

3. There has, to date, been no Staatsvertrag among the Länder because the issue of DBS broadcasting is tied to the controversial question of whether or now private broadcasting should be allowed. It seems that a Staatsvertrag on private broadcasting would need to be reached before or concurrently with one on DBS services. This condition precedent will be difficult to achieve in the current political climate. *See infra* Section VII.H.

4. In attempting to conclude a Staatsvertrag on satellite usage, the Prime Ministers of the Länder have met several times over the last two years, most recently in early 1985. Prime Minister Bernhard Vogel of Rheinland-Pfalz had earlier proposed that there be two private channels, one to be used by the consortium already using the West Beam of the ECS-1 satellite, and a public channel allocated to the two state broadcasters. The SPD Länder rejected this compromise. Negotiations are continuing.

5. The debate could be forced by exploiting the jurisdictional split. The DBP might launch the satellite and then, because the public will be compelled to start paying for the DBP's expenditure, pressure might be applied to the Länder to conclude a Staatsvertrag or, at the least, to permit DBS programmers to have access to TV-Sat. Alternatively, or in conjunction, the CDU Länder would reach an agreement that might, for example, allow them to apply to the DBP for use of the satellite; in turn, these Länder then could decide who should program the channels.

6. A non-unanimous resolution could have some substantial constitutional ramifications, which might be raised in the SPD suit before the Federal Constitutional Court, *see supra* Section VII.F.15. Moreover, it also might impair significantly the federal principles that bind Germany. Moreover, proceeding without a Staatsvertrag where one would seem required could contribute to even greater partisanship in the debate on telecommunications and media policies and the proper role of the DBP.

7. Similar jurisdictional problems may arise in the planning of the DBP's telecommunications satellite—Deutsche Fernmeldesatellit ("DFS") Kopernikus. In December, 1983, the DBP commissioned the German telecommunications and aeronautical industries to build Kopernikus, in a project led by Siemens. The Kopernikus two-satellite system will be used for telecommunications—to transmit telephone calls, data, and videoconferencing and for traffic with Berlin—and for television distribution of up to five programs. This last service will not be direct broadcast transmission. Usage is projected for 1987. The television facilities will be offered to the Länder.

8. However, considerable preplanning with respect to programming—and construction—of the satellite will be required, and there is

some skepticism as to whether the Länder will be able to agree on these issues on a timely basis. In addition to the partisan politics that make such agreement problematic, the absence of a formal mechanism for Länder consultation with the DBP creates a significant risk of deadlock in the planning process.

9. As noted, *see supra* Section VII.F.18, an accommodation on the two German transponders on the ECS-1 was finally reached: one is being used by the Sat-1 consortium and the other by ZDF, the Swiss SRG, and the Austrian ORF. The East Beam ZDF-led program, which can be beamed to Switzerland and Austria, as well as to Germany, is a pan-German broadcasting service. Therefore, the issue of satellite programming not only raises domestic use questions, but also involves issues of transborder services.

10. The DBP view of such transborder services is likely to be that no Länder consent would be required if it decided to put, for example, another German language—but not necessarily West German—signal on the ECS transponders. The DBP's position is that it is free to provide transponder capacity—as a transmission service—to a programmer and that the nationality of the customer is not a concern falling within the competence of the Länder. The Länder contend that the DBP cannot sell transponders without obtaining their consent.

11. There is further pressure to reach a Länder agreement on satellite usage arising from the fact that six channels will be available to Germany on ECS-2. The abundance of capacity will intensify the impetus for private broadcasting and will complicate further the discussions on that issue.

H. Private Broadcasting: An Ideological Debate over Interdependent Policies

As suggested by the preceding discussion, cable and satellite policies are tied closely to the question of whether private broadcasting should be permitted. In part this is because "private" broadcasters are likely to use cable or satellite technologies before using terrestrial broadcasting facilities, which are dependent on all-too-scarce frequencies. The policies also are interdependent because public broadcasters perceive private broadcasters as a threat—both to advertising revenues and to the current near-monopoly that public broadcasting has in supplying television and radio programming to the public.

1. A Staatsvertrag will be required to implement private broadcasting on a national basis, and a welter of issues will need to be resolved by common agreement. Although the SPD has been relatively steadfast in opposing private broadcasting, there are indications that it is approaching the issue with greater flexibility. Certainly, the SPD's acquiescence in the allocation of the ECS-1 channels to a public and a private entity may be a precedent for a compromise on private broadcasting. Nevertheless, the issue remains highly partisan. Most of the Länder are, however, now

examining their media policies, with the most liberal of those being the Land of Niedersachsen. There is, of course, the possibility that the Länder with the fewest restrictions will attract the most capital, thereby creating some pressures for regulatory controversy.

2. There are two radio and television "networks" in Germany. The first—ARD (Arbeitsgemeinschaft der öffentlich-rechtlichen Rundfunkanstalten der Bundesrepublik Deutschland or the Association of Public Service Broadcasting Organizations of the Federal Republic of Germany)—is comprised of the nine regional broadcasting corporations ("Landesrundfunkanstalten") and Deutsche Welle and Deutschlandfunk, which together produce one nationwide program and one program for each region. The organization of these nine regional broadcasting corporations is as follows: they are public, but not state-owned, and are controlled by boards that have representatives from a wide spectrum of groups (*e.g.*, representatives of the political parties, unions, universities, churches, etc.)

3. In 1964, a Staatsvertrag created a separate centralized programming operation: ZDF (Zweites Deutsches Fernsehen or Second German Television). ZDF serves all of Germany.

4. Funding for ARD and ZDF is two-fold—from a license fee charged to viewers and from advertising. Commercial advertising revenues constitute twenty-to-forty percent of total income; although this is substantial, restrictions on the time of broadcast (*i.e.*, weekdays, from 6 to 8 p.m.) and the amount of advertising (20 minutes per day) limit the availability of commercial revenues. The license fees are set, are allocated by a Staatsvertrag, and are relatively nominal (DM 16.25/month); hence, as a political matter, it is extremely difficult to raise the fees. (This question is currently the subject of considerable discussion.) Thus, there is significant financial pressure on public broadcasters, a factor critical in the opposition to private broadcasting. License fees are obtained directly from viewers; collection appears not to be overly problematic.

5. The ARD and ZDF split the fees collected. The ARD gets 100% of the radio fees and seventy percent of the television fees; the ZDF gets the remaining thirty percent of the television fees. These fees are divided amongst the Länder broadcasting organizations on the basis of population. The larger organizations (*e.g.*, those of Bayern and Nordrhein-Westfalen) subsidize—to a limited extent—the smaller ones (*e.g.*, Saarland and Berlin).

6. Many of the CDU-controlled Länder (along with SPD-controlled Hamburg and Nordrhein-Westfalen) have modified or are in the process of modifying their media laws. The Länder of Baden-Württemberg, Bayern, and, especially, Niedersachsen have taken the lead in this area. It appears that cable—and satellite—will be the most significant technologies available to private broadcasters. Although over-the-air frequencies are scarce, there is some possibility that low-power television will be "private" in the northern Länder. (Hamburg, Niedersachsen, Schleswig-Holstein). There are now some private local radio stations—perhaps two channels in

each Land (as is the case in Baden-Württemberg). In Berlin, private broadcasting for the pilot project on cable transmission will be permitted.

7. The first Land that has moved ahead to implement a program for licensing a private broadcaster is Niedersachsen. In July, 1984, Niedersachsen decided to license an applicant for private television and radio broadcasting; the licensing criteria included the nature and scope of the programming promised. The applicant with the best proposal would get access to the satellite channel, to the cable system, and, if available, to any terrestrial broadcasting facilities. To date, there have been no actual licenses granted in Niedersachsen; a short while after passage of the law, Prime Minister Albrecht declared that private broadcasting would not happen because one Land, by itself, provides insufficient incentive for the production of programming. The SPD is bringing a suit against Niedersachsen before the Federal Constitutional Court to test, among other things, whether one Land can authorize private broadcasting without a Staatsvertrag.

8. As a political or ideological matter, it has proven difficult to reach a Staatsvertrag on private broadcasting issues. In significant part, this is due to two views of the appropriate "model" for ensuring diversity in broadcasting. The CDU favors a model of media diversity based on "external pluralism" ("aussen- plurales Modell"), which, as is the case in the United States, relies on the plethora of outlets to guarantee mdeica diversity. The draft media law in Baden-Württemberg states its reliance on principles of "external pluralism." In Niedersachsen, it is thought that "external pluralism" can be achieved with only three broadcasters; thus, in addition to ARB and ZDF, only one private broadcaster would need to be authorized for there to be the requisite diversity.

9. The SPD Länder believe in the principles of "internal pluralism" ("binnenplurales Modell"), which, as is the case with Germany public broadcasting organizations, depends for diversity on the representation of many groups and community sectors on the broadcasters' governing boards. Because the SPD thinks "external pluralism" is either inadequate or impossible to achieve, its position is that "internal pluralism" is required. The firmest adherent of this view is the SPD government in Hessen; its resolve may be a product of the alliance in Hessen of the SPD with the Green Party. (Hessen Prime Minister Böerner of the SPD is also resolutely opposed to private broadcasting.)

10. The Green Party is concerned about the adverse impact on children, families, and women of television and home computing technologies and will not support any government that wants private commercial broadcasting. As the Green Party gains in strength, it could replace the FDP as Germay's third party; in alliance with the SPD, it could form coalition governments in the Länder. (There could, for example, be an alliance of the SPD and the Green in Hessen.) This political development could be a major stumbling block in the movement for private broadcasting.

11. For the present, there are signs of flexibility in the approaches of three SPD Länder—Nordrhein-Westfalen, Hamburg and Bre-

men—where private broadcasting is now thinkable. Indeed, Hamburg approved a private cable bill, which became effective January 1, 1985; there is now a one-year trial, with safeguards built in to preserve the status of ARD and ZDF.

12. In arguing the question of whether private broadcasting is permitted, both the SPD and the CDU have relied on a 1981 decision of the Federal Constitutional Court, *Freie Rundfunk Aktiengesellschaft Gründung (FRAG)*, BVerfGE 57, 295, in which the Court had to determine whether private broadcasting would be permitted in the Saarland. The Saarland had passed a media law in 1967 and FRAG, a private broadcaster, had, ever since that time, been unsuccessful in its attempts to obtain a license. The Bund took the position that private broadcasting would not be permissible; the Land inquired of the Court why its law was inadequate. The Court declared the law unconstitutional, largely on the ground that it lacked the requisite specificity necessary to ensure diversity of opinion. The Court held that the vagueness of the statutory provisions for regulation of private broadcasters made conceivable the unconstitutional possibility of no state control whatsoever.

13. The Court also reviewed the statutory conditions that eventually might apply to private broadcasting. First, it held, responsibility for private broadcasting is to be vested in the Länder parliaments. The Court also set forth certain requirements that would have to be included in any Länder private broadcasting laws. From these conditions, both supporters and opponents of private broadcasting use the decision to bolster their positions. The SPD's interpretation is that private broadcasting—which relies on external pluralism—cannot meet the Court's mandate that diversity of opinion be ensured. The CDU believes that the *FRAG* decision not only permits private broadcasting, but also explicitly sanctions the "aussenplurales Modell."

14. Leaving aside the political and ideological obstacles to concluding a Staatsvertrag on private broadcasting, there also are substantial substantive questions that would need to be resolved. These issues include: regulations for the organization of private broadcasters, principles of content regulation, limitations on advertising, sanctions for violation of the laws, control of access to technologies, regulation of the concentration of control to guard against the formation of a broadcast monopoly, and the appropriate "model"—internal, external, a hybrid—to be followed.

15. In October, 1984, and in January, 1985, the Länder prime ministers met to review some of these issues. They seemed to have prepared a compromise draft Staatsvertrag, which would have permitted advertiser-supported commercial broadcasting. Advertising on private broadcasting would be limited to twenty percent of the broadcast day. To facilitate the entrance of private broadcasters into the market, public broadcasters would not have been able to increase the amount of advertising. These talks have not actually concluded a Staatsvertrag, so the status of the compromise is uncertain at best. Given the SPD position on private broadcasting—and

especially that of the Hessen government—it appears increasingly difficult to achieve the requisite consensus.

I. Länder Jurisdiction over "Enhanced" and Other "Telecommunications" Services

A panopoly of jurisdictional questions regarding telecommunications also is emerging. New Länder legislation raises a spectrum of definitional issues—what services are conceded to the DBP, what services the Länder claim are within their competence—that are far from resolved. *See, e.g., supra* Section VI.B.6. (discussing Länder attempts to regulate DBP "telebox" services).

1. The draft "Landesmediengesetz" of Baden-Württemberg presents the most complicated set of issues, being the most comprehensive of the Länder statutes now being considered. *See supra* Section VI.B.7. The draft law deals specifically with radio and television. Most significantly, it asserts jurisdiction over "enhanced" telecommunications services offered over the cable network. The draft statute is vague with respect to what are "enhanced" services in cable networks; the bill claims jurisdiction over Btx, teletext, and other cable text services and asserts the right to use the network for some telecommunications services. There needs to be more attention paid to which services are to be deemed "enhanced" for jurisdictional purposes. The statutory scheme contemplates an independent agency that will, in connection with the parliament of the Land, supervise the telecommunications planning process.

2. There also is a view in Baden-Württemberg that the telecommunications planning procedure must be coordinated with the DBP to facilitate the distribution of transmission capacities. There are no formal procedures in the bill to achieve such coordination; only informal consultation will be used, which may well turn out to be a major weakness of the proposal.

3. The Länder are interested in regulating—and offering—telecommunications services because of their economic impact in developing a telecommunications infrastructure. The Prime Minister of Baden-Württemberg is particularly keen on the notion of tying Länder development to a more liberal telecommunications policy. Located in Baden-Württemberg are the headquarters of several companies in the telecommunications and information industry (*e.g.*, SEL and IBM Germany). This telecommunications initiative is, then, in part, an attempt to make Baden-Württemberg the Land of high technology—a "Silicon Valley"; the land hopes to attract investment from all over Germany and Europe.

4. At the same time, the assertion of jurisdiction by the Länder over telecommunications services is an effort to pressure the DBP to allow or to encourage innovation. As noted previously, the Länder have

sought to assert jurisdiction over telemetry exchange (*see supra* Section III.E.1.) and other two-way services: their argument is that all new services offered by the DBP require prior Länder agreement.

VIII. SOME IMPLICATIONS OF JURISDICTIONAL LINE-DRAWING

A. Deadlock and Slow-Down in Development of Telecommunications Sector

1. The potential for Länder deadlock for new services is enormous. There is considerable question whether the Staatsvertrag process can cope with the plethora of technical, social, economic, and political issues that surround each decision. The deadlock is caused, in significant part, by partisan politics. The splits among the CDU, the SPD, and the Greens are deep and are rooted in ideology. Even where the Bund and the majority of the Länder are governed by the same party (as is the case today), the federal structure seems to require agreement among all the Länder.

2. The varying ideological approaches represent fundamental differences toward industrial policy and technology. The CDU position, in short, is that some liberalization can lead to economic growth and to a stronger posture worldwide for Germany. The SPD is concerned about threatening the viability of the present framework and the social impact of technological change. The Green party is anti-industrial in orientation and not particularly interested in the growth of Germany's competitive position.

3. There is a widely-held view that the entire federal scheme helps groups that want to slow down development. The struggle among the Länder and between the Länder and Bund not only is symptomatic of a desirable balance of power, but also can exacerbate partisan or ideological tensions. The Länder, for their part, have authority in only a few areas; among them are education, broadcasting—"culture," broadly defined. Thus, the Länder try to flex their jurisdictional muscles in these areas to achieve some negotiating strength with the Bund in others.

4. The jurisdictional deadlock poses, of course, very significant practical difficulties. Planning for transmission facilities is problematic if there is no assurance that permission will ever be granted for their use. Investment decisions by the DBP must be integrated with service planning. The DBP is faced with a dilemma: should it build facilities in order to force Länder decisionmaking, with the risk that such facilities may never be utilized or become profitable? It is, however, clear that the facilities planning process—which is driven by technology and user demand—cannot always wait until a political accommodation is reached with the Länder or until the Länder agree among themselves. The implication is, therefore, that facilities may not be built—or may be built more slowly than elsewhere.

Although the industrial policy impact of being behind developments in other nations is not obvious, some adverse impact would not be unlikely.

B. Procedural and Substantive Hurdles in Achieving Consensus

1. A major—if not the major—problem in the structure would seem to be the absence of an organizational and procedural mechanism to resolve disputes, ease tension, or carry out necessary cross-jurisdictional planning functions. There is no formal process for concluding a Staatsvertrag, and there may well be sound reasons for making the process more formal. There is no central staff among the Länder. Rather, each Land has a special staff for specific tasks in the office of the Ministerpräsident ("Staatskanzlei"). These staff members prepare for meetings of the Prime Minister, but the absence of a central organization hampers the preparation process. Hence, instead of meeting to conclude an agreement, the Prime Minister must meet repeatedly to discuss and to negotiate a Staatsvertrag.

2. Similarly, an absence of a formal consultation procedure for discussions between the Länder and the DBP makes long-term planning and short-term implementation difficult. Finally, the Länder staffs are unprepared to deal with the complex array of telecommunications issues with which they are confronted, whether by the DBP or by political initiative originating in the Länder governments. There are, for example, usually only two or three individuals on each Land's staff who may know anything about telecommunications. These people often are not trained technically; such inadequate staffing also contributes to the deadlock among the various policy-making organizations.

3. Achieving a consensus is difficult enough when only one issue is involved, but it is even more problematic when there is an interlocking series of issues: private broadcasting tied to cable, which is tied to satellite policy—all of which is wrapped together with telecommunications issues and, therefore, the fundamental DBP-Länder split of authority. Thus, there is an overwhelmingly complex set of variables, political and policy thrusts, and varying intensities of interest that affect each Staatsvertrag proceeding.

4. Nevertheless, the obstacles to achieving a unified planning process may seem to some—in the SPD and in the Green Party—as somewhat beneficial. They admit that the deadlocks and jurisdictional struggles make it less likely that liberalization will occur to stimulate German competitiveness. They note, however, that less regulation of a sector does not, without more, mean that it will be at the competitive forefront: the German consumer electronics industry is not regulated, yet it, too, is not at the vanguard of worldwide competition. The sentiment exists in the SPD and the Green Party that, in any event, international competitiveness may not be all that important. Rather, some think, Germany might be better off if it focused on the rate of unemployment or the impact of technology on family

life. Thus, they conclude, these concerns—and not just procedural or organizational mechanisms for achieving change—should be at the crux of German decisionmaking. The question for many in Germany is whether Germany can "afford to miss the 'telecommunications' boat." The answer for some is "yes, if that boat is the 'Titanic.'"

C. Länder Pressure to "Open Up" the System

The pressures from the Länder to be given more authority over telecommunications services—and to participate in the DBP planning process—may well "open up" the system.

1. The experience in the U.S. suggests that one "chink" will, almost inevitably, widen to liberalize the entire structure. If the Baden-Württemberg assertion of jurisdiction over "enhanced" cable services is successful—and withstands constitutional attack—liberalization may follow elsewhere. None of the other Länder will be particularly eager to lose the competitive edge or reputation for innovation to one of their own. Clearly, the decision in the case involving the Niedersachsen private broadcasting law could lay the predicate for this and other attempts by the Länder to erode the monopoly on provision of services, if not facilities. To that extent, therefore, constitutional litigation could play a significant role in any move toward liberalization of the monopoly—much as the AT&T litigation did in the U.S.

2. There would appear to be scant prospect of a federal constitutional convention to address some of these jurisdictional concerns. Thus, at least in the short-term, German telecommunications and media policy may have to muddle through.

IX. LONG-TERM PERSPECTIVES IN TELECOMMUNICATIONS POLICY AND STRUCTURE

A. Pricing Issues, the Role of the DBP, and the Role of Users

1. Pricing issues will be at the center of telecommunications policymaking in the DBP over the next few years. There may be some movement toward cost-based pricing, but political factors make that an unlikely development, at least in the near-term. There is, however, some indication that the network modernization program—or the implementation of an ISDN environment—may introduce some cost-based elements in pricing practices. International pressures may yet push pricing issues—as unpopular as they are—into being considered by the new governmental commission.

2. In the event that movement toward cost-based pricing does not become a greater priority, it seems quite probable that there will be

further initiative to harmonize pricing structures. There is a genuine concern about the development of arbitrage, which is seen as uneconomic and contrary to the public's interest. There is some suggestion that certain value-added services might be allowed in time, but users are anxious for the liberalization of the network—and certainly for more flexible, cost-effective access to leased lines. The DBP may find it increasingly difficult to move aggressively to "harmonize" leased line and public switched tariffs, even as leased line rates are moving closer toward costs elsewhere in Europe.

3. The success of U.S., U.K., and Japanese users in lowering the rates for leased lines may prod German users into taking a more active interest in German telecommunications policy; historically, German users have not done so. The Deutscher Industrie- und Handelstag (German Chambers of Commerce) has followed major policy developments, as has the Deutsche Telecom users group. The International Telecommunications Users Group ("INTUG") has several members who have large networks in Germany and keen interests in German policies. INTUG is, however, sometimes viewed by the DBP as representative of U.S. and U.K. multinationals more than of German companies. Beyond the user groups, there are two groups of manufacturers that are involved in the process: ZVEI (Industry Association for Electronic Products), with Siemens and ITT (SEL), and the VDMA (Machinery Equipment Association), with IBM and Nixdorf in its ranks. These two groups, led, respectively, by Siemens and IBM, have taken different stances on many issues. The lack of a common user and manufacturer perspective may have diminished their impact on German telecommunications policy.

4. The question of whether the DBP can provide terminal equipment has bedeviled the DBP for years—and looks to continue to do so. The DBP—and other observers—are concerned that forcing the DBP out of existing or future equipment markets will, in the long run, deprive the consumer of choice. The DBP probably would like to increase its presence in the equipment marketplace: the DBP would, for example, hope to be competitive in ISDN terminal equipment. Political and competitive forces may make it difficult for the DBP to enlarge significantly its market presence in terminal equipment.

B. DBP Structure and Control

1. There will, undoubtedly, be some changes in the structure of the DBP over the next five years. There may be greater separation of the postal and telecommunications services within the DBP, although there probably will remain one Ministry for Posts and Telecommunications. Pressure to segregate post and telecommunications functions may come from the Ministries of Economics and for Research and Technology; however, it is likely to be resisted by various political groups, particularly trade union groups.

2. There is some indication that the DBP may make use of its network of regional and local offices to decentralize. Services may be offered on a regional or localized basis; the DBP could, for example, look toward providing electronic mail and electronic banking services through its local post offices. Plans to do so undoubtedly will meet with opposition from both the private sector and the Länder, both of which would prefer to confine the DBP to the provision of facilities and the barest of transmission services. In fact, it is not entirely clear that, from a statutory or constitutional perspective, the DBP could offer services such as electronic banking.

3. As much as the Länder-DBP tension will tend to loosen the DBP's control over use of the network, so, too, will implementation of an ISDN. The ISDN model being urged by the DBP contemplates a plethora of services. Control over those services may well be diversified—in the hands of the DBP, broadcasters, cable operators, the press, banks, shops, and airlines. The impact of such diversification is unknown, but it would seem a major force in prying loose from the DBP monopoly control over the network. At the least, it will be difficult for the DBP to monitor which services are offered—and by which providers—and whether such providers are offering services that fall within the DBP's exclusive authority. Consequently, the DBP might—either before or after the implementation of ISDN—affirmatively recognize the practical implications of such an environment on its ability to control the network and to bring its regulatory structure into conformity with what is, or would soon be, reality.

C. The Interplay of Media and Telecommunications Policies

1. Media issues have influenced significantly the debate on telecommunications policy over the years. At one level, there is no reason why this should be the case. It might be better if the two were separated, to enable policymakers to focus on telecommunications issues. The issues of media and telecommunications policy, however, are intertwined inextricably. This entanglement is almost entirely a function of the federal scheme and the jurisdictional division of authority. The constellation of issues relevant to satellite, private broadcasting, cable, and data services are interrelated; no decisions can be made unilaterally by either the Länder or the Bund, and hope to succeed. At the same time, the issues themselves are bound together so tightly that a resolution in one sphere may be difficult—or impossible—without concurrently addressing the entire "constellation."

2. In some respects, however, the media issues themselves seem capable of being resolved. The Staatsvertrag on Btx is one example of how the system can—eventually—produce a consensus and help to introduce a new service. The telecommunications issues—pricing, liberalization, structural concerns—ultimately may be more intractable, but they also are more important. They not only involve political questions (which are, as well, at the crux of media policy), but also require a resolution in other

difficult areas: economics, concentration of control, industrial policy, and international competitiveness. The future of the German telecommunications industry in a competitive new environment may depend on moving these difficult issues, particularly the pricing issue, into greater prominence and visibility in the German political scene and making "hard decisions" more acceptable on the basis of a strategic assessment of long-term international trends.

ABOUT THE AUTHORS

Robert R. Bruce is a partner in the Washington, D.C., office of Debevoise & Plimpton, which has its principal office in New York and a European office in Paris. From October 1977 to February 1981, he served as General Counsel of the Federal Communications Commission. Before joining the FCC, Mr. Bruce practiced law in Washington, D.C., and, from 1970 to 1972, was Director of Communications Planning for the Public Broadcasting Service. He graduated *magna cum laude* in Government from Harvard College in 1966; in 1970, he received a J.D. from Harvard Law School and an M.P.A. from the John F. Kennedy School of Government, Harvard University. He is the author of numerous articles on communications law and policy.

Jeffrey P. Cunard is an associate in the Washington, D.C., office of Debevoise & Plimpton. He graduated *summa cum laude* in English and Political Science from the University of California at Los Angeles in 1977 and received a J.D. in 1980 from Yale Law School, where he was an Editor of the *Yale Law Journal*. After graduation from law school he clerked for Judge Wm. Matthew Byrne, Jr., in Los Angeles, California. He is the author of and a contributor to various articles on communications law.

Mark D. Director is an associate in the Washington, D.C., office of Debevoise & Plimpton. He graduated *magna cum laude* in English and American Literature and Languages from Harvard College in 1980 and received a J.D. in 1984 from Harvard Law School, where he was Comments Editor of the *Harvard Journal on Legislation*. He is a coauthor of a text on broadcast regulation.